TORT LIABILITY OF PUBLIC AUTHORITIES IN COMPARATIVE PERSPECTIVE

Edited by
DUNCAN FAIRGRIEVE
MADS ANDENAS
and
JOHN BELL

With a Foreword by
THE RT HON LADY JUSTICE ARDEN DBE

BIICL
BRITISH INSTITUTE OF
INTERNATIONAL AND
COMPARATIVE LAW
www.biicl.org

Published and Distributed by
The British Institute of International and Comparative Law
Charles Clore House, 17 Russell Square, London WC1B 5JP

© The British Institute of International and Comparative Law 2002

British Library Cataloguing in Publication Data
A Catalogue record of this book is available from the British Library

ISBN 0–903067–72–2

Typeset by Cambrian Typesetters
Frimley, Surrey
Printed in Great Britain by Biddles Ltd,
Guildford and King's Lynn

FOREWORD

In some ways, following the development of the common law is like taking a familiar country walk. The path leads in a familiar direction until one year there is a change in the direction of path for some reason. The path that used to lead one way now leads in a different way and opens up new horizons and new possible routes. This analogy is true of the common law development of the liability in tort of public authorities. Originally movement in this field of law was slow and conservative, but now it is more rapid due to the developments in Strasbourg jurisprudence and in European Community law described in this work. Moreover, English tort law is no longer developing in isolation but in a wider European setting, and consequently new horizons for study are opening up.

The collection of essays in this book is a series of reflections of distinguished scholars at different points along the way. They cover, for example, the question of how English law will have to adapt in relation to torts involving trespass to the person where the tort is committed by a public authority. Some of the essays are snapshots of the law at particular stages along the path. Others go to the very end of the path as it currently exists and present a long-term view of the various directions in which the common law could now go.

This book is a treasury of ideas. It contains a valuable set of reflections on the development of the law in this field. Contributors have thought carefully about many issues and provide stimulating arguments and views. With the law at such a sensitive stage of development there is a particular need for scholarly input, and accordingly I strongly commend this book to those concerned with this branch of the law.

Among other subjects, this book contains a discussion of the circumstances in which a claim may be made for compensation for failure by a public authority to observe a provision of Community law, and what constitutes a sufficiently serious breach for this purpose. The idea is floated that the implementation of directives may require a continuing administrative process. The suggestion is ventured that the development of liability under European Community law, drawing on national laws, may be the way in which the foundations for a pan-European tort law are laid. There is also discussion of liability for the misdiagnosis of learning disabilities in an educational setting, damages under the Human Rights Act 1998 and misfeasance in public office. In addition, there is the mind-broadening horizon of comparative law, as well as a number of chapters based on foreign law, including the law of the United States, France, Italy, Germany, Greece, Israel, Scotland, and the Netherlands.

Dutch law, it seems, is receptive to the concept of a relatively extensive liability in tort for public authorities. The suggestion is made that that has something to do with the fact that the Dutch people think that they know all about sluices and dykes. The reassuring observation is made that it is possible that 'in the end, they trust there will always be a judge who knows where to put his finger in the dyke'. This is a more measured reaction to the extension of tort law than the English preoccupation with floodgates. However, both similes highlight an obvious truth, that the development of the law in the areas covered by this work will give rise to many difficult legal issues and will require the astute exercise of judicial judgment.

MARY ARDEN
THE RT HON LADY JUSTICE ARDEN DBE
ROYAL COURTS OF JUSTICE
LONDON
MAY 2002

PREFACE

The aim of this book is to examine the rules governing compensation for administrative wrongdoing from a comparative law perspective. In all jurisdictions, the protection offered to individuals by remedies in public law and tort law is developing. In many countries, the past few years have witnessed an increasingly important European dimension to the tort liability of public authorities, of both European Union law and European Human Rights Law provenance. Contemporaneously, there has been an evolution in other countries outside Europe, often under the influence of supranational law.

It is 10 years since *Governmental Liability: A Comparative Study*, edited by John Bell and Anthony Bradley and published by the British Institute of International and Comparative Law (BIICL), in association with the United Kingdom National Committee for Comparative Law (UKNCCL). The time is thus ripe to examine the topic again.

The origin of this book was a BIICL–UKNCCL Colloquium in London in June 2001. Many of the papers published here were originally presented at that conference to an audience of academics and practitioners; others have their origins in the many lectures and seminars on the topic held at BIICL. We would like to thank the participants at these events who, through their contributions, have helped to influence the shape of the papers in this book. Some of the contributions to this collection have previously appeared in other publications. Chapter 4, Duncan Fairgrieve's paper 'The Human Rights Act 1998, Damages and English Tort Law', was first published in *Public Law*. Chapter 7, Professor Takis Tridimas's paper 'Liability for Breach of Community Law: Growing Up and Mellowing Down?', was first published in the *Common Market Law Review*. Chapter 12, Bill Atkin and Geoff McLay's paper 'Suing Child Welfare Agencies: a Comparative View from New Zealand', is an updated version of an article published in the *Child and Family Law Quarterly*. Chapter 14, Professor Basil Markesinis's paper 'Unity or Division: the Search for Similarities in Contemporary European Law', is an expanded version of an inaugural lecture delivered at University College London on 7 June 2001. It was first published in *Current Legal Problems*. Chapter 15. An earlier version of Duncan Fairgrieve's paper 'Pushing back the Boundaries of Public Authority Liability' was published in *Public Law*.

Many thanks also to the staff of the British Institute of International and Comparative Law, and particularly Olivia Skinner, without whom this publication would never have seen the light of day.

MADS ANDENAS
JOHN BELL
DUNCAN FAIRGRIEVE
June 2002

TABLE OF CONTENTS

LIST OF CONTRIBUTORS

The Rt Hon Lady Justice Arden DBE Court of Appeal

Merris Amos Lecturer, Department of Law, University of Essex.

Mads Andenas Director, British Institute of International and Comparative Law, London; Senior Teaching Fellow, Institute of European and Comparative Law, and Fellow, Harris Manchester College, University of Oxford.

Bill Atkin Reader in Law, Victoria University of Wellington.

Gert Brüggemeier Professor, University of Bremen.

John Bell Professor of Law (1973), Director of the Centre of European Legal Studies, University of Cambridge.

Douglas Brodie University of Edinburgh.

Roberto Caranta Professor, Law Faculty, University of Turin.

Judge Jean-Paul Costa Vice-President, European Court of Human Rights.

Cees C van Dam Professor of Civil Law, Vrije Universiteit Amsterdam; Deputy-Judge District Court Arnhem.

Duncan Fairgrieve Fellow in Comparative Law, British Institute of International and Comparative Law, London; Maître de Conférences invité, Université de Paris 1, Sorbonne.

Spyridon Flogaitis Director of the European Public Law Center, Athens, Greece.

Walter van Gerven Emeritus Professor of Law at the Universities of Leuven and Maastricht.

Israel Gilead Dean, Bora Laskin Professor of Law, Faculty of Law, Hebrew University of Jerusalem.

Helene M Goldberg Director, Torts Branch, US Department of Justice.

TR Hickman Selwyn College, Cambridge.

Basil Markesinis Professor of Common Law and Civil Law, University College London; Jamail Regents Chair, University of Texas School of Law.

Geoff McLay Senior Lecturer in Law, Victoria University of Wellington.

Adrian R Stewart Law Clerk to the Hon. Matthew F Kennelly, District Judge, US District Court for the Northern District of Illinois.

Ralph-Andreas Surma Attorney-at-Law and Legal Counsel Jungheinrich-Group, Hamburg, Germany.

Takis Tridimas Professor of European Law, University of Southampton.

Jane Wright Professor, Department of Law and Human Rights Centre at the University of Essex.

INTRODUCTION

In the collection *Governmental Liability: A Comparative Study*,[1] Tony Bradley and I wrote that governmental liability was widening (immunities were declining and the grounds for obtaining compensation were expanding) and the trend was likely to continue. This volume shows that, in the subsequent 10 years, this prediction has been fulfilled.

In that study, we focused primarily on the rules of liability and how these were changing. But it is necessary to look more broadly at the context. The liability procedure may be used for a number of ancillary processes. It may serve to vindicate rights (as in English law), or be the focus of public accountability. The proper role of compensation may be rather muddled in such circumstances. More profoundly, there have been significant changes in the expectations of the public in relation to public sector services and their providers. In addition, basic values are leading to some convergence of approach across the different European legal systems.

I. THE ROLE OF LIABILITY LAW

To understand governmental liability, it is necessary to appreciate the context within which its rules operate. Two parts of the context are the objectives served by parties in bringing liability actions in courts, and the general character of the relationship between the citizen and the administration.

In Latin languages, the terms 'liability' and 'responsibility' are closely connected. The word '*responsabilité*' (or equivalent) covers both. There is an unfortunate attempt in many systems to use the process of legal liability in order to attribute blame and to establish political or administrative responsibility, In some systems, criminal liability has performed this role, especially where victims can interplead as civil parties. In other systems, the liability process serves to blame officials or public bodies. This is most obvious in England, where certain torts are actionable per se, without proof of loss. The use of particular mechanisms for dealing with such complaints depends both on the existence of various complaints institutions and processes, and traditions for using them. The following chapters frequently discuss complaints about poor schooling or poor performance by social services, which have taken the form of actions for damages, even though it is often difficult to quantify a loss. Such complaints might have

---

[1] UKNCCL 1991, p. 15

been taken to the Ombudsman in a country like Sweden.[2] We have to ask about the value-added of the legal process in such circumstances. The enforceability of the legal remedy and the quantum are clearly important. But there is also a sense in which 'justice' is associated in the minds of many people with 'a court judgment'. Being vindicated in a public forum plays an important social role, over and above the receipt of compensation.

The criminal process was used in France to prosecute officials in relation to the Furani football stadium disaster.[3] But in England, the similar Hillsborough football disaster led to several civil law actions against the officials (the police) and a public inquiry, but only to two unsuccessful prosecutions.[4] There are, thus, cultural particularities related to the use of civil liability as a public process for establishing blame. In truth, the sanctioning role of liability law remains low, and the compensatory role remains high, but there has been a change in the balance, perceptibly different in different countries.[5] The increasing use of law to attribute blame has contributed to the expansion of the role of governmental liability law. Cases such as *Osman* and *Z* are predominantly about attributing blame, rather than compensating for identifiable monetary losses which have been sustained. The Osman parents had a legitimate grievance, but suffered no monetary loss. Similarly, as is well noted in many of the papers in this collection, it is difficult to quantify the losses of the parents of abused children or even of poorly educated children. The court process is predominantly performing the role of a public inquiry and allocation of blame. Damages are secondary. We must ask, therefore, what is the place of tort in a particular legal system as a vehicle for airing grievances. The answer will not be the same in each legal system.

The chapters in this volume of Atkin and McLay and of Caranta specifically raise the issue about how far the law on liability interferes with the primary functions allocated to the administration. In their view, the administrator should not be given differing messages by different parts of the legal system. If the administration is treated by administrative law as legitimately engaged in the exercise of discretion, then this should not be the subject of actions for damages in other courts. The concern not to inhibit the administration has also been a pre-occupation of the English courts in *Hill* (police), *X* (social services), and *Rondel* (barristers

[2] See Annual Report of the Justitieombudsman 2001/2, 377–84 (available on <http://www.riksdagen.se/debatt/0102/forslag/jo1/jo1.pdf>). See also complaints to the Local Government Ombudsman for England and Wales: <http://www.lgo.org.uk/pdf/digest00/sectb00.pdf>.
[3] J Bell, *French Legal Cultures* (London, 2001), 107.
[4] The Hillsborough disaster: see generally <http://news.bbc.co.uk/hi/english/special_report/1999/04/99/hillsborough/newsid_319000/ 319303.stm>. On the unsuccessful criminal trial of police officers initiated by the victims, see *The Guardian*, 24 July 2000.
[5] See C Guettier, *La responsabilité administrative* (Paris, 1993), 181.

in court).[6] Yet, as is also remarked, there is very limited evidence that liability will have an impact on administrators. To begin with, the administrator will not have to pay personally—the employer will pay. Often the official will have moved post before the liability action is tried. In many cases, the budget for paying damages is not the budget out of which the relevant public service is operated, although the trend for decentralised budgets may increase the pressure on services which are subject to lawsuits. The incentives for the administrator to perform well are more likely to relate to come from the potential for disciplinary action or complaints, rather than the slower liability process. To take the example of social workers,[7] the criticism which arises from inquiries into the mishandling of cases involving vulnerable children is likely to have far more of an impact that the award of damages. That said, the arguments of Atkin and McLay remain important. We ought to be consistent in the way we encourage officials to act not only in relation to liability law, but also in relation to other comments on administrative action. Are they to be encouraged to experiment, and thus to reach the wrong result in some situations, or are we holding them responsible for not achieving the right result?

II. POLICY TRENDS: THE CITIZEN AND THE STATE

A critical change in recent years has been in the relationship of the administration and the citizens. During much of the twentieth century, the public administration moved from simply policing respect for public order and basic public hygiene to providing a range of essential services: education, housing, health, and so on. The framework of services thus established made an offer to the public as a whole (a universal service) and was designed according to the estimations of pubic need made by public officials. In French terminology, the individuals were 'users' of these public services. In the 1980s, this picture began to change. Services were run less by public enterprises and more by private or privatised organisations. In addition, the culture changed in that the public were no longer passive recipients of the beneficence of public bodies, but were seen as much more active 'clients' or 'customers' whose needs had to be met.[8] The most striking examples have been in the core powers of the state, such as policing and taxation, in which

---

[6] *Hill v Chief Constable of West Yorkshire* [1989] AC 53; *X (Minors) v Bedfordshire CC* [1995] 2 AC 633; *Rondel v Worsley* [1969] 1 AC 191. But now compare *Barrett v Enfield LBC* [2001] 2 AC 550; *Phelps v Hillingdon LBC* [2001] 2 AC 59 ; *Arthur J S Hall & Co v Simons* [2000] 3 All ER 673.

[7] See generally H Brayne and G Martin, *Law for Social Workers*, 6th edn (London 1999), pp 20-3.

[8] See D Truchet in F Tiphine (ed), *Administration: droit et attentes des citoyens* (La documentation française, Paris 1997), 23–35.

'service' concepts have been used to characterise relationships. A recipient of public largesse has not much standing to complain if the benefit received is less than he hoped, or even less than the donor intended. But the disappointed 'customer' of a public service would feel fully justified in complaining if the service purchased on his behalf turns out to be less than satisfactory. In more recent years, public sector train service providers in many countries have begun to offer 'compensation' for late or deficient services. In some systems, the relationship of the customer to the public service is a matter of contract, in others it is a matter of non-contractual liability. Guettier argues that the specificity of governmental liability is to be found in the balance which has to be struck between protecting the interests of the citizen and preserving the ability of the administration to act in the public interest.[9] This has led, in some systems like the French, to a limitation of liability to cases in which there is serious fault (*faute lourde*) or, as in EU law, to liability for legislative actions only where there is *manifest* illegality. In the English system, this concern has led to a finding that no duty of care is owed in certain categories of case.[10] Such an approach is well suited to the relationship of the public 'authority' and a 'user' of services. It is much less suited to the relationship between a 'customer' and a 'service provider'. The reconceptualisation of the public sector has called in question attitudes towards the extent to which citizens can expect to be compensated when the system fails them. In particular, the re-positioning of the state as regulator or as the 'purchaser' of services from the private sector calls into question the specific nature of public sector liability. In that the person regulated or the provider of a service is the first person to be blamed if things go wrong, the public authority has often only a secondary liability—usually a failure to supervise or to check. But this is not significantly different from positions of responsibility in the private sector. Basil Markesinis captures the change in mood in his inaugural lecture. He talks of a 'consumerist vision of public liability' under which 'compensating the damages suffered by citizens because of administrative activities can never be a wrong use of public money'.[11]

Furthermore, when the public sector provides the service directly, then the tendency is to treat it as holding out its ability to deliver a similar quality of service to the private sector, eg in hospitals or education. These changes undermine the claim to special treatment from the state. The public–private divide is less sharp than it once was. For instance, in France, blood transfusions might be provided in one region by the public hospital and in the next region by a private service. The incongruity of different rules for compensation between public and private sectors is stark.

---

[9] Op cit, 97.
[10] *Hill* and *X* , above n 6, serve as good examples of the concern not to compromise the administrative effectiveness of the public service.
[11] Below, p. 451.

III. BASIC VALUES

A. *Are there distinct duties to avoid causing loss?*

Rules on liability constitute the secondary or remedial rules of administrative law. The primary rules set out the powers and duties of the administration.[12] If these primary rules identify a duty owed to an individual, then it is usually straightforward to accept that there is both a secondary rule about enforcement and a secondary rule about compensation for breach, the rules on government liability. The standard of the primary duty is thus clearly established and can be the basis for criticism in disciplinary, liability or ombudsman proceedings. The problem lies in the many situations in which it is unclear from the primary rules to whom a duty is owed. That issue is one which falls to be determined as an integral issue for liability proceedings.

Where the basis of liability is breach of a protective norm, as in German law or the English breach of a statutory duty, then there will be a coincidence between the view of administrative law on who owes the duty and the law on liability. But where there is a more generic liability for administrative fault, then there is scope for a difference between who is protected for the purposes of enforcing a duty, and who can be compensated for harm caused.

The difficulty is to determine whether there should be one set of protected persons for the purposes of the enforcement of the administrative duty, and another for liability purposes. On one scenario, the law could provide that there is a primary duty to act and anyone adversely affected should be able to claim compensation. In the alternative, there could be a primary duty, enforceable through secondary rules on judicial review, but compensation rules might be distinct. There may be duties to compensate when there is no breach of a primary duty, and, correspondingly, there may be no duty to compensate in some situations of breach of a primary duty. Within the law on liability, the question arises whether it should determine independently to whom a duty is owed, or whether the range of people able to claim compensation is simply a matter of causation. The English model is that the law on governmental liability sets up its own tests of duty, to run alongside public duty issues under the enforcement procedure, judicial review. The French model is to use causation to identify who has suffered sufficiently from a breach in order to be able to claim. Italian civil law has expanded to provide compensation not only for interference with rights, but also with legitimate expectations. As a result, a diverse range of affected individuals can claim compensation, where the administration does not perform correctly. Where illegality is taken as a

---

[12] See J Bell, *AJDA* 1995, spécial, 99 at 100–3

sufficient basis for awarding compensation to those directly affected, then causation will inevitably play a controlling function. The English model is more complex in that the law on liability seeks to establish both primary duties and then secondary rules on remedies.

If anything, the trend is towards adopting the French model. A difference between the scope of a primary duty to achieve administrative outcomes and a duty not to cause loss in the process is hard to sustain in the modern 'consumerist' climate noted above. Although the English cases struggle to maintain this in a formal way, the recent raft of cases studied in this volume reveal that, in practice, the 'duty' concept is waning as a control on the scope of liability.

B. Fault

So what are the basic values in compensation and how are they developing? There seem to be two broad bases. The first is fault and the second is the principle of unjust burden, which underlies no-fault. In the case of fault, we are dealing with a failure by a public authority to conduct itself in a way which can be reasonably expected. As Van Gerven points out, fault and reasonable expectation go hand-in-hand. How different is this from private law, where the concept of the 'reasonable man' or the 'bonus paterfamilias' stands as an objective standard against which the performance of the specific defendant is measured.[13] Now such a standard has to be situated. The objective person has to be performing the same kind of role. So we have the reasonable car driver, the reasonable parent, the reasonable occupier of land, the reasonable policymaker and so on. In this way, the specific difficulties of the situation in which a public official is placed are taken into account. Structured in this way, it is hard to argue that public authorities should owe no duty to avoid causing loss by their fault. But it may be reasonable to say that it will be hard to show that they are in breach of their duty unless the fault is particularly glaring or the illegality is manifest. This perspective is set out in the first principle of the Council of Europe's Recommendation of 1984:[14]

Reparation should be ensured for damage caused by an act due to a failure of a public authority to conduct itself in a way which can reasonably be expected from it in law in relation to the injured person.

This statement offers a good perspective from which to understand the problems seen by European courts with English law. Much of the ECHR's problem with the English law lay in the suggestion that there was no duty owed to certain victims at all, rather than that the duty had not been

---

[13] Below p. 125.
[14] Recommendation N° R (84) 15 on Public Liability, adopted by the Council of Ministers of the Council of Europe on 18 Sept 1984 (Strasbourg, 1985).

breached in the kinds of facts before the court.[15] As Markesinis and Fairgrieve point out, there are ways of achieving the similar result by the use of concepts of causation or to identify losses that are difficult to recover. But to deny any recovery on the basis of the absence of a duty of care goes against the principles from which the Council of Europe starts. If there is a primary duty to achieve an outcome in conformity with principles of good administration, then this establishes what the citizen can reasonably expect the administrator should do. If damage results from this failure, to deny liability on the basis that there was no duty owed and to say this in the absence of written texts smacks of opportunism, rather than principle. In short, once it is established that the administration is supposed to act in a specific way, then it is hard to resist the view that a failure to act like a reasonable administrator is fault. More recent developments lead to a more casuistic and less wide-ranging approach to exceptions.

C. *No fault*

Much less has been said in this book about the second principle enunciated by the Council of Europe:

Reparation should be ensured if it would be manifestly unjust to allow the injured person alone to bear the damage, having regard to the following circumstances:
—the act is in the general interest;
—only one person or a limited number of persons have suffered damage, and
—the act was exceptional or the damage was an exceptional result of the act.

This is a less common basis for liability, and is not recognised in all jurisdictions to the same extent.

This principle is based on spreading the social risk of administrative policies. We are not concerned about the misperformance of policies, but merely with the ancillary costs of implementing the policy properly. To that extent the German idea of an exceptional sacrifice (*Sonderopfer*) captures the idea well. All systems find it easy to accept this principle in relation to the *planned consequences* of a policy. The administration (and through it society as a whole) is asked to internalise the cost of a particular policy. If it is planned that a road will be driven through my house, then it is accepted that compensation will be paid. In relation to property, the first protocol to the European Convention has an abundant case-law to elaborate this idea. The more problematic cases are those of *unplanned conse-*

---

[15] The approach of adopting prima facie rights and then finding reasons not to apply them may be rationally sound, but politically naive in a system of fundamental rights: cf R Mullender, in M Kramer (ed), *Rights, Wrongs and responsibilities* (Basingstoke, 2001), ch 6.
[16] CE Sect, 29 Apr 1987, *AJDA* 1987, 488.

quences. To take the case of the *Banque Populaire de Strasbourg*,[16] prisoners were released on parole or licence and they committed a bank robbery during their period of freedom. Could the bank claim compensation? The planned policy of release of prisoners increased the risk of offences, but it was not the purpose of the policy. The French Conseil d'Etat decided that this loss was a sufficiently direct part of the policy as to come within the duty to compensate for exceptional losses. This has also seemed an appropriate basis for medical risks. Few other legal systems use the rules on liability to deal with this problem. In constitutional terms, this ought to be part of the legislative design. Compensation for established interests is something which any constitution recognises and which the European Convention reinforces. But the logic of this principle stops when the harm suffered is of a type which was unforeseeable. At that point, there is no conscious risk taking by a public body. If our concern is to internalise the costs of policies, then that is a logical point to stop. On the other hand, if our concern is the fairness of leaving the loss where it lies, then we might be driven to look further.

At this point we need to distinguish *liability* from *social solidarity*. Liability is based on a principle of justice that a public body which has acted in a certain way ought to bear the consequences of its actions (whether these are the result of fault or of risk-taking). Social solidarity gives us a reason to offer assistance to those who find themselves in an unfortunate position. It is a principle of compassion, not justice. If there is a flood and many houses are damaged, then society as a whole might provide support to the victims, or might leave such support to private initiative through charity. Most systems acknowledge this principle in relation to riots (the public purse picks up the cost of riots. You do not have to show any fault in the policing of an event. Compensation systems for vaccine damage, or the effects of defective blood, or industrial disease fall into this category. I have argued elsewhere that the French willingness to provide compensation for the effects of protests or of medical experiments would be better based on social solidarity, rather than liability (even no-fault liability).[17] Under both principles, the government pays, but the reasons for paying are fundamentally different.

IV. THE SPHERES OF LIABILITY

There are four major areas in which liability is invoked: the protection of rights, the exercise of discretion, the regulation of the activities of others, and the implementation of policy.

---

[17] J Bell, 'Governmental Liability in Tort' (1996) 6 *National Journal of Constitutional Law* 85, at 90–2.

A. Rights

The European Convention has given an added impetus to the existence of liability for the interference with rights. Article 13 of the Convention requires signatory states to provide a remedy where convention rights have been interfered with, and it is this (rather than Article 6) which provided the basis for the finding of breach in Z. The result is that there can be no immunity for interference with rights, and there must be adequate compensation.

B. Discretion

Many of the more complex cases involve discretion. As has been said, there is a widespread concern not to interfere with the legitimate sphere of discretion of the administration. First, this means that the administrators must be allowed to make mistakes without incurring liability. Secondly, the difficulty and complexity of administrative decision-making has to be recognised. The mere fact of making a wrong decision or weighing up the alternatives wrongly is insufficient to give rise to liability. Particular seriousness is needed in the error. But such latitude only applies in the sphere of legitimate discretion—not where the action is unlawful. In addition, the deference to the administration is shown only where there is complex decision-making

C. Regulation

An important area for the exercise of discretion discussed in this volume is regulation. In particular, the chapter by Andenas and Fairgrieve discusses its importance. A major role of the administration in recent years has been to be a regulator, rather than a direct provider of services. The processes of 'privatisation' and 'deregulation' have been intended to enable private initiative to provide more responsive and higher quality services to the public than would have been possible from the public sector, particularly in the light of the constraints it faces on raising money for investment.[18] But a major consequence of this shift has been to increase the monitoring responsibility of the state for the actions of private-law persons and bodies.[19] In addition, there is the increased pressure on the state to provide security in preventing harm, such as child abuse, or in protecting the less aware, such as consumers in financial services. The state has an agenda in some areas to improve social behaviour, such as respecting the rights of

---

[18] G Majone, 'The Rise of the Regulatory state in Europe' (1994) 17 *West European Politics*, 77. R Baldwin, C Scott and C Hood, *A Reader on Regulation* (Oxford, 1998), 8–34.

[19] See J Richardson, 'Doing Less by Doing More: British Government 1979–1993' (1994) 17 *West European Politics*, 178.

the child, prisoners or other groups, or in improving the environment. In other areas, it wishes to encourage participation in financial investment markets, and offers the guarantee of supervision to provide a level of comfort to the hesitant new consumer. The net result is a major increase in supervision and regulation. Major concerns are expressed about how such regulation is performed, and how to handle regulatory failure. To what extent is the regulator setting and enforcing standards (a 'policeman role'), and to what extent is the regulator underwriting the system of compliance ('a guarantor role')? Concerns expressed in public about food safety, the solvency of banks and life insurance companies, or supplies of blood for transfusion have all proceeded on assumptions that it is not enough for the regulator to demonstrate that he has performed a policeman role. There is an increasing expectation that the regulator guarantees the outcomes which the system of regulation is intended to secure. The regulator is expected by the public to be pro-active in ensuring that regulatees are complying. This policy change has a major impact on the expected role of tort liability. Of course, the moral duty to pay compensation has been recognised for some time.[20] But the legal duty is one with which the various legal systems in this volume (German, Dutch, French, Italian, and English) have all struggled. On the whole, the trend will be towards some form of liability, but only for the direct victims of serious maladministration. Perhaps it is necessary for the government to contain expectations.

D. *Implementation*

By contrast with discretionary decisions, decisions on implementation require limited choices and are relatively less complex. As a result, the implementation of policy requires less deference. It is for this reason that, in spheres such as the assessment of taxation or the operation of the postal service, the French have moved away from requiring *faute lourde* to establish liability and are content to base it on simple fault. No great and complex policy choices are involved in most taxation cases. All the same, it has to be recognised that there is no sharp line between the decision to make a policy and its implementation. Indeed, incremental decision making may involve a gradual development of a policy on a case-by-case basis. Situations such as dealing with special educational needs or the handling of delicate child protection cases are complex decisions, and there needs to be deference to the administrator in such cases. The discussions in this volume reflect the difficulty of making the basis of liability depend on an artificial distinction between policy and operational decisions.

---

[20] See R Gregory, 'Barlow Clowes and the Ombudsman' [1991] *PL* 191 and 408.

V. EUROPEAN LAWS AS STANDARDS

Comparative lawyers in Europe are interested in the mechanisms and character of any convergence in the rules and principles of legal systems. Compared with the volume which I edited with Professor Bradley in 1991, this volume of essays is far more pre-occupied with the European Convention and European Union law as standards for national laws. Both have direct application in one form or another in the European legal systems discussed here. The concern of national systems is to ensure compatibility between national rules and these European standards, where the two cover the same case. In addition, national laws seek to ensure what Van Gerven calls 'homogeneity', ie to ensure that national rules are similar, whether they cover situations also governed by European rules or not. The result of this latter process is what is frequently described as the 'spillover' effect of European rules—that they have an impact beyond the sphere in which they are directly applicable. In both direct application and in spill over, European standards are having an appreciable impact on the character of national rules.

As Van Gerven points out, the process is not one-sided. EU law and the ECHR base themselves on the most protective standards in European national legal systems. These are then applied to EU institutions, as well as to member states. As he suggests, there is a process of dialogue between the legal orders. On the whole, this passes through the central courts, rather than horizontally, though the work of Markesinis does note the way in which national legal systems influence each other. The chapter by Jane Wright in this volume also notes the way in which there is scope for dialogue between the national courts and Strasbourg in developing the law. Although Strasbourg may appear to be the final court, a more European attitude to precedent, viz a process of respectful disobedience, may ensure a more sensible outcome.

But what kind of standards do the European Convention and EU law represent? As far as the European Convention is concerned, the papers in this collection identify three areas of impact. The first is that there should be effective remedies for breaches of Convention rights. If, as in Z, there is no effective remedy for a breach of a right, such as the right not to be subjected to inhumane and degrading treatment, then the liability law systems of the country will have to be changed to provide a remedy. In this situation, the Convention identifies a gap in the system of protection. The second area of impact is the adequacy of compensation. This matter is discussed in Judge Costa's paper. The Convention and the European Court of Human Rights establish areas in which compensation will be awarded. Where a national legal system fails to match such compensation, it may be guilty of a breach of the Convention's Article 13. The third area is Article

6, and the provision of access to the courts. At first sight, this is a negative provision in that it removes obstacles to access to the courts, but does not prescribe the remedy that should be made available. But, as *Osman* and *Z* show, the finding that certain rules constitute barriers to access to the court effectively encourages a legal system to create a direct, if limited, remedy. The careful renegotiation of the ruling in *Hill* and *X* by the House of Lords in *Barrett* and *Phelps*, and the parallel removal of the immunity of barristers for work in court have followed from the rulings in the European Court of Human Rights.[21] The existence of a duty of care is to be determined far more on a case-by-case basis, rather than by creating blanket rules of immunity. Although the Convention is useful in dealing with the interference with rights, it has less to say on the exercise of discretion. After all, the exercise of discretion is a major feature of administrative life. In those situations in which rights are affected, decisions like *X* and *Phelps* provide some standards. But in situations in which there are no rights affected, but interests or legitimate expectations are affected, then a different standard is required. EU law offers this in that most of the decisions its liability rules relate to are the exercise of legislative or administrative discretion. In the case of legislative action, liability only arises where there has been manifest illegality. Ordinary fault is insufficient. A similar concern is reflected in the handling of administrative discretion.

The future development of public liability in Europe will depend on the ability of legal systems to adapt to and influence European-wide debates on principles of liability. The fact that liability is not merely a matter on which individual legal systems are criticised by a central body, but on which they can influence the liability of bodies like the European Commission, enables a fruitful debate to be established.

JOHN BELL

---

[21] See n 6 above.

PART I:

HUMAN RIGHTS AND LIABILITY

1. THE PROVISION OF COMPENSATION UNDER ARTICLE 41 OF THE EUROPEAN CONVENTION ON HUMAN RIGHTS

Judge Jean-Paul Costa*

The rule of 'just satisfaction' under Article 41 of the European Convention on Human Rights is a very important one, since it enables the applicant before the European Court of Human Rights, if he 'wins', to be compensated in respect of the breach of the Convention from which he or she has suffered.

However, the rule itself is not always easy to apply. I would like to enumerate a number of issues that arise when examining the basis, the content, and the effects of Article 41 of the Convention.

The main problems that I shall deal with are the following:

I.   The basis of the rule.
II.   The exact provisions thereof.
III. The determination of who is the injured party.
IV.   The various aspects of just satisfaction.
V.   The problem of *restitutio in integrum.*
VI and VI *bis*. The period allowed to the State for payment, and the sanction in the event of failure to pay within that period.
VII. The binding force of the rule, and its execution.
VIII. Other issues.

I. THE BASIS OF THE RULE

It is generally recognised that the basis of the just satisfaction rule resides in the principle of general international law which prescribes that a State responsible for having, by act or omission, injured a party, must provide

* This chapter is based upon a lecture which was delivered at the British Institute of International and Comparative Law, London, on 7 Dec 2001. The views expressed are the author's alone and do not necessarily reflect those of the Court. The author would like to thank Mr Lawrence Early, Deputy Section Registrar, for his assistance and advice on the text including on linguistic matters.

that party with adequate reparation (see, for instance, the judgment of the *Cour Permanente de Justice Internationale* in the case of the Chorzow factories, delivered in 1928). This principle has now become a rule of customary international law.

In the case of the European Convention on Human Rights, the rule is more specific insofar as, generally speaking, one respondent State is responsible in the event of a finding of a violation of the Convention, and one or several individual applicants are the 'injured party' and are therefore entitled to be awarded just satisfaction by the State concerned. The system constitutes an improvement in the area of international responsibility, both because the party is an individual (or individuals) and because of the human rights nature of the wrong done and of the damage suffered.

It is not only the European Convention on Human Rights that contains a provision regarding just satisfaction. Article 63.1 of the San José Convention, which created the Inter-American Convention of Human Rights, is not very different from Article 41 of the European Convention and there is now also a thrust towards implementing international instruments for the protection of human rights, including provisions in favour of the victims, such as provisions on just satisfaction.

II. THE EXACT PROVISIONS OF ARTICLE 41 OF THE EUROPEAN CONVENTION

The exact text reads as follows:

If the Court finds that there has been a violation of the Convention or the protocols thereto, and if the internal law of the High Contracting Party concerned allows only partial reparation to be made, the Court shall, if necessary, afford just satisfaction to the injured party.

This text is both shorter and less precise than former Article 50 of the Convention, replaced by Article 41 when Protocol no 11 to the Convention entered into force on 1 November 1998. Former Article 50 read:

If the Court finds that a decision or a measure taken by a legal authority or any other authority of a High Contracting Party is completely or partially in conflict with the obligations arising from the present Convention, and if the internal law of the said Party allows only partial reparation to be made for the consequences of this decision or measure, the decision of the Court shall, if necessary, afford just satisfaction to the injured party.

Under the former system, based on the respective competences of the Commission and the Court, only the Court was entitled to afford just satisfaction, ie to deliver a judgment 'condemning' the respondent State to provide the applicant(s) with such satisfaction. When the Commission, under former Article 31, drew up a report on the facts and stated its opinion as to whether there was a breach by the State concerned of its obligations under the Convention, and if the question was not referred to the Court, is was for the Committee of Ministers of the Council of Europe to prescribe a period within which the State had to take the measures required by the decision of the Committee of Ministers—including just satisfaction.

III. THE DETERMINATION OF WHO IS THE 'INJURED PARTY' UNDER ARTICLE 41

Obviously, if no breach of the Convention or the protocols thereto is found by the Court, no party can be said to have been injured. There is no automatic link between Article 34—according to which 'any person, non-governmental organisation or group of individuals *claiming* to be the victim of a violation . . .' may apply to the European Court—and the fact of being an injured party. It does not suffice to claim to be a victim in order to have a finding by the Court that one's rights and freedoms, as set forth in the Convention, have been violated (on the other hand, even if the Court is strict about the 'victim' requirement for the admissibility of an application,[1] the case-law has constantly held that it is not necessary to demonstrate the existence of detriment in order to be considered a victim;[2] detriment is a matter to be examined under Article 41 (former Article 50), not an admissibility criterion).

On the contrary, if the Court holds that an article (or articles) of the Convention and/or its protocols has (have) been violated, the question of the injured party arises. Usually, there is no problem: the individual applicant(s) is (are) the injured party (parties).

Two questions, however, are worth considering. The first relates to the right of legal persons to benefit from Article 41, even as regards the award of compensation for non-pecuniary damage (for pecuniary damage, no specific difficulty seems to have arisen). Having accepted the principle that such a right accrued first to an association,[3] then to a political party,[4] the Court has now extended that principle to commercial companies.[5]

The second question relates to Inter-State cases, provided for in Article

---

[1] For a recent example, see the decision on inadmissibility 'Fédération chrétienne les témoins de Jéhovah—France'. Section II, 6 Nov 2001, to be published.

[2] See, for instance, the *Johnston v Ireland* case, 18 Dec 1986, Series A—no 112, esp s 42.

[3] *Vereinigung Demokratischer Soldaten Österreichs and Gubi v Austria*, 19 Dec 1994, Series A—no 302, 21 s 62.

[4] *Özdep v Turkey*, judgment of 8 Dec 1999, to be published in the official reports of the Court, s 57.

[5] *Comingersoll S.A. v Portugal*, judgment of 6 Apr 2000, to be published in the official reports of the Court, s 35.

34 of the Convention. Since the *Ireland v the United Kingdom* case,[6] the Court has not excluded the application of Articles 50/41 to such cases, but there has not been any concrete example of that application. In the *Ireland v the United Kingdom* case, the Court considered that it was not necessary to apply former Article 50 (s 246), but this was due to the fact that the applicant Government informed the Court that they did not request it to award monetary compensation (s 245). In the *Denmark v Turkey* case,[7] the Court decided to strike the application out of the list on the basis of a friendly settlement between the two States (and which included a sum offered '*ex gratia*' by the respondent State to the applicant State). Finally, in the *Cyprus v Turkey* case,[8] the Court simply held that 'the issue of the possible application of Article 41 of the Convention is not ready for decision and adjourns consideration thereof'. It can be concluded at this stage that the question of the application of Article 41 in Inter-State cases remains open.[9]

IV. THE VARIOUS ASPECTS OF 'JUST SATISFACTION'

If we concentrate, for the time being, on the *monetary* compensation to be awarded to the injured party, the Court has progressively developed its case law by distinguishing three categories of monetary compensation:

(a) pecuniary damage,
(b) non-pecuniary damage, and
(c) costs and expenses.

Before looking at these categories, it is necessary to recall some general principles of interpretation applied by the Court in its case law. From the beginning, the Court has held that the rule of exhaustion of domestic remedies is not applicable in the context of former Article 50 (Article 41).[10] Furthermore, the Court has considered that, whenever '*restitutio in integrum*' is, either *de jure* or *de facto*, impossible, the conclusion is that the respondent State can only offer *partial* reparation under former Article 50; hence, it is for the Court to afford the applicant just reparation.[11] Thirdly, the words 'just' (satisfaction) and 'if necessary' allow the Court a *certain*

---

[6] Judgment of 18 Jan 1978, Series A—no 25.
[7] Judgment of 5 Apr 2000.
[8] Judgment of 10 May 2001, to be published in the official reports of the Court.
[9] However, the Rules of the Court invite the applicant State in such a case to indicate any claims for just satisfaction (Arts 46.1e and 60).
[10] See the *De Wilde, Ooms and Versyp* judgment of 10 Mar 1972, Series A—no 14, 7–9, ss 15 and 16.
[11] See the *König* judgment of 10 Mar 1980, Series A—no 36, 14–15, s 35.

discretion in the exercise of the power conferred by former Article 50 (Article 41).[12] Finally, the Court carefully reviews the justification given by the applicant for his claim, and in principle never decides *ultra petita* by awarding the applicant more than he has been claiming.

It may be added that that it is not necessarily the case that the Court will in the same judgment find one or several violations of the Convention and, at the same time, decide also on the issue of just satisfaction. Even if the Court, in the interest of the good administration of justice, tries to avoid having two separate judgments, it is not always possible to do so since it may happen that the issue of just satisfaction is simply not ready for decision.[13]

Returning to the three categories of monetary compensation, the assessment of compensation for *pecuniary damage* is sometimes easy, sometimes very difficult. A simple case is one in which, as a direct consequence of a violation, the injured party has lost, or has not obtained, a precise sum which he or she would have received had it not been for the violation.[14] In other cases, the award of just satisfaction is either impossible, because the victim had failed to establish any causal link between a violation of the Convention and the alleged damage, or difficult to assess, because it is likely, but not certain, that the violation had consequences on the financial situation of the victim. The Court often finds itself in a situation in which it either deems it impossible to speculate on the consequences for the applicant in the absence of the violations found,[15] or, on the contrary, takes into account the loss of real possibilities caused by the violation and awards a certain sum as compensation for pecuniary damage, even if the amount of the loss of income, for example, is necessarily somewhat speculative.[16]

Obviously some violations of the Convention or its protocols are more suitable for an assessment of compensation for pecuniary damage than others. As a general rule, Article 1 of Protocol no 1, for instance, insofar as it deals with the subject of the protection of property, allows for an easier calculation of the losses suffered, including lost earnings. On the other

---

[12] See the *Guzzardi v Italy* judgment of 6 Nov 1980, Series A—no 39, 42 s 114.

[13] For a recent—and interesting—example, see the *Beyeler v Italy* judgment on the merits of 5 Jan 2000 (to be published in the official reports of the Court): the judgment on Art 41 will be delivered at the beginning of 2002; or the *Lustig Prean and Beckett and others v United Kingdom* judgments on the merits of 27 Sept 1999, and on Art 41 of 25 July 2000.

[14] A good example is given by the *Mazurek v France* case (judgment of 1 Feb 2000): owing to a specific provision of the *Code civil*, the applicant received a quarter, instead of a half, of his dead mother's estate. The Court held that this difference of treatment was not compatible with the Convention, and the compensation for pecuniary damage was therefore equal to a quarter of the estate.

[15] See, for instance, the *Schouter and Meldrum v the Netherlands* case of 9 Dec 1994, Series A—no 304, esp, 28 s 72.

[16] See the above-mentioned *Lustig-Prean and Beckett v the United Kingdom* judgment (Art 41) of 25 July 2000, ss 26 and 27.

hand, the violation of 'procedural' rights, such as the right to a fair trial, protected by Article 6 of the Convention, either does not give rise to pecuniary damage or does give rise to such damage but the circumstances are such that they do not facilitate the assessment of compensation by the Court.

Finally, it is necessary to add that compensation for pecuniary damage can be awarded by the Court not only to the applicant himself or herself, but also to his/her estate, if that person is deceased,[17] precisely because such compensation has a pecuniary character.

As regards *non-pecuniary damage* (*le 'dommage moral'*), it is by definition difficult to translate this into a fixed amount of money. This is the area where the Court most often decides on a 'just' basis and, if I may, I think that the Court, in this context, acts more in accordance with principles of equity than strict legal reasoning. In some cases, the Court even 'merges' the claims for pecuniary and non-pecuniary damage, and affords an amount for both of them, making it clear that it takes its decision on an equitable basis.[18]

Of course, the number of elements that serve to make up the notion of non-pecuniary damage is high, and the list is rather vague. The judgments of the Court mention words such as anxiety, stress, distress, frustration, sorrow, pain, suffering. Everything depends on the circumstances of the case and on the nature, and seriousness, of the violations found by the Court. Personal injuries, usually, are assimilated to non-pecuniary damage—or added to it.[19] And, not surprisingly, the amount of the just satisfaction awarded also depends on the nature and severity of the breaches of the rights and freedoms guaranteed by the Convention.

In this respect, it is unavoidable that some arbitrariness is to be found in the case law of the Strasbourg Court, insofar as non-pecuniary damage can scarcely be translated into a monetary amount. The length of proceedings cases—which are so numerous, especially as regards certain countries—offer a good example of how difficult it is to compensate fairly the special kind of stress and dissatisfaction suffered by the person whose case has not been heard by domestic courts within a reasonable time, the more so because all persons are not in the same situation, and do not behave in the same manner. For these reasons, the Court operates in a very sophisticated manner when dealing with the length of proceedings cases. First of all, the Court tries to take into account various parameters or criteria in order to decide whether a 'reasonable time' has been exceeded—or not: the reasonableness of the length of proceeding is to be assessed having regard to the

---

[17] See the *X v the United Kingdom* judgment of 18 Oct 1982, Series A—n° 55, 14 s 12.
[18] See the *Delta v France* judgment of 19 Dec 1990, Series A—no 191–A, s 43.
[19] See, for a case of torture, the *Selmouni v France* judgment of 28 July 1999, s 123.

degree of complexity of the case, to the applicant's behaviour, to the conduct of the national authorities, and also to the importance of the interests at stake for the applicant.[20] Then, if the Court has reached the finding that Article 6 s 1 of the Convention has been violated due to the unreasonable length of the proceedings, when it assesses the amount of compensation for non-pecuniary damage, it takes into account the 'degree of unreasonableness' of the impugned period, and the consequences of the delay for the victim. In some repetitive cases, such as the applications against Italy, the Committee of Ministers (before 1998) adopted a sort of indicative scale, providing amounts of money corresponding to various durations, with increases for the most sensitive cases (such as family-law cases or employment disputes). But, of course, even in repetitive cases of this kind, the Court—which has been inspired by the 'scale' set up by the Committee of Ministers under the old system—is attached to flexibility and the specific features of particular cases.

A final element of the just satisfaction issue concerns the reimbursement of *costs and expenses* claimed by the applicant. Again, the Court has always been both flexible and autonomous when assessing such claims. The Court has said that it does not apply a domestic rule in respect of costs and expenses, and the applicant is not entitled to his costs as of right: 'just satisfaction' is to be afforded 'if necessary', and determined by the Court at its discretion, having regard to what is equitable.[21]

That means, in particular, that the Court determines 'whether the costs and expenses were actually and necessarily incurred in order to prevent or obtain redress for the matter found to constitute a violation of the Convention, and were reasonable as to *quantum*'; 'it does not consider itself bound by domestic scales and practices, although it may derive some assistance from them'.[22]

These principles apply notably, but not only, to *lawyers' fees*, the level of which varies very much from one country to another.

Three points must be made regarding lawyers' fees:

(1) the costs and expenses are awarded to the applicant and not to the lawyer: it is for the applicant to reimburse the lawyer if he has not already done so; in some cases, the Court has recognised agreements between an applicant and his or her lawyer, such as a contingency agreement ('*quota litis*'), ie an arrangement under which the lawyer

---

[20] Among many other authorities, see the *Erkner and Hofauer v Austria* judgment of 23 Apr 1987, Series A—no 117, and the *Caleffi v Italy* judgment of 24 May 1991, Series A—206–B.

[21] See the *Sunday Times* (Art 50) judgment of 6 Nov 1980, Series A—no 38, s 15.

[22] Quotation from the *Tolstoy Miloslavsky v the United Kingdom* judgment of 13 July 1995, Series A—316–B.

receives a certain percentage of the sum awarded by the Court to the party concerned.[23]

(2) applicants, on the basis of their means, may be granted *legal aid*. The decision to grant legal aid is taken by the President of the Chamber, either at the request of an applicant or *ex officio*.[24] If it is granted, legal aid fees are payable to the lawyers, not to the applicant.[25] The result is that, when just satisfaction is awarded in a judgment, the applicant receives a certain sum for costs and expenses, *less* the sums already paid by way of legal aid.

(3) as already mentioned, the *domestic costs* may be compensated, but only if, and insofar as, they were incurred in order to prevent or obtain redress for the matter found to constitute a violation. Similarly for the so-called 'Strasbourg' costs,[26] in respect of which the Court takes into account the number of complaints found to be well-founded, compared to the number of alleged violations, as well as, more generally, the amount and relevance of the work undertaken by the applicant's representatives.

Besides lawyers' fees there exists a wide variety of other costs and expenses, including the cost of telephone calls, photocopies, travel and accommodation expenses, etc. It is necessary to say a word about *experts'* remuneration. Such costs belong to the just satisfaction field if the applicants have incurred them in the domestic legal system in order to prevent a breach of the Convention, or have it rectified or, subsequently, have the breach established by the Court.[27] As regards the costs paid for an expert report produced before the Court, these normally will not be reimbursed, except if the Court itself rules that the report was essential for enabling the applicants to obtain redress for the breach found in the principal judgment.[28]

V. THE PROBLEM OF *RESTITUTIO IN INTEGRUM*

Ideally, any breach of the Convention should be fully redressed by the respondent State, and the most logical way of doing so is to place the applicant in the situation in which he or she would have been had it not been for the violation.

---

[23] See the *Kamasinski v Austria* judgment of 19 Dec 1989, Series A—no 168, s 115.

[24] For legal aid, see the Rules of the Court, rules 91 to 96.

[25] Rule 94 of the Rules or the Court.

[26] See the *Airey v Ireland* (Art 50) judgment of 6 Feb 1981, Series A—no 41, s 13.

[27] See the *Papamichalopoulos and others v Greece* (Art 50) judgment of 31 Oct 1995, Series A—330-B 63, s 52.

[28] Same judgment, same paragraph.

But, as already pointed out, this is not always possible, for either legal or material reasons. If an individual has suffered torture, or inhuman or degrading treatment or punishment in breach of Article 3, nothing will permit the suffering to be erased. If someone has been unlawfully deprived of his or her liberty, nothing will obliterate the unlawful imprisonment. Interestingly, in a case where the applicant had been imprisoned on remand, and the time spent in detention on remand had been deducted from his prison sentence, the Court held that this fact 'must no doubt be taken into consideration in assessing the extent of the damage flowing from the excessive duration of that detention; but it does not in any way thus acquire the character of *restitutio in integrum*, for *no freedom is given in place of the freedom unlawfully taken away*'.[29]

This means that in a great number of cases the Court is 'obliged' to afford just satisfaction to the applicant, because he seldom benefits from '*restitutio in integrum*'.

Notwithstanding that remark, two complementary points must be made:

(i) Many applications end in a *friendly settlement*. Before the former Commission, between 1956 and 1999, about 12 per cent of the cases were settled in this way, and the Convention, as amended by Protocol no 11, encourages the Court to secure friendly settlements whenever possible: the friendly settlement leads to either a decision or a judgment striking the application out of the list of cases.[30] Moreover, most of the friendly settlements are effected on the basis of a financial offer made by the respondent Government and accepted by the applicant. In other words, the applicant feels satisfied that just satisfaction is awarded to him/her, before the adoption of any judgment of the Court obliging the State to pay him/her sums under Article 41 of the Convention. However, under Article 37 s 1, *in fine*, the Court 'shall continue the examination of the application if respect for human rights as defined in the Convention and the protocols thereto so requires', which implies that the Court is entitled to check whether a friendly settlement proposed is both complete and fair. Such supervision is of some relevance, in view of the inequality of bargaining power between the individual and the State.

(ii) Over and above the issue of just satisfaction, the correct execution of a Court judgment often involves *legal steps* to be taken in the domestic system in order to redress the violation(s) found, and to prevent the repetition thereof. The case law shows that the Court does not consider that it has jurisdiction to direct a Government to re-open proceedings which have

---

[29] Quotation from the *Ringeisen v Austria* (Art 50) judgment of 22 June 1972, Series A—no 15, s 21 (author's emphasis).

[30] Arts 37 to 39 of the Convention.

been found to be contrary to Article 6 of the Convention,[31] nor, more generally, to direct a State found to be in breach of the Convention to ensure that similar breaches do not occur in the future, the State concerned being left the choice of the means to be utilised in its domestic legal system for ensuring performance of its obligations under Article 46 § 1 (former Article 53) of the Convention.[32]

This does not prevent States from establishing, on their own motion, mechanisms for re-opening proceedings, for example. Thus, in France, under an Act of 15 June 2000, when, as an outcome of a judgment of the European Court of Human Rights, a person is to be considered as having been sentenced in violation of the Convention, and if, by virtue of its nature or its severity, the breach causes that person a detriment which just satisfaction under Article 41 cannot redress, he or she is allowed to request the re-opening or the criminal proceedings. This new legislation is quite important, the more so because more and more High Contracting Parties to the Convention have committed themselves in that direction. It should be pointed out that this legislation has been provoked by the awareness in France of the unfair situation in which an applicant had been placed in a real case before the Commission and the Committee of Ministers. Also, the reference in the French Act to Article 41 clearly demonstrates that the problems of just satisfaction, *restitutio in integrum* (when it is feasible) and execution of the Court judgments are closely linked.

VI. THE PERIOD ALLOTTED TO THE RESPONDENT STATE FOR PAYMENT

Once the judgment of the Court had been delivered, the sums afforded under Article 41 should be paid to the applicant as quickly as possible, the more so because—in particular due to the need to exhaust domestic remedies and the length of the proceedings before an overloaded Strasbourg Court—a very long time may have elapsed between the act or omission giving rise to the violation, and the judgment affording just satisfaction. It would therefore be unacceptable to leave the State free as regards the date of payment.

In a purely pragmatic way, the Court decided in 1991 that the amount owed to the applicant had to be paid 'within the next *three months*'.[33] Since then, the Court has always prescribed a three-month period with the

---

[31] See, among other authorities, the *Pelladoah v the Netherlands* judgment of 22 Sept 1994, Series A—297–B, 36, s 44.

[32] See, for instance, the *McGoff v Sweden* judgment of 26 Oct 1984, Series A—no 83, 28, s 31.

[33] *Moreira de Azevedo v Portugal* (Art 50) judgment of 28 Aug 1991, Series A—208–C, 34, operative para 1.

indication now that the three months period starts 'from the date on which the judgment becomes final according to Article 44 s 2 of the Convention' (as amended by Protocol no 11), since there is now a possibility in exceptional cases of referral of a case to the Grand Chamber.[34] Fortunately, few States request a referral; otherwise, there could be attempts to utilise Article 43 as a means simply to delay the time of payment of just satisfaction!

VI *BIS*. THE SANCTION IN CASE OF EXPIRY OF THE THREE-MONTHS PERIOD

Soon after the change in the case law of the Court fixing a three-month period, the Court was confronted with the problem of the expiry of the said period. It did not consider it appropriate at first to require any payment of interest.[35] The case-law changed in 1996, with the adoption of a system of default interest, calculated according to the *statutory rate* (*intérêt au taux légal*) applicable in the respondent State at the date of adoption of the judgment of the Court.[36] The interest at that rate shall be payable from the expiry of the three-month period until settlement (presently the three months is computed from the date on which the judgment becomes final— see above). The possibility (practically always utilised by the Court) to 'direct that if settlement is not made within a specified time, interest is to be payable on any sums awarded' is now provided for in the Rules of the Court.[37]

One may point out that, on the one hand, the statutory rate varies greatly from one country to another—and not necessarily according to the difference in the inflation rate—and, on the other hand, that nothing happens (in principle) if a State does not pay the sums it owes even after expiry of the three-month period. It is up to the Committee of Ministers of the Council of Europe, which is in charge of supervising the execution of the final judgments of the Court,[38] to exert the moral and political pressure that normally suffices for the correct—and fast—execution of the judgments. In some (fortunately exceptional) 'sensitive' cases, the influence of that pressure has been found to be rather weak.

[34] Art 43 of the Convention, as amended by Protocol no 11.
[35] See the *Nebbio v Italy* (Art 50) judgment of 26 Feb 1992, Series A—228-A.
[36] See the *A. and others v Denmark* judgment of 8 Feb 1996, 1996–III, 85, s 90 and 86, operative para 3b).
[37] Rule 75, s 3.
[38] Art 46, s 2 of the Convention.

VII. THE BINDING FORCE OF THE RULE AND ITS EXECUTION

It is not necessary to give lengthy explanations about this problem, which is more political than legal.

According to the above-mentioned Article 46 s 1, 'the High Contracting Parties undertake to abide by the final judgment of the Court in any case to which they are parties.' This essential rule is all the more important when a judgment affords the injured party just satisfaction under Article 41, since otherwise the judgment would have a rather symbolic effect. And it is obviously a very important aspect of the *rule of law*, an underlying principle of the whole Convention,[39] that the High Contracting Parties fully execute the judgments.

As already pointed out, as regards execution, the European Convention system relies not on the judicial body—the Court—but on a political body, namely the Committee of Ministers. But the Committee of Ministers, even if its supervisory function is not negligible, and is generally effective, has no real powers of sanctions as such. A country that would seriously and permanently violate human rights could be excluded from the Council of Europe, but such a sanction is so disproportionate that it can hardly be used.[40]

Nevertheless, some resolutions of the Committee create a positive feedback on the case law of the Court. For example, the length of proceedings applications against Italy have given rise to so many resolutions of the Committee of Ministers finding a breach of Article 6 that, finally, the Court considered that accumulation to constitute a *practice* incompatible with the Convention,[41] which disclosed aggravating circumstances; indirectly but necessarily, this practice led the Court to modify its case-law and to hold that a violation of the reasonable-time rule under Article 6 s 1 may also constitute a breach of Article 13 of the Convention.[42] And, of course, a 'double' violation has some impact on the assessment of just satisfaction under Article 41.

Anyhow, limits to the execution of the Court's judgment do exist and, again, are linked with political, rather than purely legal, issues.

---

[39] See the Convention Preamble, last full paragraph.

[40] Greece left the Council of Europe in 1967 in order to avoid possible exclusion, before being reintegrated after 1974 and the fall of the dictatorship. More recently, Belarus lost its status of observer due to the lack of democracy in that State.

[41] See the *Bottazzi v Italy* judgment of 28 July 1999 (and other judgments of the same date), s 22.

[42] See the *Kudla v Poland* judgment of 26 Oct 2000, s 149.

VIII. OTHER ISSUES

Three issues (among others) can be mentioned:

(i) The question of a 'purely symbolic' just satisfaction:

in many cases, the non-pecuniary damage alleged by the applicant is not compensated by the Court in the form of monetary satisfaction. The Court simply says that 'in the particular circumstances, the finding of a violation constitutes in itself adequate just satisfaction for the purposes of Article 41' (former Article 50).[43] The issue is controversial: recently a case was referred to the Grand Chamber, the applicant having criticised the judgment of a Chamber including such reasoning.[44] In many domestic courts, it is not exceptional that a judgment provides the injured party with a symbolic indemnity, but much depends on the sort of damage suffered.

(ii) The differences in the economic and financial situations of the various States:

the Court has constantly tried to elaborate *'common standards'* for all the High Contracting Parties. However, it is true that, among four member States, there are quite important differences as regards economic and social development and the financial possibilities of the central budgeting system.

Some countries complain of the alleged huge amounts of money they are obliged to pay to applicants as a consequence of the application of Article 41. It is obviously difficult to reconcile principles of equality and equity, and no 'natural' solutions can be found. It is, rather, a question of both common sense and flexibility on the part of the Court.

(iii) Just satisfaction and the principle of subsidiarity:

The European Court of Human Rights should be dedicated to the preventing and redressing the most serious violations of the rights and freedoms protected by the Convention. Furthermore, it should more and more become a constitutional instrument in the human rights order of Europe. It is, accordingly, all the more necessary not to overlook the principle of subsidiary: it should be for the States themselves to afford just satisfaction when a breach has occurred (especially in the case of 'minor' violations, such as length of proceedings). There are various possible means to do this. For instance, by setting up *domestic systems* of financial compensation, to be exhausted as a condition of the admissibility of an application to the Court.[45] But States might and should propose more often *friendly settlements* to applicants whose application are very likely to be considered well-founded by the Court.

---

[43] See, among many other authorities, the *Boden v Sweden* judgment of 27 Oct 1987, Series A—125 B, s 41.

[44] See the *Kingsley v the United Kingdom* judgment (not final) of 7 Nov 2000, s 63; the case is pending before the Grand Chamber; a public hearing took place on 7 Nov 2001.

[45] See the 2001 'Pinto Law' in Italy, for length of proceeding cases.

VIII. CONCLUSION

The just satisfaction system under Article 41 of the European Convention on Human Rights is certainly not perfect from at least two points of view. First, it provides a satisfaction that tries to make up for the imperfections of the domestic legal system; and it compensates *ex post facto* violations, which, most of the time, are irreversible. Secondly, the way in which just satisfaction is calculated—in spite of the efforts made by the case law—does not offer full legal certainty. Nevertheless, just satisfaction is the main tool that makes it possible to alleviate the detriment suffered by victims of a breach of the Convention. Imperfect as it may be, it has a large, sometimes considerable, practical importance for persons for whom the European Court is a last recourse and an ultimate hope.

This is the reason why it is probably impossible to replace just satisfaction as a whole, and wiser to improve the conditions under which it is awarded as well as its impact. In sum, the Strasbourg Court has always tried to do so—and should continue its efforts. An internal working party of the Court has prepared a report indicating concrete improvements. Hopefully, they will be adopted and reflected in the future case law.

2. TORT LAW, PUBLIC AUTHORITIES, AND THE HUMAN RIGHTS ACT 1998

TR Hickman*

I. THE HRA AND THE COMMON LAW

A. Effects of the HRA on the Common Law

The purpose of the Human Rights Act 1998 (the HRA) is to enable United Kingdom citizens to enforce before national courts the rights embodied in the European Convention on Human Rights.[1] The primary mechanism by which this aim is achieved is the provision of a cause of action in section 7 (1) (a), which allows victims of Convention violations by public authorities to bring proceedings under the HRA itself. Section 8 provides that a court may grant such relief or remedy, including damages, as it deems just and appropriate to remedy any such unlawful act or omission. Where the violation of a Convention right is relevant in other legal proceedings the HRA, by section 7 (1) (b), allows the unlawfulness to be raised in those proceedings. Importantly, Section 11 of the HRA provides that reliance on Convention rights 'does not restrict' any other right or claim existing under statute or at common law. This paper explores some of the ways that the common law of tort may be modified in light of the HRA.[2] Much attention has already been focused on the extent to which the HRA compels, or may precipitate, the development of the common law in horizontal situations between individuals. This paper instead concentrates on vertical situations where public authorities are the potential tortfeasors and private individuals the claimants.

Drawing a distinction between vertical and horizontal situations indicates that this author does not accept that the HRA has full horizontal

---

* Selwyn College, Cambridge. An earlier version of this paper was presented at the Durham European Law Institute's Conference on Human Rights, which was held on 13–14 July 2001. The author is grateful to Jack Beatson, Duncan Fairgrieve, Ivan Hare, Janet O'Sullivan, Gavin Phillipson, and particularly Tony Weir, for their valuable comments. The author is, of course, solely responsible for the views expressed and any errors remaining.

[1] Rights Brought Home: The Human Rights Bill Cm 3782, 1.18.

[2] The term 'tort' is reserved for common law actions.

application.[3] There is no doubt that the courts, by virtue of being included in the definition of public authorities in section 6 (1), would themselves be acting unlawfully if they acted incompatibly with a Convention right.[4] They may do so in the context of granting remedies[5] or, in limited situations, where common law doctrine *conflicts* with (not merely being *different* from) individuals' Convention rights. Since the obligation under section 6 (1) is negative[6] the common law need not *secure* individual rights *unless* securing a Convention right by provision of a civil remedy is itself a positive requirement of an article of the Convention by which public authorities are bound.[7] The existence of a cause of action under the HRA, however, largely negates any requirement to develop the common law by reference to such positive obligations in vertical situations.[8] This is reinforced by the deliberate omission from the HRA of Article 13 of the European Convention, which obliges states to ensure that citizens have an effective remedy before a national authority. It was omitted because sections 7 and 8 of the HRA were deemed in themselves to satisfy this requirement.[9]

Outside these limits Convention rights should still inform the develop-

---

[3] Cf Sir William Wade, 'Horizons of Horizontality' (2000) 116 *LQR* 217, 'Human Rights and the Judiciary' [1998] EHRLR 520 and 'The United Kingdom's Bill of Rights' in Cambridge Centre for Public Law, Constitutional Reform in the United Kingdom: principles and practice (Oxford: Hart Publishing, 1998).

[4] HRA s 6 (3) (a). Beyond this statement there is little consensus amongst commentators: eg (in addition to the articles by Wade above n 3). M Hunt 'The Horizontal Effect of the Human Rights Act' [1998] PL 423; A Lester and D Pannick, *Human Rights Law and Practice* (London: Butterworths, 1999), 31–2 and 'The Impact of the Human Rights Act on Private Law: the Knight's Move' (2000) 116 *LQR* 380; R Buxton, 'The Human Rights Act and Private Law' (2000) 116 *LQR* 48; G Phillipson, 'The Human Rights Act, 'Horizontal Effect' and the Common Law: a Bang or a Whimper?' [1999] 62 MLR 824; R Clayton and H Tomlinson, *The Law of Human Rights* (Oxford: Clarendon Press, 2000), 5.74–5.99 (which reviews much of the material), and for an analysis in the light of recent developments see I Hare, 'Verticality Challenged: Private Parties, Privacy and the Human Rights Act' [2001] EHRLR 508.

[5] In relation to care orders under the Children Act 1989 see *Re W and B*; *Re W (Care Plan)* [2001] 2 FLR 582 (CA).

[6] It is unlawful for a public authority to act in a way that is *incompatible* with a Convention right.

[7] Courts cannot be under general positive obligations to ensure that the common law protects all Convention rights between individuals, since to do so would be to create full horizontality: 'the mere fact that the court must adjudicate in a dispute where one private individual claims that another is acting in breach of the rights and freedoms of the Convention does not in and of itself place the court under a duty to find in favour of the litigant who claims his rights are being violated' (Clayton and Tomlinson, above n 4 at 5.97). Although of course the court *may* so develop the common law. Finding that such a positive obligation exists will be relatively rare, the article most likely to be breached in such cases is Art 13 which does not bind English courts. See the discussion of *Z v United Kingdom* below at n 105. The problems encountered in implying positive obligations to provide common law causes of action are discussed in the text to nn 190–7.

[8] Subject to the points made below in the text to nn 190–7.

[9] See S Grosz, J Beatson, and P Duffy, *The 1998 Act and the European Convention* (London: Sweet & Maxwell, 2000), 1-06, 1-07, C13-01–C13-13.

ment of common law doctrine. The courts should interpret the law from the new constitutional perspective represented by the HRA. It would be remiss for the courts to view the Act's presence as restricting cross-fertilisation between the European Convention and the common law; in Beatson's words this would evince an unjustified 'oil and water' approach to the relationship between statute and the common law.[10] However, if one is hoping for complete coherency between tort law and the HRA, in terms of the two sources of law becoming entirely 'mutually supporting', one is likely to be disappointed. If courts drive too hard at attempting to create such a strong form of coherency they risk creating a 'self-contradictory' or 'disjointed' system; a system which fails to meet even weak standards of coherency.[11] It is probably inevitable that the law will fall between these two positions. Therefore, although this paper analyses some of the ways that the law of tort should develop symbiotically with Convention rights, despite the presence of a separate cause of action under the HRA, it will also highlight central tensions and problems that may arise if the symbiosis is pushed too far. In particular it will be argued that tensions and problems will occur on the interface between the law of negligence and the HRA.

B. Rights and Duties

The common law has traditionally preferred to define unlawfulness by reference to *duties*, and not *rights*.[12] The HRA has, however, imported a rights-based jurisprudence into English law and this is likely to form the central tension between common law jurisprudence and Convention jurisprudence, and to pose the greatest problems for cross-fertilisation between the two.[13] This distinction, between obligations based upon rights

---

[10] Beatson, 'Has the Common Law a Future?' (1997) 56 *CLJ* 291 and 'The Role of Statute in the Development of Common Law Doctrine' (2001) 117 *LQR* 247. Lord Hobhouse recognised in *R v Governor of Brockhill Prison, ex p Evans (No 2)* [2000] 3 WLR 843, 867 that statutes influence common law development. For New Zealand see *South Pacific Manufacturing Co Ltd v New Zealand Security Consultants and Investigations Ltd* [1992] 2 NZLR 282, 292 per Cooke P and for Australia see *Brodie v Singleton Shire Council* [2001] 180 ALR 145, paras. 31–2 per Gleeson CJ Cf R Dworkin, *Taking Rights Seriously*, 9th impression (London: Duckworth, 2000), 107–18.

[11] These two forms of coherency are identified and expounded in J Raz, *Ethics in the Public Domain: Essays in the Morality of Law and Politics* (Oxford: Clarendon Press, 1994), 264–5.

[12] In tort see PH Winfield, 'Duty in Tortious Negligence' (1934) 34 *Col LR* 41. German tort law by contrast is rights orientated: see BS Markesinis, *The German Law of Obligations, Volume II. The Law of Torts A: Comparative Introduction*, 3rd edn (Oxford: Clarendon Press, 1997). The common law traditionally adopted the same approach in administrative law: in 1997 Sedley J stated that '[p]ublic law is not at base about rights . . . it is about wrongs—that is to say misuses of public power' (*R v Somerset County Council, ex p Dixon* [1997] COD 323, 331).

[13] Cf T Weir, *A Casebook on Tort*, 9th edn (London: Sweet & Maxwell, 2000) 7 and JA Weir, 'Human Rights and Damages' (2001) 40 *Washburn LJ* 413, 419-221.

and those based upon duties, is drawn purely at the doctrinal level. It does not challenge the strict correlativity of claim-rights and duties;[14] nor the fact that all legally protected interests are in one sense 'rights.' The common law's affinity for duty-based reasoning does, however, have important implications. It focuses attention on the putative wrongdoer not on the victim, and it follows from this that the notion of *reasonable conduct* and *harm caused* often become central. This is so with negligence, which is easily the dominant tort at the present time.

Negligence liability has been the subject of a powerful critique by Epstein. For Epstein tort law should be exclusively concerned with protecting rights, and the notion of reasonableness puts rights at the whim of collective goals.[15] This paper will not engage with Epstein's critique, instead it will analyse the relationship *between* negligence principles and rights-based norms. The term 'right', a notoriously over-worked word,[16] will be used in a strong sense: to describe those fundamental interests which the law regards as unlawfully interfered with without the victim having to prove that the interference was unreasonable, and even though the interference caused no additional harm. It is simply enough that there has been an interference. No one of course suggests that rights, even most human rights, are absolute. It is possible to justify interferences with most of them. The difference in perspective is nonetheless crucially important. If focus is put on a right, interferences with the right are presumed unlawful and it is up to the defendant to justify their actions.[17]

The jurisprudence of the ECtHR is focused upon rights in this sense. An applicant who claims that their rights have been violated generally need not prove either unreasonable conduct or harm.[18] In *Soering v United*

---

[14] W Cook (ed), WN Hohfeld, *Fundamental Legal Conceptions as Applied in Judicial Reasoning* (New Haven, Connecticut: Yale University Press, 1923), (claims are correlative with duties).

[15] *A Theory of Strict Liability: Towards a Reformulation of Tort Law* (San Francisco: Cato Institute, 1980). Others, particularly Weinrib and Wright, have sought to justify negligence law by reference to Kantian Right: EJ Weinrib, *The Idea of Private Law* (Cambridge, MA: Harvard University Press, 1995); RW Wright, 'Right, Justice and Tort Law' and 'The Standards of Care in Negligence Law', in D.G. Owen (ed), *Philosophical Foundations of Tort Law* (Oxford: Clarendon Press, 1995); Wright, 'Principled Adjudication: Tort Law and Beyond' (1999) 7 *Cant. LR* 265. Cf Dworkin's attempts to square negligence with his rights-centred legal theory: *Law's Empire* (London: Fontana, 1987), ch 8 and *Taking Rights Seriously* above n 10, esp 294–330.

[16] 'The word 'rights' is a highly confusing word which leads to a great deal of trouble if it is used loosely, particularly when it is used loosely in a court of law' per Ormrod LJ *A v C* [1985] 6 FLR 445, 455

[17] These differences represent the differences between trespass and case (see J Fleming, *The Law of Torts*, 9th edn (Sydney: LBC Information Services, 1998), 22) combined with their later development (see *Fowler v Lanning* [1959] 1 QB 426; *Letang v Cooper* [1965] 1 QB 325).

[18] Harm may have to be proved to recover damages, although this is not always the case: eg *Halford v United Kingdom* (1997) 24 EHRR 523. How far it is suitable to transpose common law rules on recovery, particularly those from the law of negligence, is beyond the

Kingdom, which concerned Article 3, the Court stated that 'inherent in the whole of the Convention is a search for a fair balance between the demands of the general interest of community and the requirements of the protection of the individual's fundamental rights'.[19] This balance is, however, primarily struck at the justification stage. At this stage the ECtHR has expressly stated that reasonableness will be insufficient to justify most interferences with rights; the interference must be justified by reference to legitimacy and necessity. The court has said, from its earliest jurisprudence, that necessity does not have 'the flexibility of such expressions as . . . "useful", "reasonable" or "desirable"'.[20] In establishing whether the interference is necessary to satisfy a legitimate aim the ECtHR demands that the act satisfy a 'pressing social need' and be 'proportionate' to the aim pursued.

C. Rights-based and Duty-based Torts

Despite the common law's affinity for duty-based reasoning English tort law draws a distinction between actions which focus on breach of duty by the putative tortfeasor and those actions which focus on the rights of the claimant.[21] Negligence clearly falls into the former category whereas torts such as trespass and false imprisonment fall into the latter. The House of Lords in *Stubbings v Webb* expressly recognised the different nature of rights-based and duty-based actions. Lord Griffiths asked: '[i]f I invite a lady to my house one would naturally think of a duty to take care that the house was safe but would one really be thinking of a duty not to rape her?'[22] He thought not. Their Lordships held that trespass to the person was, unlike negligence, not an action for breach of duty. Rights-based torts such as trespass are actionable *per se* and claimants do not have to prove that the defendant's conduct was unreasonable. Trespass, for example, protects direct and deliberate invasions of a person's corporeal integrity, his land, and the integrity of his things. A claimant asserts that his rights have been invaded and waits to see if the invader can justify his actions.

---

scope of this paper. In the opinion of the Law Commission such common law rules could be fairly straightforwardly transposed: *Damages Under the Human Rights Act 1998* (Law Com No 266, 2000).

[19] (1989) 11 EHRR 439, para 89.

[20] *Handyside v United Kingdom* (1976) 1 EHRR 737, para 48; *Silver v United Kingdom* (1983) 5 EHRR 347, para 97; *Young, James and Webster v United Kingdom* (1981) 4 EHRR 153, para 59. The ECtHR has on occasion spoken of a 'reasonable relationship of proportionality', eg *Osman v United Kingdom* (1998) 29 EHRR 245, para 147.

[21] See Winfield above n 12. Though they do not focus on abstract rights in the same manner as the Convention. Nor is there a clear line. Nuisance, eg, is at least legislatively associated with breach of duty: Limitation Act 1980, s 11. Cf n 17 above.

[22] [1993] 1 All ER 322, 329

Negligence is, however, very different: '[l]iability in negligence depends on the duty of care to be observed by the defendant; it does not depend on the 'rights' of the plaintiff, other than the plaintiff's right not to be negligently injured.'[23]

To be sure, the common law's rights-based actions are slimmer, less clearly defined, and less comprehensive than the broad catalogue of rights found in the Convention. However, where they do apply they do much the same job;[24] or at least they should do. Weir has lamented how trespass, and other strict liability torts, have been diluted with negligence principles. He says that if 'the plaintiff's rights have been invaded it cannot be relevant that he is none the worse for the experience, nor that it was not the defendant's fault that he invaded them'.[25] The merging of negligence principles with nuisance, which has a function in protecting rights, has been documented for many years.[26]

D. *Approaching the Development of the Common Law*

Despite the introduction of the HRA, English courts are proving reluctant to consider claims directly under the HRA and remarkably adroit at finding that the common law is either sufficiently protective, or sufficiently flexible, to protect rights. Sedley LJ encapsulated the approach of the common law courts when he stated in *Douglas v Hello!* that the common law has a perennial need 'to appear not to be doing anything for the first time'.[27] The adaptation of the common law even runs to changing breaches of duties into violations of rights. This trend has been most clearly manifested in administrative law where the common law has developed a rights-orien-

---

[23] *Sidaway v Governors of Bethlam Royal Hospital* [1984] 1 QB 493, 519–20 per Browne-Wilkinson LJ.

[24] For two different analyses of the relationship between tort law and human rights: Lord Bingham, 'Tort and Human Rights' and Sir Anthony Mason, 'Human Rights and the Law of Torts' both in P Cane and J Stapleton (eds), *The Law of Obligations, Essays in Celebration of John Fleming* (Oxford: Clarendon Press, 1998).

[25] T Weir, 'The Staggering March of Negligence', in Cane and Stapleton (eds), above n 24, 110.

[26] *Sedleigh-Denfield v O'Callaghan* [1940] 3 All ER 349; *Goldman v Hargrave* [1967] 1 AC 645; *Smith v Littlewoods Organization Ltd* [1987] AC 241. See for an attempt to reconceptualise the foundations of nuisance: C Gearty, 'The Place of Private Nuisance in a Modern Law of Torts' (1989) 48 *CLJ* 214. Buckley argues that the merger has been overstated: *The Law of Nuisance*, 2nd edn (London: Butterworths, 1996), 20–2. Reasonableness does have a collateral role in rights based torts. For example, if one withdraws consent from a licensee he does not immediately become a trespasser but has a reasonable time to get off the land; or one may have a right only to a reasonable amount, say, of light. For a succinct explanation of the principle of 'reasonable user' see BS Markesinis and SF Deakin, *Tort Law* (Oxford: Clarendon Press, 1999), 422. On the 'reasonable' use of force see *A v United Kingdom* (1998) 27 EHRR 611.

[27] *Douglas v Hello!* [2001] 2 WLR 992, para 111.

tated jurisprudence which mirrors the Convention.[28] At least in some areas, the English courts have rejected a duty-based approach to common law review in which the *Wednesbury* test of reasonableness was central.[29] The HRA's effects on private law, while less immediate, may nonetheless be pronounced. Rights-based tools come more readily to hand in private law and may be the preferred implements for remedying violations of human rights where they can be utilised. Moreover, since these torts protect the *unlawful* interference with protected interests, and section 6(1) of the HRA now makes it unlawful for public authorities to act incompatibly with Convention rights, torts such as trespass will be employed to remedy such violations where they also constitute interferences with an interest protected by the law of tort. In part III we shall explore the ways in which negligence, although not a rights-based action, can be used to protect rights and, importantly, how far it should be so used.

As well as the doctrinal malleability and the accommodating methodology of the common law, there may also be real advantages for claimants in framing an action in the common law rather than under the HRA. While it may be thought more satisfactory in principle that victims of rights violations should be entitled to damages as of right, even if nominal, it is also possible that damages under the HRA will also be 'on the low side by comparison to tortious awards'.[30] The English courts are also prepared to

---

[28] *R (Daly) v Secretary of State for the Home Department* [2001] 2 WLR 1622; Cf *In re Medicaments and Related Classes of Goods (No 2)* [2001] 1 WLR 700. Compare the words of Sedley J, above n 12. English courts began to develop administrative law by reference to the European Convention well before the HRA (see eg *Wheeler v Leicester County Council* [1985] AC 1054; *R v Secretary of State for the Home Department, ex parte Simms* [1999] 3 WLR 328; *R v Secretary of State for the Home Department, ex parte McQuillan* [1994] 4 All ER 400; *R v Secretary of State for the Home Department, ex parte Pierson* [1998] AC 539; and generally M Hunt, *Using Human Rights Law in English Courts* (Oxford: Hart Publishing, 1997), 162–262). There is some pedigree for this rights orientated approach to review. In *Chester v Bateson* [1920] KB 829 the court was prepared to hold that a regulation prohibiting proceedings for the ejectment of munitions workers was 'so grave an infringement of the rights of subjects' that it could not be lawful (per Darling J, 834). Avory J (in an approach not fully rediscovered until *Daly*, or at least *Simms*) said that although the purpose was legitimate the methods employed could not be justified (835–6).

[29] See *Daly's* case and the comments of Lord Slynn in *R (Alconbury Developments Ltd) v Secretary of State for the Environment, Transport and the Regions* [2001] 2 WLR 1389, para 51. To some extent the opposite approach can be seen in the area of EU law, where violations of rights are disguised as breaches of duty: see *Bourgoin SA v Ministry of Agriculture, Fisheries and Food* [1986] QB 716; *Garden Cottage Foods Ltd v Milk Marketing Board* [1984] AC 130; *R v Secretary of State for Transport, ex parte. Factortame (No 5)* [1999] 3 WLR 1062; *R v Secretary of State for Transport, ex parte Factortame (No 7)* [2001] 1 WLR 942; and the discussion in T Weir, *A Casebook on Tort*, 8th edn (London, Sweet & Maxwell, 1996), 213, and 'Human Rights and Damages', above n 13 at 420–1. Cf M Hoskins, 'Rebirth of the Innominate Tort?', in J Beatson and T Tridimas (eds), *New Directions in European Public Law* (Oxford: Hart Publishing, 1998).

[30] Lord Woolf, 'The Human Rights Act 1998 and Remedies', in M Andenas and D Fairgrieve (eds), *Judicial Review, in International Perspective: Volume II* (The Hague: Kluwer Law International, 2000), ch 30, 434. Cf *C v Flintshire County Council* [2001] 2 FLR 33.

award punitive damages for violations of common law rights by the state, something which the ECtHR has expressly refused to do.[31] If English courts follow the ECtHR when determining awards under section 8 of the HRA there would be an incentive for litigants to frame their actions in the common law.[32] Lord Nicholls has recently acknowledged that punitive damages have 'played a significant role in buttressing civil liberties, in claims for false imprisonment and wrongful arrest' and they retain an important role in English tort law.[33] Trial by jury is also available for some actions brought at common law, but is not under the HRA.[34]

The time limits for common law actions are also much longer than under the HRA. Section 7 (5) of the Act states that proceedings brought under section 7(1) (a) must be brought within one year of the date on which the action first accrued. There is provision for the extension of time if it would be 'equitable having regard to all the circumstances'.[35] As yet there is no indication as to how readily this will be allowed. Claims in tort by comparison have much longer time limits. Rights-based torts, for example, can be brought up to six years after the action accrues.[36] For negligence actions time does not even begin to run if the victim is a minor,[37] and in any claim relating to personal injury the clock does not start until the injuries are known to have been caused by the defendant's conduct.[38]

Furthermore, since the common law is developing private causes of action in horizontal situations to reflect the value of human rights it would be odd if the courts preferred to apply section 7 directly when the claim was vertical if the common law could do the job equally well, if not better.[39] While the HRA does not require that all existing remedial channels be

---

[31] Law Com, above n 18, 3.47. Although the courts clearly could go beyond ECtHR jurisprudence (the restriction that such damages could only be awarded in cases in which awards had been made prior to *Rookes v Barnard* [1964] AC 1129 having been removed by the House of Lords: *Kuddus v Chief Constable of Leicestershire Constabulary* [2001] 2 WLR. 1789) and award punitive damages under the HRA (cf *Crossman v R* (1984) 9 DLR (4th) 588), they are unlikely to do so since it goes beyond *restitutio in integrum*.

[32] For a discussion suggesting that there may not be much advantage here see D Fairgrieve, 'The Human Rights Act 1998, Damages and Tort Law' [2001] *PL* 695, 709–10.

[33] *Kuddus v Chief Constable of Leicestershire Constabulary*, para 63, per Lord Nicholls; Cf para 79 per Lord Hutton. Lord Scott thought that the HRA reduced the need for punitive damages (para 110), and see Lord Mackay, para 36. Lord Scott doubted whether such damages should be awarded where liability is vicarious, but Lord Hutton disagreed.

[34] False imprisonment, libel, slander, and malicious prosecution: Supreme Court Act 1981 s 69. On which see: *Beta Construction v Channel Four Television Co. Ltd* [1990] 1 WLR 1042; *Ward v Chief Constable of West Midlands Police* [1997] TLR 660; *Racz v Home Office* [1994] 2 AC 45.

[35] Section 7 (5) (b)

[36] Limitation Act 1980 s 2. See *Stubbings v Webb*.

[37] Limitation Act 1980 ss 28, 38(2). If the claim is for personal injuries the limitation period is adjusted to 3 years (s28(6))

[38] Sections 11(4)(b), 14. The limitation period is then 3 years.

[39] *Douglas v Hello!* [2001] 2 WLR 992, see Hare above n 4.

exhausted, the cause of action under the Act will probably have no more than a residual role, to fill gaps which exist in, and cannot be filled by, the common law. Where the common law can provided redress it will not be 'necessary' for the courts to award damages under the HRA.[40] Certainly with regard to rights-based torts this seems particularly appropriate. English courts,[41] and English commentators,[42] have long recognised the centrality of tort law's role in vindicating individual rights. Despite the HRA (or rather, insofar as rights-based torts will be re-invigorated, *because* of it) tort law will surely retain this central role.[43] We will now turn to look at some of the ways that the law of tort could be, and should be, influenced by the Convention and the HRA. No attempt will be made to map all the possible effects of the HRA on tort doctrine; rather the emphasis will be on highlighting areas of convergence, central tensions, and future problems.

II. THE HRA AND TORTS THAT PROTECT RIGHTS

A. Past Weaknesses in Rights-based Torts

The effect of the HRA will no doubt be felt on the law of trespass. This is well illustrated by *McLeod*[44] where the Court of Appeal applied the much criticised decision of *Thomas v Sawkins* in the context of a person's home. In that case it was held, in the context of a public meetong, that the police had powers to enter and remain on private premises, against the will of the owners, if there were reasonable grounds to apprehend a breach of the peace.[45] *McLeod* is a good illustration of the way that a focus on the

---

[40] Section 8(3). See, Beatson, and Duffy, above n 9 at 6–20. Other jurisdictions have likewise viewed constitutional provisions as secondary to established common law torts: see, eg, *Simpson v A-G* [1994] 3 NZLR 667 (but see the comments of Cooke P at 678) and *Manga v A-G* [2000] 2 NZLR 65 where recovery allowed for false imprisonment and a declaration was made to emphasise the breach of a constitutional right. Other jurisdictions have taken different approaches: ML Pilkington, 'Damages as a Remedy for Infringement of the Canadian Charter of Rights and Freedoms' (1984) *Can. Bar Rev* 517, 537

[41] *Entick v Carrington* (1765) 19 St Tr 1029, 2 Wils KB 275; *Cooper v Wandsworth Board of Works* (1863) 14 CBNS 110.

[42] AV Dicey, *An Introduction to the Study of the Law of the Constitution* 8th edn (London: Macmillan, 1915).

[43] Cf *Clerk and Lindsell On Torts*, 18th edn (London: Sweet & Maxwell, 2000), 1–24.

[44] *McLeod v Commissioner of Police for the Metropolis* [1994] 4 All ER 553. Cf *McGowan v Chief Constable of Kingston Upon Hull* [1968] *Crim LR* 34; *R v Howell* [1982] QB 416, which was not cited in *McLeod*.

[45] [1953] 2 KB 249. For criticism: AL Goodhart, '*Thomas v Sawkins*: A Constitutional Innovation' (1936) 6 *CLJ* 22, 'At first sight it may seem *unreasonable* to say that a police officer cannot take steps to prevent an act which, when committed, becomes a punishable offence. But it is on this distinction between prevention and punishment that freedom of speech, freedom of public meeting, and freedom of the press are founded [citing AV Dicey. My emphasis]' (at 30); ECS Wade, 'Police Powers and Public Meetings' (1936) 6 *CLJ* 175; H Street, *Freedom,*

defendant's conduct has weakened rights-based torts such as trespass. The claimant's ex-husband, Mr McLeod, turned up at his old home to collect his belongings. He wrongly believed that his ex-wife had agreed to this, when in fact she had agreed to nothing of the sort. When he arrived, accompanied by a couple of policemen, Mr McLeod found only his frail ex-mother-in-law at home. The policemen had been told, wrongly, that the removal of the chattels was pursuant to a court order, but they were not shown the court order, nor did they ask to see it. Confronted by the strong arm of the law, the ex-mother-in-law understandably allowed the belongings to be removed.[46] In later proceedings Mr McLeod was found to have been a trespasser, but the policemen were not. Neil LJ said they 'were reasonable in coming to the conclusion that there was a danger [of an imminent breach of the peace]', and only had only to observe a duty to 'take great care'.[47] The mother-in-law herself was not felt to be threatening a breach of the peace (in fact she was taken to hospital a few hours later from the shock of the intrusion), but the absent daughter, according to the Court of Appeal, was.[48]

The ECtHR rightly held that the policemen had violated Article 8 of the Convention since their conduct could not justify the interference with the right to private and family life.[49] Their actions, while pursuing a legitimate aim (preventing a breach of the peace), had not been proportionate. They had not acted impartially and should have taken steps to ensure that the actions of Mr McLeod were indeed pursuant to a court order. In any case, there was no threat of disorder from the ex-mother-in-law who was still recovering from a stroke. The Court of Appeal ought to have asked more rigorous questions about whether the breach of the right was justified, and not simply looked at whether the conduct of the policemen was reasonable.[50] If *McLeod* were reconsidered today, the common law itself would surely be said to protect the claimant's rights and not the reasonable policemen.

Where people are arrested and interned for offences that do not exist (for example a void(ed) bye-law) one might think it could be safely asserted that the common law would protect the individual's rights. Unfortunately things

---

the *Individual and the Law* (Harmondsworth: Penguin, 1982), 49–50; D Feldman, *The Law Relating to Entry, Search and Seizure* (London: Butterworths, 1986), 324–5; and see the interpretation in D Feldman, *Civil Liberties and Human Rights in England and Wales* (Oxford: Clarendon Press, 1993), 832–4.

[46] See *Bievens v Six Unknown Federal Narcotics Agents* (1971) 403 US 388, 394 per Brennan J.

[47] *McLeod v Commissioner of Police for the Metropolis* [1994] 4 All ER 553, 560.

[48] Quite how the breach could be described as imminent is not made clear. Cf *Foulkes v Chief Constable of Mersyside Police* [1998] TLR 402.

[49] *McLeod v United Kingdom* (1999) 27 EHRR 493.

[50] In *McGowan v Chief Constable of Kingston Upon Hull* [1968] Crim LR 34 the court recognised that justification was the key, but was not particularly careful to scrutinise the need for the invasion.

are not so clear. In the infamous case of *Percy v Hall Ministry of Defence* officials were sued by protesters who were arrested for breach of a bye-law subsequently held invalid.[51] The claims for wrongful arrest and false imprisonment were rejected. The court said that since the bye-laws had not been voided when the arrests were made the officers had been acting reasonably. The case has been criticised both for failing to recognise that unlawful bye-laws should be considered void ab initio,[52] as well as for failing to recognise that the blameworthiness of the defendants' conduct 'is an immaterial consideration when the plaintiffs' liberty is in issue'.[53] The Court strained both tort law and administrative law to prevent the protesters from recovering. Had the court focused instead on the rights of the protesters the correct result would have been achieved and clarity in the law would have been preserved.

Although *Percy* has never been overruled, the courts now accept that an offence which has been unlawfully created should be treated as void and that it does not have any interim validity before it is challenged in the courts.[54] Instead they look to the governing statute to decide whether there can nonetheless be a valid prosecution, or whether a collateral action in private law can be sustained. In *Boddington* the House of Lords accepted that the invalidity of an offence could be raised collaterally as a defence to a prosecution, where the invalid norm was of general application. In contrast in *R v Wicks*[55] the defendant was prosecuted for non-compliance with an enforcement notice, but the governing statute was said to validate the prosecution, notwithstanding that the enforcement notice was itself unlawful and void. Thus the rights of individuals are bound-up in the process of statutory interpretation (which is itself subject to the obligation in section 3 HRA to read statutes compatibly, so far as possible, with Convention rights). This point needs to be openly recognised in the courts, since the process of interpretation itself is frequently unprincipled and provides an opportunity to disguise policy judgments beneath 'legislative intentions'. [56]

---

[51] [1996] 4 All ER 523.

[52] C Forsyth, '"The Metaphysics of Nullity" Invalidity, Conceptual Reasoning and the Rule of Law', in C Forsyth and I Hare (eds), *The Golden Metwand and the Crooked Cord: Essays on Public Law in Honour of Sir William Wade QC* (Oxford: Clarendon Press, 1998), 152 n 45.

[53] Weir, above n 25 at 110. The MOD officers were acting in the pursuance of their duties, and had made no mistake of law since the bye-laws appeared valid at the time.

[54] *Boddington v British Transport Police* [1999] 2 AC 143.   [55] [1998] AC 92.

[56] C Emery, 'The Vires Defence: "Ultra Vires" as a Defence to Criminal or Civil Proceedings' (1992) 51 *CLJ* 308, 333–4, notes the relevance of Convention rights to this question. In *Boddington* Lord Irvine gave some suggestions on how to balance the principles of liberty and certainty within the process interpretation at 161–2. The decision itself emphasised the fact that it was 'important for the maintenance of the rule of law and the preservation of liberty that individuals affected by legal measures . . . should have a fair opportunity to vindicate their rights'.

The House of Lords decision of *Wills v Bowley* is a good illustration of problems which are encountered when rights rest on the interpretation of statutes.[57] The issue in the case was whether a policeman had power to arrest a person who he wrongly, but reasonably, believed to be committing an offence. Their Lordships construed the governing statute in two different ways. It was construed in one way by Lords Bridge, Wilberforce, and Russell: to protect a reasonable policeman. It was construed the opposite way by Lord Elwyn-Jones and Lord Lowry: to protect the liberty of the citizen. In *Wills* the issue was not of course that the offence was non-existent in law, it just had not actually been committed. Lord Lowry acknowledged that the case disclosed a conflict between two public policy interests: individual freedom and public order.[58] Unfortunately the majority, in gliding over this issue, came to the wrong conclusion.

Article 5 of the Convention, which protects the liberty and security of the person, is clearly relevant in this context.[59] What is 'lawful' is, however, primarily a matter for domestic law to determine.[60] Nonetheless, by placing the claimant's rights at the centre of the determination and not the blameworthiness of the alleged tortfeasor's conduct, courts should avoid the kind of results reached in *Percy* and *Wills*.

---

[57] [1982] 2 All ER 654.   [58] Ibid, 658.

[59] (1) Everyone has the right to liberty and security of person. No one shall be deprived of his liberty save in the following cases and in accordance with a procedure prescribed by law:
(a) the lawful detention of a person after conviction by a competent court;
(b) the lawful arrest or detention of a person for non-compliance with the lawful order of a court or in order to secure the fulfilment of any obligation prescribed by law;
(c) the lawful arrest or detention of a person effected for the purpose of brining him before the competent legal authority on reasonable suspicion of having committed an offence or when it is reasonably considered necessary to prevent his committing an offence or fleeing after having done so; . . .
The language of reasonableness pervades sub-section (c). This does not detract from the arguments made in the text. First, the subsections are, of course, exceptions to the right itself and are strictly construed (*Quinn v France* (1996) 21 EHRR 529). Secondly, although it is likely that that the ECtHR would not consider *Percy* or *Wills* to violate Article 5 (1) (c) because the inspectors had a reasonable suspicion (*Fox, Campbell and Hartley v United Kingdom* (1990) 13 EHRR 157; *Murray v United Kingdom* (1994) 19 EHRR 193) it may be that, in terms of tort law, reasonable suspicion could be considered necessary but not sufficient to establish a defence to a tort. Of course it is not sufficient in the sense that the action must also be lawful (on which see below note 60). Thirdly, although not all constitutional provisions illustrate the dichotomy which has been drawn between rights and reasonableness (see, eg, the IV Amendment to the US Constitution), the purpose of this paper is to emphasise central tensions and convergences between common law and Convention rights, rather than map all the intricacies of these two systems, let alone others. Still less does it purport to engage with general jurisprudential enquires into the nature of rights themselves (on which see MH Kramer, NE Simmonds, and H Steiner, *A Debate Over Rights: Philosophical Inquiries* (Oxford: Clarendon Press, 1998)).

[60] *Herczegfalvy v Austria* (1993) 15 EHRR 437, para 63; *Kemmache v France (No 3)* (1995) 19 EHRR 349, para 42. DJ Harris, M O'Boyle, and C Warbrick, *Law of The European Convention on Human Rights* (London: Butterworths, 1995), 105–7, 112–15, and 119.

B. The Convergence of Convention Rights and Rights-based Torts

The issue of unlawful state detention came before the House of Lords in 2000 (but before the HRA was brought into force) and their Lordships built upon the foundations which they had laid in *Boddington*.[61] In the *Brockhill Prison* case the applicant sued for 59 days of false imprisonment. When calculating the provisional release date the prison governor, who was defending the action, had acted in accordance with settled case law. In judicial review proceedings this settled case law was held to be wrong and the applicant was released immediately, although 59 days later than she should have been. Lord Slynn stated the following:

> If the claim is looked at from the governor's point of view liability seems unreasonable; what more could he have done? If looked at from the applicant's point of view she was, it is accepted, kept in prison unlawfully for 59 days and should be compensated. Which is to prevail?[62]

Which is to prevail? The claimant's rights or the reasonableness of the defendant's conduct? The House of Lords unanimously came down on the side of rights. The detention was unlawful and could not be justified. Lord Slynn emphasised that the result could only be determined by weighing competing principles: liberty of citizen against legal certainty of officials.[63] Lord Hope stated that it 'is no answer to a claim based on a tort of strict liability to say that the governor took reasonable care or that he acted in good faith . . .'.[64]

Their Lordships refused to read a requirement of unreasonable conduct into the tort of false imprisonment, nor did they attempt to attribute any presumptive validity to the original law. Since the detention was therefore categorised as unlawful under domestic law,[65] the claimant would have had a claim for violation of Article 5 of the Convention had the HRA been in force, and their Lordships were not prepared to countenance a different result under the common law. Lord Steyn stated that not only was there

---

[61] Cf the Court of Appeal's highly questionable decision in *Mann Singh Shingara v Secretary of State for the Home Department* [1999] Imm AR 257 where a claim for false imprisonment was thrown out, and *Boddington* distinguished.

[62] *R v Governor of Brockhill Prison, ex parte Evans (No. 2)* [2000] 3 WLR 843, 846

[63] Ibid, 848 'It is a matter of judgment how the weight of the competing principles in the present case should be assessed . . . both sides assert that the justice of the case—to the wrongly detained woman and to the governor in doing his job in accordance with the law—favour their particular interpretation.'

[64] Ibid, 854

[65] Above n 60. Some ECtHR jurisprudence suggests that it would not violate Art 5 for lawfulness to be defined to include acts in accordance with powers subsequently set-aside: *Sunday Times v United Kingdom* (1979) 40 D & R 42, paras 90–1; *Benham v United Kingdom* (1996) 22 EHRR 293, para 42. *Tsirlis and Kouloumpas v Greece* (1997) 25 EHRR 198, para 58.

common law support for the result (in Australia)[66] but the provisions of Article 5 'rule out a defence that the governor acted in accordance with the law as it was then understood at that time', and 'Article 5 reinforces the view which I have accepted.'[67] Lord Hope held that the defence of justification failed 'on common law grounds', but went on to show that he would have reached the same result by reference to the Convention.[68] Lord Hobhouse reconciled English authorities with the Convention and went on to stress the common law's 'ability to develop and evolve'.[69] The case sits in marked contrast to cases such as *Percy*, and this is attributable to the fact that their Lordships approached the case from the perspective of the claimant's rights. *Percy* was distinguished, with respect, on the unconvincing basis that it concerned a bye-law.[70]

Fleming has written that 'the negligence concept in little more than a century completely transformed the basis of tort liability. The measure of its success is attested by the fact that negligence litigation today overwhelmingly occupies the attention of the courts, and has proved so pervasive as to transform even the erstwhile strict liability of trespass.'[71] It has been suggested that the European Convention has proved, in some areas, to be a welcome catalyst for the curbing of this trend, that is, the 'Staggering March of Negligence'.[72] The *Brockhill Prison* case and *McLeod v United Kingdom* illustrate that when the courts interpret statutes,[73] and defences to rights-based torts,[74] they should do so (and hopefully will now do so) from the perspective of the claimant's rights and not the conduct of the defendant. The further alignment of rights-based torts with Convention articles may prove to be simply a matter of time.[75] The HRA could have

---

[66] *Cowell v Corrective Services Commission of New South Wales* (1988) 13 NSWLR 714: M Fordham, 'False Imprisonment in Good Faith' (2000) 8 Tort LR 53.

[67] *R v Governor of Brockhill Prison, ex parte. Evans (No. 2)* [2000] 3 WLR 843, 849.

[68] Ibid, 857–9. Lord Slynn admittedly said that he did not have to consider the position under Art 5 of the European Convention.

[69] Ibid, 867. He also said that it 'is contrary to principle that the executive should not be liable for illegally interfering with the liberty of the subject' (863). Occasionally a rigid focus on individual liberty can lead to odd results: eg *Vine v Waltham Forest London Borough Council* [2000] 1 WLR 2383 (wheel clamp a trespass without actual consent); *Webb v Chief Constable of Merseyside Police* [2000] 2 WLR 546 (possession of proceeds of drug-trafficking reverted to possession of those found to have been, more likely than not, the drug-traffickers).

[70] Ibid, 854 and 865. Cf [1999] QB 1043, 1056–7 per Lord Woolf M.R., 1068 per Roch LJ, 1077–8 per Judge LJ See also the discussion above at n 59.

[71] Fleming, above n 17 at 114.   [72] Weir, above n 25.

[73] Cf *DPP v Jones* [1999] 2 AC 240, esp 259 per Lord Irvine.

[74] Ibid, 259 per Lord Irvine.

[75] In restricting nuisance to a tort to land (overruling *Khorasandjian v Bush* [1993] 3 All ER 669) the decision of the House of Lords in *Hunter v Canary Wharf* [1997] AC 655 no doubt resumed normal service, but as Janet O'Sullivan observed this was at the expense of some artificiality: 'What precisely is it about, for example, a horrible smell that is deserving of legal sanction? Surely the fact that *human beings* are adversely affected by it.' ('Nuisance in the House of Lords—Normal Service Resumed' (1997) 56 *CLJ* 483, 485). Their Lordships

replaced much of tort law's rights-based jurisprudence entirely, but instead may breathe new life into these hallowed doctrines. It is worth recalling the words of Dworkin who has urged British judges to use 'the rich and special traditions of the British common law to develop out of the Convention a particularly British view of fundamental rights of citizens in a democratic society'.[76] Tort should retain a central role in shaping that society.

C. Individual Liability

At common law individuals remain primarily liable for torts. However, even before the Crown was itself made liable in tort it would stand behind its servants, and it remains the case that when a named individual, such as the prison governor in the *Brockhill Prison* case, is held liable, 'it is in reality the State which must compensate . . .'.[77] In most cases, since the state is worth suing and their badly paid employees are not, the state will be made vicariously liable for the torts of its servants. Its servants remain primarily, albeit nominally, liable. However, the residual possibility of individual liability of public officials is, in many circumstances, now difficult to justify. The clearest example of injustice is the acts of public servants under unlawful bye-laws or *ultra vires* orders. It is the spectre of personal liability in these circumstances which is partly responsible for the manipulation, by reference to the tortfeasors' conduct, of the substantive law in cases such as *Percy*.[78] Even in other circumstances of an infringement of individual rights

---

missed an opportunity to recognise that rights-based torts can have a role in protecting human rights between individuals (in this context home and family life). Lord Cooke, dissenting, preferred to see nuisance as protecting ones' home and drew support from Art 8 of the European Convention, Art 12 of the Universal Declaration of Human Rights, and Art 16 of the United Nations Convention on the Rights of the Child. He referred to *Arrondelle v United Kingdom* (1982) 26 D & R 5 (CD) (aircraft noise) and *Lopez Ostra v Spain* (1994) 20 EHRR 277 (fumes and smells). David Feldman has argued, eg, that the courts 'might . . . conclude that they should develop the tort of nuisance or harassment so as to provide an effective remedy for the plaintiff against surveillance by the BBC even if the BBC is not regarded as a public authority' ('Remedies for Violation of Convention Rights Under the Human Rights Act' EHRLR (1998) 691, 704). On the developing law of privacy see I Hare, above n 4, and N Moreham, '*Douglas and others v Hello! Ltd*—the Protection of Privacy in English Private Law' (2001) 64 MLR 767. For the expansion of human rights into areas traditionally covered by common law nuisance see *Hatton v United Kingdom (36022/97)* (2001) 2 Oct, and *Marcic v Thames Water Utilities Ltd* [2001] 3 All ER 698.

[76] R Dworkin, 'Does Britain Need a Bill of Rights?', in R Gordon and R Wilmot-Smith (eds), *Human Rights in the United Kingdom* (Oxford: Clarendon Press, 1996), 64.

[77] *R v Governor of Brockhill Prison, ex parte Evans (No. 2)* [2000] 3 WLR 843, 846 per Lord Slynn.

[78] The possibility of personal liability has also supported, rightly or wrongly, the policy argument that liability will lead to defensive practices, which has had a major influence on substantive law. In negligence see, eg, *Whitehouse v Jordan* [1980] 1 All ER 650 (CA); *Yuen Kun Yeu v A-G of Hong Kong* [1988] AC 175; *Hill v Chief Constable of West Yorkshire* [1989] AC 53; *X (Minors) v Bedfordshire County Council* [1995] 2 AC 633; compare the recent cases cited below n 167. The fear is by no means new, in *Ashby v White* (1703) 2 Ld

by state officers, it seems wrong to maintain the possibility of individual liability for blameless conduct simply because of the weight of the constitutional dogma that everybody should be equal before the law.[79] The rule that individuals could be liable while acting for the state was no doubt once important when the Crown and superior officials[80] were immune from suit: 'The King might not be able to do any wrong, but the question was whether his servants could; and to this the English judges had no doubts.'[81] As Pannam has pointed out these rules no longer seem appropriate.[82]

The recent clarification that the principles of vicarious liability extend to cover deliberate acts of sexual abuse committed by an employee, whilst the victim was in the defendant's care, is to be welcomed so far as it goes.[83] However, the House of Lords refused to consider the difficult policy considerations that need to be addressed in this area. While they increased the chance that the state will be caught in the net of liability for acts of its servants who cause harm in their capacity as public officers, there was little consideration of the extent to which liability could be justified by the relationship between the defendant and the claimant themselves. This is a question that is particularly significant in the public sphere. More important, then, are the suggestions in *Phelps v Hillingdon London Borough Council*

Raym 938 Gould J stated 'if we should allow [the action] we shall multiply actions upon the officers at the suit of the candidates, and every particular elector too; so that men will be thereby deterred from venturing to act in such offices, when the acting therein becomes so perilous to them and their families' ([945]). By contrast Holt CJ thought if 'publick officers will infringe mens rights, they ought to pay greater damages than other men, to deter and hinder other officers from like offences' ([955]).

[79] A 'sensible answer might be that no remedy should be given against the policeman who acted in good faith but that a remedy should be given against the a Secretary of State who put into circulation invalid by-laws with the perfectly foreseeable consequence that policemen would act on the assumption that they were valid' *Percy v Hall*, 545 per Schiemann LJ See CL Pannam, 'Tortious Liability for Acts Performed under an Unconstitutional Statute' (1966) 5 *Melb LR* 113.

[80] *Bainbridge v Postmaster-General* [1906] 1 KB 178.

[81] Pannam, above n 79 at 137.

[82] Above n 79. Parliament can immunise individuals from tort liabilities reasonably easily (see *Wills v Bowley* [1982] 2 All ER 654, 670 per Lord Lowry). Some statutory provisions exist: eg Public Health Act 1875, s 265 as amended; National Health Service Act 1977, s 125; Local Government (Miscellaneous Provisions) Act 1976, s 39. The scope and effect of these provisions is extremely unclear (S Bailey, 'Personal Liability in Local Government Law' [1999] *PL* 461) and usually construed to protect authorities and employees only from bona fide non-negligent acts. An alternative construction is that it protects individuals, acting in good faith, from liability (*Southampton and Itchen Bridge Co. v Local Government Board of Southampton* (1858) 8 E & B 801; see also HRH Wade and CF Forsyth, *Administrative Law*, 8th edn (Oxford: Clarendon Press, 1999), 745).

[83] *Lister v Hesley Hall Ltd* [2001] 2 WLR 1311. 'Our law no longer struggles with the concept of vicarious liability for intentional wrongdoing. Thus the decision of the House of Lords in *Racz v Home Office* [1994] 2 AC 45 is authority for the proposition that the Home Office may be vicariously liable for acts of police officers which amounted to misfeasance in public office—and hence for liability in tort involving bad faith' per Lord Steyn, para 20.

that public bodies can be more widely held directly liable.[84] However, direct liability of public authorities for the acts, as opposed to the torts, of others remains underdeveloped.[85] Moreover, it would be preferable that public officials were shielded from the threat of personal liability altogether for what amount to public law wrongs committed in good faith.[86] The argument that there is a 'powerful symbolism' in personal liability of government servants[87] is no more persuasive than the potentially powerful symbolism in the state, upon which people increasingly rely, shouldering full responsibility for the acts of its servants who commit torts while attempting to benefit the community. This issue goes beyond the scope of this paper; for present purposes it is enough to express regret that the HRA retains the possibility of personal liability.

The definition of 'public authority' is, however, somewhat ambiguous. This is because the definition is largely omitted. According to section 6 (3) (b), it 'includes' 'any person certain of whose functions are of a public nature'. Section 6 (5) states that a person is not a public authority by virtue 'only' of section (3) (b) if the nature of the act is private. The provisions are intended to allow either individuals or organisations to be sued.[88] However, it is far from clear what the conceptual basis for this new scheme of liability is, or how it fits into the already rather complicated system of direct and vicarious liability in tort. Not only does the HRA retain personal responsibility but it also adds a new level of ambiguity to the already murky law on direct liability.

---

[84] [2000] 3 WLR 776.

[85] The courts have not clearly distinguished situations where the organisation, to which the duty attaches, is not itself at fault, from those situations where there is carelessness at the organisational or managerial level: see *Phelps v Hillingdon LBC* 813 per Lord Clyde; *X (Minors) v Bedfordshire County Council* [1995] 2 AC 633 (discussed by Cane, 'Suing Public Authorities in Tort' (1996) 112 LQR 13, 19–21); *Gold v Essex County Council* [1942] 2 KB 293; *Cassidy v Ministry of Health* [1951] 2 KB 343; *Roe v Minister of Health* [1954] 2 QB 66; *Yepremain v Scarborough General Hospital* (1980) 110 DLR (3d) 513; *Wilsher v Essex Area Health Authority* [1986] 3 All ER 801; *Ellis v Wallsend District Hospital* (1989) 17 NSWLR 553; *Bull v Devon Area Health Authority* [1993] 4 Med. LR 117; *Robertson v Nottinghamshire Health Authority* [1997] 8 Med. LR 1; *M v Calderdale and Kirklees* (1998) Lloyd's L Rep Med 157.

[86] Clearly acts of bad faith or misfeasance should not escape personal liability, as in the famous case of *Roncarelli v Duplessis* (1959) 16 DLR 2d 689 (Prime Minister of Quebec). See also M Aronson and H Whitmore, *Public Torts and Contracts* (Sydney: Law Book Co Ltd, 1982), 20–2.

[87] PW Hogg, *Liability of the Crown*, 2nd edn (Toronto: Carswell Co Ltd, Toronto, 1989), 145.

[88] Hansard, HL 24 Nov 1997, vol 583, cols 802–3. White Paper, above n 1 at 2.2. Cf Hansard HL 24 Nov 1997, vol 583, col 811.

A. Negligence and Convention Jurisprudence

Negligence liability protects a variety of interests in English law and there is clearly overlap with those interests protected by the HRA and the European Convention. Both *Osman* and the *Bedfordshire* abuse cases (*Z v United Kingdom*[89] and *TP and KM v United Kingdom*)[90] were heard as negligence actions in England[91] and ended up in Strasbourg where breaches of human rights were found. In *Z v United Kingdom* the ECtHR found that the failure of social services to remove children from parents, at whose hands they suffered appalling abuse and neglect, constituted a violation of the right not to suffer inhumane and degrading treatment (Article 3). In *TP and KM v United Kingdom* the violation was of Article 8, because the applicant was given inadequate access to the evidence which had been relied upon when taking her child into care. The fact that neither case gave rise to a duty of care in negligence, but both disclosed violations of human rights by the authorities, illustrates that negligence liability only incompletely protects human rights. This is, of course, unsurprising since the essence of negligence is reasonableness and harm, and neither is necessarily present in the violation of a right. Such examples are far from isolated. In *W v United Kingdom*[92] the ECtHR found that the United Kingdom had breached Article 8 by failing sufficiently to involve parents in decisions over the welfare and ultimate removal of their child. An action for negligence is unsuitable for protecting these kinds of process rights where harm is often at best indirect and at worst speculative.[93]

Since negligence often resembles an action for vindication of rights it is frequently argued that it is deficient when it fails to protect rights. This tendency can be discerned in the finding against the United Kingdom on Article 6 (which protects the right to a fair hearing of one's civil rights) in *Osman v United Kingdom*.[94] The Court of Appeal in *Osman v Ferguson* had decided to strike out a claim against the police for failing to prevent an obsessed teacher injuring a pupil and killing the pupil's father.[95] In *Hill v Chief Constable of West Yorkshire* the House of Lords had ruled that the police owed no duty of care in relation to their investigative activities,[96] and the Court of Appeal applied this decision. The ECtHR found that the striking out of the action in *Osman v Ferguson* denied the applicant access to a

---

[89] [2001] 2 FLR 612.   [90] [2001] 2 FLR 549.
[91] *X (Minors) v Bedfordshire County Council* [1995] 2 AC 633
[92] (1986) A 121.
[93] See also *H v United Kingdom* (1987) 10 EHRR 95 (delay in determining future of child).
[94] (1998) 29 EHRR 245
[95] *Osman v Ferguson* [1993] 4 All ER 344.   [96] [1989] AC 53.

court. One of the things that the ECtHR was concerned to ensure was that serious grievances against the police, involving one's right to life under Article 2, could be heard by domestic courts.[97] The court stated that only an action in negligence 'would have enabled [the applicants] to secure answers to the basic question which underpinned their civil action, namely why did the police not take action sooner . . . '.[98] However, there was no action in negligence in English law, the real default was the failure of English law to protect Article 2, not that negligence law did not protect that right.[99] In *Z v United Kingdom* the ECtHR did not follow their previous ruling in *Osman* on Article 6. The full implications of this ruling will be discussed later, but Judge Roziakis, dissenting, stated that 'it is difficult for me to accept that serious matters of public concern—as are all matters involving a violation of Article 3 . . . may be left outside the protection of independent and impartial tribunals...'.[100] and that 'the Court in *Osman* was mainly concerned with the fact that the applicants in a very serious case of possible substantive human rights violations did not have the opportunity to air their grievances...' and not whether an immunity had excluded the applicants' civil rights from being determined.[101] Such a view misunderstands the relationship between negligence and human rights.

At least one commentator considered it surprising that the apparent human rights violations by the local authorities in the *Bedfordshire* cases had not been mentioned by the House of Lords when determining whether a duty of care was owed.[102] However, while the law of negligence confers civil rights on individuals, it does not protect human rights any more than it protects contractual rights (which it can do from time to time).[103] This was recognised in *Z v United Kingdom* where the real issue was identified. This had earlier been identified by Wright as the 'inadequate response of English law to the plight of the Bedfordshire and Newham children'.[104] The

---

[97] Simpson has argued that the Court in *Osman* was driven by the need to establish police accountability in many of the countries now governed by the Convention, where the history of policing is not happy: *Human Rights and the End of Empire: Britain and the Genesis of the European Convention* (Oxford: Clarendon Press, 2001), 7–8.

[98] *Osman v United Kingdom* (1998) 29 EHRR 245, para 153

[99] The absence of a civil remedy may be sufficient to breach the substantive article itself (eg *Powell v United Kingdom* (1990) 12 EHRR 355 (Art 8)) or else amount to a breach of Art 13.

[100] *Z v United Kingdom* [2001] 2 FLR 612, Partly Dissenting Opinion of Judge Rozakis (joined by Judge Palm) para 2. Similar sentiments to those outlined were expressed by the Commission in *Z v United Kingdom* (1999) 28 EHRR CD 75 para 114). The argument being that the exclusion of liability was not proportionate for so grave a harm.

[101] Ibid, para 3

[102] J Wright, 'Local Authorities, the Duty of Care and the European Convention on Human Rights' (1998) *OJLS* 1, 3, and 16. In fact, it is not that surprising that these matters were not mentioned by their Lordships, since the Convention obligations do not appear to have been cited by any of counsel in the cases.

[103] *Henderson v Merrett Syndicates Ltd* [1995] 2 AC 145.

[104] Wright, above n 102 at 28.

court recognised that there was a 'gap' in English law between interests protected by the law of negligence and those protected by human rights. This gap meant that the United Kingdom had failed to provide an effective remedy before national tribunals, and had therefore violated Article 13.[105] The ECtHR recognised that the applicants were aggrieved by the failure of domestic law to protect their rights under Article 3, but this was not a failing of negligence law itself.[106]

B. Negligence Actions, Breaches of Duty, and the Protection of Rights

In some cases the action for negligence is made to do the function of a rights-based action. In the first type of case the conduct complained of cannot quite amount to an interference with a right and so negligence is relied on to provide a residual safeguard. In *R v Deputy Governor of Parkhurst Prison, ex parte Hague* the House of Lords struggled with the problem of how to allow a remedy for intolerable conditions in prisons, but where the conditions themselves could not be characterised as false imprisonment. Their Lordships said that, in the absence of a rights-based action, the claimant would have to prove that there had been a breach the duty of care.[107] The ECtHR has been confronted with similar problems. In *Ashingdane* they felt compelled to say that where a patient, detained under the Mental Health Act 1959, endured worse conditions than he ought to have done, the complaint did not raise interferences with human rights since his detention was lawful and his conditions humane.[108] The ECtHR came to the same conclusion in a case involving solitary confinement, alleged mental and physical abuse and degradation.[109]

In *Keenan v United Kingdom*, however, a different result was reached.[110] Keenan was a prisoner who suffered from severe mental illness and who killed himself in his cell. His mother claimed breaches of Articles 2 and 3 of the Convention. Whilst detained Keenan had undoubtedly been subjected to a sub-standard of care, but it could not be shown that failings of the authorities caused his death. On this occasion the ECtHR was prepared to stretch the notion of inhuman and degrading treatment to remedy the grievance. Sir Stephen Sedley, in a separate opinion, acknowledged that Article 3 had been stretched. He said 'if Mark Keenan had not killed himself it is not easy to see what his case would have been under Article 3. As the Court

---

[105] *Z v United Kingdom,* para 102.   [106] Ibid, para 103.
[107] [1992] 1 AC 58.
[108] *Ashingdane v United Kingdom* (1985) 7 EHRR 528. The Commission said that 'the present applicant's claim involves a question of suitable treatment' (A 93, para 84).
[109] *Hilton v United Kingdom* (1978) 3 EHRR 104.
[110] (2001) 33 EHRR 38.

has more than once said, all punishment is to an extent degrading'.[111] Such transmutations do no service to the coherency of the law. The ECtHR is, however, under greater pressure to perform such doctrinal manipulations since it has only rights-based tools at its disposal.[112]

It is not just rights that may be stretched, but duties too. Hampered by the fact that domestic rights-based actions are narrowly confined and largely rooted in property, and unwilling to ground new actions in modern political and human rights,[113] English courts have, it seems, been attempting to re-tailor negligence to fit a rights-orientated jacket. The gradual relaxation of the notion of 'harm' can be seen as an unstated response to pressures from litigants wanting to vindicate rights through actions in negligence.[114] For example in *W v Essex County Council* the House of Lords was prepared to countenance recovery for the 'reactive depression, sleep disturbance, nightmares, tearfulness, exacerbation of . . . diabetes and . . . hypertension' of parents whose children had been abused by a foster child.[115] What seems to underlie the case is a feeling that the local authority had violated the claimants' right to respect for their private and family life. From this perspective actionable harm is far from the 'gist' of the action.[116] Dressing these complaints up in the garb of breaches of duty and negligence not only risks distorting negligence actions, but, importantly, it also imperfectly protects the rights in issue themselves.

Another example is *Phelps v Hillingdon London Borough Council*[117] where the House of Lords countenanced recovery in negligence for failure to mitigate dyslexia although neither the schools, nor anybody else, had

---

[111] Ibid, Concurring Opinion of Sir Stephen Sedley, para 4. Cf *Peers v Greece* (2001) 33 ERHH 51; *Selmouni v France* (2000) 29 ERHH 403.

[112] The case perhaps discloses a lacuna between the two strands of jurisprudence. It seems that the authorities fell well below acceptable standards in their treatment of Mark Keenan, but an action in negligence was not pursued because it was felt that there was no mental injury sufficient to found a claim in negligence. Since negligence is founded in corrective justice courts will not enforce duties unless their breach has caused harm. Arguably, though, the ECtHR was wrong to imply a causal requirement into Art 2 (see *LCB v United Kingdom* (1998) 27 EHRR 212).

[113] See *F v Metropolitan Borough of Wirral* discussed below n 194, and *Malone v Metropolitan Police Commissioner* [1979] Ch 344. See also the discussion above n 75.

[114] *R v Deputy Governor of Parkhurst Prison, ex parte Hague* [1992] 1 AC 58, 166 per Lord Bridge (discomfort); *Waters v Commissioner of Police* [2000] 1 WLR 1607 and *Bradford-Smart v West Sussex County Council* [2000] *The Times* 8 Nov (bullying, harassment*); Spring v Guardian Assurance Ltd* [1995] 2 AC 296 (economic loss recoverable for, essentially, defamation and injury to reputation, but where the statements benefited from a defence of privilege in defamation); but see the welcome cap: *McFarlane v Tayside Health Board* [1999] 3 WLR 1301 (distress and discomfort of unwanted pregnancy, but no damages for an unwanted healthy child) and *Greenfield v Irwin* [2001] 1 WLR 1279 (no recovery for lost earnings looking after such a child).

[115] [2000] 2 WLR 601, 607.

[116] See J Stapleton, 'The Gist of Negligence' (1988) 104 *LQR* 213 and 389.

[117] [2000] 3 WLR 776.

actually harmed the claimants.[118] The real grievances in the *Phelps* cases related to the denial of fundamental social rights, viz the right to an effective education.[119] They can also be seen as rectifying the fact that a minority had been denied the chance to develop their potential and to participate fully in society. In such cases it will be extremely difficult for claimants to prove what harm has been caused, because the effects of dyslexia may not be alleviated even if the breaches of duty had not occurred. Moreover, the calculation of 'lost' future gains will be highly speculative; although this is to some extent alleviated by fictionalising the harm as personal injury, and not economic loss, which shifts the emphasis onto quantum.

On one view negligence is being stretched,[120] if not distorted by these decisions.[121] One wonders whether *X (Minors) v Bedfordshire County Council* would have been decided the same way today. By comparison, procedural fairness and due process have been said to be 'central' to the jurisprudence of the ECtHR and the Convention itself.[122] It would perhaps

---

[118] The House of Lords heard four appeals together, three concerned dyslexia (*Phelps* [1999] 1 WLR 500, *Anderton v Clwyd County Council* and *Jarvis v Hampshire County Council* [2000] ELR 36) and one was a claim that Bromley had been in breach of duty in failing to provide a boy, suffering from muscular dystrophy, with a proper education (*G v Bromley London Borough Council* [2001] LGLR 237).

[119] The right to an education is protected by Art 2 of the First Protocol of the European Convention. The *Belgian Linguistic* case (1968) 1 EHRR 252 held that there was a right to an effective education and the court recognised the centrality of being able to draw profit from the education provided. So far no claim based on special education needs by United Kingdom applicants has been successful. The cases considered (eg *Simpson v United Kingdom* (1989) 64 D & R 188; *Ford v United Kingdom* (1996) EHRLR 534; *SP v United Kingdom* (1997) 23 EHRR (CD) 139; *McIntyre v United Kingdom* (1998) 21 Oct (29046/95)) primarily relate to deliberate choices made by local authorities (often against the background of scarce resources). The common law obligation recognised in *Phelps* goes beyond this jurisprudence, both in relation to the positive obligation on the state to assist children with special educational needs and in relation to the provision of civil remedies for any violations. Cf *R v East Sussex County Council ex parte Tandy* [1998] AC 714; *R (Holub) v Home Secretary* [2001] 1 WLR 1359.

[120] See PS Atiyah, *The Damages Lottery* (Oxford: Hart Publishing, 1997), chs 2 and 3. These cases stand in contrast to cases restrictive of the use of tort in the field of welfare rights: eg *X (Minors) v Bedfordshire County Council* [1995] 2 AC 633 and *O'Rourke v Camden London Borough Council* [1997] 3 WLR 86.

[121] A good example, in a different context, of the distortion of negligence when it attempts to protect (as opposed to take account of) rights, relates to the standard of care in medical negligence cases. It is best illustrated by United States cases on informed consent: *Salago v Leland Stanford Jr., University Board of Trustees* (1957) 154 Cal App 2d 560, 317 P 2d 170; *Canterbury v Spence* (1972) 464 F 2d 772. The courts attempted to utilise negligence to protect the right to autonomy, but they succeeded only in distorting it: see J Katz, 'Informed Consent: A Fairy Tale?: Law's Vision' (1977) 39 *U Pitt L Rev* 137. Cf *Sidaway v Governors of Bethlam Royal Hospital* [1985] AC 871. For discussion of the wider tension between negligence and rights in the medical context see H Teff, *Reasonable Care: Legal Perspectives on the Doctor-Patient Relationship* (Oxford: Clarendon Press, 1994); I Kennedy, *Treat Me Right* (Oxford: Clarendon Press, 1988), ch 20; Lord Irvine, 'The Patient, the Doctor, their Lawyers and the Judge: Rights and Duties' (1999) 7 *Med L Rev* 255.

[122] CA Gearty, 'The European Court of Human Rights and the Protection of Civil Liberties: An Overview' (1993) 52 *CLJ* 89, 98

be better in the future for such claims to be considered from the perspective of public and constitutional law, and not private law; and from the perspective of citizen's rights. Nonetheless, it has been suggested that the finding of a breach of Article 8 by the ECtHR in *TP and KM v United Kingdom* may compel the English courts to 'reconsider whether a duty of care may be owed, at least, in relation to the process of decision making and appeal'.[123]

C. Omissions and Article 2

We have seen how in *Keenan* the ECtHR stretched Article 3 in order to remedy a justifiable grievance, but which was hard to categorise as the violation of a right. It is, however, cases of omissions that present the clearest examples of violations of rights that amount in fact to breaches of duty. In such cases there is an apparent convergence with the law of negligence. Clearly failures to act are not protected by trespass, which requires an act, although other rights-based torts may protect failures to act. Nuisance is the clearest example, although this begins to look very much like negligence in these circumstances as well.[124] Negligence liability does have a function in imposing liability for failing to act, and is duty-based. Omissions present a convergence between rights and duties simply because one cannot talk about liability for omissions without talking about breach of a duty.[125] In negligence one may, however, owe a duty of care to a person one has, for example, assumed responsibility over, and yet not have been under a duty to act to prevent that person harm. This will be the case if the there is no fault in failing to act, or something else is significantly more causally responsible for the harm.

The ECtHR has adopted the language of 'duty' and 'reasonableness' in relation to the positive obligations imposed on states to protect individuals from violations of rights. Article 2 provides the clearest illustration and is particularly relevant to negligence. The ECtHR has held that Article 2, read in the light of Article 1 (which requires states to secure the protection of Convention rights), creates duties both to take positive operational measures to protect individuals from being killed, and to investigate any such killings properly.[126] With respect to the former duty the ECtHR has even begun to distinguish a quasi-duty criterion from a fault criterion. In

---

[123] *Clerk and Lindsell On Torts*, above n 43 at 1-77.

[124] See above n 26.

[125] HLA Hart and T Honoré, *Causation in the Law* 2nd edn (Oxford: Clarendon Press, 1985), 38 and 139–40.

[126] *Osman v United Kingdom* (1998) 29 EHRR 245; *Kaya v Turkey* (1998) 28 EHRR 1; *LCB v United Kingdom* (1998) 27 EHRR 212. Similar reasoning has led to the creation of positive obligations under other articles; *X & Y v Netherlands* (1986) 8 EHRR 235 (Art 8), *Plattform 'Ärtze fur das Leben' v Austria* (1991) 13 EHRR 204 (Art 11); *Airey v Ireland* (1979) 2 EHRR 305 (Art 6).

Osman the ECtHR said that first, 'it must be established that the authorities knew or ought to have known at the time of the existence of a real and immediate risk to life of an identified individual or individuals' (the 'quasi-duty' test). Secondly, the state authority must have 'failed to take measures within the scope of their powers which, judged reasonably, might have been expected to avoid the risk' (the 'fault' test).[127] Neither aspect of the test was made out in *Osman* itself, or in *Keenan*.[128] It is worth considering the various aspects of the test.

1. 'knew or ought to have known . . .'

In *Orange* the Court of Appeal held, on the basis of common law principles, that the police only owe a duty of care to prevent those in their custody committing suicide if they know or ought to have known that a prisoner is a suicide risk.[129] The case illustrates the tendency for courts to conflate the issues of duty, causation, and fault in omissions cases.[130] Conventionally it would be indisputable that the police owed a duty of care towards those in their custody and the question of knowledge would only be relevant to their culpability.[131] Rather than saying that there had been a duty to take care of the deceased, but that the police had not acted unreasonably, the court in *Orange* said that there was no duty of care because there was really no fault, which is not a particularly happy approach to adopt in relation to the duty of care in these circumstances. Importantly, the court considered *Keenan* and while acknowledging that it did not 'in itself' provide support for the submissions of defence counsel on this point, nonetheless stated that it 'confirms our view that the special and unusual duty is one which only arose where the authorities know, or ought to know, of a suicide risk in an individual prisoner's case'.[132] How far their Lordships were influenced by the ECtHR jurisprudence when formulating the duty of care is impossible to tell. However, they did more than merely note the convergence between the rights-based jurisprudence and that of negligence and, presumably, believed that alignment would promote coherency in the law.

---

[127] *Osman v United Kingdom*, para 116
[128] *Keenan v United Kingdom*, para 98
[129] *Orange v Chief Constable of West Yorkshire Police* [2001] 3 WLR 750.
[130] On which see D Howarth, 'Negligence After Murphy: Time to Re-think' (1991) 50 *CLJ* 58, 72–81.
[131] *Cekan v Haines* (1990) 21 NSWLR 296. Cf *Commissioner for the Police for the Metropolis v Reeves* [1999] 3 WLR 283; *Knight v Home Office* [1990] 3 All ER 237; *Kirkham v The Chief Constable of Greater Manchester* [1989] 3 All ER 882.
[132] *Orange v Chief Constable of West Yorkshire Police* [2001] 3 WLR 750, para 47.

2. 'a real and immediate risk to life of an identified individual or individuals'

Since 'duty, even more than charity, begins at home' the common law has imposed positive duties only where there exists a close relationship between the parties. However, when claimants seek to make public authorities liable for not preventing a third party causing harm, special problems arise; not least because public authorities are obliged to treat all people equally and so cannot plead 'duty begins at home'. In a case where the police were sued for failing to prevent the Yorkshire Ripper murdering the claimant's daughter, the House of Lords nonetheless denied that there was a duty of care because there was no 'special and distinctive risk' in relation to the victim.[133] The requirement limits potential claims and no doubt pre-empts a finding of no-fault (since an authority will not be at fault for not helping an enormous or indeterminate class of people). It has much in common with the approach of the ECtHR.

Palmer v Tees Health Authority[134] illustrates just how similar the common law test can seem to the ECtHR test. In *Palmer* a child was murdered by a mentally ill out-patient whom it was alleged that the defendants had failed to detain. Stuart-Smith LJ held that there was no proximity since the victim was unidentifiable, and this was so even though the patient had warned that he would murder a child. Pill LJ left open whether a duty could be owed to an unidentified victim, for example, if the authority had been told 'I will kill the first bald-headed man I meet', since one year had passed between the threat and the murder and so the question was not germane to the facts. He recognised that identifiability could also be seen as a breach point,[135] and Stuart-Smith LJ was not afraid to conflate breach and duty stressing, for example, the difficulties in committing the patient and noting that he was taking a 'somewhat novel approach to the question of proximity'.[136] It is unlikely that two tests vary much in substance; both require individual identification, or at least a degree of immediacy of risk to a defined class. In this context neither clearly separate duty from fault. They are in any case sufficiently close for courts further to align the jurisprudence in a similar manner to the *Orange* case.

This necessarily brief discussion has focused on but a fraction of the duty of care and only on its relation to Article 2, other considerations will apply in relation to other circumstances and other articles.[137] Aligning the duty of

---

[133] *Hill v Chief Constable of West Yorkshire* [1989] 1 AC 55, 62 per Lord Keith
[134] [1999] Lloyds L Rep Med 351.   [135] Ibid, 363.   [136] Ibid, 539.
[137] Art 8, eg, is founded on 'respect' (8(1)) has a separate 'duty' aspect, but the breach determination remains clearly defined in 8(2). Where 'respect' involves a positive obligation the ECtHR itself, although it should not, 'tends to collapse the inquiry as to what the duty is with the question of whether it has been breached': C Warbrick, 'The Structure of Article 8' [1998] EHRLR 32, 35. Cf *Osman v United Kingdom*, para 128.

care with the obligations imposed by Article 2, as well as the influence of positive obligations associated with other Convention articles, would certainly have far-reaching implications for the general principle that there is no liability for failing to act in the absence of a special relationship.[138] It is worth noting at this juncture that the obligations imposed by the HRA may lead English courts to bring the law on public authority liability, in relation to positive duties, somewhat closer to the approach taken in Australia. A sketch should suffice to make the point.

In *Pyrenees* a local authority was held liable for failing to warn tenants of a property and their neighbours that their fireplace was a fire hazard. The premises subsequently burnt down. The Australian High Court held that the authority owed a positive duty because the plaintiffs were 'particularly vulnerable and the authority exists and is empowered to protect them . . .'.[139] In a second case liability was imposed on the Stevedoring Industry Finance Committee who had failed to protect the plaintiff from contracting a fatal lung disease when working with asbestos fibres. McHugh J's judgment is of particular interest. He stressed that the defendants had the power to protect a specific class, that the class was vulnerable, and that the defendant knew or ought to have known of the risk.[140] The Committee was consequently held liable. Both cases put a heavier burden on the positive duties of public authorities than has been the case in England, stressing in particular their ability to prevent harm.[141] Finally, in a controversial decision of the Court of Appeal of New South Wales, a doctor was held liable

---

[138] See *Stovin v Wise* [1996] AC 923.

[139] *Pyrenees Shire Council v Day* (1998) 151 ALR 14, para 77 per Toohey J.

[140] *Crimmins v Stevedoring Industry Finance Committee* (1999) 167 ALJ 1, paras 92–3; also *Pyrenees*, para 115. Supplementing Todd's test for a duty of care in 'Liability in Tort of Public Bodies' in MJ Mullany and LA Linden (eds), *Torts Tomorrow: A Tribute to John Fleming* (Sydney: LCB Information Services, 1998), 55. Cf *Romeo v Conservation Commission* (1998) 151 ALR 263 (failure to fence a cliff); *Ryan v Great Lakes Council* [1999] FCA 177 (failure to prevent contamination of lake leading to hepatitis epidemic); but see *Cubillo v Commonwealth of Australia* [2000] FCA 1084 (no duty in removal of child applying *X (Minors) v Bedfordshire County Council* [1995] 2 AC 633).

[141] In *Capital & Counties v Hampshire County Council* [1997] QB 1004 the Court of Appeal held that fire service owed no duty of care for not preventing damage. Viewed as a blanket rule this would mean the law of negligence could easily come to different conclusions from Art 2. However, on the facts it is difficult to see that there was any risk to life to an identifiable person or class of persons in any of the cases considered. The rule could be unjust when someone is injured, killed, or when their home is destroyed (to all of which Art 8 is also relevant) because, say, the fire service are too lazy to turn up; but the court was well aware that finding a duty of care to prevent harm could lead to enormous liabilities for damage to corporate premises caused by others (The damages paid out in the one case where they were found to have increased the damage, to corporate premises, comfortably exceeded £15m.) The courts could demand that claims against the fire services are brought under the HRA as to preserve the integrity of the rule. The situation is different with regard to ambulance services whose failings will not have these effects (and so they are held liable: *Kent v Griffiths* [2000] 2 WLR 1158, even in the absence of specific reliance: see T Hickman, '"And That's Magic!': Making Public Bodies Liable for Failure to Confer Benefits' (2000) 59 *CLJ* 232).

for refusing to treat a boy, who was not his patient, who was having a seizure and who consequently suffered extensive brain damage and quadriplegia.[142] There is no doubt that the case exceeds obligations imposed by negligence law in England.[143]

It would be easy to under-play the areas of tension that exists between the quasi-duty test and the duty of care at common law. Two further examples can be given. First, the duty of care in English law is a question separate and prior to that of breach. The ECtHR's approach does not appear to maintain such a clear distinction. In *Keenan* the court found that although Keenan was not an immediate risk throughout the period of detention, his condition did require that he be monitored carefully and thus the determining factor was whether the authorities had acted reasonably. The ECtHR thereby made the duty aspect of the ECtHR test dependent on the fault aspect.[144] Although in the event they held that 'it is not apparent that the authorities omitted any step which should have reasonably been taken'.[145]

The second difference relates to the absence of negative policy considerations at the quasi-duty stage. There are many such relevant considerations[146] that English courts have considered at the duty stage. They often relate to the unfairness or injustice in holding public bodies liable for potentially enormous losses, or about the complex polycentric problems that are raised. Since violations of rights are actionable without proof of harm, damages are not available as of right, and the focus is right-specific, such considerations are not prominent at the duty stage of the ECtHR test.[147] However, the ECtHR said in *Osman*:

bearing in mind the difficulties in policing modern societies, the unpredictability of human conduct and the operational choices which must be made in terms of priorities and resources, [the positive] obligation must be interpreted in a way which does not impose an impossible or disproportionate burden on the authorities.[148]

---

[142] *Lowns v Woods* [1996] Aust. TRep. 81–376. Mahoney JA gave a strong dissent. For the controversy see K Amirthalingam and T Faunce, 'Patching Up "Proximity": Problems with the Judicial Creation of a New Medical Duty to Rescue' (1997) 5 *Tort LJ* 19; D Mendleson, 'Dr Lowns and the Obligation to Treat: Creative Law-Making in the New South Wales Court of Appeal' (1996) *Tort LR* 242; L Haberfield, '*Lowns v Woods* and the Duty to Rescue' (1998) *Tort LR* 56.

[143] *Cassidy v Ministry of Health* [1951] 2 KB 343. 'Doctors, who faithfully subscribe to the Hippocratic Oath, are not subject to civil liability if they hypocritically refuse to attend a dying patient' (AM Linden, *Canadian Tort Law*, 7th edn (Ontario: Butterworths, 2001), 267).

[144] *Keenan v United Kingdom*, paras 95–6.

[145] Ibid, para 98.

[146] J Stapleton, 'Duty of Care Factors: a Selection from the Judicial Menus', in Cane and Stapleton (eds), above n 25 at 73–87.

[147] See the discussion above n 141.

[148] *Osman v United Kingdom*, para 116.

Accordingly the court said that not every claimed risk to life could give rise to a positive obligation to take operational measures to prevent the risk from materialising. Nonetheless these considerations were felt to be sufficiently accounted for *by* the quasi-duty test and *within* the quasi-fault test.[149] These policy factors will therefore be considered primarily at the fault stage.[150] Before we turn to the test of reasonableness employed by the ECtHR it is worth dwelling on the ECtHR's employment of the word 'operational'. This distinguishes the duties at issue in *Osman* from other positive duties such as to create effective criminal law regime.[151] While its use is ambiguous, it does not seem that this reference to operational acts implies the importation of the policy-operational distinction, which is employed by Commonwealth courts to define which areas of governmental decision-making are non-justiciable in negligence.[152]

3. *'failed to take measures within the scope of their powers which, judged reasonably, might have been expected . . .'*

In *Bland* the House of Lords invoked the *Bolam* test[153] as the test of lawfulness of medical decisions to withdraw treatment from someone in a persistent vegetative state (PVS), and to determine the patient's right to life in this context.[154] In *NHS Trust A v M* the Court of Appeal had to determine whether withdrawing treatment from someone who was in a persistent vegetative state violated Article 2.[155] In holding that it did not, the court noted that the test of reasonableness employed by the ECtHR bears a remarkable similarity to the negligence standard. The court then noted an important difference. It said that since the *Bolam* reasonable man test reserved to the court the power to determine whether treatment was indeed in a patient's best interest (as opposed to deferring to what the doctors thought) the test in negligence was somewhat stronger than the test of reasonableness applied by the ECtHR.[156] Though these comments were reserved to the declaratory cases on PVS the court does retain the power in

---

[149] This helps to explain the antipathy to the Court of Appeal's rejection of the Osman claim on policy grounds, even though proximity had been found.

[150] Similarly the Commission ((1998) 29 EHRR 245 (CD)) stated that the 'range of policy decisions' would be accommodated within the standard of reasonableness applied (para 91).

[151] *Mahmut Kaya v Turkey* (2000) 28 Mar (22535/93)

[152] *Anns v Merton London Borough Council* [1978] AC 728; *Phelps v Hillingdon London Borough Council* [2000] 3 WLR 776; *Rowling v Takaro Properties Ltd* [1988] AC 633; *Just v British Columbia* [1989] 2 SCR 1228; *Crimmins v Stevedoring Industry Finance Committee* (1999) 200 CLR 1.

[153] *Bolam v Friern Hospital Management Committee* [1957] 2 All ER 118

[154] *Airdale NHS Trust v Bland* [1993] AC 885.

[155] [2001] 2 WLR 942.

[156] *Frenchay Healthcare National Health Service Trust v S* [1994] 1 WLR 601 and *In re S* [2000] 3 WLR 1288.

the wider context to disagree with a body of opinion on what, in the circumstances, is reasonable conduct.[157] The ECtHR has rejected the submission that reasonableness could be equated to wilful disregard of duty or gross negligence.[158] Even so, their test could be read in a number of ways and is at present ill-defined in comparison with its common law counterpart. Although the test does not appear to be as intrusive as the standard applied in PVS cases, it is easy to overstate the intrusiveness of the *Bolam* test which does not give the courts a particularly strong supervisory role. This point will be explained in the following section. Moreover, since *Osman* was decided in a very different context the ECtHR test may yet prove to be more than a monolithic concept. The differences between the tests of reasonableness may therefore prove to be negligible.

As noted above it seems that problems of scarce resources, and the difficult and delicate nature of the tasks faced by public servants will be primarily relevant under the determination of reasonableness. Focusing closely on the ECtHR jurisprudence would therefore lead to the erosion of the immunity in negligence afforded for policy level decisions in English courts.[159] It may be better that in non-justiciable policy areas the courts should require that claims be brought under the HRA, rather than the ambit of negligence extended. If issues are non-justiciable, or outside the scope and protection of negligence partly on constitutional grounds, then the courts may be justified in modifying their position only in cases in which there is a constitutional mandate under the HRA. If similar reasoning were applied to cases brought at common law in analogous cases it could leave the duty of care lopsided and uncertain. While comparisons may be drawn with administrative law, which has adopted a different approach in human rights cases, administrative law is better able to adapt to protect rights than negligence.[160]

We shall see, however, that the English courts have already shifted their emphasis from the duty of care to its breach in the context of public authority liability and this may well precipitate this erosion of its own accord; if not a general shift to consider policy issues under fault and not duty. Nonetheless, while the obligations imposed by Article 2 remain uncertain (the definition of 'reasonable' the meaning of 'operational' particularly) alterations to negligence by reference to ECtHR jurisprudence should be cautiously made. While this is a clear area of convergence, there remain

---

[157] *Bolitho v City and Hackney Health Authority* [1998] AC 232. See the discussion below at n 173

[158] *Osman v United Kingdom*, para 116.

[159] See *Re HIV Haemophiliac Litigation* (1990) 41 BMLR 171. This approach has long been advocated by Bailey and Bowman (see 'Negligence in the Realms of Public Law: A positive Obligation to Rescue?' [1984] *PL* 276, 'The Policy/Operational Dichotomy: A Cuckoo in the Nest' (1986) 45 *CLJ* 430, and 'Public Authority Negligence Revisited' (2000) 59 *CLJ* 85).

[160] See above n 28, and n 121.

important tensions between the two strands of jurisprudence. It is also significant and illuminating that one of the most pronounced areas of convergence between common law principles of negligence and Convention jurisprudence should involve the right to life, since traditionally the common law of negligence has not protected such an interest since it was not viewed as an actionable harm.[161] Moreover, the current scheme under the Fatal Accidents Act 1976 will usually not promise relatives with an effective remedy.

C. Further Influences on the Duty of Care

Clerk & Lindsell suggests that the finding against the United Kingdom in *Z v United Kingdom* on Article 3 and *TP and KM v United Kingdom* on Article 8 may prompt the English courts to develop less restricted duties of care to protect these rights.[162] There are several possible responses to this view. First, it must be borne in mind that damages are not *required* for breaches of human rights and monetary awards under the HRA may be less readily made than has been the practice of the ECtHR,[163] whereas they are available as of right for negligence. Secondly, it is possible that similar policy considerations to those considered within the *substance* of the negligence determination, could be considered under the HRA when determining whether *damages* are just and appropriate or whether they are necessary to afford just satisfaction.[164] In particular, reference may well be had to considerations of distributive justice (which seems to be the currently preferred approach to considerations of fairness and justice) as a way to balance demands for compensation with the wider public interest.[165] Thirdly, unlike the re-invigorating effect that the HRA may have on rights-based torts, its presence could be a good reason for *reversing* the trend of expanding negligence, particularly to make public authorities liable where

---

[161] 'In a civil court the death of a human being cannot be complained of as an injury' *Baker v Bolton* (1808) 1 Camp 493 per Lord Ellenborough. *Admiralty Commissioners v SS Amerika* [1917] AC 38. The present law is to be found in the Fatal Accident Act 1976 (as amended); *Hicks v Chief Constable of South Yorkshire* [1992] 1 All ER 690, 2 All ER 65. See *Keenan v United Kingdom*, para 128.

[162] *Clerk and Lindsell On Torts*, above n 43 at 1–73, 1–77.

[163] See the discussion by Sir Stephen Sedley in his Concurring Opinion in *Keenan*, although he felt that the hands of the United Kingdom's courts were tied somewhat by the failure to include Art 13 in the HRA. Also *R (K) v Camden and Islington Health Authority* [2001] 3 WLR 553, para 54 (Sedley LJ).

[164] HRA s 8(1) and (3). For discussion of this point see D Fairgrieve, above n 32 at 700–2; Law Commission, above n 18, para 4.4.1.

[165] Rights Brought Home: above n 1, para 2.6. Particularly relevant may be the cases about ineffective sterilisation and careless family planning services: *McFarlane v Tayside Health Board* [2000] 2 AC 59 (financial expenses of healthy child not recoverable); *Greenfield v Irwin* [2001] 1 WLR 1279 (loss of employment while looking after healthy child not recoverable. Discussed below n 196).

private persons would not be. In such cases the HRA itself is likely to prove a sufficient deterrent,[166] and comes with a more satisfactory jurisprudence for dealing with grievances relating to violations of fundamental rights. So, for example, rather than drawing negligence into line with the obligations imposed by Article 2, the courts could apply the rights-based jurisprudence directly. This may reduce tensions and ensure compatibility.

Such an approach seems, however, unlikely to occur. There are already signs that policy considerations which point against the existence of a duty of care, particularly defensiveness, will be treated with more circumspection by the courts.[167] This trend will no doubt be fuelled by the pressure to adapt negligence to protect human rights, and the residual nature of the HRA action. The recent House of Lords cases of *Phelps, Barrett* and *W v Essex County Council* signal a move towards a less restrictive duty of care in actions against public bodies, and place emphasis instead on what is for claimants a demanding test of fault.[168] The courts have stressed that public officials will be subject to the *Bolam* test,[169] and fault will not be easy to prove.[170] Far from allowing the court to 'substitute its own view of the appropriate means for that of the department or authority . . .'[171] Lord Hutton has stated that 'the discretion is to be exercised by the authority . . . and not by the court'.[172] In relation to an established practice, a body of professional opinion will not be departed from unless the court feels that it is without a logical basis or that the experts have failed to properly direct their minds to the risks and benefits of their actions.[173] Demanding requirements for proving fault have been used to overcome problems of complexity and policy in the area of medical negligence[174] and in future this may be

---

[166] See D Howarth, *Textbook on Tort* (London: Butterworths, 1995), 187–91.

[167] See, eg, the remarks of Lord Slynn and Lord Clyde in *Phelps v Hillingdon London Borough Council* [2000] 3 WLR 776 (792 and 808–9), those of Lord Hutton and Lord Slynn in *Barrett v Enfield London Borough Council* [1999] 3 WLR 79 (98 and 113–14), and generally *Arthur JS Hall & Co. v Simons* [2000] 3 WLR 543.

[168] See Bailey and Bowman, 'Public Authority Negligence Revisited' (2000) 59 *CLJ* 85; P Craig and D. Fairgrieve, 'Barrett, Negligence and Discretionary Powers' [1999] *PL* 626.

[169] *Bolam v Friern Hospital Management Committee* [1957] 2 All ER 118; *X (Minors) v Bedfordshire County Council* [1995] 2 AC 633, 763.

[170] *Phelps*: 'The professionalism, dedication and standards of those engaged in the provision of educational services are such that cases of liability for negligence will be exceptional' per Lord Slynn, 792, also see Lord Clyde, 809.

[171] *Dorset Yacht v Home Office* [1970] AC 1004, 1067 per Lord Diplock.

[172] *Barrett v Enfield London Borough Council* [1999] 3 WLR 79, 115.

[173] *Bolitho v City and Hackney Health Authority* [1998] AC 232.

[174] Eg, *Wilsher v Essex Area Health Authority* [1986] 3 All ER 801, 809 per Mustill LJ; *Sidaway v Board of Governors of the Bethlam Royal Hospital* [1985] AC 871, 887–9 per Lord Scarman, 892–3 per Lord Diplock; *Whitehouse v Jordan* [1980] 1 All ER 650 (CA); [1981] 1 All ER 267 (HL). S McLean, 'Negligence: A Dagger at the Doctor's Back?', in P Robson and P Watchman (eds), *Justice Lord Denning and the Constitution* (Farnborough: Gower, 1981); Lord Woolf, 'Are the Courts Excessively Deferential to the Medical Profession?' (2001) 9 *Med. LRev* 1, 2. The courts have been compelled to utilise the test of fault in this way since it is

the approach taken in the wider context of public authority liability. One can speculate as to how far this trend has been prompted by the demands of the Convention,[175] but it may also enable easier integration, at least in relation to omissions.[176] In many circumstances, of course, rights-based analysis will be far more rigorous.[177]

We saw in the previous section how the positive obligations imposed by the HRA will affect the proximity between individuals and public authorities. The duty of care and its ambit must always be 'profoundly influenced by the statutory framework';[178] and the statutory framework now has to be read to impose positive obligations on public bodies to protect human rights. In *Phelps* Lord Slynn stated that it is 'clear that the loss suffered by a child who has not been treated in accordance with statutory intent can often be said to be foreseeable, proximate and serious'.[179] It is worth adverting to one further concrete example, in the context of Article 8. In the *Bedfordshire* litigation the Court of Appeal dismissed the claim against the child psychiatrist partly because the mother had no rights and so the psychiatrist's duty was only to consider the best interests of the child.[180] Social workers must now respect the rights of parents and their private and family life. While negligence principles should not themselves extend to protect parental rights *per se*,[181] courts will no longer be able to assert that the functions of social services are restricted to protecting the welfare of the child. This may make it easier to find that social workers owe a duty of care to parents.

D. Approaches to the Development of Negligence Law

At least three roads, which the law of negligence could take, can be

---

undeniable that doctors owe patients a duty of care. Cf *A-B John Wyeth & Bros. Ltd* [1994] 18 BMLR 38.

[175] The most likely influence is Art 6, on which see below text to nn 182–9.

[176] The duty of care has been criticised as otiose (WW Buckland, 'Duty to Take Care' (1935) 51 *LQR* 637) but is used to stabilise the law of negligence and to demarcate its boundaries. It acts as a control device over lower courts and, in other jurisdictions, juries. It is intrinsically connected to the common law method and the doctrine of precedent. It is thus axiomatic that its application to deny an action may deprive an otherwise worthy claimant of a remedy. If negligence is to be used by English courts to protect human rights (for which such an approach is unsuitable) the structure of negligence could well be fundamentally altered. Cf Craig and Fairgrieve, above n 168 at 638 ff on the shift in *Barrett* from duty to fault, and the discussion above at n 141.

[177] It is also to be queried how favourably the ECtHR would look on the *Bolitho* test, which seems to have much in common with *Wednesbury* (see *Herczegfalvy v Austria* (1992) 15 ECHR 437, para 82). Cf [1993] 4 *Med LRev* 241, 243 per Dillon LJ.

[178] *X (Minors) v Bedfordshire County Council* [1995] 2 AC 633, 739.

[179] *Phelps v Hillingdon London Borough Council* [2000] 3 WLR 776, 789

[180] See the discussion below n 194.

[181] Ibid.

discerned from the foregoing discussion. One approach would be to consider the negligence enquiry without reference to the fact that the authority owed an obligation to protect the individual's substantive rights, and simply apply negligence principles in strict isolation to the modified relationship between the parties and the existence of the HRA. This would be a mistake and an 'oil and water' approach to common law development. A second approach would be to maintain a clear separation between the negligence enquiry and any enquiry into whether a Convention right had actually been violated. These enquiries may well reach different conclusions, but the presence of the HRA would permeate the underlying policy considerations intrinsic to the negligence determination. Negligence *might* then recoil from the public sphere leaving the HRA to define the obligations of the state; but, perhaps unfortunately, this seems unlikely. A third approach would amalgamate the rights issue into negligence, or strongly align the two strands of jurisprudence. The case of *Orange* can perhaps be seen as signalling a move in this direction. The approach adopted by English courts will also depend largely on context, the jurisprudence relating to Article 2, for example, seems particularly relevant to negligence. It has, however, been suggested that even in such areas of apparent convergence there remain important tensions. There is a danger for the coherence of negligence law in pushing cross-fertilisation too far. The second approach identified is clearly preferable.

E. The Future Influence of Article 6

Much academic and judicial attention has been focused on the implications of the finding in *Osman* that the Court of Appeal had violated Article 6 by striking out the claim in negligence against the police.[182] The background to this aspect of the decision has been explained above. Thankfully, the court in *Z v United Kingdom* as has resiled somewhat from its earlier decision in *Osman*. It recognised that negligence should not be faulted for failing to protect human rights:

---

[182] Criticism: Lord Hoffmann, 'Human rights and the House of Lords' (1999) 62 *MLR* 159; Sir R Buxton, above n 4; Craig and Fairgrieve, above n 168; T Weir, 'Down Hill-All The Way?' (1999) 59 *CLJ* 4; M Lunney, 'A Tort Lawyer's View of *Osman v UK*' [1999] *KCLJ* 238; G Monti, '*Osman v UK*: Transforming English Negligence Law into French Administrative Law' (1999) 48 *ICLQ* 757. Compare: BS Markesinis, J-B Auby, D Coester-Waltjen, and S Deakin, *Tortious Liability of Statutory Bodies A Comparative and Economic Analysis of Five English Cases* (Oxford: Hart Publishing, 1999), 96–104. For judicial discussion see in particular: *Barrett v Enfield Borough Council* [1999] 3 WLR 79, 84–6 per Lord Browne-Wilkinson; *Kent v Griffiths* [2000] 2 WLR 1158, 1168–9 per Lord Woolf MR; *Palmer v Tees Health Authority* [1999] Lloyds L Rep Med 351, 354–6 per Stuart-Smith LJ and 362 per Pill LJ; *S v Gloustershire County Council* [2001] 2 WLR 909.

It is not enough to bring Article 6 (1) into play that the non-existence of a cause of action under domestic law *may be described* as having the same effect as an immunity, in the sense of not enabling the applicant to sue for a given category of harm.[183]

The ECtHR acknowledged that it had been mistaken in concluding that the public policy factors were not an integral part of the duty of care in English law, implying that Article 6 could not bite on such matters at all.[184] We have seen that the court held that the real failing was the 'gap' in English law, which constituted a breach of Article 13. However, the ECtHR was not altogether clear. It continued: 'the ruling of law concerning [the policy considerations] *in this case* does not disclose the operation of an *immunity*' (my emphasis).[185] The ECtHR seems to be suggesting that *some* adverse rulings on policy grounds (perhaps those of a 'sweeping or blanket nature')[186] would still have to be justified, and that *Osman v Ferguson* was wrong in not sufficiently 'weighing in the balance the competing considerations of public policy', in particular the policy that wrongs should be remedied, as was done in *X (Minors) v Bedfordshire County Council*.[187]

Given the recent trend of cases which reassert this balancing approach on domestic principles (although influenced by *Osman*) the implications of this reservation (if indeed it is one) may be limited.[188] It would also retain the influence of Article 6 on the content of substantive rights, despite the ECtHR's assertion that Article 6 does not guarantee any particular content for civil rights. It sits uneasily with the recognition that policy considerations, as part of the duty of care, are integral to the substantive determination of liability; as well as the observation that the cases had been 'litigated with vigour up to the House of Lords'.[189] The reservation would be best seen, if biting on the duty of care at all, as attaching to new immunities or the extension of existing ones, and requiring justification at that stage.

---

[183] *Z v United Kingdom*, para 98 (my emphasis).

[184] On this the ECtHR had been mislead by the Court of Appeal who had said that the policy considerations were 'a separate point which is not reached at all unless there is a duty of care' (*Osman v Ferguson* [1993] 4 All ER 344, 354 per McCowen LJ).

[185] *Z v United Kingdom*, para 100.

[186] Ibid, para 98.

[187] This is difficult to square with the suggestion (ibid, paras 96 and 101) that once the claim was determined against the applicants in *X (Minors) v Bedfordshire County Council* there was no arguable civil right under English law. How could there be such a right regarding the investigative activities of policing after *Hill v Chief Constable of West Yorkshire Police* [1989] AC 53? Surely the ECtHR is not suggesting that it reserves the right to ensure whether precedent has been properly applied (see, eg, *Bellet v France* (1995) A 333B).

[188] *Barrett v Enfield London Borough Council*; *Phelps v Hillingdon London Borough Council*; *Arthur JS Hall & Co. v Simons*; cf *Waters v Commissioner of Police* [2000] 1 WLR 1607; *Darker v Chief Constable of the West Midlands* [2000] 3 WLR 747.

[189] *Z v United Kingdom*, para 95

F. The Problem of Positive Obligations to Allow a Civil Remedy

Courts will not be compelled to develop civil remedies for violations of human rights unless failure to do so would itself violate a positive obligation derived from a Convention article by which they are bound.[190] The danger with too readily inferring these mandatory obligations is evident from analysing one vertical situation in which this issues may arise, namely violations of substantive rights by public authorities (other than the courts themselves) before the introduction of the HRA.

Since the House of Lords threw out the claims in negligence of the *Bedfordshire* children it would seem that claimants in an analogous position would have no remedy under the common law, nor would they under the HRA since the cause of action for unlawfulness is not retrospective. Since the courts are not bound to ensure that there is an effective remedy for violations of human rights, they will not be in violation of Article 13 by not so ensuring.[191] Claimants will have to go to the government, or in default to Strasbourg. If we assume *arguendo* that the courts would be in breach of Article 3 (by which they *are* bound) in refusing a civil remedy, then they would be *compelled* either to adapt the law of negligence to allow recovery, or fashion a new common law remedy.[192] The danger with the former for the coherency of private law can be seen if, instead of negligence, we imagine that the action was brought in contract to avoid the apparently binding authority of *X (Minors) v Bedfordshire*. Should the court allow recovery in the absence of consideration or even a formal agreement between the parties, by developing the common law of *contract*? And to do so on an ad hoc basis? Surely not.[193] For those who dislike the House of Lords' decision in *X (Minors) v Bedfordshire County Council*, overruling it may not appear unappetizing, but the more general point remains: fashioning remedies to protect rights out of existing common law actions may have serious repercussions for the wider coherency of private law. It may be preferable in some cases to fashion *new*

---

[190] Grosz, Beatson, and Duffy, above n 9 at 4-49.

[191] Sedley LJ has, however, recently stated that the requirement of Art 13 'reflects the long-standing principle of our law that where there is a right there should be a remedy' (*R (K) v Camden and Islington Health Authority* [2001] 3 WLR 553, para 54). Not all rights, however, need be protected in tort. Many 'rights' are also no more than 'freedoms' or 'privileges'. His statement should, therefore, be used cautiously.

[192] See Clayton and Tomlinson, above n 4 at 5.95–5.98.

[193] N Mole, 'Local Authorities and Human Rights' [2001] FL 487, 488 states that if faced with an *X (Minors) v Bedfordshire* 'lookalike' case occurring before the HRA, the 'logical answer appears to be to permit a strike out' but a 'more sensible approach would seem to be to apply the spirit of the finding of a violation of Art 13 [in *Z v United Kingdom*] . . . so as to allow the matter to be decided by English courts'. This view overlooks the wider implications in adapting the common law on an ad hoc basis.

remedies,[194] despite the fact that the HRA is not thought to compel the creation of new causes of action and to do so in these circumstances would be to give the HRA, in substance, retrospectivity which was not intended.[195]

A variant of this sticky problem arose in *Greenfield v Irwin*[196] in which it was alleged that the bar in tort on recovery for the costs incurred and loss of employment in bringing up a healthy but unwanted child, breached Article 8 of the Convention. The Court of Appeal wasted little time in throwing out this aspect of the claimant's case, noting that this was in essence a claim for welfare benefits, which were not required to be supplied by national authorities. Article 8 had not been interfered with, let alone unjustifiably so. Buxton LJ added, '[e]ven if it were the case on these facts that a breach of article 8 arose by the failure of the domestic legal system to grant damages in these circumstances, the way in which such a failure can be asserted in domestic private law proceedings is not wholly clear, to put it at its lowest'.[197]

IV. CONCLUSIONS

In a recent lecture Lord Woolf stated:

Like it or not, we have moved from a society which was primarily concerned with

---

[194] *Ashby v White* (1703) 2 Ld Raym 938 stands for the proposition that new rights-based torts can be developed. Claimants attempted to argue that the Court of Appeal should recognise the tort of infringement of parental rights in *F v Metropolitan Borough of Wirral* [1991] 2 FLR 114 but the court declined the invitation and considered that the first instance judge had been 'indulgent' and 'generous' in allowing the 'obscure' point to be argued as an amendment to the pleadings (121 and 128 per Purchas LJ). Admittedly it is by no means clear what conduct counsel was alleging had interfered with the alleged right, but the court held that there was no right under the common law beyond a father's right in the property of his child's services (*A v C* [1985] FLR 445, 455; *Re KD* [1988] AC 806). It is at least arguable that this case could be reconsidered since several of the reasons given by the court for denying an action have now been somewhat undermined (eg reliance on *A v Liverpool City Council* [1982] see now *Barrett v Enfield London Borough Council* [1999] 3 WLR 79, 110; reliance also on *R v Secretary of State for the Home Department, ex parte Brind* [1991] AC 696. Cf *R v A* [2001] All ER (D) 222; *Re W* and *Re D*; *Re W (Care Plan)* [2001] 2 FLR 582).

[195] There is at least one possible argument to justify a refusal by a court to alter the common law in these particular circumstances. Since Art 1, by which states must secure the rights contained in the Convention, has not been given effect by the HRA (because the HRA itself is thought to fulfil it) it could be argued that the courts are themselves under no obligation by virtue of the HRA to secure human rights beyond what has been mandated by Parliament, viz those situations in which actions can be brought prospectively for unlawfulness. However, Hare has pointed out the ECtHR has not always connected positive obligations to Article 1 (above note 4 at 517). From a practical perspective it may be extremely difficult for applicants to prove that the absence of a civil remedy in itself violates a substantive Convention right (Grosz, Beatson, and Duffy, above n 9 at 4-49–4-51).

[196] [2001] 1 WLR 1279.   [197] Ibid, para 33.

the *duty* individuals owed to society to one which is concerned primarily with the *rights* of the individual . . . judges do move with the times, even if more slowly that some would like. The move to a rights-based society has fundamentally changed the behaviour of the courts.[198]

The search for coherency in the common law now that rights play a central role is likely to occupy English courts for years to come. The objective of this paper has been to contrast negligence, based as it is on reasonableness and harm, with rights-based norms that are actionable *per se*, largely irrespective of fault and where interferences are presumed unlawful. In doing so areas of convergence and tension between Convention jurisprudence and the common law have been highlighted. It has been suggested that in the post-HRA era rights-based torts should be reinvigorated by reference to the Convention. Negligence law too will have to adapt, but attempts to stretch negligence in pursuit of strong coherence with the HRA risks negligence law becoming disjointed or incoherent. One possible way to avoid this would be to ask whether a Convention right had been infringed *before* one turned to the question of negligence. Such an approach would, however, depend on the willingness of the courts to promote the HRA, in some circumstances, from being a safety net for the common law.

---

[198] The Provost's Lecture at University College London, 17 Jan 2001, above n 174 at 3.

3. THE RETREAT FROM *OSMAN*: *Z v UNITED KINGDOM* IN THE EUROPEAN COURT OF HUMAN RIGHTS AND BEYOND

Jane Wright*

I. INTRODUCTION

Osman v United Kingdom[1] was a seminal case for English tort law, arguably producing a change in the judicial mindset[2] that had for the previous decade and more refused to countenance an expansion to public authority liability. Prior to *Osman*, a raft of cases had confirmed that English courts would be slow to recognise new areas of public authority liability in tort. The trend that gradually emerged from these cases was that a significant factor in fixing the boundaries of public authority liability was an appeal to considerations of public policy.[3] Thus, in *Hill v Chief Constable of West Yorkshire*,[4] the House of Lords held that the police did not owe a duty of care to the final victim of a psychopathic murderer because there was no proximity of relationship between herself and the

---

* Professor, Department of Law and Human Rights Centre at the University of Essex. I am extremely grateful to all those who participated in the discussion of *Z v United Kingdom* at the Annual Meeting of the British Institute of International and Comparative Law on 22 June 2001 and with whom some of the ideas expressed here have been discussed. Needless to add, the responsibility for errors is mine alone.

[1] [1999] 1 FLR 193.

[2] See, eg, *Barrett v Enfield London Borough Council* [2001] 2 AC 550 where the House of Lords refused to strike out the claimant's claim for damages for personal injury arguably caused by the mismanagement of his childhood while in the care of the local authority. Although the House of Lords' decision in *Phelps v London Borough of Hillingdon* [2001] 2 AC 619 was not based upon the direct liability of the local education authority, but rather upon the vicarious liability of the local authority for the negligent failure of an educational psychologist to diagnose dyslexia, it can be seen as part of a judicial willingness to recognise the liability of public authorities in appropriate cases. In *Phelps*, the House of Lords upheld the trial judge's award of damages for the failure to diagnose and thus ameliorate the condition of dyslexia. It was also held in *Anderton v Clwyd County Council* (appeal consolidated with *Phelps*), on an application for discovery, that failure to mitigate the effects of dyslexia was a claim for personal injury under s 33(2) Supreme Court Act 1981.

[3] A point made forcefully by B Markesinis, J-B Auby, D Coester-Waltjen, and S Deakin, in *Tortious Liability of Statutory Bodies* (Oxford: Hart Publishing, 1999), 43.

[4] [1989] AC 53.

police force. However, in what was arguably *obiter dictum*, Lord Keith also held that the police force did not owe a general duty of care to potential victims of crime when they undertook their public duty to investigate and suppress crime for policy reasons. These policy reasons were set out in some detail and included the following: performance of their public duty would not be enhanced by fear of litigation (what might be termed the deterrence factor); far from improving professional standards, the imposition of liability might lead to a detrimentally defensive frame of mind; many decisions relate to appropriate deployment of resources and are unsuitable for adjudication; and defending legal actions would divert manpower and resources from the important function of suppression of crime. As the author has observed elsewhere, such policy considerations are really no more than matters of impression and are very rarely supported by empirical evidence.[5] Lord Keith's views were elevated to the status of *ratio* by the Court of Appeal in *Osman v Ferguson*,[6] the English proceedings that led to the Strasbourg hearing in *Osman*. In *Elguzouli-Daf v Commissioner of Police for the Metropolis*,[7] the Court of Appeal held by analogy with *Hill* that, for policy reasons, in the absence of an assumption of responsibility, the Crown Prosecution Service owed no duty of care to those in custody and the subject of potential criminal proceedings. Finally, in *X (Minors) v Bedfordshire County Council ('Bedfordshire')*,[8] the English proceedings that led to the Strasbourg hearing in *Z v United Kingdom*,[9] the House of Lords held that it would not be fair, just and reasonable to recognise a duty of care on the part of a local authority to children in respect of whom it was discharging statutory welfare functions. In his leading speech, which is discussed below, Lord Browne-Wilkinson set out in detail the policy reasons that argued against finding a duty of care.

There were exceptional cases of course, such as *Swinney v Chief Constable of Northumbria*,[10] in which the police were held to owe a duty of care to a police informer who was threatened and suffered psychological damage as a result of the failure by the police to guard the identity of the informer with sufficient care. On the facts, the police had thereby assumed a responsibility to protect the identity of the informant. In that case the public interest arguments argued in favour of liability: it is clearly in the public interest that those who help the police to apprehend criminals should be protected appropriately.

---

[5] See J Wright, 'Local Authorities, the Duty of Care and the European Convention on Human Rights' (1998) 18 *OJLS* 1. See also Wright, *Tort Law and Human Rights* (Oxford: Hart Publishing, 2001), 'Introduction' and *passim*.

[6] [1993] 4 All ER 344: see M Tregilgas-Harvey, '*Osman v Metropolitan Police Commissioner*: The Cost of Police-Protectionism' (1993) 56 *MLR* 732.

[7] [1995] 2 WLR 173.

[8] [1995] 2 AC 633.

[9] [2001] 2 FLR 612.

[10] [1997] QB 464.

In view of the wide ranging appeals to public policy made by defendants, it might reasonably have been expected that counsel for claimants would have countered the non-liability arguments with appeals to 'policy' of a different kind: many of the cases described above implicate the rights laid down in the European Convention on Human Rights ('the Convention'). *Osman* concerned the right to life (Article 2), *Elguzouli-Daf* the right to liberty and security of the person (Article 5) and *Bedfordshire* concerned, at the very least, the right to respect for private life (Article 8) and as Strasbourg later decided the right to be free from inhuman and degrading treatment (Article 3). The author argued prior to *Osman* coming before Strasbourg that the courts should take account of convention rights in the development of the tort of negligence.[11] Such argument might have been anticipated in the light of *Derbyshire County Council v Times Newspapers Ltd*,[12] where all members of the Court of Appeal were agreed that in the case of uncertainty in the common law the court should have regard to the Convention. In the House of Lords the only speech was given by Lord Keith who reached the same conclusion as the Court of Appeal (a local authority could not sue in libel), but he reached this decision without 'finding any need to rely upon the European Convention'.[13] However, Lord Keith did not cast any doubt on the correctness of the Court of Appeal's views as to when it would be appropriate to have recourse to the Convention.

It was against this background, generally favouring non-liability on the part of public authorities in new areas, that the European Court of Human Rights stepped into the fray, first in *Osman* in 1999 and then in 2001 with Z, a decision that marked a retreat from *Osman* and one that will now ensure that English courts are forced once again to reassess their approach to public authority liability. At the same time, the Human Rights Act 1998 has come into force and it is necessary to consider also the impact that this alternative framework of remedies may have upon the nascent expansion of public authority liability in tort. The picture that emerges is one where the boundaries of liability in tort seem to ebb and flow, but at this juncture it is difficult to predict what impact Z and the Human Rights Act will have on the liability of public authorities at common law.

This chapter will present a critique of the Strasbourg decision in Z and examine the implications for English tort law that flow from this decision. Z is a decision that is on its face impenetrable and it is also impossible to understand without revisiting the Court's reasoning in *Osman*. The following discussion will therefore begin with a brief résumé of the European Court of Human Rights' decision in *Osman* and will then move on to examine the decision in Z.

---

[11]   Wright, 'Local Authorities'.   [12]   [1992] QB 770.
[13]   *Derbyshire County Council v Times Newspapers Ltd* [1993] AC 534, 551.

II. *OSMAN V UNITED KINGDOM*: WHAT DID THE EUROPEAN COURT OF HUMAN
RIGHTS DECIDE?

In *Osman v Ferguson*,[14] the Court of Appeal held that the police force
owed no duty of care in negligence to the Osman family who had the
misfortune to be targeted by a dangerous obsessive who ultimately killed
one member of the family and injured another. The offender was well
known to the claimants who had pleaded for assistance from the police over
a period of months. Thus, the case was markedly different from *Hill v Chief
Constable of West Yorkshire*,[15] where the House of Lords had found that
there was no proximity of relationship between the police force and the last
victim of the Yorkshire Ripper. There was nothing on the facts of *Hill* that
would lead to the police force being able to single out the unfortunate Miss
Hill from the rest of the female population who could fall prey to the
psychopathic murderer. In contrast, two members of the Court of Appeal in
Osman v Ferguson considered that the facts did disclose sufficient proximity on which to found a duty of care; however, all members of the Court
were agreed that it would not be fair, just and reasonable to recognise a
duty of care for the policy reasons articulated by Lord Keith in *Hill* and the
action was struck out on the basis that no duty of care was owed. The
Osmans then instituted proceedings in Strasbourg alleging, *inter alia*, that
the decision to strike out by the House of Lords amounted to a violation of
the Article 6 right to a fair trial, which includes the right of access to a
court. The Osmans also complained that the United Kingdom had violated
Article 2 of the Convention (the right to life) and Article 13 (the right to an
effective remedy). These Articles are not however relevant to the immediate
discussion which will focus on the Article 6 complaint.

The European Court of Human Rights held that the Court of Appeal's
decision to strike out the Osmans' claim amounted to a restriction on the
right of access to a court that violated Article 6. Article 6 provides that, 'In
the determination of his civil rights and obligations...., everyone is entitled
to a fair and public hearing within a reasonable time . . . ' This right
includes the right of access to a court. In *Golder v United Kingdom*, the
Court held that 'the Article embodies the "right to a court", of which the
right of access, that is the right to institute proceedings before courts in civil
matters constitutes one aspect only'.[16] In order for Article 6 to bite, it is
necessary that an applicant can show that he has an arguable claim in
domestic law. Article 6 might properly be described as embodying a procedural right to determine the effect of substantive national rules. It is not a
vehicle through which Strasbourg can dictate what domestic law should be.

---

[14] [1993] 4 All ER 344.   [15] [1989] AC 53.   [16] Series A no 18 (1975) para 36.

However, the Court's decision in *Osman* was subsequently to be reviled by members of the English academic and judicial communities because it was perceived as an attack upon, or an attempt to shape, English substantive law.

The Court found that Article 6 was applicable because it accepted the government's argument that the principle of *Hill* did not doom an action to failure. Therefore, the applicants had a right, deriving from the law of negligence, to seek an adjudication on the admissibility and merits of an arguable claim that they were owed a duty of care by the police on the basis of the criteria laid down in *Caparo Industries plc v Dickman*.[17] The effect of the strike out decision was therefore to restrict the right of access to a court and that restriction must be examined to determine whether it was lawful. This required to Court to satisfy itself that the limitation applied did not 'restrict or reduce the access left to the individual in such a way or to such an extent that the very essence of the right is impaired. … a limitation will not be compatible with Article 6(1) if it does not pursue a legitimate aim and if there is not a reasonable relationship of proportionality between the means employed and the aim sought to be achieved'.[18] The Court found that while the restriction pursued a legitimate aim, namely, the maintenance of an effective police force, it nevertheless violated the proportionality principle. The Court of Appeal had proceeded on the basis that *Hill* provided an immunity and the fact that the Court of Appeal had not weighed in the balance public policy arguments that pulled in the direction of liability amounted to an unjustifiable restriction on the applicant's right to have a determination on the merits. The Court of Human Rights held that if such competing policy considerations are not considered 'there will be no distinction made between degrees of negligence or of harm suffered or any consideration of the justice of a particular case'.[19]

The message from *Osman* was clear: English courts should proceed cautiously before striking out a claim on the basis that no duty of care was owed. However, *Osman* did not decide that English courts could not strike out claims in negligence. As a number of commentators have observed on a strikeout application the facts are assumed to be as pleaded so that in one sense the form of hearing favours an applicant. The correct interpretation of *Osman*, as was subsequently made implicit in the Commission decision in *Z v United Kingdom*, was that English courts must be mindful of the balancing process that should be undertaken in cases that engage fundamental rights. The problem in *Osman* was that the Court of Appeal had not

---

[17] [1990] 2 AC 605.

[18] *Osman* [1999] 1 FLR 193 citing *Tinnelly & Sons Ltd and McElduff v United Kingdom* (1998) 27 EHRR 249 as the most recent authority. See also *Ashingdane v United Kingdom*, Series A no 93 (1985) from which this test derives.

[19] *Osman* [1999] 1 FLR 193 para 151.

undertaken such a consideration of *competing* policy considerations. As the
Commission stated in *Z*, when examining the House of Lords' decision in
Bedfordshire, 'the exclusionary rule gave no consideration to the seriousness or otherwise of the damage or the nature or degree of the negligence
alleged or the fundamental rights of the applicants which were involved'.[20]

Osman was not without its critics. Lord Hoffmann was not alone when
he appeared infuriated by this perceived attempt to interfere with the
content of English substantive law.[21] Lord Browne-Wilkinson confessed
that he found the decision difficult to understand.[22] Auld LJ remarked on
the state of uncertainty in the law engendered by the *Osman* decision.[23]
Nevertheless, its impact was immediate, both in terms of procedure and
substance. The response of English courts was to display a marked reluctance to strike out claims in negligence, emphasising that decisions should
be made on the basis of certain facts. As described above this was an over-
reaction to *Osman*. Unsurprisingly, the courts also began to shy away from
findings of non-liability. The most significant decisions during the immediate post-*Osman* phase were *Barrett v Enfield London Borough Council*[24]
and *Phelps v London Borough of Hillingdon*.[25] Both decisions have been
subject to extensive academic analysis and it is beyond the scope of this
chapter to go into detail here.[26] Suffice to observe that in *Barrett*, the House
of Lords distinguished *Bedfordshire* on the narrow basis that the relevant
policy considerations were different when a child had been taken into care:
therefore, the action for damages for personal injury should proceed to
trial. *Phelps* is less significant in the sense that it was an action against a
local education authority that was held vicariously, rather than directly,
liable for the failure of an educational psychologist to diagnose dyslexia. A
sceptical observer might have argued that *Phelps* is no more than an example of a successful claim for pure economic loss that was contingent upon
the discovery of an assumption of responsibility. It was found after all in
Phelps that the relevant educational psychologist had made an assumption
of responsibility to the claimant. However, in *Anderton v Clwyd County
Council*,[27] a claim for failure to mitigate the effects of dyslexia was treated
as a claim for personal injury for the purposes of discovery under section
33(2) Supreme Court Act 1981. The decision in *Phelps* can be seen as reflective of a welcome trend towards individualised justice rather than a contin-

[20] (1999) 28 EHRR CD 65 para 114.
[21] Rt Hon Lord Hoffmann, 'Human Rights and the House of Lords' (1999) 62 MLR 159.
[22] *Barrett v Enfield London Borough Council* [2001] 2 AC 550, 558.
[23] *Gower v Bromley London Borough Council* [1999] ELR 356.
[24] 2001] 2 AC 550.   [25] [2001] 2 AC 619.
[26] See P Craig and D Fairgrieve, '*Barrett*, Negligence and Discretionary Powers' [1999] *PL*
626 and D Fairgrieve and M Andenas, 'Tort Liability for Educational Malpractice: the *Phelps*
Case' [1999] 10 *KCLJ* 210.
[27] [2001] 2 AC 619.

uation of attempts to constrain the demands on the public purse through the application of arbitrary rules in the form of blanket immunities from suit. By way of contrast, it should be recalled that in *M (A Minor) v Newham London Borough Council*,[28] the plaintiff's claim that the local authority was vicariously liable for the negligence of a social worker and psychiatrist was denied not only on the grounds that there was no assumption of responsibility to the claimants, but also for the same policy reasons that applied in *Bedfordshire*. The clear implication was that public authority liability should be denied at all costs.

In the light of *Osman* and indeed the Commission decision in Z (which were both unanimous), it was reasonable to anticipate that the European Court of Human Rights would find that the House of Lords decision in *Bedfordshire* to uphold the strike out order was also a disproportionate restriction on the right of access to a court contemplated by Article 6 and, therefore, unlawful. However, in a complete volte-face the European Court of Human Rights has effectively overruled *Osman*, and has decided that when English courts determine the scope of negligence through the duty of care device that is a substantive law issue upon which Article 6 scrutiny does not bite. The following discussion will therefore provide an analysis of the Court's decision in Z and then consider the implications for English law that flow from this retreat from *Osman*.

III. Z *V UNITED KINGDOM* IN THE EUROPEAN COURT OF HUMAN RIGHTS[29]

It will be recalled that this case concerns the application to Strasbourg by the children whose action in negligence was struck out by the House of Lords in *Bedfordshire*[30] for the reason that no duty of care was owed to them for policy reasons. In *Bedfordshire*, five children attempted to mount an action in negligence against the local authority charged with responsibility for their welfare under a range of statutes. They had suffered appalling neglect by their parents over a period of almost 5 years at the end of which they were taken into care. The leading judgment for a unanimous House of Lords was given by Lord Browne-Wilkinson who held that the action should be struck out on the basis that a direct duty of care was not owed to the children by the local authority, because it would not be 'fair, just and reasonable' to recognise a duty of care for a range of policy reasons. To summarise[31] these reasons included: the interdisciplinary nature

---

[28] Appeal consolidated with *Bedfordshire* [1995] 2 AC 633.

[29] This discussion draws substantially on the author's previous work: Wright, *Tort Law*, xxiii–xxxvii.

[30] [1995] 2 AC 633.

[31] For the author's critique of the House of Lords decision see Wright, 'Local Authorities'.

of responsibility for child welfare, involving social workers, the police, educational bodies, and doctors, which would make it unfair to single out one defendant; the task is delicate; a fear of defensive practice; fear of vexatious and costly litigation and the consequent diversion of human resources and money from the performance of the requisite service. The children then petitioned Strasbourg alleging violations of Article 3 (the right to be free from inhuman and degrading treatment), Article 6 (the right of access to a court), Article 8 (the right to respect for private life) and Article 13 (the right to an effective remedy). The subsequent discussion will focus largely on the Article 6 issue, because it is that part of the decision that constitutes a rejection of *Osman*.

The Commission had found that Articles 3 and 6 had been violated. The Commission considered first of all whether Article 6 was applicable to the claim. In line with its constant jurisprudence, the Commission stated that Article 6 does not guarantee any particular content of substantive law and that the obligation in Article 6 extends to obligations that can be said 'at least on arguable grounds to be recognised by domestic law'.[32] The Commission saw no reason to distinguish Z from *Osman* (the applicants must be taken to have had a right, derived from the law of negligence to seek an adjudication on the admissibility and merits of a claim that they were owed a duty of care). The Commission then proceeded to examine whether the decision of the House of Lords, since it amounted to the deprivation of access to the court (the strike out meant that no hearing took place on the merits), satisfied the requirements of legitimacy and proportionality laid down by *Ashingdane*[33] and *Lithgow v United Kingdom*.[34] In other words, did the restriction pursue a legitimate aim and was there a reasonable relationship of proportionality between the means employed (the denial of a duty of care) and the aim sought to be achieved. The aim of preserving the efficiency of the public service was found to be legitimate, but the restriction was a disproportionate interference with the Article 6 right, because there was no consideration of the seriousness of the damage or the degree of negligence or the fundamental rights of the applicants which were involved.[35]

After the Commission had delivered its Report, the United Kingdom government conceded that Article 3 had been breached, but contested the Article 6 complaint before the Court of Human Rights.

The decision of the Court in Z is of immense significance because it apparently marks a rejection of the application of one strand of Article 6 jurisprudence relating to the right of access to a court to English common

---

[32] Citing *James v UK* Series A no 98 (1986) para 81 and *Ashingdane v United Kingdom*, Series A no 93 (1985) para 55.

[33] Ibid.   [34] Series A no 102 (1986).

[35] *Z v United Kingdom* (1999) 28 EHRR CD 65, para 114.

law decisions regarding the scope of negligence: in this sense it is an over-ruling of the Court's decision in *Osman v United Kingdom*.[36] In summary, the Court has decided that where English courts refuse to recognise a duty of care in relation to a class of actors and/or a class of harm under the third head of *Caparo Industries Plc v Dickman*[37] (it would not be fair, just and reasonable to recognise a duty of care) and thereupon strike out a claim, that is not to create an immunity or an exclusionary rule that should then be evaluated for compliance with Article 6 jurisprudence regarding propor-tionality and legitimacy. Instead, what English courts are doing in such cases is to deny that (henceforth) there is an *arguable* claim the existence of which would engage Article 6 obligations.[38] Taking the decision to its logi-cal conclusion, the Court seems to be saying that the determination of the scope of the negligence action is purely within the prerogative of the English courts and the development of these substantive rules does not engage Article 6. The decision is difficult to follow and inherently contradictory. It is understood that the arguments put forward by Gearty in his article 'Unravelling Osman'[39] were put to the Court[40] and have influenced the outcome. With that in mind the analysis will also make reference to those views, where relevant.

In contrast with the decision of the Court in *Osman* and the Commission in Z, which were both unanimous, the Court's decision in Z was a major-ity decision (12–5) and Sir Nicholas Bratza, the elected English judge, voted against the United Kingdom government in the Commission. His place in the Court was then taken by Lady Justice Arden as an ad hoc judge. The hearing took place on 28 June 2000, but almost eleven months elapsed before judgment was pronounced. It might reasonably be surmised that agreement was difficult to reach and the appended dissents reveal a signifi-cant level of dissatisfaction with the outcome of the Article 6 complaint. What the Court seems to have done is to endeavour to retain the integrity of its supervisory jurisdiction as laid down in *Ashingdane v United Kingdom*,[41] but to deny that the control tests of legitimacy and propor-tionality deriving from that case were applicable to Z. It is extremely diffi-cult to grasp precisely why the House of Lords' decision in *Bedfordshire* did not amount to the creation of an exclusionary rule effecting a restriction on access to the court. That is, however, what the Court in Z decided. The

---

[36] [1999] 1 FLR 193. [37] [1990] 2 AC 605.

[38] On the question of 'arguability' see discussion below.

[39] (2001) 64 MLR 159.

[40] I am grateful for the comments on this point made by D Anderson QC, Counsel for the Government in Z, at a Seminar held on 19 July 2001 on the subject of 'Human Rights and Tort Remedies in English Public Law' at the British Institute of International and Comparative Law.

[41] Series A no 93 (1985) para 55.

decision in *Osman v United Kingdom* provoked a great deal of criticism, both judicial and academic, but it seems unlikely that *Z* will lay the *Osman* ghost to rest, because it in turn has created its own litigation-provoking uncertainties.

In *Z*, the United Kingdom Government conceded that both Articles 3 (the right not to suffer inhuman and degrading treatment) and 13 (the right to an effective remedy) had been breached. The European Court of Human Rights made the highest ever awards of just satisfaction (compensation) under Article 41 for psychological and physical damage totalling £320,000, with one child receiving £132,000. The awards comprised sums in respect of pecuniary damage to include the cost of psychiatric treatment and loss of employment opportunities. Sums (£32,000) in respect of non-pecuniary damage for the pain and suffering of each of the children were included in the award.

The Court began its analysis by recalling its jurisprudence to the effect that the guarantees encompassed by Article 6 extend only to disputes that can be said 'at least on arguable grounds', to be recognised by domestic law.[42] Therefore, the Court held that, at the outset, in the proceedings before the English courts, there was a genuine dispute about the existence of the right to sue in negligence and the applicants therefore arguably had a claim in domestic law.[43] It was agreed by the parties that, prior to *Bedfordshire*, there was no precedent that determined whether a local authority could be liable in the tort of negligence for the improper performance of child protection duties. Therefore Article 6 was engaged. In a remark heavy with significance for future claims to Strasbourg, the Court stated that: 'The Government's submission that there was no arguable (civil) right for the purposes of Article 6 once the House of Lords had ruled that no duty of care arose has relevance rather to any claims which were lodged or pursued subsequently by other plaintiffs.'[44] Thus far, the Court's approach accorded with what it had said in *Osman*. It is at the next stage of the analysis that the Court parted company with *Osman*.

The Court recalled its decision in *Golder v United Kingdom*[45] which laid down the principle that, where a person does have an arguable claim, there should be access to a court: without access to court 'the procedural guarantees laid down in Article 6 concerning fairness, publicity and expeditiousness would be meaningless'. However, at paragraph 93 of the judgment, the Court relying on established authority, recalled that the right enshrined in Article 6 is not absolute; it may be subject to limitations such

---

[42] Art 6 is expressed to apply '[in] the determination of his civil rights and obligations . . .': see discussion accompanying n16 above.

[43] [2001] 2 FLR 612.   [44] Ibid.

[45] Series A no 18 (1975) para 36.

as statutory limitation periods, security for costs orders and so on. The Court then went on to refer to its judgment in *Ashingdane* and stated that:

Where the individual's access [to a court] is limited either by operation of law or in fact, the Court will examine whether the limitation imposed impaired the essence of the right and in particular whether it pursued a legitimate aim and there was a reasonable relationship of proportionality between the means employed and the aim sought to be achieved.[46]

Clearly, the effect of this statement is that the question of whether English law requires to be evaluated for legitimacy and proportionality will depend upon whether the applicant's access to the court has been 'limited'. It is on this crucial issue that Z differs from *Osman v United Kingdom*. It will be recalled that in *Osman*, the Court of Human Rights took the view that the decision of the House of Lords in *Hill v Chief Constable of West Yorkshire*[47] (no duty of care in negligence in relation to the investigation/suppression of crime) had created an exclusionary rule in favour of the police force which acted as a restriction on the right of access to a court. The Court (applying the *Ashingdane*[48] and *Tinnelly*[49] line of jurisprudence) concluded that the decision of the Court of Appeal in *Osman v Ferguson*[50] had violated Article 6, because, although the aim of the exclusionary rule (maintenance of an effective police service) could be regarded as legitimate, the principle of proportionality was not satisfied, in that there was no consideration of degrees of harm or degrees of negligence.

In Z, the applicants contended that the decision of the House of Lords in *Bedfordshire* deprived them of access to a court (as a result of the claim being struck out on the basis of no duty, there was no determination on the merits) because it was effectively an exclusionary rule. The Court rejected this argument, stating that the procedural guarantees laid down in *Golder* had been observed because the case had been litigated with vigour up to the House of Lords and the applicants had not been prevented in any practical manner from pursuing their claim: no procedural rules or limitation periods had been invoked. In a complete rejection of its conclusion in *Osman*, the Court stated that it was not persuaded 'that the House of Lords' decision that there was no duty of care may be characterised as either an exclusionary rule or an immunity which deprived [the applicants] of access to a court.'[51] In *Osman*, of course, the Court had come to the very opposite conclusion. How then could the Court justify its departure from the reasoning employed in *Osman*? Ironically, the justification lay in part in the case law that has emerged from the English courts subsequent to *Osman* and which clearly manifested the imprint of *Osman*, if not always explicitly,

---

[46] [2001] 2 FLR 612, para 93. [47] [1989] AC 53. [48] Series A no 93 (1985).
[49] (1998) 27 EHRR 249. [50] [1993] 4 All ER 344.
[51] [2001] 2 FLR 612, para 96.

certainly implicitly. In *Z*, the Court stated that its decision in *Osman* was based on an understanding of the law of negligence that now had to be

> reviewed in the light of the clarifications subsequently made by the domestic courts and notably the House of Lords. The Court is satisfied that the law of negligence as developed in the domestic courts since the case of *Caparo* and as recently analysed in the case of *Barrett v Enfield LBC* includes the fair, just and reasonable criterion as an intrinsic element of the duty of care and that the ruling of law concerning that element in this case does not disclose the operation of an immunity. In the present case, the Court is led to the conclusion that the inability of the applicants to sue the local authority flowed not from an immunity but from the applicable principles governing the substantive right of action in domestic law. There was no restriction on access to court of the kind contemplated in the *Ashingdane* judgment.[52]

Putting it at its crudest, the court has justified a retraction of its reasoning in *Osman*, because English courts have demonstrated in cases such as *Barrett v Enfield London Borough Council*,[53] that in some instances there may in fact be liability. *Bedfordshire* was distinguished in *Barrett* on the thinnest of grounds, namely, that the arguments in *Bedfordshire* did not apply with the same force to children where the decision had been made to take them into care and the House of Lords clearly felt the pressure of the Strasbourg decision in *Osman*. It is of course illogical to say that because one class of persons may bring proceedings in negligence against a public body there can, therefore, be no immunity in relation to another class of persons. The dissent on this point by Judge Thomassen (joined by Judges Casadevall and Kovler) makes this very point:

> To reach its conclusion that the decision by the House of Lords was no immunity, the Court's majority observes, in para 99, that in cases concerning the liability of local authorities in child care matters brought after the applicants' case the domestic courts have held that a duty of care may arise. But this does not change the fact that an immunity was conferred on the authorities in the applicants' case. Apparently the immunity applied in the applicants' case was found no longer appropriate in subsequent cases, the national courts taking into account, amongst other factors, the Court's approach in the *Osman* case.[54]

In the author's view, the House of Lords in *Bedfordshire* clearly applied an exclusionary rule to prevent the children pursuing their claims to trial. Public policy arguments, as perceived by the House of Lords, meant that those children could not sue. In a common law system where the judiciary is responsible for the delineation of civil responsibility no distinction should be drawn between Immunities (exclusionary rules) that are laid down and circumscribed by Parliament on the one hand (Ashingdane)[55] and the

---

[52] [2001] 2 FLR 612, para 101.   [53] [2001] 2 AC 550.   [54] [2001] 2 FLR 612.
[55] *Ashingdane* Series A no 93 (1985) concerned immunity from suit created by Mental Health Act 1959, s 141, see discussion accompanying n 58, below.

courts on the other. Both statutory and common law rules are capable of creating immunities that constitute a restriction on the right of access to the court.

It is also apparent that the Court was not entirely convinced by its own reasoning. The Court states, without explaining adequately why, that the application of the fair, just and reasonable criteria in *Bedfordshire* did not disclose the operation of an immunity and there was therefore no restriction on the right of access to a court. As described above, it has been held in the constant jurisprudence of the court that where there *is* such a restriction, then such should be assessed to ensure that it pursues a legitimate aim and accords with the principle of proportionality. Having reached its decision that no exclusionary rule had been applied in *Bedfordshire*, the corollary must be that these tests were quite clearly irrelevant and should logically have been disregarded. However, this is not what the Court did, thus manifesting an obvious discomfiture with its own finding. For the Court stated that the House of Lords' decision in *Bedfordshire* was reached after a careful balancing of the policy reasons for and against the imposition of liability, because Lord Browne-Wilkinson weighed the principle that wrongs should be remedied, which requires very potent counter considerations to be overridden, against other public policy concerns. In this part of its judgment, the Court was attempting to establish that, although there was no exclusionary rule, the House of Lords had, in any event, satisfied the standards against which such a rule would be evaluated. This is a complete misrepresentation of Lord Browne-Wilkinson's speech in *Bedfordshire*. To adopt the terminology of the Court of Human Rights in *Osman* and the Commission in Z, Lord Browne-Wilkinson gave no consideration to the degree of harm, the degree of negligence or the fact that fundamental rights were engaged. It is indeed scarcely conceivable (even taking account of the then general hostility to negligence actions against public authorities) that had Convention arguments been put before the court,[56] the House of Lords could have reached its decision with such alacrity.

The outstanding question from the Court's decision in Z, which is not answered clearly by the judgment, is why did the refusal to recognise a duty of care in *Bedfordshire* not constitute a restriction on access to the court of the kind contemplated in the *Ashingdane* judgment? This question requires us to revisit that authority and to examine the arguments put forward by Gearty as to how the line of authority stemming from *Ashingdane* should be interpreted.

---

[56] See Wright, 'Local Authorities'.

IV. *ASHINGDANE V UNITED KINGDOM*

Ashingdane was an offender patient who had suffered from paranoid schizophrenia and been detained in Broadmoor Hospital. Several years after his detention he was no longer considered to pose the threat of violence that he previously did and the Home Secretary gave consent for his transfer to a local psychiatric hospital. The staff at the most suitable hospital took the view that they did not have the resources to care for an offender patient such as Ashingdane and refused to admit him, warning that industrial action might be taken were he to be transferred. He consequently wanted to challenge the failure of the Secretary of State and health authority to provide appropriate hospital care for his mental health.

Having obtained legal aid, Ashingdane instituted proceedings to challenge the legality of his continued detention at Broadmoor. Various relief was sought in the form of declarations that, *inter alia*, the Department of Health and Social Security and the local health authority were acting ultra vires in refusing to transfer him, as well as declarations that the members and officers of the union were acting unlawfully. The matter was litigated up to the Court of Appeal where the proceedings were stayed because there was no allegation of bad faith or lack of reasonable care and it was found that the acts complained of fell within the immunity created by the Mental Health Act 1959. The Court of Appeal found that Ashingdane's civil action against the local health authority and the Department of Health and Social Security was barred by operation of law on account of section 141 of the Mental Health Act 1959 which provides that:

(1) No person shall be liable . . . to any civil . . . proceedings to which he would have been liable apart from this section in respect of any act purporting to be done in pursuance of this Act . . .unless the act was done in bad faith or without reasonable care.

(2) No civil . . . proceedings shall be brought against any person in any court in respect of any such act without the leave of the High Court, and the High Court shall not give leave under this section unless satisfied that there is substantial ground for the contention that the person to be proceeded against has acted in bad faith or without reasonable care.

Thereupon Ashingdane took his case to Strasbourg alleging that the United Kingdom had breached its obligations under Article 5 paragraphs (1) and (4), which are not relevant for present discussion, and Article 6(1).

The Government contended that Article 6 (1) was not applicable because the claims did not relate to a 'civil right'. The Court of Human Rights declared that it was not necessary to settle this issue, because assuming that Article 6(1) was applicable, the requirements of the Article had not been violated. The Court referred to the *Golder* holding that Article 6(1) secured the right of access to a court. In *Ashingdane*, the applicant did have access to the court, both the High Court and the Court of Appeal, where he was told, predictably enough, that his actions were barred by the statute. The Court stated that '[to] this extent, he thus had access to the remedies that existed within the domestic system. . . . This of itself does not necessarily exhaust the requirements of Article 6(1). It must still be established that the degree of access afforded under the national legislation was sufficient to secure the individual's "right to a court", having regard to the rule of law in a democratic society.'[57] In the passage that has come to assume enormous significance the Court declared that the right of access to a court under Article 6 is not absolute and may be subject to limitations. Such limitations must not:

restrict or reduce the access left to the individual in such a way or to such an extent that the very essence of the right is impaired . . . a limitation will not be compatible with Article 6(1) if it does not pursue a legitimate aim and if there is not a reasonable relationship of proportionality between the means employed and the aim sought to be achieved.[58]

The Court took the view in *Ashingdane* that these tests were satisfied. It is difficult to see why it was appropriate to apply these criteria to the staying of proceedings in *Ashingdane*, but not to the strike-out in *Bedfordshire*. It is emphasised also that the Court in Z evinces no explicit willingness to cast doubt on the authority of *Ashingdane*; rather, the Court has taken the view that those principles do not apply in Z. The perspective adopted by Gearty provides illumination on this question.

In *Unravelling Osman*,[59] Gearty traces the development of Strasbourg supervision in relation to Article 6 and suggests an alternative interpretation of *Ashingdane* that would have led to different outcomes in both *Tinnelly*[60] and *Osman*.[61] Gearty's thesis is that the appropriate interpretation of *Ashingdane* (but not the one adopted in *Osman* or *Tinnelly*) is that Strasbourg supervision under Article 6 operates at two levels that are *mutually exclusive*. First, where a person can show that she has an arguable civil claim in domestic law, that will engage Article 6 and secure the procedural guarantees laid down in *Golder*. This he describes as the 'threshold' test for the engagement of Article 6 guarantees. Thus, in Z, the Court found that the threshold of arguability was satisfied and then moved on to ensure that the procedural guarantees had been observed. Gearty then suggests that, where a person cannot show an arguable claim, the tests of legitimacy and proportionality should be applied as a 'fallback' test in order to ensure that Strasbourg retains a proper supervisory jurisdiction over states. He has

[57] Series A no 93 (1985) para 57.   [58] Ibid.
[59] (2001) 64 MLR 159.   [60] (1998) 27 EHRR 249.
[61] [1999] 1 FLR 193.

argued that the fact that Ashingdane's claims were barred by operation of law should naturally have led the Court to conclude that, therefore, Article 6 was not applicable as the threshold test of arguability had not been satisfied. He suggests that the further evaluation of the degree of access for compatibility with principles of legitimate aim and proportionality should rightly be regarded as a 'European fallback test' that would only apply when the threshold test of establishing an arguable claim in domestic law (thus engaging Article 6) had not been met. Gearty has argued that:

> it was clear enough from the Court's reasoning [in *Ashingdane*] that this test could only apply where the threshold test had not been passed and that, once it was brought into play, it would take effect notwithstanding that the impugned deprivation or restriction of access had been clearly set out in national law, and in respect of which therefore no issue of unlawfulness could have arisen at the domestic level (and thus by definition no arguable case): indeed this was the whole point of the test.[62]

In the author's view, this interpretation is at odds with the express words of the Court in *Ashingdane*: it is not clear at all from the reasoning of the Court that this was intended to be only a fallback test. Indeed, a substantial leap of inference is required to make this assertion. The Court did not find that Ashingdane had no arguable case. It spoke instead of degrees of access and the court's fallback position applies, *whatever* the degree of access. Gearty does not suggest that there can be degrees of arguability: either an applicant is within Article 6, or they are not in which case the fallback test will apply. It is suggested that such an approach is also unduly formalistic: can it really be said that a claimant has access to a court when (as in *Bedfordshire*) all argument in favour of liability is rejected peremptorily on the grounds of judicially conceived notions of public policy that mean certain claims cannot be entertained, whatever their merits. The corollary of the Gearty interpretation is that the degree of scrutiny applied by Strasbourg differs depending upon which route an applicant takes into Article 6. Where an applicant can show an arguable claim simpliciter, Article 6 is simply a guarantee of the procedural requirements of a fair trial. If a claimant cannot show an arguable claim the stricter level of supervision which requires an evaluation of exclusionary rules and hence, possibly, a pronouncement on the legitimacy of substantive law comes into play. Adopting Gearty's perspective, though, the children in *Bedfordshire* did have an arguable case so that the threshold for entry to Article 6 was satisfied, and in view of that there was no mandate for invoking the fallback test. It is presumably this thinking that led the Court to conclude that the applicants had had access to a court with all the procedural rights enshrined

---

[62] (2001) 64 MLR 159, 169.

in Article 6: as the Court of Human Rights observed, the case had been litigated with vigour all the way up to the House of Lords.

Thus, according to Gearty, a claimant cannot on the one hand have both an arguable case that engages Article 6 and then also seek to engage another level of supervision, the jurisprudence relating to the right of access (proportionality and legitimacy) that is properly the fallback test. This approach is unduly restrictive and out of tune generally with Strasbourg jurisprudence which eschews narrow formalism. There is also no support for this view in the case law, apart from Z itself. There is jurisprudence in which as Gearty puts it this second limb of *Ashingdane* is 'jettisoned without explanation',[63] but this is rather more indicative of the Court of Human Rights' haphazard approach to the use of precedent rather than a concerted effort to develop doctrine. Subsequent authority, beginning with *Fayed v United Kingdom*[64] picked up the *Ashingdane* level of supervision in its entirety, paving the way for *Tinnelly* and *Osman*. It should finally be emphasised that the Court of Human Rights in Z seemed scarcely convinced by its own reasoning, in light of the fact that it (ostensibly) satisfied itself in any event that the criteria applicable under the fallback position (legitimacy and proportionality) had been fulfilled by the House of Lords decision in *Bedfordshire*.

The sceptic might argue, however, that the Court had its eye to the future when it observed that the control tests of legitimacy and proportionality had been satisfied. The point was made above that in Z the Court observed that *henceforth* claimants in the position of the Bedfordshire siblings will not have 'an arguable case' in domestic law: thus, the threshold test for engaging Article 6 would not be satisfied. It might be thought then that the fallback test as it has been described by Gearty would apply in full rigour. However, by ostensibly scrutinising Lord Browne-Wilkinson's speech in *Bedfordshire* for compliance with the tests of legitimacy and proportionality, the Court has effectively closed off that argument.

V. ARTICLE 13: THE RIGHT TO AN EFFECTIVE REMEDY

Before the Court, the Government accepted that, in the 'particular circumstances of the case', the range of available remedies (compensation from the Criminal Injuries Compensation Board, invocation of the complaints procedure under the Children Act 1989 and complaint to the Local Government Ombudsman) was insufficient to satisfy the demands of Article 13. In view

---

[63] Ibid, 171, citing *James v United Kingdom* Series A no 98 (1986) and *Lithgow v United Kingdom*, Series A no 102 (1986).
[64] Series A no 294 (1994).

of the seriousness of the violation of one of the most important Convention rights, the Government accepted that a legally enforceable right to compensation should be available and pointed out that such a right would exist on the coming into force of the Human Rights Act 1998.

In its observations on Article 13, the Court began by highlighting the principle of subsidiarity: it is for states to enforce Convention rights in 'whatever form they happen to be secured in the domestic legal order'.[65] However, there is a limit to the discretion afforded to the state and the scope of the Article 13 obligation will vary depending upon the nature of any violation. The Court held that where an allegation is made that there has been a failure to protect someone from the acts of others there should be a mechanism for establishing liability and in the case of breaches of Articles 2 and 3 compensation should in principle be available for non-pecuniary damage. However, the Court declined to make any finding as to whether on these facts only court proceedings could provide effective redress, 'though judicial remedies indeed furnish strong guarantees of independence, access for the victim and enforceability in compliance with the requirements of Article 13 (see . . . *Klass v* Germany)[66, 67]

Nevertheless, the Court held that the applicants did not have available to them an appropriate mechanism for determination of their allegations that they had suffered inhuman and degrading treatment and nor did they have any possibility of obtaining an enforceable award of compensation. Therefore, Article 13 had been breached. In view of the fact that the only realistic means of securing damages was the tort action, this finding gives a strong signal to the English courts that on analogous facts, where proceedings under section 7 of the Human Rights Act 1998 are unavailable, the common law must fill the breach.

VI. BEYOND *Z* v *UNITED KINGDOM*: WHITHER THE COMMON LAW?

For the reasons described above, *Z* is an unsatisfactory decision and one that is out of step generally with recent Strasbourg jurisprudence.[68] In the period since *Osman*, as the Court in Z observed, the starkness of the legal landscape has been relieved by a number of cases being permitted to go to trial with facts that may lead to an expansion of common law obligations. In relation to acts occurring after 2 October 2000 (Human Rights Act 1998, section 22(4)), claimants will have the right to take proceedings against a public authority (other than a court) under section 7 of the

---

[65] [2001] 2 FLR 612, para 108.   [66] Series A no 28 (1978).
[67] [2001] 2 FLR 612, para 109.
[68] See *Ashingdane* Series A no 93 (1985), *Tinnelly* (1998) 27 EHRR 249 and *Osman* [1999] 1 FLR 193, discussed in Wright, *Tort Law*, ch 4.

Human Rights Act, where it is considered that a public authority has acted incompatibly with Convention rights. In *Z*, it was conceded by the Government that the state had acted incompatibly with its positive obligation under Article 3 to protect the children from inhuman and degrading treatment. However, the decision of the House of Lords did not amount to a violation of Article 6; rather, the United Kingdom had failed to ensure that the claimants had an appropriate remedy in accordance with Article 13. The question remains then as to how English law will accommodate claims brought in relation to acts of public authorities that occurred before 2 October 2000, of which there are many in the judicial system, and which may now legitimately be the subject of strike-out orders on the basis that the third limb of *Caparo* is not satisfied.

The effect of Z is that striking out claims in negligence will not amount to a violation of Article 6. Although the Court of Human Rights relied in part on post-*Osman* English cases to find that there was no immunity, in the author's view that does not alter the fact that Z effectively upheld an immunity recognised by the House of Lords in *Bedfordshire*. It is arguable that it has been the threat of proceedings against the United Kingdom in Strasbourg under Article 6 that has resulted in English courts being rather less willing to strike out claims in negligence against public bodies and to uphold awards of damages.[69] The question that arises is whether English courts are likely to regard Z as the green light to revert to a general pattern of hostility towards negligence actions against public authorities. A number of arguments outlined in the following brief observations suggest that this outcome may be unlikely.

The immediate impact of *Osman* on the English legal mind was to highlight awareness of the requirements of Article 6 of the Convention and, as previously described, English courts sought to ensure that *Osman* type claims would no longer be taken to Strasbourg. However, English lawyers continued, in the period between the Human Rights Bill receiving Royal Assent and the Act coming into force, to disregard other Articles of the Convention in legal proceedings. It might be argued that there was in the immediate post-*Osman* period (ie prior to the Human Rights Act coming into force on 2 October 2000) no legal obligation at domestic level whereby English courts should take account of Convention obligations. But that argument is equally true of the Article 6 right to a fair trial. The fact that Strasbourg found against the United Kingdom in *Osman* in October 1998 did not alter the status of the Convention in English law. However, the effect of *Osman* was immediate. Thus, in a number of cases Article 6

---

[69] See, eg, the speech of Lord Browne-Wilkinson in *Barrett v Enfield LBC* [2001] 2 AC 550 and the House of Lords' decision in *Phelps* [2001] 2 AC 619 and see Wright, *Tort Law*, ch 4 and *passim*.

loomed large; however, other articles of the Convention were disregarded. For example, in *Kent v Griffiths*,[70] which concerned the question of whether an ambulance answering an emergency call owed a duty of care to an ill person, no argument was made in relation to Article 2 (the right to life). In *W. v Essex County Council*,[71] which concerned the psychiatric damage caused to a family by a foster child who sexually abused the children of the foster family, no argument was made in relation to either Article 3 or Article 8 of the Convention. The focus of the English legal mind remained firmly upon Article 6. In this author's view, the impact of *Z* is likely to be that argument in relation to the development of the common law shifts to the substantive obligations on the state that are created under alternative articles of the Convention.

Z is a case in which on the one hand a positive obligation under Article 3 arose[72] and was breached but on the other the fact of inability to sue in negligence did not amount to a violation of Article 6. In such cases there is therefore, English precedent aside, nothing to prevent English courts from rejecting claims in negligence. However, where such claims engage Convention rights, other than Article 6, petitions will continue to be made to Strasbourg unless an effective remedy is given in this country. It is therefore appropriate that the common law should be reflective of Convention standards (as a minimum, the Convention is after all a floor of rights) and that a remedy should be available for breaches at domestic level, where a claimant cannot avail herself of the Human Rights Act 1998. Although the Strasbourg Court declined to indicate that a judicial process was necessary to vindicate the rights concerned, the only possible remedy at that time other than the remedies effectively discounted, was the action in negligence. This will continue to be the case in relation to claims based upon acts occurring before 2 October 2000, where the gist of the action is negligence.[73] It should also be borne in mind that limitation periods do not begin to run against a child until he or she reaches the age of majority so that claims in relation to pre-Human Rights Act acts will be brought before the courts for many years to come.

Apart from the direct action against a public authority (other than a court)[74] under section 7 Human Rights Act 1998, section 6(1) also casts an obligation upon the court to act compatibly with Convention rights by virtue of the inclusion of a court within the definition of public authority.[75]

---

[70] [2000] 2 WLR 1158.   [71] [2001] 2 AC 592.

[72] The government conceded and the Commission and Court found that the children were subject to a real and immediate risk of inhuman and degrading treatment of which the local authority ought reasonably to have been aware and that the local authority had failed despite measures reasonably available to take steps to end that treatment.

[73] Human Rights Act 1998, s 22(4).

[74] Proceedings in relation to judicial acts are governed by Human Rights Act 1998, s 9.

[75] Human Rights Act 1998, s 6(3).

There is now clear authority for the proposition that the common law should be rendered compatible with Convention rights.[76] If English courts do not adapt to this role applications will continue to be made to Strasbourg where an effective remedy is not given at domestic level. The obligation upon the court under section 6 applies whether a defendant is public or private, although the scope of positive obligations is much weaker in relation to private parties.[77]

However, there is an unresolved issue relating to retrospectivity regarding the court's obligation under section 6. It has been argued above that where a remedy is unavailable under the Human Rights Act because the act of a public authority (other than a court) took place before 2 October 2000, as would be the case on the facts of *Bedfordshire*, for example, then the courts, in fulfilling their obligation, must act compatibly with the Convention in judicial proceedings that take place after 2 October 2000. The House of Lords has recently held in *R v Lambert*[78] (by a 4–1 majority, Lord Steyn dissenting) that where the 'act' complained of (in that case an act of the court) occurred before 2 October 2001, then section 22(4) of the Act applies: thus, the Human Rights Act 1998 was not intended to have any retrospective effect. This means that decisions of courts or tribunals made before the Act came into force cannot be impugned under section 6 on the ground that the adjudicating body has acted incompatibly with Convention rights. In *R v Lambert* the appellant argued that he should not have been convicted under the Misuse of Drugs Act 1971, because the requirement to establish a defence on the balance of probabilities conflicted with the presumption of innocence in Article 6(2) of the Convention. At issue was the 'act' of the court in the direction given to the jury at the trial. Clearly, the effect of the House of Lords deciding that a conviction could be open to challenge post October 2001 for incompatibility with the Convention would have the potential to reopen many cases. It is not clear from the authorities how the Act should be interpreted and applied when a claimant comes before the court and argues that the court must develop the common law to achieve compatibility with Convention rights but the impugned act/omission of a public authority (other than a court) occurred before 2 October 2000. In *Reynolds*[79] (pre-Act), *Douglas*[80] and *Venables*[81] the court has been in no doubt regarding its own obligation to ensure that the

---

[76] On the role of the court under s 6 see: *Reynolds v Times Newspapers Ltd.* [1999] 3 WLR 1010 (pre-Human Rights Act), *Douglas and others v Hello Limited* [2001] 2 All ER 289 and *Venables and another v News Group Newspapers Limited* [2001] Fam 430. See Wright, *Tort Law*, 21–33.

[77] It is beyond the scope of the present chapter to go into detail here. For detailed discussion, the reader's attention is drawn to Wright, *Tort Law*, ch 5.

[78] [2001] 3 WLR 206. I am particularly grateful to my colleague Merris Amos for discussion on this point.

[79] [1999] 3 WLR 1010.   [80] [2001] 2 All ER 289.   [81] [2001] Fam 430.

common law is compatible with the Convention. However, *Reynolds* was decided before the Act came into force and in *Douglas* and *Venables* the impugned conduct (in both cases of the press) took place after the Act came into force. The author would suggest that courts should act compatibly with Convention principles in developing the common law whenever the impugned conduct took place. It was unacceptable prior to the introduction of the Human Rights Bill for the common law to develop in isolation from the Convention and the effect of section 6 is that the interpretative approach set out in *Derbyshire* has been elevated from a 'may' to a 'must.' Even if it is not accepted that a degree of retrospectivity is indirectly achieved through the medium of the court's role under section 6 of the Human Rights Act, the culture of English law has changed sufficiently to highlight the role that the Convention should play in shaping the common law.[82]

It can forcefully be argued that if English courts are to act in a manner that is compatible with Convention rights they must ensure that, where appropriate (and this would arguably be the case in relation to Articles 2 and 3 of the Convention, which require a mechanism for establishing any liability of State officials or bodies and an enforceable right to compensation)[83] a judicial remedy is available for the violation of Convention rights, where a claim under the Human Rights Act is not available. One option would be for courts to continue the trend we have seen in cases such as *Barrett v Enfield London Borough Council*[84] which signify an expansion of the circumstances in which claims may be brought in negligence in terms of both the identity of defendants and recognised harms. It seems highly unlikely that the courts will ignore the steer given to them in Z, that it was the prevailing trend to open up negligence that reassured the Court of Human Rights that immunities were not being applied to public authorities.

The effect of the ruling regarding Article 6 in Z is likely to be that claimants will now focus their attention on other articles of the Convention. The task for English courts will be to ensure that the common law accommodates Convention requirements in appropriate cases. While tort law and Convention law serve different aims, these aims do overlap. It is through tort law that Convention rights are potentially vindicated, as would have been the case in Z, if the House of Lords in *Bedfordshire* had recognised a duty of care. In practical terms the types of case that are likely to exercise English courts are those concerning the liability of public authorities in relation to omissions. Strasbourg has developed an extensive jurisprudence the nub of which is that the state may have a positive obligation, for example,

---

[82] *R v Daly* [2001] 3 All ER 433.
[83] See *Z v United Kingdom* [2001] 2 FLR 612, para 109.
[84] [2001] 2 AC 550.

to protect the right to life and to protect an individual from inhuman and degrading treatment.[85] Clearly, where a public authority acts incompatibly with these obligations a claim will lie against a public authority under section 7 of the Human Rights Act in relation to acts occurring after 2 October 2000. In other cases it will be for the courts to adapt the common law.

There is no necessary equivalence between the criteria used to establish whether a duty of care at common law exists and when a positive obligation to protect a person from the criminal acts of another arises under Articles 2 and 3 of the Convention, although the tests for liability under English and Convention law, respectively, reveal common themes. Under English law where the act/omission of a public authority arises in connection with the performance of statutory powers/duties the statutory framework will be relevant to the issue of liability. The imposition of liability on public authorities in relation to the performance of statutory obligations requiring the exercise of discretion is particularly problematic and it is impossible to do justice to this important issue here, but some brief observations will be made. As far as Strasbourg is concerned, what matters is that states fulfil their positive obligations: the vehicle by which that is achieved is irrelevant and will afford no excuse (for example, that performance of a statutory obligation was contingent upon the exercise of discretion) for non-performance.

The test for establishing a positive obligation to act to protect an individual from threat to life (Article 2) or inhuman and degrading treatment (Article 3) in Convention law is knowledge of a 'real and immediate risk' to the victim of which the authorities 'knew or ought reasonably to have had knowledge'.[86] Policy issues are taken into account by Strasbourg in determining whether a positive obligation has been breached, because such obligations should not be interpreted so that they would impose 'an impossible or disproportionate burden on the authorities'.[87] The fact that English courts seem now more likely to consider policy issues at the breach stage of the negligence inquiry[88] is in tune with the Strasbourg approach where it

---

[85] See Wright, *Tort Law*, ch 5.

[86] *Osman v United Kingdom* [1999] 1 FLR 193; *Z v United Kingdom* [2001] 2 FLR 612, and see Wright, *Tort Law.*

[87] *Osman*, op cit, para 116.

[88] See Craig and Fairgrieve, '*Barrett*'. If the general trend that emerges in relation to public authority liability is that issues of liability are determined at the breach rather than the duty stage, the consequences for the public purse will be significant. Not only will many cases proceed to trial but the combined operation of *hindsight* bias and *outcome* bias will lead to proportionately greater findings of liability. The work of psychologists in this area is significant. Fischhoff's work (B Fischoff, 'Hindsight (foresight: the effect of outcome knowledge on judgement under uncertainty' (1975) 1 *Journal of Experimental Psychology: Human Perception and Performance* 288–99, cited in A Merry and A McCall Smith, *Errors, Medicine and the Law* (Cambridge: Cambridge University Press, 2001)) demonstrates that when a group

would seem that a failure to perform a positive obligation might be excused where the underlying cause is a lack of resources. According to Strasbourg jurisprudence, positive obligations to protect the right to life should not impose an impossible or disproportionate burden on authorities and the necessity to make operational choices in terms of priorities and resources has been acknowledged.[89]

The effect of *Barrett* seems to be that the requirement generally to establish *Wednesbury* unreasonableness (introduced by Lord Browne-Wilkinson for a unanimous House of Lords in *Bedfordshire*) in relation to decisions involving the exercise of discretion, as a precondition to bring an action in negligence, has been rejected. Instead, the court will refuse to consider issues that it regards as non-justiciable. The difficulty is to determine what precisely are non-justiciable issues. In *Barrett*, Lord Slynn stated that: 'The greater the element of policy involved, the wider the area of discretion accorded, the more likely it is that the matter is not justiciable so that no action in negligence can be brought.'[90] The types of example frequently given are those involving the allocation of scarce resources or the distribution of risks. Arguments relating to allocation of resources may be acceptable to Strasbourg, but as indicated previously they would be considered in relation to whether a right has been violated (or in negligence terminology breached), not whether there was any positive duty to act. Strasbourg would never say that a decision of an organ of the United Kingdom was not justiciable, but it might conclude that there had been no breach of a positive obligation in the light of resource considerations. The tone of English judgments suggests that courts are unlikely to challenge the deployment of resources; Strasbourg is perhaps less likely to be so wary.

The criteria applied by Strasbourg for determining when a positive obligation to act arises (real and immediate risk of which there is/should be knowledge) are reminiscent of the public law test of *Wednesbury* unreasonableness introduced by Lord Browne-Wilkinson in *Bedfordshire*. To paraphrase, according to Strasbourg, a positive duty to act arises where it is obvious that action should be taken: in *Wednesbury* language no reasonable authority could possibly have come to the conclusion that action was not required. If public authority defendants do attempt to take advantage of the ruling in Z it seems likely that they will argue in novel cases engaging positive obligations that the standard *Caparo* criteria (overlaid with the

---

of people know what happened in any series of events they are much more likely to consider a result predictable. The effect of outcome bias is that where very serious harm occurs it is more likely that the court will find that there has been a breach of duty than where a consequence is of a minor nature.

[89] *Osman* [1999] 1 FLR 193 and *Kilic v Turkey*, App no 22492/93, judgment dated 28 Mar 2000.

[90] [2001] 2 AC 550, 571.

test of justiciability laid down in *Barrett*) are unsuitable for circumscribing the parameters of responsibility where Convention rights are engaged. Positive obligations to act are recognised in English law, *inter alia*, where a defendant has made an assumption of responsibility for the well-being of the claimant. An assumption of responsibility *per se* would not engage Articles 2 or 3 of the Convention. In cases such as Z, something in the nature of knowledge of 'real and immediate risk' is required. On the facts of *Osman* this was not satisfied because there was, according to the Court of Human Rights, no decisive stage at which the police knew (ought to have known) of the risk to the Osman family.

It would seem that the application of the *Wednesbury* test has survived *Barrett* in cases concerning the failure to exercise statutory powers simpliciter. It will be recalled that in *Stovin v Wise*[91] a 3–2 majority of the House of Lords held that there were two minimum pre-conditions for establishing a duty of care where a local authority failed to exercise a statutory power: it must have been irrational to fail to exercise the power so that there was a public duty to act and there must be exceptional grounds for holding that compensation should be paid. *Stovin v Wise* was distinguished recently by the Court of Appeal in *Kane v New Forest DC*[92] on the basis that the local authority had created a source of danger on the highway, but the decision itself cast no doubt on the authority of *Stovin*.

It is anticipated that in novel cases, indicative of the engagement of positive obligations under the Convention, English courts will be invited to construct proximity criteria designed to accommodate the urgency conveyed by the concepts of real and immediate risk. An analogy could be drawn with the specificity of the proximity criteria that have been developed in cases concerning pure economic loss and psychiatric damage suffered by secondary victims. In these types of claim the notion of proximity is shorthand for a clutch of indicators that determine whether in principle liability may lie. Further, a *Wednesbury* type of pre-condition to establishing liability might be required. It is of course difficult to separate notions of duty and breach, but it should be noted that in *Osman* the Court of Human Rights rejected the government argument that only gross negligence should found liability.[93] Liability would flow from a failure to take reasonable measures in the face of a real and immediate risk. It is important, therefore, in this context to separate clearly the duty to act and the measures required to discharge that duty. Any introduction of a test for liability that is more stringent than the current *Caparo* criteria must not have the effect of excusing all but the most negligent decisions. This would

---

[91] [1996] 3 All ER 801.   [92] [2001] 3 All ER 914.
[93] *Osman* [1999] 1 FLR 193 para 116.

seem to have been the effect of Lord Browne-Wilkinson's speech in *Bedfordshire.*[94]

VII. CONCLUSION

It is regrettable that the European Court of Human Rights has effectively overruled *Osman* and decided that when English courts develop the tort of negligence they do so unencumbered by the prospect of scrutiny under the principles laid down by *Ashingdane.* In the author's view, the House of Lords quite clearly recognised an immunity in *Bedfordshire,* and that fact cannot be displaced by decisions taken after *Osman,* according to which liability in principle may be found. The avowed intention of the Human Rights Act 1998, as described in the Bill,[95] is that rights should be brought home so that citizens in the United Kingdom have the full enjoyment of all the rights enshrined in the Convention without the need to take the long expensive road to Strasbourg to secure justice. The reality is that if English courts do not take seriously their obligation under section 6 of the Human Rights Act or alternatively the common law, that intention will be frustrated. In *Z,* the abused children suffered an appalling violation of their human rights for which no domestic remedy was available. In future, if an action under the Act itself is not available the courts must ensure that the common law is reflective of Convention rights, so that Convention rights really are brought home.

[94] See Wright, 'Local Authorities', and see also Cane who has described the standard of care applied to public authorities through the application of *Wednesbury* principles as 'extraordinary unreasonableness': P Cane, *The Anatomy of Tort Law* (Oxford: Hart Publishing, 1997), 41.
[95] *Rights Brought Home: The Human Rights Bill* (Cm 3782).

4. THE HUMAN RIGHTS ACT 1998, DAMAGES AND ENGLISH TORT LAW

*Duncan Fairgrieve**

I. INTRODUCTION

The means for gaining redress for administrative wrongs in the English legal system are extremely heterogeneous. The focus of most legal literature has naturally been upon the tort of negligence, which until recently has provided precious little succour for litigants.[1] However, one should not forget that the English courts commonly allow claims based upon other torts. Assault, and false imprisonment are particular favourites in actions against the police.[2] Even before the recent revisionist negligence cases,[3] the courts did allow claims in negligence for ordinary operational carelessness, for instance in the case of road accidents.[4] The police paid over £10 million to claimants for public liability claims and road traffic accident claims in 1999/2000.[5]

Moreover, aggrieved claimants are not restricted to actions before the courts. Non-judicial means of grievance-resolution, although often over-looked, play an important role on a day-to-day basis in procuring compensation for the victims of administrative wrongdoing.[6] This is most clearly

---

[*] Fellow in Comparative Law, British Institute of International and Comparative Law; Maître de Conférences invité at l'Université de Paris 1, Sorbonne.

[1] For claims concerning the exercise of statutory functions, the English courts adopted a protectionist approach in cases such as *Elguzouli-Daf v Commissioner of Police* [1995] QB 335; *Hill v Chief Constable of West Yorkshire* [1989] AC 53; *Stovin v Wise and Norfolk CC* [1996] AC 923; *X(Minors) v Bedfordshire CC* [1995] 2 AC 633.

[2] For further discussion, see R Clayton and H Tomlinson, *Civil Actions Against the Police* (London: Sweet & Maxwell, 1992), ch 4.

[3] In a series of recent cases, the courts have shown a more liberal approach to claims in negligence in respect of the discretionary statutory functions of public bodies: *Barrett v Enfield LBC* [2001] 2 AC 550; *Phelps v Hillingdon LBC* [2001] 2 AC 619.

[4] See, eg, *Gaynor v Allen* [1959] 2 QB 403.

[5] Public liability (malfeasance) is said to include assault, false imprisonment, and malicious prosecution: see Report of Her Majesty's Chief Inspector of Constabulary 1999/2000, ch 2 (Oct 2000).

[6] See C Harlow and R Rawlings, *Law and Administration*, 2nd edn (London: Sweet & Maxwell, 1997), ch 18.

illustrated by the intervention of the public law ombudsmen in the United Kingdom, which often facilitate the payment of redress.[7]

Another element has recently been added to this complex pattern of remedies. Under the Human Rights Act 1998 (HRA), the courts will gain a power to grant damages as a remedy for the breach of a Convention right[8] by a public authority.[9] In shaping the elements of this remedy, the courts are statutorily obliged to take account of the principles of the European Court of Human Rights in making reparation.[10] In this paper it will be argued that in some respects the Strasbourg case law is different to the orthodox English law approach. However, it will be suggested that the English courts are generally well placed to take account of these new considerations.[11] The very notion of public law liability in tort has been evolving recently, and reference will be made to these developments, as well as to non-judicial methods of redress for administrative wrongdoing. It will also be argued that the HRA may also prove to be a conduit for comparative law influences.

This analysis of the new damages remedy under the HRA will be structure in the following manner. The statutory provisions of the HRA will first be examined. Then, there will be an investigation of the type of action which has been created by the HRA. This will be followed by a detailed discussion of the factors which may be relevant in shaping the new damages remedy. The issues of loss and quantum will then be broached in a separate section, followed by a presentation of how the domestic courts will conceive the causal link between the human rights violation and the applicant's damage.

II. THE STATUTORY PROVISIONS

The HRA makes it unlawful for any public authority to act in a way which is incompatible with Convention rights.[12] The Act lays down remedies for

---

[7] *Ex gratia* payments for maladministration may be made by public bodies after investigation by the Health Services Commissioner, the Parliamentary Commissioner for Administration, and the Commission for Local Administration (or Local Government Ombudsman). Note also that payments are now systematically made (without intervention of an ombudsman) by certain public bodies for loss caused by maladministration: see, for instance, Department of Social Security, *Financial Redress for Maladministration* (Sept 1998).

[8] The Convention rights which are protected by the HRA are laid down in s 1(1) HRA.

[9] The exact statutory mechanism for the award of damages under the HRA will be examined in the next section.

[10] S 8(4) HRA.

[11] The focus of this article is upon damages under the HRA. The effect of the HRA and the ECtHR's case law on orthodox torts will not be covered in this piece. See further P Craig and D Fairgrieve, '*Barrett*, Negligence and Discretionary Powers' [1999] PL 626.

[12] S 6(1) HRA.

such unlawfulness. Section 8(1) HRA provides that the court 'may grant such relief or remedy, or make such order, within its powers as it considers just and appropriate'. This confers a broad discretion upon the courts in fashioning an armoury of remedies, amongst which a grant of damages will take its place. In developing the damages remedy, the HRA lays down some significant requirements. Section 8(3) asserts that a pre-condition of the award of damages is that taking account of all the circumstances of the case, the 'court is satisfied that the award is necessary to afford just satisfaction to the person in whose favour it is made.' Those circumstances which must be taken into account by the court include 'any other relief or remedy granted, or order made, in relation to the act in question'[13] and 'the consequences of any decision (of that or any other court) in respect of that act.'[14]

In terms of the forum in which the damages claim can be made, the HRA provides that only those courts and tribunals which have the power to award damages or compensation in civil proceedings may award damages for breach of a Convention right.[15]

III. TYPE OF ACTION

There has been some debate about the exact categorisation of the damages remedy under the HRA. The Law Commission has argued in its recent report entitled *Damages under the Human Rights Act 1998* that the HRA creates a new form of action for breach of statutory duty.[16] Lester and Pannick have described this remedy under the HRA as 'a new public law tort of acting in breach of the victim's Convention rights'.[17] Lord Woolf is, on the other hand, unhappy with the description of this remedy as a new government tort.[18] As there is no automatic right to damages for unlawfulness, and the courts retain a discretion as to the remedy they award, it is perhaps more accurate to describe this as a new *power* to award damages for unlawfulness. It is difficult to describe this new action as a public law tort if there is no *right* to monetary compensation.[19]

---

[13] S 8(3)(a) HRA. [14] S 8(3)(b) HRA. [15] S 8(2) HRA.

[16] Law Commission and Scottish Law Commission, *Damages under the Human Rights Act 1998* (Law Com No 266, 2000; Scottish Law Com No 180, 2000) [hereafter referred to as *Damages under the HRA*] para 4.20 (although this analogy is qualified with the reservation that 'the remedy is discretionary, rather than as of right').

[17] 'The Impact of the Human Rights Act on Private Law: the Knight's Move' (2000) 116 *LQR* 380, 382.

[18] Lord Woolf, 'The Human Rights Act 1998 and Remedies', in M Andenas and D Fairgrieve (eds), *Judicial Review in International Perspective: Volume II* (The Hague: Kluwer Law International, 2000), 432.

[19] See, eg, the definition of a tort given by Toulmin QC (Official Referee) in *R v Secretary of State for Transport ex p Factortame Ltd (No 7)* The Times, 10 Jan 2001 as '[a] breach of

The brevity of the statutory language means that the primary duty of setting the parameters of the damages remedy falls upon the courts. In this task, they are statutorily obliged to take into account the principles applied by the Strasbourg Court, both in determining whether liability arises and, if so, in setting the quantum of damages which should be awarded.[20] The jurisprudence of the European Court of Human Rights (ECtHR) will provide some help, but it is well known that (as we shall see) the Strasbourg principles are by no means crystal clear.[21] In effect, this confers a broad discretion upon the domestic courts to develop their own principles within the statutory framework of the HRA.[22]

IV. FACTORS IN AWARDING DAMAGES UNDER THE HUMAN RIGHTS ACT

In order to gain an award under the HRA, the claimant will have to show that the breach of the Convention caused him or her compensatable loss. These issues of loss and causation will covered in the next sections. Prior to that, we will look at some of the factors that might influence the courts in exercising their discretion to award damages for loss caused by a breach of human rights.

A. Residual Remedy

The damages remedy under the HRA is a *residual* remedy in the sense that damages may only be awarded if, after consideration of the effects of 'any other relief or remedy granted, or order made, in relation to the act in question,'[23] the award is necessary to afford just satisfaction.[24] The reference to non-pecuniary remedies could be interpreted to mean that the courts should achieve just satisfaction primarily through non-pecuniary remedies,[25] such as requirements to make apologies[26] or changes to administrative practice.[27] From one perspective, it would make sense for the courts to achieve full reparation, where possible, by using non-pecuniary remedies, and adapting their remedial powers in imaginative ways.[28] Indeed, inspiration

---

noncontractual duty which gives a private law *right* to the party injured to recover compensatory damages at common law from the party causing the injury' (emphasis added).

[20] S 8(4) HRA.

[21] S Grosz, J Beatson, and P Duffy, *Human Rights: The 1998 Act and the European Convention* (London: Sweet & Maxwell, 2000), para 6-21; A Mowbray, 'The European Court of Human Rights' Approach to Just Satisfaction' [1997] *PL* 647.

[22] See Lord Woolf, 'The Human Rights Act 1998 and Remedies', 433.

[23] S 8(3)(a) HRA.

[24] I Leigh and L Lustgarten, 'Making Rights Real: the Courts, Remedies and the Human Rights Act' [1999] *CLJ* 509, 527.

[25] Grosz, Beatson, and Duffy, op cit, para 6-22.   [26] Ibid.

[27] *Damages under the HRA*, para 5.4 (in respect of just satisfaction under Scots Law).

[28] Grosz, Beatson, and Duffy, op cit, para 6-22.

may be found in this respect from the public law ombudsmen who, in accordance with their general ethos, have adopted a great degree of flexibility in formulating the remedies to redress maladministration.[29]

There seems to be a tension between the residual nature of the damages remedy as expressed in the statute and the overriding principle of full reparation as expressed in the ECtHR's case law.[30] In a great many cases, especially for past failures, it will simply be impossible to remedy the consequences of infringements of Convention rights other than by an award of damages.[31]

B. Fault

At present, the great majority of torts which apply to public authorities require proof of fault in the sense of negligent or intentional wrongdoing. Cases in which public bodies may be found strictly liable are rare.[32] In English law, exceptional cases aside,[33] there is no equivalent of the French administrative law doctrine of liability based upon risk or equality before the public burdens.[34]

So, an important issue in respect of the damages remedy under the HRA is the relevance of *fault*. Will it be necessary for the claimant to show that the breach of the Convention rights was the result of a lack of reasonable care on the part of the public body?

Some guidance may be derived from the wording of the HRA, and the Convention rights for which it affords protection. In one specific case, the mental state of the wrongdoer is crucial. Under section 9(3) HRA, it is provided that damages may not be awarded in respect of a judicial act done in good faith.[35] In other words, bad faith is a pre-condition of a right in

---

[29] The Local Government Ombudsman (LGO) emphasises that 'practical action' might provide a remedy, and gives the example of taking action to make the provision specified in a statement of special educational needs: see Commission for Local Administration in England, *Guidance on Good Practice 6: Remedies* (London, 1997), para 10.

[30] See, eg, *Ringeisen v Austria* (1979–80) 1 EHRR 504 (just satisfaction).

[31] The LGO has also recognised that in many circumstances financial compensation will be the only appropriate remedy for maladministration: see Commission for Local Administration in England, *Guidance on Good Practice 6: Remedies*, para 7.

[32] The principle in *Rylands v Fletcher*, which could have been developed into a broad principle of risk-based liability, has been severely restricted in actions against public bodies: see Craig, *Administrative Law*, 4th edn (London: Sweet & Maxwell, 1999), 884.

[33] See, eg, *Burmah Oil v Lord Advocate* [1964] 2 All ER 348, 355.

[34] For discussion of the French doctrine of liability without fault, see R Errera, 'The Scope and Meaning of No-Fault Liability in French Administrative Law' (1986) 39 *CLP* 157; LN Brown and J Bell, *French Administrative Law*, 5th edn (Oxford: Oxford University Press, 1998), 193 ff.

[35] Otherwise than to compensate a person under Art 5(5) of the Convention which provides for an enforceable right to compensation for victims of arrest or detention in contravention of Art 5.

damages by an individual who considers that his or her Convention rights have been violated by a judicial act. Proving bad faith will present a significant obstacle to reparation.[36]

Beyond this specific case, the courts would seem to have move room for manoeuvre in shaping the role of fault.[37] There have been some indications as to how they might proceed. In a recent extrajudicial piece, the Lord Chief Justice argued that the existence of fault should neither be a pre-condition of an award of damages nor should it be ignored:[38] rather the presence of fault should be a factor making it more appropriate to award damages. Such an approach has much in common with Community law, an analogy which was explicitly made by Lord Woolf.[39] This makes it appropriate to investigate briefly the EC law position.

The conditions of state liability under Community law are well known,[40] but the element of most relevance in this context is that the breach of the Community provision must be 'sufficiently serious.' This test, and its two constituent components, manifest and grave breach,[41] depends upon a balancing of many different factors, including:[42] the clarity and the precision of the rule breached; the measure of discretion left by the rule to the national authorities; and whether any error of law was excusable or inexcusable. It should be underlined that no further fault, such as negligence, on the part of the Member State, above and beyond a sufficiently serious breach of Community law, is a necessary pre-condition for liability.[43] In certain circumstances, mere illegality may even suffice to constitute a sufficiently serious breach.[44] Nonetheless, this does not mean that the mind of the infringing party is always irrelevant. As Lord Clyde held in the latest judgment of the *Factortame* litigation before the House of Lords: 'A delib-

---

[36] A Olowofoyeku, 'State Liability for the Exercise of Judicial Power' [1998] *PL* 444, 460.

[37] Art 5(5) ECHR seems to provide for an enforceable right to compensation for breach of the provisions of Art 5 ECHR (ie regardless of fault). However, the ECtHR has not interpreted this as necessitating a *right* to compensation, and has often held that a finding of a violation of the Convention is sufficient just satisfaction: *Damages under the HRA*, para 6.80.

[38] Lord Woolf, 'The Human Rights Act 1998 and Remedies', 433.

[39] Ibid.

[40] In summary, state liability will arise if the rule of Community law breached was intended to confer rights upon individuals, the breach was 'sufficiently serious', and there was a direct causal link between the breach and the damage sustained. See Cases C-6/90 and C-9/90 *Francovich and Bonifaci v Italy*; Cases C-46/93 and C-48/93 *Brasserie du Pecheur SA v Germany; R v Secretary of State for Transport, ex p Factortame Ltd* [1996] QB 404.

[41] Namely, whether the Member State has 'manifestly and gravely' disregarded the limits on its discretion: Cases C-46 and 48/93, *Brasserie du Pecheur SA v Germany*, ibid, 499.

[42] Ibid.

[43] See *R v Secretary of State for Transport ex p Factortame Ltd (No 5)* [2000] 1 AC 524, 541, 554.

[44] Where the Member State is not called on to make any legislative choices and had only considerably reduced or no discretion, the mere infringement of Community law might be sufficient to establish the existence of a sufficiently serious breach: see, eg, Case C-5/94 *R v MAFF, ex p Hedley Lomas LTD* [1997] QB 139.

erate intention to infringe would obviously weigh heavily in the scales of seriousness. An inadvertent breach might be relatively less serious on that account. Liability may still be established without any intentional infringement.'[45]

It would be desirable to adopt a similarly flexible approach to fault under the HRA. In some circumstances, the presence of fault may be relevant, in others areas—as in EC Law—[46] it may be felt that unlawfulness *per se* suffices. For violations of the fundamental provisions of the European Convention on Human Rights (ECHR), such as Article 2[47] or Article 3,[48] it may be felt that it is unnecessary to require anything over and above the elements which are required by the substantive provisions of the Convention themselves.[49] Thus, unlawfulness will be the determining factor. In cases of less serious human rights breaches, the presence or absence of fault on the part of the public authority may well be relevant in deciding whether the public authority should be financially responsible for the consequences of the unlawfulness, for instance in case of breach of procedural guarantees laid down in Article 6 of the ECHR.

Objections may however be made to the adoption of such a liberal approach in respect of the fundamental provisions of the Convention. Some may argue that it diverges from the traditional rule of public law that liability in damages should not arise merely from unlawfully caused loss.[50] Various points should, however, be borne in mind. The rule would be relaxed only in the specific case of the breach of the most fundamental Convention rights. Furthermore, it should be observed that the traditional resistance to the parity between illegality and fault has not been without its critics.[51] Indeed, it may well be that the dangerousness of this parity has been overstated. The ombudsmen have been presiding over a de facto mechanism for awarding compensation for loss caused by administrative wrongfulness *per se*,[52] with the general consent of public bodies[53] and this has worked without major problems. If this should be acceptable in the case of

---

[45] *R. v Secretary of State for Transport ex p Factortame Ltd (No 5)* [2000] 1 AC 524, 555.

[46] See n 44 above.

[47] The right to life.

[48] The right to freedom from torture and inhuman or degrading treatment or punishment.

[49] Subject of course to showing that the breach caused loss to the applicant.

[50] Reiterated in the cases of *R v Knowsley MBC, ex p Maguire*, The Times, 26 June 1992; *X(Minors) v Bedfordshire CC* [1995] 2 AC 633, 730.

[51] See, eg, Sir Robert Carnwath, 'The *Thornton* Heresy Exposed: Financial Remedies for Breach of Public Duties' [1998] *PL* 407, 422.

[52] See M Amos, 'The Parliamentary Commissioner for Administration, Redress and Damages for Wrongful Administrative Action' [2000] *PL* 21, 28.

[53] It is now generally accepted by Central Government that where maladministration has caused injustice, then those affected should be put back in the position they would have been in had the maladministration not taken place: see *Government Accounting*, ch 36 (The Stationery Office, 1998), para 36.3.5.

administrative errors, then it might seem illogical that breaches of the more fundamental, and restricted, human rights should not receive the same protection before the courts.

A final point should be made in respect of unlawfulness and fault in the sphere of human rights. A damages remedy may only be sought if the defendant has acted unlawfully according to the HRA, and thereby has breached a Convention right. Breach of a Convention right might itself involve an element of fault. An illustration of this is found in the right to life guaranteed by Article 2, which provides *inter alia* that 'no one shall be deprived of his life intentionally.' Although Article 2 has been interpreted so that intentionally wrongdoing is not an *essential* requirement of this provision,[54] many of the cases do in fact involve deliberate or negligent wrongdoing.[55] There are other examples of an 'in-built' element of fault. The commission of torture or inhuman treatment in contravention of Article 3 will often have occurred deliberately by the public body, its employees or agents.[56] In these case, the elements of the Convention right themselves will thus provide effective control mechanisms upon the existence of unlawfulness prior even to a claim for damages.

C. Policy Concerns

Traditionally, the negligence liability of public authorities in the exercise of their statutory activities has been rather limited.[57] Until the recent spate of liberal decisions,[58] various policy concerns have been used by the courts under the third limb of the *Caparo* test[59] as a formidable obstacle to claims. The most frequently invoked policy concerns against the recognition of duties of care have been:[60] the multi-disciplinary nature of administrative decision-making; the possibility of causing liability-avoiding defensive prac-

---

[54] It covers the accidental deprivation of life by the use of lethal force: K Reid, *A Practitioner's Guide to the European Convention on Human Rights* (London: Sweet & Maxwell, 1998), 361.

[55] See, eg, *Salman v Turkey*, Application no 21986/93, Judgment of 27 June 2000.

[56] Many of the principal Art 3 cases have occurred in the context of direct physical ill-treatment by agents of the State: Reid, op cit, 377.

[57] See, eg, the cases of *Elguzouli-Daf v Commissioner of Police* [1995] QB 335; *Hill v Chief Constable of West Yorkshire* [1989] AC 53; *Stovin v Wise and Norfolk CC* [1996] AC 923; *X(Minors) v Bedfordshire CC* [1995] 2 AC 633.

[58] *Barrett v Enfield LBC* [1999] 3 WLR 79; *Phelps v Hillingdon LBC* [2000] 3 WLR 776.

[59] *Caparo Industries plc v Dickman* [1990] 2 AC 605: was the injury foreseeable; were the parties sufficiently proximate; was it fair, just and reasonable to impose a duty of care?

[60] See, eg, *X(Minors) v Bedfordshire CC* [1995] 2 AC 633, 749–51. For further discussion of these policy factors see P Craig and D Fairgrieve, '*Barrett*, Negligence and Discretionary Powers' [1999] *PL* 626, 633–6; B Markesinis, J-B Auby, D Coester-Waltjen, and S Deakin, *Tortious Liability of Statutory Bodies: A Comparative and Economic Analysis of Five English Cases* (Oxford: Hart Publishers, Oxford, 1999); SH Bailey and MJ Bowman, 'Public Authority Negligence Revisited' [2000] *CLJ* 85, 95 ff.

tices; the sensitive and delicate nature of public bodies' activities; the existence of alternative remedies for claimants.[61]

One issue of importance therefore is whether the traditional judicial penchant for protectionist policy factors will manifest itself in respect of claims for damages under the HRA. The wording of the HRA would certainly seem to allow for account to be taken of policy factors. Section 8(3) HRA states that the domestic court must take into account 'the consequences of any decision (of that or any other court) in respect of that act'. A number of commentators have interpreted this as an implicit reference to the need to avoid an opening of the 'floodgates' to claims.[62] Over and above the implications of this specific provision, the general discretion accorded to the courts in formulating remedies which are 'just and appropriate' does give some scope to refer to public policy factors.[63]

Lord Woolf has argued that the ECHR should not be used to promote a public law damages culture, using phraseology echoing the aforementioned policy considerations: the courts must avoid 'creating dangers of "preventive administration"'; that the 'days when public bodies could be regarded as having purses of bottomless depth are now past'; account should be taken of the fact that '[t]here can be numerous victims of the same unlawful act.'[64] On the other hand, however, Lord Woolf drew an explicit analogy with state liability for breach of Community law, which would seem to suggest a more limited role for policy concerns.[65] Indeed, the courts have adopted the Community law test with equanimity, and have avoided resorting to the protectionist language that has often marked the domestic law. This has sometimes resulted in a juxtaposition of very different attitudes to similar cases. This is perhaps best illustrated by Lord Hoffmann's views of the tort liability of the state. When the Factortame litigation returned to the House of Lords on the issue of liability for damages, Lord Hoffmann boldly upheld the lower court's decision that the enactment of the Merchant Shipping Act 1988 constituted a sufficiently serious breach of Community law.[66] In a crucial part of his judgment, his Lordship declared that 'I do not think that the United Kingdom . . . . can say that the losses caused by the

---

[61] Such as statutory appeal mechanisms, judicial review, and the ombudsmen schemes.

[62] M Amos, 'Damages for Breach of the Human Rights Act 1998' [1999] EHRLR 178, 186; M Supperstone, J Goudie, and J Coppel, *Local Authorities and the Human Rights Act 1998* (London: Butterworths, 1999), 25.

[63] Sir Robert Carnwath, 'ECHR Remedies From a Common Law Perspective' (2000) 49 *ICLQ* 517, 525.

[64] Lord Woolf, 'The Human Rights Act 1998 and Remedies', 433.

[65] Although, policy concerns are by no means absent from Community law. Indeed, one of the reasons for the need to show a sufficiently serious breach in order to gain reparation for breach of EC Law is to avoid 'an excessive chilling factor' upon the legislative discretion of the Member States: Cases C-46 and 48/93, *Brasserie du Pecheur SA v Germany, R v Secretary of State for Transport, ex p Factortame Ltd (No 4)* [1996] QB 404, 498.

[66] *R v Secretary of State for Transport ex p Factortame Ltd (No 5)* [2000] 1 AC 524, 548.

legislation should lie where they fell. Justice requires that the wrong should be made good.' However, in another well-known case on the same topic of public authority liability in tort, a few years earlier, Lord Hoffmann was in less liberal mode. *Stovin v Wise*[67] concerned an allegedly negligent failure of a local authority to exercise a statutory power to direct a private landowner to remove an obstruction from his land in order to improve visibility at a dangerous road junction. In rejecting the claim, Lord Hoffmann held in a notably restrictive judgment that 'the trend of authorities has been to discourage the assumption that anyone who suffers loss is prima facie entitled to compensation from a person (preferably insured or a public authority) whose act or omission can be said to have caused it. The default position is that he is not.'[68]

The lesson to draw from this is that attitudes to policy considerations depend greatly upon the context within which a cause of action is framed. It may well be that the influence of policy factors under the HRA will be diluted, in common with Community law. The Law Commission has argued that to have regard to policy considerations would be difficult to reconcile with the general principle of *restitutio in integrum* adopted by the Strasbourg Court.[69] Although this seems to confuse the issues of quantum and liability, it is perhaps true that if public interest considerations, rather than those of the victim, were to prevail in a significant number of cases, then the effectiveness of the remedy may be called into question.[70] This does not mean that it is inappropriate to take account of wider considerations in exercising the discretion to award damages under the HRA. Indeed, the Government's White Paper entitled *Rights Brought Home*, indicates that the appropriate remedy under s 8(1) depends 'on a proper balance between the rights of the individual and the public interest'.[71] But in striking the correct balance, the public interest concerns must not systematically trump those of the individual, and should rather complement the search for a just and appropriate remedy to ensure the securing of civil liberties.

V. LOSS AND QUANTUM OF DAMAGES

Having identified some of the factors which may be of relevance in establishing whether the discretion to award damages should be exercised, we

---

[67] [1996] AC 923.   [68] Ibid, 949.

[69] Damages under the HRA, para 4.4.1.

[70] And thus may give rise to recourse to Strasbourg for a breach of Art 13 ECHR (which has not been included in the HRA). The European Court of Human Rights found that the restrictive provisions of tort law in relation to child abuse claims as expounded in *X(Minors) v Bedfordshire* CC [1995] 2 AC 633 fell foul *inter alia* of Art 13 (*Z v UK*, [2001] 2 FLR 612 and *TP and KM v UK* [2001] 2 FLR 549).

[71] *Rights Brought Home: The Human Rights Bill*, Cmnd 3782 (1997) para 2.6.

will now look more closely at the types of loss which may be recoverable under the HRA, and the rules adopted for calculating the quantum.

In the case law of the ECtHR, damages are generally awarded for three main heads of loss: pecuniary loss, non-pecuniary loss, and costs.[72] Under the HRA, the issue of costs will be determined by the ordinary domestic rules.[73] However, in terms of pecuniary and non-pecuniary loss, the domestic courts will have to take account of the Strasbourg case law both in determining compensable damage and in devising the rules of quantum.[74] It will be argued in this section that the ECtHR, in parallel with the French Law tradition, has taken a broad approach to the types of loss recoverable, including economic loss, moral harm, and loss of opportunities (the latter analysed under the heading of causation). An initial point to investigate however is whether the English courts are restricted to the award of compensatory damages under the HRA.

A. Solely Compensatory Damages?

Damages in the common law are by no means exclusively compensatory. English courts are accustomed to awarding non-compensatory damages such as nominal damages, contemptuous damages, and exemplary damages.[75] It is thus interesting to speculate whether non-compensatory damages should be available under the HRA. Two issues are of particular relevance in this sphere: the possibility of making a mere declaration of a breach rather than a damages award and the award of punitive damages.

First, the ECtHR often asserts that a judgment declaring that a human rights violation has occurred is enough to constitute just satisfaction in respect of claims for non-pecuniary damage without any further monetary award.[76] It is legitimate to ask whether the English courts might adopt a practice under the HRA of refusing damages, and instead simply make a declaration of unlawfulness.[77] We have seen above that the provisions of the HRA indicate that damages are a *residual* remedy, and that there are many other potential orders that can be made by the court, for instance a change in administrative practice.[78] Nonetheless, where there is a *proven*

---

[72] See generally *Damages under the HRA*, para 3.22 ff; Starmer, *European Human Rights Law* (London: Legal Action Group, 1999), para 2, 48 ff.

[73] S 8(4) HRA refers to the taking account of the ECtHR case law in respect of 'damages' and not costs. See Lord Woolf, 'The Human Rights Act 1998 and Remedies', 434.

[74] S 8(4) HRA.

[75] See A Burrows, *Remedies for Torts and Breach of Contract*, 2nd edn (London: Butterworths, 1994), ch 5.

[76] Reid, op cit, 402. See, eg, *Nikolova v Bulgaria,* Application no 31195/96, Judgment of 25 Mar 1999.

[77] As it would seem free to do under s 8(1) HRA.

[78] See text accompanying n 27 above.

loss caused by a human rights violation, which satisfies the other ingredients of a damages remedy outlined above,[79] it is likely to be rare that an English Court will decide that a mere declaration would be enough to constitute just satisfaction.[80]

Secondly, there is the question of punitive damages. Received opinion is that—exemplary or punitive damages are not awarded by the ECtHR.[81] At first sight, this would seem to be borne out in the case law. In two recent cases, where applicants sought exemplary damages, the court explicitly rejected the claims for both punitive and aggravated damages.[82] However, a closer look at the Strasbourg case law reveals a more complex picture. The Court has often referred to the seriousness of the State's violation of the Convention when making awards for non-pecuniary loss frequently when punitive damages have been sought, and ostensibly rejected.[83] This reference to the conduct of the state seems hard to reconcile with the stated aim of purely compensatory damages. Indeed, an approach which goes beyond merely *restitutio in integrum* seems to have received some confirmation in the case of *Gaygusuz v Austria*,[84] where Judge Matscher dissented from the majority judgments awarding 200,000 Austrian Schillings (£11,000) in damages as he felt that this exceeded by twofold the amount that the applicant could possibly have sustained.

Another case which illustrates a dislocation between the quantum of damages and the scope of loss is that of *Halford v UK*.[85] In this well-known case, a former Assistant Chief Constable complained of the taping of phone conversations in order to gather information for use in a sex discrimination claim she was bringing against the police. Although the court found that the damage of which she complained, stress, had not been shown to derive from the interception of her calls rather than from the wider conflict at work, it nonetheless awarded her £10,000 as a 'just and equitable amount of compensation'. One way of seeing this award is as a recognition of the harm caused to her personality right, the right to privacy. Another, and perhaps nearer to the truth, would be that the award of damages in respect of a loss for which there was no proven causal link with a human rights violation is simply a disguised form of punitive damages.[86]

---

[79] See text accompanying n 12 *et seq* above for an indication of the exact statutory requirements.

[80] *Damages under the HRA*, para 4.50.

[81] K Starmer, *European Human Rights Law*, para 2.45; Supperstone, Goudie, and Coppel, op cit, 25.

[82] *Mentes v Turkey*, 1998-IV, 1686, para 21 (just satisfaction); *Selcuk v Turkey* (1998) 26 EHRR 477, para 119.

[83] See, eg, *Mentes v Turkey*, 1998-IV, 1686; *Aksoy v Turkey* (1997) 23 EHRR 553.

[84] 23 EHRR 364.

[85] *Halford v UK* (1997) 24 EHRR 523.

[86] See *Damages under the HRA*, para 6.160, n 276.

Such an approach would not be surprising to those familiar with civil law jurisdictions. As Professor von Bar has observed in his authoritative study of comparative tort law, punitive damages are by no means unique to the common law, which merely imposes them more openly than civil law jurisdictions.[87] A good example of this phenomenon is found in French Law. Non-compensatory damages are *prima facie* contrary to the underlying principles of *responsabilit(administrative*.[88] But principle and practice diverge. The lower courts' 'sovereign power of assessment'[89] in awarding damages provides a veil behind which, as in French civil law,[90] a punitive element for egregious fault may be included.[91]

Therefore, one should be careful in concluding that the damages awards of the ECtHR are solely compensatory. Indeed, as a former Secretary of the European Commission of Human Rights has recognised, in some cases where large awards have been made 'it cannot be excluded that the Court imposes some "punitive" element on the respondent State'.[92]

In light of this, how should the English courts approach the question of punitive damages under the HRA? In English law, punitive damages are designed to express the court's disapproval of the defendant's exceptionally bad conduct, and may be awarded *inter alia* for oppressive, arbitrary or unconstitutional action by servants of the government.[93] Until recently, the award of exemplary damages was limited by means of the 'cause of action test', restricting the grant of such damages to those causes of action for which exemplary damages have been awarded prior to the case of *Rookes v Barnard*[94] in 1964.[95] This rule precluded the awarding of such damages for negligence,[96] public nuisance,[97] and breach of statutory duty.[98]

---

[87] C Von Bar, *The Common European Law of Torts*, Volume 1 (Oxford: Oxford University Press, 1998), para 611.

[88] See generally R Chapus, *Droit Administratif Général*, Volume 1, 13th edn (Paris: Montchrestien, 1999), para 1405.

[89] See further C Pollmann, 'Contrôle de Cassation du Conseil d'Etat', *Revue du Droit Public* (1996), 1653.

[90] R David, *English Law and French Law: A Comparison in Substance* (London, 1980), 166; J Bell, S Boyron, and S Whittaker, *Principles of French Law* (Oxford: Oxford University Press, 1998), 396.

[91] On sanctions theory in French administrative law see Harlow, 'Francovich and the Problem of the Disobedient State' (1996) 2 *ELJ* 199, 206. More open derogations from the *restitutio in integrum* principle may be found in the practice of the administrative courts in levying punitive damages when a public body delays executing a court's judgment: Laws of 16 July 1980 and 8 Feb1995. See generally Chapus, op cit, para 1035.

[92] Krüger, 'Reflections on some Aspects of Just Satisfaction under the European Convention on Human Rights', in *Liber Amicorum Marc-André Eissen* (Brussels: Bruylant, 1995), 268.

[93] *Rookes v Barnard* [1964] AC 1129.

[94] Ibid.   [95] See *AB v South West Water Services Ltd* [1993] QB 507.

[96] Ibid.   [97] Ibid.

[98] *R v Secretary of State for Transport ex p Factortame (No 5)* The Times, 11 Sept 1997 (CA).

However, in a recent case the House of Lords refused to strike out an action for the award of exemplary damages for misfeasance in public office, rejecting the 'cause of action test' as a limiting factor upon the award of such damages.[99] Their Lordships specifically left open the question of the availability of exemplary damages under the Human Rights Act.[100]

In light of the surreptitious practice of the Strasbourg court, it might be argued that the English courts should be allowed to include a penal element in damages awards under the Human Rights Act. If exemplary damages serve a purpose in stigmatising, punishing and deterring oppressive conduct by public servants, then they should be available in the cases of breaches of fundamental rights. The serious breach of human rights would seem to be an example *par excellence* of the need to single out egregious behaviour for particular censure. On the other hand, there are arguments for excluding punitive damages in this sphere.[101] The language of the HRA instructs the English courts to take account of the 'principles' of the ECtHR. And whatever the surreptitious practice of the ECtHR might be, it has made it clear that *in principle* it will not award punitive and aggravated damages.[102]

We will now look more closely at the specific heads of loss for which damages have been awarded by the Strasbourg Court, as well as the method for measuring these claims

B. Pecuniary Loss

The Strasbourg court has awarded compensation for various types of pecuniary loss.[103] Many of these will present little difficulty for the English courts, as they are replicated in domestic law, such as loss of past and future earnings,[104] and medical expenses.[105]

The ECtHR has also been prepared to make awards for pure economic loss.[106] In contrast, the English courts have been cautious when faced with tort claims for such loss. In respect of the tort of negligence, the courts have generally been reluctant to allow recovery of financial loss which is uncon-

---

[99] *Kuddus v Chief Constable of Leicestershire Constabulary* [2001] UKHL 29.

[100] Ibid., at paras. 46 (Lord Mackay) and 92 (Lord Hutton). Lord Scott argued that exemplary damages should not be awarded for breach of statutory duty unless expressly authorised (see para 122), but as has already been argued, the remedy under the HRA is not exactly akin to classical tort actions, see text accompanying n 19 above.

[101] For the arguments against the award of exemplary damages in civil proceedings generally see Lord Scott's judgment in *Kuddus v Chief Constable of Leicestershire Constabulary* [2001] UKHL 29.   [102] See cases in n 82 above.

[103] See generally *Damages under the HRA*, para 3.23.

[104] See, eg, *Young, James and Webster v UK* (1983) 5 EHRR 201.

[105] See, eg, *Ilhan v Turkey*, Application no 22277/93, judgment of 27 June 2000.

[106] See, eg, *Allenet de Ribemont v France* (1995) 20 EHRR 557 (compensation *inter alia* for loss of business opportunities); *Pine Valley Developments Ltd v Ireland* (1993) 16 EHRR 379 (loss of value in land).

nected with physical damage to the plaintiff's person or property.[107] Torts other than negligence are of limited use in gaining damages for economic harm caused by a public body.[108]

Under the Human Rights Act, the courts will be required to adopt a different approach. Despite the reticence about the recovery of purely financial loss, this will not necessarily present an insurmountable obstacle. The nature of the Convention rights means that this is unlikely to result in a large extension of liability. In any case, in the sphere of damages for breach of Community law, the courts have quickly overcome their caution in respect of purely economic losses.[109] Public bodies themselves are not unused to paying damages for economic losses in other areas.[110]

C. Non-pecuniary Loss

The European Court of Human Rights has made monetary awards for non-pecuniary loss[111] covering diverse intangible injuries,[112] including anguish,[113] anxiety,[114] 'feelings of frustration and helplessness',[115] harassment, humiliation and stress[116], as well as cases of serious mental distress.[117]

How will the English courts take account of these principles? Many of these types of loss may be accommodated by ordinary tort law principles. So, the awards for non-pecuniary loss for unlawful detention are replicated by damages for the tort of false imprisonment.[118] Awards which the

---

[107] See, eg, *Murphy v Brentwood District Council* [1991] 1 AC 398. The major exception to the wariness of claims in respect of purely financial loss is the rule laid down in the case of *Hedley Byrne & Co Ltd v Heller & Partners* [1964] AC 465.

[108] For a restrictive approach to the recovery of economic loss for breach of statutory duty, see *Feakins Ltd v Dover Harbour Board*, The Times, 9 Sept 1998.

[109] See, eg, *R v Secretary of State for Transport ex p Factortame Ltd (No 5)* [2000] 1 AC 524, in which Lord Hoffmann—not generally known for his enthusiasm for state liability—held that in respect of the pure economic loss sustained that '[j]ustice requires that the wrong should be made good.'

[110] Including areas that might be affected by the Human Rights Act. So, in the planning sphere, when planning permission is revoked or modified, compensation can be claimed for the expenditure, loss or damage suffered by a person who is 'interested in the land' (Town and Country Planning Act 1990, s 107(1)). Moreover, there are numerous examples of the Local Government Ombudsman recommending, and local authorities accepting, to pay compensation for economic loss, eg, compensation gained for financial loss caused by the irregular grant of planning permission (Report 93/195, Blaenau Gwent BC [1995] JPL 1055).

[111] Also referred to by the ECtHR, in civil law terminology, as 'moral damage', eg *Gillow v UK*, A124-C (1987).

[112] For further examples, see K Starmer, *European Human Rights Law*, para 2.57 ff.

[113] *Loizidou v Turkey*, judgment of 28 July 1998.

[114] *Cazenave de la Roche v France* [1998] *Human Rights Case Digest* 620.

[115] *H v UK* (1991) 13 EHRR 449 (just satisfaction).

[116] *Young, James and Webster v UK* (1983) 5 EHRR 201.

[117] For instance 'bouts of depression'—*Estima Jorge v Portugal*, 1998-II 762, para 52.

[118] For discussion of this tort, see B Markesinis and S Deakin, *Tort Law*, 396 ff.

Strasbourg Court has made for distress which is consequential upon other compensatable loss should not pose a problem: the English courts will willingly grant damages for non-pecuniary loss consequent upon personal injury, such as pain and suffering and loss of amenity.[119]

In other ways, the ECtHR's approach is very different from that found at present in English law. Indeed, the Strasbourg Court does seem on the whole to take a more generous view of compensable moral damage than the English Courts. The English courts have been reluctant to countenance recovery for grief and distress unconnected with the claimant's own physical injury. A claim for mental distress by itself is unlikely to succeed.[120] In contrast, the ECtHR has been willing to provide compensation for free-standing 'moral damage'.[121] The Strasbourg Court has allowed claims in respect of 'loss of relationship', an injury which encompasses the emotional harm caused by the disruption to a relationship.[122]

In its broad recognition of moral damage, and its apparently open attitude to the heads of loss for which compensation can be awarded, the ECtHR is probably closer to the French law tradition than the common law.[123] In any case, it would seem that if account is taken of the Strasbourg jurisprudence then the English courts may have to revise their erstwhile cautious approach to the circumstances in which recovery can be made for moral damage, at least in making awards under the Human Rights Act. There are a number of reasons why the English system is well placed to take account of these new considerations. First, there are indications that the courts have already quietly adjusted their attitude to damages for mental distress in certain circumstances. The major exception to the non-recovery of 'free-standing' mental injury is psychiatric harm,[124] and there are signs that the courts are moving slowly towards a widening of the recognised heads of psychological injury. In the recent case of *Phelps v Hillingdon LBC*, concerning public authority liability for failure to diagnose and treat educational difficulties, Lord Slynn recognised that 'psychological damage and a failure to diagnose a congenital condition and to take appropriate action as a result of which a child's level of achievement is reduced . . . may constitute damage' in a negligence claim.[125] Indeed, in a recent bullying

---

[119] See recent discussion of this in *Heil v Rankin* [2000] 2 WLR 1173.

[120] *McGregor on Damages* 16th edn (London: Sweet & Maxwell, 1997), para 90; *Clerk & Lindsell on Torts*, 17th edn (London: Sweet & Maxwell, 1995), para 1-22.

[121] See, eg, *H v UK* (1991) 13 EHRR 449 (just satisfaction).

[122] For instance where there has been disruption to a relationship between a parent and child due to human rights violations: *H v UK* (1991) 13 EHRR 449; *O v UK* (1991) 13 EHRR 578.

[123] Bell, Boyron, and Whittaker, op cit, 393.

[124] For a comparative law study see M Janssens, 'Nervous Shock Liability' (1998) 6 *European Review of Private Law* 77.

[125] *Phelps v Hillingdon LBC* [2001] 2 AC 619, 664.

case, the judge accepted that the boundaries of negligence had been moved forward by the judgment in *Phelps*, and held that 'a moderate depressive episode' could constitute the gist of a negligence action in education cases.[126] In respect of claims relating to the 'loss of relationship', there is also an interesting, albeit isolated, case in which it was held that the act of denying an adult mentally handicapped daughter access to her mother, where such an act was contrary to the daughter's will or against her best interests, could constitute a tortious act.[127] In any case, the courts could perhaps draw parallels with the previous head of damages for 'loss of consortium'.[128] Again, it may be helpful to make reference to Continental legal systems, where culpable infringements of the right to parental care commonly give rise to a delictual claim in damages.[129]

Secondly, it is instructive to set the position of the courts in a wider perspective. The ombudsmen have adopted a broad approach to loss, often recommending financial reparation for a broad category of 'distress', including stress, anxiety, frustration, and inconvenience.[130] Indeed, a close examination of the Local Government Ombudsman's work reveals interesting parallels with the Strasbourg case law.[131] The UK has been found in violation of the ECHR in proceedings relating to children in care, in which 'feelings of frustration and helplessness' have been identified as a head of compensable damage.[132] Leigh and Lustgarten have argued that these cases illustrate the fact that the HRA will necessitate an 'important extension of compensation'.[133] And yet, local authorities are already familiar with providing monetary compensation for just such intangible loss in similar spheres. For instance, the Local Government Ombudsman found maladministration in the investigation of child abuse and recommended that West

---

[126] *Bradford-Smart v West Sussex County Council* (QBD, 8 Nov 2000).

[127] In *Re C (Adult Patient) (Access: Jurisdiction)* [1994] 1 FCR 705. But in another case, it has been held that there is no right of action in tort for interference with parental rights: *F v Wirral Metropolitan BC* [1991] *Fam* 69.

[128] Abolished by Law Reform (Miscellaneous Provisions) Act 1970, ss 4 and 5; Administration of Justice Act 1982, s 2. Note however that the action for loss of consortium was restricted to a relationship between spouses; there was never any action in common law for the loss of consortium of a child: *F v Wirral Metropolitan BC* [1991] *Fam* 69, 88, 115 ff. 'Loss of consortium' is the term actually used in the ECtHR's case law: *W v UK* (1991) 13 EHRR 453.

[129] C von Bar, *The Common European Law of Torts*, Volume 2, para 108.

[130] Commission for Local Administration in England, *Guidance on Good Practice 6: Remedies* (London, 1997), para 30.

[131] A point also made by Sir Robert Carnwath, 'Welfare services-liabilities in tort after the Human Rights Act' [2001] *PL* 210.

[132] See, eg, *H v UK* (1988) 13 EHRR 449; *O v UK* (1988) 13 EHRR 578; *R v UK* (1988) 13 EHRR 457.

[133] I Leigh and L Lustgarten, 'Making Rights Real: the Courts, Remedies and the Human Rights Act' [1999] *CLJ* 509, 529.

Sussex County Council make an *ex gratia* payment of £1,000 to the complainants to reflect their time, trouble, and anxiety.[134]

D. Rules of Quantum

Finally, a word should be said about the rules governing the measure of damages. In terms of quantum, the general principle of *restitutio in integrum* prevails in the Strasbourg case law as it does in English tort law.[135] However, the fact that a legal system espouses the notion of *restitutio in integrum* is significant, but not particularly explicative. *Restitutio in integrum* is not a self-executing concept. It relies upon much subjective evaluation on the part of the courts; particularly in terms of non-pecuniary loss.[136] More important than the principle of *restitutio in integrum* is how the individual rules for determining quantum are conceived. The difficulty with the European case law is that these rules are not spelt out.[137] Indeed, on many occasions the ECtHR merely states that the compensation to be awarded has been assessed on an equitable basis.[138] This less structured method of analysis in granting damages awards does, as noted by the Law Commission,[139] echo the French law approach.[140]

In terms of the level of damages before the ECtHR, the Government in its official guidance to public authorities on the HRA has observed that this 'tends to be modest'.[141] Although this may well be a product of wishful thinking, this view has been confirmed by other commentators.[142] Examples may indeed be found of cases in which the damages awards seem low,[143] but there are also other cases in which the Court has been more generous.[144]

---

[134] West Sussex CC (98/B/1350) (available from the LGO). See also Report 97/A/2293 published in The Commission for Local Administration in England, *Digest of Cases 1998, Section J: Social Services* (London, 1998), 108.

[135] *Ringeisen v Austria* (1979–80) 1 EHRR 504 (just satisfaction); *Papamichalopoulos v Greece* (1996) 21 EHRR 439.

[136] T Hill, 'Litigation and Negligence: A Comparative Study' (1986) 6 OJLS 183, 212; D Shelton, *Remedies in International Human Rights Law* (Oxford: Oxford University Press, 1999), 261.

[137] The Court even refused the Commission's request to provide clarification of a damages award in *Allenet de Ribemont v France* (1996) 22 EHRR 582 (interpretation).

[138] A Mowbray, 'The European Court of Human Rights' Approach to Just Satisfaction' [1997] PL 647, 649.

[139] *Damages under the HRA*, para 3.8.

[140] See, eg, Bell, Boyron, and Whittaker, op cit, 396; C Von Bar, *The Common European Law of Torts*, Volume 2, para 16.

[141] *Human Rights Task Force Core Guidance For Public Authorities* (Home Office), para 89.

[142] Mowbray, op cit, 658.

[143] *Johnson v UK* (1999) 27 EHRR 296: £10,000 awarded to applicant who had spent an excessive amount of time in a maximum security psychiatric hospital after it was conclusively shown that he was no longer suffering from mental illness ($3\frac{1}{2}$ years).

[144] *Guillemin v France* (1998) 25 EHRR 435: FF 250,000 awarded for the applicant living

Regardless of the Strasbourg approach, Lord Woolf has argued that damages awards under the HRA should be moderate, and that they should be 'on the low side by comparison to tortious awards'.[145] However, there may well be serious problems in adopting a dual-track approach to the measure of damages. The same factual situation may give rise to an action in tort law, as well as a damages action under the HRA. It would be wrong to make the quantum of the damages award dependent upon the cause of action, especially when both are designed to effect *restitutio in integrum*. The courts may be acting in breach of Article 14 of the ECHR prohibiting discrimination if they systematically undervalue awards given under the HRA in comparison with comparable tort claims.[146]

VI. CAUSATION

Finally, we will look at how the notion of causation is applied by the European Court, and the way in which account may be taken of this in English Law. According to the case law of the ECtHR, there must be a 'direct'[147] and 'clear'[148] causal link between the damage suffered by the applicant and the violation of the Convention. Although the approach of the Court sometimes mirrors the but-for test of causation found in English law,[149] the Court has never articulated clearly the principles of causation which it uses.[150] No general test of causation has been laid down.

This discretionary approach has led to uneven results. In general, the test of causation has been developed by the ECtHR to become an important control mechanism,[151] and many claims are rejected for want of causation.[152] And yet the Court has sometimes taken a more liberal approach to

'in a state of uncertainty and anxiety' due to an unlawful expropriation procedure and unreasonable length of the proceedings to challenge the expropriation. See also the recent case of *Z v UK* [2001] 2 FLR 612.

[145] Lord Woolf, 'The Human Rights Act 1998 and Remedies', 434.

[146] Art 14 prohibits the different treatment of those in a comparable position in the enjoyment of one of the rights guaranteed under the Convention. In this situation, the substantive provision breached would be Art 13 (effective remedy before national authority). However, it might be argued that such discrimination would not be unlawful under the HRA as Art 13 has not been included in the Act.

[147] See, eg, *Sekanina v Austria* (1994) 17 EHRR 221.

[148] See, eg, *Barberà, Messegué and Jabardo v Spain* (1994) A 285-C.

[149] See, eg, *König v Germany*, A 36 (1980) para 18. For English law, see Rogers, *Winfield and Jolowicz on Tort*, 15th edn (London: Sweet & Maxwell, 1998), 199.

[150] See Sharpe, 'Article 50', in Pettiti, Decaux, and Imbert, *La Convention Européenne des Droits de l'Homme* (Paris: Economica, 1995), 816.

[151] M Supperstone, J Goudie, and J Coppel, *Local Authorities and the Human Rights Act 1998* (London: Butterworths, 1999), 26.

[152] Especially for claims concerning pecuniary loss, for a recent example see *Asan Rushiti v Austria*, Application no 28389/95, judgment of 21 Mar 2000. See comments of Sharpe, 'Article 50', 815; Shelton, op cit, 242.

causality. In some cases, it has been prepared to presume that causation existed,[153] and in others it has even appeared to award compensation whilst admitting that the link of cause and effect was not present.[154]

The relative opacity of these principles should give the domestic courts ample room to fashion their own principles of causation, no doubt based upon those used in ordinary tort law. There is one issue that might prove to be more challenging for the courts, namely damages for lost opportunities or chances. We will examine this in more detail.

A. Loss of a Chance

The award of damages for loss of a chance is a thorny issue which has exercised the minds of many jurists.[155] It has also occupied the time of the ECtHR on many occasions and has been particularly prevalent in respect of breach of Article 6 (fair hearing), where applicants have alleged that a procedural impropriety has reduced their chances of gaining a benefit or avoiding a loss. How will the English courts take account of the Strasbourg case law concerning lost chances?

One thing that is clear is that the Strasbourg case law is not clear. In some cases, the ECtHR has insisted upon proof of a direct causal link between the human rights violation and the applicant's damage, whereas in others it has been satisfied with proof of merely a lost opportunity of avoiding that loss. There seem to be no criteria guiding when a lost chance will do. So, in adopting a 'strict'[156] approach to causation, the ECtHR has rejected some claims for compensation for breach of Article 6 by proceedings of national law, on the basis that it would not speculate as to the outcome of the national proceedings had the violations not occurred.[157] On the other hand, in other cases, the Court has been more liberal. In *Tinnelly & Sons Ltd v UK*, the ECtHR awarded sums of £10,000 and £15,000 for the applicants' lost opportunity to have an adjudication on the merits of

---

[153] Grosz, Beatson, and Duffy, op cit, para 621. See, eg, *Open Door Counselling and Dublin Well Woman v Ireland* (1993) 15 EHRR 244.

[154] *Halford v UK* (1997) 24 EHRR 523: the court found that the stress of which the applicant complained had not been shown to derive from the breach of the Convention right but nonetheless awarded her £10,000 as 'just and equitable amount of compensation'. This might be an example of the award of punitive damages: see text accompanying n 85 above.

[155] The lost chance doctrine has inspired a vast amount of academic writing (worldwide), but for a recent selection of common law contributions, see J Fleming, 'Probabilistic Causation in Tort Law' (1989) 68 *Can Bar Rev* 661; M Lunney, 'What Price a Chance' (1995) 15 LS 1; H Reece, 'Losses of Chances in the Law' (1996) 59 MLR 188; J Stapleton, 'The Gist of Negligence, Part II: the Relationship between "Damage" and Causation' (1988) 104 LQR 389.

[156] *Damages under the HRA*, para 3.60.

[157] *Ruiz-Mateos v Spain* (1993) 16 EHRR 505 (national proceedings in violation of Art 6(1) due to their unreasonable length and non-adversarial nature); *Saunders v UK* (1997) 23 EHRR 313 (violation of the right not to incriminate oneself during criminal proceedings).

their claims before the domestic courts due to the application of public interest immunity certificates.[158] Similarly, lost opportunities were found to stem from violations of Convention rights due to procedural defects in respect of local authority child protection proceedings and the lack of a judicial remedy.[159]

Given the ECtHR's discretionary and equitable approach to the award of monetary compensation generally, it is perhaps unsurprising that it has adopted a flexible method for determining causation. It may be that the Court is simply influenced by equitable considerations, such as sympathy for the applicants' circumstances, in deciding whether to award compensation for lost opportunities.[160] Its specific position as an international court may also contribute to the uneven approach in the sense that the judges may not always feel that it is appropriate for an international court to speculate upon what the outcome of national proceedings would have been if a breach of the Convention had not occurred.[161]

It should also be noted that there is by no means an unanimous approach to the lost chance doctrine in the European jurisdictions which the ECtHR judges represent.[162] In fact, the present position of the English courts in respect of tort actions[163] for recovery of 'pure loss of a chance'[164] is far from crystal clear itself.[165] This will exacerbate the process of taking account of the conflicting strands of the Strasbourg case law.

In terms of domestic law, in the leading English case of *Hotson v East Berkshire AHA*, the House of Lords rejected a claim for damages for the lost chance of avoiding avascular necrosis.[166] Although their Lordships did

---

[158] *Tinnelly & Sons Ltd v UK; McElduff v UK* (1999) 27 EHRR 249.

[159] *W v UK* (1991) 13 EHRR 453 (violation of Arts 6(1) and 8).

[160] J Coppel, *The Human Rights Act 1998: Enforcing the European Convention in the Domestic Courts* (Chichester: Wiley, 1999), para 2.133.

[161] In light of these difficulties, it has been argued by Judge Zupancic in his partly dissenting judgment in *Hood v UK* (2000) 29 EHRR 365, that Art 41 ECHR ought to be interpreted so as to require the respondent State to permit the retrial of cases.

[162] See N Jansen, 'The Idea of a Lost Chance' (1999) 19 *OJLS* 271, who draws a contrast between English and German law, where loss of a chance is not accepted as a general type of damage giving rise to a tort claim, and French and Dutch law where the concept of damages for loss of a chance is recognised more broadly.

[163] It is a well-established principle that damages for loss of a chance are recoverable in contract: *Chaplin v Hicks* [1911] 2 KB 786.

[164] P Cane, *Tort Law and Economic Interests*, 2nd edn (Oxford: Oxford University Press), 137. This is to be distinguished from a lost chance consequential upon physical injury. The probabilistic calculation of damages is generally accepted where the plaintiff has proved some compensatable damage on the balance of probabilities, eg, where damages are awarded for loss of future income in a personal injury action. This issue goes to quantification rather than liability: *Doyle v Wallace*, The Times, 22 July 1998.

[165] Thus, it is somewhat strange that the Law Commission concluded that given the inconsistencies in the Strasbourg case law, damages for loss of a chance should be based 'upon normal common law principles' (*Damages under the HRA*, para 4.86).

[166] *Hotson v East Berkshire Area Health Authority* [1987] AC 750.

not explicitly deny the possibility of claiming damages for lost chances,[167] they actually left very little opportunity for its future application in personal injury cases.[168] On the other hand, there has been a sprinkling of successful damages actions for the lost opportunity of financial gain.[169] In *Allied Maples Group Ltd v Simmons & Simmons*,[170] it was indicated that claimants could gain damages from their solicitors for the lost chance of negotiating proper protection against contingent liabilities in a contract for the takeover of assets.[171] It would also seem that lost chance damages may be awarded for lost employment opportunity.[172]

There is also a related line of cases concerning lawyers' negligence that may be of assistance in formulating lost chance claims under the HRA. It is well established that lawyers may be liable to their clients for negligently causing a loss of opportunity to bring or defend proceedings.[173] The most common blunder is the failure to institute proceedings in time,[174] such as failure to issue a writ within the limitation period.[175] In these cases, damages are calculated by taking the value of the plaintiff's primary (but elapsed) claim, which is then discounted in accordance with the risk of failure of the action. These lawyers' cases may be relevant to damages claims under the HRA in the following manner. Parallels may be drawn between a claim that was not heard by the courts due to lawyers' negligence, and a grievance for which access to court was unlawfully restricted in breach of Article 6(1) of the ECHR. In the human rights cases, the courts may, following the example of the lawyers' negligence cases, accept to evaluate the chances of the claimant having obtained a favourable result had his or her Convention rights been respected. The lawyers' negligence cases show how effective control mechanisms may be developed. A precondition of such a claim is that the claimant's litigation must have had some prospect of success, rather than just a nuisance value.[176] Other lost chance cases have indicated that the plaintiff must show a real or substantial chance has been

---

[167] 1987] AC 750, 782-3, 786.

[168] J Stapleton, 'The Gist of Negligence, Part II: the Relationship between "Damage" and Causation"' (1988) 104 *LQR* 389, 394. See, eg, *Richardson v Kitching* [1995] 6 Med LR 257.

[169] M Lunney and K Oliphant, *Tort Law: Text and Materials* (Oxford: Oxford University Press, 2000), 184; B Markesinis and S Deakin, *Tort Law*, 183.

[170] *Allied Maples Group Ltd v Simmons & Simmons* [1995] 1 WLR 1602.

[171] The use of the lost chance doctrine in this case has been explained by some commentators on the basis that the loss depended upon the hypothetical action of a third party: Rogers, *Winfield and Jolowicz on Tort*, 205.

[172] *Spring v Guardian Assurance* [1995] 2 AC 296, 327.

[173] See *Jackson & Powell on Professional Negligence* (London: Sweet & Maxwell, 1997), paras. 4-222 ff.

[174] Evans, *Lawyer's Liabilities* (London: Sweet & Maxwell, 1996), 124.

[175] For instance, *Kitchen v Royal Air Force Association* [1958] 1 WLR 563 (solicitors negligently failed to issue a writ before the limitation period expired).

[176] Ibid, 575.

lost rather than a purely speculative one.[177] A robust approach of the courts to compensable lost chances under the HRA would both do much to circumvent worries that there might be a flood of groundless claims for imaginary chances, and do something to reflect the more cautious strand of the ECtHR judgments on probabilistic causation.

In some ways, however, the analogy with the lawyers' cases may be imperfect. The claims under the HRA will often concern an unlawful administrative procedure that has already occurred and the chance lost, for instance a licensing procedure in breach of Article 6 of the ECHR that has already taken place and the licence awarded to another applicant. All the lawyers' negligence cases have concerned the situation in which the lawyer's negligence has *entirely* deprived the client of bringing or defending proceedings. The claimant has thus claimed damages for the lost chance of success in a *hypothetical* court case. The only relevant judicial statement as to whether lost chance damages can be awarded when the lawyer's negligence has caused an actual case to be lost is the *obiter dictum* of Lord Diplock in *Saif Ali v Sydney Mitchell & Co*.[178] His Lordship seemed to express preference for the all-or-nothing approach,[179] thus excluding the use of the lost chance doctrine.[180] According to this view, it would have to be shown on the balance of probabilities that, but for the negligent act, the case would have been won. In the recent case of *Arthur JS Hall & Co v Simons*,[181] in which the House of Lords finally abandoned the immunity of advocates in respect of the conduct of legal proceedings, and thus increased the possibility of this conundrum facing the courts, their Lordships did not clearly indicate their view of this problem.[182] It is submitted that despite Lord Diplock's dictum the courts are likely to adopt a more liberal approach and apply probabilistic analysis in these cases rather than insist upon the all-or-nothing test of causation. Indeed, the ECtHR has itself granted compensation for lost chances even where the negative outcome of which there was a risk has actually materialised.[183]

---

[177] *Allied Maples Group Ltd v Simmons & Simmons* [1995] 1 WLR 1602, 1614. See Burrows, *Remedies for Torts and Breach of Contract*, 34.

[178] [1980] AC 198.   [179] Ibid, 222D-E.

[180] See *Jackson & Powell on Professional Negligence*, para 5-38.

[181] [2000] 3 WLR 543.

[182] This problem reflects a deeper debate concerning lost chance damages, which is whether they should be available in those cases in which the negative outcome of which there was a risk has actually materialised: (see P Cane, *Tort Law and Economic Interests*, 140–1). Connected to this is whether such damages can be awarded in respect of past facts as well as future or hypothetical ones (see discussion in A Burrows, *Tort Law and Economic Interests*, 2nd edn (Oxford: Oxford University Press, 1996), 31 ff; H Reece, 'Losses of Chances in the Law' (1996) 59 *MLR* 188)

[183] See, for instance, *Bönisch v Austria* (1991) 13 EHRR 409 (national proceedings in which the applicant was convicted did not adhere to the principle of equality of arms and so were in breach of Art 6(1)).

Another potential difficulty is of a constitutional nature. Where claims are brought for lost chances of gaining a favourable decision from a public authority, the courts will be required to investigate the decision-making process of the authority, and to speculate upon the chances of a decision having been taken in the claimant's favour if the Convention right or rights had been respected. Constitutional objections may be made to such an approach on the basis that it would involve the courts adjudicating upon matters which had been entrusted to administrative authorities by statute.[184] Practical difficulties may also be encountered by the courts in deciding what the authority would have done if it had acted lawfully. Thus it might be argued that the courts will be hampered by the lack of experience, tools, and knowledge that the authority itself has when it takes such decisions.[185]

In response to these concerns various points should be made. The constitutional difficulties should not be overstated. The courts will not be imposing a solution upon the administrative bodies. In many cases, it will be possible for the courts to resubmit the decision to the public authority, which will retake the decision this time in conformity with the Convention, and on that basis it can be decided what compensation will be required. In other cases, where it is not possible for redetermination to occur, the courts will merely be asked to determine the percentage chance that the administrative body would have acted in a certain way: not stipulate what it *should* have done. The practical difficulties of requiring a court to shadow an administrative authority's decision-making process have been surmounted in other areas without undue difficulties. This is exemplified by damages actions for the breach of public procurement rules.[186] If a tendering procedure is run incorrectly, then the unsuccessful bidder may gain damages from the awarding authority, the quantum of which will be calculated by the chance lost of winning the contract and making a reasonable degree of profit.[187]

There is also another important reference point. In line with their flexible approach to redress, the ombudsmen have also recognised the usefulness of focusing upon chances as well as outcomes. The Local Government Ombudsman states in its informative guidance on remedies that it will recommend compensation for lost opportunities, for instance where a complainant has been deprived of a right of appeal because the council did

---

[184] Arrowsmith, *Civil Liability and Public Authorities* (Earlsgate: Winteringham, 1992), 31; P Craig, 'Compensation in Public Law' (1980) 96 *LQR* 413.

[185] Arrowsmith, n 184 at 31.

[186] See generally S Arrowsmith, *The Law of Public and Utilities Procurement* (London, 1996), 891–5

[187] See, eg, *Harmon Façades Ltd v The Corporate Officer of The House Of Commons* (Technology & Construction Court, 28 Oct 1999).

not inform him or her of that right.[188] Several concrete cases illustrate the application of these principles in practice. In one instance, the LGO recommended that a substantial *ex gratia* payment should be made to the owner of a mushroom farm who had lost the chance to make representations to the local council planning committee in order to gain protection from the development of an open-cast mine on neighbouring property.[189]

VII. CONCLUSION

The means for gaining compensation for administrative wrongs in England are extremely diverse. Not only do many different institutions provide or facilitate the payment of redress (the courts, the ombudsmen, the public bodies themselves) but they rely on different principles governing payment (fault, public law unlawfulness,[190] maladministration,[191] and—on rare occasions—liability without fault).[192] In terms of formulating the new remedy under the HRA, this feature of the English system may be particularly useful. We have already seen that reference to Community law may be helpful in shaping this remedy. It is also submitted that it may be useful to have reference to less orthodox legal sources, such as the ombudsmen. In many areas, their approach has been far more radical than the courts.[193] This not only shows that the English system is open to different approaches, but that this has been achieved with the acquiescence of public bodies themselves.[194]

A final point to make is that this new remedy serves to underline another characteristic of the English system in this sphere, that it is essentially very porous and open to many different influences. We have already noted the influence of European Community law; under the Human Rights Act there is now a direct route into the domestic legal system for European Human rights law. The HRA may prove to be a conduit for comparative law influences in a wider sense. The jurisprudence of the ECtHR has been influenced by the civil law system, for instance in taking a broad approach to the loss that may be recoverable in damages. In formulating the rules governing

---

[188] Commission for Local Administration in England, *Guidance on Good Practice 6: Remedies* (London, 1997), para 28.

[189] Report 94/B/4608 cited in the Commission's *Digest of Cases 1996, Section J: Planning* (London, 1997), 101. See also Report 90/C/2581 Harrogate BC [1996] JPL 776.

[190] See n 44 above.

[191] *Ex gratia* payments for maladministration may be made by public bodies after investigation by the Health Services Commissioner, the Parliamentary Commissioner for Administration and the Commission for Local Administration (or Local Government Ombudsman).

[192] See nn 32 and 33 above.

[193] See, eg, text accompanying n 52 above.

[194] See n 53 above.

damages under the HRA, the English courts will take account of this more liberal attitude. In turn, this might prompt a more general re-evaluation of the present stance of the courts in respect of pure economic loss and moral damage in the light of comparative law, through the first-hand application of concepts shaped by foreign law influences.

PART II:

EUROPEAN COMMUNITY LAW INFLUENCES

5. EUROTORTS AND UNICORNS: DAMAGES FOR BREACH OF COMMUNITY LAW IN THE UNITED KINGDOM

*Merris Amos**

The development of the remedy in damages for breach of Community law before United Kingdom courts is framed by two events almost 30 years apart. In 1974, when deciding whether a respondent could amend its defence on the ground that there were additional defences available to it under the EC Treaty, Lord Denning, allowing the application, held that Articles 85 and 86 of the Treaty[1] were part of our law. In his view, they created 'new torts or wrongs' and the English courts could deal with any breach.[2] In July 2001, Elliot Morley, Parliamentary Under-Secretary at the Department for Environment, Food and Rural Affairs, revealed that settlement had been reached with 91 of the 93 claimants in the *Factortame* litigation. Under the terms of the settlement, the total sum of damages the State is to pay for its breach of the EC Treaty[3] is £55 million including interest but excluding costs.[4]

Lord Denning said it was possible and the claimants in *Factortame* have succeeded. It is clear that the 'Eurotort' has well and truly arrived in United Kingdom national law although the path from 1974 to 2001 has not been smooth. In this chapter the development of this remedy in damages before United Kingdom courts will be examined and assessed in particular the characterisation of the remedy, the domestic courts' interpretation of its constituent elements, and prospects for the future.

I. A BRIEF HISTORY

Although Lord Denning bravely foresaw the future in 1974, it took many

---

* Lecturer, Department of Law, University of Essex.
[1] Now Arts 81 and 82.
[2] *Application des Gaz SA v Falks Veritas Ltd* [1974] 3 All ER 51, 58.
[3] *R v Secretary of State for Transport, ex p Factortame Ltd (No 3)* [1992] QB 680.
[4] HC Deb., vol. 372, col. 399, 19 July 2001. See also HC Deb., vol 366, cols 126–8, 3 Apr 2001.

years before UK courts fully accepted that it was possible for a litigant to be awarded damages for a breach of Community law in circumstances wider than those countenanced by existing private law remedies. To some extent, this was understandable given that in contrast to many other European legal systems,[5] English law remains unwilling to accept that 'a subject should be indemnified for loss sustained by invalid administrative action'.[6] Such action 'by itself, gives rise to no claim for damages'.[7] The classic example of this lacuna in the English legal system is the case of *R v Metropolitan Borough of Knowsley, ex p Maguire*[8] where the applicants suffered economic loss as a result of the respondent's ultra vires refusal of taxi licences.[9] Although the decision of the Council was eventually quashed and licences issued to the applicants, when they sought compensation for the damage they had suffered, their claims failed 'because we do not have in our law a general right to damages for maladministration'.[10] Any compensation sought, 'must be based on a private law cause of action'[11] such as negligence, breach of statutory duty, or misfeasance in public office.

It is clear that this principle was operative in the decision of the Court of Appeal in *Bourgin SA v Ministry of Agriculture Fisheries and Food*[12] in 1985. The claimants, French turkey producers, had suffered significant losses when the Minister for Agriculture Fisheries and Food revoked their general import licence. When the European Court of Justice found that the revocation was in breach of Article 30[13] of the EC Treaty, the claimants sought damages in the UK courts.

Parker LJ concluded that a breach of Article 30 by the government should be regarded as a 'simple excess of power' which was 'closely akin to the right of an individual in English domestic law not to be subjected to an ultra vires measure.' It was therefore open to the individual to seek a declaration that the measure was invalid but damages would only be available if he or she could establish misfeasance.[14] The judgment of Nourse LJ was even clearer:

---

[5] eg France.

[6] *Hoffmann-La Roche v Secretary of State for Trade and Industry* [1975] AC 295, 359 per Lord Wilberforce. For the purposes of this chapter 'invalid administrative action' is defined as administrative action or omission tainted by illegality, irrationality, or procedural impropriety which is thereby liable to be declared illegal, quashed, or held void or voidable. See further *Council of Civil Service Unions v Minister for the Civil Service* [1985] AC 374, 410–11 per Lord Diplock.

[7] *X (Minors) v Bedfordshire County Council* [1995] 2 AC 633, 749 per Lord Browne-Wilkinson.

[8] 31 July 1989, Unreported, Divisional Court.

[9] Otton J also found that the Council had acted irrationally and that each applicant had a legitimate expectation that a licence would be issued as they had met the criteria outlined in a letter from the Council.

[10] *R v Knowsley Metropolitan Borough Council, ex p Maguire* (1992) Times, 26 June, DC per Schiemann J.

[11] Ibid.

[12] [1986] 1 QB 716.

[13] Now Art 28.

[14] [1986] 1 QB 716, 788.

In this country the law has never allowed that a private individual should recover damages against the Crown for an injury caused to him by an ultra vires order made in good faith. Nowadays this rule is grounded not in procedural theory but on the sound acknowledgement that a minister of the Crown should be able to discharge the duties of his office expeditiously and fearlessly, a state of affairs which could hardly be achieved if acts done in good faith, but beyond his powers, were to be actionable in damages. What then can be the interest of Community law in endangering the continuation of this system?[15]

In the years that followed, this judgment severely restricted the ability of those who possibly had a claim for damages for breach of Community law to obtain redress. For example, in *An Bord Bainne Co-operative Ltd v The Milk Marketing Board*[16] the Court of Appeal held that an application to join the Ministry of Agriculture Fisheries and Food to the claim was unarguable as the decision in *Bourgin* was binding. Although it was possible for a claimant obtain a remedy in damages if he or she could show the breach of Community law amounted to a breach of statutory duty[17] or a misfeasance in public office,[18] the elements of both of these torts were very difficult to prove.[19]

The deadlock was finally broken in November 1991 with the decision of the European Court of Justice in *Francovich & Bonifaci v Italy*.[20] The ECJ held that the full effectiveness of Community rules would be impaired if individuals were unable to obtain compensation when their rights were infringed by a breach of Community law for which a Member State could be held responsible.[21] It specified that there should be a right to compensation when three conditions were met:

The first of those conditions is that the result prescribed by the directive should entail the grant of rights to individuals. The second condition is that it should be possible to identify the content of those rights on the basis of the provisions of the directive. Finally, the third condition is the existence of a causal link between the breach of the State's obligation and the harm suffered by the injured parties.[22]

Soon after, in the light of this decision, the House of Lords cast doubt on whether *Bourgin* was correctly decided.[23] It was concluded that a cross-undertaking in damages was not required from a local authority seeking an injunction to restrain the defendants from trading on Sundays. Lord Goff,

---

[15] Ibid, 790. [16] [1988] 1 CMLR 605.
[17] *Garden Cottage Foods Ltd v Milk Marketing Board* [1984] 1 A. 130 distinguished in *Bourgin*.
[18] *Bourgin SA v Ministry of Agriculture Fisheries and Food* [1986] 1 QB 716.
[19] See further, J Convery, 'State Liability in the United Kingdom After Brasserie du Pecheur' (1997) 34 *Common Market Law Review* 603.
[20] [1993] 2 CMLR 66. [21] Ibid, para 33.
[22] Ibid , para 40.
[23] *Kirklees Metropolitan Borough Council v Wickes Building Supplies Ltd* [1992] 3 WLR 170.

with whom the other Lords agreed, stated that if section 47 of the Shops Act 1950 was found to be in conflict with Article 30[24] of the EC Treaty 'the United Kingdom may be obliged to make good damage caused to individuals by the breach of Article 30 for which it is responsible'.[25]

In 1992, the claimants in *Factortame*, having succeeded in establishing that provisions of the Merchant Shipping Act 1988 were in breach of articles of the EC Treaty,[26] sought damages for the losses they had suffered. Finding that there was a discrepancy between the decisions in *Bourgin* and *Francovich*, the Divisional Court referred to the ECJ questions concerning the conditions under which a Member State may incur liability for damage caused to individuals by breaches of Community law attributable to that State. As it took the ECJ almost four years to answer, the status of damages for breach of Community law in the UK remained in limbo.

In 1993 in *Chisholm v Kirklees Metropolitan Borough Council*[27] Ferris J in the Chancery Court, following *Bourgin*, held that it was 'doubtful' whether under Community law there was a right to recover loss suffered by the enforcement of a domestic law found incompatible with Community law. The following year, in *R v Secretary of State for Employment ex p Seymour-Smith*[28] McCullough J in the Divisional Court commented that there was no procedure in the UK whereby the individual may claim damages from the state for failure to legislate in accordance with Community law. In 1995 in *R v Ministry of Agriculture Fisheries and Food ex p Live Sheep Traders Limited*[29] Simon Brown LJ in the Divisional Court noted that the applicants were unable to cite a single instance of a *Francovich* claim being successfully invoked in our courts.

Again the impetus came from the ECJ. In March 1996 it gave its judgment in *Brasserie du Pecheur S.A. v Federal Republic of Germany; R v Secretary of State for Transport, ex p Factortame Ltd (No 4)*.[30] The Court concluded that the right to reparation is the necessary corollary of the direct effect of the Community provision whose breach caused the damage sustained.[31] It clarified the conditions for liability:

Community law confers a right to reparation where three conditions are met: the rule of law infringed must be intended to confer rights on individuals; the breach must be sufficiently serious; and there must be direct causal link between the breach of the obligation resting on the State and the damage sustained by the injured parties.[32]

---

[24] Now Art 28.   [25] [1992] 3 WLR 170, 189.
[26] *R v Secretary of State for Transport ex p Factortame Ltd (No 3)* [1992] QB 680.
[27] [1993] ICR 826.   [28] [1994] IRLR 448.
[29] Unreported, Divisional Court, 12 Apr 1995.   [30] [1996] ECR I-1029.
[31] Ibid, para 22. See further, J Steiner, 'The Limits of State Liability for Breach of Community Law' (1998) *European Public Law* 69; P Craig, 'Once More Unto the Breach: The Community, the State and Damages Liability' (1997) 113 *LQR* 67.
[32] Ibid, para 51.

A clarification of the availability of the remedy before United Kingdom courts soon followed. One of the first decisions was that of the Commercial Court in *Three Rivers District Council v Bank of England (No 3).*[33] Although the claim was struck out, the Community law element on the ground that the First Council Banking Co-ordination Directive 1977 did not confer rights upon savers, Clarke J commented on the recent decisions of the ECJ:

> the court has now laid down clear rules as to the criteria which must be met. Those criteria are different from the criteria which must be established on any view of the English tort of misfeasance in public office . . . in such a case the claim should not be regarded as claim for damages for the tort of misfeasance in public office, but rather as a claim of a different type not known to the common law, namely a claim for damages for breach of a duty imposed by Community law or for the infringement of a right conferred by Community law.[34]

Soon after, in *R v Secretary of State for the Home Department ex p Gallagher,*[35] the Court of Appeal directly applied the test set out by the ECJ in *Brasserie du Pecheur.* In the cases that followed, there was little controversy over the availability of damages for a breach of Community law.[36] Nevertheless, attention was devoted to new problems, in particular, characterisation of the cause of action, the existence of a duty, whether or not rights had been conferred on individuals, and the meaning of sufficiently serious breach.

II. CHARACTERISATION OF THE CAUSE OF ACTION

Characterisation of the cause of action for damages for breach of Community law has always been an issue for concern in domestic law. As noted in the introductory paragraphs, in 1974 Lord Denning accepted that directly effective treaty articles created 'new torts or wrongs'.[37] However, when the issue was next to arise, ten years later in *Garden Cottage Foods,*[38] Lord Diplock characterised a breach of Article 86[39] as a breach of statutory duty. His Lordship could see 'no other categorisation that would be capa-

---

[33] [1996] 3 All ER 558.   [34] Ibid, 624.   [35] [1996] 2 CMLR 951.
[36] See, eg, *R v Secretary of State for Transport, ex p Factortame (No 5)* [1997] Eu LR 475; *R v Department of Social Security, ex p Scullion,* Unreported, Divisional Court, 25 Mar 1998; *R v Secretary of State for Transport, ex p Factortame (No 5)* [1998] Eu LR 456; *Three Rivers District Council v Governor and Company of the Bank of England (No 3),* Unreported, Court of Appeal, 4 Dec 1998; *Bowden v South-West Services Ltd* [1999] 3 CMLR 180. See further, T de la Mare, 'Bringing a Francovich Claim in English Courts' [1997] *Judicial Review* 143.
[37] *Application des Gaz SA v Falks Veritas Ltd* [1974] 3 All ER 51, 58.
[38] *Garden Cottage Foods Ltd v Milk Marketing Board* [1983] 3 WLR 143.
[39] Now Art 82.

ble of giving rise to a civil cause of action in private law on the part of a private individual'.[40]

The problem UK courts have had with characterisation of the remedy essentially stems from the fact that it represents an attempt to marry a public law wrong with a private law remedy.[41] As discussed in preceding paragraphs, in English law there is no general statutory or common law right to damages where a person suffers loss as a result of a public law wrong *per se*. It is possible that the situation may have been different had the remedy been developed through cases brought against private respondents. However, the nature of Community law is such that these cases are rare. More often than not, it is only possible to bring a claim against a public body for a breach of Community law.[42] When confronted with what is essentially an ultra vires act committed by a public body, UK courts have been loath to make an award of damages, unless of course a private law wrong can also be made out.

The problems with characterising the cause of action as a breach of statutory duty or misfeasance in public office soon became apparent. The ECJ had specified that national remedies must meet the requirements of equivalence[43] and effectiveness.[44] Although UK courts could justify the unavailability of damages on the ground of equivalence, often it was not possible to obtain damages for a similar domestic wrong,[45] the test of effectiveness was impossible to meet.[46]

For example, in *Bourgin* the majority of the Court of Appeal, unlike the Divisional Court,[47] found that a breach of Article 30 did not represent a breach of statutory duty as it did not meet the specific requirements of that tort. Although it did leave open the question of a possible misfeasance in public office, this is a tort notoriously difficult to prove. It was beyond question that Article 30 was of direct effect and had been breached yet the applicants were to have no effective remedy before a national court.[48] The only real disincentive to further breach was the prospect of an infringement action brought by the Commission although this was not recognised by the majority who maintained that judicial review combined with breach of

---

[40] [1983] 3 WLR 143, 149–50.

[41] See the judgment of Sir John Donaldson MR in *An Bord Bainne Co-operative Limited v Milk Marketing Board* [1984] 2 CMLR 584.

[42] But see *Courage Ltd v Crehan* [1999] 2 EGLR 145.

[43] *Rewe-Zentralfinanz eG and Rewe-Zentral AG v Landwirtschaftskammer fur das Saarland* [1976] ECR 1989.

[44] *Von Colson and Kamann v Land Nordrhein-Westfalen* [1984] ECR 1891.

[45] See *Bourgin SA v Ministry of Agriculture Fisheries and Food* [1986] 1 QB 716.

[46] See further, Convery, op cit 603 and Craig, op cit 67.

[47] *Bourgin SA v Ministry of Agriculture Fisheries and Food* [1986] 1 QB 716.

[48] The majority in *Bourgin* dealt with the question of effectiveness by finding that the ECJ had not specified that an effective remedy must be dissuasive of further breaches.

statutory duty and misfeasance in public office effectively protected individual rights.

Following the decision of the Court of Appeal in *Bourgin*, considerable confusion surrounded the remedy and there was little discussion of whether or not the characterisation of the remedy had been correct.[49] Even after the decision of the ECJ in *Brasserie du Pecheur* the issue of characterisation was rarely discussed as often the claim was defeated on other grounds.[50] However, as the *Factortame* litigation progressed, it became increasingly evident that the character of the claim would have to be determined as exemplary damages were sought.

Following the guidance of the ECJ in *Brasserie du Pecheur* the Divisional Court had to determine whether or not in principle a similar claim made under English law would qualify for an award of exemplary damages. Somewhat confusingly, the Divisional Court stated that liability for a breach of Community law was 'best understood as a breach of statutory duty' though later in the judgment described the cause of action as *sui generis* although 'of the character of a breach of statutory duty'.[51] It concluded that exemplary damages were therefore not available.

The issue arose again at the end of 2000 when it was sought to add additional parties to the proceedings and obtain damages for injury to feelings and distress and aggravated damages. Toulmin J in the Technology and Construction Court concluded that although the nature of the breaches of Community law could be characterised as breaches of duty or obligations, the assessment of those breaches was undertaken in a way which was novel under English law.[52]

His Lordship defined a tort as 'a breach of non-contractual duty which gives a private law right to the party injured to recover compensatory damages at common law from the party causing the injury'.[53] His conclusion was that action by an individual against a government for breach of Community law was an action founded on tort within the meaning of the Limitation Act 1980 and that the term 'Eurotort' may be apt.[54] 28 years

---

[49] See *Kirklees Metropolitan Borough Council v Wickes Building Supplies Ltd* [1992] 3 WLR 170, 227; *Ministry of Defence v Meredith* [1995] IRLR 539.

[50] See, eg, *R v Ministry of Agriculture Fisheries and Food, ex p Lay and Gage* (1998) COD 387; *R v Secretary of State for the Home Department, ex p Gallagher* [1996] 2 CMLR 951.

[51] *R v Secretary of State for the Home Department, ex p Factortame (No 5)* [1997] EuLR 475, 531. Toulmin J in *R v Secretary of State for Transport, ex p Factortame (No 7)* [2001] 1 WLR 942 found the exposition helpful but not conclusive.

[52] *R v Secretary of State for Transport, ex p Factortame (No)* [2001] 1 WLR 942, 958.

[53] Ibid, 965.

[54] Ibid, 966. His Lordship also concluded that the government was not liable in principle to pay damages to the claimants for injury to feelings and aggravated damages although this is not a rule of general application and will depend on the provision of Community law breached, ibid, 985.

after the United Kingdom joined the Community, the birth of the Eurotort in its national law has been confirmed, what remains is for its constituent elements to be fleshed out.

III. DUTY

When seeking damages for commission of a Eurotort, the claimant must first establish that a duty is imposed on the respondent by Community law[55] and second that the law imposing this duty is intended to confer rights on individuals. These two elements do not necessarily go hand in hand.

A treaty article imposes duties on public bodies and private bodies if it is unconditional in the sense that it leaves no discretion to Member States, and it is sufficiently clear and precise.[56] Following his detention on his return from France for refusal to show his passport, Mr Flynn sought judicial review of the Secretary of State's decision to maintain passport control and also damages for his detention. He based his claim on Article 7a of the EC Treaty. His claim failed at the first hurdle, the Divisional Court concluding that Article 7a imposed no obligation on Member States, let alone one that was clear and precise.[57]

Regulations impose duties on public bodies and private bodies. Article 249 of the EC Treaty provides that a regulation 'shall be binding in its entirety and directly applicable in all Member States'.[58] Far more complicated is the position of directives. If the articles of a directive are sufficiently clear, precise and unconditional, they impose duties on public bodies only.[59] However, the duty does not arise until the date for implementation of the directive has expired.[60]

It is also possible that a directive may continue to impose duties on a public body even if it has been fully and correctly transposed into national

---

[55] In other words, that the Community law is of direct effect.

[56] *NV Algemene Transporten Expeditie Onderneming van Gend en Loos v Nederlandse Administratie der Belastingen* [1963] ECR 1; *Defrenne v Societe Anonyme Belge de Navigation Aerienne* [1976] ECR 455.

[57] *R v Secretary of State for the Home Department, ex p Flynn*, Unreported, Divisional Court, 9 Mar 1995 per McCullough J.

[58] *Commission v Italy* [1973] ECR 101.

[59] *Van Duyn v Home Office* [1974] ECR 1337; *Marshall v Southampton and South-West Hampshire Area Health Authority (Teaching)* [1986] ECR 723. It is not necessary to show that individual rights are also conferred, see Lenz, 'Horizontal What? Back to Basics' (2000) 25 ELR 509. See also the speech of Lord Hope in *Three Rivers District Council v Governor and Company of the Bank of England (No 3)* [2000] 2 WLR 1220.

[60] *Pubblico Ministero v Tullio Ratti* [1979] ECR 1629; *Becker v Finanzamt Munster-Innenstadt* [1982] ECR 53.

law.[61] In *Three Rivers*,[62] Lord Hope, giving the judgment of the House of Lords on the Community law question, did not decide the issue one way or the other. However, it was noted that the Court of Appeal had found some support in the decision of the ECJ in *Norbrook*[63] for the view that there may be category of directives in relation to which a Member State's obligation of proper implementation is not restricted to a once and for all legislative process, but also requires a continuing administrative process.[64]

Lord Hope also stated that great weight should be attached to Auld LJ's reasons, given in the Court of Appeal, for rejecting the Bank's argument that implementation of the directive deprived the claimants of recourse to the directive.[65] Auld LJ, in his dissenting judgment, held that it was possible that there had been a mis-implementation of the directive. More importantly, he noted that recent decisions of the ECJ indicated that in the main the court is indifferent to the precise route by which it gives effect to a directive.[66] This is undoubtedly correct. Although there is no direct authority on the point, the ECJ has held that where an obligation to pursue a particular course of conduct is imposed by a directive on a Member State, this obligation is strengthened where individuals are able to rely on the directive before their national courts.[67] Surely this obligation is strengthened even more by the ability of an individual to claim damages for breach of the directive in certain circumstances.

Whilst the question is an important one, yet to be directly answered by national courts or the ECJ, it is likely that in future cases a similar approach to that taken by the House of Lords and Court of Appeal in *Three Rivers* will be followed. Assuming the directive continues to impose a duty, the claimant must still prove the other elements of the Eurotort, in particular, that the directive confers rights on individuals. If these other elements are satisfied, given the principle of effective protection[68] it is difficult to imagine that the mere fact a directive has been fully implemented in

---

[61] Although not direct authorities on this point, see *Verbond van Nederlandse Ondernemingen (VNO) v Inspecteur der Invoerrechten en Accijnzen* [1977] ECR 113; *Officier van Justitie v Kolpinghuis Nijmegen* [1987] ECR 3969; *Inter-Environment Wallonie ASBL v Region Wallonie* [1998] 1 CMLR 1057.

[62] *Three Rivers District Council v Governor and Company of the Bank of England (No 3)* [2000] 2 WLR 1220. For comment, see Allott, 'EC Directives and Misfeasance in Public Office' [2001] CLJ 4.

[63] *Norbrook Laboratories v Ministry of Agriculture Fisheries and Food* [1998] ECR I-1531.

[64] [2000] 2 WLR 1220, 1241.

[65] Ibid.

[66] *Three Rivers District Council v Governor and Company of the Bank of England (No 3)*, Unreported, Court of Appeal, 4 Dec 1998.

[67] *Van Duyn v Home Office* [1974] ECR 1337.

[68] *Francovich and Bonifaci v Italy* [1991] ECR I-5337, paras 32–3. See also *R v Secretary of State for the Home Department, ex p Gallagher* [1996] 2 CMLR 951, para 10 per Lord Bingham CJ.

national law would stand in the way of a claimant being awarded damages for its breach.

Finally, Article 249 of the EC Treaty imposes one further duty on the State:

A directive shall be binding, as to the result to be achieved, upon each Member State to which it is addressed, but shall leave to national authorities the choice of form and methods.

Member States are thereby under a duty to take all measures necessary to achieve the result prescribed by a directive.[69] If it is not possible for an individual to establish the existence of a duty otherwise, or a private body has committed the breach of directive, this may be a claimant's only recourse.

IV. CONFERRAL OF RIGHTS ON INDIVIDUALS

Having established that a duty is imposed on the respondent by Community law, it does not necessarily follow that the Community law in question is also intended to confer rights on individuals.[70] In *Bowden*,[71] the Court of Appeal had to determine whether the rule of law relied upon conferred rights upon individuals. It framed the question as follows: was the provision adopted in order to protect the interests of the person who claims to be entitled to a right under the directive, and did the result prescribed entail the grant of rights to individuals. It concluded that Mr Bowden, a mollusc fisherman, was conferred rights by the Shellfish Waters Directive as the State's failure to implement the directive, or to comply with the directive, meant that the water was polluted, a fact which directly affected him as a mollusc fisherman.

The House of Lords took a far more restrictive approach to the interpretation of this element of the tort in *Three Rivers District Council v Governor and Company of the Bank of England*.[72] The case arose from the collapse of the Bank of Credit and Commerce International (BCCI) in 1991. Those who had placed money on deposit with BCCI through the UK branches of the Bank for the most part lost their money. In May 1993 6,019 depositors, directed and financed by the liquidators, commenced an action against the Bank of England for misfeasance in public office. Their original claim was that the Bank did not discharge its duty properly—it should not have granted a licence to BCCI or it should have revoked it. £550 million plus interest was sought.

[69] *Francovich and Bonifaci v Italy* [1991] ECR I-5357.
[70] See Lenz, 'Horizontal What? Back to Basics' (2000) 25 ELR 509.
[71] *Bowden v South West Water Services Ltd* [1998] Env LR D15.
[72] [2000] 2 WLR 1220.

The Community law element of the claim was introduced in August 1995. In October 1997, Clarke J, in the Commercial Court, struck out the entire claim.[73] In December 1998, a majority of the Court of Appeal dismissed the appeal.[74] By the time the appeal reached the House of Lords, the Community law argument had developed considerably. The claimants claimed that they were entitled to damages for losses caused by breach of Community law for the following three reasons:

In June 1980 the Bank granted BCCI a full licence to carry on business as a deposit taker contrary to the First Council Banking Co-ordination Directive of 1977 and the Banking Act 1979.

After the grant of the licence until the eventual closure of BCCI, contrary to the 1977 Directive, Banking Act 1979 and Banking Act 1987, the Bank concluded it had no discretion or power to revoke the licence. This was the case, it was alleged, even thought it knew that BCCI had conducted and was conducting its affairs in a way which threatened the interests of depositors.

Throughout this period the Bank failed to supervise BCCI to the detriment of the depositors and contrary to the 1977 Directive and Banking Acts 1979 and 1987.

Lord Hope, giving the judgment of the House of Lords on the issue, held that the question of conferral of rights, had to be answered by examining the recitals and the articles of the Directive itself without any preconception as to its purpose based upon extrinsic materials. Although the claimants relied in particular on the 3rd, 4th, 5th, and 12th recitals, and on Articles 3, 6, 7, and 8, Lord Hope held it was necessary to have regard to some of the other recitals and articles in order to understand the overall effect of the Directive.[75]

His Lordship stated that the claimants did not need to show that depositors were the only persons in whose favour obligations were imposed or on whom the Directive conferred rights:

But in order to satisfy the *Dillenkofer* conditions they must be able to demonstrate that the result to be achieved by the Directive entailed the grant of rights to depositors and potential depositors as well as to the credit institutions operating in several member states whose activities were to be authorised and supervised by the competent authorities.[76]

Lord Hope described the Directive as the first step in a process of harmonisation of provisions for the regulation of credit institutions carrying on business within the Community and concluded as follows:

[73] [1996] 3 All ER 558.   [74] [1999] EuLR 211.
[75] [2000] 2 WLR 1220, 1247.   [76] Ibid.

It is not possible to discover provisions which entail the granting of rights to individuals, as the granting of rights to individuals was not necessary to achieve the results which were intended to be achieved by the directive.[77]

In reaching this conclusion, Lord Hope made clear that the question whether provisions in a Directive create rights and obligations for individuals depends in each case on the subject matter of the Directive, and on the context and the nature and purpose of the provisions which are in issue. Whilst the potential width of the class of persons granted rights did not preclude the conclusion rights had been created, the fact that there was no definition of any expression referring to individuals in whose favour rights might be said to have been created was fatal:

the absence of a definition of that kind from the Directive suggests that it was not the intention when the directive was being drafted to grant rights under the directive in favour of individuals or any group or class of individuals.[78]

Lord Hope's speech can be contrasted with the dissenting judgment of Auld LJ in the Court of Appeal. At the end of a lengthy judgment, Auld LJ concluded that the Directive 'imposed clearly defined obligations on Member states and on their regulatory bodies and, in doing so, gave rise to corresponding Community law rights in individuals in the position of the plaintiffs to enforce those obligations'.

The reasoning of Auld LJ is far more in keeping with the teleological approach of the ECJ. In reaching his conclusion, his Lordship kept in mind the close connection in Community law between the imposition of obligations on Member States and making those obligations effective by the conferment on individuals of rights corresponding to them. His Lordship was particularly influenced by the fact that the Directive would not achieve its purpose if it did not also confer corresponding rights on depositors to enforce that obligation against the regulator by actions for damages where appropriate.

His Lordship was also influenced by the fact that the grant of rights requirement has been 'broadly and flexibly interpreted by the European Court'. A number of ECJ decisions on the 1977 Directive were examined and it was found that the Directive imposed a supervisory role on regulators and that one of its underlying purposes was the protection of savers. His Lordship also looked at analogous cases before the ECJ, in particular *Dillenkofer*,[79] and concluded that he did not see much difference between the directive in that case and the 1977 Directive.

Given the strong dissenting judgment of Auld LJ in the Court of Appeal

---

[77] [2000] 2 WLR 1220, 1257. However, it was found that the Directive conferred rights on the credit institutions affected by it.
[78] Ibid, 1249.
[79] *Dillenkofer v Germany* [1996] ECR I-4845.

and the particular difficulty of the issue, it is surprising that Lord Hope concluded it would not be appropriate for a reference to the ECJ as he considered the matter *acte clair*.[80] Considering that every major step forward in the development of the Eurotort before United Kingdom courts has been as a result of decisions of the ECJ, it is hoped that this new found national confidence will not result in a few steps back.

V. BREACH

The third element in establishing commission of a Eurotort is breach. A breach of duty may arise from a legislative act[81] or administrative act[82] or from the non-implementation[83] or mis-implementation[84] of a directive. Many claims fail when the applicant is unable to show that there has actually been a breach of Community law. For example, in *Boyd Line*[85] the claimant fishermen were unable to show that the Ministry of Agriculture, Fisheries and Food had breached a Community regulation concerning fishing in Norwegian waters.

As the tort is not one of strict liability, it must also be demonstrated that the breach was sufficiently serious. With respect to this element of the tort, UK courts have followed closely the decisions of the ECJ.[86] It appears from the judgments so far that regardless of whether the breach is occasioned by an administrative act or a legislative act, a basket or global approach is adopted to determining sufficient seriousness. For example, in *Lay and Gage*[87] the claimants had successfully established before the ECJ that the Ministry of Agriculture Fisheries and Food had misinterpreted a Community regulation concerning the milk quota. In determining that this

---

[80] [2000] 2 WLR 1220, 1258. The parties were unanimous in the Divisional Court and Court of Appeal in asking the court not to make a reference to the E.C.J. However, in the House of Lords the plaintiffs asked for a reference on the question whether the Directive conferred rights, and if so what rights, on depositors.

[81] See, eg, *Brasserie du Pecheur SA v Germany* [1996] ECR I-1029.

[82] See, eg, *R v MAFF, ex p Hedley Lomas* [1996] ECR I-2553; *R v Ministry of Agriculture Fisheries and Food, ex p Lay and Gage* (1998) COD 387.

[83] See eg *Dillenkofer v Germany* [1996] ECR I-4845; *R v Department of Social Security, ex p Scullion* [1993] 3 CMLR 798; *R v Attorney General for Northern Ireland, ex p Burns* [1999] IRLR 315.

[84] See, eg, *R v H.M. Treasury, ex p British Telecommunications* [1996] ECR I-1631; *R v Secretary of State for the Home Department, ex p Gallagher* [1996] 2 CMLR 951.

[85] *Boyd Line Management Services Ltd v Ministry of Agriculture, Fisheries and Food,* Unreported, Court of Appeal, 30 Mar 1999. See also *R v Ministry of Agriculture, Fisheries and Food, ex p Astonquest Ltd,* Unreported, Court of Appeal, 21 Dec 1999.

[86] Including *Brasserie du Pecheur SA v Germany* [1996] 1 CMLR 889; *R v HM Treasury, ex p British Telecommunications PLC* [1996] 2 CMLR 217; *R v Ministry of Agriculture, Fisheries and Food, ex p Hedley Lomas (Ireland) Ltd* [1997] QB 139.

[87] *R v Ministry of Agriculture Fisheries and Food, ex p Lay and Gage* (1998) COD 387.

was not a sufficiently serious breach, the Divisional Court took into account the complexity of the applicable legislation, the bona fides of the Ministry and the fact that the legitimate expectation of the claimants was not clear and obvious.[88]

This approach was also evident in the judgment of the Divisional Court in *Factortame (No 5)*[89] where argument centred predominantly on the issue of sufficiently serious breach. The Court added quite a bit to the bare bones of the decision of the ECJ,[90] although not with a great degree of clarity. With respect to the meaning of manifest and grave disregard it adopted the opinion of Advocate General van Gerven in *Mulder*.[91] Four matters must be taken into account: the particular importance of the principle infringed; the fact that disregard of that principle affected a limited and clearly defined group; the fact that the damage went beyond the bounds of the economic risks inherent in the operators' activities in the sector concerned; and the fact that the principle was infringed without sufficient justification.

One to three were easily shown. The remaining issue was whether or not there was sufficient justification. The Court decided there was not for four reasons. First, discrimination on the ground of nationality was the intended effect of the domicile and residence conditions. Secondly, the government intended to injure the applicants. Thirdly, the government decided to achieve its object through primary legislation making it impossible for the applicants to obtain interim relief without the intervention of the ECJ. Finally, the Commission was hostile to the proposed legislation. A manifest and grave disregard of the limits of the UK's discretion was found and liability to compensate the applicants established.[92]

The Secretary of State appealed to the Court of Appeal and then to the House of Lords. The Court of Appeal[93] adhered far more to the decision of the ECJ. Far less prescriptive that the Divisional Court it did not find it necessary to rely on the opinion of Advocate General van Gerven in *Mulder* although it did state that that opinion was supportive of its conclusion. It concluded, looking at the position overall, that it would not be right to deprive the respondents of a remedy for the wrong which has been done to them. In adopting this view, the court regarded itself as merely applying the approach of the ECJ.[94]

---

[88] See also *R v Secretary of State for the Home Department, ex p Gallagher* [1996] 2 CMLR 951; *R v Department of Social Security, ex p Scullion* [1999] 3 CMLR 798.

[89] *R v Secretary of State for Transport, ex p Factortame Ltd (No 5)* [1997] EuLR 475.

[90] *Brasserie du Pecheur SA v Germany* [1996] 1 CMLR 889.

[91] *Mulder v Council and Commission* [1992] ECR I-3061.

[92] See further, NP Gravells, 'Part II of the Merchant Shipping Act 1988: A sufficiently serious breach of European Community Law?' [1998] PL 8.

[93] [1998] EuLR 456.

[94] Ibid, 475.

The House of Lords[95] was also far less prescriptive than the Divisional Court as to the meaning of sufficient seriousness and manifest and grave disregard. Lord Clyde noted that it would be premature to attempt a comprehensive analysis[96] and this is very clear from the speeches given. Reflecting the decision of the Divisional Court, in finding a sufficiently serious breach, the following factors were important. First, this was a direct breach of a clear and fundamental provision of the Treaty. Secondly, what was done was done deliberately with full knowledge of the risks. Thirdly, it was clear that once the law took effect it would almost certainly cause serious and immediate loss to those affected by it. Fourthly, the Commission had told the government that the proposed conditions were prima facie contrary to Article 52. Fifthly, the use of primary legislation made it impossible for the claimants to obtain interim relief. Finally, the provisions of the Act went beyond anything necessary to deal with the situation. It is likely that this comprehensive list of factors will prove influential in any future assessments of sufficiently serious breach.

VI. CAUSATION

Of all the elements of the Eurotort, the one that has caused the least controversy in UK courts so far has been causation. In *Gallagher*[97] the Court of Appeal considered the question of causation and held that the claimant must show on the balance of probabilities that the injury for which he seeks compensation was caused by the unlawful conduct of which he complains. Although Mr Gallagher had established a breach of Community law, he could not show that that breach probably caused him to be excluded from the United Kingdom when he would not otherwise have been excluded.[98]

VII. THE FUTURE

The existence of the remedy and its characterisation are no longer pressing issues in domestic law but it is clear that as more claims are brought, problems with the interpretation and application of the Eurotort will become more complex. This was very evident in the *Three Rivers* litigation and also arose in *Courage Ltd v Crehan*[99] where the tenants of 'tied' public houses sought damages from their landlords for breach of Article 81 of the EC Treaty. The ECJ is yet to give its answers to the questions referred to it by

---

[95] [1999] 3 WLR 1062.   [96] Ibid, 1087.   [97] [1996] 2 CMLR 951.
[98] See also *R v Attorney General for Northern Ireland, ex p Burns* [1999] IRLR 315.
[99] [1999] 2 EGLR 145.

the Court of Appeal, but Advocate General Mischo has concluded that Community law precludes a rule of national law which prevents a party subject to a clause in a contract which infringes Article 81 from recovering damages for the loss suffered by it on the sole ground that it is a party to that contract.[100] If the ECJ reaches a similar conclusion, a whole new stage in the development of the Eurotort will begin.

The future may also hold the possibility of reform of non-Community law spurred on by the development of the Eurotort. Although those suffering loss as a result of breach of Community law now have an avenue for redress, it is anomalous that those suffering loss as a result of invalid administrative action not involving an element of Community law remain without a remedy. In 1988 the Committee of the JUSTICE–All Souls Review of Administrative Law in the United Kingdom recommended that a remedy in damages should be available where 'a person suffers loss as a result of wrongful administrative action not involving negligence'.[101] The development of the Eurotort in national law will only add to the existing support for a general right to compensation for invalid administrative action.[102]

But despite these possible developments in the reach and momentum of the Eurotort, it is important to remember that it will remain a very difficult tort to prove. In particular, the concept of sufficiently serious breach essentially means that only the most flagrant violations of Community law will result in a damages award. UK courts, perennially reluctant to create apprehension in the administration, impose delays or a financial burden on the State that will be passed on to the tax payer, should be very pleased with the way things have turned out.[103]

---

[100] Mar 2001. Advocate General Mischo also concluded that a defence of contributory fault may be possible: 'Community law does not preclude a rule of national law which provides that courts should not allow a person to plead and/or rely on his own illegal actions as a necessary step to recovery of damages, provided that it is established that this person bears more than negligible responsibility for the distortion of competition.'

[101] *Administrative Justice, Some Necessary Reforms*, Report of the Committee of the JUSTICE–All Souls Review of Administrative Law in the United Kingdom (Oxford: Clarendon Press, 1988), 361 and 364. The Committee did not extend this recommendation to the decisions of courts and tribunals: 363.

[102] See, eg, Lord Wilberforce's dissenting speech in *Hoffmann-La Roche v Secretary of State for Trade and Industry* [1975] AC 295 and the judgment of Lord Woolf MR in *R v Secretary of State for Transport, ex p Factortame (No 5)* [1998] EuLR 456, 469. See further ME Amos 'Extending the Liability of the State in Damages' (2001) 21 *LS* 1.

[103] *Cullen v Morris* (1819) 2 Stark 577, 587; *Bourgoin SA v Ministry of Agriculture Fisheries and Food* [1986] QB 716, 790 per Nourse LJ; *Rowling v Takaro Properties Ltd* [1988] AC 473, 502 per Lord Keith; *X v Bedfordshire County Council* [1995] 2 AC 633, 749–51 per Lord Browne-Wilkinson; *Stovin v Wise* [1996] AC 923, 958 per Lord Hoffman.

6. THE EMERGENCE OF A COMMON EUROPEAN LAW IN THE AREA OF TORT LAW: THE EU CONTRIBUTION

Walter van Gerven *

The emergence of a common European tort law is brought about by three factors, or driving forces, each of which has its own rationale. First, there is European Community (EC) law where the rationale for developing tort rules is to make a remedy in compensation available for individuals whose 'Community rights' have been infringed by Community Institutions, Member States or other individuals. Secondly, there is the law of the European Convention of Human Rights (ECHR) where the rationale is the preservation, through the award of damages, of 'Convention rights' of individuals against infringements by Contracting States. Third, there is comparative law. Today one rationale of comparative law beyond understanding one anothers' legal systems is to promote convergence and homogeneity between legal systems of States which, as the Member States of the European Union, are engaged in a process of integration. Within such a framework of integration comparative law has become an instrument, in the area of tort law as in others, to prepare legislation and to enforce it, through remedies before domestic courts, in a sufficiently uniform manner in all of the Member States.[1] In this contribution I will deal with the first factor of convergence only.

I. THE DIRECTIVES ON PRODUCT LIABILITY AND E-COMMERCE: EUROPEAN COMMUNITY LEGISLATION AS A SOURCE OF COMMON RULES

The most obvious and direct impact of EC law on the domestic laws of the Member States is

---

* Professor em K U Leuven and U Maastricht. Former Advocate General at the Court of Justice to the European Communities.

[1] See further W van Gerven, 'Comparative Law in a regionally integrated Europe', in *Comparative Law in the 21st Century*, WG Hart Legal Workshop Series (London: Kluwer Academic Publishers, 2002), 155.

when the EC legislature expressly requires Member States to include in their national tort law specified rules that prescribe certain conditions as giving rise to tortious liability on the part of all or some defined class of persons toward other persons ... who are to enjoy the benefit of the required rules. Such legislation may leave Member States with some latitude in relation to the conditions that are to be prescribed in the definition of the required tortious liability (...).[2]

A prime example of Community *legislation* is Directive 85/374 concerning liability for defective products[3] which so far has brought about the most far-reaching change in the tort law of the Member States as a result of EC harmonisation measures.[4] Obviously, the alterations are limited to the specific issues covered by the Directive and, even then, subject to a number of elements which are left to the discretion of the Member States. The most important of these elements is whether a Member State wants to make available to producers the so-called 'product liability risk defence' allowing the producer to escape liability if 'the state of scientific and technical knowledge at the time when he put the product into circulation, was not such as to enable the existence of the defect to be discovered' (Article 7(e); in combination with Article 15(b) of the Directive). The defence was finally included in the national implementing legislation of, for instance, Germany, France and the UK. That does, of course, not preclude the European Court of Justice (ECJ) from interpreting the directive provision on which the defence is based, if the issue is raised before the Court *either* directly in an action, under Article 226 (ex 169) EC, against a Member State which has not correctly or not completely implemented the Directive, *or* by way of a preliminary ruling, under Article 234 (ex 177) EC, when the Directive needs interpretation in a litigation pending before a national court between public or private parties.

The former occurred in case C-300/95, *Commission v UK*, which was decided by judgment of 29 May 1997.[5] In that judgment the Court held that the state of scientific and technical knowledge of which the producer

---

[2] J Lever, 'Mutual Permeation of Community and National Tort Rules', in J Wouters and J Stuyck, (eds), *Principles of Proper Conduct for Supranational, State and Private Actors in the European Union: Towards a Ius Commune* (Antwerp: Intersentia, 2001), 91 ('Principles of Proper Conduct').

[3] The relevant extracts from text of the directive as modified by directive 1999/34, can be found in W van Gerven, J Lever, and P Larouche, *Cases, Materials and Text on National, Supranational and International TORT LAW*, 2nd enlarged edn (Oxford: Hart Publishing, 2000), (*Casebook on TORT LAW*), 645–6 with comments 646–9.

[4] In the area of car accidents, only directives concerning compulsory liability insurance have been adopted which have no direct impact on national laws (whether based on strict liability, as in France or Germany, or on fault liability, as in England). They have an indirect impact, though, in that the law of tortious liability will tend to evolve in step with compulsory insurance coverage: see *Casebook on TORT LAW*, at 596.

[5] [1997] ECR I-2649. Extracts of the judgment are reproduced also in *Casebook on TORT LAW* at 670–2 with comments at 672–3.

must *prove* that it was *not* such as to enable him to discover the defect, includes the *most advanced* level of knowledge *generally*, and not only in the industrial sector concerned; that such knowledge must be taken in an *objective* (and not merely a subjective) sense, ie, knowledge 'of which the producer is presumed to have been informed'; provided, the Court added, that such knowledge was *accessible* to the manufacturer at the time when the product was put into circulation.[6] Although the UK legislation implementing the Directive was not unambiguous[7], the ECJ dismissed the EU Commission's contention that Article 7(e) had not been properly implemented by the UK. To reach that conclusion the Court took into account that no material was produced to the Court indicating that the courts in the UK would not interpret the national implementing act in accordance with the wording and the purpose of the Directive.[8]

The *Commission v UK* case illustrates the way in which EC legislation, in conjunction with case law of the ECJ, influences the development of national tort law.[9] That is obviously the case when a directive is properly transposed *but also*, as follows from the above judgment, when a directive is not transposed in a fully unambiguous manner, in that situation because of the duty for national courts to interpret domestic legislation in conformity with Community law. French legislation, which was long overdue to implement Directive 85/374,[10] offers an example of how that duty may take effect even when the national legislator has not implemented the Directive at all. For indeed, 'French courts, under the lead of the *Cour de cassation* took it upon themselves to interpret French law in such a way as to introduce Directive 85/374 in the case law', mainly by extending 'the contractual *obligation de sécurité* incumbent upon the manufacturer and trade seller beyond the contractual realm to third-party victims of defective products'.[11] The *Cour de cassation,* in a judgment of 9 July 1996, went even so far that it used itself the discretion which the Directive had left to the Member States' legislature, by holding that the defence of *Article 7(e)* was *not* available under French law.[12] Insofar as it related to contaminated blood, the judgment was confirmed by Law of 19 May 1998: indeed, although the defence was introduced in Article 1386-11(4) of the French

---

[6] Para 26–9 of the judgment.

[7] Art 7 (e) of the Directive was implemented by Consumer Protection Act 1987, s 4 (1) (e).

[8] Para 38 of the judgment. In the meantime see *A and Others v National Blood Authority and Others,* 26 Mar 2001, briefly commented on in the Editorial on 'Product liability and the effect of directives' [2001] *ELRev* 213–14.

[9] Thus Lever, n 2, at 94.

[10] It was only by law of 19 May 1998 that the directive was implemented by inserting Arts 1386-1 to 1386-18 into the Civil Code.

[11] *Casebook on TORT LAW,* at 659.

[12] Cass. Civ 1re, 9 July 1996, D.1996.Jur.610; excerpts reprinted in *Casebook on TORT LAW,* at 630.

Code civil, Article 1386-12 did not make it available to the producer 'if the injury was caused by a part of the human body or parts taken from the human body'.

Harmonisation of national laws is far from perfect: it is often based on a compromise between national systems and, once effected, does not, of itself, guarantee convergence to remain for ever. An analysis of English, French and German law before and after the implementation of Directive 85/374[13] shows for instance that: 'Product liability...provides an excellent case-study of the interaction between Community and national laws. Against the background of fairly different national laws..., Directive 85/374 purported to create a harmonised regime, whose coherence was however affected by the specific dynamics of Community law-making, including the need to compromise'. Moreover, *caveat emptor*: 'Its implementation nevertheless shows how quickly a harmonised text can start to be 'de-harmonised' again...'.[14]

A judgment of the German *Bundesgerichtshof* of 9 May 1995 offers an unfortunate example of such 'de-harmonisation' or 're-nationalisation'.[15] In that judgment the German Supreme Court decided that the defence of *Article 7(e)* of the Directive, as included in § 1(2), under 5, of the *Produkthaftungsgesetz* of 15 December 1989, can be raised only where the loss arises from a design defect, not where it arises from a manufacturing defect. The Court made that decision of its own initiative, refusing to submit any question of interpretation to the ECJ, on the ground that, since Member States had been left free not to introduce the product development risk at all, a national court, when asked to interpret implementing legislation, could also of its own initiative determine whether that legislation had adopted the defence and to what extent.[16]

More recently the ECJ rendered another judgment, this time in a preliminary ruling procedure brought at the request of the Danish Supreme Court. The judgment concerns the interpretation of *Article 7(a)* of Directive 85/374, which excludes liability for a defective product that is 'not put ... into circulation'.[17] The main question submitted to the ECJ was whether a

---

[13] At 598–683 of the *Casebook on TORT LAW*.

[14] Both passages at 682.

[15] *BGHZ* 129, 353 of which excerpts are reproduced in *Casebook on TORT LAW*, at 655–6 with comments at 657–9.

[16] Both the summarising statement and the *caveat* (with a reference to the German judgment) in the quotation above, show the strategic importance of comparative law research in a perspective of EC harmonisation: such research is needed, first, to uncover the national laws in a specific field and to provide the background against which a useful harmonisation can take place, and, secondly, once it has been effected, to protect harmonisation against national reflexes of legislators and judges in the Member States who are called upon to apply the harmonised rules in a national context.

[17] Judgment of 10 May 2001, Case C-203/99, *Henning Veedfald* [2001] ECR I-3569.

defective product must be held to have been put into circulation where the product (in that case a perfusion fluid produced and prepared for use in hospitals owned by a municipality) was used in one of the hospitals in the course of a specific medical service (ie in preparing a kidney for transplantation) and where the damage caused (the kidney becoming unusable for the operation) resulted from the preparation of the product. The ECJ answered that question in the affirmative adding, in reply to a second question, that the exemption from liability referred to in *Article 7(c)* of the Directive (concerning activities having no economic purpose) does not cover the use of a defective product in the course of a medical service just because that service in the municipal hospital is entirely financed from public funds.

When liability arises in consequence of the Directive, as implemented in national law, the producer 'shall be liable for damage caused by a defect in his product' (Article 1), which means, according to Article 9, that he must compensate 'damage caused by death or by personal injuries' and 'damage to, or destruction of, any item of property other than the defective product itself, with a lower threshold of 500 [Euro]'. In the same judgment referred to above, the ECJ pointed out, replying to further questions from the Danish Supreme Court, that, although it is left to the national courts to determine the precise content of these two heads of damage (and without prejudice to non-material damage which is a matter, according to Article 9, last sentence, of the directive, to be decided by national law), the application of national rules should not be allowed to impair the effectiveness of the Directive. Accordingly, national rules may not restrict the categories of recoverable material damage nor may national courts decline to award damage on the ground that the damage concerned (damage to the kidney) does not fall under the heads of damage mentioned in Article 9 (a) and (b) of the Directive (or under the head of non-material damage mentioned in the last sentence of Article 9). It appears from this that Community directives may curtail the discretion of Member States not only with respect to the conditions for liability to arise in a specific instance covered by the directive but also with respect to the actual extent of the duty to compensate.[18]

Another area where European harmonisation has had a direct impact on

---

[18] For another and even more far-reaching example, see the judgment of the ECJ of 2 Aug 1993 in Case C-271/91, *Marshall II* [1993] ECR I-4367, where the Court held, in relation with Art 6 of Directive 76/207/EEC concerning equal treatment of men and women regarding working conditions, that interest for delayed payment of compensation is a head of damage that must be compensated for. See also, for a recent example, the Court's judgment of 12 Mar 2002 in case C-168/00, *Leitner v TUI Deutschland*, where the Court interpreted Art 5 of the Travel and Vacation Directive 90/314/EEC to also award, in principle, non-material damage in case of non-performance under the contract.

national tort law relates to electronic commerce.[19] In order not to discourage the development of e-commerce, providers of electronic services have been exempted, within limits, from (civil and penal) liability. That is the purpose of Articles 12–15 of the Electronic Commerce Directive 2000/31/EC[20] which contain certain exemptions, so-called 'safe harbours', for intermediaries providing or facilitating access to Internet-based services.[21] Exemptions from liability for the content of the information handled are, under certain conditions, granted to providers of 'mere conduit' services, that is transmission of information in, or provision of access to, a communication network (Article 12), for providers of 'caching', which is temporary storage of information for the purpose of making access easier and faster for other recipients and for providers of 'hosting', that is permanent storage of information on behalf of clients who want to make a website available to the public. It is not the place here to deal with these provisions any further.[22] It may suffice to mention that the directive does not affect the possibility for national courts or authorities to require from an intermediary, within the limits of their national law, to stop a violation or to prevent one; that the directive refers to national law for issues of liability outside the exemptions, particularly under what conditions liability arises for a violation which cannot benefit from an exemption; and that the generality of the conditions for an exemption to apply may require intermediaries of services to make delicate judgments, for instance as to which degree of knowledge will put them under an obligation to act, by taking down the offending information or taking other appropriate steps.[23] Obviously, it will be for the national courts, with the help of the ECJ in preliminary ruling procedures, to clarify the scope of the directive exemptions.

---

[19] For a comprehensive overview, see A Lopez-Tarruellla 'A European Community Regulatory Framework for Electronic Commerce' [2001] CMLR, 1337–84.; I Walden, 'Regulating Electronic Commerce: Europe in the global E-economy' [2001] ELR 529–47.

[20] Directive on certain legal aspects of information society services, in particular electronic commerce, in the Internal market, OJ L 178/1.

[21] See also Art 5 (1) of Directive 2001/29/EC, OJ L 167/10 on harmonisation of certain aspects of copyright and related rights in the information society which provides an exemption under certain circumstances from copyright infringements for temporary reproductions. On this subject, see M Buydens, 'Droit d'auteur et droits voisins dans la société de l'information', *JT droit européen*, 2001, 217–26.

[22] On that subject see A Strowel, N Ide, and F Verhoestraete, 'La directive du 8 juin 2000 sur le commerce electronique: un cadre juridique pour l'internet', *Journal des Tribunaux*, 2001, 133–45 and T Verbiest and E Wéry, 'La responsabilité des fournisseurs Internet: derniers développements jurisprudentiels', in ibid, at 165–72.

[23] Thus A Cruquenaire and J Herveg, 'La responsabilité des intermediaries d'internet et les procédures en référé ou comme en référé', *Journal des tribunaux*, 2002, 309–11, at 310.

II. LIABILITY OF COMMUNITY INSTITUTIONS AND MEMBER STATES FOR BREACHES
OF COMMUNITY LAW: ARTICLE 288 EC AND *FRANCOVICH* CASE LAW IN SEARCH
OF COMMON PRINCIPLES

Case law of the Community courts, the ECJ and the CFI, has also a direct impact on the shaping of tort law. Although rendered at the occasion of specific cases, that case law interprets the Community Treaty and has therefore the same rank as the Treaty itself, that is higher than Community regulations or directives and higher than implementing national laws.

In the area of tort liability extensive case law has been developed by the Community courts in two respects: one line of cases concerns the non-contractual liability of Community institutions towards individuals who have suffered damage as a result of a breach of Community law for which one of those institutions is responsible either directly, through one of its members, or vicariously, as an employer of civil servants acting in the performance of their duties (Article 288, para 2 EC);[24] another line of cases concerns the non-contractual liability of Member States towards individuals who have suffered damage as a result of a breach of Community law for which a Member State is responsible because of action of one of its divisions, bodies (including the legislator proper)[25] or public authorities,[26] or of a civil servant of one of those. The second form of liability (ie, of a Member State)—called *Francovich* liability after the ECJ's judgment[27] where the principle was first stated—is not based on an explicit Treaty provision but was held by the Court to be 'inherent in the system of the Treaty'.

It is not the place here to go deeper into the case law of the Community courts in both those areas.[28] It may suffice to point out: (i) that it is for the

---

[24] See also para 4 of Art 288 EC which provides in personal liability of civil servants towards the Community.

[25] ECJ, Joined cases C-46/93 and C-48/93, *Brasserie du Pêcheur and Factortame* [1996] ECR I-1029, para 32.

[26] It is for national law to decide which branch, organ, or authority is liable to provide compensation provided however (i) that a Member State may not escape liability by pleading the distribution of powers and responsibilities as between bodies which exist within the national legal order, particularly in a federal State (see ECJ, Case C-302/97, *Konle v Austria* [1999] ECR I-3099, para 62), or by claiming that the public authority responsible for the breach of Community law does not have the necessary power, knowledge, means or resources (see ECJ, Case C- 424/97, *Haim II*, [2000] ECR I-5123, para 27); and moreover, (ii) that the national law concerned may not be contrary to the principles of effectiveness and equivalence: see T Tridimas, 'Liability for breach of Community law: growing up and mellowing down?' [2001] CMLR, at 317–21. For a comprehensive analysis, see G Anagnostaras, 'The allocation of responsibility in State liability actions for breach of Community law: a modern gordian knot?', in [2001] ELR 139–58.

[27] Case C-6/90 and 9/90, *Francovich v Italy* [1991] ECR I-5357.

[28] See *Casebook on TORT LAW*, at 889–930. Also, with references to the most recent case law, Tridimas, see n 26, 301–32.

ECJ and the CFI to determine the tort liability of *Community institutions* in accordance with, as stated in the second paragraph of Article 288 EC, 'the general principles common to the laws of the Member States'; (ii) that the tort liability of *Member State* divisions, bodies and authorities on the basis of the *Francovich* doctrine is to be determined by the national courts, in accordance with case law of the ECJ as laid down, mainly, in preliminary rulings; case law which also refers to 'the general principles common to the laws of the Member States, from which, in the absence of written rules, the Court ... draws inspiration ...';[29] (iii) that, accordingly, 'in the absence of particular justification', 'the conditions under which the State may incur liability for damage caused to individuals by a breach of Community law ... cannot differ from those governing the liability of the Community in like circumstances';[30] as a result the tort rules laid down in the two lines of case law, one relating to Community institutions and the other relating to Member States, are used by the Court, *back and forth*, as a source of inspiration;[31] (iv) that for non-contractual liability of both the Community and the Member States to arise, especially in an area where the authority concerned has a wide discretion, *three conditions* must be fulfilled: the rule of law infringed must be intended to confer rights on individuals; the breach must be sufficiently serious (in French: 'suffisamment caractérisée'); and there must be a causal link between the breach of the obligation resting on the authority and the damage sustained by the injured parties;[32] (v) that the content of the condition of *serious breach* does not depend on the general or individual nature of the act but on the circumstance that the authority concerned had a *wide discretion* or, to the contrary, only a considerably *reduced* discretion *or no discretion* at all;[33] in the case of wide discretion the decisive test is whether the authority manifestly and gravely disregarded the limits on its discretion whilst in the case of (almost) no discretion the mere infringement of Community law *may* be sufficient to establish a sufficiently serious breach;[34] (vi) that it is for the national court to decide

---

[29] *Brasserie du Pêcheur*, above, n 25, para 41.

[30] Ibid, para 42.

[31] See ECJ, Case C-352/98 P, *Bergaderm* [2000] ECR I-5291, para 39–44 where the rules developed by the ECJ for the liability of the Member States were now applied to the liability of the EU Commission. In earlier case law the reverse had been true.

[32] *Brasserie du Pêcheur*, above n 25, para 51. Of these three conditions only the first is decided conclusively by the ECJ itself as it pertains fully to the interpretation of Community law (see Joined cases C-178, 179, 188-190/94, *Dillenkofer* [1996] ECR I-4845, and Case C-127/95, *Norbrook Laboratories* [1998] ECR I-1531). The other two conditions are to be determined by the national courts, however in accordance with the guidelines given by the ECJ (as indicated further in the text): Tridimas, see n 26, at 316.

[33] *Bergaderm*,above n 31, para 43.

[34] *Dillenkofer*,above n 32, para 25. It follows from the *Brinkmann* judgment, below n 37, that, where a Member State fails to adopt implementing measures to transpose a directive into national law, the national administrative authorities may present as a valid defence that,

whether there is a serious breach in a *situation of wide discretion*, for which it must however, according to case law of the ECJ, take the following factors into consideration: 'the clarity and precision of the rule breached, the measure of discretion left by that rule to the national or Community authorities, whether the infringement and the damage caused was intentional or involuntary, whether any error of law was excusable or inexcusable, the fact that the position taken by a Community institution may have contributed towards the omission, and the adoption or retention of national measures or practices contrary to Community law';[35]   fault, subjective or objective, is not a condition except where the aforementioned factors include an element of fault;[36] (vii) that it is also for the national court to determine whether there is a direct *causal link*; that does not mean, however, that causation fully depends on national law: in recent case law the ECJ has given some guidelines which a national court must comply with in determining the question of causation;[37] (viii) that, where the three conditions referred to under (iv) are satisfied, *reparation* commensurate with the loss or damage sustained must be made in accordance with national law, provided that the national rules concerned do not treat Community law claims less favourably than similar domestic claims (the principle of equivalence) and that they do not make it impossible or excessively difficult to obtain reparation (the principle of effectiveness).[38]

In addition to the foregoing two particularities deserve to be mentioned. They are both drawn primarily from case law of the CFI concerning the non-contractual liability of Community institutions under Article 288, para 2, EC, but also apply, according to the ECJ's judgment in *Bergaderm*,[39] to the liability of Member States if there is no particular justification to provide in a different regime. The first particularity concerns situations where the public authority concerned enjoys no, or only a reduced, discretion. In that

---

despite the lack of implementing measures, they have endeavoured themselves to comply with the requirements of the directive: see Tridimas, see n 26, at 306; also Anagnostaras, see n 26, at 143–4.

[35] *Brasserie du Pêcheur,* above n 25, para 56.

[36] Ibid, para 75–80.

[37] See ECJ, Case C-319/96, *Brinkmann Tabakfabriken* [1998] ECR I-5255; Case C-140/97, *Rechberger* [1999] ECR I-3499. Also Tridimas, see n 26, at 310.

[38] *Brasserie du Pêcheur,* above n 25, para 67 and 82 with further specifications. Under Art 43 of the Protocol on the ECJ's Statute an action on the basis of 288 EC shall be barred after a period of 5 years from the occurrence of the event giving rise to the liability: on this provision, see M Broberg, 'The calculation of the period of limitation in claims against the European Community for non-contractual liability' [2001] ELR, 275–290. In this respect the ECJ in its case law relating to Francovich liability does not pursue homogeneity between the two liability regimes: for Member State liability it is for the national legal systems to determine the time limit for bringing an action, albeit subject to the principles of equivalence and effectiveness. See further Tridimas, *The General Principles of EC Law* (Oxford: Oxford University Press, 1999), 338–42.

[39] Above, n 27.

situation a serious breach of Community law may be established on the basis of a mere infringement of Community law (as mentioned in point 7, under (v) above). That will be the case, obviously, in a situation where the act committed by the public authority, or a civil servant acting in the performance of his/her duties, is of a purely factual nature as well as in a situation where a legal (administrative or legislative) act is concerned that not involve wide discretion. In such a situation, the conditions for liability to arise—whether under Article 288, para 2, EC or under the *Francovich* doctrine—are: illegality or wrongfulness of the act (or omission), actual damage and a causal link between the illegality and the damage.[40] Furthermore, the decisive test to establish illegality or wrongfulness in such a situation is, as repeated by the CFI in its *Fresh Marine* judgment, whether the public authority, in that case the Commission, had committed an error which would not have been committed by an administrative authority exercising ordinary care and diligence.[41] That is in line with earlier case law of the ECJ where the test was whether the authority concerned acted as a reasonable authority would have behaved under the circumstances.[42] I will revert to that issue later in the article.

The second particularity relates to the issue of State liability for *lawful* conduct. The question came up in the *Dorsch Consult* where the CFI was led to examine whether the EU Council could be held non-contractually liable on the basis of Article 288, para 2, EC for lawful conduct causing harm to the applicants. To support their damage claim the latter relied on French and German law where such claims are allowed under special circumstances.[43] Quoting earlier case law of the ECJ,[44] the CFI did not reject the claim forthwith but carefully examined the conditions for such claims to be granted (special and abnormal injury sustained and direct causation). It concluded nevertheless that the claim could not be admitted

---

[40] For a recent judgment of the CFI, see case T-277/97, *Ismeri Europe* [1999] ECR II-1825, para 95 and 100 which was upheld by the ECJ by judgment of 10 July 2001 in case C-315/99 P [2001] ECR I-5281. That case related to alleged defamatory statements by the Court of Auditors. Both Community courts dismissed the claim for damages brought on the basis of Art 288, then 215, para 2, EC.

[41] Judgment of 24 Oct 2000, Case T-178/98 [2000] ECR II-3331, para 61. For a comment, see J Wakefield [2001] *CMLRev*, at 1043–57. See also Tridimas, see n 26, at 330–1. In that judgment the CFI continues to attach importance to the nature of the wrongful act; but in my view, in line with *Bergaderm* to which the Court refers explicitly, seen as an element to assess the existence of discretion, which in the case of an administrative act has less chances to exist than in the case of a normative act.

[42] *Casebook on TORT LAW*, 901.

[43] On that subject see P Larouche, 'The Brasserie du Pêcheur Puzzle', in *Principles of Proper Conduct*, above n 2, 111, at 115–17, who argues that also the *Brasserie* judgment could be fitted in the framework of 'objective liability of the State' of which the German and French doctrines of *Aufopferung* and *Egalité devant les charges publiques* are illustrations.

[44] Para 59 of the judgment.

in the circumstances of the case.[45] The judgment was upheld by the ECJ.[46]

It has been mentioned that to establish non-contractual liability under Article 288, para 2, but also (as accepted by the ECJ) under the *Francovich* doctrine, the Community courts are required to draw inspiration from general principles which the Member States' legal orders have in common. In a short extrajudicial statement which he wanted to be 'radical and perhaps provocative', Advocate General Francis Jacobs put the question forward whether there are such general principles in the area of tort law (as Article 288, para 2 EC assumes) and 'if there are, (whether) they exist at a level of generality so broad as to be of little practical use'; 'in practice', he adds, 'the Court has had itself to fashion the principles of Community liability'.[47]

The answer to that question obviously depends on what is meant by 'common principles'. In that respect, no one holds the view that, for a principle to be 'common', it must exist in all of the Member States. That would already have been difficult in a Community of six Member States, and would be virtually impossible in a Community of fifteen and more to come. 'Common' means in this context, I would think, that the principle is accepted (by a prevailing opinion) in a sufficiently large number of Member States in which the issue concerned has arisen in similar terms. Furthermore, the notion of 'principle' does not refer to precise rules but to maxims or concepts with a considerable degree of abstraction which, in concrete cases, may nonetheless result in similar solutions. In some States such principles may have been reduced to writing, in others they may find support in legislation or in case law.

Given this broad understanding, it is clear for instance that the conditions for non-contractual liability to arise, those are illegality (with some ingredients of objective, or even subjective, fault), occurrence of damage and causation, are principles common to the laws of the Member States, just like the principle that adequate, or even full, reparation must be made for the injury caused constitutes a common principle, at least insofar as injury is concerned which is sustained by a plaintiff belonging to the group of persons which the infringed rule intends to protect. Of course, even then there will remain differences between the legal systems—which 'functional' comparative law research (that is looking for common *solutions*) may, however, be able to reduce in number and in size[48]—for which the Community courts will need

---

[45] Case T-184/95, *Dorsch Consult* [1998] ECR II-688.

[46] Case C-237/98P, [2001] ECR I-4549.

[47] In *Principles of Proper Conduct*, see n 2, at 129–31.

[48] For a general discussion of similarities and dissimilarities in the major European legal systems with respect to the concept of unlawfulness (however, in a distant perspective of creating a civil code), see D Howarth, 'The general conditions of unlawfulness', in *Towards a European Civil Code* (ed A Hartkamp), 2nd and expanded edn, 1998, at 397–430.

to find a proper solution having regard to the particularities of Community law. But even then, the composition of those Courts (with judges coming from all Member States) is such as to enable them to 'fashion' an underlying principle that fits in sufficiently well with the legal systems of the Member States where it may have been unknown so far.

An example of disparities that the ECJ was called upon to straighten out, within the framework of the principle of State liability, concerns the condition of 'serious' breach in a situation of wide discretion. The Court did so by understanding it to mean that the public authority had 'manifestly and gravely disregarded the limits on its discretion', an understanding for which support could be found in the laws of the Member States insofar as all courts tend to take a deferential attitude towards the exercise of discretion by public authorities.[49] Actually, it would have been possible, I believe, to find an even more comprehensive common principle, to be applied regardless of discretion, by using the test of 'a reasonable authority acting under similar circumstances' as a general standard to establish the wrongfulness of a public authority's conduct. Whereby the words 'under similar circumstances' would then include, among other circumstances, the more or less discretionary nature of the competences attributed to the authority concerned, meaning that the conduct of an authority enjoying wide discretion in a concrete situation would be assessed by comparing it with that of a reasonable authority having the same kind of wide discretion.[50] As a matter of fact, such a comprehensive standard seems to be more in line with the original French terminology still used for serious breach, ie, a 'violation suffisamment caractérisée'. It also corresponds better with the ECJ's ruling in *Francovich* according to which the conditions for liability must depend on the nature, or character, of the violation, in other words must depend on the type of circumstances under which the violation has occurred.[51]

Less certainty exists, to use a euphemism, as to whether it is also a common principle which the Member States share, that breaches of Community law attributable to a national legislator are to give rise to *Francovich* liability. That solution was acknowledged by the ECJ in its

---

[49] Cf F Schockweiler, G Wivenes, and J M Godart, 'Le régime de la responsabilité extra-contractuelle du fait d'actes juridiques dans la communauté européenne', *Rev trim dr eur*, 1990, 27 ff.

[50] See my contribution 'Taking Article 215 (2) EC seriously', in J Beatson and T Tridimas (eds), *New Directions in European Public Law* (Oxford: Hart Publishing, 1998), 35, at 43–4. See also, for a tentative typology of possible breaches, my earlier contribution 'Bridging the Unbridgeable: Community and National Tort Laws after *Francovich* and *Brasserie*', in (1996) *ICLQ*, 507–44, at 521. Compare with the similar position taken by J Bell, 'Governmental Liability in Tort', in *National Journal of Constitutional Law* (1996), 85, at 96–7.

[51] *Francovich*, above n 27, para 38. See further D Edward and W Robinson, 'Is there a place for Private Law Principles in Community law?', in T Heukels and A McDonnell (eds), *The Action for Damages in Community Law* (Dordrecht: Kluwer, 1997), 339–49, at 344–5.

Brasserie judgment,[52] despite the fact that hardly any support can be found for it in the laws of the Member States.[53] In that regard, only international law—to which the ECJ refers indeed[54]—can be relied on, in addition to Community law itself, that is Article 288, para 2, EC where all institutions of the Community, including the Council and the Parliament, are subjected to the obligation to repair damage resulting from a breach of Community law by those institutions. That in itself might seem to be a strong argument, as it cannot be denied—Community law being an integral part of the Member States' legal systems—that a principle embodied in Community law is also a principle common to the laws of the Member States.[55] However, the ECJ has followed another (and better) line of reasoning in accepting, in accordance with international law, that, in a situation where a provision of a higher legal order is infringed, the State 'must be viewed as a single entity, irrespective of whether the breach...is attributable to the legislature, the judiciary or the executive'.[56]

As appears from the above quotation from *Brasserie*, not only wrongful acts of a national legislator may give rise to *Francovich* liability on behalf of the Member State concerned, but also breaches committed by the national judiciary.[57] Actually, like for the Community legislator, that holds also true for the Community courts which are Community institutions in the sense of Article 288, para 2, EC. And in fact, with regard to tortious liability resulting from wrongful conduct of domestic courts, more support can be found in the laws of the Member States than for liability of the legislator proper,[58] albeit under conditions which differ from Member State to Member State. Indeed, where all national laws tend to recognise personal liability of judicial officers (and as a result 'vicarious' liability of the State) for gross negligence, denial of justice, or criminal offence, only some admit liability of the State for less blameworthy judicial acts as well.[59] The most far-reaching example in that regard is Belgian law where

---

[52] Above, n 24.

[53] See *Casebook on TORT LAW*, at 392.

[54] Para 34 of the judgment referred to above, n 29. The Court could also have referred to the case law of the ECHR: see in that respect JL Sharpe, in LE Pettiti, E Decaux, and PH Imbert (eds), *La Convention Européenne des droits de l'homme* (Paris: Economica, 1995), at 811.

[55] But that may not have been what the Contracting Member States had in mind when adopting the wording of Art 288 EC which obviously refers to the Member States' (own) legal orders.

[56] See para 35 of the *Brasserie* judgment, above, n 25.

[57] Cf also Anagnostaras, see n 26, at 140 with further references in n.8.

[58] *Casebook on TORT LAW*, at 392.

[59] See, eg, Art L.781-1 of the French *Code de l'organisation judiciaire*, reproduced in *Casebook on TORT LAW*, 384, where in the comments under the Article reference is made to case law interpreting gross negligence as 'such a fundamental error that no conscientious judge could have made it'.

the Court of cassation acknowledged, in a judgment of 19 December 1991, that liability of the State—but not that of the judge personally (which would be inconsistent with the principle of independence of the judiciary)— can be engaged for wrongful conduct generally, however under certain restrictive conditions as to the definitive character of the judicial act concerned. Interestingly enough, the Court of Appeal of Liège, to which the case was remanded, applied as a test to establish the wrongfulness of the act, whether the judge concerned had acted in a way that 'a normally careful and circumspect judge placed in the same circumstances at the relevant point in time would not have acted'.[60] That standard is actually the same, *mutatis mutandis,* as the one used in Belgian law with regard to conduct of civil servants (for which the State is vicariously liable as well as the civil servant personally but then only in case of a serious or non-occasional fault) but also with regard to conduct of private persons generally. In all of these situations the concept of a 'careful and circumspect person' (or 'bonus pater familias') will be used to establish wrongfulness.[61]

Finding general principles which the legal systems have in common, in view of fashioning Community legislation and case law, is the result of a dialectical interaction between national laws and Community law. In that regard, it can hardly be overlooked that in Community institutions such as the Council, the Commission and the Court—where lawyers from all Member States work closely together—'law making' and 'solution finding' are unavoidably activities in which all national legal backgrounds play a role. That is most obvious, of course, where normative legal instruments are elaborated, as is exemplified by the Directive on Product Liability. But also in the preparation of judgments of the Community courts (and opinions of Advocate Generals) legal systems of the Member States are, so to speak, omnipresent in the minds of all those involved (court members, legal secretaries, researchers, translators). Moreover, when new or important issues arise, internal memoranda will be prepared by the research department of the Court in which the legal systems of the Member States are thoroughly analysed. After the AG's opinion has been submitted and after the Court's judgment has been rendered, both will be published in the official languages

---

[60] The judgment of the Court of cassation is reproduced in excerpt in the *Casebook on TORT LAW,* 385–6 and the reference to the Court of Appeal's judgment is in note (3) under it, at 388.

[61] It is worthwhile to note that Belgian tort law, like English law and unlike French law, applies the same norms (to be assessed by the same courts) to private and public defendants, and this by virtue of a set of rules which has been developed incrementally by the Court of Cassation over a period of 70 years. It is worthwhile to mention this because it contradicts a widespread belief that legal systems belonging to the same legal family like the Belgian and the French have 'automatically' more in common between themselves than with legal systems belonging to another legal family. Comparative research shows that such is often not the case, at least not in the area of tort law.

of the Community. Those documents will be used in proceedings before the domestic courts, and will be extensively discussed and analysed in scholarly writings, throughout (and outside) the Community. All these factors have for result that Community legislation and case law is the outcome *and* the source of a long process of cross-fertilisation, back and forth, between the national legal orders and the Community legal order. In that context convergence of legal systems and legal mentalities is part of an ongoing process.

Cross-fertilisation does not only occur within the realm of Community law in a legislative or judicial context as described above, it also occurs as a result of voluntary 'spill-over' in neighbouring areas of domestic law which, although remaining 'purely' national, give rise to similar issues as those arising in areas governed or affected by Community law.[62] Well-known examples are legislations enacted by national legislatures in the area of competition law which, although covering purely national (no 'inter-State') situations are made to conform as much as possible to the corresponding Community rules (for 'inter-State' trade). Other illustrations of that phenomenon are the acceptance in the Member States of principles, like the equality and proportionality principle, and of remedial rules, such as the defence of immunity of the State, which domestic courts borrow from Community law for application in purely national situations. Such spill-over effect which is not, or only partially, imposed by Community law itself,[63] takes place for reasons of good governance (keeping the legal system manageable by avoiding useless discrepancies) or of equal protection (putting plaintiffs, or defendants, on the same footing in similar situations). Another area where spill-over may occur, sooner or later, is with regard to liability of national legislatures, as laid down in *Brasserie* for breaches of Community law, if it were to lead in a domestic legal system to the acceptance of liability also for breaches of their own Constitution.[64]

Cross-fertilisation is not a one-way-street and Community law is not eternal law. In other words, even when a rule or solution of Community law may be firmly established, it may still undergo the influence of developments on the national scene. An illustration thereof in the area of State liability is the re-allocation of *Francovich* liability away from the central State towards the regional divisions of a Member State, as was allowed,

---

[62] On such 'spill-over' effect, see G Anthony, 'Community Law and the Development of UK Administrative Law: Delimiting the "Spill-over" Effect' in [1998] EPL 253–76.

[63] Spill-over would be imposed by Art 10 EC if homogeneity is necessary 'to facilitate the achievement of the Community's tasks', eg where and insofar as convergence between domestic and Community competition rules would be needed to facilitate compliance or enforcement of the Community rules.

[64] The ECJ's *Francovich* and *Brasserie* case law has, of course, also other consequences for the laws of the Member States, particularly in the area of compensation for pure economic loss: see *Casebook on TORT LAW*, 951–3.

within limits, in the recent judgment in *Konle*.[65] Clearly, that judgment reflects difficulties, arising especially in federalised Member States, when it comes to determine which division of a State (*Land* or region) is responsible, also financially, for a particular breach of Community law. As advocated by some,[66] the *Konle* ruling might be relied on in the future to re-arrange the liability of the legislator proper, this time away from the legislative towards the executive branch. That may occur in instances where the executive could, and should, have used its competence to undo the failure of 'its' legislator to comply with Community law—a tendency already recognised in the ECJ's judgment in *Brinkmann*.[67] It would show how national legal systems continue to play a role in shaping Community law, more particularly in this instance how their reluctance as to direct liability of the legislator proper might lead to a 'mellowing down'[68] of that liability, not with respect to the principle as such but in terms of ultimate responsibility for the financial consequences thereof. And indeed, a precedent therefore may be seen in the *reglement écran* theory of French administrative law according to which the administration is held to be at fault (thus breaking the causal link with the legislature's fault) when it implements a legislative measure adopted in violation of Community law.[69]

III. PRIVATE ENFORCEMENT OF COMMUNITY LAW: SHAPING A COMMON TORT LAW ALSO IN RELATIONS BETWEEN PRIVATE PERSONS

The ECJ's *Francovich* and *Brasserie* case law relates to non-contractual liability of Member States, and their public authorities (in the broadest sense of the word). The question has obviously arisen whether the principle should also apply, as a matter of Community law, to breaches committed by private persons. That can only be the case of course if and insofar as the infringed Community law provision contains directly applicable obligations for the alleged wrongdoer, such as e.g. Article 81 (ex 85) or Article 82 (ex 86) EC.[70] The question came up in *Banks* with regard to the application of

---

[65] Above, n 26.

[66] See the article of G Anagnostaras, see n 26, at 142 ff.

[67] Above, n 37; see also the comment by Anagnostaras, see n 26. But also when that were not to occur, that same result is achieved already now if, under national law, an action in damages against the State for breach of Community law by the legislator proper must be brought against the Minister of Justice as the legal representative of the State in legal matters: thus under Belgian law as illustrated by a judgment of the Court of Appeal of Brussels of 5 Jan 2000, Rechtsk Weekbl, 2002, 1103.

[68] The term is taken from Tridimas, see n 26.

[69] For excerpts from, and references to, relevant case law, see *Casebook on TORT LAW*, 380–3. See also Anagnostaras, see n 26.

[70] See ECJ, Case 127/73, *BRT* [1974] ECR 51.

Articles 65 and 66 (old) of the Coal and Steel Community Treaty—those are the competition provisions applying to the coal and steel sector. However, in its judgment the ECJ regarded those articles, unlike Articles 81 and 82 EC, not to be directly applicable.[71] In my Opinion, as Advocate General,[72] I took the opposite position. Having taken that position, I had to examine the question of liability of the defendant company for anti-competitive practices under directly applicable Treaty provisions, and came to the conclusion that the reasons for the ECJ to have decided in *Francovich* and *Brasserie* that Member States are liable for breaches of Treaty provisions, equally apply to private persons.[73] Those reasons are that '(t)he full effectiveness of Community rules would be impaired and the protection of the rights which they grant would be weakened if individuals were unable to obtain redress when their rights are infringed by a breach of Community law...'.[74] In *Banks* the ECJ did not rule on the issue because, as mentioned, of its refusal to attach direct effect to the relevant Treaty provisions.

It was only recently that the ECJ was given the occasion to examine the liability of private persons for breach of Article 81 (ex 85) EC. That was in *Courage v Crehan*, a case relating to an exclusive dealing agreement between a pub tenant and a brewer.[75] In his Opinion delivered on 22 March 2001 Advocate General Mischo, although not giving an explicit answer to the question of principle, nonetheless concluded that the direct effect of Article 81 EC in relations between private persons is 'to include (...) the right, for individuals, to be protected from the harmful effects which an agreement which is automatically void may create', adding that '(T)he individuals who can benefit from such protection are, of course, primarily third parties, that is to say consumers and competitors who are adversely affected by a prohibited agreement.'[76]

In its judgment of 20 September 2001 the ECJ comes to the same conclusion, however (and fortunately) taking a more principled and straightforward approach. Recalling that Article 81 EC, like Article 82 EC, constitutes a fundamental provision for the functioning of the internal market and that it produces direct effects in relations between individuals and creates rights for individuals which national courts must safeguard, it concludes, as to the principle of liability, that '(t)he full effectiveness of Article 8[1] of the Treaty and, in particular, the practical effect of the prohibition laid down [in the first paragraph thereof] would be put at risk if it were not open to any individual to claim damages for loss caused to him by contract or by conduct liable to restrict or distort competition.'[77]

---

[71] Case C-128/92, *Banks v National Coal Board*, [1994] ECR I-1209, para 15–19.
[72] [1994] ECR I-1212.   [73] Paras 36–45 of the Opinion.
[74] ECJ in *Francovich*, n 27, para 33.
[75] Case C-453/99 [2001] ECR I-6297.
[76] Opinion at [2001] ECR I-6300, paras 37 and 38.   [77] Para 26 of the judgment.

The judgment is of crucial importance for the development of common principles of both contractual and non-contractual liability between private persons, first because it will require the ECJ to flesh out the principle of 'private law' liability in subsequent case law, and secondly because it will help to level the playing ground between countries, like the common law countries (but also some civil law countries),[78] where private and public entities are subjected to the same liability rules, and those where public and private liability are subjected to different rules.[79] That the ECJ will not be able to escape the task of giving precise guidelines as to how to apply the liability principle in concrete situations (like it was brought to do in its 'post-*Francovich*' case law for State liability), is illustrated by the *Courage v Crehan* judgment itself. Indeed, answering the concrete question raised by the referral court (the English Court of Appeal) concerning the possibility *for a contracting party* to the prohibited agreement to ask for damages, the ECJ held that there should not 'be any absolute bar to such an action'.[80] However, that should not prevent a national legal system, subject to the principles of equivalence (between Community and national claims) and of effectiveness (not making claims practically impossible or excessively difficult), 'from taking steps that the protection of the rights guaranteed by Community law does not entail the unjust enrichment of those who enjoy them'.[81] Nor does it preclude national law 'from denying a party who is found to bear responsibility for the distortion of competition the right to obtain damages from the other contracting party' for which the Court refers to 'a principle which is recognised in most of the legal systems of the Member States and which the Court has applied in the past' (reference omitted), according to which 'a litigant should not profit from his own unlawful conduct, where this is proven'.[82] In the following paragraph the Court then enumerates some factors which a national court should take into consideration to apply that principle.[83] Convergence, at the initiative of the Community courts, also in matters of private law has thus started with regard to Community law breaches emanating from private persons.

When the ECJ will be asked in later case law to flesh out the principle of liability of private parties for breaches of Community law, it can—and most likely will, at least in instances where non-contractual liability is at stake (ie, when an infringement is complained of by a *third party*, eg, a competitor)[84]—draw inspiration from its earlier case law concerning liability of

---

[78] Cf above, n 61 where Belgian law is quoted as an example.

[79] In countries where the distinction is not made, case law relating to conduct of public authorities automatically influences the rules applicable to private persons.

[80] Para 28 of the judgment.   [81] Para 29 and 30.

[82] Para 30–1.   [83] Paras 33–5.

[84] It is clear from para 26 of the judgment, as quoted above in the text accompanying n 77, that 'any individual' may claim in damages.

Community institutions (Article 288, para 2, EC) and of Member States (*Francovich*). And in fact, in *Courage v Crehan*, the Court already referred to earlier case law, on the one hand, to avoid unjust enrichment on behalf of the plaintiff and, on the other hand, to prevent the defendant from drawing profit from his own (as compared with the plaintiff's more significant) unlawful conduct.[85] However, with regard to the condition of serious breach, the case law to be taken into account here will be not so much the ECJ's judgments concerning situations where public authorities possess wide discretion but rather those concerning situations where only a limited or no discretion is involved. For indeed, Articles 81 and 82 EC contain precise prohibitions which, over the years, have been clarified in many judgments of both Community courts, and which therefore leave hardly any (other than a merely interpretative) discretion to the undertakings participating in anti-competitive conduct.[86] That would imply that, in such a situation, it is sufficient for liability to arise, that three conditions are fulfilled: unlawful conduct existing in a breach of Article 81 or 82 EC,[87] the existence of actual damage sustained by the plaintiffs (either a contracting party or third parties, such as competitors or consumers)[88] and a link of direct causation between the illegality and the damage.[89]

On the contrary, with regard to the concepts of causation and damages, and the duty of reparation, much more guidance can be drawn from the ECJ's case law concerning the liability of public authorities under either Article 288, para 2, EC or *Francovich*. In that case law *causality* is deemed to exist when the link between the violation and the injury sustained is 'direct, immediate and exclusive' which can only occur if the damage arises directly from the conduct of the wrongdoer and does not depend on the intervention of other causes, whether positive or negative.[90] That means that the cause may not be too remote and not too broad and unspecific. It

---

[85] See the quotations to, eg, Case 238/78 *Ireks-Arkady* [1979] ECR 2955, para 14 (first principle named in the text, referring to Art 288 (ex 215)) and Case 39/72 *Commission/Italy* [1973] ECR 101, para 10 (second principle, referring to Art 226 (ex 169) EC).

[86] The *Courage/Crehan* judgment relates to a breach of Art 81 EC. It is not unlikely, on the contrary very probable, that in later cases breaches will be at issue of other EC Treaty provisions of which the ECJ has held that they have also *horizontal* direct effect (eg Art 39 (ex 48) EC on free movement of workers: see case C-281/98, *Angonese* [2000] ECR I-4139). Also in such instances Treaty provisions are concerned which have been so often interpreted in earlier case law that little scope for interpretation is left to the persons obliged to comply.

[87] In para 35 of the *Courage v Crehan* judgment the ECJ points out that the conditions for application of Art 81 (or 82) must not necessarily be the same as for certain civil law consequences to apply.

[88] In its Opinion Advocate General Mischo refers explicitly to consumers; see para 38 of his Opinion in *Courage and Crehan*.

[89] Above, by n 40.

[90] Thus A Toth, 'The concepts of damage and causality as elements of non-contractual liability', in T Heukels and A McDonnell (eds), *The Action for Damages in Community Law* (Dordrecht: Kluwer, 1997), 179–98, at 186.

also means that intervening cause, such as contributory negligence of the applicant, may break the chain if causation.[91] And indeed, in *Brasserie/Factortame*, the ECJ stated that, in accordance with a general principle which the legal systems of the Member States have in common, 'the national court may inquire whether the injured party showed reasonable diligence in order to avoid the loss or damage or limit its extent and whether, in particular, he availed himself in time of all the legal remedies available to him'.[92] As for *damage*, inspiration can be drawn from the ECJ's judgments in *Mulder v Council*[93] and *Mulder v Commission*[94] (relating to Article 288 EC), where issues of burden of proof, heads of damage and the assessment thereof, and the award of pre- and post-judgment interests, were dealt with explicitly.[95]

However that be, rather than to leave it to the Community courts to flesh out the conditions under which liability might arise in relations between private persons, it would be advisable, as I have submitted elsewhere,[96] that the Community legislature itself would enact regulations or directives to that effect. That would be particularly, and urgently, needed in the field of competition law where private enforcement should be made more effective than it is now when—pursuant to the Commission's pending modernisation proposals to make domestic courts fully responsible to apply Articles 81 and 82 EC[97]—adequate remedies must be made available to private plaintiffs initiating procedures before national courts. At that occasion rules should be provided not only with regard to the remedy of compensation but also regarding the remedies of nullity, restitution (and restitutionary damages), interim relief and, possibly, collective claims on the part of consumers.

IV. EUROPEAN COMMUNITY LAW PROVIDING STEPPING-STONES TOWARDS A MORE COMPREHENSIVE PUBLIC AND PRIVATE TORT LAW

As the foregoing shows, the contribution of EU law to the emergence of a common European law in the area of tort, whether effected through legisla-

---

[91] Ibid, at 193 ff.   [92] Para 84 and 85 of the judgment.
[93] Joined Cases C-104/89 and C-37/90 [1992] ECR I-3061 (interlocutory judgment).
[94] Same Joined cases [2000] ECR I-203 (definitive judgment).
[95] The award of interests may have a similar deterrent effect as treble damages under US law. See further W van Gerven, 'Substantive Remedies for the Private Enforcement of EC Antitrust Rules Before National Courts', in CD Ehlermann and I Atanasiu (eds), *European Competition Law Annual 2001* (Oxford: Hart Publishing, 2002) in the text accompanying n. 54–61, with further references.
[96] Ibid, text accompanying n 157.
[97] Concerning this proposal see CD Ehlermann, 'The Modernization of EC Antitrust Policy: a legal and cultural Revolution' [2000] CMLR 537–90.

tive measures, mainly directives, or through case law of the Community and domestic courts, is based on a 'piece-meal' approach: directives pursue harmonisation in limited areas of the law; case law relates to compensation seen as a specific remedy to protect Community rights. Such fragmented approach is unavoidable because of the basic principle of attribution of (limited) competences which the Member States have agreed to transfer to the European Community and its (legislative, executive and judicial) institutions. That is *a fortiori* so in areas of private law, whether contract law or tort law, which are matters for which the Member States have chosen to retain primary responsibility.

To deal with the piece-meal character of Community legislation and of implementing national legislation, the Commission has recently published two documents, one in the form of a Communication, dated 11 July 2001, on European Contract Law—which contains, in Annex I, an impressive list of Community directives and regulations, constituting the Community 'acquis' in the area of private law (and thus not only of contract law) and the other in the form of a Green Paper, dated 2 October 2001, on Consumer Protection.[98] In the second document the Commission explores the direction which consumer law should take in the future and how the existing Community legislation could be made less fragmented. In that respect the Commission proposes a 'mixed approach' of comprehensive regulation laid down in a framework directive based on a general clause of good market behaviour, and supplemented by targeted directives where necessary and, at the same time, leaving room for 'formal stakeholder participation in the regulatory process'.[99] The first document is even more ambitious, at least in one of its options where it provides in comprehensive legislation in the area of contract law. In that respect the Communication invites 'stakeholders, including businesses, legal practitioners, academics and consumer groups' to submit information and comments 'on the need for farther-reaching EC action in the area of contract law, in particular to the extent that the case-by-case approach might not be able to solve all the problems which might arise'.[100] This initiative is seen by some as a first step towards codification, at the European level, of large parts of private patrimonial law, including the law of tort, and must therefore be seen, and examined, in that broader perspective (as I have done elsewhere).[101] Let me only state here, as my personal view, that in the present state of Community law there is no legal basis for such comprehensive legislation (outside the realm of

---

[98] The Communication on European Contract Law is published in OJ [2001] C 255/1; the Green Paper on European Union Consumer Protection is Com (2001), 531.

[99] Para 3.4 of the Green Paper.

[100] Para 10 of the Communication.

[101] See my article on 'Codifying European Private Law? Yes...if' [2002] ELR 156–76.

consumer or competition law) and that, even if there were a legal basis, it would still be desirable to achieve codification with the involvement of national parliaments. That should of course not prevent comprehensive codification from being prepared nor, and even more importantly, should it prevent European lawyers from being educated in a perspective of such codification to (gradually) come into existence.

As mentioned at the outset of this contribution, EU law is only one of the driving forces towards convergence of (parts of) private law. With regard to tort law, the law of the ECHR is another important factor in two respects: first, by guaranteeing individual plaintiffs to have full access to domestic courts in the Contracting States; and, secondly, by contributing to the emergence of common rules as a result of the application of Article 41 ECHR which allows the Human Rights Court 'if necessary (to) afford just satisfaction to the injured party' where internal law 'allows only partial reparation to be made'.[102] The first aspect is particularly highlighted by the evolution in English law 'pushing back the boundaries of public authority liability'.[103] That evolution illustrates perfectly well the interaction which occurs between national and supranational case law. Indeed, after the Strasbourg's Court judgment in *Osman v UK*[104] which had raised considerable criticism in the U.K, the Court 'adroitly... responded to the domestic disquiet' in its later *Z v UK* judgment[105] in which it reviewed its earlier reasoning (but not the result) in light of the 'clarification' made by domestic courts after *Osman*.[106] The second aspect is to be seen in case law of the Strasbourg Court concerning loss and quantum of damages and concerning causation.[107] In that respect it remains to be seen whether that case law may sooner or later lead to regarding a violation of a plaintiff's personality right to constitute harm in itself or *per se*.[108]

A third driving force mentioned at the outset of this article is comparative law undertaken in legal writings and reflected in case law of the national courts. Again, the phenomenon seems to be more conspicuous in the case law of UK courts than in that of courts of the other Member

---

[102] See further D Fairgrieve, 'The Human Rights Act 1998, Damages and Tort Law', in [2001] *PL*, 695–716.

[103] Thus Fairgrieve's still more recent article 'Pushing back the Boundaries of Public Authority Liability: Tort Law enters the Classroom', in [2002] *PL*, 288–308.

[104] 1 ELR 193, referred to and discussed in Fairgrieve's article mentioned in the preceding note, at 299.

[105] [2001] 2 ELR 612, referred to ibid, at 300, where the quotation figures at 301.

[106] Fairgrieve, ibid, at 300–1.

[107] Fairgrieve, see n 102, at 702–15.

[108] On this development, see C von Bar, 'Damage without Loss', in *The Search for Principle, Essays in Honour of Lord Goff of Chieveley* (Oxford: Oxford University Press, 2000), 23–43; W van Gerven, 'Remedies for infringements of Fundamental Rights', lecture held in Bremen on 12 Apr 2002, nyp.

States.[109] That may be due to the fact that UK judges are, because of their familiarity with the legal systems of the former Commonwealth, more inclined to look at case law in other countries, and to the fact that the common law, because of the incremental and inductive way of reasoning, is more flexible than other laws and also more apt to include foreign law sources in its reasoning. It may also be due, however, to the fact that, because of the 'fair, just and reasonable criterion' which is one of the elements to establish a duty of care in the law of negligence, there have been more public policy minded exclusionary rules than in other legal systems which now come gradually, and fiercely, under attack,[110] frequently as a result of EU and/or ECHR law.

Not much of a conclusion is needed here except that contemporary law, also in core subjects of private law, can no longer be understood in the Member States of the EU—which at the same time are   among the Contracting States of the ECHR—without recognising and understanding the importance of socio-economic and legal integration and the phenomenon of mutual permeation to which it gives rise, back and forth.[111]

---

[109] A most prominent example is Lord Goff's speech before the House of Lords in *White v Jones* [1995] 2 AC 207, also reproduced in part and discussed in *Casebook on TORT LAW*, 219–24 and 244–7.

[110] Apart from the development in public authorities' liability rules, already mentioned and discussed by Fairgrieve in the article mentioned in n 103, another example is the immunity of advocates which has been successfully challenged in *Arthur JS Hall & Co v Simons* [2000] 3 WLR 543.

[111] See also my article on 'Mutual permeation of public and private law at the national and supranational level', *Maastricht Journal of Eur Comp Law* (1998), 7–24 and 'The invader invaded or the need to uncover general principles common to the laws of the Member States', in GC Rodriguez Iglesias, *et al* (eds), *Mélanges en hommage à Fernand Schockweiler* (Baden-Baden: Nomos, 1999), 593–603.

7. LIABILITY FOR BREACH OF COMMUNITY LAW: GROWING UP AND MELLOWING DOWN?

Takis Tridimas *

I. INTRODUCTION

This article seeks to discuss the recent case law of the European Court of Justice pertaining to liability for breach of Community law. After placing State liability in damages in the context of the Court's policy on remedies, it reviews the second-generation cases on State liability focusing successively on causal relationship, the requirement of serious breach, and the question which authority is responsible to pay reparation. It then discusses the judgment in *Bergaderm*[1] and the attempt to unify the conditions of State and Community liability using the first as a model for the second.

II. STATE LIABILITY AND SELECTIVE DEFERENCE

The recognition of a right to reparation for breach of Community law in *Francovich*,[2] signalled the apotheosis of judicial intervention in the law of remedies and provided the most evocative illustration of the principle *ubi jus, ibi remedium*. The Court's approach in *Francovich* incorporated all signs of constitution-building. In terms of reasoning, it relied on Article 10 (ex 5) EC and the principle of effectiveness to cover the remedial deficit of constitutional rights.[3] The Court pronounced that the principle of State liability 'is inherent in the system of the Treaty',[4] thus asserting functional inseparability between rights and remedies. Indeed, one of the key features of judicial constitutional building at Community level has been the way the Court of Justice has derived from the general principles of primacy and direct effect a specific duty on national courts to provide full and effective

* Professor of European Law, University of Southampton.
[1] Case C-352/98 P, *Laboratoires Pharmaceutiques Bergaderm and Goupil v Commission*, judgment of 4 July 2000.
[2] Joined Cases C-6 and C-9/90 *Francovich and others* [1991] ECR I-5357.
[3] See *Francovich*, ibid, paras 33–6.
[4] Ibid, para 35.

protection of Community rights.[5] The recognition of a right to reparation became a constitutional imperative because it was supported by a strong instrumental rationale. As the internal market began to take shape in the aftermath of the Commission's White Paper of 1985, it became increasingly clear to political and judicial actors alike that reliance on traditional means of enforcement, mainly the doctrine of direct effect and the tardy procedure of Article 226 (ex 169), were inefficient. The right to reparation came to close the gap between rights and remedies and reduce the under-enforcement of Community rights that the Court perceived to be constitutional in nature.

In a first generation of cases, the Court developed the legal basis of liability and the conditions which must be fulfilled in order for a right to reparation to arise.[6] *Brasserie du Pêcheur and Factortame*[7] took the law forward by establishing the universality of the right to reparation,[8] introducing the notion of 'serious breach' as a pivotal condition of liability, and modelling State liability on the liability of the Community institutions. The tenet of the first generation case law was that Member States who make no effort to implement directives could expect no sympathy. Failure to implement a directive is *per se* a serious breach.[9] By contrast, Member States who transpose directives but do so unsuccessfully will be invited to a dialogue. Liability ensues only if the breach is serious, which in turn involves an enquiry revolving around discretion, good faith, reasonableness, and the behaviour of related actors, namely, the Commission and other Member States.[10]

---

[5] See T Tridimas, 'Enforcing Community Rights in National Courts: Some Recent Developments', in D O'Keeffe and A Bavasso (eds), *Judicial Review in European Union Law, Liber Amicorum in Honour of Lord Slynn of Hadley* (The Hague: Kluwer Law International, 2000), 465–79, at 466.

[6] See for an extensive discussion, Tridimas, *The General Principles of EC Law* (Oxford: Oxford University Press, 1999), ch. 9, where further bibliography is given. In recent years, attention has focused also on the liability of public authorities in a comparative perspective. See B Markesinis *et al*, *The Tortious Liability of Statutory Bodies* (Oxford: Hart Publishing, 1999); Van Gerven *et al*, *Cases, Materials and Text on Tort Law, Jus Communae Casebook* (Oxford: Hart Publishing, 2001).

[7] Joined Cases C-46 and 48/93 *Brasserie du Pêcheur v Germany and the Queen v Secretary of State for Transport ex parte Factortame* [1996] ECR I-1029.

[8] In *Brasserie*, the Court held that the principle of State liability is inherent in the system of the Treaty and therefore 'holds good for any case in which a Member State breaches Community law, whatever be the organ of the State whose act or omission was responsible for the breach' (para 32). Liability may therefore arise as a result of action by the legislature, the administration, or the judiciary. For the latter, see H Toner, 'Thinking the Unthinkable? State Liability for Judicial Acts after Factortame III' 17 *YEL* (1997) 165.

[9] Joined Cases C-178, 179, 188-190/94 *Dillenkofer and others v Germany* [1996] ECR I-4845, paras 27–8.

[10] For incorrect implementation of directives, see Case C-392/93 *The Queen v HM Treasury ex parte British Telecommunications plc* [1996] ECR I-1631, Joined Cases C-283, C-291 and C-292/94 *Denkavit Internationaal BV et al v Bundesamt für Finanzen* [1996] ECR I-5063. For breach by the national administration, see Case C-5/94 *The Queen v Ministry of Agriculture, Fisheries and Food ex parte Hedley Lomas (Ireland) Ltd* [1996] ECR I-2553.

We now seem to witness a second generation of cases. Since 1998, the Court has delivered six judgments on State liability.[11] These do not contain any innovations. The Court, rather, has concentrated on developing and refining the remedy. It can be said that the second generation cases present two distinct features: in terms of legal analysis, the Court has concentrated on elaborating the condition of causation, whereas hitherto it had focused mainly on the condition of seriousness of the breach. In terms of judicial policy, the cases evince a tendency to leave more matters to the national courts and, perhaps, in some respects a tactical relaxation of liability. Both these features are consistent with the general approach of the Court in the field of remedies that can best be described as one of selective deference.

The present author has argued[12] that the case law concerning the protection of Community rights in national courts has successively gone through three phases: in the early years, the Court relied on the national laws for the protection of Community rights in national courts subject to the requirements of equivalence and effectiveness.[13] In a second phase, the case law sought more exacting standards from the national legal systems.[14] More

---

[11] These are the following in reverse chronological order: Case C424/97 *Salomone Haim v Kassenzahnärztliche Vereinigung Nordrhein (Haim II)*, judgment of 4 July 2000; Case C-140/97 *Rechberger and Greindl v Austria* [1999] ECR I-3499; Case C-321/97 *Ulla-Brith Andersson and Susanne Wåkerås-Andersson v Swedish State* [1999] ECR I-3551; Case C-302/97 *Konle v Republic of Austria* [1999] ECR I-3099; Case C-319/96 *Brinkmann Tabakfabriken GmbH v Skatteministeriet* [1998] ECR I-5255; Case C-127/95 *Norbrook Laboratories Limited v Ministry of Agriculture* [1998] ECR I-1531. In a number of other cases, the Court has referred to State liability as a possible remedy without examining it in detail. See, eg, Joined Cases C-192 to C-218/95 *Comateb and Others v Directeur Général des Douanes et Droits Indirects* [1997] ECR I-165; Case C-90/96 *Petrie* [1997] ECR I-6527. For a critique of this trend, see M Dougan, 'The Francovich Right to Reparation: The Contours of Community Remedial Competence' (2000) 6 *European Public Law*, 103. Note also that in a distinct but related development the Court delivered its first judgment under Art 228 (x 171) C imposing a periodic penalty payment on Greece for failure to comply with Directive 75/442 on waste and Directive 78/319 on toxic waste: Case C-387/97 *Commission v Greece*, judgment of 4 July 2000.

[12] See Tridimas, 'Enforcing Community Rights in National Courts'. See also the classification of A Arnull, *The European Union and its Court of Justice* (Oxford: Oxford University Press, 1999), at 143 et seq., and the critique of Dougan, op cit.

[13] According to the classic approach, in the absence of Community rules, it is for the domestic legal system of each Member State to designate the courts and tribunals having jurisdiction and to lay down the detailed procedural rules governing actions for safeguarding the rights which individuals derive form Community law, provided that such rules satisfy two conditions: they are not less favourable that those governing similar domestic actions (the principle of equivalence); and they do not render virtually impossible or excessively difficult the exercise of rights conferred by Community law (the principle of effectiveness). See Case 33/76 *Rewe v Landwirtschaftskammer für das Saarland* [1976] ECR 1989. Case 45/76 *Comet v Productschap voor Siergewassen* [1976] ECR 2043.

[14] This phase is exemplified, apart from Francovich, by judgments such as Case 222/84 *Johnston v Chief Constable of the Royal Ulster Constabulary* [1986] ECR 1651 (national laws must make available effective judicial review for the protection of Community rights); Case C-213/89 *Factortame* [1990] ECR I-2433 (interim relief against the State must be available in national courts for the protection of Community rights).

recently the Court has followed a policy of selective deference, involving the directed use of judicial power. In some areas, the Court appears to defer to the standards of protection applicable in the national legal systems, or even restrict the application of previous case-law.[15] In others, it seems to prefer a more robust approach leading to the striking down of national rules pertaining to procedure and remedies.[16] All in all, the Court appears to leave more discretion to the national courts and be more selective in its interventions. This reflects perhaps a wider tendency in the case law. The determining criterion is that an individual must have an effective opportunity to protect his rights deriving from Community law. In one view, the judicial policy on procedures and remedies reflects the corresponding policy on the internal market: the Court of Justice will strike down the national rules which prevent effective access to remedial protection.[17] The Court however has not articulated any specific criteria and its interventions are not necessarily predictable. This is an area of law where the art of casuistry prevails.[18]

This article reviews the second generation of State liability cases, dealing respectively with causation, seriousness of breach, and the question which authority is liable to make reparation. Before embarking on a discussion of the cases, it will be recalled that individuals have a right to reparation where three conditions are fulfilled: the rule of law infringed must have intended to confer rights on individuals; the breach must be sufficiently serious; and there must be a direct causal link between the breach of the obligation resting on the State and the damage sustained by the injured parties.[19] These conditions must be fulfilled in all cases[20] but their application may vary depending on the nature of the breach.[21]

---

[15] The primary example of this is the demise of *Emmott*. See the following line of cases: Case C-208/90 *Emmott* [1991] ECR 4269; Case C-338/91 *Steenhorst-Neerings v Bestuur van de Bedrijfsvereniging voor Detailhandel, Ambachten en Huisvrouwen* [1993] ECR I-5475; Case C-188/95 *Fantask and Others v Industriministeriet* [1997] ECR I-6783. Cf Case C-246/96 *Magorrian v Eastern Health and Social Services Board* [1997] ECR I-7153.

[16] See, eg, Case C-312/93 *Peterbroeck v Belgian State* [1995] ECR I-4599, Case C-326/96 *Levez v Jennings (Harlow Pools) Ltd* [1998] ECR I-7835, and more recently, Case C-78/98 *Preston and Other v Wolverhampton Healthcare NHS Trust and Others and Fletcher and Others v Midland Bank plc*, judgment of 16 May 2000.

[17] See S Prechal, 'Community law in National Courts: The Lessons from Van Schijndel' (1998) 35 *CMLRev* 681, 691 and see also A Biondi, 'The European Court of Justice and Certain National Procedural Limitations: Not Such a Touch Relationship' (1999) 36 *CMLRev* 1271.

[18] See further Van Gerven, 'Of Rights, Remedies, and Procedures' (2000) 37 *CMLRev* 501.

[19] See, eg, Joined Cases C-178, 179, 188-190/94 *Dillenkofer and others v Germany* [1996] ECR I-4845, para 20–1; Case C-140/97 *Rechberger and Greindl v Austria* [1999] ECR I-3499, para 21; Case C424/97 *Haim II*, judgment of 4 July 2000, para 36; Case C-127/95 *Norbrook Laboratories Limited v Ministry of Agriculture* [1998] ECR I-1531, para 107.

[20] Note however that a Member State may make liability of public authorities for breach of Community law subject to less strict conditions: see Joined Cases C-46 and 48/93 *Brasserie du Pêcheur v Germany and The Queen v Secretary of State for Transport ex parte Factortame* [1996] ECR I-1029, para 66.

[21] See Joined Cases C-178, 179, 188-190/94 *Dillenkofer and others v Germany* [1996] ECR I-4845, para 24, and Opinion of AG Mischo in Haim II, at para 42.

III. CAUSATION: THE CASES

The condition of causation was examined in *Brinkmann* and *Rechberger* both of which raised interesting issues hitherto unexplored in the case law.

In *Brinkmann*[22] the applicant in the main proceedings was a German company that produced 'Westpoint', a patented tobacco product. That product consists of tobacco rolls enveloped in porous cellulose that needs to be wrapped in cigarette paper in order to be smoked. In Germany, Westpoint was taxed as smoking tobacco but on importation in Denmark, the Danish authorities decided to tax it at the higher rate applicable to cigarettes. The applicant brought an action claiming that the Danish authorities should tax Westpoint as smoking tobacco and seeking compensation for the loss suffered. The Court upheld the applicant's contention that Westpoint must be classified as smoking tobacco within the meaning of the Second Directive on taxes other than turnover taxes which affect the consumption of manufactured tobacco.[23] It then turned to examine whether the erroneous classification of the product gave rise to liability in damages. The Court found that Articles 3(1) and 4(1) of the Directive, which contain the definitions of cigarettes and smoking tobacco, were not properly transposed into national law since the competent Minister authorised to introduce the relevant provisions had not adopted any implementing measures. The Court recalled that failure to implement a directive is *per se* a serious violation.[24] It found however that, in the circumstances, there was no direct causal link between the breach of Community law and the damage allegedly suffered by the applicant. This was because, despite the failure to implement the directive by ministerial decree, the Danish authorities gave immediate effect to the relevant provisions of the directive.[25] The Court proceeded to examine whether the Danish authorities had committed a sufficiently serious breach of the directive and found that they had not. It came to that conclusion on the following grounds. Westpoint did not correspond exactly to either of the definitions of the Directive, being a new product that did not exist at the time the directive was adopted. In view of the nature of Westpoint, the classification made by the Danish authorities was not manifestly contrary to the wording or the aim of the Directive. Notably, the Commission and the Finnish Government had supported the same classification.[26]

---

[22] Case C-319/96 *Brinkmann Tabakfabriken GmbH v Skatteministeriet* [1998] ECR I-5255.

[23] Council Directive 79/32, OJ 1979, L 10/8.

[24] Case C-319/96 *Brinkmann Tabakfabriken GmbH v Skatteministeriet* [1998] ECR I-5255, para 28.

[25] Ibid, para 29.

[26] Ibid, para 31.

Brinkmann is the first case where the Court relied on causation to restrict State liability. In doing so, it was able to limit liability without technically qualifying its strict approach that failure to implement is *per se* a serious breach.[27] This has important repercussions. It means that, where a Member State fails to adopt implementing measures in order to transpose a directive into national law, the national administrative authorities may present as a valid defence that, despite the lack of implementing measures, they themselves endeavoured to comply with the requirements of the directive. In such a case, the State would incur liability only if their failure to comply with the directive was serious, ie, not excusable within the *BT* sense.[28] This inserts an important *caveat* on State liability and provides an exit route in cases of non-transposition. It also offers an incentive to public authorities to observe the requirements of directives even where the legislature has failed to take implementing measures. It is possible that, in the absence of implementing measures, separate administrative authorities in one and the same Member State may understand the meaning of a directive differently. It is conceivable then that some of them might be found to have committed a serious breach but others might not.[29]

A criticism which might be levelled against *Brinkmann* is that it is not based on a structured view of causation. Why was the alleged loss of the applicants more attributable to the erroneous interpretation of the directive by the Danish administration rather than the failure to adopt implementing measures? After all, proper transposition requires binding measures of general application and, if the Minister authorised by national law to adopt implementing provisions had done so, the authorities would not have had to improvise. The approach of the Court was pragmatic. In the circumstances, it was satisfied that the Member State, through the administrative authorities, had paid due respect to its obligations under Community law and intended to comply with the requirements of the directive in its dealings with the affected traders. Also, the Directive in issue lent itself to application by administrative action. The absence of transposing legislation did not make it impossible for the authorities to give effect to the requirements of the directive. The outcome in *Brinkmann* seems correct. It is submitted however that *Brinkmann* applies only to cases where it is possible for the national administration to apply the provisions of a directive in the absence of implementing legislation. In some cases, the requirements of a directive

---

[27] See Joined Cases C-178, 179, 188-190/94 *Dillenkofer and others v Germany* [1996] ECR I-4845.

[28] Case C-392/93 *The Queen v HM Treasury ex parte British Telecommunications plc* [1996] ECR I-1631.

[29] This begs the question which authority would be the appropriate defendant in an action for damages, ie whether it would be the Member State itself or the agency that made the decision on the specific circumstances. On this issue, see below.

may be such that the administration may not be able to cover the failure to adopt implementing measures of general application, in which case liability will ensue automatically irrespective of any efforts made by the authorities to accommodate the requirements of Community law.

The cautious generosity shown in *Brinkmann* was not forthcoming in *Rechberger, Greindl and Others v Austria*,[30] a case which raised issues pertaining both to the requirement of serious breach and causation. *Rechberger* concerned Directive 90/314 on package travel,[31] which was in issue also in *Dillenkofer*. It will be remembered that the purpose of the Directive is to protect the purchaser of package travel. To that effect, Article 7 requires the package tour organiser to provide sufficient security for the refund of money paid over and for the repatriation of the consumer in the event of the organiser's insolvency. In *Dillenkofer* the Court had decided that Article 7 confers on individuals rights whose content is determinable with sufficient precision, and therefore the first condition for the right to reparation to arise was fulfilled.[32] In *Rechberger*, an Austrian newspaper offered to its subscribers a holiday trip at substantially reduced prices as a gift to thank them for their loyalty. The offer proved more popular than it had been anticipated. This caused the travel organiser who had undertaken the organisation of the trips logistical and financial difficulties which, in turn, led to bankruptcy proceedings being initiated against it. The plaintiffs in the main proceedings were subscribers who had taken part in the newspaper's offer. They had all paid the travel costs in advance but their trips were cancelled and, as a result, they suffered financial loss. Since they were unable to recover against the travel organiser, they brought an action against Austria claiming that their loss was attributable to the State's failure to implement the Package Travel Directive in full.

The first issue raised in the case concerned the temporal limitation of protection. The Austrian regulation which intended to implement Article 7 of the Directive applied to travel packages booked after 1 January 1995, the date of Austria's accession to the EU, but limited protection to those with a departure date of 1 May 1995 or later. The Court accepted that the financial guarantees provided for by Article 7 do not extend to contracts of package travel concluded before 1 January 1995, which was the date prescribed for the transposition of the Directive. It held however that the protection of Article 7 must be applied to all package travel booked after that date irrespective of the departure dates of the travel. Neither Article 7 nor any other provision of the Directive granted Member States a right to limit protection

---

[30] Case C-140/97 *Rechberger and Greindl v Austria* [1999] ECR I-3499.

[31] Council Directive 90/314/EEC of 13 June 1990 on package travel, package holidays, and package tours, OJ 1990 L 158/59.

[32] Joined Cases C-178, 179, 188-190/94 *Dillenkofer and others v Germany* [1996] ECR I-4845, para 44.

to trips taken on a date later than the time-limit prescribed for transposition. Since Article 7 was clear and precise and the Directive conferred no margin of discretion on Member States, the temporal limitation of protection amounted to a scrious breach.[33]

The second issue raised in *Rechberger* concerned the method by which Austria gave effect to Article 7. The implementing measures required a travel organiser to have a contract of insurance or a bank guarantee covering at least 5 per cent of the organiser's business turnover in the corresponding quarter of the previous calendar year. In the first year of business, the amount of cover was to be based on the estimated turnover from the intended business of the organiser.[34] Some of the plaintiffs in the main proceedings had suffered loss because the bank guarantee issued by the travel organiser in accordance with the implementing measures was insufficient to reimburse their travel costs. The referring court asked whether the Austrian legislation correctly transposed Article 7. It also asked whether there was a direct causal link between the late or incomplete transposition of Article 7 and loss or damage caused to the consumer.

The Court interpreted Article 7 strictly as imposing an obligation of result. It held that national legislation transposes properly that provision only if it achieves the result of providing the consumer with an effective guarantee.[35] The guarantee required by the Austrian legislation was limited both in terms of its amount and in terms of the basis on which the cover was calculated. It was therefore 'structurally incapable' of catering for events in the economic sector in question, such as a significant increase in the number of bookings in relation to either the turnover for the preceding year or the estimated turnover.[36] The Court concluded that the Austrian legislation did not transpose properly Article 7 but, curiously, did not express a view on whether the incorrect transposition of the Directive was a serious breach. This is presumably because the referring court did not ask that question *expressis verbis*. The issue of seriousness, however, appeared

---

[33] Case C-140/97 *Rechberger and Greindl v Austria* [1999] ECR I-3499, para 51. The Court also confirmed that it has no jurisdiction to rule on whether a Member State is liable under the EEA Agreement for failure to implement a Community directive prior to its accession to the European Union, where the obligation to implement arises under the EEA Agreement. The issue arose because, under the terms of the EEA Agreement, Austria was required to transpose the Package Travel Directive into domestic law on 1 Jan 1994. See also on the same point, Case C-321/97 *Ulla-Brith Andersson and Susanne Wåkerås-Andersson v Swedish State* [1999] ECR I-3551. The liability of an EFTA State for infringement of a directive referred to in the EEA Agreement was examined in the EFTA Court's judgment E-9/97 Sveinbjörnsdóttir, 10 Dec 1998.

[34] In some cases, the Austrian rules required the amount of cover to be no less than 10 percent of the organiser's turnover or estimated turnover. See para 3(2) of the regulation on security provided by travel agencies, *Reisebüro-Sicherungsverordnung*, BGB1, No 881 of 15 Nov 1994, 6501.

[35] Case C-140/97 *Rechberger and Greindl v Austria* [1999] ECR I-3499, para 64.

[36] Ibid, para 62.

to be crucial for determining whether the plaintiffs in the main proceedings had a right to reparation. As we shall see, in answering the final question posed by the national court, the Court of Justice held that there was direct causal link between Austria's failure to transpose and the loss suffered by the plaintiffs. This finding in itself does not settle the outcome since liability would ensue only if the loss was causally connected to a serious breach. It may seem surprising then that no attempt was made to address the issue of the seriousness of the breach in the judgment. Arguably, the Court left the glass half-full in circumstances where the spirit of cooperation of the preliminary reference procedure invited it to fill it.[37]

Turning now on the issue of causation, the Austrian Government argued that there was no direct causal link between late or incomplete transposition of Article 7 and the loss or damage suffered by consumers, because the unsuccessful transposition had contributed to the damage only as a result of a chain of wholly exceptional and unforeseeable events. By this, the Government meant that the loss of the plaintiffs was due to the imprudent conduct of the travel agent and the atypical character of the case. The Court declined to accept that argument. It pointed out that Article 7 requires a guarantee specifically aimed at arming consumers against the consequences of bankruptcy, whatever the causes of bankruptcy may be. State liability for breach of Article 7 cannot be precluded by imprudent conduct on the part of the travel organiser or by the occurrence of exceptional and unforeseeable events.[38] This is correct: the chain of causation cannot easily be broken by the conduct of the travel organiser since it is against the financial risks associated with that very trader that the Directive is intended to safeguard the consumer.[39]

---

[37] By contrast, AG Saggio expressly stated that Austria's defective transposition amounted to a sufficiently serious and clear breach: see paras 46–8 of the Opinion. Cf the Austrian government's submissions in paras 56–8 of the judgment.

[38] Case C-140/97 *Rechberger and Greindl v Austria* [1999] ECR I-3499, paras 74–5.

[39] In some cases, however, the imprudent conduct of the person on whom the obligation is imposed may expose that person to other types of proceedings. The issue then could be raised whether the injured party should pursue first an available form of action against that person rather than a claim against the State for compensation if the first form of action provides an effective alternative. This issue did not appear to be relevant in Rechberger and, more generally, it has not been raised in the case-law. Note however that in Brasserie, the Court held that, in order to determine the right to reparation, the national court may enquire whether the injured party showed reasonable diligence in order to avoid or limit the loss and whether, in particular, he availed himself in time of all the legal remedies available to him: see para 84 of the judgment: Joined Cases C-46 and 48/93 *Brasserie du Pêcheur v Germany* and *the Queen v Secretary of State for Transport ex parte Factortame* [1996] ECR I-1029.

IV. CAUSATION: SOME CONCLUSIONS

It may be helpful at this juncture to attempt to draw some conclusions regarding causation as they emerge from the case law. The starting point is that there must be a direct causal link between the breach of an obligation resting on the State and the damage sustained by the injured parties.[40] It is for the national court to determine whether such link exists.[41] This means that the national court must determine whether causation exists on the facts. It does not mean that the rules governing causation depend on national law. Although the case law is equivocal on this point, this view is supported by *Brinkmann* and *Rechberger* and derives also from the nature of State liability as a Community remedy. Causation, as the others conditions of liability, must be determined in the first place by Community law. At the very least, the Court will discard the national rules of causation which do not provide an effective standard of protection. So far, however, the Court has not elaborated any systematic principles of causation but has approached the issues that arise on a case by case basis. It may be noted that, despite the general pronouncement in *Brasserie du Pêcheur* that State liability in damages is based on principles analogous to those governing the liability of Community institutions, so far no apparent attempt has been made by the Court to borrow from its case law on Article 228(2) (ex 215(2)) EC with regard to causation.[42]

V. SERIOUSNESS OF BREACH AND MEMBER STATE DISCRETION

A breach of Community law is not actionable in damages unless it is sufficiently serious. For this to be established, a Member State must have manifestly and gravely disregarded the limits on the exercise of its discretionary powers.[43] In *Brasserie du Pêcheur* the Court laid down a number of guidelines to be taken into account by the national court with a view to determining whether the threshold of seriousness has been reached.[44] Suffice it

---

[40] See, eg, Brasserie, ibid, para 51; Case C-127/95 *Norbrook Laboratories Limited v Ministry of Agriculture* [1998] ECR I-1531, para 107; Case C-319/96 *Brinkmann Tabakfabriken GmbH v Skatteministeriet* [1998] ECR I-5255, para 25; Case C-140/97 *Rechberger and Greindl v Austria*, [1999] ECR I-3499, para 72.

[41] Brasserie, ibid, para 65; *Norbrook*, ibid, para 110; *Rechberger*, ibid, para 72.

[42] See the criticism by Van Gerven, 'Taking Article 215(2) EC Seriously', in J Beatson and T Tridimas (eds), *New Directions in European Public Law* (Oxford: Hart Publishing, 1998), 35–48.

[43] Joined Cases C-46 and 48/93 *Brasserie du Pêcheur v Germany and The Queen v Secretary of State for Transport ex parte Factortame* [1996] ECR I-1029, para 55.

[44] Ibid, paras 56–7. These considerations are the following: the clarity and precision of the rule breached; the measure of discretion left to the national authorities; whether the infringe-

to make two points in this context. Other things being equal, the margin of discretion enjoyed by the Member State is in an inverse relationship with the likelihood of establishing a serious breach. The less the margin of discretion left to the national authorities by the Community rules, the easier it would be to establish that a breach of those rules is serious. In *Hedley Lomas*, it was held that, where a Member State has no discretion, or where its discretion is considerably reduced, the mere infringement of Community law might be sufficient to establish the existence of a serious breach.[45]

The second point is this. According to established case-law, in determining whether a breach is serious, the precision and clarity of the provision breached is of cardinal importance.[46] We saw above that in *Rechberger* the Court considered the temporal limitation of protection a serious breach since no provision of the Travel Package Directive gave Member States any discretion to limit the guarantees of Article 7 in time. In that case the Court also confirmed that the seriousness of breach is a qualitative rather than a quantitative concept: the fact that Austria had implemented all the other provisions of the Directive did not exonerate it from liability for breach of Article 7.[47]

The case law declares that it is for the national court to establish whether a breach is serious. But how much freedom does the Court of Justice leave to the national court? The Court's intervention is highly selective. In *Rechberger* it made no effort to examine whether Austria's incomplete transposition of the Package Travel Directive amounted to a serious breach. *Konle v Austria*[48] favoured also a hands-off approach.

Mr Konle, a German national, brought an action before the Regional Civil Court of Vienna seeking to recover damages for the loss that he sustained as a result of the alleged infringement of Community law by the Tyrol legislation on land transactions. The Tyrol Law on the Transfer of Land of 1993[49] made the acquisition of building land in the Tyrol region by foreign nationals subject to prior authorisation. As a condition for the

---

ment and the damage caused was intentional or involuntary; whether any error of law was excusable or inexcusable; the fact that the position taken by a Community institution may have contributed towards the omission; the adoption or retention of national measures or practices contrary to Community law. In any event, a breach of Community law will be sufficiently serious if it has persisted despite a judgment of the Court which establishes the infringement in question.

[45] Case C-5/94 *The Queen v Ministry of Agriculture, Fisheries and Food ex parte Hedley Lomas (Ireland) Ltd* [1996] ECR I-2553, para 28; Joined Cases C-178, 179, 188-190/94 *Dillenkofer and others v Germany* [1996] ECR I-4845, para 25; Case C-127/95 *Norbrook Laboratories Limited v Ministry of Agriculture* [1998] ECR I-1531, para 109.

[46] See especially Case C-392/93 *The Queen v HM Treasury ex parte British Telecommunications plc* [1996] ECR I-1631.

[47] Case C-140/97 *Rechberger and Greindl v Austria* [1999] ECR I-3499, para 52.

[48] Case C-302/97 *Konle v Republic of Austria* [1999] ECR I-3099.

[49] *Tiroler Grundverkehrsgesetz* 1993, Tiroler LGB1. 82/1993.

granting of authorisation, the prospective acquirer had to prove that the land would not be used for the purposes of establishing a secondary residence. By contrast, acquisition of building land by Austrian nationals was subject to a simple declaration that the land would not be used as secondary residence. The 1993 Law was replaced with effect from 1 October 1996 by a new Law which abolished the declaration procedure and extended the authorisation requirement to Austrian and foreign nationals alike.[50] Subsequently, by a judgment of 10 December 1996, at a time when the 1993 Law was no longer in force, the Austrian Constitutional Court declared it unconstitutional on the ground that it was in breach of the fundamental right to property.

In 1994, Mr Konle sought to acquire a plot of land in the Tyrol region but was refused authorisation by the Land Transfer Commission pursuant to the 1993 Law. The refusal was subsequently annulled by the Austrian Constitutional Court on the ground that 1993 Law had been declared unconstitutional. The effect of the Constitutional Court's judgment was to bring Mr Konle's application back before the Land Transfer Commission but, without waiting for the Commission's new decision, he brought an action for State liability in damages.

On a reference for a preliminary ruling, the Court held that the 1993 Law discriminated against nationals of other Member States in respect of inter-State capital movements and that such discrimination was prohibited by Article 56 [ex 73b] EC unless it was justified on grounds permitted by the Treaty. The Austrian government sought to rely on Article 70 of the Act of Accession which states that 'Notwithstanding the obligations under the Treaties on which the European Union is founded, the Republic of Austria may maintain its existing legislation regarding secondary residences for five years from the date of accession.' The question arose whether the 1993 Law could be considered as 'existing legislation' on the date of accession, ie, 1 January 1995, given that it was subsequently declared unconstitutional by the Constitutional Court. The Court of Justice held that the concept of 'existing legislation' is based on a factual criterion and does not require an assessment of the validity in domestic law of the legislation in issue. Any rule of Austrian law concerning secondary residences which was in force on the date of accession is, in principle, covered by the derogation of Article 70 unless it was withdrawn subsequently with retroactive effect.[51] The Court added, uncontroversially, that it is for the national court to assess the temporal effects of declarations of unconstitutionality made by the Austrian constitutional court.[52]

---

[50] *Tiroler Grundverkehrsgesetz* 1996, Tiroler LGB1. 61/1996.
[51] Case C-302/97 *Konle v Republic of Austria* [1999] ECR I-3099, paras 28–9.
[52] Ibid, para 30. Notably, the Court also found the 1996 Tyrol Law incompatible with the

The answer to the national court's question was inconclusive since it was inter-linked with matters of national law. If the 1993 Law were deemed to be in force on 1 January 1995, it would be covered by the derogation of Article 70. If, by contrast, the 1993 Law was deemed not to be in force on that date because of its subsequent annulment by the Constitutional Court, then it could not benefit from Article 70. In the latter case, the Law would be in breach of Community law, but would it be a serious breach for the purposes of State liability in damages?

By its second and third questions, the referring court asked respectively whether it is for the Court of Justice to assess whether a breach of Community law is sufficiently serious, and if so whether the breach met that condition in the circumstances of the case. The Court provided a laconic response. Referring to previous case law, it held that it is, in principle, for the national courts to apply the criteria to establish the liability of Member States in damages.[53] In view of that reply, it was not necessary to respond to the third question.

It may perhaps seem surprising that the Court did not give any guidelines to the national court and, in effect, made no attempt to engage in a dialogue. This readiness to delegate more competence to the national courts does not follow inevitably from *Brasserie du Pêcheur*. One may argue that the Court's reticence is understandable given that, in the circumstances, the seriousness or otherwise of the breach was to a good extent dependent on interlinking issues of national law. The judgment however is liable to give the impression that the notion of seriousness is for national law to decide. This is not a correct reading. 'Serious breach' is, as a legal notion, a matter of Community law and therefore ultimately for the Court of Justice to determine.

It is notable that Advocate General Sazzio was more forthcoming. His starting point was the same as that of the Court, namely that it is for the national court to verify whether the conditions governing State liability for breach of Community law are fulfilled. He argued however that the Court of Justice has the task of providing 'centralised supervision' through the dialogue facilitated by the preliminary reference procedure. It is thus for the Court to define the scope of a sufficiently serious breach by establishing the conditions in which an individual may claim protection of the right to reparation, and for the national court to determine whether those conditions are met on the facts of the case.[54] The Advocate General took the view that, in

---

EC Treaty. As stated above, that Law gave an end to the differential treatment of foreigners and extended the requirement of prior authorisation also to Austrian citizens. The Court however found that the procedure of authorisation was liable to work to the disadvantage of Community nationals and was also disproportionate. See paras 40 et seq. of the judgment.

[53] Case C-302/97 *Konle v Republic of Austria* [1999] ECR I-3099, paras 58–9.

[54] Ibid, Opinion of AG La Pergola, para 24.

the circumstances, the breach was not sufficiently serious. This is because the Community rules in issue where not clear and precise, since the scope of the derogation provided in Article 70 of the Act of Accession could not be ascertained easily. That analysis appears correct. The 1993 Law was overtly discriminatory; but what would make it infringe Community law, if it was finally established that there was an infringement, would not be its substantive content, which benefited from the temporal derogations provided for in the Act of Accession, but the fact that it turned out not to be 'existing legislation' because it was annulled with retroactive effect for breach of Austrian constitutional law. That does not appear, in principle, to be a serious breach.[55]

In contrast to *Konle* which concerned liability arising from legislation, *Haim II*[56] raised issues pertaining to liability arising from acts of the administration. Mr Haim was an Italian national who, after obtaining a diploma in dentistry from the University of Istanbul and practising in Turkey, obtained permission to practise as a self-employed dentist in Germany. His diploma was also recognised as equivalent to the domestic dentistry qualification in Belgium where, for a period, he worked as a dental practitioner under a social security scheme. When however he applied to the KVN, the German competent authority,[57] to become eligible for appointment as a dental practitioner under a social security scheme, his application was refused. The applicable German regulations made such eligibility subject to completion of a preparatory training period of at least two years. Under the regulations, that condition did not apply to dental practitioners who had obtained in another Member State a qualification recognised under Community law and who were authorised to practice dentistry there. The KVN refused to apply that exemption to Mr Haim since he did not hold a qualification from another Member State but only a diploma from a non-member country recognised by a Member State as equivalent to it own diplomas. In *Haim I*[58] the Court held that Directive 78/686 on the mutual recognition of dentistry qualifications[59] could not assist a person in the position of Mr Haim since he did not possess a diploma from another Member State. It held however that such a person had a right under Article

---

[55] Save perhaps for the exceptional case where it could be said that the Law was so manifestly against the right to property that, on the basis of the rules of domestic law, it could be foreseen with reasonable certainty that it would be annulled with retroactive effect.

[56] Case C424/97 *Haim II*, judgment of 4 July 2000.

[57] Kassenzahnärztliche Vereinigung Nordrhein (Association of Dental Practitioners of Social Security Schemes in Nordrhein).

[58] Case C-319/92 *Haim* [1994] ECR I-425.

[59] Council Directive 78/686/EEC of 25 July 1978 concerning the mutual recognition of diplomas, certificates and other evidence of the formal qualifications of practitioners of dentistry, including measures to facilitate the effective exercise of the right of establishment and freedom to provide services, OJ 1987 L 233, p. 1.

52 (now Article 43) EC to have his practical experience in another Member State taken into account for the purposes of establishing whether he has completed the preparatory period required by German law.

Following the judgment in *Haim I*, the German authorities enrolled Mr Haim on the register of dental practitioners eligible for appointment as dentists under a social security scheme. On account of his age, Mr Haim did not seek appointment but brought an action against the competent authority seeking compensation for the loss of earnings he had allegedly suffered in the past by its refusal to enrol him in the register. The Landgericht Düsseldorf before which the action was brought, absolved the KVN from liability on the ground that, although it had erred in refusing enrolment, it had acted in good faith. The regulations did not provide for a derogation from the obligation to complete a 2-year preparatory training period on account of professional experience acquired abroad. The decision of the KVN turned out to be unlawful on grounds of incompatibility with Article 52 EC. At the time the decision to refuse enrolment was taken, the question whether the freedom of establishment required professional experience gained in another Member State to be taken into account had not been decided. That question was only decided subsequently in *Vlassopoulou*.[60] On those grounds, the Landgericht Düsseldorf concluded that Mr Haim's action for damages had no basis in domestic law but sought a preliminary ruling in order to determine whether Mr Haim could derive a right to reparation directly from Community law.

The reference gave rise, *inter alia*, to issues pertaining to administrative discretion. The national court asked in particular whether, where a national official has applied national law in a manner not in conformity with Community law, the mere fact that the official did not have any discretion in taking his decision gives rise to a serious breach of Community law. Recalling its judgment in *Hedley Lomas*, the Court held that where, at the time when it committed an infringement, a Member State had only considerably reduced, or even no discretion, the mere infringement of Community law may be sufficient to establish the existence of a serious breach.[61] In *Haim II* the Court clarified that what matters is the discretion left to the Member State by Community law. The existence and scope of that discretion are determined by reference to Community law and not by reference to national law. The discretion which may be conferred by national law on the official or the institution responsible for the breach of Community law is, in this respect, irrelevant.[62]

---

[60] Case C-340/89 [1991] ECR I-2357.

[61] Case C424/97 *Haim II*, judgment of 4 July 2000, para 38.

[62] Ibid, para 40. It will be noted however that the discretion conferred by national law on a public authority may be relevant for the purposes of determining which body is responsible for making reparation, and therefore for identifying the proper defendant. See below.

It is interesting that in *Haim II* the Court was more forthcoming than in *Konle*. Although it reiterated that it was for the national court to examine whether there was a serious breach of Community law in the circumstances of the case, it recalled the factors laid down in *Brasserie* and gave some guidelines as to how those factors were to be applied. It stated that, when the German legislature adopted the regulation in question and the competent authority refused to enrol Mr Haim, the Court had not yet given judgment in *Vlassopoulou*, where it held for the first time that the host Member State must take into consideration the diplomas, certificates and other evidence of qualifications which the person concerned has acquired in another Member State.[63] The implication of the judgment appears to be that neither the German legislature nor the KVN had committed a serious breach.[64] That view was shared by Advocate General Mischo and also the Commission and the governments who submitted observations in the proceedings.

Given the allocation of competence between the Court of Justice and the national courts in the context of the preliminary reference procedure, the Court's input in some cases will be limited perforce. Thus, whilst the general direction of the remedy depends on the Court of Justice, its application on the facts depends on the referring court. Of the three conditions of liability, the only one which will be decided conclusively by the Court is the first, namely whether the provision breached is intended to grant rights to the injured party. That condition pertains to the interpretation of Community law which falls squarely within the jurisdiction of the Court of Justice. The other two conditions may be left to the national court, depending on the circumstances of the case. This point is reiterated by *Norbrook*.[65] The Ministry of Agriculture, Fisheries and Food refused to issue Norbrook with an authorisation for marketing a veterinary medicinal product before being supplied with further information concerning the supply, manufacturing process, and testing methods of a substance used by Norbrook for its manufacture. Norbrook argued that, under the terms of Directives 81/851 and 81/852,[66] the Ministry did not have the power to require the informa-

---

[63] Case C424/97 *Haim II*, judgment of 4 July 2000, para 46.

[64] The law was clarified in *Haim I* and, as we saw, the KVN revised its decision following that judgment. Clearly, if the German authorities had insisted in refusing to recognise Mr Haim's practical experience after that judgment, they would have committed a serious breach. Should the German authorities have revised their view already after Vlassopoulou which was delivered before *Haim I*? In other words, did the breach become serious as from Vlassopoulou? The answer is probably not. Vlassopoulou did not concern qualifications from third countries and the law did not become crystal clear until *Haim I*. Notably, after *Haim I*, the Commission proposed a corresponding amendment to Directive 78/686.

[65] Case C-127/95 *Norbrook Laboratories Limited v Ministry of Agriculture* [1998] ECR I-1531.

[66] Council Directive 81/851/EEC on the approximation of the laws of the Member States relating to veterinary medicinal products (OJ 1981, L317/1) and Council Directive

tion requested. Directive 81/851 seeks to harmonise the national laws relating to veterinary medicinal products and, inter alia, specifies the conditions for the issue, suspension and withdrawal of marketing authorisation. It provides that no such product may be marketed in a Member State unless authorisation has previously been issued by its competent authorities. Directive 81/852 lays down details concerning the particulars and documents to be submitted with an application for marketing authorisation. The Court interpreted Directive 81/851 as meaning that the competent authority is not authorised to require particulars and documents other than those expressly listed in its provisions. It held however that Directive 81/852 allows national authorities to require particulars of the manufacturing process and control testing methods used by the manufacturer, subject to certain conditions being fulfilled, which was for the national court to determine. The Court then proceeded to examine the issue of possible State liability in damages arising as a result of the refusal to issue authorisation. It held that the directives granted a right to obtain authorisation if certain conditions were fulfilled. Since those conditions were laid down precisely and exhaustively in their provisions, the scope of the right conferred on applicants was sufficiently identified. As regards the other two conditions of liability, the Court simply referred to its previous case law, and left it to the national court to determine whether they were fulfilled.

VI. WHICH AUTHORITY IS RESPONSIBLE FOR PROVIDING REPARATION?

In *Konle* and, especially, in *Haim II* the Court had the opportunity to provide some guidance on the question which national authority bears the obligation to provide reparation and is the proper defendant in an action for damages. This issue had not been examined hitherto in the case-law. The principles which emerge from *Konle* and *Haim II* can be summarised as follows.

As a general rule, the question which authority is liable to provide compensation is for national law to decide. Community law imposes limitations which derive, in the first place, from the right to reparation itself and, in the second place, the principles of effectiveness and equivalence. The basic obligation incumbent on Member States is to ensure that individuals obtain reparation for loss or damage caused to them by non-compliance with Community law. This principle must be honoured whichever public authority is responsible for the breach and whichever public authority is,

81/852/EEC on the approximation of the laws of the Member States relating to analytical pharmaco-toxicological and clinical standards and protocols in respect of the testing of veterinary medicinal products (OJ 1981 L 317/16).

under national law, responsible for making reparation.[67] In *Haim II* the
Court declared that a Member State may not escape liability by pleading the
distribution of powers and responsibilities as between the bodies which
exist within the national legal order or by claiming that the public authority responsible for the breach of Community law does not have 'the necessary power, knowledge, means or resources'.[68] A further obligation derives
its origins from the *Rewe* and *Comet* case-law.[69] The procedural arrangements and the conditions from reparation laid down by national law must
not be less favourable than those relating to similar domestic claims (principle of equivalence) and must not be so framed as to make it excessively
difficult to obtain reparation (principle of effectiveness).[70]

The dictum that a Member State may not avoid liability by claiming that
the body responsible for the breach of Community law did not have the
necessary power, knowledge, means or resources is of considerable importance. It is phrased in general terms and appears to be a minimum requirement deriving from the principle of effectiveness. If that is correct, it must
be honoured in all cases, ie, even if national law does not guarantee an
equivalent degree of protection for comparable claims based on national
law. The issue may be crucial in relation to independent public bodies
which enjoy budgetary autonomy.

Subject to the requirements stated above, it is up to each Member State
to ensure the way individuals obtain reparation. Thus, in Member States
with federal structure, reparation for damage need not necessarily be
provided by the federal State.[71] Analogous principles apply to States with
unitary structure. In *Haim II*, it was held that where a Member State
devolves legislative or administrative tasks to a public law body legally
distinct from the State, reparation for loss caused by measures taken by that
body may be made by it and not by the State.[72] Similarly, Community law
does not preclude a public law body from being liable to make reparation
in addition to the State itself.[73]

It follows from *Haim II* that a Member State may devolve liability to an
independent public law agency responsible for the breach or be jointly

---

[67] Case C-302/97 *Konle v Republic of Austria* [1999] ECR I-3099, para 62; Case C424/97
Haim II, judgment of 4 July 2000, para 27.
[68] Case C424/97 *Haim II*, judgment of 4 July 2000, para 28.
[69] Case 33/76 *Rewe v Landwirtschaftskammer für das Saarland* [1976] ECR 1989; Case
45/76 *Comet v Productschap voor Siergewassen* [1976] ECR 2043.
[70] Case C424/97 *Haim II*, judgment of 4 July 2000, paras 30, 33; Case C-302/97 *Konle v
Republic of Austria* [1999] ECR I-3099, para 63; Joined Cases C-6 and C-9/90 *Francovich and
others* [1991] ECR I-5357, paras 41–3; Case C-127/95 *Norbrook Laboratories Limited v
Ministry of Agriculture* [1998] ECR I-1531, para 111.
[71] Case C-302/97 *Konle v Republic of Austria* [1999] ECR I-3099, para 64.
[72] Case C424/97 *Haim II*, judgment of 4 July 2000, para 31.
[73] Ibid, para 32.

liable with such an agency. Although the judgment is phrased in terms of facilitation, the requirement of equivalence may in fact fetter, or even remove altogether, national discretion. If domestic law provides for the liability of a public body for a comparable breach of national law, the principle of equivalence requires that the body must also be held responsible for the breach of EC law. The converse is also true: an action for damages against the State for breach of Community law by an independent public authority must be available if it is available for comparable breaches of national law.

The crucial consideration here is that the claims must be comparable. But what is a comparable claim?[74] The requirement of equivalence applies 'where the purpose and cause of actions are similar.'[75] In principle it is for the national court to establish the similarity of claims and, in doing so, it must consider 'the purpose and essential characteristics' of allegedly similar domestic actions.[76] This is by no means a mechanical exercise. Some intricate questions may arise in this context. What if there are more than one comparable claims in national law? Does the individual have a choice? In some cases, it may not even be possible to specify in general terms which alternative cause of action is more favourable to the individual because an action may be more favourable in some respects but less so in other respects. It is submitted that the individual is not necessarily entitled to choose the most favourable treatment in the circumstances. The objective of the case law is not to treat claims based on Community law preferentially over claims of domestic law. It suffices if the national legal system affords the injured party an effective opportunity to seek reparation. If a claimant under Community law had unlimited choice or were allowed to 'cherry pick' and combine elements from different causes of action, that would lead to uncertainty and disrupt the national systems of procedure and remedies.[77]

The issue whether an independent administrative authority as opposed to the State itself is liable may depend on whether it had any discretion in taking the decision which amounted to a serious breach of Community law.

---

[74] For a detailed analysis, see Tridimas, 'Enforcing Community Rights in National Courts', 468–71.

[75] See Case C-78/98 *Preston and Other v Wolverhampton Healthcare NHS Trust and Others and Fletcher and Others v Midland Bank plc*, judgment of 16 May 2000, para 55; Case C-326/96 *Levez v Jennings (Harlow Pools) Ltd* [1998] ECR I-7835, para 41; Case C-231/96 *Edis v Ministero delle Finanze* [1998] ECR I-4951, para 15.

[76] Case C-78/98 *Preston and Other v Wolverhampton Healthcare NHS Trust and Others and Fletcher and Others v Midland Bank plc*, judgment of 16 May 2000, para 56; Case C-326/96 *Levez v Jennings (Harlow Pools) Ltd* [1998] ECR I-7835, para 43; Case C-261/95 *Palmisani v Istituto Nazionale della Previdenza Sociale (INPS)* [1997] ECR I- 4025, paras 34-8.

[77] See also M Hoskins, 'Rebirth of the Innominate Tort?', in Beatson and Tridimas (eds), *New Directions in European Public Law*, 100.

If the administrative authority was bound by national legislation in taking the decision, it might be more difficult to hold it liable for the ensuing breach of Community law. If, by contrast, it enjoyed discretion under national law and could have exercised it in such a way as not to commit a serious breach, it would be easier to allocate liability to the authority itself. These are, however, considerations to be taken into account by national law. Community law does not appear to impose any hard and fast rules in this respect.[78]

What if a Member State has delegated functions to a private body? Although *Haim II* refers to the liability of 'public-law bodies', it is submitted that national law is not in principle precluded from devolving liability to a body governed by private law to which public functions have been delegated and which, in the exercise of those functions, is responsible for an actionable breach of Community law. A host of consequential issues arise from *Haim II*. If an individual successfully brings an action for reparation against an independent public agency, may in turn that agency seek to recover its loss against the State on the ground that the breach of Community law was in fact attributable to the latter? This question acquires importance where the authority is independent from central government and enjoys budgetary autonomy, for example a professional association enjoying public law status. A further question relates to causation. What happens in cases where the applicant has successfully established a breach of Community law but there is uncertainty as to whether the breach is attributable to the State or an independent public authority? In other words, is it a condition for the success of the action that the applicant must be able to establish firmly a direct causal link with the action of a specific body? In principle, the question should be answered in the affirmative. In some cases, however, it may not be easy determine which body should be sued and failure to identify the proper defendant may cost the success of the action. A claim for reparation against an independent public agency may need to be brought in a different court from a claim against the State. The danger is that an applicant who decides to bring an action against the agency and finds his claim rejected on the ground that the action should have been brought against the State, may find his action against the latter time-barred. It should be emphasised here that, in addition to the requirements laid down above, Community law imposes an

---

[78] See the Opinion of AG Mischo in *Haim II*, para 32. In a different context, the Court has declared that all national authorities are under an obligation to uphold the principle of primacy and ensure the effective protection of Community rights, if necessary, by setting aside any obstacles posed by national law, including national legislation. See, eg, Case 106/77 *Simmenthal* [1978] ECR 629 and Case 103/88, *Fratelli Costanzo v Comune di Milano* [1989] ECR 1839. The Court recently reiterated the application of this principle in relation to administrative authorities: see Case C-224/97 *Ciola v Land Vorarlberg*, judgment of 29 Apr 2000.

additional requirement founded on the principle of legal certainty. The rules of national law pertaining to the right of reparation for breach of Community law must give to individuals an effective opportunity to claim reparation and must be clear and precise so that citizens are able to understand them.[79]

Finally, if national law makes the right to reparation for loss suffered as a result of breach of domestic law subject to less stringent conditions than those laid down in the Court's case-law, the principle of equivalence requires that those conditions must also apply to a claim for reparation based on breach of Community law. The issue of comparability of claims arises here once again and, with it, some interesting questions. For example, the law of a Member State may provide for a right to damages for the breach of the general principle of non-discrimination as guaranteed in the national constitution or, more specifically, for discrimination on grounds of race, including nationality.[80] Would then an applicant who had suffered loss as a result of discrimination contrary to a fundamental freedom, such as the right of establishment, be able to rely on that cause of action and thus avoid the requirement of a 'serious' breach? This of course assumes that the 'comparable' cause of action under national law is more favourable to the individual but this may not be excluded in some cases. Suffice to point out here the unexploited potential of the principle of equivalence. This principle penetrates the fabric of national law and, in some ways, is more onerous for the Member States than the principle of effectiveness. It penetrates the fabric national law. Effectiveness and equivalence together force the national courts to revisit national rules, unveil the inter-relationship of national remedies, and unearth inconsistencies hidden in the evolution of national legal systems.

VII. REVERSING THE INFLUENCE: THE CONDITIONS OF COMMUNITY LIABILITY
RE-VISITED

In parallel to the developments discussed above, there has been a renewed effort to unify the conditions of Community and State liability and redefine the former on the basis of the latter.

In *Brasserie*, the Court declared that the conditions under which a Member State may incur liability for breach of Community law cannot, in the absence of particular justification, differ from those governing the liability of the

---

[79] Cf the case law on national measures transposing directives: Case 29/84 *Commission v Germany* [1985] ECR 1661; Case C119/92 *Commission v Italy* [1994] ECR I-393; Case C-236/95 *Commission v Greece* [1996] ECR I-4459.

[80] This is the case with the Race Relations Act in the United Kingdom.

Community institutions in like circumstances.[81] On that basis, the Court proceeded to define serious breach, in cases where the national authorities enjoy wide discretion, by reference to the test of 'manifest and grave disregard'.[82] Despite this general pronouncement of principle, the Court did not pursue the analogy consistently. It is not clear from *Brasserie* that the conditions of State liability correspond in substance to those of the Community institutions under Article 215(2) (now 288(2)) EC.[83] A further criticism is that, as the case law on State liability developed, it did not seem to pay much attention to the case-law under Article 215(2).[84]

Despite these criticisms, the basic premise that the liability of Community and national authorities must be governed by similar principles is well founded. As the Court expressly stated, the protection of the rights of the individual cannot vary depending on whether a national or a Community authority is responsible for the damage.[85] In *Brasserie*, the correlation between State and Community liability served a dual rationale: it underlined the affinity between State liability and the rule of law, and served as a source of legitimacy for the Court's bold move to recognise a right to reparation against Member States. It should of course be borne in mind that, as there are strong similarities between Community and State liability, so there are important disparities between the two. Suffice it to refer here to the different constraints under which the Community and the national legislature operate within the bounds of the Community legal order: whilst the first act as primary legislature, the second are bound by the principle of primacy.[86]

Be that as it may, the Court's dicta in *Brasserie* inevitably opened the way for the dialectical development of the law: If Community liability is capable of influencing State liability, the reverse must also be true. Indeed, in its recent judgment in *Laboratoires Pharmaceutiques Bergaderm and Goupil v Commission*[87] the Court reversed the correlation by relying, for the first time, on its case law on State liability to determine the conditions applicable to the liability of the Community institutions.

---

[81] *Brasserie*, para 42. Already, in his Opinion in *Francovich*, AG Mischo had sought inspiration from the case law under Art 215(2) (now 288(2)) EC to establish the right to reparation against the State. In its judgment, the Court did not draw any analogy between Community and Member State liability, probably because the type of breach in issue, namely failure to implement a directive, did not lend itself to such a comparison.

[82] *Brasserie*, para 45.

[83] See further Tridimas, *The General Principles of EC Law*, 333.

[84] Van Gerven, 'Taking Article 215(2) EC Seriously'.

[85] *Brasserie*, para 42.

[86] This was expressly recognised in *Brasserie*: see para 46 of the judgment.

[87] Case C-352/98 P, *Laboratoires Pharmaceutiques Bergaderm and Goupil v Commission*, judgment of 4 July 2000 confirming on appeal the CFI's judgment in Case T-199/96 *Bergaderm and Goupil v Commission* [1998] ECR II-2805.

Before examining this case, it is helpful to recall briefly the conditions under which the Community institutions may incur liability pursuant to Article 288(2) EC.[88] In general, a right to reparation arises where the injured party has suffered damage causally connected with an unlawful act attributable to a Community institution.[89] In relation to administrative acts, it is accepted that any kind of illegality may give rise to liability. The case law states that, in the field of administrative action, any infringement of law constitutes illegality which may give rise to liability on the part of the Community.[90] Liability arising as a result of legislation is subject to much stricter conditions. Under the *Schöppenstedt* formula, there are three crucial considerations: there must be violation of *a superior rule of law*; that rule must be intended *for the protection of the individual*; and the violation must be *serious*.[91]

The most troublesome requirement is that the violation must be serious. But what does that mean? According to the test first enunciated in *HNL v Council and Commission*,[92] in areas where the Community legislature enjoys wide discretion, the Community may not incur liability 'unless the institution concerned has manifestly and gravely disregarded the limits on the exercise of powers'. The requirement of manifest and grave disregard applies to all legislative measures in relation to which the institution concerned enjoys wide discretion, whether or not they are measures of economic policy.[93] By contrast, where the Commission does not enjoy wide discretionary powers, the requirement that the violation must be sufficiently serious is not exemplified by the condition that it must have manifestly and gravely disregarded the limits of its powers.[94] The case law, however, is not

---

[88] For a detailed analysis, see TC Hartley, *The Foundations of European Community Law*, 4th edn (Oxford: Oxford University Press, 1999), ch 17, and T Heukels and A McDonell (eds), *The Action for Damages in Community Law* (The Hague: Kluwer, 1997).

[89] See, eg, Case 4/69 *Lütticke v Commission* [1971] ECR 325, para 10; Case T-575/93 *Koelman v Commission* [1996] ECR II-1, para 89.

[90] Case 145/83 *Adams v Commission* [1985] ECR 3539; Case T-390/94 *Aloys Schröder et al v Commission* [1997] ECR II-501, para 51. For an extensive discussion, see MH Van der Woude, 'Liability for Administrative Acts under Article 215(2) EC', in Heukels and McDonell (eds), *The Action for Damages in Community Law*, 109–28. An administrative act in this context is defined as one 'by which the administration applies general rules in individual cases or otherwise exercises its executive powers in an individual manner'. See Van der Woude, at 112 where further references are given.

[91] Case 5/71 *Zuckerfabrik Schöppenstedt v Council* [1971] ECR 975. And see also, eg, Joined Cases 83 and 94/76, 4, 15 and 40/77 *HNL v Council and Commission* [1978] ECR 1209.

[92] Joined Cases 83 and 94/76, 4, 15 and 40/77 *HNL v Council and Commission* [1978] ECR 1209, para 6.

[93] See, eg, Case C-63/89 *Assurances du Crédit v Council and Commission* [1991] ECR I-1799. In any event, what is a measure of economic policy is difficult to define. See Tridimas, *The General Principles of EC Law*, 320.

[94] See, eg, Case C-152/88 *Sofrimport v Commission* [1990] ECR I-2477; cf the Opinion of AG Tesauro at 2502; Joined Cases 44-51/77 *Union Malt v Commission* [1978] ECR 57.

consistent. In the *Live Pigs* case, for example, the CFI seemed to suggest that the requirement of serious breach applies only where the measure is legislative in character *and* the author of the act enjoys wide discretion.[95] Also, in some cases the Court has not even referred to the *Schöppenstedt* formula even though the alleged loss arose as a result of legislative action.[96] Also, it is notable that the test of manifest and grave disregard applies only in relation to legislative measures. The case law has not applied it to administrative measures, even where such measures entail the exercise of wide discretionary powers.[97]

The factual background to *Bergaderm* was defined by the Cosmetics Directive[98] which requires Member States to prohibit the marketing of cosmetic products containing the substances specified in Annex II to the directive. It also sets up an Adaptation Committee, consisting of representatives of the Member States and a representative of the Commission acting as chairman, whose task is to propose the amendments necessary to adapt Annex II to technical progress. The procedure to be followed for the introduction of amendments is provided for in Article 10 of the Directive.

Bergaderm SA brought an action against the Commission seeking to recover compensation for the loss that it had allegedly suffered by the adoption of a directive restricting the use of a carcinogenic molecule used by Bergaderm in the manufacture of a sun oil called Bergasol. The directive in issue was an adaptation directive adopted by the Commission following the recommendation of the Adaptation Committee. Bergaderm claimed that the Adaptation Directive concerned exclusively Bergasol and therefore was to be regarded as an administrative act. It claimed that the Commission had adopted the Directive in breach of the procedural requirements laid down in Article 10 of the Cosmetics Directive and also Bergaderm's rights of defence.[99] Further, it argued that the Commission had committed a mani-

---

[95] Joined cases T-481 and T-484/93 *Vereniging van Exporteurs in Levende Varkens and Another v Commission* [1995] ECR II-2941, para 81.

[96] See Case 81/86 *De Boer Buizen v Council and Commission* [1987] ECR 3677 and the Christmas Butter cases (Joined Cases 279, 280, 285 and 286/84 *Rau v Commission* [1987] ECR 1069, Case 27/85 *Vandemoortele v Commission* [1987] ECR 1129, Case 265/85 *Van den Bergh en Jurgens v Commission* [1987] ECR 1155). See further MH Van der Woude, 'Liability for Administrative Acts under Article 215(2) EC', in Heukels and McDonell (eds), *The Action for Damages in Community Law*, 113–14.

[97] See Van der Woude, op cit, and see Joined Cases T-458 and T-523/93 *ENU v Commission* [1995] ECR II-2459, para 67 (loss allegedly arising from the Commission's failure to guarantee disposal of the applicant's uranium production pursuant to Art 53 Euratom). That case however does not provide authority that the CFI rejected the test of manifest and grave disregard in relation to administrative acts.

[98] Council Directive 76/768 of 27 July 1976 on the approximation of the laws of the Member States relating to cosmetic products (OJ 1976 L 262/ 169). The Directive has been amended, inter alia, by Council Directive 93/35/EEC of 14 June 1993, OJ 1993 L 151/32.

[99] Art 10 of the Cosmetics Directive requires that, when the Adaptation Committee delivers an unfavourable opinion on the draft measures submitted by the Commission, the latter

fest error of assessment and a breach of the principle of proportionality in considering that Bergasol posed a risk to public health, and also had misused its powers.

The CFI held that the Adaptation Directive was a measure of general application and therefore, under the established case law, liability would ensue only if, in adopting it, the Commission had disregarded a superior rule of law for the protection of the individual. It held that it was not necessary to examine whether the provisions governing the procedure for the adoption of the Adaptation Directive were such rules since, in any event, the Commission had not infringed them. It also rejected Bergaderm's other arguments.

On appeal, Bergaderm argued, *inter alia*, that the CFI had erred in law by considering the Adaptation Directive as a legislative measure and also that the CFI was incorrect in deciding that there was no breach of a superior rule of law. The Court rejected the appeal. The importance of the judgment lies not so much on the outcome reached on the facts but on certain pronouncements of principle made by the Court sitting in plenum. The Court began by referring to *Brasserie* as an authority on the interpretation of Article 215(2) EC (now 288(2)).[100] It then reiterated the principle that the conditions under which a State may incur liability should not, in the absence of particular justification, differ from those governing the liability of Community institutions in like circumstances, and re-stated the conditions which must be fulfilled in order for State liability to arise. Referring to *Hedley Lomas*, it held that, where the Member State 'or the [Community] institution in question' has only considerably reduced discretion, the mere infringement of Community law may be sufficient to establish the existence of a sufficiently serious breach.[101] The Court then proceeded to examine whether the CFI had erred in law in its examination of the way in which the Commission exercised its discretion in adopting the Adaptation Directive. Crucially, it held that the general or individual nature of a measure taken by an institution is not a decisive factor for identifying the limits of the discretion enjoyed by the institution in question.[102] On that

---

must without delay propose measures to the Council, which acts by a qualified majority. If, within three months of the proposal being submitted to it, the Council has not acted, the proposed measures are to be adopted by the Commission. Bergaderm argued that the Commission breached Art 10 because instead of returning to the Council when the Adaptation Committee delivered an unfavourable opinion on 1 June 1992, concerning its proposal to restrict the maximum level of the substance in issue, it submitted the same proposal some years later.

[100] Case C-352/98 P, *Laboratoires Pharmaceutiques Bergaderm and Goupil v Commission*, judgment of 4 July 2000, para 40.

[101] Ibid, para 44; *Brasserie*, para 43.

[102] Case C-352/98 P, *Laboratoires Pharmaceutiques Bergaderm and Goupil v Commission*, judgment of 4 July 2000, para 46.

basis, it rejected the appellant's first ground which was based exclusively on the categorisation of the Adaptation Directive as an individual measure.[103] After rejecting the other arguments presented by Bergaderm, the Court turned to examine its final ground of appeal. By that the appellant claimed that, contrary to what the CFI had found, there was breach of higher-ranking rules of law for the protection of the individual. The Court rejected once more the appellant's arguments but what matters more is its reasoning. In the light of the unified conditions of liability laid down earlier on in the judgment, the Court interpreted the last ground of appeal as alleging that the CFI misinterpreted the legislation in considering that the Commission did not infringe a rule of law intended to confer rights on individuals.[104] The absence of the *Schöppenstedt* formula in paragraph 62 of the judgment is conspicuous and deliberate.

Bergaderm unifies the conditions of liability. For a right to reparation against a national authority or a Community institution to arise, the conditions of liability are the same, namely, the rule breached must be intended to grant rights to individuals, the violation must be serious, and there must be a direct causal link. This derives from paragraphs 41, 42, and 62 of the judgment. In *Brasserie* the Court had already declared in the context of State liability that the above conditions 'correspond in substance' to those defined in relation to Article 288(2) (ex 215(2)) EC.[105] The new elements in *Bergaderm* are two: first, the express unification of the conditions of liability in relation to both legislative and administrative Community acts and, secondly, the fact that this time the influence was reverse: the Court sought inspiration from *Brasserie* to determine the conditions of liability under Article 288(2) EC. It is notable that the Court linked Community liability to State liability at its own instigation without being prompted by the Advocate General who, in his Opinion, proposed the rejection of the appeal following a classic approach.[106] No such trend was evident in any other case on Community liability decided recently.[107]

---

[103] Case C-352/98 P, para 47.   [104] Ibid, para 62.   [105] *Brasserie*, para 53.

[106] AG Fennelly opined that the Directive in issue was a legislative and not an administrative measure for the purposes of determining the applicable conditions of liability. The requirement therefore that there must be violation of a superior rule of law for the protection of the individual had to be satisfied. He found that the Commission had not committed a violation. Furthermore, in his view, the alleged breach of the procedural requirements of the Cosmetics Directive were not superior rules of law for the protection of the individual since their aim was to protect the division of powers between the various Community institutions and not to protect individuals. See, also in this context, Case C-282/90 *Vreugdenhil v Commission* [1992] ECR I-1937.

[107] See, eg, Case C-13/99 P *TEAM Srl v Commission*, judgment of 15 June 2000; Case C-237/98 P Dorsch, *Consult Ingenieurgesellschaft mbH*, judgment of 15 June 2000. The legal context of neither case lent itself to the unification of the conditions of liability and reversal of influence. Both judgments were delivered by a five-member chamber.

Bergaderm places particular emphasis on the degree of discretion enjoyed by the author of the act for the purposes of determining whether the breach is serious. The degree of discretion is critical both in relation to Community and to national authorities,[108] and both in relation to administrative and legislative acts.[109] The most important aspect of *Bergaderm* is precisely this, ie, that it links liability with discretion irrespective of the administrative or legislative character of the measure. In doing so, it does away with the need to draw artificial distinctions between legislative and administrative measures.[110] It also recognises that, in certain cases, the Community administration may enjoy ample discretion and may be called upon to make choices which are equally difficult, complex and sensitive as those of the legislature, and its liability should therefore be governed by the same conditions. It thus opens the way for the test of manifest and grave breach to be applied as a condition governing liability for administrative acts, where the administration enjoys wide discretion.

Bergaderm seems to lay down the requirement of serious breach as a general condition of liability. In its case law under Article 288(2) (ex 215(2)) EC, the Court has not expressly articulated that requirement as a condition of liability arising as a result of administrative action. The reason why seriousness has not featured as a condition in this context is probably that there has not been much need to develop such a conceptual tool. The cases where a natural or legal person suffers loss directly as a result of Community action are relatively few because Community law is administered mainly at national level. By contrast, in the context of normative injustice, the notion of seriousness has served both a constitutional and an economic rationale by underscoring the exceptional character of liability. It is submitted however that the introduction of seriousness as a general condition of liability is helpful both from the methodological and the substantive point of view. In terms of methodology, it serves to structure better the judicial enquiry. In terms of substance, it recognises the growth in Community administrative powers and that in certain cases the Community administration may be called upon to make difficult policy choices entailing the exercise of broad discretion.

---

[108] *Bergaderm*, para 40.

[109] Ibid, para 46. On that basis the Court proceeded to find that the first ground of appeal, which was based exclusively on the categorisation of the Adaptation Directive as an individual measure, had in any event no bearing on the issue and should be rejected. See para 47.

[110] Notably, the Court treats as a legislative measure for the purposes of determining the conditions of liability in an action for damages under Art 288(2) any measure of general application irrespective of whether it may be of individual concern for the purposes of Art 230(4) (ex 173(4)) EC: see Case C-152/88 *Sofrimport v Commission* [1990] ECR I-2477; See Joined Cases T-480 and T-483/93 *Antillean Rice Mills and Others v Commission* [1995] ECR II-2305, confirmed on this point on appeal C-390/95 P [1999] ECR I-769. See also the Opinion of the AG in *Bergaderm*.

The introduction of seriousness as a condition of liability does not mean that it will now be more difficult to render the Community administration liable. In fact, so far very few actions under Article 288(2) (ex 215(2)) against administrative acts have succeeded[111] and it is submitted that in those cases the breach was sufficiently serious. If *Bergaderm* was applicable, the result would not have been affected.

With regard to legislative acts, *Bergaderm* seems to replace the previous formula that there must be *a violation of a superior rule of law for the protection of the individual* with the condition that the defendant institution must have infringed *'a rule of law intended to confer rights on individuals'*.[112] Despite the difference in phraseology, the requirement that the rule must intend to protect the individual is conceptually the same. It appears, however, that there is no longer reference to breach of a 'superior' rule of law. To appreciate the significance of this aspect of the judgment, we need to examine briefly the previous case-law under Article 288(2) (ex 215(2)).

The requirement that there must be violation of a superior rule of law for the protection of individual resembles the German *Schutznormtheorie*, according to which the State is liable only where it breaches a legal norm which protects a subjective public right of the injured party. The legal norm in issue must be intended to protect a specific group to which the injured party belongs rather than merely the public in general.[113] Under Community law, the condition that the rule must be for the protection of the individual is not difficult to satisfy. It suffices that the rule is intended to protect interests of a general nature, for example the interests of producers in a certain sector. The test is therefore less stringent than the requirement of direct and individual concern applicable to establish *locus standi* in actions for judicial review under Article 230(4) (ex 173(4) EC).[114]

Certain principles are fundamental to the Community legal order but do not have as their purpose the protection of individual rights. In *Vreugdenhil*, it was held that the objective of the rules governing the division of powers between the institutions is not to protect the individual but to maintain a balance between the institutions. Therefore, illegality of a

---

[111] Case 145/83 *Adams v Commission* [1985] ECR 3539; Case T-514/93 *Cobrecaf v Commission* [1995] ECR II-624.

[112] *Bergaderm*, para 62. Emphasis added.

[113] See Arnull, 'Liability for Legislative Acts under Art 215(2) EC', in Heukels and McDonell (eds), *The Action for Damages in Community Law*, 129, 136 and see AG Darmon's Opinion in Case C-282/90 *Vreugdenhil v Commission* [1992] ECR I-1937.

[114] See Joined Cases 5, 7 and 13-24/66 *Kampfmeyer v Commission* [1967] ECR 245, at 263; See also Case 5/71 *Zuckerfabrik Schöppenstedt v Council* [1971] ECR 975; Joined Cases 9 and12/60 *Vloeberghs v High Authority* [1961] ECR 195; Case 9/56 *Meroni v High Authority* [1958] ECR 133; Joined Cases 9 and 11/71 *Compagnie d'Approvisionnement v Commission* [1972] ECR 391.

measure which arises from failure to observe the institutional balance, as for example where the Commission exceeds its implementing powers, is not sufficient on its own to give rise to liability in damages.[115] The Court has also held that breach of the duty to state reasons may not give rise to liability in damages,[116] even though in a different context it has asserted the importance of Article 253 (ex 190) EC for enabling individuals to protect their rights and the Court to exercise its judicial function.[117]

By contrast, the Court has not placed much importance on the requirement that the rule of law must be superior. The omission of this term in *Bergaderm* does not seem to make a great deal of difference. Save in very exceptional circumstances,[118] a Community legislative act cannot give rise to liability unless it is illegal, namely, unless it breaches a higher-ranking rule of law. Such a rule may fall into one of three categories:[119] (a) It may be a provision of the Treaty or other primary Community law; (b) It may be a general principle of law, such as equal treatment or protection of legitimate expectations; (c) It may be a Community act which in formal ranking stands higher than the Community act which caused damage, as for example where a Commission regulation breaches the terms of its parent Council regulation. It seems then that, in principle, the breach of a 'superior' rule of law is implicit in the concept of unlawfulness which normally is a condition for Community liability to arise. Following *Bergaderm*, the requirement that there must be manifest and grave disregard continues to apply where a legislative act has been adopted in the exercise of wide discretionary powers. This will usually, but not invariably, be the case.[120]

Finally, it should be noted that the unification of the conditions of liability in *Begarderm* has implications also for State liability. It reiterates the view that, in the context of State liability, the notions of seriousness of breach and causal relationship are for Community law and not for national law to determine, although in most cases their application on the facts will be left to the national court.

---

[115] Case C-282/90 *Vreugdenhil v Commission* [1992] ECR I-1937.

[116] Case 106/81 *Kind v EEC* [1982] ECR 2885, para 14, and see more recently the CFI's case law: Case T-167/94 *Nölle v Council and Commission* [1994] ECR II-2589, para 57; Case T-390/94 *Aloys Schröder et al v Commission* [1997] ECR II-501, para 66.

[117] See, eg, Case 294/81 *Control Data v Commission* [1983] ECR 911, para 14, Case 250/84 *Eridania v Cassa Conguaglio Zucchero* [1986] ECR 117, para 37.

[118] In exceptional circumstances, an applicant may be entitled to compensation for 'unusual' and 'special' damage occurring as a result of a valid legislative act. See Case T-184/95 *Dorsch Consult Ingenieurgesellschaft v Council* [1998] ECR II-667; confirmed on appeal: Case C-237/98 P Dorsch *Consult Ingenieurgesellschaft mbH*, judgment of 15 June 2000. So far, however, no such action has been successful.

[119] See Craig and De Burca, *EU Law, Text, Cases, and Materials*, 2nd edn (Oxford: Oxford University Press, 1998), 518.

[120] See above.

Despite the renewed attempt to unify the conditions of liability in *Bergaderm* important gaps in the analogy between Community and State liability remain. In its case law under Article 288(2) (ex 215(2)), the Court refers to two elements in determining whether there is a manifest and grave disregard of discretionary powers, namely, the extent to which the law has been violated and also the effect of the measure on individuals. The latter element is exemplified by the requirement that the damage alleged by the applicants must go beyond the bounds of the economic risks inherent in the activities in the sector concerned.[121] That requirement, however, was not mentioned in *Brasserie* as a prerequisite for the establishment of State liability in damages and has not been mentioned by the Court in subsequent cases on the liability of national authorities.

Also, in *Brasserie* the Court drew an analogy between State and EC liability only as far as the basis and the conditions of liability are concerned, not as regards the remedy of reparation. On the contrary, in *Haim II* it reasserted that it is for the Member States to establish that remedy subject to the principles of equivalence and effectiveness. There is here a lack of consistency: The case law under Article 215(2) has in fact much to teach State liability and it is somewhat surprising that the Court has not made more use of it.[122]

VIII. THE RESPONSE OF THE CFI

In *Fresh Marine Company AS v Commission*,[123] decided only (a) few months after *Bergaderm*, the CFI somewhat muddled the waters by following the traditional case law under Article 288(2) (ex 215(2)) and attributing importance to the nature of the measure from which the alleged damage arose. The applicant was a Norwegian company which, in order to avoid the imposition of anti-dumping and anti-subsidy duties, had given the Commission an undertaking that it would not sell salmon in the Community below a certain price. On the basis of a report submitted by the applicant, the Commission took the view that, during the third quarter of 1997, the applicant had failed to observe its undertaking, and adopted a regulation imposing a provisional anti-dumping duty. Subsequently, following clarifications provided by the applicant, the Commission concluded that it had not broken its undertaking and repealed the provisional duties. The applicant brought an action seeking to recover the damage which it had allegedly suffered by not being able to export salmon to the Community

---

[121] See above, eg, Joined cases C-104-89 and C-37/90, *Mulder* [1992] ECR I-3061, para 13.

[122] See Van Gerven, 'Taking Article 215(2) EC Seriously'.

[123] Case T-178/98 *Fresh Marine Company AS v Commission*, judgment of 24 Oct 2000.

during the period when the provisional duties were in force. It argued that the Commission's decision to revoke the undertaking and impose provisional duties should not be regarded as an administrative act but as a bundle of individual decisions targeted against it and therefore the *Shoppenstedt* test should not apply. The Commission counter-argued that the alleged damage was caused by a legislative act and therefore the higher level of gravity provided by the case law in relation to legislative acts had to be satisfied.

Referring to its earlier case law, the CFI reiterated that, in principle, anti-dumping measures are legislative acts involving choices of economic policy and therefore the Community may incur liability only if there is a sufficiently serious rule of law for the protection of the individual.[124] It pointed out however the special features of that case. Although the anti-dumping duties had been imposed by a regulation, by adopting that measure the Commission was not in fact exercising economic policy but giving effect to the conclusions drawn from its analysis of the report submitted by the applicant.[125] In view of those distinct characteristics, the CFI held that, in the circumstances, there was no need to satisfy the *Shoppenstedt* test and that the mere infringement of Community law would be sufficient to lead to liability. It referred in support of that proposition to *Bergaderm*.[126] It held that 'a finding of an error which, in analogous circumstances, an administrative authority exercising ordinary care and diligence would not have committed will support the conclusion that the conduct of the Community institution was unlawful in such a way as to render the Community liable under Article (288 (ex 215)) of the Treaty.[127] On that basis, it proceeded to examine whether the Commission had committed such an error when monitoring compliance by the applicant with its undertaking. It came to the conclusion that the Commission had breached its duty of diligence, although it also found contributory negligence on the part of the applicant.

Fresh Marine Company reiterates that the test of manifest and grave disregard does not apply in relation to legislative acts, whose adoption does not entail the exercise of wide discretionary powers. This was already established in previous case law[128] and conforms to *Bergaderm*. The judgment of the CFI, however, does not reflect the tenor of *Bergaderm*. The latter links the gravity of the breach primarily with discretion whereas *Fresh*

---

[124] *Fresh Marine*, ibid, para 57, and see Case T-167/94 *Nölle v Council and Commission* [1995] ECR II-2589.

[125] *Fresh Marine*, ibid, paras 58–60. The CFI also distinguished previous case law, ie T-167/94, *Nolle* [1995] ECR II-2589 and C-122/86, *Metallefticon* [1989] ECR 3959.

[126] *Fresh Marine*, ibid, para 61.

[127] Ibid.

[128] See text accompanying n 94 above.

Marine continues to be dominated by the distinction between legislative and administrative acts. The starting point of the analysis of the ECJ in *Bergaderm* seems to be that the legislative or administrative nature of the act is not necessarily crucial, whereas the starting point of the CFI in *Fresh Marine* seems to be the opposite.

IX. CONCLUSIONS

The second generation cases on State liability in damages do not introduce any innovation although they do clarify some important points. In some respects, the cases appear to provide evidence of retreat from the law of remedies. *Brinkmann* used, for the first time, causation to limit liability and *Konle* left the issue of seriousness entirely to the national court. In *Rechberger* and *Haim II*, by contrast, the Court was prepared to give more guidance to the national court. The allocation of liability among the various national authorities is left to national law to decide. Such responses are in conformity with the judicial policy of selective deference which underlies recent developments in the law of remedies. Having established State liability as a new remedy, the Court is now prepared to leave more discretion to the national courts. At this stage, it seeks to embrace the national legal systems rather than provide leadership through quantum leaps, restricting its interventions in perfecting the art of casuistry. The more the case-law leaves matters to the national courts, the more that it encourages the internalisation[129] of Community law and cross-fertilisation between the Community and the national legal orders. There is no denying that the case law of the Court of Justice acts as a catalyst to national law reform. It should be remembered however that notions of serious breach and direct causal link are products of Community law of which the Court itself is the final arbiter. There is no mellowing down, but consolidation and studied deference.

Bergaderm confirms the tendency to view the Community and national institutions as separate organs of the same constitutional order.[130] It unifies the conditions of liability and, in doing so, signals a shift of emphasis on the conceptual framework which governs the liability of the Community. It

---

[129] The term 'internalisation' is used to connote the process by which doctrines of Community law, such as direct effect and liability in damages, are assimilated by the national legal orders and are applied by the national courts as an integral part of national law. This is a two-way process. On the one hand, it means that national rules of substantive law, procedure, and remedies are reformed in line with Community requirements. On the other hand, principles of EC law are supplemented by, and applied within, the framework of national law.

[130] For a similar tendency with regard to the standards of judicial review, see Case C-120/97 *Upjohn Ltd v The Licensing Authority established by the Medicines Act 1968 and Others* [1999] ECR I-223.

stresses the degree of discretion enjoyed by the institution rather than the administrative or legislative character of the act. In a welcome development, it opens the road for the test of 'manifest and grave disregard' to be extended to administrative acts which entail the exercise of broad discretion. As the judgment in *Fresh Marine Company* illustrates, however, *Bergaderm* is not crystal clear, and one would wish for a more lucid statement on the part of the Court regarding the importance to be attributed to the legislative or administrative character of the measure giving rise to damage.

Overall, the recent case law on liability of Community and national authorities evinces an interesting realignment through which a new balance will emerge. On the one hand, the prescriptive approach evident in the field of remedies in an earlier phase of the case law has given way to selective deference. With regard to State liability the Court leaves more matters to be decided by the national courts. On the other hand, it is prepared to use State liability, which may itself be subject to influences from national laws, as a model for the liability of the Community. The fruitful dialectical interaction between Community and national law continues but, at in this current phase, there are signs that, to some extent, convergence 'from above' is being replaced by convergence 'from below'.

8. MISFEASANCE IN PUBLIC OFFICE, GOVERNMENTAL LIABILITY, AND EUROPEAN INFLUENCES

Mads Andenas* and Duncan Fairgrieve**

I. INTRODUCTION

The protection offered to individuals by remedies in public law and tort law is developing in all jurisdictions. The past few years have witnessed an increasingly important European dimension to the tort liability of public authorities. European Union law and European Human Rights law have added to the constitutional protection of tort claims against public authorities already established as a matter of domestic law in many European countries.

In this setting, English, French, and Italian courts have dealt with the liability of banking regulators for lack of supervision of banks. Moreover, there has been parallel litigation before the English and French courts concerning liability of the respective regulators for the failure of the Bank of Credit and Commerce International ('BCCI').

In this article it is argued that the expansion of tort liability for misfeasance in public office in the House of Lords' recent decisions in *Three Rivers District Council v Bank of England*[1] may contribute to resolving possible conflicts with the European Convention of Human Rights. It may also reduce the differences in the protection offered under English law and EU law. Finally, it is argued that when it comes to establishing limiting mechanisms replacing the ones that have been eroded, English law may make good use of French and EU law.

This article is organised in the following way. In Section II, the framework for banking supervision in the United Kingdom is examined, and the requirements for liability under English law are set out. Liability under EU

* Director, British Institute of International and Comparative Law, London; Senior Teaching Fellow, Institute of European and Comparative Law, and Fellow, Harris Manchester College, University of Oxford.
** Fellow in Comparative Law, British Institute of International and Comparative Law, London; *Maître de Conférences invité*, Université de Paris 1, Sorbonne.

[1] *Three Rivers District Council and others v Governor and Company of the Bank of England* [2000] 2 WLR 1220; *Three Rivers District Council and others v Governor and Company of the Bank of England* [2001] UKHL 16.

law in the BCCI case is discussed in Section III. Comparative law material is introduced in Section IV, with reference to parallel proceedings and developments in other European jurisdictions. In Section V, some EU law issues are revisited. In Section VI, in the light of the EU and European discussion, we return to consider the broader implication of misfeasance in public office and its role in relation to English negligence liability.

II. ENGLISH LAW: STATUTORY IMMUNITY AND MISFEASANCE

The case of *Three Rivers District Council v Bank of England*[2] arose out of alleged misfeasance by the Bank of England in supervising the Bank of Credit and Commerce International (BCCI). After BCCI went into liquidation depositors brought damages claims which were struck out in the High Court and Court of Appeal.[3] In the House of Lords, the first hearing was restricted to two questions of law.[4] The first question concerned the exact ingredients of the tort of misfeasance in public office. The way the relevant elements of this tort were dealt with, in four separate speeches, has not aided the process of clarification. The second question was whether the Bank of England was capable of being liable in damages to the claimants for violation of Community law as laid down in the First Banking Directive.[5] The House of Lords held that the claimants did not have a damages remedy under Community law.

The second hearing before the House of Lords dealt with the question whether it was right to strike out the claimants' action on the basis that there was no reasonable prospect of the claim succeeding at trial.[6] The strike out application made by the Bank of England was rejected by a majority of the House of Lords.[7] A crucial factor in their decision was the reliance, of the judge at first instance and the majority in the Court of

---

[2] *Three Rivers District Council* [2000] 2 WLR 1220; *Three Rivers District Council* [2001] UKHL 16.

[3] At first instance, after initial proceedings concerning various preliminary issues of law, Clarke J acceded to the Bank of England's application to strike out the action (Judgment of 30 July 1997 (unreported)). The Court of Appeal upheld Clarke J's decision in a joint majority judgment of Hirst and Robert Walker LJJ; Auld LJ dissented: *Three Rivers DC v Bank of England* [1999] EuLR 211

[4] *Three Rivers District Council* [2000] 2 WLR 1220.

[5] First Council Banking Co-ordination Directive of 12 Dec 1977 (77/780/EEC).

[6] Under the transition arrangements guiding the introduction of the Civil Procedure Rules (CPR) in 1999, the question whether the misfeasance claim should be struck out was determined according to the CPR: *Three Rivers District Council* [2001] UKHL 16, paras 12–13.

[7] The Bank of England asked the House of Lords to give summary judgment against the claimants under Rule 24.2 CPR. Lords Steyn, Hope and Hutton allowed the appeal against the striking out of the claim. Lords Hobhouse and Millett dissented.

Appeal, on the findings of the Bingham Report into the supervision of BCCI.[8] Lord Hope said that Bingham LJ was not in a position to conduct a fair trial of the issues relating to the tort of misfeasance in public office.[9] He agreed with the dissenting opinion of Auld LJ in the Court of Appeal that it would not be right to treat the Bingham Report as effectively conclusive on the questions that arose in the litigation.[10] Lord Hutton also agreed. He held it impermissible for the judge and the majority of the Court of Appeal, in deciding at this interlocutory stage whether there was no real prospect of the action succeeding, to be influenced by the findings and conclusions of Bingham LJ.[11] Disregarding for this reason, the conclusions in the Bingham Report, the majority held that it could not be said the claim had no real prospect of succeeding. The claim had to proceed to trial.

The main features of the UK model of banking supervision are briefly set out below. It is followed by an outline of the law on tort liability applying to the Bank of England as banking supervisor. The scene is then set for the discussion of the *Three Rivers* case.

A. The Reluctant and Immune Supervisor

The UK model of banking supervision remained a minimalist one under the responsibility of the Bank of England. Until the adoption of the Banking Act 1979 supervision was implemented on an informal basis[12] with no comprehensive legislative backing.[13] The Banking Act 1979 created a statutory system for authorisation of all deposit-taking institutions. This was modernised by the Banking Act 1987 which increased the Bank of England's power to regulate, vet controlling shareholders and require information.[14] In 1988 the Bank published a Statement of Principles.[15] The Statement lays down in some detail the grounds for using the powers to revoke and restrict an authorisation under the 1987 Act.

---

[8] Inquiry into the Supervision of the Bank of Credit and Commerce International (HC Paper (1992–3), No 198.

[9] *Three Rivers District Council* [2001] UKHL 16, para 33 and 80.

[10] Ibid, para 33 and 86.

[11] Ibid, para 132.

[12] Banking supervision was not without bureaucracy: there were many administrative permits and dispensations which had to be obtained if a full range of banking activities were to be attained. This served more as a barrier to entry than a basis for real supervision. 'The underlying idea was to await the development of a new financial institution and then make a judgment', W Möschel, 'Public Law of Banking' (1991) *Int Enc Comp Law*, vol IX, ch III at para 20.

[13] The Bank never formally invoked the power of recommendation and direction contained in s 4(3) of the Bank of England Act 1946. The Bank's approach to supervision was that of a gentleman's code of ethics and self regulation. See G Penn, *Banking Supervision* (London: Butterworths, 1989), 10–11.   [14] See ibid, 15.

[15] The current Statement of Principles from 1998 was issued by the Financial Services Authority and is complemented by the very extensive Guide to Banking Supervisory Policy.

The protection of depositors was set out, in the long title of the 1979 and 1987 Acts, as the prime objective of banking supervision. In contradiction to this, the focus of a new ideology of banking supervision, prudential supervision, became the solidity of financial institutions and payments systems. Supervision should prevent contagion and systemic risk that could threaten the stability of the banking system.[16] The Bank of England developed this over the years, partly in response to criticism over its handling of the different banking crises,[17] and partly in interaction with international standard setting. In this new perspective, individual bank insolvency could be acceptable. Indeed, under certain circumstances, it might even promote the soundness of the financial system.[18] This redefinition created a clear tension in relation to the Bank of England's statutory duties, both under domestic and EU law.

The change to modern methods of banking supervision[19] and the development of formal powers was a long and gradual process. This added another tension: the continued reliance on informal supervision after the establishment of a formal framework with legal duties and sanctions for breach of those duties. In the Bank's practice, omissions to make use of formal sanctions could for instance be justified with market reactions.[20] The Bank could omit to use sanctions where its 'moral suasion' failed, even though this contrasted with the philosophy of the legislation and the Bank's own Statement of Principles.[21]

The Bank of England Act 1998 followed yet another banking crisis, this time ushering in radical reform. The 1998 Act transferred banking supervision from the Bank of England to the Financial Services Authority, an independent financial services regulator. The Bank of England retained certain functions in relation to the supervision of banks' liquidity.

In terms of potential liability, a statutory immunity from damages liabil-

---

[16] See the discussion of systemic risk in R Cranston, *Principles of Banking Law* (Oxford: Oxford University Press, 1997), 71–2.

[17] See, for instance, the submissions by the Governor of the Bank of England and its other representatives to parliamentary committees and the annual reports by the Bank on banking supervision.

[18] The advantages for a banking supervisor are obvious. Compare systemic risk, which has not yet ever materialised in a systemic collapse, as the only standard of accountability with loss for depositors which occur with most individual bank failures.

[19] See the discussion of these issues in Cranston, op cit, 91–2.

[20] For instance it could be claimed that that the market would withdraw from a bank whose activity was restricted. This could bring about the collapse of the bank with possible consequences for the stability of the banking market.

[21] This is well documented in the Rt Hon Lord Justice Bingham's *Inquiry into the Supervision of the Bank of Credit and Commerce International* (HC Paper (1992–3), No 198) and in see *Report of the Board of Banking Supervision Inquiry into Circumstances of the Collapse of Barings* (1995). As mentioned above, at 260 of the latter Report it was noted that no such inspection ('visit') to Barings Bank was ever undertaken before its collapse in 1995.

ity was introduced under the Banking Act 1987.[22] Under the terms of the statute, liability may only arise if the impugned act or omission 'was in bad faith'.[23] Regardless of the statutory provisions, regulators have traditionally been well protected by the common law. The cases concerning liability in negligence have been restrictive and not imposed any duty of care upon regulators in respect of economic loss.[24] The cases concerning the supervision of financial institutions confirm this restrictive approach.[25] The statutory immunity may well have been superfluous in 1987. But as the common law develops, and tort liability expands, the immunity may become more important.

The statutory immunity is not applicable to acts taken in bad faith. This exception allowed for claims based on the tort of misfeasance in public office. Misfeasance in public office is the only specifically 'public law' tort in English law.[26] In the BCCI case the claims against the Bank of England were thus based on the tort of misfeasance in public office, and the remedies under Community law.

B. Misfeasance in Public Office: The Mental Requirements

The essence of misfeasance is the exercise of power by a public officer in bad faith which causes loss to the claimant.[27] The crucial element of this tort is the mental requirement, which may be divided into two alternatives. First, the most stringent form of this tort is known as targeted malice. It requires proof that a public officer has acted with the intention of injuring

---

[22] Banking Act 1987, s 1(4). See now Schedule 1, s 19(1) of the Financial Services and Markets Act 2000. For an in-depth analysis of UK law, see C Hadjiemmanuil, *Banking Regulation and the Bank of England* (London: LLP 1996) and the more general discussion in Cranston, op cit, 91 et seq.

[23] This immunity reaches further than restricting mechanisms in other European jurisdictions. It is for instance undisputed that German regulators will be liable in negligence to the banks they supervise. The possible restrictions in German tort liability are in relation to depositors, other creditors and shareholders.

[24] See, eg, *Lam v Brennan* [1997] PIQR P488 (planning control); *Reeman v Department of Transport* [1997] 2 Lloyd's Rep 648 (health and safety regulation). See discussion in H McLean, 'Negligent Regulatory Authorities and the Duty of Care' [1988] OJLS 442; PP Craig and D Fairgrieve, 'Barrett, Negligence and Discretionary Powers' [1999] *Public Law* 626, 646.

[25] *Yuen Kun Yeu v Attorney General of Hong Kong* [1988] AC 175; *Davis v Radcliffe* [1990] 2 All ER 536.

[26] See *Bourgoin S.A. v MAFF* [1986] QB 716, 776. See also *Dunlop v Woollahra Municipal Council* [1982] AC 158, 172; *Jones v Swansea CC* [1990] 3 All ER 737.

[27] Generally, see PP Craig, *Administrative Law*, 4th edn (London: Sweet & Maxwell, 1999), 875–80; S Arrowsmith, *Civil Liability and Public Authorities* (Winteringham: Earlsgate, 1992), 226 ff; W Wade, *Administrative* Law, 8th edn (Oxford: Oxford University Press, 2000), 765 ff; McBride, 'Damages as a Remedy for Unlawful Administrative Action' [1979] CLJ 323.

the claimant.[28] The second form, untargeted malice, is made out when a public officer acts in the knowledge that he exceeds his powers, and that this act would probably injure the claimant.[29]

The focus of the litigation before the House of Lords in the *Three Rivers* case was upon the second less stringent form, untargeted malice. In the House of Lords, the debate over the mental element in misfeasance concerned two separate questions. The first question is the public officer's knowledge of the unlawfulness of his or her act. Must it be shown that the defendant knew or suspected that the act was unlawful? Or is it sufficient to show that he *ought* to have known that such was the case? Which of these differing standards is applicable?

The second question concerns the awareness of the *consequences* of that unlawful act. What is the requisite state of mind of the public officer concerning the likelihood of the claimant being damaged by the unlawful act? The manner in which these elements are framed by the courts is an essential part of understanding the role of this tort in controlling public wrongdoing. The mental element of the tort is its main control-mechanism.

The first judgment of the House of Lords in *Three Rivers* resolved these questions in the following way. On the knowledge of illegality, it was held that the claimant must show either that the officer had *actual knowledge* that the impugned act was unlawful or that the public officer acted with a state of mind of *reckless indifference* to the illegality.[30] On the awareness of consequences, counsel for the claimants had argued that that there was no need for it to be shown that the public officer had actually known that his actions would probably injure the claimants, arguing that recovery should be made for all reasonably foreseeable loss.[31] This had been supported by Lord Justice Auld's dissenting judgment in the Court of Appeal.[32] In the first judgment of the House of Lords, the test of reasonable foreseeability was rejected. The relevant test was subjective. It was necessary to show that the public officer knew that his act would probably injure the claimant. As with the knowledge as to the unlawfulness of the act, it would seem that reckless indifference as to the consequences, in the sense that the officer acted without caring whether the consequences happened or not, was sufficient.

---

[28] *Bourgoin SA v MAFF* [1986] QB 716, 776. See also *Dunlop v Woollahra Municipal Council* [1982] AC 158, 172.

[29] *Three Rivers District Council* [2000] 2 WLR 1220 and [2001] UKHL 16.

[30] *Three Rivers District Council* [2000] 2 WLR 1220. See also [2001] UKHL 16, para 121 (Lord Hutton)

[31] See argument in the Court of Appeal: *Three Rivers District Council v Bank of England* [1999] EuLR 211, 243.

[32] *Three Rivers District Council* [1999] EuLR 211, 270–2, 370 (CA).

The second judgment of the House of Lords applied the test to rule on the question whether the claim should be summarily dismissed. The House of Lords stated that the correct test for misfeasance was that laid down in the first judgment.[33] But the second judgment did more than illustrate the practical application of the requirements of the tort. The second judgment provided some clarification of two aspects of the action, the necessary knowledge as to consequences in terms of untargeted malice, and the exact meaning and role of bad faith.

1. *Knowledge as to Consequences*

The formulation of the requirement to show knowledge as to consequences will be a crucial point when the case goes to trial. The exact articulation of these consequences cover disputed territory but essentially entail the knowledge or recklessness of the failure of BCCI, the lack of a rescue package to save it, and the resultant loss of the depositors' money.

In the second judgment of the House of Lords in *Three Rivers*,[34] it was reiterated that what is required is recklessness in a subjective sense of awareness of risk by the defendant.[35] Inadvertent recklessness, in the sense of reasonable foreseeability, was not enough. But it was again repeated at various stages that the test as to knowledge of the consequences covers reckless indifference to the risk of loss,[36] which extends to 'recklessness about the consequences, in the sense of not caring whether the consequences happen or not, will satisfy the test'.[37]

The 'couldn't care less' test for recklessness as to consequences is elastic. On one interpretation, it could imply advertence to the risk of the consequences occurring but accompanied by entire indifference to whether that happened or not. This combines awareness with a lack of concern. Another interpretation is more radical, and would cover the circumstances where the defendant had not thought about the particular consequence of certain acts or omission and thus showed a practical indifference to their occurrence. This has sometimes been used in criminal law cases of alleged rape where the defendant has been convicted on the basis that he 'couldn't care less' whether the victim was giving consent or not.[38] There are those who believe that it hard to reconcile such an approach with the label of advertent or subjective recklessness.[39]

---

[33] *Three Rivers District Council* [2001] UKHL 16, para 41.

[34] Ibid, 16.

[35] Ibid, 16, paras 44, 46, 62, and 76.

[36] See, eg, ibid, para 58.

[37] Ibid, para 62. Another variant of this is referred to in Lord Hobhouse's judgment as 'blind eye knowledge'—see para 164 ff.

[38] See *Satnam and Kewal S* (1984) 78 Cr App R 141.

[39] Ashworth, *Principles of Criminal Law*, 179.

Could there be grounds for arguing in favour of the broader interpretation in the context of misfeasance in public office? There are some indications in Lord Hope's decision of a recognition of the inherent problems in taking too narrow a view of foresight of consequences. This is highlighted in two particular features of his judgment. First, counsel for the Bank had argued that the claim should be struck out on the basis that the statement of claim did not support an allegation of 'knowledge, belief or suspicion of likely or probable loss'. Lord Hope refused to strike out the claim on this basis, and emphasised the importance of discovering the facts at trial before making specific definitions of the state of mind required.[40] This suggests that the trial judge will have a certain amount of room to manoeuvre in framing the exact test. Secondly, a later aspect of Lord Hope's judgment is also revelatory about the required state of mind of the public officer. Lord Hope admitted that he saw much force in a section of Auld LJ's dissenting judgment in the Court of Appeal which underlined the iniquity of allowing the defendants to rely upon the reason for their unlawfulness—the failure to fulfil its supervisory obligations properly—to defeat the misfeasance claim on the basis that this very failure—its 'self-imposed ignorance'—precluded them from suspecting that the depositor's would probably suffer loss.

Auld LJ's argument strikes right at the heart of requirement of foresight. Does Lord Hope's recognition of the force of Auld LJ's comment imply a more indulgent approach to claimants meaning that subjective awareness of risk might not always be required? Most probably not. Given Lord Hope's basic definition of recklessness for untargeted malice in which he emphasised the awareness of risk, it would seem that the narrower interpretation of the 'couldn't care less test' is right: it has to be shown 'that the public officer was aware of a serious risk of loss due to an act or omission on his part which he knew to be unlawful but chose deliberately to disregard that risk'.[41] But at the very least, the approval of Auld LJ's statement suggests that at trial the judge should draw the necessary inferences from any attempt that is made by the bank to make use of its self-imposed lack of prescience as to the effects of its supervisory activities to defeat a claim for lack of foresight of consequences.

A related issue is the degree of awareness of risk which will have to be averred by the claimants. The defendants had argued that there needed to be proof of awareness of *probable* loss. In response to this, Lord Hope underlined that in the end this question was a matter of fact and degree to be determined by the judge at trial.[42] In giving guidance for that process his

---

[40] *Three Rivers District Council* [2001] UKHL 16, para 60.
[41] Ibid, para 46.
[42] Ibid, para 60.

Lordship acknowledged that an important consideration was that supervision was conferred by statute in order to protect depositors. The First Banking Directive was premised upon this policy. Underpinning the supervisory system is the fact that in the absence of proper supervision, deposits are likely to be at risk. In that context, Lord Hope expressed the test to be applied at trial as whether the risk of loss was *sufficiently serious* to warrant a finding of reckless on the part of the supervisor.[43]

2. The Role of Bad Faith

Another important aspect of Lord Hope's judgment is the clarification of the exact meaning and role of bad faith. The first House of Lords' judgment had left this question somewhat open. Counsel for the Bank of England argued that the action should be struck out because the pleadings did not make specific allegations of dishonesty in the sense of subjective bad faith on the part of officials of the bank.[44] Lord Hope flatly rejected this argument.[45] In effect he held that proof of the elements of the tort in terms of knowledge of unlawfulness of the act or omission and its consequences was enough.[46] This is particularly important in terms of recklessness as to the consequences. It would seem that proof that the defendant did not care whether the consequences happened or not is enough. Bad faith is demonstrated by recklessness on the part of the administrator in disregarding the risk.[47] Lord Hope emphasised that no additional element of dishonesty or bad faith was required.[48]

This is a significant point in favour of the claimants in the *Three Rivers* case. It would probably have been difficult to show outright bad faith on the part of the officials in dealing with BCCI. Now, according to the majority judgment of their Lordships this is no longer necessary. This clarification of the role of bad faith is also significant in a wider sense. It is sufficient to show disregard of a sufficiently serious risk of loss, coupled with unlawfulness. This is clearly a very broad interpretation of bad faith. This will serve to make the tort of misfeasance more broadly applicable for compensating administrative wrongs.[49] Reckless administrators are a more common phenomenon than outright dishonest ones.

---

[43] Ibid, paras 60 and 76. He also expressed this in terms of the following test: 'the public officer was aware of a serious risk of loss due to an act or omission on his part which he knew to be unlawful but chose deliberately to disregard that risk' (para 46).

[44] Ibid, paras 57 and 62. [45] Ibid, para 62.

[46] Ibid, paras 44 and 62. [47] Ibid, para 44. [48] Ibid, para 62.

[49] For a restrictive interpretation of the bad faith requirement in the Court of Appeal, see *Greville v Sprake* [2001] EWCA Civ 234; *Thomas v Chief Constable of Cleveland* [2001] EWCA Civ 1552.

We will examine the ramifications of the reshaping of the tort of misfeasance in a later section. We turn now to examine the House of Lords decisions in respect of Community Law.

III. THE EU LAW ISSUES BEFORE THE ENGLISH COURTS

A. EU Law in the UK Courts: the General Issues

Banking supervision in the UK was for a long while fundamentally different from other EU member states. Even after many years of EU harmonisation, UK banking supervision remained minimalist, with the Bank of England as a reluctant supervisor. As we have seen, banking supervision was first put on a statutory footing in the Banking Act 1979. The 1979 Act[50] transposed into English Law the newly adopted EU First Banking Directive.[51] It was first after the secondary banking crisis of the early 1970s that the Bank of England had to accept some degree of formalisation of banking supervision in EU legislation. The UK had blocked the First Banking Directive but the objections to the proposal were then withdrawn.[52]

In the BCCI case, the different standards of banking supervision in the UK compared with those applicable in other European countries could potentially have been an issue both in the context of the misfeasance claim and the claim for breach of EU law. The tension between the requirements of the First Banking Directive and UK banking supervision could only have been appreciated fully with this in mind. But this tension never became an issue in the proceedings or in the judgments.

Liability under EU law was evidently attractive to the claimants as it would have avoided many of the restrictive mental elements required in misfeasance. In the event, all three courts confirmed that misfeasance in public office is a narrower tort than that based on a sufficiently serious breach of Community law. There was extensive discussion of the Community law issues. Only the dissenting judge in the Court of Appeal, Lord Justice Auld, held that a claim could be based on Community law. He held that EU legislation did impose duties on the Bank of England. The purpose was to protect depositors. The obligations imposed upon the Bank by the EU legislation could give depositors a right of redress against it for breach of those obligations.

---

[50] See the useful overview of the regulatory system in *Three Rivers District Council* [2000] 2 WLR 15 (abridged), [1999] EuLR 211 (in full) CA.

[51] In particular, the First Banking Directive of 1977: First Council Banking Co-ordination Directive of 12 Dec 1997 (77/780/EEC).

[52] See Cranston, op cit, 70.

In the House of Lords, Lord Hope of Craighead gave the main speech on Community law issues.[53] He relied on Lord Justice Auld for the formulation of the two critical questions.[54] First, did the First Banking Directive entail the grant of rights to individual depositors and potential depositors? Second, was the content of those rights identifiable on the basis of the provisions of the Directive?

Lord Hope reviewed the European Court's case law on the First Banking Directive and he found little support there. He relied on an examination of the terms of the Directive itself. He pointed out that the recitals showed that it was intended to be the first step in a continuing process to co-ordinate the supervision of credit institutions. He concluded that the protection of savings was merely a matter to which regard had to be had, along with the creation of equal conditions of competition, in the process of coordination.

Lord Hope further held that the only duty which the First Banking Directive imposed was a duty to cooperate. When the Directive allowed the withdrawal of authorisation in limited circumstances, its terms were restrictive rather than obligatory: it could not place a duty to act on the Bank of England. Various issues arising from this judgment merit examination in greater depth.

B. The Purpose of the Directive and the Duties on the Supervisor

The BCCI failure was the very type which the First Banking Directive was intended to prevent. BCCI operated in several member states at a stage when the coordination of banking supervision was being developed at a Community level. It is well documented that the BCCI was allowed to continue its business for a long period due to coordination problems between the banking supervisors in different member states.

The First Banking Directive was initiated to secure non-discriminatory treatment of banks from other Member States. This was effected by removing certain forms of direct discrimination against foreign banks or initiating procedures, and by introducing the right to judicial review, for instance in the authorisation of banks. The opening up of the banking markets in the Directive was accompanied by certain safeguards to protect the interest of depositors. Depositors were to be protected by certain supervisory measures that should be undertaken by national authorities. In particular they were to protect depositors from the problems of coordination between different national banking supervisors.

This was the first step in establishing a new supervisory system in the Community. It is hard to accept the position taken in the judgment by the House of Lords that the Bank of England could not have a duty to make

---

[53] [2000] 2 WLR 1220, 1236.   [54] [2000] 2 WLR 1220, 1242.

use of the powers to revoke an authorisation. It is hard to do so on the basis of a literal interpretation. On the basis of the background for, and context of, the Community regulation of banking supervision it is even more difficult. The provisions of the Directive must also be read in light of the supervisory systems of the other member states that in effect were adopted as the Community model with these particularly fundamental consequences in the UK.[55]

Lord Justice Auld in the minority in the Court of Appeal interpreted the provisions of the Directive on supervisory duties in a way that is wholly consistent with this context. He also made use of the case law of the Court of Justice on the Directive, including the ruling in the *Parodi* case.[56] The other judges attempted to explain away these cases, one by one,[57] with brief and mostly formal arguments.

C. Damages and Direct Effect

The discussion of liability was in all three instances, from Mr Justice Clarke to the House of Lords, closely linked to the requirements for direct effect. Lord Hope in the House of Lords let liability depend on two uncontroversial questions.[58] First, did the First Banking Directive entail the grant of rights to individual depositors and potential depositors? Secondly, was the content of those rights identifiable on the basis of the provisions of the Directive? But there are several places in Lord Hope's speech, as it is in the majority judgments of the lower courts, where it seems as if the requirements for tort liability include precision and unconditionality, which of course are the basic requirements for direct effect.[59]

The condition for tort liability that the directive conferred rights on individuals[60] does not go that far. The condition is that the result prescribed by

---

[55] See the discussion of the supervisory systems of other member states by M Andenas and D Fairgrieve, 'To Supervise or to Compensate', in ead, *Judicial Review in International Perspective* (2000).

[56] *Societe Civile Immobiliere Parodi v Banque H. Albert de Bary et Cie* (Case C-222/95) [1997] ECR I-3899; [1997] All ER (EC) 946, ECJ. Another interesting point concerns the French courts' application of the ECJ's preliminary ruling which arguably is inconsistent with that of the House of Lords. That should have resulted in a new reference to the ECJ by the House of Lords.

[57] In *Dillenkofer* [1996] ECR I-4845 para 22 the condition that the directive conferred rights on individuals was formulated in the following way: the result prescribed by the directive must entail the grant of rights to individuals and the content of those rights must be identifiable on the basis of the directive. This formulation does not allow a national court to disregard the European Court's case law on the interpretation of a directive!

[58] [2000] 2 WLR 1220, 1242.

[59] Directly effective EU law can be relied on in national courts. Member States can be held liable in tort for breach of EU law whether the provisions of EU Law are directly effective or not.

[60] This condition is established in the European Court's judgment in *Dillenkofer* [1996] ECR I-4845 para 22 and was referred to in the judgments as 'the *Dillenkofer* condition'.

the directive must entail the grant of rights to individuals, and that the content of those rights must be identifiable on the basis of the directive. This is different from the precision and unconditionality required for direct effect.

In the majority decisions of the English courts in the *Three Rivers* litigation the requirement of the granting of rights to individuals has become materially different from what is required according to the authoritative case law of the European Court.

It could be noted here that the German Government proposed, under the negotiations on the First Banking Directive, the inclusion of a clause stating that the Directive did not give rise to liability in damages to depositors for the national regulator. The European Commission opposed this limitation of liability. The Commission's view was that it would be inappropriate to limit in the directive the remedies provided in national law. Damages liability for breach of Community law (as a matter of Community law) has of course been established later.[61] The choice was made not to limit a possible liability to depositors based on the requirements of the Directive.[62]

IV. PARALLEL PROCEEDINGS AND DEVELOPMENTS IN OTHER EUROPEAN JURISDICTIONS

A. Proceedings in France

The English legal system is by no means the only system to have considered the question of the liability of regulatory authorities. The French administrative courts have also been grappling with similar issues, and the case law has been developing swiftly.

Due to the complex and sensitive nature of bank supervision, the French *Conseil d'Etat* traditionally required claimants to show *faute lourde*, or grave fault, in state liability actions concerning the activities of the main agency responsible for banking supervision, the *Commission Bancaire*.[63] The standard of liability applied by the courts was particularly high,[64] and only one claim had ever satisfied this *faute lourde* requirement.[65]

---

[61] See Section V below.

[62] This was not brought to the attention of the English courts in the *Three Rivers* litigation.

[63] *Conseil d'Etat* 29 Dec 1978, *Darmont*, [1978] *Recueil des Décisions du Conseil d'Etat* 542. Other agencies also exercised supervisory functions: see further D Fairgrieve and K Belloir, 'Liability of the French State for Negligent Supervision of Banks' (1999) 10 *European Business Law Review*, 17. It should be noted that the reason for the *Darmont* case law is that the Commission Bancaire in its disciplinary function is acting as a court not as an administration.

[64] Cliquennois, 'Essai Sur La Responsabilité de l'Etat du Fait de Ses Activités de Contrôle et de Tutelle' [1995] *Les Petites Affiches*, No 98, 4.

[65] This case is itself over 35 years old and relates to facts that took place in the 1950s. *Conseil d'Etat* 24 Jan 1964, *Achard*, [1964] *Recueil des Décisions du Conseil d'Etat*, 43.

This restrictive approach has however recently been challenged by claimants in a series of cases. In the case of *Kechichian*, depositors brought an action against the state alleging that the *Commission Bancaire* had failed to supervise properly a bank, the United Banking Corporation, thereby contributing to its failure and the consequent loss of their deposits. At first instance, the claims were rejected. On appeal, the *Cour Administrative d'Appel de Paris* reiterated the principles enunciated in an earlier decision concerning the Bank of Credit and Commerce International,[66] in which it had abandoned the traditional prerequisite of *faute lourde* and decided that the standard of *faute simple* applied to the supervisory role of the *Commission Bancaire*.[67] The *Cour Administrative d'Appel* thus continued the seemingly inexorable shift from graded fault standards in French administrative law[68] towards a unified standard of *faute simple*.[69]

An appeal was made to the *Conseil d'Etat*. The case was assigned to the *Assemblée de Contentieux*, the Plenary Chamber of the *Conseil d'Etat* denoting the importance of the issues raised by the claims. In an extremely significant judgment, the *Conseil d'Etat* overturned the *Cour Administrative d'Appel's* decision on the standard of fault.[70] The claimants needed to show that the *Commission Bancaire* had committed a *faute lourde* in its supervisory activities. Nonetheless, the *Conseil d'Etat* upheld the lower *Cour Administrative d'Appel's* finding of liability. The *Commission Bancaire's* failure to act decisively to ensure that the bank was re-capitalised within a short space of time,[71] and its willingness to back-track on initial requirements amounted to a *faute lourde*. For only the second time in its history, the state was found liable in damages by the administrative courts for the loss caused to investors by the collapse of a credit institution. However, the state was not found liable for the full loss of these depositors. As the primary causal contributor of the bank's failure was the fraudulent activities of its directors, the *Conseil d'Etat* held the state solely liable for the part it played in the failure of the bank, which was held to represent 10 per cent of the lost deposits.

Various conclusions can be drawn from this case. The *Conseil d'Etat* decided that in this sensitive area of governmental activity the time was not

---

[66] *Cour Administrative d'Appel de Paris* 30 Mar 1999, *El Shikh*, AJDA.1999.951. See discussion in Andenas and Fairgrieve, 'To Supervise or to Compensate?', s 348 et seq.

[67] Cour Administrative d'Appel de Paris 25 Jan 2000, Kechichian, Req 93PA01250.

[68] See Errera [1990] Public Law 571; Raynaud and Fombeur, AJDA 1998.418, 424.

[69] *Conseil d'Etat* 20 June 1997, *Theux, Recueil des Décisions du Conseil d'Etat* 253 concl. Stahl (emergency services); *Conseil d'Etat*, 29 Apr 1998, *Commune de Hannappes, Recueil des Décisions du Conseil d'Etat* 185, RDP 1998.1001 n X. Prétot, JCP 1999.II.10109 note Genovèse (fire-services).

[70] *Conseil d'Etat* 30 Nov 2001, *Kechichian*.

[71] Subsequent to the issuing of a formal 'lettre de suite', which had been motivated by an inspection which had uncovered weaknesses in the bank's finances.

right for a shift from *faute lourde* to *faute simple*. The protective role of *faute lourde* was still deemed necessary in order to provide a 'margin of manoeuvre' for the public body.[72] But it would be wrong to view this case as a simple restatement of the previous case law. Indeed, it is possible to perceive it as a significant step forward. The traditional approach to claims in this area was very restrictive and the standard of liability very high.[73] It would not be exaggerated to say that a form of quasi-immunity applied.[74] The approach of the *Conseil d'Etat* in the most recent case strikes a different note. *Faute lourde* was maintained but the judges sent a signal that they are prepared to look closely at the regulator's activities and will impose liability if the appropriate standards are not met. The shift is illustrated by the difference in approach between the *Tribunal Administratif* and the *Conseil d'Etat*. Both applied the standard of *faute lourde* but only the latter found that it had been made out.[75]

The French case law also affords an opportunity to reflect upon the control mechanisms. The means of controlling the existence and extent of liability are by no means limited to the notion of fault. The French cases show that various other mechanisms exist. In the case of *El Shikh*, concerning the BCCI failure, depositors complained that the French regulators had been at fault in the way they supervised BCCI. It was alleged *inter alia*[76] that the BCCI's banking licence should have been withdrawn, and that the primary supervisory body, the *Commission Bancaire*, had failed to act promptly and in an appropriate manner to irregularities it had discovered during investigations at the Bank. The *Cour Administrative d'Appel's* decision to apply *faute simple* in this case must now be viewed as erroneous. Nonetheless, the case is still instructive in other respects. Despite the shift in the standard of fault, the claim against the French state by the BCCI depositors failed. Indeed, the court did not even decide whether or not the *Commission Bancaire's* actions constituted a *faute simple*.[77] It instead

---

[72] Chapus, *Droit Administratif Général*, vol 1, 13th edn (Paris: Montchrestien, 1999), para 1463.

[73] Cliquennois, 'Essai Sur La Responsabilité de l'Etat du Fait de Ses Activités de Contrôle et de Tutelle' [1995] *Les Petites Affiches*, no 98, 4.

[74] Only one claim had previously satisfied the traditional *faute lourde* requirement. This case is itself over 35 years old and relates to facts that took place in the 1950s: *Conseil d'Etat* 24 Jan 1964, *Achard* [1964] *Recueil des Décisions du Conseil d'Etat*, 43. For discussion of this, see generally Fairgrieve and Belloir (1999) 10 *European Business Law Review* 13.

[75] *Tribunal Administratif de Paris*, 7 July 1993 (unreported).

[76] For a fuller examination of the facts of the case, see Andenas and Fairgrieve, 'To Supervise or to Compensate?'

[77] In respect of the parallel claim concerning the exercise of the *Commission Bancaire's* disciplinary power, the French courts maintained the pre-requisite of *faute lourde* laid down in the case of *Darmont* in 1978 (see n 63 above). The Court held that on the facts of the case the Commission Bancaire did not commit a *faute lourde*. It should again be noted that the reason for the *Darmont* case law is that the Commission Bancaire in its disciplinary function is acting as a court not as an administration.

rejected the claims on the basis that the causal link between the alleged faults and the claimants' loss was not established.[78] The Bank's collapse was primarily due to fraudulent activities of its employees at the BCCI group level, and particularly at the Bank's principal place of business in London. There was no direct causal link between the allegedly deficient supervision of the French branches of BCCI for which the French supervisory authorities were responsible, and the claimants' loss.

The *Conseil d'Etat's* recent decision in *Kechichian* also illustrates that creative solutions at the level of causation can allay fears of, in common law terminology, the opening of a floodgates of claims. The *Conseil d'Etat* reduced the liability of the State in line with the part it played in the failure of the bank, which represented 10 per cent of the ultimate loss. Moreover, the lower court's solution—though it proved unattractive to the *Conseil d'Etat*—might be of interest from a comparative law perspective. In *Kechichian*, the *Cour Administrative d'Appel* found that the inadequate supervision of the bank had played a causally significant role in its failure. But it considered that that had only deprived the investors of a *chance* of avoiding the bank's collapse. So, the damages award was assessed as 20 per cent of the losses of each depositor.

B. Parallel Issues in German and Italian Law: Are Depositors Protected?

In traditional German doctrine,[79] supervision of financial institutions was undertaken in the interest of the public at large and not to protect individuals.[80] Consequently, individual depositors could not have any tort claim against the banking regulator. This doctrine was premised upon a decision by the *Bundesgerichtshof* (Supreme Court) in a case concerning the supervision of insurance companies.[81] But in two decisions from 1979, *Wetterstein*[82] and *Herstatt*[83], the Supreme Court departed from this doctrine. The Court recognised that individual bank creditors (*Gläubiger*), and this included depositors, represented a protected interest.[84] Banking

---

[78] For a more detailed examination of this point, see Andenas and Fairgrieve, 'To Supervise or to Compensate?'

[79] F Ossenbühl *Staatshaftungsrecht* (Munich: CH Beck, 1998), 64.

[80] German law is of interest here as a background to the First Banking Directive. It is also necessary to understand a point based on the legislative history of the directive concerning a proposed article in the Directive limiting liability to depositors (see under Section IV below).

[81] BGH Z 58, 96 at 98.   [82] BGHZ 74, 144 at 147.

[83] BGHZ 75, 120 at 122. In the *Herstatt* case the claimants were a group of private depositors. The *Gemeinschaftsfonds bzw. Feuerwehrfonds* proved insufficient at the insolvency of the Herstatt-Bank in 1974. The response was the establishment in 1976 of the *Einlagesicherungsfonds des Bundesverbands der deutschen Banken,* as an industry initiative to pre-empt legislation establishing a public deposit guarantee scheme. See further Schimansky, Bunte, Lwowski, and Bunte, *Bankrechts-Handbuch*, vol 1 (Munich: CH Beck, 1997), para 25 at 3, 25.

[84] F Ossenbühl *Staatshaftungsrecht* (Munich: CH Beck, 1998), 63–4.

supervision was undertaken not only in the general interest but also in the interest of individuals. In response to these cases, new legislation was introduced in 1984, stating expressly that banking supervision is undertaken in the public interest only. This was intended to exclude claims from individuals. A statutory immunity directly barring tort claims would be unconstitutional as Article 34 of the German Constitution prohibits such immunities.[85] The only way open to the legislator was to limit the purpose of banking supervision.

It is no surprise that the new legislation has been criticised by commentators as both unconstitutional and contrary to EU law.[86] If the 1984 legislation is primarily a limitation of liability, it cannot be constitutional. The question may be more doubtful if the 1984 legislation is considered to be a real limitation of the primary functions and purpose of banking supervision. The limitation of liability that was intended by the 1984 legislation will not affect those who are directly affected by an unlawful administrative act of the *Bundesaufsichtsamt* such as banks or their management. Here the ordinary liability rules apply.[87]

There is also interesting litigation before the Italian courts. In Italy, depositors have an unusual constitutional protection. Article 47 of the Italian Constitution (1948) provides that the state shall encourage and supervise saving in all its forms. This article was adopted to impose a duty on the state to supervise banks in the interest of depositors. It influenced the language of the Treaty of Rome which in Article 57(2) required unanimity for the adoption of Community measures concerning the protection of savings. But it is only in a series of recent judgments that the way has been paved for tort remedies against banking supervisors.

The Italian *Corte di Cassazione* (Supreme Court) decided in two judgments that the *Banca d'Italia* in principle can be held liable in damages to investors and depositors for negligent supervision of banks.[88] Recently, the

---

[85] It is interesting to note that Art 34 GG also bars legislation that qualifies the degree of fault required for liability. French distinctions such as *faute lourde* could not be expected to pass review under Art 34 GG. The Constitution does not, on the other hand, bar a limitation of the right of recourse against the civil servant personally to a qualified form of negligence.

[86] See also the discussion by WR Schenke and J Ruthig 'Amtshaftungsansprüche von Bankkunden bei der Verletzung staatlicher Bankenaufsichtspflichten'NJW 1994, 2324; and Ossenbühl op cit, 64 with extensive references.

[87] V Szagunn, U Haug, and W Ergenzinger, *Gesetz über das Kreditwesen* 6th edn (Stuttgart: Ferlag W Kohlhammer, 1997), 170. The parallel UK immunity excludes also this kind of liability; this was indeed the main purpose of the immunity.

[88] Although the *Corte di Cassazione* did not actually decide on the issue of liability. After the Supreme Court's ruling of 22 July 1993, n 8181 in the case following the liquidation of the Banca Popolare di Fabrizia, the Tribunale di Roma, on the facts of the case, did not find in favour of the claimant. The Supreme Court held again in *Cassa di Risparmio di Prato—Landini* (27 Oct 1994, n 8836) that the Banca d'Italia could be liable in damages to investors for lack of supervision and that such claims fall within the competence of the civil courts. The case is still pending before the Tribunale di Firenze.

Corte di Cassazione has applied the doctrine of protection of legitimate interests and held the securities commission *Consob* liable for investors' losses.[89] The principles enunciated in this decision might be extended to the sphere of banking supervision. Accordingly, the supervisory authority must act in accordance with general principles of fairness and good administration, and must use its powers whenever necessary in order to protect interests safeguarded by law. In the *Consob* case, the *Corte di Cassazione* clearly overturned old jurisprudence and extended the tort remedies available to depositors and investors.

V. TORT LIABILITY UNDER EUROPEAN COMMUNITY LAW

The impact of European Community law, even if it did not give rise to a damages claim in this case, is of importance. In *Brasserie du Pecheur and Factortame*[90] the European Court of Justice clarified the conditions for liability: 'Community law confers a right to reparation where three conditions are met: the rule of law infringed must be intended to confer rights on individuals; the breach must be sufficiently serious; and there must be a direct causal link between the breach of the obligation resting on the State and the damage sustained by the injured parties.'[91]

The notion of a 'sufficiently serious breach' was thus introduced by the ECJ as the core condition of liability. In a second generation of cases,[92] the ECJ has developed and refined the remedy, concentrating on elaborating the condition of causation.[93]

In *Three Rivers*, the House of Lords held that there was no Community right for depositors to be breached. There was no need to deal with issues of causation. However, in the context of expanding liability as a matter of English law, one issue is the guidance that can be found in Community law, as in the French case law, on causation as a limiting mechanism. One starting point may be the rather stringent principles governing the liability of

---

[89] Cass. Sez. I, 3 marzo 2001 n 3132.

[90] In *Brasserie du Pecheur SA v Federal Republic of Germany; R v Secretary of State for Transport, ex p Factortame Ltd (No 4)* [1996] ECR I-1029.

[91] At para 51.

[92] See Case C-424/97 *Salomone Haim v Kassenzahnärztliche Vereinigung Nordrhein*, judgment of 4 July 2000; Case C-140/97 *Rechberger and Greindl v Austria* [1999] ECR I-3499; Case C-321/97 *Ulla-Brith Andersson and Susanne Wåkerås-Andersson v Swedish State* [1999] ECR I-3551; Case C-302/97 *Konle v Republic of Austria* [1999] ECR I-3099; Case C-319/96 *Brinkmann Tabakfabriken GmbH v Skatteministeriet* [1998] ECR I-5255; Case C-127/95 *Norbrook Laboratories Limited v Ministry of Agriculture* [1998] ECR I-1531.

[93] See T Tridimas, 'Liability for Breach of Community Law: Growing up and Mellowing Down?', in Ch 7 above.

Community institutions,[94] the other the evolving causation rules for Members States' breach of Community law. Causation, as with the other conditions of liability for breach of Community law, is determined in the first place by Community law. National rules of causation that do not provide an effective standard of protection, will be discarded.

Neither did the House of Lords have to revisit the test of 'sufficiently serious breach'. When Lord Hope uses the 'sufficiently serious risk', this is at an evidentiary level.[95] However, the way in which this is done does bring misfeasance liability under English law closer to the level of protection offered by liability under Community law.

VI. THREE RIVERS: THE BROADER PERSPECTIVE

The decision in *Three Rivers* should be placed in the context of general developments of tort law. Domestic tort remedies have been developing under the influence of European Human Rights Law and European Community Law,[96] and the *Three Rivers* decision may be seen as part of this process. Comparative Law may also be of assistance in this gradual development. The broadening of the elements of misfeasance in public office may make this tort more attractive to claimants.

A. The European Context

We have already analysed the rejection of the Community law damages claim in *Three Rivers*. Despite this position, and the questionable way in which the European cases were interpreted and the preliminary reference avoided, the European law influence on the development of the English law tort of misfeasance in the *Three Rivers* case should by no means be regarded as negligible. There are signs of the influence of both European Community and Human Rights law in the decision.

There must scarcely be an area of English law that is untouched by the domestication of European Human rights law. The financial services law

---

[94] However, so far no apparent attempt has been made by the Court to borrow, in developing causation rules for Member States' liability for breach of Community law, from its case law on Art 228(2) and liability for Community institutions with regard to causation, see the criticism by Van Gerven, 'Taking Article 215(2) EC Seriously', in Beatson and Tridimas (eds), *New Directions in European Public Law* (Oxford: Hart Publishing, 1998), 35–48.

[95] *Three Rivers District Council* [2001] UKHL 16, para 60.

[96] J Wright, *Tort Law and Human Rights* (Oxford: Hart Publishing, 2001); B Markesinis, J-B Auby, D Coester-Waltjen, and S Deakin, *Tortious Liability of Statutory Bodies: A Comparative and Economic Analysis of Five English Cases* (Oxford: Hart Publishing, 1999); Amos, 'Extending the liability of the state in damages' [2001] LS 1; Craig and Fairgrieve, 'Barrett, Negligence and Discretionary Powers' [1999] *Public Law*, 626.

might be seen as a rare exception. The *Three Rivers* case shows how untrue this is. Procedural guarantees enshrined in Article 6 have already made their mark on the architecture of financial services regulation,[97] and it would seem that their effect is being felt in the most recent *Three Rivers* judgment. In the judgments of the majority in the House of Lords concerning the improper use of the Bingham Report, repeated reference is made to the claimant's right to a fair trial.[98] Similar concerns are present when Lord Hope expresses his hesitance in striking out claims concerning complex issues of fact and law without examination at trial. An explicit analogy was drawn with the right to a fair trial guaranteed by Article 6 of the European Convention when emphasising the overriding objective of the new procedural rules.[99] Moreover, a statutory immunity will of course be subject to a proportionality review under Article 6 ECHR about the right to a fair trial.[100]

Also, Community law influences can be detected within Lord Hope's judgment. In various key areas of his judgment, he acknowledged the influence of European law in shaping the elements of the cause of action. In response to the fact-sensitive issue of the degree of risk of which the regulator must have been aware, Lord Hope instinctively latched upon the test of a *sufficiently serious* risk of loss.[101]

Supranational law is not the extent of potential European influence in this sphere. Developments at a national level in European jurisdictions may also have a role to play. The international and cross-jurisdictional nature of the regulation of banks makes this sphere, as we have already seen, particular open to the influence of comparative law.

B. Role of Misfeasance in Governmental Liability

In controlling governmental wrongdoing, the tort of misfeasance has generally been distinguished from other torts by the need to show egregious intentional wrongdoing. This high level of required fault has limited its attractiveness to potential claimants who have instead preferred to rely upon the torts of assault, false imprisonment, and more particularly, negligence.

A consideration of the future role for the tort of misfeasance must be placed in the context of the broadening of its constituent elements; devel-

---

[97] J McDermott, 'Commercial Implications of the Human Rights Act 1998' (2000) BJIBFL 449, 453.
[98] *Three Rivers District Council* [2001] UKHL 16, para 6 (Lord Steyn), 33 and 80 (Lord Hope).
[99] *Three Rivers District Council* [2001] UKHL 16, para 92.
[100] See, for instance, the recent decision by the European Human Rights Court in *Al-Adsani v United Kingdom*, Application no 35763/97, Judgment of 21 Nov 2001.
[101] *Three Rivers District Council* [2001] UKHL 16, paras 60 and 76.

opments which we have already examined above. Misfeasance is now an intentional tort for which recklessness suffices. Although the form of recklessness proscribed in the recent cases is by no means objective, and some awareness on the part of the defendant would seem to be required, the gap between this tort and the tort of negligence, premised upon the all-pervading notion of reasonable foreseeability, has undoubtedly been narrowed.

This broadening of the mental element of the tort of misfeasance is not the only explanation for its enhanced appeal to litigants. Three further points should also be made.

1. *Requirement of Proximity*

In order to succeed in an action based upon the tort of negligence, the claimant must show that he or she was in a proximate relationship with the defendant. This can prove to be a significant obstacle to recovery.[102]

The exact role of proximity within the tort of misfeasance has been contested. In the Court of Appeal decision in *Three Rivers*, the majority indicated that proximity was of relevance to misfeasance in public office,[103] that it might play a limiting role where the number of claimants was large and alleged 'range of duty' was wide.[104] However, the House of Lords took a different view. The Court of Appeal's approach to proximity was rejected by Lord Steyn and Lord Hutton.[105]

This might make the tort of misfeasance in certain circumstances a more realistic option to claimants than the tort of negligence, particularly where the class of the potential claimants to which a duty of care in negligence would be owed is very broad. Indeed, in the case of banking supervision, the common law approach of the courts to negligence claims has been restrictive. In a number of cases, it has been held that no duty is owed by regulators to depositors for want of proximity.[106] So, no duty may arise at common law, even if the regulators are shown to have acted in flagrant breach of their duties. In such circumstances, misfeasance presents an alternative action against the wrongdoers. There will no doubt be other areas of public authority activity in which proximity has traditionally posed an obstacle to recovery in damages on the basis of negligence, and in which misfeasance in public office may therefore provide a remedy.[107]

---

[102] See, eg, *Capital & Counties plc v Hampshire County Council* [1997] QB 1004.

[103] *Three Rivers District Council* [1999] EuLR 211, 270–2 (CA).

[104] Ibid, 270.

[105] *Three Rivers District Council v Bank of England* [2000] 2 WLR 1220, 1233 and 1267.

[106] In the regulatory sphere, see *Yuen Kun Yeu v Attorney General of Hong Kong* [1988] AC 175 (Privy Council); *Cooper v Hobart*, 2001 SCC 79 (Supreme Court of Canada).

[107] For instance, in actions against the police.

2. The Recovery of Economic Loss

The reluctance of the courts to allow the recovery of pure economic loss for negligent wrongdoing is well known. Other than in restricted circumstances, the English courts preclude the recovery of financial loss which is unconnected with physical damage to the claimant's person or property.[108]

Reluctance to allow claims concerning pure economic loss is one of the reasons for which the actions in negligence against financial regulators have foundered.[109] However, this policy of caution has not—as yet—been extended to the tort of misfeasance in public office. It is no coincidence therefore that many of the leading misfeasance cases concern economic loss,[110] of which *Three Rivers* is an example *par excellence*. Although the size and extent of the loss suffered by the BCCI depositors may have had some impact on the framing of the tort in *Three Rivers*, it certainly did not have an exclusionary effect. This characteristic of the tort might draw its attention to those who traditionally would have difficulties in availing themselves of a negligence claim, such as disappointed applicants for commercial licences, or those who have suffered loss due to adverse planning decisions.

3. Exemplary Damages

In exceptional cases, the English courts can award punitive damages which are designed to express the court's disapproval of the defendant's exceptionally bad conduct.[111] Until recently, the award of exemplary damages was limited by means of the 'cause of action test', restricting the grant of such damages to those causes of action for which exemplary damages have been awarded prior to the case of *Rookes v Barnard*[112] in 1964.[113] This rule precluded the awarding of such damages for negligence,[114] breach of statutory duty,[115] and misfeasance in public office. However, in a recent case the House of Lords refused to strike out an action for the award of exemplary damages for misfeasance in public office, rejecting the 'cause of action test' as a limiting factor upon the award of such damages.[116]

---

[108] The major exception to this is the rule laid down in the case of *Hedley Byrne & Co Ltd v Heller & Partners* [1964] AC 465.

[109] See references to the spectre of indeterminate liability in *Cooper v Hobart*, 2001 SCC 79 (Supreme Court of Canada).

[110] *Bourgoin SA v MAFF* [1986] QB 716; *Roncarelli v Duplessis* (1959) 16 DLR (2d) 689 (Canadian Supreme Court).

[111] *Rookes v Barnard* [1964] AC 1129.   [112] Ibid.

[113] See *AB v South West Water Services Ltd* [1993] QB 507.

[114] Ibid.

[115] *R. v Secretary of State for Transport ex p Factortame (No 5)* The Times, 11 Sept 1997 (CA).

[116] *Kuddus v Chief Constable of Leicestershire Constabulary* [2001] 2 WLR 1789.

It is not entirely clear what the position now is in respect of the other torts which previously were not eligible for the award of punitive damages. Should the position remain that negligence is excluded, then there would be an added reason for bringing an action in misfeasance: the potential for a greater quantum of damages.

VI. CONCLUSION

The House of Lords judgment in *Three Rivers* is an important one for the domestic law of governmental liability. It is illustrative of a gradual liberalising of the conditions for state liability which has been a feature of recent cases on the tort of negligence.[117]

We have seen that liability for financial market supervisors is under discussion in several EU member states, and there are recent developments in the case law and legislation of a number of member states including France, Germany, and Italy. The House of Lords made no reference to any of this.[118] Neither did it make any reference, in the discussion of the system of the relevant directive, to the systems of banking supervision in other member states with one exception.[119]

It is unfortunate that account was not taken of the European developments. The cases from other national European jurisdictions indicate a perceptible shift towards a more liberal approach to actions brought by investors. The French courts have recognised liability of the regulator, the *Commission bancaire*, whilst still maintaining a strong protection at the fault level. The Italian courts have extended their case law in favour of governmental liability for inadequate supervision in the sphere of financial supervision. The German doctrinal critique of the 1984 legislation, limiting the case law in favour of depositors, has become increasingly vocal.

The comparative law material could serve a number of purposes. This backdrop of European cases may perhaps assist in the comprehension of the developing English case law. The developments in the House of Lords are

---

[117] See, in particular, *Barrett v Enfield LBC* [2001] 2 AC 550; *Phelps v Hillingdon LBC* [2001] 2 AC 619.

[118] But the House of Lords extensively discussed cases from different Commonwealth jurisdictions which were recognised as persuasive authorities. Lord Bingham foresees that judgments from other European countries will be dealt with in a similar way, see for instance his highly convincing and elegant argument in 'A New Common Law for Europe', in Markesinis, *The Coming Together of the Common Law and the Civil Law. The Clifford Chance Millenium Lectures* (Oxford: Hart Publishing, 2000), 27. A predecessor as Senior Law Lord, Lord Goff of Chieveley introduced a use of comparative legal materials in the House of Lords which today is more extensive than in any other European court. But not in the present case.

[119] This one exception is the statement about there being no supervisory authorities in the UK or Denmark before the First Banking Directive [2000] WLR 1220 at 1254. It is based on a factual misunderstanding.

not taking place in isolation: they are occurring within a broader European trend.

The comparative law dimension is not only helpful in allowing one to place the English developments in a wider context. It may also provide practical guidance for the domestic courts. In particular, the French litigation allows one to challenge the assumption that changes at the fault level may result in uncontrollable extension of liability in general. The approach of the French administrative courts illustrates a creative attitude to the control mechanisms in these cases. In particular, the doctrine of loss of a chance may well be a useful tool for the English courts in evaluating the quantum of loss suffered by depositors. Although the courts have been reluctant to apply this doctrine in personal injury cases for lost chances of recovery,[120] there have been a number of successful damages actions for the lost opportunity of financial gain,[121] in spheres a diverse as lost employment opportunities,[122] loss of opportunity to bring civil proceedings.[123] Comparative material could serve other purposes. It could provide a better understanding of the supervisory regime under the two banking directives in force at the relevant time. This is of course crucial for the determination of liability under Community law.

---

[120] *Hotson v East Berkshire Area Health Authority* [1987] AC 750.
[121] *Allied Maples Group Ltd v Simmons & Simmons* [1995] 1 WLR 1602. See M Lunney and K Oliphant, *Tort Law: Text and Materials* (Oxford: Oxford University Press, 2000), 184; Markesinis and Deakin, *Tort Law*, 4th edn (Oxford: Oxford University Press, 1999) 183.
[122] *Spring v Guardian Assurance* [1995] 2 AC 296, 327.
[123] *Kitchen v Royal Air Force Association* [1958] 1 WLR 563

PART III:

COMPARING SYSTEMS

9. TORTIOUS LIABILITY FOR NEGLIGENT MISDIAGNOSIS OF LEARNING DISABILITIES: A COMPARATIVE STUDY OF ENGLISH AND AMERICAN LAW

Basil Markesinis* and Adrian R Stewart**

I. INTRODUCTORY REMARKS

George Bernard Shaw once remarked that 'England and America are two countries separated by a common language.'[1] That statement could be modified to read that England and America are two countries separated by a common legal heritage. The comparison of the two systems in the area of negligent misdiagnosis of learning disabilities suggests as much. For though it reveals no significant difference—not at least until the very recent decision of the House of Lords in *Phelps v Hillingdon LBC*[2]—in their approach towards liability at *common law*, it does bring into relief the backdrop differences which produce the real divergence between English and American law. These include, inter alia, the existence in America of civil jury trials, contingency fee arrangements, punitive damages, and dual court systems of overlapping jurisdiction at the state and federal levels. The imposition of liability in America thus brings with it unusually high transaction costs of defending and prosecuting claims, as well as the possibility (albeit rare) of awards that are so large that defendants could be bankrupted. None of these factors exist in England to such a pronounced extent.

That the true differences between English and American law must be

---

* QC, LL D (Cantab), DCL (Oxon), Professor of Common Law and Civil Law, University College London; Jamail Regents Chair, University of Texas School of Law; Fellow of the British Academy; Member of the American Law Institute.

** BA, 1995, The University of Arizona; MFA, 2000, The University of Houston; JD, 2000, The University of Texas School of Law. Law Clerk to the Hon Matthew F Kennelly, District Judge, US District Court for the Northern District of Illinois. Opinions expressed herein are exclusively the responsibility of the authors.

[1] *The Oxford Dictionary of Quotations* (ed Elizabeth Knowles 5th edn) (Oxord: Oxford University Press, 1999), 521.

[2] [2000] 3 WLR, 776.

sought in fundamental differences in the 'backdrop' of the two systems was the main thesis of the late Professor Fleming in his stimulating monograph *The American Tort Process*, published in 1987.[3] But this imaginative thesis has often been forgotten on both sides of the Atlantic; and in England, where references to American law have, if anything increased in recent times, they have been accompanied by some unfortunate misunderstandings. Thus, the House of Lords has been castigated by an eminent New Zealand judge,[4] who subsequently joined the Lords, for erroneously believing a decision of the United States Supreme Court[5] in a matter of federal jurisdiction as representing the tort law in the various states. And in the *Phelps* case, to be discussed further down, we shall see that neither Counsel nor the judges who heard the dispute seemed to be aware of the intricate richness of American federal and state law, which complement the solutions of pure common law. In particular, the American Individuals with Disabilities Education Act (IDEA) seems never to have been mentioned.[6]

By contrast, the United States Supreme Court has apparently felt less and less inclined to cite foreign cases. This was not always so since that Court at one time felt compelled to fit its decisions into a broader Anglo-American jurisprudence. For instance, in the 1953 *Dalehite v United States* decision[7] the Court cited English, Canadian, Australian, and New Zealand authorities for support of a 'discretionary function' exception to the federal government's waiver of sovereign immunity.[8] The 1999 case *Alden v Maine*,[9] however, is perhaps representative of the Court's current reluctance to cite contemporary English case law. It would seem that the law of England is nowadays of interest to today's justices only to the extent that eighteenth-century authorities influenced the Founders and their understanding of the Constitution.[10] Similarly, state courts often refer to the common law of England, but increasingly confine their citations to English

---

    3 John G Fleming, *The American Tort Process* (1988)

    4 Lord Cooke of Thorndon, 'An Impossible Distinction' (1991) 107 *LQR* 46, esp 60, agreeing with the late Professor John Fleming who spoke—(1990) 106 *LQR* 525, 530—of 'one-sided and misleading references' to American case law.

    5 *East River SS Corp v Transamerica Delaval* 476 US 858, 106, S Ct Rep 2295 (1986).

    6 Discussed below in s 3(b)(i).

    7 346 US 15, 73 S Ct 956 (1953).

    8 346 US at 33, 73 S Ct at 967, n 27 (citing the English Crown Proceedings Act of 1947 and cases such as *Enever v The King* (1906) 3 Com LR 969, 988). See also ibid at 36 n 31 (Justice Reed, writing for the majority, cited *East Suffolk Rivers Catchment Board v Kent*, (1941) AC 74, and other cases to buttress his reliance on American state cases that articulated the discretionary function immunity).

    9 527 US 706, 119 S Ct 2240 (1999).

    10 527 US at 715, 119 S Ct at 2247–8 (citing 1 W Blackstone, *Commentaries on the Laws of England*, 234–5 (1765), for proposition that there was a 'close and necessary relationship understood to exist between sovereignty and immunity from suit' at the time of the Founding).

cases from before their establishment as separate courts.[11] One of the purposes of this article is therefore to remind the reader that in these days of increasing globalisation awareness of how sister courts have handled similar issues may be a source of inspiration and benefit. At the same time, however, one must also undertake such endeavours conscious of the dangers of the comparative use of foreign material. This article is thus as much an attempt to inform American judges about developments in English law as it is to suggest to academics and practitioners—on both sides of the Atlantic—a way of using foreign law before national courts.

In keeping with the views advocated over many years by the first of us,[12] our study begins by comparing a narrow factual situation, which has been litigated in both systems. The situation we have chosen is the negligent misdiagnosis of learning disabilities in educational settings. From there we move on to show how one must progressively widen the scope of one's research and understanding of a foreign legal system before one can begin to make constructive comparative comments. The result of our survey shows, not unexpectedly, an American law as complex as it is abundant. It is complex because of the existence of two parallel systems of compensation, federal and state,[13] and abundant because the various states and federal circuits are free to adopt differing legal stances. This richness holds out lessons for the English of what to do and what to avoid. But as we shall point out later on, the English material also has a lesson or two for American judges provided it reaches them in a usable way.

In accordance with our belief that one should widen one's research as one deepens one's inquiry, we then move on to the question of quantum of damages. At this stage, we suggest that here, as in so many other areas of tort law, the differences in awards between the English and American systems, coupled with the ability (or inability) of judges to control them effectively, may go a long way towards explaining the long-established hostility towards these claims. At the same time, we are mindful of both the methods used for limiting damages, such as statutory caps on damages or qualified official immunity, and those legal principles, such as *respondeat superior* or 'bad faith', which allow liability to find, sooner rather than later, a sufficiently 'deep pocket'.

---

[11] See, eg, Kilmer *v* Mun, 17 SW 3d 545, 551 (Mo 2000) (citing *Scott v Shepard*, 96 Eng Rep 525 (1773) for an early discussion of causation).

[12] See B Markesinis, *Foreign Law and Comparative Methodology: A Subject and a Thesis* (1997); id, *Always on the Same Path: Essays in Foreign Law and Comparative Methodology* (Oxford: Oxford University Press, 2000).

[13] In America, federal courts apply and interpret federal statutes and the federal constitution, while applying state law as interpreted by state courts. See *Erie RR Co v Thompkins*, 304 US 64, 58 S Ct 817 (1938). State courts do the reverse, interpreting and applying state law, while being bound to merely apply federal law as interpreted by federal courts.

But in making these assertions we tread carefully for we readily admit that an over-simplified, broad-brush, comparison of levels of awards may not do full justice to such a complicated subject. For a simple comparison of figures does not adequately reflect such things as the American contingency fee system (which can swallow 20 to 45 per cent of any award). Nor does it say anything about the (effective) absence (in the United States) of a generous social compensation system which often explains (if not justifies) the making of a large award. The final reason why we tread gently on this subject is because judicial references to the impact that damages have on the rules of substantive law are neither frequent nor sophisticated in their presentation.

This kind of approach to the subject also led us to compare the style and method of reasoning adopted on both sides of the Atlantic. We regard this a fascinating subject for a number of cultural reasons that need not be explained here since they must be obvious to most. But the difference of judicial styles has led many American courts, unlike some of their most recent English counterparts, to hide behind legal screens the real reasons that seemed to be troubling the judicial mind. The invocation of 'magic words' such as educational malpractice, public duty doctrine, or discretionary function immunity, is all-too-often sufficient to dismiss an American claim. Here, we find the English judges have, in recent times at any rate, been more open—if not always very convincing. But whatever the deficiencies in the English reasoning the open discussion of the main policy concerns has facilitated a meaningful discussion of the underlying issues. More importantly, perhaps, it has also allowed in recent times a number of leading members of the House of Lords—notably Lords Nicholls, Hutton, and Clyde—to confront in two recent cases these concerns in an equally open manner. If, as we suggest, these concerns are largely shared by judges on both sides of the Atlantic, then the latest decision of the House of Lords may warrant careful scrutiny on the western side of the divide. In short, we feel that here, as in so many other sections of our paper, there is plenty of room for give and take. For anyone who believes that comparative law is a two-way street, this is but yet another confirmation that the study of foreign law can make one humble and proud.

One last word about our topic. For the reasons already stated, our subject is, at first glance at least, deliberately narrow. Nonetheless, we venture to suggest that this does not mean that its interest is a limited one. For, as the study of the English cases shows most clearly, the recent litigation is the culmination of years of litigation that has affected a wide range of statutory bodies, such as the police,[14] local authorities,[15] the public pros-

---

[14] *Hill v Chief Constable of West Yorkshire* [1989] 1 AC 53.
[15] *X(Minors) v Bedfordshire County Council* [1995] 2 AC 633; *Stovin v Wise* [1996] AC 923; *W v Essex County Council* [1998] 3 WLR 534.

ecution service,[16] the fire services,[17] and the public rescue services.[18] In England, all of the above have, at one stage or another, been sued for allegedly failing to discharge their duties properly; and, as in the United States, in most (but not all) cases the defendants have gone scot-free.[19] The reasoning common to both legal regimes is discussed below.

But in England, unlike the United States, a new and outside factor is prompting a re-appraisal of internal law. This factor is Europe in the form of the Court of the European Communities and, most relevant in our case, the Court of Human Rights in Strasbourg. This 'outside' influence has proved, for political but also technically legal reasons, highly controversial, often bringing to the fore the Europhobic tendencies that so many in modern Britain share. But what is probably most significant about the Strasbourg interventions is that they have challenged the repeated reliance on the notion of duty of care in order to strike out actions at an early stage in the legal proceedings. This, in other words, is a superb example of modern human rights law challenging and influencing internal private law.[20] Because of lack of space, this aspect of modern, English law will be omitted from this paper. Fortunately, it can be omitted without damaging the presentation of the *Phelps* judgment to an American audience since Strasbourg is, on the surface of things, mostly absent from the opinions in *Phelps*.[21]

With that introduction, we turn to the presentation of our research. In section 2, we survey and analyse the English common law governing the liability of statutory bodies in tort—both in general and as it applies to the specific example of the negligent misdiagnosis of learning disabilities. Section 2 focuses largely on the recent English decision in *Phelps* and the important distinction it draws between generalised claims of poor education and the narrow situation of negligent misdiagnosis. Section 3 covers the diverse 'American' position and attempts to ascertain whether the current consensus against liability will continue. Section 3 also describes the unique features of American federal statutory law relating to children with learning disabilities, including a sharp limitation on damages. As we shall

---

[16] *Elguzouli-Daf v Commissioner of Police of the Metropolis* [1995] 2 WLR 173.

[17] *Capital & Counties plc v Hampshire County Council* [1997] QB 1004 [1997] WLR 331.

[18] *Skinner v Secretary of State for Transport, The Times*, 3 Jan 1995, QBD.

[19] The English courts have been most restrictive in respect of negligence actions against public authorities. It should be noted however that actions based on other torts have had more success. In civil actions against the police, the torts of assault, battery, false imprisonment, and malicious prosecution are commonly applied. See, eg, *Thompson v Commissioner of Police of the Metropolis* [1998] QB 498.

[20] On this point, see Markesinis 'Der wachsende Einfluß der Menschenrechte auf das englische Deliktsrecht', *Festschrift für Hans Stoll zum 75 Geburstag* (2000).

[21] Visible rather than absent is probably the best way to describe the above. For like Banquo, Strasbourg dominated the thinking that has lead to the reappraisal even if its judgments are hardly visible in the opinions of the House of Lords.

see, there are arguments common to both systems for denying liability. However, both systems have managed to provide some sort of remedy to the learning disabled child. Sections 4 and 5 present our arguments in detail.

II. THE LAW IN ENGLAND

A. *The Law until* Phelps

The ruling in *Phelps* is best understood if it is set against the background of a number of important decisions of the House of Lords (and the Court of Appeal) which set the parameters of the possible tortious liability of statutory bodies. Of these decisions, three cases stand out for special attention because of their detailed discussion of the underlying policy issues. They are: *Hill v Chief Constable of West Yorkshire,*[22] *Stovin v Wise,*[23] and *X (Minors) v Bedfordshire County Council, and M (A Minor) v Newham London Borough Council.*[24]

Hill v Chief Constable of West Yorkshire[25] involved a claim by the mother of a deceased woman (suing for damages to the daughter's estate) against the police on the grounds that because of their alleged negligence they failed, during their investigations of the commission of a series of similar crimes, to apprehend the perpetrator. This failure allowed the criminal to remain at large for a further period of time, during which he murdered the plaintiff's daughter. The action against the police failed on the grounds of no duty of care.

In *Stovin v Wise*[26] a local authority failed to exercise its statutory power to direct a private landowner, on whose property lay an obstruction, to have it removed in order to improve visibility at a nearby road junction which was known to have caused traffic accidents in the past. The plaintiff, who was injured at this junction by the defendant's car, claimed damages against him for his injuries. The defendant, in turn, joined the council as a third party. The action against the defendant having been settled, the battle shifted to the council's potential liability. By a majority of three to two, the House of Lords ruled in favour of the council.

Finally, *X(Minors) v Bedfordshire County Council*[27] was one of two

---

[22] *Hill v Chief Constable of West Yorkshire* [1989] 1 AC 53.
[23] *Stovin v Wise* [1996] AC 923.
[24] *X(Minors) v Bedfordshire County Council* [1995] 2 AC 633.
[25] *Hill* [1989] 1 AC 53.   [26] *Stovin* [1996] AC 923.
[27] *X(Minors)* [1995] 2 AC 633. For the rich American law, largely in line with the *Bedfordshire* ideas, see Michael R Flaherty, 60 *ALR* 4th 942 (1998), 'Tort Liability of Public Authority for Failure to Remove Parentally Abused or Neglected Children from Parents' Custody'.

'child-abuse' actions (consolidated and heard together with three other cases dealing with alleged failures in the provision of education to children with special needs). In the first child abuse case, one finds most of the general discussion of the law. It arose in connection with a claim that a local authority negligently and in breach of its statutory obligations failed to exercise its powers to institute care proceedings after it had received serious reports that the plaintiff/child had been the subject of parental abuse and neglect. The second child abuse case, *M (a Minor) v Newham London Borough Council*, was the mirror image of the first. For here the claim was for negligently removing the child from maternal care on the basis of an unfounded belief that the abuse had taken place by the mother's co-habitee and the conclusion that the mother was unable to protect her child. Both the actions against the local authority for alleged negligence and/or breach of statutory duty failed.

In all of these cases the plaintiffs failed partly because the courts took the view that no action under the relevant statute was available to the plaintiff but also because the courts believed that the defendants owed no duty of care to the plaintiffs and thus their liability could not be engaged under the ordinary rules of negligence. This result was reached partly on the application of the usual, legalistic devices of foreseeability, proximity, and the like, but mainly by reliance being placed upon a complex series of policy arguments. We shall examine these factors in a subsequent section. Here it will suffice to set them out in summary form. They are four.

(i)   *Economic*: imposing liability on the public bodies in question would make bad economic sense;
(ii) *Inhibition*: liability would inhibit the freedom of action of the officials who took the relevant decisions;
(iii) *Discretionary*: it would be inappropriate for the courts to control elected officials/bodies and tell them how to exercise their discretionary powers; and
(iv) *Alternatives*: the victims in these cases had alternative remedies that made a tort remedy in the form of damages not only superfluous but dangerous (mainly for the economic reason).

In the *Bedfordshire* cluster of cases that were tried together, the claims flowing from the negligent misdiagnosis of learning disabilities by the relevant psychology services were seen in a more favourable light than the child abuse claims. Lord Browne-Wilkinson, speaking for the entire House, thus thought that the position in these three cases could be 'wholly different'.[28] Liability under the ordinary rules of negligence might be engaged, so long as the psychology service was not 'part and parcel of the system established

---

[28]   *X(Minors)* [1995] 2 AC at 762.

by the defendant authority for the discharge of its statutory duties'.[29] Even more relevant to the *Phelps* litigation was the fact that Lord Browne-Wilkinson left open the question of the local authority's vicarious liability. Indeed, one reason for rejecting its *primary* liability in all of the *Bedfordshire* cluster of cases, and in line with alternative remedy policy argument, above, was the view:

> that in almost every case . . . there will be an alternative remedy by way of a claim against the authority on the grounds of its vicarious liability for the negligent advice on the basis of which it exercises its discretion.[30]

One more brief observation is needed before we come to the *Phelps* litigation.

After the *Bedfordshire* decision was handed down, and as a result of dissatisfaction with another 'police' case,[31] a complaint was lodged before the Court of Human Rights in Strasbourg. This was accepted by the court, *inter alia*, on the grounds that the dismissal of the plaintiff's action for lack of a duty of care amounted to a denial of justice and was thus in breach of Article 6 of the Convention.[32] This reasoning of the Strasbourg court, though subsequently accepted by the Commission in a complaint concerning *Bedfordshire* itself,[33] has proved highly controversial in England and it

---

[29] *X(Minors)* [1995] 2 AC, at 763.

[30] Ibid, at 762.

[31] *Osman v Ferguson* [1993] 4 All ER 344. The case involved a schoolteacher who, in 1987, developed a 'unhealthy' obsession with one of his charges. Both the boy, who rejected these advances, and his parents, complained to the school and its head teacher. This led to a number of interviews with the teacher who became increasingly hostile and engaged in a series of menacing acts affecting the young boy's family. The police, who had been informed of the teacher's behaviour, apparently remained inactive, even after it became known that the dejected and depressed teacher 'threatened to do a Hungerford'. (In 1987 the city of Hungerford in England became the scene of a massacre in which a gunman burst into a school, killed sixteen persons, and then committed suicide.) A year later, as the acts of criminal violence intensified, the police were, apparently, putting together a file with a view of prosecuting the mentally deranged teacher. But, alas, he acted first, by killing the father and injuring the brother of the boy who was the subject of amorous advances. The judge at first instance refused to strike out the action—not least because in this instance it was arguable that some kind of relationship had come into being between the complainant's family and the police through their repeated reporting of the murderer's activities. But his decision was reversed by the Court of Appeal that relied on the *Hill* judgment to justify its conclusion. Once again, the reader must consult the lengthy narrative of the facts as given by the Strasbourg judgment in *Osman* to evaluate the proximity that had been created in this case between police and the victim and his family and also to appreciate the extent of the police inactivity. Such legal results would not be tolerated by other European legal systems. Thus, for Germany, see BGH 30 Apr 1953 LM, s 839 [Fg] BGB, no 5. For France, see, Conseil d' Etat, 29 juillet 1948, *Recueil des arrêts du Conseil d' Etat*, 213; Conseil d'Etat, 26 juin 1985, *Recueil des arrêts du Conseil d' Etat*, 254. Absent a special relationship, American law, like English law, is very reluctant to impose any liability on the policy and the statutory bodies that are answerable for it.

[32] *Osman v UK* (1998) 5 BHRC 293.

[33] *Z and Others v the UK*, Report of the Commission, 10 Sept 1999. The very detailed narration of the facts contained in the Commission's Report underlies how lawyers can go too

is unclear whether it will stand or not in the future. At the time of writing, the future of the *Osman* ruling remains in some doubt even in Strasbourg. But in England, the post *Osman* era witnessed a House of Lords staying almost aloof of the controversy while the Court of Appeal barely concealed its dislike of the Strasbourg decision. Nonetheless, in practice all major cases that ended in the House of Lords since *Osman* have resulted in a reversal of the lower courts' striking out actions.[34] *Osman*, like Banquo in Macbeth's dinner for Duncan,[35] has thus played an invisible yet crucial role to the entire proceedings.

B. The Law after Phelps

The *Phelps* litigation concerned a school failure to diagnose dyslexia in one of its children and thus leaving it without appropriate educational training. Dyslexia is, nowadays, a medically recognised disorder manifested by difficulty in learning to read despite conventional instruction.[36] It is dependent upon fundamental cognitive disabilities, which are frequently of constitutional origin. Until comparatively recently, the disorder was not medically recognised and the courts, here as in cases of psychiatric injury, took a sceptical attitude towards this disability, often associating its deleterious effects to environmental factors connected with the child/claimant's life or to lack of intelligence.[37] The difficulties of diagnosis also delayed its admission into

---

far in tolerating horrific behaviour for the sake of preserving the intellectual neatness of their system. It could be argued that, in its bluntness, the notion of duty of care does just that. Note, however, that the European Court of Human Rights has subsequently taken a different view of this question, see further Ch 3 above, J Wright, 'The Retreat from *Osman: Z v UK* in the European Court of Human Rights and Beyond.'

[34] *Barrett v Enfield London Borough Council* [1999] 3 WLR 79, [1999] 3 All ER 193 started this trend. It was repeated in *W v Essex County Council* [2000] 2 WLR 601. *Barrett*, in one sense, is a factual variant to *Bedfordshire*. For in the newer case the plaintiff had been in the care of the local authority from a young age and complained that because of their neglect, they had failed, inter alia, to organise for his adoption and, instead, proceeded to make many and inappropriate placements with foster parents. The Court of Appeal struck out his action on the grounds that it was not 'fair, just and reasonable to impose a duty of care' in relation to the authority's statutory discretion in these matters. But the House of Lords took the view that a duty should not be ruled out *a priori* and set about doubting the policy reasons which had hitherto prevailed and negated the imposition of a duty of care. In this sense, *Phelps* must be seen as a decision that completes this process.

[35] The appropriate imagery comes from Paul Craig and Duncan Fairgrieve, '*Barrett*, Negligence and Discretionary Powers' [1999] *Public Law*, 626, 631.

[36] See American Psychiatric Ass'n, Diagnostic and Statistical Manual of Mental Disorders, 4th edn (1995), 46–53.

[37] This is not the first time that medical uncertainties have encouraged judicial timidity. Thus, the ability to claim damages for negligently inflicted psychiatric harm (in the United States usually referred to as emotional distress) has, on the whole, been very restrained. This is partly because, until recently, this type of harm was seen as one that was unreal, easily faked, and, generally, not deserving the protection of the law. The medical view on the matters has changed; but the law is still lagging behind.

the law as a plausible cause of tortious harm. It is thus not entirely surprising that the Court of Appeal, which under its presiding judge Lord Justice Stuart-Smith had become involved in a number of such cases, was once again, to take a hostile view to such claims. Thus, invoking a barrage of arguments, ranging from the opinion that the claimant had suffered no recognisable harm to the view that the educational psychologists, who had failed to discover the child's disability, owed no duty to the child, itself,[38] the Court of Appeal refused to allow the claims to go to trial. In its *opposition* to these claims the Court, however, arguably went a step too far. For it attempted to modify Lord Browne-Wilkinson's view in *Bedfordshire* that vicarious liability might, in appropriate circumstances be possible and held that this, too, should be categorically excluded if the purpose of the primary immunity of the Council was to be respected. In its *Phelps* judgment, the House of Lords would have none of all this. And what in our view makes it particularly significant is the fact that it reviewed and rejected the policy reasons, which had hitherto militated against the imposition of liability. Thus, though the House of Lords left open for future reconsideration the question of *primary* liability of the authority, its rejection of the policy arguments put forward to bolster vicarious immunity, makes it difficult to see how, in a future decision, the very same reasons can be resurrected to support primary immunity. Equally noteworthy is the fact that by not making *Osman* the centre of the decision, their lordships seem to have opened the road for reconsideration of the immunity cases irrespective of what happens to *Osman* in the years to come. For present purposes, therefore, it will suffice to make two points about this important decision, which may be relevant to future American practice.

The first concerns some of the arguments advanced by the two most thoughtful opinions of the House of Lords delivered by Lords Nicholls and Clyde concerning the policy fears underpinning the non-liability rule. They will be discussed in section 5, below where the validity of these oft-expressed fears will be reviewed. Here, suffice it to say that they do not seem to carry much weight with the law lords who decided *Phelps*. The second pointer, which one must lay down, relates to a fine distinction drawn mainly in Lord Nicholls' judgment between misdiagnosis cases and general claims based on poor teaching. For the learned Law Lord, the latter

---

[38] This is a well-known technique for defeating a claim based on statute where the statute itself gives no clue on the matter. In this case, however, it was particularly dubious given that the psychology profession that carries out these tests inclines to the view that their duties are as much towards the child as to the authorities that had commissioned their services. See D Galloway, 'Special Education in the UK' (1998) 15 (1) *Educational and Child Psychology*, 100, 106; G Lindsay, 'Sheffield Psychological Service', *Educational Psychology in Practice*, Apr 1995: Special Issue, 39.

would not attract liability. This distinction, no doubt difficult to draw in some cases, could, nonetheless, prove attractive to future American courts since it could allow them to preserve their hostility towards the tort of educational malpractice while setting aside the misdiagnosis cases for separate treatment.[39] Few American courts have recognised this distinction, and then only in dissent.[40] Most courts have simply characterised claims of negligent misdiagnosis as 'failure to teach properly' and dismissed them without extended discussion.[41]

III. THE LAW IN AMERICA

A. State Tort Law

As is well known, in the United States the highest court of each state is almost always the last resort for plaintiffs in tort litigation. Although this decentralised system of adjudication has led to a somewhat fragmented and diverse picture, sometimes a consensus among the various courts can be found to exist. With respect to the public duty doctrine, qualified official immunity, and the tort of educational malpractice, such a consensus seems, on the whole, to have emerged. The picture one gets is not one favourable to plaintiffs. In denying liability, most American courts cite the public duty doctrine. Many states grant public officials immunity for discretionary acts. Virtually all of the states reject the tort of 'educational malpractice'. Such chance as there is for success, can be found in the various exceptions that have grown around these doctrines. These include special relationships that overcome the public duty doctrine objection, and 'bad faith' or 'non-discretionary' exceptions to immunity.

1. The Public Duty Doctrine

Education in America is predominately a local affair. Nearly 15,000 school districts, most co-extensive with city or county governments, administer the nearly 90,000 schools in the American public education system.[42] These entities do not benefit from total sovereign immunity, but the common law

---

[39] See, eg, *Doe v Board of Education of Montgomery County*, 453 A 2d 814 (Md 1982); *Donohue v Copiague Union Free School District*, 407 NYS 2d 874 (NY App, 1979).

[40] *Doe*, 453 A 2d at 820 (Eldridge, J, dissenting); *Donohue*, 407 NYS 2d at 883 (Suozzi, J, dissenting).

[41] *Johnson v Clark*, 418 NW 2d 466, 468 (Mich App 1987).

[42] National Center For Education Statistics, *Overview of Public Elementary and Secondary Schools and Districts: School Year, 1997–98*, May 1999. <http://nces.ed.gov/pubs99/1999322/> (last visited 21 May 2001).

has long recognised[43] a limited immunity for municipalities,[44] including school districts.[45] Based on the fact that these entities engaged in both run-of-the-mill corporate activities as well as certain activities that were uniquely governmental, courts protected their governmental but not the corporate (or proprietary) activities. In the post-Second World War era, more than half of the states abrogated sovereign immunity, either by statute or judicial decision,[46] and municipal immunities were likewise affected if not always eliminated. The American Law Institute even went as far as stating that the rule should be that municipalities have no general immunity at all.[47]

However, the jettisoning of the doctrine has not been followed by the abandonment of immunity. No duty has ever been 'discovered' that did not require its own control mechanisms. As in the English cases,[48] American courts have relied upon 'legalistic' arguments as well as policy reasons for limiting or denying liability. Thus, courts have retained and developed old formalisms and spawned new ones designed to limit or eliminate liability. The English policy arguments, including the economic, inhibition, discretionary, and alternative relief arguments,[49] have also been reproduced in American decisions,[50] although without cross-citation. To be sure, given the plethora of decisions, it is not surprising also to find American courts that have articulated some countervailing arguments in order to impose liability. One such argument, for example, has stressed the inconsistency of applying

---

[43] W Page Keeton, *et al*, *Prosser & Keeton on the Law of Torts*, 5th edn (1984), s 131 (citing *Russell v Men of Devon* [1798] 2 Term Rep 667, 100 ER 359) [hereinafter Prosser and Keeton].

[44] For the purposes of this article, we use the terms 'local authority,' 'municipality', and 'school district' interchangeably. It should be noted that private schools (either religious or secular) are not protected by sovereign immunity, and their administrators are not cloaked with qualified immunity. In those cases, the only protection is the defence that plaintiff/students are seeking to advance a discredited 'educational malpractice' claim. However, private schools and undergraduate institutions are more susceptible to liability sounding in contract, especially where there has been a complete failure to educate. See, eg, *Lemmon v U of Cincinnati*, 750 NE 2d 668, 671 (Ohio Ct Cl 2001) (finding a contract between student and university but finding no breach thereof); *Ross v Creighton U* , 957 F. 2d 410, 415–17 (7th Cir 1992) (dismissing negligence action but reinstating a narrow contract claim); *Zumbrun v U of Southern Cal*, 25 Cal App 3d 1, 101 Cal Rptr 499 (1972).

[45] See, eg, *Bang v Independent School Dist. No 27 of St Louis County*, 225 NW 449, 450 (Minn 1929) ('A school district in the exercise of its governmental functions is not liable for negligence unless liability is imposed by statute').

[46] *Prosser & Keeton*, at 1052.

[47] *Restatement of Torts* (2d) s 895C. (1979).

[48] *See Hill v Chief Constable of West Yorkshire* [1989] 1 AC 53; *X(Minors) v Bedfordshire County Council* [1995] 2 AC 633 (HL); *Elguzouli-Daf v Commissioner of Police of the Metropolis*, [1995] 2 WLR 173; *Stovin v Wise*, 1996] AC 923; and *W v Essex County Council* [1998] 3 WLR 534.

[49] See Markesinis, *et al*, *Tortious Liability of Statutory Bodies* (1999), 45–50. [Hereinafter Markesinis, *Tortious Liability*.]

[50] See below s 3 (a)(i) 'Policy Arguments'.

formalistic limitations on liability after abrogating sovereign immunity since such attempts only succeed in re-introducing the sovereign immunity doctrine through the back door.[51] Other courts have also taken the view that governmental immunity from tort actions may be nullified *pro tanto*, by the existence of liability insurance.[52] But the majority of jurisdictions still take the view that the procurement of liability or indemnity insurance by a governmental unit does not affect its immunity from tort liability.[53] On the whole, therefore, these attempts to break loose from the mentality that reigned during the days of sovereign immunity have not met with wide success.

As a general rule,[54] American courts have not, in this area of the law, made extensive use of amorphous concepts such as 'foreseeability' or 'proximate cause' to deny liability.[55] Nevertheless, the use of other 'legalisms' still tends to obscure the policy preferences of individual judges even when these make an appearance in the judgments. However, as we see in some English cases and American decisions, 'appeal to 'policy' can serve no less as a brake than as an accelerator of legal change',[56] and it has to be attempted in a sophisticated and empirically supported manner if it is to be convincing. In the United States, such attempts as there are to explore the policy reasons that lie behind the decisions of the courts can be found more in academic literature, than in court decisions.[57]

---

[51] See, eg, *Adams v State*, 555 P 2d 235, 241–2 (Alaska 1976) ('[W]e consider that the "duty to all, duty to no-one" doctrine is in reality a form of sovereign immunity'); *Schear v Board of County Commissioners of Bernalillo Co*, 101 NM 687 P 2d 728, 734 (NM 1984) ('We will not now breathe new life into a rule which, as a ghost of sovereign immunity, operates as a denial of a cause of action'); *Coffey v City of Milwaukee*, 247 NW 2d 132, 137 (Wis 1976).

[52] See, eg, *Crowell v School Dist. No 7*, 805 P 2d 522, 533 (Mont 1991); *McGaha v Board of Regents of Univ of Oklahoma*, 691 P 2d 895, 898 (Okla 1984) (noting that authority to purchase liability insurance, along with an actual purchase of such insurance, acts as an effective limited waiver of immunity).

[53] *American Law Reports* 2d 1437, vol 68 (1959), RD Hursh, 'Liability or Indemnity Insurance Carried by Governmental Unit as Affecting Immunity from Tort Liability' (with references).

[54] One of the earliest 'educational malpractice' cases—*Peter W v San Francisco Unified School District*, 131 Cal Rptr 854 (Cal App 1st Dist 1976)—did, indeed, approach the problem by applying the multi-criteria test which the Supreme Court of California first developed in the case of *Biakanja v Irving* 320 P 2d 16 (Cal 1958). But *Biakanja* was a case concerned with the question whether a notary who had negligently attested a will could be liable to the frustrated beneficiary and its proposed tests look awkward when applied to the dyslexia cases and the kind of policy issues that they raise.

[55] Leon Green would no doubt be pleased. See Leon Green, *Foreseeability in Negligence Law*, 61 *Colum L Rev* 1401, 1403 (1961) (noting that such vague terms will 'doubtless remain in our legal system to serve and to plague the profession as long as the common law is recognised as a means of settling disputes').

[56] John G Fleming, *The American Tort Process* (Oxford: Clarendon Press, 1988), 34.

[57] See, eg, Barbara Armacost, 'Affirmative Duties, Systemic Harms, and the Due Process Clause', 94 *Mich L Rev* 982, 1002 (1996).

(a) Legalistic Arguments

A primary 'legalistic' control mechanism is the public duty doctrine.[58] Others include the proprietary/governmental[59] and discretionary/operational[60] distinctions, as well as the invocation of the various immunities granted by statute[61] or found in the common law.[62] Legislatures have also intervened with comprehensive government tort claims acts, most of which have included caps on compensatory damages and/or prohibitions on punitive damages.[63]

Reading the American cases one is often left with the impression that the public duty doctrine has in many cases been deployed mechanically to deny liability. This doctrine, first enunciated in 1855 by the US Supreme Court in *South v Maryland ex rel Pottle*,[64] states that a duty to the public does not create liability to an individual person, in the absence of a special relationship. For example, a police officer is generally responsible for law enforcement. However, he does not owe each person a legally enforceable duty. The primary exception to this rule is when a special relationship exists (or has arisen) between an official and a citizen. The test for special relationship varies from state to state but, generally speaking, includes assumption of a duty by a government official, contact with a plaintiff-victim, reliance by a plaintiff-victim on a government official, and knowledge of that reliance on the part of the official.[65] An influential articulation of this exception was stated by the New York Court of Appeals in *Cuffy v City of New York*.[66] There, the court held that the 'special relationship' exception required four things:

[58] For the first American articulation, see *South v Maryland*, 59 US 396 (1855). For academic approval, see Thomas Cooley, *The Elements of Torts*, vol. III, 4th edn (1895), s 300.

[59] See, eg, *Catone v Medberry*, 555 A 2d 328, 333 (RI 1989) (approving of liability 'when governmental employees engage in activities normally undertaken by private individuals').

[60] See, eg, *Hill v City of Charlotte*, 72 NC 55 (NC 1875); *Prosser & Keeton*, s 131 at 1052 (noting that courts properly refuse to review decisions 'involv[ing] the dilemma of policy intended to be resolved by the legislative or executive branches.') See also *Dalehite v United States*, 346 US 15, 34, 73 S Ct 956, 967 (1953) (exempting from liability the 'discretion of the executive or the administrator to act according to one's judgment of the best course').

[61] See, eg, Mass Gen L Ann 258, s 10(c) (granting immunity for intentional torts).

[62] See, eg, *Jungerman v City of Raytown*, 925 SW 2d 202 (Mo 1996) (applying immunity to officers as well as the municipalities for which they work).

[63] See, eg, New Jersey St Ann, s 59:9-2(c) (1937) ('No punitive or exemplary damages shall be awarded against a public entity'); 51 Okl St Ann, s 154 (1910) (limiting personal injury liability to $100,000 per person and $1,000,000 for any single occurrence or accident).

[64] *South v Maryland* 59 US 396 (1855). This decision, while not binding on state courts, has had significant doctrinal influence.

[65] See, eg, *Downey v Wood Dale Park Dist*, 675 NE 2d 973, 981 (Ill App 1997) (municipality must be uniquely aware of a particular danger or risk and there must be specific wilful acts or omissions on the part of the municipality that cause or allow the injury while the plaintiff is under the direct and immediate control of municipal employees or agents).

[66] *Cuffy v City of New York* 505 NE 2d 937 (NY 1987). *Followed by* White v Beasley, 552 NW 2d 1 (Mich 1996).

(1) an assumption by the municipality, through promises or actions, of an affirmative duty to act on behalf of the party who was injured; (2) knowledge on the part of the municipality's agent that inaction could lead to harm; (3) some form of direct contact between the municipality's agents and the injured party; and (4) that party's justifiable reliance on the municipality's affirmative undertaking.[67]

Thirteen States have expressly rejected[68] the public duty doctrine as the prevailing rule, holding that 'duty to all [amounts to] duty to no-one'.[69] However, the majority of states retain it.[70] In two states, Rhode Island and Florida, the public duty doctrine was expressly rejected,[71] but has since reappeared.[72] In some states, the doctrine is retained, but confined solely to cases related to law enforcement.[73]

---

[67] Cuffy, 505 NE 2d at 940.

[68] See *Adams v State* 555 P 2d 235 (Alaska 1976); *Ryan v State* 656 P 2d 597 (Ariz 1982); *Leake v Cain* 720 P 2d 152, (Colo 1986); *Calloway v Kinkelaar*, 659 NE 2d 1322, 1336 (Ill 1995); *Wilson v Nepstad* 282 NW 2d 664 (Iowa 1979); *Gas Service Co, Inc v City of London*, 687 SW 2d 144, 149 (Ky 1985); *Stewart v Schmieder*, 386 So 2d 1351 (La 1980); *Doucette v Town of Bristol* 635 A 2d 1387 (NH 1993); *Schear v Board of County Comm'rs*, 687 P 2d 728 (NM 1984); *Brennan v City of Eugene* 591 P 2d 719 (Or 1979); *Hudson v Town of East Montpelier*, 638 A 2d 561 (Vt 1993); *Coffey v Milwaukee* 247 NW 2d 132, 137 (Wis 1976); *Soles v State* 809 P 2d 772, 774 (Wyo 1991).

[69] *Adams v State* 555 P 2d 235, 241 (Alaska 1976).

[70] See *Donahoo v* State 479 So 2d 1188, 1190–1 (Ala 1985); *Thompson v County of Alameda*, 27 614 P 2d 728 (Cal 1980); *Gordon v Bridgeport Housing Authority*, 544 A 2d 1185, 1189 (Conn 1988); *Turner v District of Columbia*, 532 A 2d 662 (DC 1987); *Dept. of Transp v Brown*, 471 SE 2d 849 (Ga 1996); *Ruf v Honolulu Police Dept*, 972 P 2d 1081, 1088 (Hawaii 1999); *Gary Police Dept v Loera*, 604 NE 2d 6 (Ind Ct App 1992); *Robertson v Topeka*, 644 P 2d 458, 463 (Kan 1982); *Brum v Town of Dartmouth*, 704 NE 2d 1147 (Mass 1999); *White v Beasley* 552 NW 2d 1 (Mich 1996); *Cracraft v St. Louis Park* 279 NW 2d 801 (Minn 1979); *Jungerman v City of Raytown* 925 SW 2d 202 (Mo 1996); *Nelson v Driscoll*, 983 P 2d 972, 977 (Mont 1999); *Coty v Washoe County* 839 P 2d 97, 99 (Nev 1992); *DeLong v County of Erie*, 457 NE 2d 717 (NY 1983); *Isenhour v Hutto* 517 SE 2d 121 (NC 1999); *Brodie v Summit County Children Services Bd.* 554 NE 2d 1301, 1308 (Ohio 1990); *Houle v Galloway Sch. Lines, Inc* 643 A 2d 822, 826 (RI 1994); *Whatt v Fowler* 484 SE 2d 590 (SC 1997); *Gleason v Peters* 568 NW 2d 482, 484 (SD 1997); *Matthews v Pickett County* 996 SW 2d 162, 164–5 (Tenn 1999); *Day v State* 980 P 2d 1171, 1175 (Utah 1999); *Burdette v Marks* 421 SE 2d 419, 421 (Va 1992); *Ravenscroft v Washington Water Power Co*, 969 P 2d 75, 84–5 (Wash 1998); *Walker v Meadows* 521 SE 2d 801, 806 (WVa 1999); see generally, McQuillan on Municipal Corporations, s 53.04.25, 3rd edn, Perkowitz-Solheim, *et al* (eds) (1993).

[71] *Commercial Carrier Corp. v Indian River County* 371 So 2d 1010 (Fla 1979) (rejecting public duty doctrine in a highway case); *Catone v Medberry* 555 A 2d 328 (RI 1989) (applying proprietary/governmental distinction).

[72] *Sams v Oelrich* 717 So 2d 1044 (Fla Dist Ct App 1998); *Houle v Galloway Sch Lines, Inc* 643 A 2d 822 (RI 1994).

[73] See, eg, *Thompson v Waters*, 351 NC 462, 526 SE 2d 650 (NC 2000); *EP v Riley*, 604 NW 2d 7, 13–14 (SD 1999) ('[W]e now specifically clarify that the public duty rule extends only to issues involving law enforcement or public safety'); *Conner v James*, 981 P 2d 1169, 1171 (Kan 1999) ('[T]he public duty doctrine expresses a general rule that law enforcement duties are owed to the public at large and not to any specific person'); *Dept. of Transp. v Brown*, 471 SE 2d 849, 852 (Ga 1996) ('We believe that difference in the duties warrants limitation of the public duty doctrine [to] the provision of police services').

Despite its prevalence, the public duty doctrine has been attacked as legally dubious. As already stated, after abrogating sovereign immunity for state and local governments, many courts have viewed reliance on the doctrine as a way of resurrecting sovereign immunity in the obscuring form of a syllogistic legal argument. For example, the Minnesota Supreme Court denied it was citing sovereign immunity, even as it refused to impose liability on state and local governments. It said:

> By abolishing the distinction between public duty and special duty, the court would depart from vast precedent and traditional common-law principles of negligence. The distinction is not merely a relic of the verbiage used by courts in days of sovereign immunity. Instead, it is a corollary of the basic tenet of negligence law: general duties owed to the entire public rather than a specific class of persons cannot form the basis of a negligence action.[74]

It is arguable that the public duty doctrine is a legal formalism designed to tilt the scales in favour of the municipal defendant. Abolishing the public duty doctrine does not necessarily increase the liability of municipal defendants;[75] it merely changes the starting point of a court's liability analysis. Instead of a rule that says 'find no duty unless an exception applies' American courts, without the public duty doctrine, take the realistic position that 'policy determines duty'.[76] The judicial role in this arena is well stated by the Supreme Court of New Mexico in *Torres v State*:

> With deference to constitutional principles, it is the particular domain of the legislature, as the voice of the people to make public policy. Elected executive officials and executive agencies also make policy, to a lesser extent, as authorized by the constitution or the legislature. The judiciary, however, is not as directly and politically responsible to the people as are the legislative and executive branches of government. Courts should make policy in order to determine duty only when the body politic has not spoken and only with the understanding that any misperception of the public mind may be corrected shortly by the legislature.[77]

Thus the traditional factors that are weighed in a duty/risk analysis are brought into play. These include 'convenience of administration, capacity of the parties to bear the loss, a policy of preventing future injuries, the moral blame attached to the wrongdoer',[78] 'the consequences to the community of imposing a duty to exercise care with resulting liability for breach, and

---

[74] *Cracraft v City of St Louis Park* 279 NW 2d 801, 804 (Minn 1979). But see, *Gas Service Co v City of London*, 687 SW 2d 144, 148 (Ky 1985) ('The concept of liability for negligence expresses a universal duty owed by all to all. The duty to exercise ordinary care commensurate with the circumstances is a standard of conduct that does not turn on and off depending on who is negligent').

[75] *Coffey v Milwaukee* 247 NW 2d 132, 137 (Wis 1976).

[76] *Torres v State* 894 P 2d 386 (NM 1995).

[77] Ibid.

[78] *Prosser & Keeton*, 5, 359.

availability, cost, and prevalence of insurance for the risk involved'.[79] To these, one most also add the more overtly policy-oriented reasons to which allusion has already been made. There is, in short, no shortage of reasons (valid or invalid) for denying liability if that is what a judge wishes to do. The question is to decide the starting point: liability unless there is a reason to deny it, or the reverse?

This divide in American courts thus seems similar to the doctrinal conflict echoed in Lord Bingham's dictum that the 'first claim on the loyalty of the law [is] that wrongs should be remedied'[80] and Lord Hoffmann's riposte that 'the default position' in tort law is that an injured party is not entitled to compensation from his tortfeasor.[81] One suspects that Lord Bingham would reject the public duty doctrine as unjustly denying compensation to victims whose harm was caused by a municipal defendant. And Lord Nicholls, judging from his recent pronouncements in *Phelps*, might well find himself in the same camp. Lord Hoffman, on the other hand, might embrace it as a legitimate starting point.

As stated, what is the 'default position'? Should a court start from a perspective that municipal bodies in their governmental capacity are immune from tort liability and then seek to find an exception? Or should a court treat a municipal defendant like any other tortfeasor at first but take care to hear their special defences? The answers depend largely on the policy concerns that accompany these disputes.

(b) Policy Arguments

While it is true that some American opinions simply apply the public duty doctrine without reference to policy, others are also willing to consider policy arguments for liability, if only to refute them. But our research does reveal that American courts rely broadly on the same arguments to deny liability as those prevalent in England (at least pre-*Phelps*), albeit without cross-citations. This is significant because it demonstrates the enduring similarities in English and American tort law, particularly in terms of the anti-liability arguments. The significance of *Phelps* is that it has largely refuted all of them. Whether this reasoning will come to the United States, only time will tell.

So what is the position in the United States?

In at least six states, courts have articulated an 'economic rationale' for applying the public duty doctrine. In North Carolina, the Supreme Court has stated that the public duty doctrine 'recognises the limited resources of

---

[79] Ibid. at 359 n 24 (quoting *Vu v Singer Co* 538 F Supp 25, 29 (ND Cal 1981).
[80] *M v Newham London Borough Council and X v Bedfordshire County Council* [1994] 2 WLR 554.
[81] *Stovin v Wise* [1996] AC 923, 949.

law enforcement and refuses to impose judicially an overwhelming burden of liability'.[82] In Michigan, the Supreme Court approached the problem from a different angle when it said that the public duty doctrine 'protects governmental employees from unreasonable liability'.[83] In Washington, the Supreme Court thought that the doctrine avoids 'making municipalities insurers for every harm that might befall members of the public interacting with such municipalities'.[84] And the New York, Rhode Island, and West Virginia courts have expressed similar concerns.[85]

The 'inhibition' argument has been made by the Michigan Supreme Court in the case of *White v Beasley*.[86] The court held that liability for failure to enforce an ordinance would create 'tremendous liability' that would 'certainly dissuade the city from enacting ordinances designed for the protection and welfare of the general public, and thereby the general public would lose the benefit of salutary legislative enactments'.[87] Courts in Kentucky and New York have also included the inhibition argument in their reasoning.[88]

The Michigan court also made use of the 'discretionary' argument in *White* by holding that the public duty doctrine could be justified on the basis of avoiding 'unreasonable interference with policy decisions'.[89] Similarly, the Alabama Supreme Court held that imposing liability on the police would require the unpredictable re-allocation of limited resources.[90] The Montana Supreme Court adopted the public duty doctrine to prevent 'excessive court intervention into the governmental process'.[91] Other courts have likewise taken the view that the allocation of tax-payers' money should be left to the legislature or the executive and should not be subject to court interference[92] though, as Professor Dobbs has argued,[93] little judicial attention seems to have been paid to the fact that not all cases involve allocation of substantial resources.

In the United States, the 'alternative relief' argument has not been articulated as frequently as by English judges, yet illustrations of it can be found even in the kind of cases currently under review. Thus, in *Hunter v Board*

---

[82] *Isenhour v Hutto*, 517 SE 2d 121, 124 (NC 1999).

[83] *White v Beasley*, 552 NW 2d 1, 3 (Mich 1996).

[84] *Taylor v Stevens County* 759 P 2d 447 (Wash 1988).

[85] See *Boland v Town of Tiverton*, 670 A 2d 1245 (RI 1996); *Benson v Kutsch*, 380 SE 2d 36 (WVa 1989); *O'Connor v New York*, 447 NE 2d 33 (NY 1983).

[86] *White v Beasley* 552 NW 2d 1 (Mich 1996).

[87] Ibid, at 4.

[88] *Grogan v Commonwealth of Kentucky* 577 SW 2d 4 (Ky 1979); *O'Connor v New York* 447 NE 2d 33 (NY 1983).

[89] *White*, 552 NW 2d at 3 (Mich 1996).

[90] *Calogrides v City of Mobile* 475 So 2d 560 (Ala 1985).

[91] *Nelson v Driscoll* 983 P 2d 972, 977 (Mont 1999).

[92] *Tipton v Town of Tabor*, 567 NW 2d 351 (SD 1997).

[93] Dan Dobbs, *The Law of Tort*, (2000) 727.

of Education of Montgomery County,[94] the court felt that 'an award of money damage [was] a singularly inappropriate remedy for asserted errors in the educational process'.[95] This did not leave the aggrieved parents without a remedy since their children were not without recourse because of the presence of a number of administrative procedures. It should also be noted that, although it has never been cited in this way, the federal IDEA law provides, in effect, an alternative remedy.[96]

B. Educational Malpractice

The tort of 'educational malpractice' apparently first appeared as an idea in the early 1970s. Some have traced the idea to a 1970 article on fraud in education.[97] The broad conception of educational malpractice is a cause of action that allows students and their parents to sue a school district for an 'alleged failure of its general duty to educate'.[98] From the outset, authors such as Mark Yudof expressed concern at overly aggressive judicial intervention and argued that 'it is inappropriate for the courts to intervene in the educational process in an effort to equalise schooling outcomes'.[99] Although Yudof's comments were made in the context of equal protection and constitutional judicial review, many of his arguments seem also to be applicable when negligence actions are brought under the rubric of educational malpractice.

Since that time, nearly every state court presented with this tort has rejected it and this despite nearly universal support by those who have

---

[94] *Hunter v Bd of Educ of Montgomery County*, 439 A 2d 582 (Md 1982). This, too, was a case involving the negligent evaluation of a young boy's learning abilities, the complaint alleging that the school 'caused him to repeat first grade materials while being physically placed in the second grade'. It was further alleged that this 'misplacement . . . caused the student to feel 'embarrassment', to develop 'learning deficiencies', and to experience 'depletion of ego strength' [*sic*]. Ibid at 583.

[95] Ibid, at 487–8 and 586. See also, *Hoffman v Board of Education of the City of New York*, 400 NE 2d 317, 320 (NY 1979) ('In our view, any dispute concerning the proper placement of a child in a particular educational program can best be resolved by seeking review of such professional educational judgment through the administrative processes provided by statute'), *Accord, DSW v Fairbanks North Star Borough School District*, 628 P 2d 554, 557 (Alaska 1981). See, likewise, Professor Dobbs's critique of this 'minor' (as he calls it) argument in *The Law of Torts*, 726.

[96] See below Section III(B)(1).

[97] *See* Kevin P McJessy, Comment, *Contract Law: The Proper Framework for Litigating Educational Liability Claims*, 89 Nw U L Rev 1768, 1769 and n 4 (1995) (citing Stuart A Sandow, *Emerging Education Policy Issues in Law: Fraud* (1970)).

[98] Eldridge J, dissenting in *Doe v Board of Education of Montgomery County* 453 A 2d 814, 820 (Md 1982); *Donohue v Copiague Union Free School District*, 391 NE 2d 1352, 1353 (NY 1979).

[99] Mark G Yudof, *Equal Educational Opportunity and The Courts*, 51 *Texas L Rev* 411, 418 (1973).

written on the subject.[100] The notable exception to this rule of wide application is the Supreme Court of Montana.[101] General claims of substandard teaching have thus been dismissed.[102] And educational malpractice has also been taken to include cases of misdiagnosis of learning disabilities such as those discussed in this article. Thus, in cases where students were negligently misdiagnosed with a mental disability and placed in special education classes when it was unnecessary and harmful to their education, courts denied liability.[103] And conversely, when learning disabled students were not diagnosed and the suffered from remaining in a regular class, courts have also denied liability.[104]

Four arguments have been made by state courts in denying liability for educational malpractice.

First, it has been argued that the prospect of a flood of litigation coun-

---

[100] See, eg, Frank D Aquilla, *Educational Malpractice: A Torte En Ventre*, 39 *Clev St L Rev*, 323 (1991); John Elson, 'A Common Law Remedy for the Educational Harms Caused by Incompetent or Careless Teaching', 73 *Nw UL Rev* 641 (1978); Richard Funston, 'Educational Malpractice: A Cause of Action in Search of a Theory', 18 *San Diego L Rev* 743 (1981); Patrick D Halligan, 'The Function of Schools, the Status of Teachers and the Claims of the Handicapped: An Inquiry into Special Education Malpractice', 45 *Mo L Rev* 667 (1980); Robert H Jerry, 'Recovery in Tort for Educational Malpractice: Problems of Theory and Policy', 29 *U Kan L Rev* 195 (1981); Johnny C Parker, *Educational Malpractice: A Tort is Born*, 39 *Clev St L Rev* 301 (1991); Gershon M. Ratner, 'A New Legal Duty for Urban Public Schools: Effective Education in Basic Skills', 63 *Tex L Rev* 777 (1985); Sanford F Remz, 'Legal Remedies for the Misclassification or Wrongful Placement of Educationally Handicapped Children', 14 *Colum JL & Soc Probs* 389 (1979). But see John S Elson, 'Suing to make Schools Effective, or How to Make a Bad Situation Worse: A Response to Ratner', 63 *Tex L Rev* 889 (1985); Mark G Yudof, 'Effective Schools and Federal and State Constitutions: A Variety of Options, 63 *Tex L Rev* 865 (1985).

[101] See *BM by Burger v State* 649 P 2d 425 (Mont 1982); *Parini v Missoula County High Sch Dist No 1*, 944 P 2d 199 (Mont 1997).

[102] See, eg, *Doe v Town of Framingham*, 965 F Supp 226 (D Mass. 1997); *Blane v Alabama Comm. College*, 585 So 2d 866 (Ala 1991); *Moore v Vanderloo*, 386 NW 2d 108 (Iowa 1986); *Wickerstrom v North Idaho College*, 725 P 2d 155 (Idaho 1986); *Donohue v Copiague Union Free Sch Dist*, 391 NE 2d 1352 (NY 1979); *Peter W v San Francisco Unified Sch Dist*, 60 Cal App 3d 814, 131 Cal Rptr 854 (Cal Ct App 1976). See also Gershon M Ratner, 'A New Legal Duty for Urban Public Schools: Effective Education in Basic Skills', 63 *Texas L Rev* 777 (1985); Mark G Yudof, 'Effective Schools and Federal and State Constitutions: A Variety of Opinions', 63 *Texas L Rev* 865 (1985); John S Elson, 'Suing to Make Schools Effective, or How to Make a Bad Situation Worse: A Response to Ratner', 63 *Texas L Rev* 889 (1985).

[103] See, eg, *Doe v Board of Educ of Montgomery County*, 453 A 2d 814 (Md 1982); *Smith v Alameda County Social Servs Agency*, 153 Cal Rptr 712, 718–19 (Cal Ct App 1979); *Hoffman v Board of Educ of the City of New York*, 400 NE 2d 317, 319 (NY 1979).

[104] See, eg, *Brantley v District of Columbia*, 640 A 2d 181, 184 (DC 1994) (finding that no cause of action existed, even for negligent misdiagnosis, because of inherent uncertainties regarding the nature of damages, the potential for a flood of litigation, and the threat of interfering with day-to-day operations of the schools); *Rich v Kentucky Country Day*, 793 SW 2d 832 (Ky Ct App 1990) (denying the existence of educational malpractice claims against private as well as public schools; *Hunter v Board of Educ of Montgomery County*, 439 A 2d 582 (Md 1982) (denying negligence claim but permitting claim for intentional tort of misplacement); *DSW v Fairbanks North Star Borough Sch Dist*, 628 P 2d 554 (Alaska, 1981).

sels against liability.[105] This is an economic/administrative convenience kind of rationale. Secondly, courts are mindful of the separation of powers doctrine and therefore reluctant to allow themselves to enter the critical area of policymaking by the executive branch.[106] This is similar to the 'discretionary' argument. Thirdly, courts claim to have no satisfactory standard of care for judging the conduct of teachers and school officials.[107] Finally, courts argue that calculation of damages is difficult if not impossible.[108] These arguments represent variations of views also found in English cases.

A commonly cited case in the field of 'educational malpractice' is the California Court of Appeal's opinion in *Peter W v San Francisco Unified School District*.[109] The court dismissed the claims of a high school senior that he had been negligently educated throughout his youth. The court held that claims of 'educational malpractice' present (a) no conceivable workability of a rule of care against which defendants' alleged conduct may be measured; (b) no reasonable degree of certainty that a plaintiff suffered injury within the meaning of the law of negligence; and (c) no such perceptible connection between the defendant's conduct and the injury suffered, as alleged, which would establish a causal link between them.[110]

The court basically said that the plaintiff's claim presented no duty, no causation, and no injury. But this cannot be universally true for every claim against a school. A school has a duty to take care to prevent physical injuries. It has obligations created by federal and state statutes specifically for the benefit of disabled students. It is certainly true that defining the minimum standard of education would be difficult, if not impossible. But the duty to detect and diagnose learning disabilities is reducible to simple elements. Were the signs indicative of a learning disability? Was it reasonable that the signs could have been detected by a professional exercising the common standards of her profession? No court would be asked to pass judgment on whether a school's curriculum was reasonable, whether a teacher made the correct pedagogical selection, or any other vague question. But a court may properly review cases of misdiagnosis.

---

[105] See, eg, *Peter W*, 60 Cal App 3d at 825 (predicting that liability would produce 'tort claims—real or imagined—of disaffected students and parents in countless numbers').

[106] See, eg, *Donohue*, 391 NE 2d at 1354 (arguing that educational malpractice claims would 'require the courts not merely to make judgments as to the validity of broad educational policies . . . but, more importantly to sit in review of the day-to-day implementations of those policies').

[107] See, eg, *Peter W*, 60 Cal App 3d at 824 ('Unlike the activity of the highway or the marketplace, classroom methodology affords no readily acceptable standards of care, or cause, or injury').

[108] Ibid (holding that no court could achieve any reasonable degree of certainty that a plaintiff student had suffered injury within the meaning of the law of negligence).

[109] 60 Cal App 3d 814 (Cal 1976). The case has been cited by courts more than 100 times.

[110] Ibid. at 824–5.

This distinction is crucial and often overlooked. The dissenting opinion of Judge Eldridge in *Doe v Board of Education of Montgomery County*.[111] from 1982 bears much resemblance with the views expressed by Lord Nicholls in *Phelps v Hillingdon LBC*.[112] Both make the crucial distinction advanced by this article between educational malpractice and negligent misdiagnosis of learning disabilities. Judge Suozzi of the New York Appellate Division has also dissented by pointing out that traditional principles of malpractice are easily adapted to the educational testing context, especially when the school district completely fails to even attempt testing.[113]

The *Peter W.* court also claimed that the plaintiff had not suffered any injury under the law of negligence.[114] Misdiagnosis of a learning disability is neither a physical nor a pecuniary injury. It produces a harm that is difficult to quantify and could result in awarding excessive and speculative verdicts to sympathetic plaintiffs. Divining 'what might have been' seems to be a task beyond the powers of a judicial system; a difficulty also noted in the *Phelps* litigation in England (and addressed below). Would a learning disabled student have done better? In what manner and to what extent does the misdiagnosis make the student worse off? How has the misdiagnosis harmed the learning disabled student, except that he received a general public benefit (free schooling) but not the one best tailored to his needs (special education).

The answer to these concerns is that learning disabilities can worsen over time. They are amenable to certain special techniques that, if not given promptly, may preclude any possibility of recovery.[115] In the case of a negligent misdiagnosis, the failure to treat learning disabilities in a timely fashion can worsen their impact and severity. The defendant is liable for the injury because parents rely on the misdiagnosis and therefore nothing is done to cure the learning disability. The school district's misdiagnosis is the cause-in-fact and proximate cause of the worsening state of the child's learning disability (whereas they were not causally linked to the disability in its original state). The fact that such injuries may be psychological does

---

[111] *Doe v Bd of Educ of Montgomery County*, 453 A 2d 814 (1982).

[112] *Phelps v Hillingdon LBC* [2000] 3 WLR 776, at 804–5 (HL).

[113] *Donohue v Copiague Union Free School District*, 407 NY S 2d 874, 885 (NY App 1978) (Suozzi, J, dissenting) ('In my view, the negligence alleged in the case at bar is not unlike that of a doctor who, although confronted with a patient with a cancerous condition, fails to pursue medically accepted procedures').

[114] *Peter W v San Francisco Unified Sch Dist*, 60 Cal App 3d 814, 824, 131 Cal Rptr 854, 861 (Cal Ct App 1976) ('Substantial professional authority attests that the achievement of literacy in the schools, or its failure, are influenced by a host of factors which affect the pupil subjectively, from outside the formal teaching process, and beyond the control of its ministers').

[115] See generally, American Psychiatric Ass'n, *Diagnostic and Statistical Manual of Mental Disorders*, 4th edn (1995), 46–53.

not remove them from the realm of tort law. The task of assigning dollar values to such damages (especially when the cost of remedial education is clearly defined) is not beyond the power of the courts.[116]

The *Peter W* court also noted that causation could barely be theorised, much less established to the degree that would satisfy a court. The overall success or failure of a student is largely the product of the student's efforts, and a school's pedagogical choices and management styles are obviously discretionary government decisions beyond the scope of justiciable inquiry. The knot of causation that produces a troubled child is very complex and separating the school's fault out of a vast array of other possible suspects is likely to prove impossible. However, it is conceivable that a school's failure to properly diagnose a learning disability could be a cause-in-fact and legal cause of an irremediable harm. Once allowed to reach adulthood without specialised education tailored to his disability, a student has dysfunctionally developed in a manner that cannot be undone. When a school professional gives an opinion that denies the existence of a learning disability, it is clear to him that the parents of a child will be relying on his opinion, perhaps to their regret. Under those circumstances, it seems that the negligent misdiagnosis would be the cause of injuries in a manner cognisable by the courts.

It should be noted that in America the principal exception to the public duty doctrine is when a special relationship has been found to exist between a government official and a plaintiff-victim. As suggested above,[117] the test for a special relationship commonly includes at least four factors: (1) assumption of duty by the government; (2) knowledge of possible harm on the part of the government; (3) direct contact between the government official and the plaintiff-victim; and (4) reliance by the plaintiff-victim on the government's actions. In most states that accept the public duty doctrine, the hypothetical addressed by this article would appear to qualify for this exception. School districts and their psychologists examine students on an individual basis, satisfying the assumption of duty requirement. They do not examine every student, just those who are failing to achieve minimal results on standardised tests. In doing so, the schools are aware that any misdiagnosis could have irremediable consequences. This satisfies the knowledge requirement. Students are entrusted every day to the care of school districts. This satisfies the contact requirement. Parents of students with learning disabilities can be expected to rely on their school psychologists' diagnoses. This satisfies the reliance requirement. There is no greater wrong-doer in these situations. In each of these ways, negligent misdiagnosis of learning disabilities is distinguishable from the usual public duty

---

[116] The question of damages for the incurable student, however, is admittedly difficult to ascertain. This issue is discussed below.
[117] See above Section III.A.1.(a), 'Legalistic Arguments'.

doctrine case involving police protection or investigation. No one suggests that 'do duty' is the appropriate response when doctors in government hospitals commit malpractice.

Even though a special relationship might be tenable, some American courts have nevertheless held that even harm directly caused by educational malpractice would not be legally recognised. This is because:

even where the chain of causation is complete and direct, recovery may sometimes be denied on grounds of public policy because (1) the injury is too remote from the negligence; or (2) the injury is too wholly out of proportion to the culpability of the negligent tortfeasor; or (3) in retrospect it appears too highly extraordinary that the negligence should have brought about the harm; or (4) because allowance of recovery would place too unreasonable a burden on the defendant; or (5) because allowance of recovery would be too likely to open the way for fraudulent claims; or (6) allowance of recovery would enter a field that has no sensible or just stopping point.[118]

Alongside these concerns, there are other 'legalisms' that serve to deny plaintiffs their recovery in state tort law. Even when a special relationship is proven, and even if an American court could be persuaded to recognise the distinction advanced by this article between educational malpractice and negligent misdiagnosis of learning disabilities, there are other obstacles. The next section covers them.

C. Immunity of Officials

As with the public duty doctrine, qualified official immunity in America is not uniformly articulated or enforced in the various state courts. Furthermore, immunity of local governments and their officials against federal claims is a matter of federal law, separate and apart from state law immunities.[119] While the public duty doctrine protects municipalities, themselves, their culpable officers may not be that lucky. In Pennsylvania, for instance, local public entities may be immune to suits for false arrests,[120] and though the individual officer may himself be liable for that or other intentional torts,[121] the public entities may still end up by being liable for the torts of their employees, either on vicarious liability grounds or because of internal practices. But such a result, just about tolerable in cases of intentional activities by officials, becomes grossly unfair in cases of negligently inflicted harm. So in practice, even where the authority enjoys

---

[118] *Page v Klein Tools, Inc*, 610 NW 2d 900, 905 (Mich, 2000) (quoting *Wilson v Continental Ins Cos*, 274 NW 2d 679 (Wis, 1979)).
[119] Except in those cases brought under diversity jurisdiction, where a federal court applies state law as interpreted by the state court of last resort.
[120] *Burger v Borough of Ingram*, 697 A 2d 1037 (Pa Commonwealth, 1997).
[121] *Renk v City of Pittsburgh*, 641 A 2d 289, 293–4 (Pa, 1994).

immunity, it may, indirectly, end up by footing the bill by indemnifying the officer and providing for the costs of his defence.[122]

Public employees, however, are often protected by immunity; and where this is the case, the liability of the employer will often also be foreclosed. Section 815.2 of the California Government Code offers an illustration. It states:

Except as otherwise provided by statute, a public entity is not liable for an injury resulting from an act or omission of an employee of the public entity where the employee is immune from liability.[123]

Officials may also be given immunity based upon their 'discretionary' acts or those actions taken in 'good faith.' Public official immunity protects public officers who act tortiously while performing discretionary acts in the furtherance of his duties, without malice.[124] Ministerial or administrative acts not involving 'discretion' are, on the other hand, often subject to liability. A statutory waiver of immunity by the state can be limited to a local government's vicarious liability through an action against its employees, such that actions filed against the government itself are defeated.[125]

In some states, government employees are immune from suit arising from the performance of their: (1) discretionary duties in; (2) good faith as long as they are; (3) acting within the scope of their authority.[126] The test for 'good faith' is whether a reasonably prudent officer under the same or similar circumstances would have acted in the same or similar manner.[127]

Qualified official immunity for discretionary acts covers 'weighing of public policy considerations, such as potential risks and benefits to public', not low-level decisions about how to accomplish a ministerial task.[128] As one court put it:

Qualified official immunity serves primarily to shield government employees from exposure to tort liability that would (1) hamper or deter those employees from vigorously discharging their duties in a prompt and decisive manner, and (2) unfairly subject employees who have a duty to exercise discretion regarding matters of public policy to the judgment of those acting within a judicial system that is ill-suited to assess the full scope of factors involved in such decision making.[129]

---

[122] Dobbs, *The Law of Torts*, 717.

[123] But see *Thomas v City of Richmond*, 892 P 2d 1185 (Cal 1995), recognising limited exceptions.

[124] *James v Prince George's County*, 418 A 2d 1173, 1178–80 (Md, 1980). See also *Restatement, 2d, Torts*, s 895D (1979).

[125] *Williams v Prince George's County*, 685 A 2d 884, 897 (Md, 1996); Md Ann Code, Courts and Jud Proc, s 5-302(a) (1973).

[126] *Harris County v Garza*, 971 SW 2d 733, 736 (Tex App—Houston [14th Dist.] 1998, no pet h).

[127] *City of San Antonio v Garcia*, 974 SW 2d 756, 758 (Tex App—San Antonio, 1998, no pet h).

[128] *Hudson v Town of East Montpelier*, 638 A 2d 561 (Vt, 1993).   [129] Ibid, at 564.

The crux of qualified official immunity is finding that a certain activity is 'discretionary'. Under the *Restatement (Second) of Torts*,[130] this analysis entails consideration of several factors namely: (1) the nature and importance of the function that the officer is performing; (2) the extent to which evaluating tort liability will amount to passing judgment on the conduct of a co-ordinate branch of government; (3) the extent to which liability would inhibit the discretion of the official; (4) the extent to which the ultimate financial responsibility will fall on the officer; (5) the likelihood of harm because of the official's action; (6) the nature and seriousness of the type of harm that may be produced; (7) the availability of alternate forms of relief.

These factors are not likely to be present in a case of negligent misdiagnosis. A school psychologist is not a high-level executive-branch official responsible for making policy decisions. Nonetheless, the apparently widespread tendency of local authorities to indemnify their public employees in the (rare) event of their being sued and being held liable means that the threat of litigation against them is unlikely to influence their behaviour. Incidentally, one of the underlying ideas behind immunity is that official ardour is desirable and that the threat of liability would dampen it. But, as Professor Dobbs has so rightly remarked, 'The first point is a question of values; the second is a question of data. Neither point is demonstrated in most of the case discussions.'[131] Finally, the availability of alternative relief under the IDEA scheme, described below, also means that many of these claims will be channelled down this route and this may also take off some of the pressure for ordinary tort litigation.

Phelps is not a perfect analogue to the American state law cases. There, the lords held that vicarious liability attached to local authorities based on the tortious conduct of their educational psychologists, regardless of primary liability. In the American state law cases, the consensus appears to be that local authorities will indemnify officers for conduct within the course and scope of their employment. However, the point is generally moot in America, as the judicial hostility is almost universal to educational malpractice claims, whether predicated upon direct or vicarious liability.

D. Federal Statutory Law

In addition to common law remedies, usually sought in state courts, a plaintiff may also have recourse to federal courts under several federal statutes. These include the Individuals with Disabilities Education Act (IDEA), the Rehabilitation Act, the Americans with Disabilities Act, and the Civil Rights Act of 1871 (42 USC s 1983). The most important of these statutory

---

[130] *Restatement, 2d, Torts*, s 895D, comment e (1979).
[131] Dan Dobbs, *The Laws of* Torts, 733.

remedies is the relief available under the IDEA: reimbursement for private school tuition.

1. Relief Under IDEA

Congress enacted the Individuals with Disabilities Education Act[132] (IDEA) to 'ensure that all children with disabilities have available to them a free appropriate public education. . . .'[133] The Supreme Court has interpreted this clause to require an education that confers some educational benefit on the disabled child.[134] The IDEA was designed to create a 'basic floor of opportunity,'[135] not to mandate the 'best education money can buy'.[136] A child is considered disabled not only if he or she is blind, deaf, or mentally impaired, but also if he or she has a serious emotional disturbance or a learning disability that requires special education.[137] State and local governments are required to identify and assess disabling conditions.[138]

Enacted under Congress's Spending Clause power, the IDEA provides federal funding to states and local governments who meet certain requirements,[139] such as procedural safeguards.[140] These safeguards include informing the parent or guardian of all procedures available and providing a 'due process' hearing when a parent or guardian complains that his or her child has been denied the rights secured by the IDEA.[141] States must also provide procedures for administrative review of decisions regarding the 'identification, evaluation, or educational placement of the child, or the provision of free appropriate public education to such child'.[142] These administrative procedures must be exhausted before parents are allowed to file a civil action in state or federal court under the IDEA.[143]

In civil IDEA actions, judicial review of a state's administrative procedure is not as deferential as normal review of agency actions, 'in which courts are generally confined to the administrative record and are held to a highly deferential standard of review"[144] A reviewing court decides based on a 'preponderance of the evidence' standard, with the admission of new

---

[132] See Individuals with Disabilities Education Act (IDEA), 20 USC s 1400 et seq (2000). In 1975, Congress enacted the Education for All Handicapped Children Act, Pub L No 94–142, 89 Stat 773 (1975). In 1990, Congress amended and renamed the Act to the IDEA. Education of the Handicapped Act, Amendments of 1990, Pub L No 101–476, s 901(a), 104 Stat 1103 (1990).

[133] See 20 USC s 1400 (d) (1)(A)(2000).

[134] See *Board of Educ. v Rowley*, 458 US 176, 200, 102 S Ct 3034, 3047 (1982).

[135] Ibid 458 US at 201.   [136] *Ahern v Keene*, 593 F Supp 902, 912 (D Del, 1984).

[137] See 20 USC s 1401(3)(A) (2000).

[138] See ibid ss 1412(a)(3)(A) and 1414 (2000).   [139] See ibid s 1412 (2000).

[140] See ibid s 1412(5)(a)(6) (2000).   [141] Ibid s 1415(b)(6) and (f) (2000).

[142] See ibid s 1415(b)(1)(2000). See also ibid s 1415(g) (2000).

[143] See 20 USC s 1415(i)(2) (2000).

[144] *Ojai United Sch Dist v Jackson*, 4 F 3d 1467, 1461 (9th Cir 1993).

evidence allowed.[145] Courts 'must decide independently whether the requirements of the IDEA were met'.[146] The IDEA permits a reviewing court to 'grant such relief as the court determines is appropriate'.[147] However, as a matter of statutory construction, this section has been construed narrowly. Thus, only limited monetary damages are usually available under the IDEA 'appropriate relief' section. Circuit (and other) courts have declined to allow recovery of damages for pain and suffering because the IDEA does not provide for such damages.[148] At least one circuit court has noted that the clause does not limit relief 'in any way',[149] but the majority view is that only a single element of damages is available under the IDEA, *viz.* reimbursement expenses for the cost of private school paid for by parents of a learning disabled child.[150] Thus, in *Hall v Knott County Board. of Education,*[151] the US Court of Appeals for the Sixth Circuit held that plaintiffs can obtain reimbursement for past or future educational expenses under the IDEA but not general damages, such as compensation for lost earning power.[152] Moreover, reimbursement expenses are available if only the private school selected by the parents was appropriate and equitable considerations support the parents claim.[153] Additionally, counsel may receive legal fees from school districts and state governments.[154] It is important to note that the US Supreme Court has yet to interpret the 'appropriate relief' section, so the quantum of possible damages remains an open question.

The IDEA has no corollary in English law. In a sense, this federal remedy acts as 'alternative relief.' It reduces the pressure on state courts to recognise negligent misdiagnosis, whether that pressure is from litigants or progressive judges. The IDEA also appears comprehensive enough to

---

[145] *Board of Educ v Rowley*, 458 US 176, 102 S Ct 3034 (1982).

[146] *Board of Educ v Illinois State Bd*, 41 F 3d 1162, 1167 (7th Cir 1994).

[147] See 20 USC s 1415(i)(2)(B)(iii) (2000).

[148] See *Kelly K. v Town of Framingham*, 633 NE 2d 414, 418 (Mass Ct App 1994); *Crocker v Tennessee Secondary Sch. Athletic Ass'n*, 980 F 2d 382, 385–6 (6th Cir 1992).

[149] *WB v Matula*, 67 F 3d 484, 494 (3rd Cir 1995).

[150] See *Florence County School Dist v Carter*, 510 US 7, 13–14 (1993) (holding that parents may unilaterally place their child in a private school and receive reasonable reimbursement); *Sabatini v Corning-Painted Post Area Sch. Dist.*, 78 F Supp 2d 138, 145–6 (WDNY 1999) (authorising payment of college tuition to assist a 22-year-old disabled student in obtaining a high school diploma).

[151] *Hall v Knott County Bd of Educ* 941 F 2d 402 (6th Cir 1991).

[152] Ibid, at 406–7.

[153] See *School Comm of Burlington, Mass v Department of Educ*, 471 US 359, 374, 105 S Ct 1996 (1985); *Ft Zumwalt Sch Dist v Clynes*, 119 F 3d 607, 614–15 (8th Cir 1997) (declining to award damages for the consequences of a poor education or emotional distress damages); *Heidemann v Rother*, 84 F 3d 1021, 1033 (8th Cir 1996) (refusing to allow general or punitive damages under the IDEA).

[154] See 1415(i)(3)(B)–(G) (2000); *Board of Educ of Oak Park v Kelly E*, 207 F 3d 931 (7th Cir 2000); *Zak L v Cambridge School Comm*, 44 F Supp 2d 395, 399 (D Mass, 1999).

dissuade most courts from entertaining creative alternatives, such as those described in the next section.

2. Litigation Under 42 USC Section 1983

Violations of the IDEA may also be independently actionable under federal civil rights law. The Civil Rights Act of 1871 provides a federal remedy for the 'deprivation of any privileges, or immunities secured by the Constitution and laws [of the United States] by any person acting under color of [state] law'.[155] This Reconstruction-era statute lay dormant until 1961, mainly because of restrictive interpretations by the Supreme Court.[156] However, since that time, the Court has fashioned an elaborate scheme of litigation in federal and state courts that impacts American local authorities directly.[157] Liability for negligent misdiagnosis as a violation of constitutional rights is very unlikely given the current, fairly conservative judicial climate in the United States. Liability for violations of the IDEA is a possible avenue for relief, but, as we will discuss below, is less preferable than a state tort law cause of action, for both doctrinal and pragmatic reasons.

The seminal decisions of *Monroe v Pape*[158] in 1961 and *Monell v Department of Social Services of New York*[159] in 1978 invigorated the constitutional tort cause of action and applied it to municipal corporations.[160] Federal and state courts will now enforce the due process guarantees of the Fourteenth Amendment to the Constitution, as well as those substantive rights delineated in the Bill of Rights that have been incorporated against the States

[155] Civil Rights Act of 1871, 42 USC s 1983 (2001). See generally, Sheldon H Nahmod, 1 *Civil Rights and Civil Liberties Litigation: The Law of Section 1983*, 4th edn (1999). The expression—strange to English eyes—of 'acting under color of law' means that the actor exercises power 'possessed by virtue of state law and made possible only because [of] the authority of state law . . .' See *West v Atkins*, 487 US 42, 49, 108 S Ct 2250 (1988). Private individuals can, only rarely, act under colour of law: *Adickes v SH Kress & Co*, 398 US 144, 90 S Ct 1598 (1970).

[156] See, eg, Civil Rights Cases, 109 US 3 (1883) (interpreting narrowly the 'state action' requirement); *Slaughter-House Cases*, 83 US (16 Wall) 36 (1873) (applying the 'privileges and immunities' clause to national citizenship only); *Twining v New Jersey*, 211 US 78 (1908) (finding that the Bill of Rights is not a privilege of national citizenship).

[157] Given that the statute is short and requires, on its face, only causation, the Supreme Court has judicially created the remainder of the cause of action, including the elements, state-of-mind, joint and several liability, compensatory damages, proximate cause, mitigation of damages and class actions.

[158] *Monroe v Pape*, 365 US 167 (1961).

[159] *Monell v Dept of Soc Serv of New York*, 436 US 658 (1978).

[160] State governments are immune from suit under the protections of the Eleventh Amendment. US Const. Amend. XI (holding that 'the judicial power of the United States shall not be construed to extend to any suit in law or equity, commenced or prosecuted against one of the United States by Citizens of another State'). But local governments do not benefit from this immunity. See *Lincoln Co v Luning* 133 US 529, 530, 10 S Ct 363, 363 (1890) (holding that counties are only parts of a state in a 'remote sense.').

via the Fourteenth Amendment.[161] In addition, section 1983 provides a remedy for deprivation of statutory rights (such as those found in the IDEA).[162]

Monroe, for example, found that the Chicago Police had violated the Fourth Amendment[163] when they burst into the plaintiff's home and forced him and his family to stand naked while their house and possessions were ransacked. The plaintiff was arrested but then released without being charged.[164] Although the police officers were liable, *Monroe* interpreted 'person' under section 1983 to exclude municipalities, and the Court accordingly dismissed the City of Chicago as a defendant. That specific holding was distinguished in 1978 by *Monell*, which held that section 1983 applied with equal force to local authorities, given that they were 'persons' under the statute.[165] However, liability exists only for official policies, not vicariously for the unauthorised wrongdoing of government officials.

Since 1978, civil rights litigation against local authorities, particularly arising out of law enforcement activities has expanded dramatically.[166] Recent reports have noted, for example, that Los Angeles County paid $106 million in damages related to police misconduct over the last ten years.[167] A police misconduct scandal commonly known as 'Rampart' (after the name of the corrupt division) is predicted to cost Los Angeles at least $125 million.[168] Although the Rampart litigation may produce the largest civil rights award ever, it should be noted that this estimate is less than1 per cent of a $15 billion annual budget[169] and still half the budget allocation in Germany for such expenses.[170]

The elements of a section 1983 claim are a matter of federal law.[171]

---

[161] Virtually all of the Bill of Rights has been incorporated. The Second Amendment right to keep and bear arms, however, is one of the few rights not yet incorporated and therefore has not been enforced. See, eg, *Love v Pepersack*, 47 F 3d 120, 123, 4th Cir 1995).

[162] See *Maine v Thiboutot*, 448 US 1, 100 S Ct 2502 (1980).

[163] 'The right of the people to be secure in their persons, houses, papers, and effects, against unreasonable searches and seizures, shall not be violated . . . ' US Const amend. IV.

[164] Monroe, 365 US at 183.

[165] Monell, 436 US at 662. See generally, McQuillan on Municipal Corporations, s 53.04.25, 3rd edn, Perkowitz-Solheim, *et al* (eds) (1993), s 53.172.

[166] See Nicholas Riccardi, *County's Costs Adding Up in Rampart Probe*, LA Times B1 (17 Mar 2000); BJ Palermo, 'Rampart Liability Figure Grows with Scandal', 22 *Nat'l LJ* (28 Feb 2000 at A5); Paul Elias, *Rampart Scandal Spurs Civil Suit*, The Recorder (13 Oct 1999), available on Westlaw at 10/13/1999 RECORDER-SF 8; Paul Elias, *O'er Rampart They Watch*, The Recorder (11 Oct 1999, at 1.)

[167] Elias, ibid (quoting figures from City Attorney James Hahn).

[168] Palermo, 'Rampart Liability Figure Grows with Scandal', at A5).

[169] Nicholas Riccardi, *County's Costs Adding Up in Rampart Probe*, LA Times B1 (17 Mar 2000).

[170] Markesinis, *Tortious Liability* (1999), 61. Of course, this is a highly tentative estimate and does not include the cost of defending cases. Nevertheless, the comparison is illuminating.

[171] See, eg, *Scheuer v Rhodes*, 416 US 232 (1974). See also Christina Brooks Whitman, 'Emphasizing the Constitutional in Constitutional Torts', 72 *Chi Kent L Rev* 661 (1997).

However, the Court in *Monroe* noted that section 1983 does not require specific intent, that it would be interpreted against a 'background of tort liability',[172] and that it was enacted to remedy the lack of State enforcement of Fourteenth Amendment rights 'by reason of prejudice, passion, *neglect*, intolerance, or otherwise'.[173] This dissonance between constitutional standards and tort principles has led to great confusion.[174] A lower court noted that 'the common law . . . may create immunities that do not apply to an action under section 1983 [and] conversely the developing law of torts may extend potential liability to some defendants beyond the reach of the federal statute'.[175]

A major issue is the requisite state of mind in the defendant that must be shown by the plaintiff. While it is unclear if mere negligence is ever sufficient for the purposes of section 1983, the Court has held that different standards apply to different constitutional rights, as a matter of textual and historical interpretation. Equal protection, for example, requires 'purposeful discrimination,'[176] Eighth Amendment violations require 'deliberate indifference',[177] and due process violations require more than mere negligence.[178] In substantive due process cases, the Court has uttered extremely limited decisions, such as a 'conscience-shocking' standard applicable only to police pursuit cases that requires showing a 'purpose to cause harm unrelated to the legitimate object of arrest'.[179]

This maze of variegated liability standards for various violations results from the constitutional dimension. Section 1983 does not itself contain a state-of-mind requirement; the requisite standards flow from the text of the Constitution.[180] The Supreme Court requires a close fit between the constitutional provision at issue and the allegedly wrongful conduct of the defendant. The Court has stated that the due process clause 'does not transform every tort committed by a state actor into a constitutional violation'.[181]

Proving the liability of municipal bodies generally requires that: (1) a policy or custom existed; (2) it was attributable to the municipal defendant on non-vicarious grounds; (3) a constitutional deprivation occurred; and (4) the policy or custom caused the constitutional deprivation.[182] The tort

---

[172] *Monroe*, 365 US at 187.
[173] Ibid, at 180 (emphasis added).
[174] Nahmod, op cit, s 3:2.
[175] *Carter v Carlson*, 447 F 2d 358, 361 (DC Cir 1971), *rev'd on other grounds*, 409 US 418 (1972).
[176] *Washington v Davis*, 426 US 229, 244 (1976); Nahmod, op cit, s 3:83.
[177] *Estelle v Gamble*, 429 US 97, 104 (1976); Nahmod, op cit, s 3:27.
[178] *Daniels v Williams*, 474 US 327, 329–30 (1986); Nahmod, op cit, s 3:51.
[179] *County of Sacramento v Lewis*, 118 S Ct 1708 (1998).
[180] *Parratt v Taylor*, 451 US 527, 534–35 (1981); Nahmod, op cit, s 3:2.
[181] *DeShaney v Winnebago County Dept. of Social Services*, 489 US 189, 201–2 (1989).
[182] *Bordanaro v McLeod*, 871 F 2d 1151 (1st Cir 1989); McQuillan on Municipal Corporations, s 53.04.25, 3rd edn, Perkowitz-Solheim, *et al* (eds.) (1993), s 53.172.

doctrine of *respondeat superior* does not exist under section 1983,[183] and punitive damages are not available against a municipal defendant.[184] However, punitive damages are available against individual defendants, many of whom are indemnified by municipalities.[185] Given these limitations, it would be hard to obtain a remedy under section 1983 for negligent misdiagnosis. The Supreme Court has adopted restrictive interpretations of 'policy' and 'custom' in recent years, requiring plaintiffs to prove, for example, that the defendant municipality was the 'moving force' that caused the alleged violation of rights.[186] The Court has also held that a single act of a policymaker is usually insufficient as a matter of law,[187] thereby cutting down on negligent hiring and training cases.[188]

The constitutional tort described above has brought municipalities into court for almost 30 years. This 'backdrop' of American human rights law may explain courts' hostility to educational malpractice, even if the explanation is counter-intuitive. For it seems that if a municipality can be sued for constitutional violations (as well as torts that result in physical injury), then the imposition of liability for negligent misdiagnosis will not result in speculative and unpredictable jury verdicts. After all, civil juries in section 1983 cases select supposedly 'arbitrary' dollar amounts every day to compensate injured plaintiffs for their pain and suffering and punish defendants for their outrageous behaviour. And the sky has not fallen. This experience would seem to illustrate the capacity of municipalities to bear the burden of litigation.

To the contrary, however, the multiple sources for liability that currently exist may counsel against more liability. From this perspective, educational malpractice seems to resemble the 'straw that broke the camel's back'. Federal courts may also be reluctant to find liability under a federal statute where state courts have so often declined to do the same.[189]

---

[183] *St Louis v Praprotnik*, 485 US 112 (1988); Pembaur *v* Cincinnati, 475 US 469 (1986).
[184] *City of Newport v Fact Concerts, Inc.*, 453 US 247 (1981).
[185] See, eg, *Cornwell v City of Riverside*, 896 F 2d 398 (9th Cir 1990) (holding that when individual defendants are indemnified, a plaintiff may not refuse payment by an employer city); Nahmod, op cit, s 6:64.
[186] *Board of County Com'rs of Bryan County, Okl. v Brown*, 520 US 397, 117 S Ct 1382 (1997) (defining 'moving force' as a 'municipal action . . . taken with the requisite degree of culpability [that] demonstrates [a] direct causal link between the municipal action and the deprivation of federal rights').
[187] Ibid 520 US at 405 (limiting liability predicated upon single acts to cases 'where the evidence that the municipality had acted and that the plaintiff had suffered a deprivation of federal rights also proved fault and causation').
[188] See, eg, Canton *v* Harris, 489 US 378, 109 S Ct 1197 (1989) (limiting liability for failure to train to a narrow set of factual situations).
[189] *Hall by Hall v Vance County Bd. of Educ*, 774 F 2d 629, 633 and n 3 (4th Cir 1985) (holding that the Education for All Handicapped Children Act (EAHCA), an earlier version of IDEA, 'does not create a private cause of action for damages for educational malpractice') (citing *Anderson v Thompson*, 658 F 2d 1205, 1211–13 (7th Cir 1981).

3. Violations of the IDEA as Deprivation of Right Under Section 1983

This theory of liability is a hybrid of the two just described. 42 USC section 1983 provides that any person who, under colour of state law, causes any citizen to be deprived of any right under the Constitution or federal law, 'shall be liable to the party injured in an action at law, suit in equity, or other proper proceeding for redress'. Although section 1983 is often associated with constitutional torts, both the text of the statute and the interpretations of the US Supreme Court make it clear that violations of statutory rights are actionable.[190] Plaintiffs have sued under section 1983 for violations of the IDEA, claiming that, by failing to provide a free appropriate public education, local school boards are liable.[191]

In *Smith v Robinson*,[192] the US Supreme Court interpreted the IDEA as a comprehensive remedial scheme that 'should not be supplemented by the remedial apparatus of § 1983'.[193] Although the plaintiffs had asserted other legal theories for recovery, the Court found that plaintiffs should not be allowed to 'circumvent the requirements or supplement the remedies'[194] provided under the IDEA, which are exclusive. Accordingly, it did not allow for the recovery of attorney's fees in a civil action filed to secure a 'free appropriate public education.'

Shortly thereafter, Congress disagreed. In matters of statutory interpretation, Congress is free to overrule the Supreme Court. In the Handicapped Children's Protection Act of 1986, Congress expressly provided for attorney's fees under the IDEA, and also added a provision confirming that the IDEA was not exclusive of other remedies.[195] The legislative history confirms that 'Congressional intent was ignored by the US Supreme Court ... in *Smith v Robinson*' and that § 1983 suits remained viable as sources of law for 'securing the rights of handicapped children and young.'[196]

---

[190] *See Maine v Thiboutot*, 448 US 1, 100 S Ct 2502 (1980).

[191] As is often the case, plaintiffs plead all causes of action in the alternative.

[192] *Smith v Robinson*, 468 US 994, 104 S Ct 3457, 82 L Ed 2d 746 (1984).

[193] Ibid 468 US at 1003.   [194] Ibid 468 US at 1019.

[195] See Individuals with Disabilities Education Act (IDEA), 20 USC s 1415(l) (2000). ('Nothing in this title shall be construed to restrict or limit the rights, procedures, and remedies available under the Constitution [or statutes] protecting the rights of children with disabilities . . .').

[196] See HR Rep No 296 (1985). But see, *Charlie F. v Board of Educ*, 98 F 3d 989, 991 (7th Cir 1996) ('the structure of the statute—with its elaborate provision for educational services and payments to those who deliver them—is inconsistent with monetary awards to children and parents'); *Heidemann v Rother*, 84 F 3d 1021, 1033 (8th Cir 1996) ('[P]laintiffs' claims based upon defendants' alleged violations of the IDEA may not be pursued in this s 1983 action because general and punitive damages for the types of injuries alleged by plaintiffs are not available under the IDEA'); *Sellers v School Bd*, 141 F 3d 524, 530 (4th Cir 1998) (interpreting the IDEA savings clause—'Nothing in this chapter shall be construed to restrict or limit the rights, procedures, and remedies available . . . under other Federal statutes protecting the rights of children and youth with disabilities'—to preclude suit under s 1983).

Since the addition of the non-exclusive section, some federal courts have allowed damages broader than mere reimbursement for private school expenses. In *Walker v District of Columbia*,[197] the US District Court for the District of Columbia held that a student alleging deprivation of special education services could bring an action for monetary damages. In *Charlie F. v Board of Education of Skoakie School District*,[198] the US Court of Appeals for the Seventh Circuit noted in dictum that 'appropriate relief' could include services in kind vice monetary compensation. In *WB v Matula*,[199] the US Court of Appeals for the Third Circuit held that 'certainly the plain language of § 1983 . . . compels the conclusion that, as a matter of law, an aggrieved parent or disabled child is not barred from seeking monetary damages'.[200] In *Jackson v Franklin County School Board*,[201] the US Court of Appeals for the Fifth Circuit remanded a section 1983 and IDEA suit to the district court for a determination of damages, including money damages for any injury resulting from the defendant's acts or omissions. And a recent decision of the District Court for the Southern District of New York expressly authorised money damages in a section 1983 suit for violations of the IDEA as well as even allowing punitive damages in such an action.[202]

3. Negligence Causes of Action

American courts often appear to apply the label of 'educational malpractice' to a broad range of cases. First, and most appropriately, they decline to hear cases that claim that liability should be imposed merely for bad teaching.[203] If they entertained cases such as that, courts would be making policy decisions in a field about which they know little. Furthermore, it would be difficult if not impossible to apportion blame among the student, teacher, parents, and society in general. Secondly, cases are denied where a physical injury has resulted to a third party because of allegedly bad teaching. For example, someone injured in a car wreck brings a cause of action against the school that poorly taught and licensed a disabled driver.[204]

---

[197] *Walker v District of Columbia*, 969 F Supp 794, 796–7 (DDC 1997).

[198] *Charlie F v Bd. of Educ of Skokie Sch Dist*, 98 F 3d 989, 991–3 (7th Cir 1996).

[199] *W.B. v Matula*, 67 F 3d 484 (3d Cir 1995). *See also Mrs W v Tirozzi*, 832 F2d 748, 753–4 (2nd Cir 1987).

[200] *Matula*, 67 F 3d at 495.

[201] *Jackson v Franklin County Sch Bd*, 80 F 2d 623, 631–2 (5th Cir 1986). But see, *Sellers v School Bd*, 141 F 3d 524, 529–30 (4th Cir 1998) (dismissing a s 1983 action for violation of the IDEA).

[202] *RB ex rel LB v Board of Educ of City of New York*, 99 F Supp.2d 411, 417 (SDNY 2000) (citing *Franklin v Gwinnett County Pub Schs*, 503 US 60, 112 S Ct 1028 (1992)).

[203] *Peter W v San Francisco Unified School District*, 60 Cal. App 3d 854, 131 Cal Rptr 854 (Cal Ct App, 1976).

[204] See, eg, *Moss Rehab v White*, 692 A 2d 902 (Del, 1997).

These cases present difficult issues of causation and standards of care. Thirdly, courts dismiss cases brought by learning disabled children and their parents, claiming that a school did not diagnose the disability and, consequently, failed adequately to provide special education services.[205] This type of case is the least susceptible to the anti-liability arguments.

Holding schools and psychologists liable for misdiagnosis of learning disabilities would not present many of the arguments used to deny 'educational malpractice' claims. The standard of care applied to educational psychologists is well developed. A flood of litigation would not be likely to flow from the small percentage of students who are learning disabled. The operation of other legal doctrines, such as immunity for discretionary acts and the public duty doctrine, would prevent cases that would require courts to second-guess the policy judgments of local governments. And compensatory damages are measurable by the cost of remedial education and would, in any event, be severely limited by issues of causation (as we explain below).

IV. THE TRUE REASONS OF IMMUNITY

In Section II, above, we summarised the policy arguments that have been advanced by some courts, both English and American though we also stated that they seem to have received a more elaborate treatment in the hands of some British judges. For convenience's sake we restate them here and then we would like to question their validity by drawing on the more extensive critique that was attempted in a recent book which was co-authored by the first of us.[206] Thus the policy arguments used against the imposition of liability are:

(i)   An economic argument: imposing liability on the public bodies in question would make bad economic sense;

(ii)   An inhibition argument: liability would inhibit the freedom of action of the officials who took the relevant decisions;

(iii) A discretionary argument: it would be inappropriate for the courts to control elected officials/bodies and tell them how to exercise their discretionary powers; and

---

[205] *Doe v Board of Education of Montgomery County*, 453 A 2d 814, 820 (Md 1982); *Donohue v Copiague Union Free School District*, 391 NE 2d 1352, 1353 (NY 1979). But see, *BM by Burger v State of Montana* 649 P 2d 425, 430 (Mont 1982) (finding liability for negligent misdiagnosis).

[206] Markesinis, Auby, Coester-Waltejn, and Deakin, *Tortious Liability of Statutory Bodies* (Oxford: Hart Publishing, 1999).

(iv) An 'alternative relief' argument: the victims in these cases had alternative remedies which made a tort remedy in the form of damages not only superfluous but dangerous (mainly for the reason (i) above).

A. Economic Arguments

Economic arguments in favour of the immunity rule have taken various forms. Here we shall look at (and question) two. One must, however, also alert the reader that these economic arguments have not, to our knowledge, been advanced in the factual context that is examined in this article. Instead, they figure mainly in the context of local authority liability for defective building foundations or highway accidents caused by (removable) obstructions that impede the view of drivers. Though their application to misdiagnosis cases seems doubtful in the extreme, their underlying assumptions could, one day, be used by those who favour an economic approach to law so they must briefly be addressed.

1. First Party Insurance is a More Effective Way of Spreading the Loss than Imposing Liability upon Public Bodies

Insurance arguments feature in a number of English judgments such as Lord Hoffman's opinion in *Stovin v Wise* as well as in some of the other cases under consideration here. The broader case for reducing the role of liability and, by extension, of liability or third party insurance, in favour of loss or first party insurance, has been made by Professor Patrick Atiyah. In *The Damages Lottery*,[207] Atiyah argues that the liability system *is* both inefficient, because it gives rise to wasteful double insurance—first party and third party—and regressive, in the sense that higher prices and inefficient public services hit the poor hardest. First party insurance, he claims, would be preferable because only those who considered it worthwhile to insure would pay the premiums to do so.[208]

It is often assumed that the existence of liability insurance creates waste within the third category of accident costs identified by Calabresi, those relating to the administration of the system, while doing little to promote efficient precautions in relation to the second category. However, there is some empirical evidence to suggest that the abolition of liability and its replacement by private loss insurance (even if such a practice was conceivable in our factual pattern) leads to an increase in accident rates. This can be seen from 'before and after studies' that looked at jurisdictions which abolished liability in tort for road traffic accidents and replaced it with a

---

[207] Patrick S Atiyah, *The Damages Lottery* (Oxford: Hart Publishing, 1997).
[208] Ibid, at 134.

system based on first party insurance. In Quebec, the rate of increase in accidents was, according to various accounts, between 10 per cent and 30 per cent.[209] Insurance can, it seems, have a deterrent effect if premiums and bonuses are related to the experience of individual policyholders. This is true even of first party insurance. If first party insurance is 'experience rated'—in other words, the less experienced pay higher premiums—the system incorporates an incentive to improve the standard of care.

In general, it is not at all clear from the present state of research in this area that we should prefer a tort regime in which fault plays no role. The system of fault plus liability insurance will often be a more effective deterrent than a no-fault scheme. Liability insurance is important from an economic point of view because it attaches implicit prices to dangerous activities. In this way, 'the direct incentives of the liability system may be translated into the terms of insurance policies'.[210] Insurers have an incentive to monitor the activities of the insured and set premiums according to how far they act to reduce the risk of harms to third parties. While this implicit pricing will not work well if insurance societies operate on the basis of 'knock for knock'—effectively allowing claims to cancel each other out—this practice is, it seems, fading away in Britain for the very reason that it involves the cross- subsidisation of dangerous activities by the less dangerous, and hence is not in the long-term interests of insurance companies.[211] Hence, it is not necessarily the case that defendants can simply pass on the costs of liability if they have third party insurance. It seems that both the level of activity and the degree of care taken by defendants can be affected through the operation of liability when coupled with insurance.

This is demonstrated by the studies of North American workers' compensation schemes. In such schemes, it is the employers who have to take out insurance, not the employees. Insurance premiums end up being varied by industry and, more rarely, by firm. The most carefully constructed empirical studies—those which control for the fact that the introduction of no-fault compensation leads to an increase in the number of injuries which get *reported*—found that increases in workers' compensation benefits led to a reduction in injury rates, and that the reduction was most substantial for

---

[209] Don Dewees *et al.*, *Exploring the Domain of Accident Law* (Oxford: Oxford University Press, 1996), 25, citing M Gaudry, 'The effects on road safety of the compulsory insurance, flat premium rating and no-fault features of the 1978 Quebec Automobile Act', in Osborne Commission, *Report of Inquiry into Motor Vehicle Accident Compensation in Ontario*); R Devlin, 'Liability versus no-fault Automobile Insurance Regimes: An Analysis of the Experience in Quebec' (unpublished PhD dissertation, University of Toronto) (on file with the University of Toronto Library).

[210] Steven Shavell, 'Economic Analysis of Law' (1999) *NBER Reporter* (Spring), 12, 13.

[211] This has been extensively reported in the insurance and financial press. See, for instance, Nigel Richardson, 'Motor Insurance. Myth Hits the Crash Barrier', *The Independent* (London), 23 Mar 1996, at 26. We are grateful to Mr David Howarth of Clare College, Cambridge, for this reference and for a most helpful discussion on this point.

high-risk industries and high-risk firms.[212] This evidence supports the claim that risk-related liability insurance helps reduce accident rates, in addition to providing for a degree of loss spreading.

In short, to argue that liability insurance necessarily involves waste and inefficiency within the system of accident compensation as a whole is to fail to understand the complex economic effects to which this form of loss-spreading gives rise. The optimal or ideal form of insurance depends in practice on a range of factors that include the relative wealth of the parties concerned (how effectively can they meet claims in the absence of insurance?) and the ability of insurers to observe and verify the risk-reducing activities of the insured. In some circumstances, it may be economically efficient to impose a statutory obligation on certain parties to take out liability insurance, as is currently the case in many areas of accident law. This would be so, for example, if those taking part in risk-creating activities would not, in the absence of insurance, have the means to meet claims against them. In some cases, economists suggest that the legislator should intervene to make liability insurance unlawful—this would be efficient where insurers could not effectively monitor risk-reducing activities and vary premiums accordingly. The legislature also has an interest in regulating attempts by potential defendants to render themselves 'judgment-proof' by various devices aimed at evading liability (we return to this point below in the context of our discussion of the 'defendant of last resort' argument).

To resolve these questions is a complex matter. As Professor Steven Shavell has suggested: '[t]o understand when and how to regulate liability insurance, these points need to be explored, and data needs to be developed and analysed on the nature of the judgment-proof problem and of liability insurance coverage in various areas of risk.'[213] These are issues which probably require the kind of systematic consideration of policy options which only the legislature can effectively engage in. What, then, is the message for the courts? The issue for them is not whether and how to regulate liability insurance, but whether to create a demand for this type of insurance in the first place by imposing liability. As we have seen, the economic arguments for and against liability insurance are finely balanced; but they certainly do not point towards it being necessarily inefficient and wasteful. On the contrary, it may play a vital role in signalling to potential defendants the means by which they can reduce risks of harm to third parties.

This insight is just as relevant to the behaviour of statutory bodies and public authorities as it is to manufacturers, occupiers, and employers.

---

[212] M Moore and WK Viscusi, *Compensation Mechanisms for Job Risks: Wages, Workers' Compensation and Product Liability* (1990); Don Dewees, *et al, Exploring the Domain of Accident Law* (Oxford: Oxford University Press, 1996), 25

[213] Shavell, 'Economic Analysis of Law', at 14.

Where public bodies carry third party insurance, we would expect insurance companies to monitor their internal processes for assessing and managing risk, in this way contributing to improved effectiveness in the delivery of public services. Where, alternatively, public bodies operate on the basis of self-insurance—in other words, carrying sufficient funds to meet potential claims—they have just as strong an incentive to avoid incurring liability for negligence. As David Howarth has pointed out,[214] negligent local authorities in this position will either have fewer recourses to meet their policy objectives, or will have to raise taxes to make up the difference and explain to voters why they are doing so. If, therefore, the courts were to grant sweeping immunities to public bodies, they would, in effect, be negating one of the principal mechanisms by which overall costs within the accident compensation system—not just the costs of accidents themselves but also the costs of precautions and the costs of administering compensation—are minimised. These arguments seem to us to be particularly apposite to the situation examined in this article.

This is not to suggest that the practice of liability insurance is always efficient. However, the answer to inefficiency, in this context, lies not in the abolition of liability, but rather in the regulation of insurance practices, as we have just explained. The history of liability insurance suggests that the legislator is ready to intervene to make insurance compulsory where this is socially and economically desirable. There is no valid economic reason for courts to short-circuit this process by denying liability on the part of whole classes of defendants through the use of the duty concept. Indeed, from an economic viewpoint there is every reason for them not to take this step.

2. *Public Bodies Deserve Special Protection as 'Defendants of Last Resort.'*

An argument which did not figure prominently in the judgments of the English cases, but which has been discussed in the context of the academic debate and is implicit in some of Lord Hoffmann's comments in *Stovin v Wise*, is the idea that public bodies are at risk of speculative litigation in a way which most individuals and private-sector companies are not. The idea is that public authorities are liable to become 'defendants of last resort' since they are unable to escape liability in ways which are open to other types of defendants. The most obvious way in which other defendants do this is through bankruptcy or insolvency.

This practice does not appear so widespread in Britain, but we are certainly familiar with the idea that public authorities may end up as resid-

---

[214] D Howarth, 'Towards a Guilt-Free Society, Lottery', review of PS Atiyah, *The Damages Lottery*, in *The Times Literary Supplement*, 5 June 1998, at 11.

ual defendants when all else fails. Thus it has been suggested that the difficulty which home owners have in tracking down and obtaining damages from negligent builders explains why, in the line of cases culminating in *Murphy v Brentwood District Council*,[215] it was local authorities which bore the force of litigation in respect of defective premises. Even where a builder can be traced and has sufficient assets to be worth suing, contribution between joint tortfeasors means that the builder's negligence is, to some extent, underwritten by the resources of the local authority: the activities of negligent private sector defendants are then subsidised by the public purse.[216]

In our view, this is the *only* 'economic' argument, which could justify treating public authorities as a special case through the device of the duty of care. All the other arguments considered here either fail to stand up to close economic scrutiny (such as the insurance argument), or, insofar as they survive such scrutiny, could be applied with equal force to cases involving private-sector defendants (such as the defensive administration argument).

However, in accepting that the danger of speculative litigation against public bodies is a real one, we do not need to accept a near-blanket denial of liability of the kind which the law appears to have reached after the decisions in *X(Minors)* and *Stovin v Wise*. Control devices may continue to be available to the courts even if the possibility of a duty of care in some cases is admitted. A control device is clearly present in the form of the special pre-tort relationship which existed in each of the *Essex*, *Osman*, and *Elguzouli-Daf* cases, where there were clear elements of reliance and (in the *Essex* case) of undertakings given by the defendant to the plaintiff. In none of these cases could the need to discourage 'last resort' litigation realistically be invoked as a reason for defeating the claim. And a series of control devices were suggested by some of their lordships in the *Phelps* judgment which, in England at least, are likely to work. We return to this point in our conclusions where we question whether these same devices can also work in the United States.

Stovin v Wise was not a case involving a pre-tort relationship; there was no element of specific reliance and no undertaking given by the defendant to the plaintiff as an individual. Lord Hoffmann's concerns about the implications of joining highway authorities to litigation involving road traffic accidents raise similar issues to those, which we have considered under the heading of 'last resort' litigation. Was the majority correct, therefore, to reject the possibility of liability in this case? There are in fact several features of *Stovin v Wise* which make it a special case and which could have

---

[215] *Murphy v Brentwood District Council* [1991] 1 AC 398 (HL 1990).
[216] See Tony Weir, 'Governmental Liability' [1989] *Public Law* 40.

been used as control devices. As Lord Nicholls of Birkenhead explained in his judgment, the defendant not only had the resources to take the action necessary to remove the hazard, but had failed to do so only because of internal mismanagement, and not because of a decision of policy concerning the allocation of resources. It is true that, in this case, the result of making the highway authority liable would have been to benefit the first defendant's liability insurers. From an economic point of view, however, there may have been nothing wrong with this. As we suggested earlier, where liability follows fault, the workings of the insurance system can ensure that a price is attached to negligent activity (or non-activity), thereby providing incentives for it to be minimised. It is far from clear that the *full* consequences of the accident in *Stovin v Wise* should have been borne by the first defendant's liability insurance, given that the situation of danger in this case was one for which the highway authority was to a certain degree responsible.

In many ways the *X(Minors)* case is the most complex and difficult one from the point of view we are considering here. Nevertheless, it is possible to see how this case, like *Stovin*, could have turned on the presence or absence of fault, rather than being decided on the issue of duty of care (with the result that the issue of fault was never considered). The decision to initiate childcare proceedings (or not) is, in nearly all cases, one involving a high element of professional judgment which the courts could review only with some difficulty. Very similar issues therefore arise as in the context of other situations where the courts must assess whether professional negligence has occurred; and here, as there, it does not seem implausible to suggest that some protection against frivolous claims could have been achieved by the application of the *Bolam*[217] test. Certainly, some of their lordships in the *Phelps* judgment seemed to think that this is so.

A. The Inhibition Argument: Imposing Liability on Public Authorities Will Lead to Inefficiency in the Form of 'Defensive Administration' and the Diversion of Expenditure

In his judgment in *Stovin v Wise*,[218] Lord Hoffmann argued that:

the creation of a duty of care upon a highway authority, even on grounds of irrationality in failing to exercise a power, would inevitably expose the authority's budgetary decisions to judicial inquiry. This would distort the priorities of local authorities, which would be bound to try to play safe by increasing their spending on road improvements rather than risk enormous liabilities for personal injury accidents.

---

[217] *Bolam v Friern Hospital Management Committee* [1957] 1 WLR 582 (QB); Basil Markesinis and S F Deakin, *Tort Law* (4th edn, 1999), 164–5 [hereinafter *Tort Law*].
[218] *Tort Law* at, 419.

They will spend less on education or social services. I think that it is important, before extending the duty of care owed by public authorities, to consider the cost to the community of the defensive measures which they are likely to take in order to avoid liability.

As we saw above, similar arguments were made by Lord Brown-Wilkinson in the *Bedfordshire* case, by Lord Justice Steyn in *Elguzouli-Daf,*[219] and by Lord Keith in *Hill.*

The claim that negligence liability leads to 'defensive practices' is often made in this and related contexts. However, the evidence on which it rests remains slim. Some US studies have found evidence that expenditure on bureaucratic and administrative procedures designed to avoid liability for medical negligence, such as various kinds of form-filling and checking, has grown considerably in recent years and now amount to billions of dollars across the system as a whole.[220] No extensive studies have been carried out for the United Kingdom or its public services. The authors of a recent empirical study, however, conducted in England in order to determine the effects of the recognition of a duty of care—albeit a very limited duty—upon the fire services,[221] cautiously concluded that 'the imposition of liability has not led to wide-spread defensive fire-fighting'.[222]

Lord Hoffmann's suggestion that, after *Anns,*[223] local inspectors insisted on 'stronger foundations than was necessary' is therefore just speculation. Brandeis and amicus briefs are unknown in English law;[224] and counsel rarely, if ever, cite empirical data to support their arguments. One could thus answer Lord Hoffmann's hunch, with a counter hunch namely, that while it is possible that the post-*Anns* regime led to unnecessarily strong and expensive foundations, the post-*Murphy* situation may be encouraging sloppy verification of building calculations. But what the law must, surely, be striving to achieve is neither excessive caution nor unnecessary sloppiness; and the latter may well follow a signal from the courts that they are opposed to any form of civil liability. Legal arguments cannot be solved, and litigation cannot be determined, on the basis of hunches, however eminent and experienced their source may be. Moreover, hunch or intu-

---

[219] See *Elguzouli-Daf v Commissioner of Police of the Metropolis* [1995] 2 WLR 173 (CA 1994).

[220] See generally Don Dewees *et al, Exploring the Domain of Accident Law* (Oxford: Oxford University Press, 1996), ch 5 (reviews this evidence).

[221] Due to the case of *Capital & Counties PLC v Hampshire County Council* [1997] QB 1004 [1997] WLR 331 (CA).

[222] Hartshorne, Smith, and Everton, 'Caparo Under Fire: A Study into the Effects upon the Fire Service of Liability in Negligence' (2000) 63 *MLR* 502, 521.

[223] *Anns v Merton London Borough Council* [1978] AC 728 (HL), overruled by *Murphy v Brentwood District Council* [1991] 1 AC 398 (HL).

[224] Although third party intervention in English courts may increase under the Human Rights Act 1998, as envisaged by the Lord Chancellor. See HL Deb, vol 583, cols 832–3 (24 Nov 1997).

ition, the dividing line between what is prudent and what becomes excessive, is a fine one. At present, we do not have enough empirical evidence to guide us in the matter of foundation inspections; and what we do have from another area of the law—medical malpractice—may suggest that one person's excessive caution is another's prudent practice. In another case,[225] Lord Hoffmann was prepared to be more candid and admit that the absence of empirical evidence makes it difficult to predict the economic consequences of a pro-liability decision; so why not show the same candour here and avoid alarmist statements? In short, we submit that an economic analysis of a decision requires more than the English judges have so far been able to produce. Our impression is that the position in the United States is not much better.

What is also problematic for this argument is that it could apply with equal force to well-established areas of tortious liability, such as employers' liability and product liability. The argument is not unique to the liability of public authorities. Indeed, from this point of view the case for granting immunity to public authorities (via the concept of duty of care) is weaker still, since they are not subject to the forces of competition, nor to the same damaging reputational effects of litigation that affect private sector organisations. If they are immune from liability, then there are few (if any) outside forces acting upon them. It may be argued that local governments are indispensable agencies such that their failure, unlike a private corporation, would leave the market without a supply of the relevant services (in this case, special education). However, it seems unlikely, if not unthinkable, that local authorities would shutter their public schools because of the imposition of liability.

In other contexts, the courts have been sceptical of arguments about the inhibitive effect that civil liability would have on the actors. In *Dorset Yacht*, Lord Reid had no time for such arguments.[226] In *Spring*, the House of Lords unanimously rejected a variant of this argument, and the sky has not yet fallen on our heads. Yet another variant of this point appeared in *Rondel v Worsley*[227] and there it won the day until, in the summer of 2000 this citadel of immunity succumbed to the current reforming zeal of the House of Lords.[228] The signs are that Strasbourg, again, may remind us that continental European advocates are also subject to duties towards their courts and judges along with their duties to their clients. Their potential liability for negligent conduct has not caused them to be less honest, less forthright, or less effective than our barristers; and compulsory insurance

---

[225] *White v Chief Constable of South Yorkshire Police* [1998] 3 WLR 1510, 1556 (HL).
[226] *Dorset Yacht Co. Ltd v Home Office* [1970] 2 WLR 1140, 1151 (HL).
[227] *Rondel v Worsley* [1969] 1 AC 191 (HL 1967).
[228] *Phelps v Hillingdon LBC* [2000] 3 WLR 776 (HL).

has ensured that they have not suffered financial ruination as a result of a liability rule. The brief comparative survey done by the first of us in a recent book[229] suggests that the potential of civil liability has not made Continental European police forces, local authorities, or social security agencies less prompt, less efficient or less effective. The judges' arguments that apocalyptic consequences would follow if our system went the same way may thus sound attractive on paper but, in their extreme form, they are, once again, unsupported by any empirical evidence. The most recent pronouncement on this type of case—*Barrett v Enfield London Borough Council*[230]—may provide some evidence that this point is getting through to some judges. Thus, in *Barrett* Lord Hutton opined that he 'would not give this consideration great weight'.[231] This statement was preceded, however, by the words, 'In the circumstances of this case', and this could be seen as an important proviso given that Lord Hutton was keen to stress that the *Bedfordshire* arguments carried 'insufficient weight' in the case which he was actually deciding. On the other hand, the learned Lord coupled his 'dislike' of the 'inhibition argument' with an express approval of a wider *dictum* by Lord Justice Evans in the Court of Appeal phase of the *Barrett*[232] hearing, and this could give a wider significance to Lord Hutton's phrase.

C. *The Discretionary Argument: The Division of Powers Between the Courts and the Executive: The Dangers of Controlling Elected Bodies*

A further category of reasons relates to the division of powers between the courts and the executive when controlling the activities of public bodies. In our view, the current talk of the need to shield public bodies may be going too far in the direction of stating that the only real control is political and not legal. As one leading public lawyer has observed in his classic textbook,[233] 'Public authorities, including ministers of the Crown, enjoy no dispensation from the ordinary law [of the land] This is an important aspect of the rule of law.' Echoes of this can be found in Lord Nicholls's dissent in *Stovin* where he reminded us that '[t]he law must recognise the need to protect the public exchequer *as well as the private interests*.'[234] In the light of what will be said below about the validity of the 'alternative remedies'

---

[229] Markesinis, *Tortious Liability*.

[230] *Barrett v Enfield London Borough Council* [1999] 3 WLR 79 (HL).

[231] Ibid, 114.

[232] There, the Lord Justice had argued that 'if the conduct in question is of a kind which can be measured against the standards of the reasonable man, placed as the defendant was, then I do not see why the law in the public interest should not recognise those standards to be observed' *Barrett v Enfield London Borough Council* [1998] QB 367, 380.

[233] Sir William Wade, in Wade and Forsyth, *Adminstrative* Law, 7th edn (Oxford: Oxford University Press, 1994), 763.

[234] *Stovin v Wise* [1996] AC 932, 934 (HL). (Emphasis added.)

argument, one might be forgiven for believing that our judges seem to be losing sight of this aspect of the matter. This is becoming particularly apparent where serious human rights are being violated as a result of this protective stance. All that such statements really betray is the fact that for as long as we do not have a set of morally (if not legally) superior rules, there is a serious risk that human rights values will be sacrificed to traditional tort reasoning. In this context it is interesting to note the contrast with the law in France and Germany where judicial control of public bodies is seen as a legitimate way of additional control and not as a dangerous and unacceptable interference with their decisional powers.

In the context of misdiagnosis cases such as *Phelps*, the argument that a court's intervention in such matter would amount to trespassing into the domains of political and municipal discretion is also unsustainable. For, as an American judge once put it:

permitting a suit by the plaintiffs because of the misdiagnosis of health care professionals . . . would not interfere with . . . school board judgments. It is a matter which does not involve education policy. A court would not be asked to 'evaluate conflicting theories of how best to educate' . . . [it] would merely determine whether the psychologist adhered to that standard of care in diagnos[is] that the average clinical psychologist would have employed under similar circumstances.[235]

In this type of case, therefore, the court is not faced with the kind of 'polycentric' problems which are best left to political organs but with a straightforward adjudication between the rights and duties of two opposing parties: the psychiatrist (and his employers) and the victim of the misdiagnosis. That this is so can be seen from the fact that if a private psychologist had engaged in the same conduct the question of his liability would have been treated as a straight forward case of medical malpractice without any talk about floodgates, unbearably economic consequences, or judicial usurpation of the decision-making powers of others. By analogy, if a doctor in a public hospital commits medical malpractice on a patient, no one thinks to shout 'no duty!'

D. The Alternative Remedies Argument

The question of alternative remedies is also relevant in this context. In a few instances, newly invented remedies—for instance an Ombudsman's report—have provided remedies to wronged victims which the tort system could either not produce or might produce after a lengthy and costly litigation. In a handful of other cases, from the group here reviewed, the non-liability rule can be justified by the existence of *truly* alternative and

---

[235] *Doe v Board of Education of Montgomery County*, 453 A 2d 814, 823 (Md, 1982) (Eldridge, J, dissenting).

effective remedies.[236] We submit, however, that these cases are, in numerical terms, very much the exception.[237] So, how serious are judges when they tell us that a poor, under-privileged and, probably, uneducated citizen who has found himself unjustly held in custody for over three months can bring a successful action for malicious prosecution or misfeasance in public office? It is not just that his social and economic position makes it almost impossible for him even to contemplate taking on the governmental apparatus responsible for his misery—especially in these days of reduced generosity on the part of the Legal Aid Board; it is also that the torts in question have ingredients that make it very difficult to invoke them with any real chance of success. Finally, the availability of purely administrative law type of remedies (eg, judicial review) is attractive only in theory. In practice, they hardly achieve any (moral) satisfaction; they promote no deterrent function; and they bring about no compensation whatsoever. On the contrary, the conclusion reached in cases such as *Elguzouli-Daf* and *Essex County Council*, to the extent that they are (partially) justified by the argument that in all of these instances there is an alternative remedy, can only provoke moral outrage, even among hardened lawyers.

Although this way of testing the validity of 'the alternative remedy' argument is not shared (yet?) by the majority of our judges, the *Barrett* decision in the House of Lords provides some signs that not all of them are convinced by the prevailing argumentation we are here criticising. Thus, it is submitted that Lord Hutton was right to go beyond what we are stating, and not merely test the effectiveness of the alternative remedy (as we are suggesting), but assert boldly that 'the jurisdiction of the court should not be excluded because of the existence of other avenues of complaint'.[238] As stated, this argument becomes even stronger when one bears in mind the exceptional paucity of 'alternative remedies' asserted to be open to disgruntled plaintiffs. Because of its strong human rights implications, *Elguzouli-*

---

[236] *Olotu v Home Office* [1997] 1 WLR 328 (CA 1996), where the remedy of *habeas corpus* was available to the illegally (over)-detained plaintiff and where, one also finds hints, that he might, additionally, have grounds for complaint against those who failed to alert him as to his possible remedies. Similarly, in *Hill v Chief Constable of West Yorkshire* [1989] AC 53 (HL) the availability of compensation under the Criminal Injuries Compensation Board obviously weighed on the minds of some of the judges in the Court of Appeal. In this context, however, one must note two things: first, the generosity of the Criminal Injuries Compensation awards is, nowadays, considerably reduced. The effectiveness of this 'alternative' remedy must be looked at very carefully. Secondly, in many of the cases mentioned in this article this particular, alternative remedy was simply not available.

[237] The Ombudsman's report in the Barlow Clowes affair is, possibly, one of the finest example of such intervention since it led to the government paying out to investors who lost their life saving a sum in the order of £16 million. Several ombudsmen schemes are currently in operation and are described briefly by Professor Peter Cane, *Tort Law and Economic Interests*, 2nd edn (Oxford: Oxford University Press, 1996), 366 ff.

[238] *Barrett v Enfield London Borough Council*, [1999] 3 WLR 79, 114 (HL).

Daf[239] is the case that stands out most clearly in our minds. And it is certainly true in the misdiagnosis cases. For as a learned American judge put it:

Whether or not administrative remedies are useful in the context of educational malpractice, they clearly are not helpful in the context of a misdiagnosis by a health care professional, the cure for which necessitates the expenditure of a large sum of money.[240]

In the United States, the alternative remedy is the IDEA, a federal scheme that requires states to implement testing, provide special education, and submit to judicial review in federal court. The IDEA attempts to prevent misdiagnosis of learning disabilities, but also to provide a remedy in the event that misdiagnosis occurs. This remedy is unclear, but the majority view is that reimbursement for private school tuition is the appropriate relief. The IDEA provides some relief, but has at least three disadvantages. First, the statute does nothing for children who have slipped through the educational system undiagnosed and ill-educated. No reimbursement would be due, as they and their families would not have paid private-school tuition. Secondly, the IDEA is unlikely to ever produce full compensatory damages that a tort lawsuit should recover (eg, lost wages or pain and suffering).[241] And third, the remedy under the IDEA would only come after the fact and with extremely high transaction costs, as administrative exhaustion is a prerequisite to judicial review in federal court. There are other flaws in the statute, including federalism and vagueness concerns inherent in the burdens imposed upon state and local governments, but the question of quantum of damages remains the unanswered question. A state law cause of action is preferable in the sense that local jurisdictions could fashion a remedy that best suits them, and in a more straightforward manner than via strained interpretations of a federal statute.

---

[239] *Elguzouli-Daff v Commissioner of Police of the Metropolis* [1995] 2 WLR 173 (C.A. 1994). involved the Crown Prosecution Service. Torts actions were brought by two persons who were detained in custody for suspected crimes. After a long periods in detention—22 and 85 days respectively—the Crown Prosecution Service (CPS) discontinued proceedings against them on the grounds that there was insufficient evidence. The plaintiffs' statement of claim against the CPS for alleged negligence in the handling of their case was struck out by the judge who held that they disclosed no reasonable cause of action. The Court of Appeal unanimously rejected the plaintiffs' appeal, on the ground that the CPS owed no duty of care to those it was prosecuting.

[240] *Doe v Board of Education of Montgomery County*, 453 A 2d 814, 824 (Md, 1982) (Eldridge, J, dissenting).

[241] Admittedly, some may not view this fact as a disadvantage.

V. BANKRUPTING LOCAL AUTHORITIES

After reading many cases on both sides of the Atlantic, one is inclined to the view that all the concerns, expressed and unexpressed, against possible liability largely boil down to one fear: the imposition of liability might bankrupt the local authority. If avoiding this risk means sacrificing all other values, including that of fairness and compensation of unjustly caused harm, so be it. Yet matters need not be viewed in such apocalyptic terms. Let us explore this thought further, first by looking at some key passages of *Phelps* and then by elaborating some of its ideas with the help of academic literature.

A. *Some Views from* Phelps

In his thoughtful judgment Lord Nicholls of Birkenhead said:

I can see no escape from the conclusion that teachers do, indeed, owe such duties. The principle objection raised to this conclusion is the spectre of a rash of "gold-digging" actions brought on behalf of under-achieving children by discontented parents, perhaps many years after the events complained of. If teachers are liable, education authorities will be vicariously liable, since the negligent acts or omissions were committed in the course of the teachers' employment. So, it is said, the limited resources of education authorities and the time of teaching staff will be diverted away from teaching and into defending unmeritorious legal claims . . . I am not persuaded by these fears. I do not think they provide sufficient reason for treating work in the classroom as territory, which the courts must never enter. 'Never' is an unattractive absolute in this context. This would bar a claim, however obvious it was that something had gone badly wrong, and however serious the consequences for the particular child. If a teacher carelessly teaches the wrong syllabus for an external examination, and provable financial loss follows, why should there be no liability? Denial of the existence of a cause of action is seldom, if ever, the appropriate response to fear of its abuse. Rather, the courts, with their enhanced powers of case-management, must seek to evolve means of weeding out obviously hopeless claims as expeditiously as is consistent with the court having a sufficiently full factual picture of all the circumstances of the case.[242]

Lord Clyde completed the onslaught on the arguments of the timorous when he said:

In the present case I am not persuaded that there are sufficient grounds to exclude these claims even on grounds of public policy alone. It does not seem to me that there is any wider interest of the law which would require that no remedy in damages be available. I am not persuaded that the recognition of a liability upon employees of the education authority for damages for negligence in education would

---

[242] *Phelps v Hillingdon LBC* [2000] 3 WLR 776, 804 (HL).

lead to a flood of claims, or even vexatious claims, which would overwhelm the school authorities, nor that it would add burdens and distractions to the already intensive life of teachers. Nor that it should inspire some peculiarly defensive attitude in the performance of their professional responsibilities. On the contrary, it may have the healthy effect of securing that high standards are sought and secured. If it is thought that there would only be a few claims and for that reason the duty should not be recognised, the answer must be that if there are only a few claims there is less reason to refuse to allow them to be entertained. As regards the need for this remedy, even if there are alternative procedures by which some form of redress might be obtained, such as resort to judicial review or to an ombudsman or the adoption of such statutory procedures as are open to parents, which might achieve some correction of the situation for the future, it may only be through a claim for damages at common law that compensation for the damage done to the child may be secured for the past as well as the future.[243]

These extracts contain their lordships responses to some of the policy fears discussed earlier on in this paper. But, read with the rest of their opinions and in conjunction with the views expressed by academics who have written extensively on these cases, they suggest that some important members of the current House of Lords are not persuaded by these nightmarish fears. Here are then are some of the ways that could help contain liability to manageable bounds.

B. Ways of Avoiding the Nightmare Scenario

1. Negligence Levels

The House of Lords in *Phelps*—and academic writers before it—have always argued that the standard of care that English courts would require before they found that a duty of care had been breached would be high and would, in any event, act as one (of many) controlling devices against an open-ended liability. Lord Clyde in *Phelps* expressed this idea in the following words when he said[244]

Any fear of a flood of claims may be countered by the consideration that in order to get off the ground the claimant must be able to demonstrate that the standard of care fell short of that set by the *Bolam v Freiern*[245] test. That is deliberately and properly a high standard in recognition of the difficult nature of some decisions which those to whom the test applies require to make and of the room for genuine differences of view on the propriety of one course of action against another.

---

[243] Ibid, at 809.   [244] Ibid.

[245] *Bolam v Freiern* [1957] 1 WLR 582 (QB). The case involved medical malpractice and the crucial words of McNair J. held that '[A doctor] is not guilty of negligence if he has acted in accordance with a practice accepted as proper by a responsible body of medical men skilled in that particular art . . .'

As stated, British academics have shared this view even before it was espoused by Lord Clyde. Professor Craig and Dr Fairgrieve for instance, in an article[246] written shortly after the first of the revisionist decisions was handed down,[247] argued that 'The *Bolam* test gives a good degree of protection to defendants.' In *Phelps*, Lord Slynn of Hadley agreed.[248] Overall, the Craig/Fairgrieve article, written in measured language, refuses to accept the alarmist, traditional position that any shift from duty to breach would court disaster. It must, however, be admitted that in the United States, where so much more power vests in the hands of juries, such degree of security might be diluted. We shall return to this point in our conclusions.

2. Causation

Causation could also raise formidable problems for future plaintiffs, especially since the absence of records and delay in bringing such claims might make it very difficult for plaintiffs to substantiate them. But even leaving problems of evidence aside, the hurdles of *Phelps* on causation for plaintiffs are formidable. They would have to satisfy the court first, that if their difficulties had been discovered in time, the school ought to have taught them in a different way and then, if this had happened, their ultimate educational attainment would have improved. These are not insubstantial hurdles; and, overcoming them still leaves open the question of the extent, in financial terms, of the plaintiff's future loss. The quantum problems are thus also likely to be formidable.

The point was well made by Garland J at First Instance and Lord Justice Otton at the Court of Appeal hearings in *Phelps*. For even if a duty is recognised and the inadequacy of the educational training received by the plaintiff is proven, it does not mean that his or her claims for lost earnings can be made on the basis that he or she would have grown up to have the earnings of a Bill Gates. As the judge at First Instance in the *Phelps* case said:[249]

It is quite impossible to make any specific findings as to the plaintiff as she might have been. I have commented that the attempt to do so is to enter deeply into the realm of hypothesis. Clearly, she would be somewhat, perhaps substantially, more literate than she is now. She would probably have greater self-confidence and self-esteem which would improve her employment prospects. Whether she could ever have become a computer operator I regard as pure speculation.

---

[246] Craig and Fairgrieve, 'Barrett, Negligence and Discretionary Powers' [1999] *Public Law* 626.
[247] *Barrett v Enfield LBC* [1999] 3 All ER 193 (1999).
[248] 'courts should not find negligence too readily . . .' *Phelps*, 3 WLR, at 792.
[249] *Phelps v Hillingdon LBC* [1999] 1 WLR 500, 529 (CA).

3. Controlling the Levels of Awards

This heading, related to the previous one, presents further reasonable opportunities for controlling the size of awards in a legally reasonable manner. The question of the proper measure of damages has thus far not been adequately addressed by the courts. No doubt, this is because the focus on duty has prevented the courts from reaching this point of the enquiry. But whatever the reason for this omission, we are presented with a chance of defining these limits in as rational a manner as we can. [250] Perhaps, the following two propositions can serve as starting points to such an examination.

Let us begin by remembering that in the words of Lord Justice Otton of the English Court of Appeal:[251]

Any plaintiff with a congenital condition faces formidable difficulties in proving a causal link between failure to diagnose and/or to treat appropriately and outcome, particularly in relation to future earning capacity.

We see this as a legitimate, serious, but not in all cases as a insurmountable obstacle, the difficulties varying on the facts of each case, the nature and extent of the disability, the age of the plaintiff, and the availability of any kind of employment history to assist in the evaluation of future earnings.

Let us then also recall that judges and psychiatrists accept that while the effects of proper diagnosis and resultant different education are largely speculative, both seem to agree that failing to improve the plaintiffs' condition, however slightly, often leaves them suffering in self-confidence and self esteem. This non-pecuniary heading of harm needs to be compensated though, again, the most likely result (in countries not dependant on jury quantification)[252] would be to award a small and conventional amount.

Finally, though the ultimate result of a proper education designed for those suffering from this neurological dysfunction is uncertain, all concerned accept that it can have a (variable) effect on the plaintiff's literacy. Thus the cost of providing such an education privately, if not made available under the state system, should also be recoverable since it can have a beneficial effect on the plaintiff, albeit an unquantifiable one. This

---

[250] In his judgment in *Phelps* Lord Slynn admitted that 'there is room for much debate as to quantum in this type of case', *Phelps v Hillingdon LBC* [2000] 3 WLR 776, 794 (HL).

[251] Ibid [1999] 1 WLR 500, at 530.

[252] In countries such as America this effect could only be attained through some kind of capping regime. Many states have adopted statutes that specify absolute limits on damages awarded against local authorities. See, eg, New Jersey St Ann's 59:9-2(c) (1937) ('No punitive or exemplary damages shall be awarded against a public entity'); 51 *Okl St Ann's* 154 (1910) (limiting personal injury liability to $100,000 per person and $1,000,000 for any single occurrence or accident).

result, apparently accepted in German law[253] lies also at the basis of the IDEA scheme. It does, however, represent one potentially serious problem. Put simply, it is this: What happens if the plaintiff's parents or guardian do not move swiftly to supply private education, initially at their expense? This may well be the case since incurring such an expenditure may be impossible for particular plaintiffs or too risky for others. Given the time of resolving these issues through litigation, this risk is, in fact, a very high one. Plaintiffs should be able to obtain a preliminary injunction if they can make a clear showing of probable success and probable irreparable injury.[254] An injunction could be issued in federal court that would, for example, require a local authority to pay for private-school tuition during the pendency of the trial.

One final thought is called for under this heading of measure of damages.

The facts of the litigated cases are meagre on this point; but from what can glean from them most of these plaintiffs came from modest to poor environments and could not normally be predicted to be high earners. If this is, indeed, the prevalent pattern it may be due to the fact that middle class parents seem to be more effective in getting services up-front or, otherwise, convincing their schools to provide such services. This would also mean that the long-after-the-fact damage claims come disproportionately from the poorer and the most needy.

Taken individually, the above arguments seem to us to be quite compelling. But taken cumulatively, they become even more persuasive to those at least who do not share the apocalyptic view that the discovery of a duty of care in such cases will ruin many local authorities. This over all assessment is supported by the evidence that exists—admittedly not complete or detailed enough to warrant complete confidence but, nonetheless of considerable interest. And, as we have seen, this evidence suggests that the total amounts awarded against local authorities for all sorts of violations of their statutory duties remains a small fraction of their total budget. Of course, some would argue, that even these amounts are too high; and one dollar spent on the compensation of a dyslectic child or a falsely imprisoned citizen may be one dollar too many. But that is precisely where we take issue with this school of thought. For example, take the English case of *Elguzouli* discussed above.[255] In these days when human rights dominate the legal and political discourse to the extent that they do, we find

---

[253] OLG Hamm, 11th Civil Senate, 23 Mar 1990, 11 U 108/89 (unpublished report, reprinted in Markesinis, *The German Law of Obligations*, vol II, *The Law of Torts: A Comparative Introduction*, 4th edn (forthcoming 2002).
[254] In the United States, this would be possible under Federal Rule of Civil Procedure 65.
[255] *Elguzouli-Daff v Commissioner of Police of the Metropolis* [1995] 2 WLR 173 (CA 1994).

it unacceptable that someone can be negligently detained in prison for eighty days and, when released without being charged, fail to get any redress on the grounds that such costs might be financially crippling to the state.

4. Court Management

This is another safety valve that would allow English courts, after the recent Woolf reforms,[256] to manage the case before them more actively and weed out unmeritorious or vexatious claims.

5. Misdiagnosis v Inadequate Education

If it be objected that the previous arguments might help keep matters under control in England but not in the United States because of structural differences in the background and the procedures of American (mainly state) courts, the same objection cannot be levied against the distinction advocated under this heading. The distinction is contained clearly in Lord Nicholls opinion in *Phelps*. He elaborated in three steps thus:

Let me consider three instances. Take a case where an educational psychologist is employed by an education authority . . . When carrying out the assessment and advising the education authority, [does] he owe a duty of care to the child? . . . I confess I entertain no doubt on how that question should be answered . . .This seems to me to be, on its face, an example par excellence of a situation where the law will regard the professional as owing a duty of care to a third party as well as his own employer. The duty to the pupil would march hand in hand with the professional's responsibilities to his own employer . . . My second illustration concerns a teacher. Does a teacher owe a common law duty of care to a pupil who is obviously having difficulty and not making the progress he should? Teachers are not educational psychologists, and they are not to be treated as though they were. But they, too, are professionals. It would make no sense to say that educational psychologists owe a duty of care to under performing pupils they asked to assess, but teachers owe no duty of care to under-performing pupils in their charge or about whom they give educational advice under a statutory scheme . . . A teacher must exercise due skill and care to respond appropriately to the manifest problems of such a child . . . [and] if he does not do so, he will be in breach of the duty he owes the child . . . My third illustration raises a particularly controversial issue. It cannot be that a teacher owes a duty of care only to children with special educational needs. The law would be in

---

[256] They are set out in detail by his Lordship in his Access to Justice, Final Report to the Lord Chancellor on the Civil Justice System in England and Wales, HMSO (1996), available at <http:// www.law.warwick.ac.uk/Woolf/report> (last visited 7 July 2001). The relevant rules will now be found in the Civil Procedure Rules 1998 r 3.4(2). How this works in the post-Phelps era can be seen in S v Gloucestershire County Council; L v Tower Hamlets London Borough Council [2001] 2 WLR 909.

an extraordinary state if, in carrying out their teaching responsibilities, teachers owed duties to some for their pupils but not to others. So the question which arises, and cannot be shirked, is whether teachers owe duties of care to all their pupils in respect of the way they discharge their teaching responsibilities . . . I can see no escape from the conclusion that teachers do, indeed owe such duties . . . This is not to open the door to claims based on poor quality of teaching. It's one thing for the law to provide a remedy in damages when there is manifest incompetence or negligence comprising specific, identifiable mistakes. It would be an altogether different matter to countenance claims of a more general nature, to the effect that the child did not receive an adequate education at the school . . . proof of under performance by a child is not by itself evidence of negligent teaching. There are many, many reasons for under performance. A child's ability to learn from what he is taught is much affected by a host of factors which are personal to him and over which the school has no control. Emotional stress and the home environment are two examples. Even within a school, there are many reasons other than professional negligence. Some teachers are better at communicating and stimulating interest than others, but that is a far cry from negligence . . . The list of factors could continue,[257] suffice it to say, the existence of a duty of care owed by teachers to their pupils should not be regarded as furnishing a basis on which generalised 'educational malpractice' claims can be mounted.

Given the small number of learning disabled children (perhaps 5 per cent),[258] and the irrelevance of theoretical challenges to negligent misdiagnosis (such as the *Peter W* arguments that no justiciable injury exists, etc.), we are left to quibble regarding the amount of damages. The resolution of that question must be left for other articles; suffice to say that American courts are well equipped to limit damages via capping statutes that eliminate punitive damages and reduce compensatory damages to legislatively specified amounts. We are asserting here negligent misdiagnosis presents a cognizable injury that is demonstrably caused by tortfeasor school districts who owe a duty of care to their learning disabled students.

VI. COMPARATIVE CONCLUSIONS

As one might expect, the study of English and American law shows that the two systems have, for a long time, traversed the same path as far as liability in common law is concerned. To be sure, English judgments have

---

[257] Cf *Hunter v Board of Education, Montgomery Co*, 485, A 2d 582, 584 (1982) ('Substantial professional authority attests that the achievement of literacy in the schools, or its failure, is influenced by a host of factors which affect the pupil subjectively, from outside the formal teaching process, and beyond the control of its ministers. They may be physical, neurological, motional, cultural, environmental; they may be present but not perceived, recognised but not identified').

[258] See *Diagnostic and Statistical Manual of Mental Disorders*, 4th edn (1995), 46–53.

perhaps shown a more detailed consideration of precedents and embarked on a much more detailed consideration of the statutory instruments they had to apply. As a result, and not surprisingly, they tend to be longer than the comparable American decisions. More recently, a number of English judges have also shown a greater willingness to discuss openly the policy considerations which, in their view, militate against the imposition of liability and they have done so in a fairly elaborate manner. Again, so far as we have been able to ascertain, this has not been matched in the American decisions. For example, the only American case to accept educational malpractice did so in an opinion that barely fills seven pages of the Pacific Reporter.[259] In the main, however, the two systems have coincided, both in their unwillingness to impose liability and, broadly speaking, in the reasons invoked for taking this stand. In this respect, the contrast with the major Continental European systems could not have been greater. For in the latter systems a philosophy very different to the English and the American seems to dictate almost as an imperative that society, which obtains the benefit of these activities, should also bear their costs rather than saddle them on ordinary and, on the whole, weak citizens. In very recent times, however, English and American law seem, in a narrow area of the law, to have parted company; and the *Phelps* decision has opened up a road which may also be available to the United States. Whether American judges can or will take it, remains to be seen. But one thing must be stressed here with a measure of some conviction: the 'Nicholls' type of reasoning is not, in a technical, legal sense, un-transplantable to the United States. A number of citations have already been given to show that the analysis of the learned Law Lord, though not yet widely shared in the United States has, nonetheless, been independently advocated by a number of American judges[260] and academics. So, the legal ground for receiving it in the United States is not hostile; if such a reception fails to make any headway, it will be due to the wider backdrop factors which give American law its particular flavour.

As already stated, it is arguable that the impetus behind *Phelps* was provided by the Strasbourg court's rulings that the unrestricted use of the notion of duty of care amounted to a violation of Article 6 of the European Convention on Human Rights. This approach, as has also been noted, is controversial; and it may not withstand for long a sustained critical examination. Yet *Osman* prompted the House of Lords in *Barrett* to back-track somewhat from the *Bedfordshire* high watermark and, perhaps, take this process a step further in its *Phelps* judgment as it repulsed the Court of

---

[259] *BM by Burger v State of Montana*, 649 P 2d 425 (Mont 1982).
[260] Albeit in dissent. See, eg, *Doe v Board of Education of Montgomery County*, 453 A 2d 814, 820 (Md 1982) (Eldridge, J, dissenting); *Donohue v Copiague Union Free School District*, 407 NYS 2d 874, 883 (NY App, 1979) (Suozzi, J, dissenting).

Appeal's attempts in the same case to widen the non-liability rule. Thus, as a result of all these cases, the *Bedfordshire* policy assumptions, already beleaguered by Strasbourg, may have ended up even weaker than they appeared to be after *Barrett*. In that sense, the Court of Appeal's attempt in *Phelps* to extend the scope of immunity has, most certainly, backfired. For though in their *Phelps* judgment their Lordships only decided the vicarious liability option, and reversed the Court of Appeal's attempt to foreclose it, the hearing gave to two of the three judges who wrote reasoned judgments the opportunity to challenge and, effectively, reject all the policy grounds invoked in favour of immunity. Though *Phelps* left the question of primary liability open, it is difficult to see how the *Bedfordshire*, and *Stovin*, policy arguments, rejected in the context of vicarious liability, can be revived in the context of primary liability under common law. If such a revival of the non-liability stance were thus to be attempted, it would probably have to come from a differently composed panel of the House of Lords[261] including such high priests of immunity as Lord Hoffmann. But such a shift, if it happened, would inevitably have to be carefully phrased and watered down for otherwise it would contain the seeds of great uncertainty for the future since it would reveal the members of the House of Lords as being divided on important matters of principle.

Phelps, we have argued all along, may also prove of interest to American lawyers. To the extent that the same policy arguments enunciated against the imposition of liability can also be found in the corresponding American decisions, *Phelps* must now cast a shadow over the analogous American cases, as well. For, prima facie, only ignorance of the *Phelps* judgements or unjustified chauvinism could ever justify any American judge worth his salt from at least considering the validity of the new arguments that challenge the no-liability policy grounds. We stress prima facie, however, for we acknowledge that some of the arguments as to the efficacy of alternative controlling devices, found explicitly or implicitly in *Phelps*, may prove more questionable within the broader American framework. It is thus open to discussion whether the American court-management techniques, especially at the state level, are or can be made to be as effective as the new Woolf reforms appear to be. Likewise, controlling the bounds of liability through the notions of breach and causation[262] may be less easy in a system where

---

[261] For though one has all along been focusing on the judgments of Lords Nicholls and Clyde one must not forget that Lords Slynn and Hutton were also involved in *Barrett* in the gradual weakening of *Bedfordshire* and its arguments.

[262] In our statement we bracket causation together with carelessness since so many colleagues have so often warned of how 'things can get out of control' in a system that is so dependant on civil juries. Yet, many of the American judges who have tried and dismissed claims of educational malpractice (including dyslexia cases) have included in their judgments dicta about the difficulties of linking the damages claimed to the alleged negligent misdiagnosis that strike us as remarkably similar to the ideas put forward by Garland J and Otton LJ in

the jury trial so radically affects negligence litigation. On the other hand, Lord Nicholls's distinction between misdiagnosis and ordinary educational malpractice can less easily be pushed aside as inappropriate to the American setting. Anyway, this is not the place to pronounce definitively on all these issues. The comparatist can do no more than suggest new avenues to his foreign colleagues and alert them to the desirability to see foreign decisions and their arguments within the wider context of the system in which they were rendered. He must then leave it to the local lawyers to draw their own conclusions about the persuasive value of the foreign ideas. Yet, even with these caveats, we submit that the dislike shown by some of the law lords towards the use of devices that exclude liability in a blanket way merits careful consideration. Lord Nicholls sentences that 'Never is an unattractive absolute' and that 'Denial of the existence of a cause of action is seldom, if ever, the appropriate response to fear of its abuse' have special, and we submit transatlantic, resonance.[263] Thus we do not accept the view that the law in the United States, especially at state level, is so firmly set that it is incapable of change. For, although we recognise that often these decisions are predetermined by the stances of the judges deciding the case, we hope that the current judicial climate is not universally opposed to liability for negligent misdiagnosis. As stated by Cardozo, 'Some theory of liability, some philosophy of the end to be served by tightening or enlarging the circle of rights and remedies, is at the root of any decision in novel situations when analogies are equivocal and precedents are silent.'[264] We refuse to admit that English and American courts have grown so far apart that the 'theory of liability' found in *Phelps* will not find at least a few receptive judges.

The above points must also be accompanied by one additional observation. This new, critical evaluation of the reasons against liability has been made possible only because judges such as Lord Browne-Wilkinson, Hoffmann, Stein (and one or two others) were willing to bring them out into the open and expose them to the purifying effect of the public gaze. So, even if we disagree with their policy reasons, we must be grateful to them for making them public. Yet the danger of invoking policy arguments, with-

---

the *Phelps* case. One should therefore not rush to claim that the controlling devices that may be available to the English judges are not also there to be used by their American counterparts. Thus, see for instance: *DSW v Fairbanks North Star Borough School District*, 628 P 2d 554, at 556 (1981); *BM by Burger v State of Montana*, 649 P 2d 425, 430 (Mont 1982).

[263] 'It is the business of the law to remedy wrongs that deserve it, even at the expense of a 'flood of litigation', and it is a pitiful confession of incompetence on the part of any court of justice to deny relief on such grounds.' W Prosser, *Handbook of the Law of Torts*, 4th edn (1971), s 12, at 51.

[264] Benjamin N Cardozo, *The Growth of the Law* 102 (Yale: Yale University Press, 1924) (cited by *Dalehite v United States*, 346 US 15, 49, 73 S Ct 956, 975 (1953) (Jackson, J, dissenting).

out any attempt to substantiate them with the backing of empirical evidence, must also not be forgotten nor must it be underestimated. In this sense, we entirely agree with the robust refusal of Lord Justice Buxton of the English Court of Appeal to listen to policy arguments put forward by counsel if not backed by some kind of hard fact evidence.[265] Here, and in a different work,[266] we tried to adduce some evidence and some arguments of the kind that a judge might regard as useful to fill this vacuum. But we readily acknowledge that much more empirical work remains to be done before one proves that the fears about imposing liability are real or unreal. Some of the thoughts put forward in this paper could provide guidelines for future empirical research.

The change of direction signalled by the House of Lords in *Phelps* should not be seen as a green light to plaintiffs to pin on these misdiagnoses unjustified claims to riches. If the American position remains unaltered, and *Phelps* fails to find imitators in the United States, it will, we think, be partly due to two fears. The first is that weak cases may have to be litigated all the way up to the stage of directed verdict; the second, the danger of uncontrolled jury awards, coupled perhaps by exorbitant punitive damages. If the first danger is as great as many might think it to be, this may be partly due to the lack of court-management techinques which English judges are nowadays given under the Woolf reforms. In any event, it could be partly addressed by the distinction between a claim of bad education and misdiagnosis, which found such favour with Lord Nicholls. If the second fear were to be proved correct, it would be ironic in the extreme. For the greed of plaintiffs (or their lawyers), if proved unmanageable, would prove the decisive cause of their continued failure to recover even fair and reasonable amounts.[267] Yet this need not be so. For, even setting aside the controlling devices that seem to be available in England, American law has shown the

---

[265] In *Perrett v Collins* [1998] 2 Lloyd's Rep 255, 276–7, he thus argued that '[t]here was no evidence to support any of these [policy] contentions. . . . In my respectful view, the Court should be very cautious before reaching or acting on any conclusions that are not argued before it in the way in which technical issues are usually approached, with the assistance of expert evidence.'

[266] Markesinis, Auby, Coester-Waltejn, and Deakin, *Tortious Liability of Statutory Bodies* (Oxford: Hart Publishing, 1999).

[267] Yet it is this greed, coupled with a 'lust to sue', that has arguably contributed to the devaluation of the tort of educational malpractice and, in turn, led to its whole-hearted rejection by the American courts. *Ross v Creighton University*, 957 F 2d 410, 415 (7th Cir 1992) strikes us a case that, arguably, comes under this category. For there the plaintiff argued that Creighton University 'owed him a duty to recruit and enrol only those students reasonably qualified and able to academically perform at Creighton and that they breached that duty by admitting him, not informing him how unprepared he was for studies there, and then not providing tutoring services . . . to enabl[e] him to receive a meaningful education', ibid, at 415. Apparently, the kind of courses that he was advised to take—possibly because his 'academic level was far below that of the average Creighton student'—included 'markmanship' and the 'theory of basketball', ibid, at 412.

way forward in another way. The IDEA scheme for instance is, in theory, based on the notion that the appropriately limited amounts can and should be awarded to deserving victims. Thus, if all else failed, capping statutes might well be the only answer available in the United States; and one hopes that their enactment might be favoured even by the plaintiff's lobby on the grounds that half a loaf is better than none.

A further lesson that flows from *Phelps* and, on the whole, ignored thus far in the United States, is the distinction between educational malpractice and misdiagnosis. We mentioned this several times and we repeat it again in our conclusions since we see mileage in this distinction. Yet the only judgment that we found in the United States that explored it fully was the dissent in *Doe v Board of Education of Montgomery County*.[268] The dissenting judgment of Justice Eldridge[269] and Lord Nicholls speech in *Phelps* deserve to receive both in the United States and in England more attention and elaboration. For between them they provide the germs of a workable compromise to this problem even though the distinction it proposes is, at its fringes, likely to bring into relief demarcation problems.

On the stylistic front we have already noted the difference that we found between the English judgments—especially the most recent ones—and those found in the parallel American cases. How a judge writes tells us much about what is going through his mind. These differences of style raise issues which deserve to receive more attention in the classroom than they have hitherto done. But we have also suggested why the open English invocation of policy has also made it easier to challenge if not refute the arguments that underpinned the non-liability rule. One would be most disappointed with any future decision of a major American court, which retained the existing non-liability rule without saying why the arguments advanced in England against liability are unconvincing. Thus, is it really right to say that a liability rule would bankrupt a local authority given that the total bill for the liability rule in Germany amounts to 1.5 per cent of the annual budget? And does not the same kind of picture emerge from the admittedly insufficient American figures available to us at present despite the magnitude of American awards?[270] Of course, one could argue that X million of dollars is X millions too many; and that such sums would be better spent on more schools, hospital beds, better equipment or, at any rate, the provision of the kind of services that elected officials—not judges and juries—believe should

---

[268] *Doe v Bd. of Educ of Montgomery County*, 453 A 2d 814 (Md 1982).

[269] Ibid, at 819.

[270] The *Los Angeles Times*, 17 Mar 2000, estimated that the ramifications of the 'Rampart scandal' would cost the County government at least $6 million. The county's annual budget is $15 billion. During the years 1989–99, the LA tax-payers paid an estimated $106 million to settle abuse and lawful arrest cases. The infamous Rodney King incident cost it $3.8 million of which 1.4 per cent went to legal fees and costs. See Nicholas Riccardi, *County's Costs Adding Up in Rampart Probe*, LA Times B1 (17 Mar 2000).

be made available.[271] There is force in such reasoning and nothing is gained by denying it. However, it totally ignores the fact that in many—not all— of these cases innocent victims have suffered serious harm as a result of undoubted negligence and, at times, intentional activities on the part of public officials. The 'Rampart scandal',[272] currently plaguing Los Angeles County is, if substantiated, monumentally embarrassing as it suggests a very wide corruption in the local police department. In such and other similar cases, should the harm suffered by ordinary citizens always be subordinated to the book-keeping argument of local authority budgetary surpluses come what may? Or is it right to argue that the imposition of liability will make officials reluctant to act? Or, on the contrary, is a measured degree of responsibility likely to contribute to the maintenance of high standards of public service? One is inclined to agree with Lord Bingham[273] that it would be too rash to ignore any deterrent value to a liability rule; and one is thus pleased to note that this argument most recently found favour with a least one judge in the *Phelps* case.[274] In this context, one must also add as a postscript that most if not all of the mega-awards are found in the most egregious forms of police abuse and not in the context of negligent misdiagnosis discussed in this paper.[275]

One way or another, the study of this topic also shows how many of the rules of negligent liability are really rules related to quantum of damages and procedure. Find a satisfactory solution to the latter problems and you may find that the former disappears or, at any rate, becomes less frighten-

---

[271] The *Los Angeles Times* article referred to in the previous note, estimated that the $6 million costs would cover the expense of 180 extra beds in the county's six public hospitals. See ibid.

[272] The Rampart police station, situated some forty blocks west of the downtown area of Los Angeles covers a mostly Latino community. According to the confessions of one of the police officers arrested in the process of trying to steal cannabis in the possession of the police, local policemen engaged regularly in routine beatings and unjustified shootings of suspects and the falsification of evidence which led to many wrongful convictions. No outside observer can comment meaningfully on such accusations. What can, however, be noted is that some 100 convictions have thus far been overturned as a result of the Rampart scandal; and numerous claims are currently pending against the Los Angeles Police Department. Henry Weinstein, Judge Oks Use and Racketeering Law in Rampart Suits, *Los Angeles Times*, 29 Aug 2000, at A1. The Federal Department of Justice has recently been given supervisory authority over the Los Angeles Police Department. Tina Daunt, City Agrees to US Reforms for LAPD, *Los Angeles Times* A1 (20 Sept 2000). The enormity of American damages must be weighed against the enormity of the alleged criminal activities carried out (by a fraction) of the law enforcement agencies.

[273] *X v Bedfordshire* [1994] 2 WLR 554, 662G.

[274] *Phelps v Hillingdon LBC* [2000] 3 WLR 776, 809 (HL) (per Lord Clyde).

[275] The plaintiff in *Phelps* received approximately £ 40,000 (around $60,000). The figures claimed that we have seen in the misdiagnoses cases range around the half a million dollar mark; but in none have the causation and quantum tests enunciated in this paper seem to have been applied. In the absence of contrary evidence, we thus remain of the view that the absolute fears about damages remain to be substantiated.

ing. After all, is this not one of the reasons—the main reason —why we fear so much tort compensation of pure economic loss? And is this also not true with compensation for emotional distress or, as it is nowadays called in England, psychiatric damage? Yet such a connection seems rarely to be addressed in court and even less discussed in the classroom where the mind-twisting arguments of causation seem to take up more time than the case law suggests they deserve. A simple examination of litigated parallels thus reveals that there is much to be learned from looking at what is happening in other systems. The challenge that the study of foreign law and comparative methodology presents is more relevant today than it ever was before. But it will also be useful if it teaches lawyers how to factor into the purely legal reasoning the wider backdrop factors which make American law so intriguing and yet so difficult to grasp.

10. PUBLIC LAW ILLEGALITY AND GOVERNMENTAL LIABILITY

*Roberto Caranta**

I. THREE DIFFERENT FACTUAL SITUATIONS

The issue of public law illegality can arise with reference to governmental liability cases in three different situations. First, loss may be considered as directly and primarily flowing from an illegal administrative decision; thus damages are not the only remedy available in that 'public law remedies' such as judicial review can effectively or, at least in part, redress the damage caused. Secondly, illegal administrative decisions may be merely part of the factors which led to the causing of the loss and judicial review, even if available, does not provide an effective remedy. Thirdly, administrative decisions are far removed in the background, and the loss flows from the way in which a given task is performed or a service is provided. In such cases too, as Lord Nicholls quite rightly pointed out in *Stovin v Wise*, public law has difficulties 'to afford a remedy matching the wrong'.[1]

Examples of the three situations are, respectively, the cases dealt with by English courts in *R v Secretary of State for transport, ex p Factortame*,[2] *Three Rivers District Council v Bank of England*,[3] and *Phelps v Hillingdon London Borough Council*.[4]

The relationship between public law illegality and governmental liability is structured differently in each of these situations. In sum, the relevance of illegality decreases gradually from the first to the last situation. The additional conditions that are necessary to establish liability depend upon which of the three cases apply.

These three situations will be analysed in turn with reference to the French, Italian,and English laws. Since common lawyers do not normally divide their case law according to the lines here proposed, it will at times be necessary to anticipate the discussion of some cases to allow a better understanding. This will be noted whenever appropriate in the text.

---

* Professor Dr, University of Turin, Law Faculty. This contribution was made possible by CNR and MURST funding.
[1] [1996] AC 923 (HL) 933.
[2] [1991] AC 603 (ECJ and HL).
[3] *Three Rivers District Council v Bank of England (No. 3)* [1996] 3 All ER 558 (QB); [2000] WLR 15 (CA); [2000] WLR 1220 (HL).
[4] [2000] WLR 776 (HL).

A. Reviewable Administrative Decisions

The issue of illegality is quite evidently in the foreground when loss flows from an administrative decision. Under certain conditions, administrative decisions can legally encroach on citizens' rights. When certain conditions are absent, the citizens can be legally refused benefits. Public authorities have legal powers to harm citizens in many different circumstances. Harm alone cannot therefore be sufficient to establish liability. Illegality is going to be a most relevant issue.

The idea of administrative decisions is very much at the centre of administrative law as developed on the Continent. According to nineteenth-century private law conceptual models focusing on Rechtsgeschäft (legal acts), administrative bodies were supposed to act through a system of highly formalised decisions. Procedural law contributed also to the same outcome. An aggrieved citizen had to be addressed a formal administrative decision to be able to seek judicial review (what the French called a *décision préalable*). The duty to give reasons, soon to become a general principle in many Continental legal systems, also required formal administrative decisions.

Administrative decisions were, and still are, at the core of many cases concerning governmental liability. This is possibly so also because on the Continent most private activities, from land development to the retail sector are highly regulated. To pursue any economic activity, authorisations or licences of some kind are normally needed. The denial or withdrawal of such decisions can deprive a person of his or her livelihood. Administrative decisions are thus very much litigated and remedies in damages are often sought.[5]

Judicial review is also normally available, albeit under more or less restrictive conditions. Judicial review can be an effective remedy, but at times it is not. Once illegality is established, further conditions may be required before imposing liability. Liability claims can moreover be allowed in cases where administrative decisions are not illegal.

Administrative decisions enjoy a much less central role in English law. Two non-mutually exclusive explanations are possible. On the one hand, administrative law is much less pervasive in everyday life; on the other hand, judicial review is still in its infancy; courts are not yet used to give administrative decision the hard look necessary to ensure that there are a large number of cases in which illegality is found and damages can be sought.

---

[5] CE 27 July 1988, *Leon*, D. 1989, somm 122, concerned the case of a sailor forbidden to sail; in France, sailors need a licence to sail.

1. French Ésprit Cartésien

Before going into the details of French law on this topic, a procedural point has to be made. Jurisdiction for deciding damages claims against public authorities is normally accorded to administrative courts.[6] In the early 1870s, Agnes Blanco, a 5-year-old girl, was run over by a vehicle owned by the local tobacco making plant while playing in a street. Tobacco was manufactured by a State subsidiary and the Tribunal de conflits held that damage actions were to be adjudicated according to rules different from those laid down in the Code civil for the relationships as between individuals.[7] The *Conseil d'Etat* gained jurisdiction over the claim and held the State responsible and ordered it to pay Agnes a life rent for her disabilities.[8] The procedural choice has led to a case law where questions concerning administrative decisions and their legality have a central role.

(a) Toute illégalité est constitutive d'une faute

As a rule, fault is the general precondition to liability, and this applies equally to private and public law.[9] In administrative law, this has evolved into a general principle of fault liability know as *faute de service*. It should be underlined that French administrative courts, and the *Conseil d'Etat* first among them, have developed a notion of fault that is closely linked to the realities of administrative action.

Concerning liability due to the adoption or to the failure to adopt an administrative decision, the general rule is that *toute illégalité constitue par elle-même une faute*;[10] illegality itself amounts to a fault which in principle is sufficient to establish liability.[11] Said the other way round, fault is 'treated as equivalent to illegality'.[12]

---

[6] There are exceptions, for instance concerning road accidents involving State and other public authorities vehicles: full analysis in C Bréchon-Moulènes, *Les régimes législatifs de responsabilité publique* (Paris: LGDJ, 1974).

[7] TC 8 Feb 1873, *Blanco*, D 1873, II, 20; the most relevant passage of the short judgments states: 'Cons. que la responsabilité qui peut incomber à l'Etat pour les dommages causés aux particuliers par le fait des personnes qu'il emploie, ne peut être regie par les principes qui sont établis dans le Code civil pour les rapports de particulier à particulier'. The theoretical elaborations leading to this outcome have been analysed in detail by M Deguergue *Jurisprudence et doctrine dans l'élaboration du droit de la responsabilité administrative* (Paris: LGDJ, 1994), 43 ff.

[8] CE 8 May 1874, *Blanco*, Rec 1874, 416.

[9] BS Markesinis *et al*, *Tortious Liability of Statutory Bodies: A Comparative and Economic Analysis of Five English Cases* (Oxford: Hart Publishing), 1999), 16.

[10] M Paillet, *La faute de service en droit administratif français* (Paris: LGDJ, 1980), 284; some comments on the rights vindicated through liability actions are to be found in I Poirot-Mazères, 'La notion de préjudice en droit administratif français' (1997) *Rev dr publ* 519, 547 ff.

[11] The development of this idea has been traced by M Deguergue, *Jurisprudence et doctrine dans l'élaboration du droit de la responsabilité administrative* (Paris: LGDJ, 1994), 185 ff.

[12] P Craig, 'Once More Unto the Breach: The Community, the State and Damages Liability', in M Andenas (ed), *English Public Law and the Common Law of Europe* (London: Key Haven, 1998), 151.

The principle has been affirmed in a number of cases.[13] To name a few relatively recent examples: the non-admission to the *Ordre des architectes* of a person having the statutory requirement needed for admission was sufficient to give rise to liability;[14] the administrative organ which denied a citizen access to certain documents was found liable once the right of access of the said citizen had been established;[15] liability arose when a bid to a public procurement procedure was unlawfully rejected;[16] a sailor who was prevented from sailing due to the mistaken decision as to the existence of an illness was entitled to compensation for loss of income.[17]

In respect of (substantive) legitimate expectations, the claimant is not asked to show beyond any reasonable doubt that, but for the illegality, he or she would have been in a better position.[18] For instance, an applicant for a public sector job whose application has been unlawfully rejected is not asked to show that he or she would have been appointed if the selection had been properly conducted. All he or she has to show is that there was a serious chances (*chances sérieuses*) of getting it.[19] This case law, originally confined to competitive selection procedures for posts within the civil service, was later extended to public procurement procedures.[20] In the case of recovery for such a lost chance, the amount of compensation is normally reduced commensurate with the chance forfeited.[21]

In a way, illegality makes a strong prima facie case for finding the defendant authority liable. There are however various ways the defendant can escape or mitigate its liability.

In case of purely procedural and formal illegalities, that is irregularities which have no effects on the substantive adjudication of a given case, liability is normally excluded for lack of causation between illegality and damage.[22] For instance, if no reasons are given for refusing an application

---

[13] Further cases are listed by I Poirot-Mazères, 'La notion de préjudice en droit administratif français' (1997) *Rev dr publ* 519, 547.

[14] CE 10 Dec 1993, *Min. Équipement c/ Durand, D.* 1994, somm 361, obs P Bon and P Terneyre (in that case, the evaluation of the claimant's requirements was found to have been illegal due to an *erreur manifeste d'appréciation*); CE 1 Oct 1993, *Meignan, D.* 1994, somm 360, obs P Bon and Ph Terneyre.

[15] CE 10 July 1992, *Touzan, Act. jur Dr adm* 1992, 766, obs J-P Théron; the claimant was awarded 5000 FF.

[16] CE 23 Mar 1994, *Syndacat intercommunal à vocation unique pour l'étude et la réalisation du golf de Cognac, D* 1994, somm 123, obs Ph Terneyre.

[17] CE 27 July 1988, *Leon, D* 1989, somm 122.

[18] I Poirot-Mazères 'La notion de préjudice en droit administratif français' (1997) *Rev dr publ* 519, 549.

[19] One of the most recent case is CE 24 Jan 1996, *Collins, Dr Adm* 1996, no 112.

[20] CE 23 Mar 1994, *Syndacat intercommunal à vocation unique pour l'étude et la réalisation du golf de Cognac, D* 1994, somm 123, obs Ph Terneyre.

[21] Poirot-Mazères, 'La notion de préjudice en droit administratif français' (1997) *Rev dr publ* 519, 549, n 142.

[22] This trend has emerged at the same time as the cquivalence between illegality and fault

for a licence, but good reasons in fact exists to support a negative decision, no liability will occur.[23] Again, when a physician working with a local authority was fired due to breaches of disciplinary rules without prior advice of a commission where trade unions were represented, he was not awarded damages since there was no doubt about the existence and gravity of the disciplinary breaches and the illegality was thus merely procedural in nature.[24]

Exclusion of liability is not always the case. For instance, in the Meignan case a licence to sell spirits to the public was suspended for 21 days owing to the fact that spirits had been served to an already drunken person; the suspension was signed by an officer not competent to take those kind of decisions and was therefore unlawful, but as the claimant, Meignan, was in breach of the relevant regulations all the same; the *Conseil d'Etat* reduced the damages due to him on the basis of contributory negligence.[25]

Cases where public defendants are found liable are also limited by the fact that French courts are very demanding as to the proof of the existence of actual damage.[26] For instance, in Sté Les Briqueteries Joly, the claimant was unlawfully denied a quarrying licence; its claims in damages however failed since the *Conseil d'Etat* held that no proof had been given both as to the actual intention to exploit the quarry and as to the existence of the necessary financial resources at the time the licence was refused.[27]

Liability is excluded or mitigated when the damaged person has in some way contributed to the illegality, by giving the administrative authority incorrect statements, false representations and so on.[28]

The principle *toute illégalité constitue par elle-même une faute* has been called to play a role with reference to building certificates. Under the relevant French legislation, to be able to sell or to lease houses built pursuing a land development scheme, the developer has to get a certificate stating that all the works provided for in the project (but some concerning the road

---

has been made more stringent: M Deguergue, *Jurisprudence et doctrine dans l'élaboration du droit de la responsabilité administrative* (Paris: LGDJ, 1994), 193 ff.

[23] CE 14 July 1964, *Prat-Flottes et Sté des instituts de plein air*, Rec CE 438.

[24] CE 22 Jan 1988, *Samuel*, D 1989, somm, 114.

[25] CE 1 Oct 1993, *Meignan*, D 1994, somm, 360, obs P Bon and P Terneyre.

[26] A review of both the doctrinal developments and the relavant case law may be found in Poirot-Mazères, 'La notion de préjudice en droit administratif français' (1997) *Rev dr publ* 519, 535 ff.

[27] CE 10 June 1992, *Sté Les Briqueteries Joly*, in *Rev dr publ* 1993, 261.

[28] CE 28 July 1993, *SARL Bau-Rouge*, Rec CE 1993, 249; D 1994, somm 365, obs P Bon and P Terneyre; in that case, a company which asked for permission to develop a site had produced an environmental impact assessment which was not sufficient; the *Conseil d'Etat* found contributory negligence stating that intention to deceive the authority is not necessary. On this case also C Pollmann, 'L'étendue du contrôle de cassation du Conseil d'État en matière de responsabilité extra-contractuelle des personnes publiques' in (1996) *Rev dr publ* 1653, 1684 f.

system) have been executed. If the works have been executed and the certificate is refused or delayed, the authority will be liable to the builder.[29] If the certificate is endorsed notwithstanding the fact that the works have not been completed, the authority is liable to those having bought or leased the buildings.[30]

In some specific sectors, such as taxation, damage claims have to meet higher standards. Gross negligence is required to hold the fiscal administration responsible for mistakes made in situations where they meet special difficulties in performing their tasks.

It has however been pointed out that 'the dividing line between ordinary and grave fault is neither obvious nor great'.[31] Moreover, the scope allowed to gross negligence has constantly shrunk even with reference to decisions taken by the fiscal service.[32]

(b) Liability for Legal Decisions

In certain situations, French public administration can be held liable even if no illegality is present.[33] Of course, some form of compensation for legal decisions infringing individual rights is provided for in the legislation of many countries. This is normally the case with expropriation. French courts, however, have elaborated a fairly general rule based on the equality principle according to which, where an administrative body makes an individual suffer a prejudice both special and abnormal in the pursuit of the common good, that individual is entitled to compensation.[34]

The leading case is *Couitéas*. A group of indigenous people squatted on Mr Couitéas's land. For fear of widespread unrest, the police refused to dislodge them. The refusal was not considered to be illegal, since it was in the public interest to avoid confrontation with armed indigenous people.[35] However, Mr Couitéas was held to be entitled to compensation for the

---

[29] CE 22 Dec 1936, *Sté Le Parc de Cachan, Rec CE* 1936, *tables,* 1139.

[30] CE 8 Sept 1993, *Ass syndacale des propreétaires du lotissement de l'Eden Lorrain,* D 1994, somm. 360, obs P Bon and P Terneyre; damages were considerable reduced as the limitation period barred most of the heads of claims. The local authority was surrogated into the rights (if any) of the claimants against the builder: CE 12 Jan 1983, *Tondu, Rec CE, tables,* 853.

[31] Markesinis *et al*, op cit, 31.

[32] In CE 27 July 1990, *Bourgeois, Rec CE* 1990, 242, it was held that *faute simple* was enough to establish liability in case of mistakes affecting uncomplicated decisions, such as those due to mere calculation mistakes; if the mistake concerns the way the fiscal services have appreciated the incomes of the interested parties, then *faute lourde* is still required: also CE 29 Dec 1997, *Commune d'Arcueil, Rec.* 512; *Rev fr dr adm* 1998, 97, concl G Goulard.

[33] P Fombeur, 'Les évolutions jurisprudentielles de la responsabilité sans faute', in *Act jur Dr adm* 1999, num spéc 100, 101.

[34] M Deguergue, *Jurisprudence et doctrine dans l'élaboration du droit de la responsabilité administrative* (Paris: LGDJ, 1994).

[35] Had the refusal been illegal, liability would have been established under the rule equating illegality and fault: CE 21 Aug 1948, *Husson et Dame Chiffre, Rec* 1948, 173.

harm suffered in the general interest.[36] It has been remarked that in doing so administrative courts give a remedy in damages in cases where they are not ready to strike down administrative decisions which, although not in line with the duties placed upon the administrative authority, are nonetheless reasonable on the circumstances.[37]

These cases normally go under the label of *responsabilité sans faute*. The label ceases to be misleading as soon as one recalls the equation between illegality and fault; what is missing here is rather illegality than fault. As a rule, to avoid opening too much the gates of liability, damages are awarded only in so far as the loss suffered is both abnormal and special.[38]

It is doubtful whether some strands of this case law are in line with the decision taken by the European Court of Justice in an infringement proceeding brought against France.[39] The Court held that by refraining from taking forceful actions against road blockades aimed at imported good from other member States (Spanish strawberries in the instance) the French Republic was in breach of Article 5 (now Article 10) of the EC Treaty.[40]

(c) Liability for Legislative Acts

Under certain (and normally restrictive) conditions, French administrative courts have been ready to hold the State liable for decisions taken by the legislature. This is the more remarkable since judicial review of legislation is still today in its infancy in France. Also these cases can be considered to fall under the heading of '*responsabilité sans faute*'. The proviso here is that fault-illegality cannot be established missing a legal institutions, such as a supreme court, empowered to annul legislation for breach of a superior rule of law.

In the well-known case of *La Fleurette*, the claimant had to stop manufacturing certain milk products following the enactment of a statute prohibiting the production of such a good for public health considerations. The *Conseil d'Etat* held that it was entitled to compensation.[41] The ground

---

[36] CE 30 Nov 1923, *Couitéas*, S 1923, III, 57, and *Rec* 1923, 789.

[37] Recently, J Moreau, 'Responsabilité administrative et sécurité publique', in *Act jur Dr adm* 1999, num spéc, 96, 97.

[38] Generally P Amselek, 'La responsibilité sans faute des personnes publiques d'après la jurisprudence administrative' in *Recueil d'études en hommage à Ch. Eisesmann* (Paris: LGDJ, 1975), 234.

[39] Case C-265/95 *Commission v France* [1997] ECR-6959.

[40] According to J-C Bonichot, 'Devoir d'agir ou droit de ne pas agir: l'Etat entre les exigences de l'order public et celles du droit européen' *Act jur Dr adm* 1999, no spéc, 86, 88, the generous liability system can make up for the shortcomings in promptly restoring law and order; a different view is voiced by E Souteyrand, 'La responsabilité de l'administration' in *Act jur Dr adm* 1999, num spec, 92, 93, according whom the freedom of police forces is now limited.

[41] CE 14 Jan 1938, *Sté La Fleurette*, *Rec* 1938, 25.

for finding the State liable was the *rupture de l'égalité devant les charges publiques*. A very heavy burden was imposed on a specific firm in the general interest. The equality principle militated in favour of compensation as is the case, for instance, with expropriation or with damages flowing from the construction of public works.[42]

Cases on liability for legislative decisions have been rare. A recent one concerned a law that validated a posteriori the procurement procedure followed to build a new soccer stadium in Paris on the occasion of the 1998 World Cup. The administrative procedure followed was illegal in many respects and the final administrative decision awarding the contract was annulled by a first instance administrative court. The French Parliament intervened with a statute validating the choice of the contractor. Mr Sarfati, who had seen his offer rejected during the procurement procedure, sued the State for damages. His claim was upheld in principle, since the *Cour administrative d'appel* in Paris held that the validation had been in breach of the principle of *égalité devant les charges publiques*; the action however failed because, according to the court, the bid submitted by the claimant had been rejected also for sound reasons; thus, he was not able to show serious enough chances to get the procurement.[43]

(d) Breaches of Community Law

Given their rather generous approach to governmental liability, French courts would not be expected to have any problem in accepting liability for breaches of Community law.

Actually, some problem arose from a deep-rooted reluctance to accept the *primauté* of Community law over national law. Alivar, an Italian firm, was refused by the French authority a licence to export potatoes from France; the refusal was based on a regulation forbidding such exports which was at odds with the Community principle of free movements of goods then embodied in Article 30 of the (then) EEC Treaty. Alivar was awarded damages by the French administrative courts. The ground,

---

[42] The development of this idea has recently been traced by Deguergue, *Jurisprudence et doctrine dans l'élaboration du droit de la responsabilité administrative* (Paris: LGDJ, 1994) 137 ff.

[43] CAA Paris, 4 Dec 1997, *M Sarfatti, Act jur Dr adm* 1998, 254, concl Lambert; the relevant part of the decision states: 'la responsabilité de l'Etat est en principe susceptible d'être engagée à l'égard des achitectes qui, comme M. Sarfat, ont été privés, par l'effet des dispositions de ladite loi, des possiiblités d'accès à l'octroi de la concession, sur le fondement du principe de l'égalité des citoyens devant les charges publiques; que, toutefois, il ne résulte pas de l'instruction que M Sarfati, dont le project qui comportait deux stades, n'a pas donné satisfaction, tant au regard de objectfs de la polyvalence que de celui de la qualité achitecturale et de l'insertion dans le site, ait eu, nonobstant le fait que son projet prévoyait un prix particulièrement bas, une chance suffisamment sérieuse d'obtenir la concession.'

however, was *responsabilité sans faute*, since the *Conseil d'Etat* stopped short from declaring the regulation illegal.[44]

Later, however, in the famous *Nicolo* case, the *Conseil d'Etat* accepted the *primauté* of Community law if not the direct effects of directives.[45]

The most important French case concerning liability for breach of Community law was decided a few months after the European Court of Justice judgment in Francovich.[46] Two tobacco manufacturers, Arizona Tobacco Products and Philip Morris, claimed damages in respect of loss flowing from decisions of the French Finance Ministry fixing the price of cigarettes and cigars. The *Conseil d'Etat* found the decisions illegal and in breach of Community law provisions effecting the gradual elimination of State monopolies and forbidding Member States from setting the price of tobacco products in a discriminatory way towards imported products. It then applied the well-known equation between illegality and fault and found the State liable.[47]

French administrative courts have since been ready to offer compensation for breaches of Community law.[48]

More recently, some British whisky producers brought actions concerning the loss flowing from an instruction issued by the Justice ministry to public prosecutors to prosecute advertisements of foreign spirits. The instruction had been purportedly issued to comply with a European Court of Justice judgement finding that French regulations forbidding advertising foreign spirits were in breach of Community law.[49] Actually, it was inconsistent with the decision of the Court.[50] Reversing the judgment of the Paris *Cour d'appel*, the *Cour de cassation* held that the breach amounted to a *faute lourde* and that the fact that no prosecution had ever been commenced against the claimants was irrelevant as to the question of liability. What the lower court had to find was rather whether, the sales of the

---

[44] CE, ass, 23 Mar 1984, *Act jur Dr adm* 1984, 396, with annotation by B Genevois; *Rev trim dr europ* 1984, 341, concl R Denoix de Saint Marc.

[45] CE, ass, 20 Oct 1989, *Nicolo*, *Rev fr dr adm* 1989, 813, concl P Frydman and annotation by B Genevois; also L Dubois 'L'arrêt Nicolo et l'integration de la règle internationale et communautaire dans l'ordre juridique français', *Rev fr dr adm* 1989, 995.

[46] Joined cases C-6 and 9/90 *Francovich and others/Italian Republic* [1991] ECR I-5357.

[47] CE, ass, 28 Feb 1992, *Arizona Tobacco Products GmbH et al*, *Act jur Dr adm* 1992, 210, concl M Laroque.

[48] In CE, ass, 30 Oct 1996, *Sté Dangeville*, *Act jur Dr adm* 1996, 1045; *Rev trim dr europ* 1997, 171, and *Rev fr dr adm* 1997, 1067, concl G Goulard, the claim for damages money unduly paid was not met, but this was because a previous unjust enrichment action had already been rejected under the pre-*Nicolo* case; *res judicata* thus meant that the action for damages was dismissed.

[49] Case 152/78 [1980] ECR-2289.

[50] Also Joined Cases 314, 315, and 316/81 and 83/83 [1982] ECR-4337.

claimant's products had been affected as they had refrained from advertising their products out of fear of criminal prosecution.[51]

The case law on Member States liability is not quoted in the judgment of the *Cour de cassation*. Here again, however, national requirements are applied in a way which is consistent with the approach of the European Court of Justice.

2. Italian Uncertainties

Italian law is at present in a state of flux. Old rules that made it very difficult to gain compensation in cases of illegal administrative decisions have undergone momentous, and at times contradictory, changes in the past few years.[52]

(a) Starting with a Catch 22 Situation

As was the case with French law, to understand Italian law on governmental liability one has to start with the question of which courts have jurisdiction to entertain actions against public bodies. Both civil courts and administrative courts enjoy such jurisdiction. According to Article 2 of l. 20 March 1865, n 2248, All E, which is still the rule of general application even if challenged by a growing number of exceptions, civil courts are competent when civil and political rights are at stakes. Administrative courts, on the contrary, are competent with reference to *interessi legittimi*. The distinction between rights (*diritti soggettivi*) and *interessi legittimi* has some bearing with the English dichotomy distinguishing private and public law rights. To make simple a matter that has been a subject of hot dispute for well over a century, two broad rules can be given. First, the person asking for a decision from an authority has no right, just an *interesse legittimo*. For instance, those asking for a licence to open a shop, a building permission, a school grant or any other benefit, or submitting a bid to a public procurement procedure, all are said to be entitled to an *interesse legittimo*. Since most economic activities in Italy are, or at least were until fairly recently, made conditional upon the delivery of a licence or permission, *interessi legittimi* are widespread. Secondly, even a *diritto soggettivo* turns into an *interesse legittimo* when confronted with an administrative decision, quite independently from the question whether the decision is legal or not.[53]

---

[51] Cass. 21 Feb 1995, *SCP Celice-Blancpain et SCP Ancel-Couturier-Heller*, in *Gazette du Palais* 5, 6 juillet 1996, no 187, 188, pp 366 f, with note by J-C Fourgoux; the *Cour de cassation* had jurisdiction since the decision whose legality was challenged was an instruction issued by the Justice ministry to the public prosecutors.

[52] An instant picture of the present position is given in R Caranta, *Attività amministrativa ed illecito aquiliano* (Milano: Giuffré, 2001).

[53] This last judge-made rule has been subject to strong scholarly criticism but still stands: E

The overall consequence of the system just sketched is that administrative courts are usually competent when administrative decisions have been adopted and when a public body has failed to address a request. The problem, as far as governmental liability is concerned, is that traditionally administrative courts had only the power to annul administrative decision but no power to award damages. At the same time, civil courts had no jurisdiction whatever to deal with *interessi legittimi*. From this procedural straitjacket, a seemingly catch 22 situation, the *Corte di cassazione*, having the last word in matters of jurisdiction, distilled the rule that no claim for damages was available for the infringement of *interessi legittimi* by illegal administrative decisions; judicial review was to be the only remedy.[54]

Later, this exclusionary rule was abandoned in two situations. First, if a licence or permission was illegally withdrawn, and this decision was annulled, one could ask for damages.[55] From the substantive law point of view, this led to the confusing situation that no action for damages laid when a licence was illegally refused, but liability could attach if the licence was illegally withdrawn. From the procedural point of view, this meant that one had first to ask administrative courts to annul the withdrawal decision, then, if successful, ask civil courts for damages. The explanation for this was that *interesse legittimo* turned into a *diritto soggettivo* upon the grant of the licence, then turned again into an *interesse legittimo* when the licence was withdrawn, and lastly resurrected as a *diritto soggettivo* once the withdrawal decision was annulled.[56]

Secondly, damages could be asked when the administrative decision or

---

Cannada Bartoli, 'Affievolimento', in *Enciclopedia del Diritto*, vol I (Milano: Giuffré, 1958) 670, e Idem 'Interesse (diritto amministrativo)', in *Enciclopedia del Diritto*, vol. XXII (Milano: Giuffré, 1972) 13; A Angeletti, *Aspetti problematici della discriminazione delle giurisdizioni e Stato amministrativo* (Milano: Giuffré, 1980).

[54] Concerning building permissions Cass, Sez un., 9 Feb 1963 n 252, in *Foro amm*. 1963, II, 225, with annotation by E Cannada Bartoli, 'In tema di tutela successiva al giudicato amministrativo'; Cass, Sez un., 12 giugno 1982 n 3541, in *Foro it* 1982, I, 1860, with note by CM Barone; Cass, Sez un., 5 dicembre 1987 n 9095, in *Cons St* 1989, II, 1347, with note by F Longo, 'Alcune considerazioni in tema di annullamento dell'illegittimo diniego di concessione edilizia e jus superveniens'; Cass, 29 Nov 1988 n 6485, in *Giust civ* 1988, I, 2810, and 1989, I, 1150, with annotation by P Stella Richter, 'Sulla irrisarcibilità del danno causato dall'illegittimo diniego della concessione di costruzione malgrado il carattere non discrezionale della stessa'. Concerning shop licencing Cass, Sez un, 31 July 1962 n 2294, in *Foro amm*. 1963, II, 475, with note by C Dal Piaz 'Illegittimo rifiuto di autorizzare la riapertura di un esercizio commerciale, e risarcibilità del danno subito dall'interessato'.

[55] The *leading cases* concerned on shop licences: Cass, Sez un, 5 Oct 1979 n 5145 e n 5146, both reported in *Giust civ* 1979, I, 1810; cases on building permissions followed: Cass, Sez un, 1 Oct 1982, n 5027, *Foro it* 1982, I, 2433, and Cass, Sez un, 1 Oct 1982 n 5028, in *Giur it* 1982, I, 1, 1663, with annotation by F Roselli, 'Recenti mutamenti legislativi e giurisprudenziali in materia di 'ius aedificandi'.

[56] This very baroque theory was the brainchild of AM Sandulli, 'In tema di provvedimenti comunali in materia edilizia e risarcimento dei danni', in *Giur it* 1972, I, 1, 103; today it does not command widespread support.

inaction after a request was made were not only illegal, but in breach of criminal law provisions. This is the case, for instance, when the illegal decision is the result of malice.[57]

(b) The Latest Developments

This situation was commonly resented as unacceptable, last but not least because it conflicted with Community law provisions providing that a remedy in damages to be available in case of breach of rules on public procurement and more generally with the European Court of Justice case law on Member States liability.[58]

In 1999, the *Corte di cassazione* made a spectacular turnaround. The *Vitali* case, or rather, to be more accurate, two of them but with the same reasoning, was rather straightforward. A local authority had assented to an urban development plan; when amending the existing urban plans, however, it failed to introduce those changes necessary to implement the development plan; the developer was successful in challenging the new urban plans and have them quashed by the administrative courts; then he went to the civil courts asking for damages. It was a case where damages could be had even according to the above mentioned case law (first exception to the exclusionary rule), but the *Corte di cassazione* preferred to overrule the exclusionary rule itself by stating that, given certain conditions as to the fault, causation and harm, infringements of *interessi legittimi* could sound in damages.[59]

---

[57] Cass, Sez un, 23 Nov 1985, n 5813, in *Giust civ* 1986, I, 734; Cass, 11 Feb 1995, n 1540, in *Dir proc amm* 1997, 358, con nota di D D'orsogna 'Danno "da reato" e comportamento illegittimo dell'amministrazione: verso l'"ingiustizia" dei danni derivanti da lesioni di interessi legittimi'.

[58] Among others G Greco, 'Interesse legittimo e risarcimento dei danni: crollo di un pregiudizio sotto la pressione della normativa europea e dei contributi della dottrina', in *Riv it dir pubbl. comunitario* 1999, 1108.

[59] Cass, Sez un, 22 July 1999, n 500; the decision has been reported and commented in most Italian law journals (and there are many of them); here is just a selection of journals: in *Foro it.* 1999, I, 2487, with observations by A Palmieri e R Pardolesi, in *Foro it* 1999, I, 3201, with notes by R Caranta, 'La pubblica amministrazione nell'età della responsabilità'; F Fracchia, 'Dalla negazione della risarcibilità degli *interessi legittimi* all'affermazione della risarcibilità di quelli giuridicamente rilevanti: la svolta della Suprema corte lascia aperti alcuni interrogativi'; A Romano 'Sono risarcibili; ma perché devono essere interessi legittimi?'; E Scoditti, 'L'interesse legittimo e il costituzionalismo. Conseguenze della svolta giurisprudenziale in materia risarcitoria'; in *Giorn. dir. amm.* 1999, 832, with note by L Torchia, 'La risarcibilità degli interessi legittimi: dalla foresta pietrificata al bosco di Birnam'; in *Riv it. dir pubbl comunitario* 1999, 1108, with note G Greco 'Interesse legittimo e risarcimento dei danni: crollo di un pregiudizio sotto la pressione della normativa europea e dei contributi della dottrina'; in *Giur cost.* 1999, 3217, with note by F Satta, 'La sentenza n 500 del 1999: dagli *interessi legittimi* ai diritti fondamentali', and in *Giur. cost* 1999, 4045, with annotations by FG Scoca, 'Per un'amministrazione responsabile', and by G Azzariti, 'La risarcibilità degli *interessi legittimi* tra interpretazioni giurisprudenziali e interventi legislativi. Un commento alla sentenza n 500 del 1999 della Corte di cassazione'.

To do so, the *Corte di cassazione* turned the question of competence on its head. It claimed that an action for infringement of *interessi legittimi* is to be considered an action vindicating the civil law right to ask for damages under the general rules laid down in Article 2043 of the Civil code. This is debatable,[60] but anyway a new statute was rather quickly passed in order to make sure that liability actions arising from positive administrative decisions or from a failure to adopt an administrative decision are litigated in administrative courts.[61]

The way was thus open to find the State and other public law entities liable for unlawful decisions infringing both *diritti soggettivi* and *interessi legittimi*. In the past two years Italian courts have scrambled to start developing coherent principles concerning governmental liability in this field. Unlike French courts, Italian judges have so far refrained to embrace any equivalence between illegality and liability. They tend to ask the claimant to show that prejudice actually had flowed from the illegal administrative act or omission complained of.

The problem can be better explained first by way of example. One of many bids in a public procurement procedure is illegally rejected, maybe for procedural reasons; the decision to reject the tender is challenged and annulled; this does not mean that, but for the illegality, the bid would have been successful; maybe the winner would not have changed, maybe another bid but not the claimant's would have prevailed. The illegal act may not have made the claimant's position worse.

The problem is fairly general. In Italy, as elsewhere on the Continent, public bodies are under a general duty to give reasons for their decisions. This also applies when the authority is granted more or less wide margins of discretion. The authority is expected to state why it decided one way rather than other possible ways. A decision can be illegal because no reason is given, or the reasons given are not sufficient, or just wrong. This is enough to have a decision quashed by way of judicial review proceedings. Good reasons can however exist; the decision could be affirmed on grounds other from those given. If so, is the person having had the decision annulled also entitled to damages?

The question cannot be given a definitive answer right now. The possibility to ask for damages in the event of infringements of *interessi legittimi* has been recognised very recently and the *Consiglio di Stato*, the highest

---

[60] For discussion and references R Caranta, *Attività amministrativa ed illecito aquiliano* (Milano: Giuffré, 2001), 35 ff.

[61] L 21 July 2000, n 205; for a commentary F Caringella and M Protto (curr), *Il nuovo processo amministrativo* (Milano: Giuffré, 2001); the matter has not ended there, since the new statute has already been challenged before the Constitutional court and a decision is pending: Trib Roma, 16 novembre 2000, in *Corr giurid* 2001, 72, with notes by *v* Carbone and A Di Majo, ''E' costituzionale il nuovo riparto di giurisdizione?'.

administrative court, has yet to address the full scope of this sort of question (moreover the *stare decisis* rule does not apply in Italy, so that lower courts are not bound by their own precedents and by rulings of higher courts).[62] What is possible is to refer to some cases so far decided at first instance.[63]

One of the most fully reasoned decision has been handed down by the *Tribunale amministrativo regionale per la Toscana*.[64] A bid had been unlawfully excluded from a public procurement procedure for works passed according to a negotiated procedure. The decision to award the procurement contract was challenged and quashed. Damages were then asked for the losses consequent to the exclusion and the failure to be awarded the procurement. The *Tribunale* distinguished claims concerning three different possible losses: (1) loss of the procurement award; (2) loss of chances to be awarded the procurement; (3) loss related to expenses made to submit the offers and to missed opportunities. To recover the loss under the first heading, the claimant has to give the proof that, but for the illegal decision, he would have been awarded the contract; as to the second heading, the claimant is expected to show the existence of some of the requirements necessary to get the contract; as to the third heading, the costs incurred as well as the specific business opportunities lost to pursue the unsuccessful procurement have to be proven. It is plain that to give the proof concerning the first heading is almost impossible or at least very difficult when there are many participants and the contract is awarded with a method different from the lowest price bid.[65] The claimant having worded its claim in a way to fit under the first heading only, the action failed. Some other decisions have pointed to technical expertise as a way to find out the potentially winning bid,[66] but most administrative courts are not ready to follow that way.[67]

---

[62] Cons St, Sez IV, 2 June 2000, n 3177, in *Foro amm.* 2000, 2096, with remarks by R Iannotta, has not tackled the most difficult issues.

[63] Further discussion in R Caranta, *Attività amministrativa ed illecito aquiliano* (Milano: Giuffré, 2001).

[64] TAR Toscana, Sez II, 13 Apr 2000, n 660, in *Foro amm.* 2000, 3679.

[65] TAR Lombardia, Sez III, 6 Apr 2000, n 2718, in *Foro amm.* 2000, 3286 (*obiter*).

[66] TAR Toscana, Sez I, 21 Oct 1999, n 766, in *Foro amm.* 2000, 2264; in *Foro it* 2000, III, 196, with note by L Carozza and F Fracchia, 'Art 35 d leg 80/98 e risarcibilità degli "interessi meritevoli di tutela": prime applicazioni giurisprudenziali', and TAR Lombardia, Sez III, 6 novembre 2000, n 6259, in *Giust civ* 2001, I, 863; given the very limited value of the respective claims, no expertise was however ordered by the courts in these cases.

[67] Eg TAR Puglia, Lecce, Sez II, 6 Novr 1999, n 753, in *Foro amm.* 2000, 1949; TAR Toscana, Sez I, 21 Oct 1999, n 766, in *Foro amm* 2000, 2264; in *Foro it* 2000, III, 196, with note by L Carozza and F Fracchia, 'Art. 35 d leg 80/98 e risarcibilità degli "interessi meritevoli di tutela": prime applicazioni giurisprudenziali'; TAR Lombardia, Sez III, 23 Dec 1999, n 5049, in *Corr giuridico* 2000, 388, with note by A Di Majo, 'Danno ingiusto e danno risarcibile nella lesione di interessi legittimi'; TAR Lombardia, Milano, Sez II, 12 aprile 2000, n 2793, in *Urbanistica e appalti* 2000, 985, with note by M Protto, 'Responsabilità della p.a.

Since damages under the second (and third) heading were not asked, the Tuscany court did not elaborated very much on how strong a claim a claimant has to make and substantiate with proof its case to show sufficient chances; many courts, in any case, just refuse to consider chances.[68]

Most cases so far litigated in Italian courts deal with public procurement. Other cases refer to delays to address requests for building permission or unlawful refusal of building permission. In one case, a firm saw many times rejected, often after considerable delay, its application for an urban development plan that was in line with the existing planning regulations. The *Tribunale amministrativo regionale per la Sicilia* found that this behaviour was characterised as *sviamento di potere* (*détournement de pouvoir* in French); since there was no doubt that the firm was entitled to have its application accepted under the relevant regulations, it was awarded damages.[69] Such a case would be probably treated as one of targeted malice in England, even if malice is only inferred by the reiteration of illegal behaviours and not proven by any declaration made by those having taken the decisions or delayed them.

One of the few cases decided by the *Consiglio di Stato* also concerned building permission. An application had been rejected and the negative decision successfully challenged by way of judicial review. The application was renewed but in the meantime the local authority had changed the planning regulations and rejected the application again with reference to the new rules. The second negative decision was in turn challenged and quashed, because the application was to be assessed according to the rules in place at the moment the judgment concerning the first negative administrative act had become *res judicata*. The damages action was affirmed in so far as the original application had to be met under the old rules.[70]

---

per lesione di interessi legittimi'; TAR Lombardia, Sez III, 16 June 2000, n 4417, in *Foro amm.* 2000, 3960, e TAR Lombardia, Sez III, 6 Nov 2000, n 6259, in *Giust civ* 2001, I, 863.

[68] Eg, TAR Lombardia, Sez Brescia, 14 gennaio 2000, n 8, e TAR Puglia, Bari, Sez II, 23 marzo 2000, n 1248, both reported in *Urbanistica e appalti* 2000, 987, with note by M Protto 'Responsabilità della p.a. per lesione di interessi legittimi'; the first decision also reported in *Foro it.* 2000, III, 197, with note by L Carrozza—F Fracchia 'Art 35 d leg. 80/98 e risarcibilità degli "interessi meritevoli di tutela": prime applicazioni giurisprudenziali'.

[69] TAR Sicilia, Catania, Sez I, 18 gennaio 2000, n 38, in *Corr giuridico* 2000, 388, with note by A Di Majo, 'Danno ingiusto e danno risarcibile nella lesione di interessi legittimi'; in *Danno e responsabilità* 2000, 306, with note by *v* Carbone, 'Rivincita del cittadino e fine di un privilegio: prime condanne della PA a risarcire la lesione di interessi legittimi'; in *Foro it.* 2000, III, 196, with note by L Carrozza and F Fracchia, 'Art 35 d leg 80/98 e risarcibilità degli "interessi meritevoli di tutela": prime applicazioni giurisprudenziali'.

[70] Cons St, Sez IV, 2 June 2000, n 3177, in *Foro amm* 2000, 2096, with remarks by R Iannotta; the decision, however, did not go so far as to affirm that the firm was entitled to get the building permission, leaving the question open for determination by the local authority.

Also concerning building permissions, Italian courts seem to look for certainty rather than just chances.[71]

In the end, unlike French administrative courts, most Italian judges are very reluctant to put themselves in the shoes of administrative authorities, to decide what the situation would have been if no illegality had happened. They rather annul the decisions taken by public bodies and then refer the matter back to the same authority for a new assessment.[72]

While assessing the substantive merits of a claim against a public body in a liability action is still a problem for Italian administrative courts, the equivalence between illegality and fault (meaning negligent behaviour) is often affirmed. The requirement of fault is spelt out in Article 2043 of the Civil code, but already the *Corte di cassazione* in the *Vitali* decision had referred to the fault of the administrative organisation and not to the fault of any named or even given public servant.[73] Consequently, administrative courts usually do not go into any depth while assessing fault, being content to find whether any administrative decision or omission to take a decision was illegal.[74] It is however fair to say that often enough public bodies are responsible of blatant and reiterated disregard of the applicable rules enough to make one think of malice.[75] In at least some cases, however, damage actions failed because the illegal decision was taken in application of rather muddled legal rules and the construction placed on them by the administration, even if admittedly wrong, was not flying into the face of the words of the rules themselves (innocent mistake).[76]

---

[71] Also TAR Puglia, Bari, Sez II, 17 Jan 2000, n 169, in *Foro it* 2000, I, 481, with note by F Fracchi, 'Risarcimento danni da c.d. lesione di interessi legittimi: deve riguardare i soli interessi a "risultato garantito"?'; in *Urbanistica e appalti* 2000, 987, with note by M Protto, 'Responsabilità della p.a. per lesione di interessi legittimi'.

[72] To some extent, this is allowed by the new statute; even if there are some doubts, however, the most acceptable position seems to be that courts should solve the question whether the authority is liable or not, leaving for discussion among the parties only the problem of the *quantum* of damages: Cons. St., Sez IV, 1 Feb 2001, n 396, to be reported in *Giur i.* 2001.

[73] R Caranta, *Attività amministrativa ed illecito aquiliano* (Milano: Giuffré, 2001) ch 5.

[74] Cons St, Sez IV, 11 Oct 2000, n 5412, in *Foro amm* 2000, 3055 (s m .); TAR Abruzzo, Sez Pescara, 23 Sept 1999, n 750, in *TAR* 1999, I, 4423; it has even been said that the requirement is not applicable: TAR Lombardia, Sez III, 6 novembre 2000, n 6259, in *Giust civ* 2001, I, 863.

[75] TAR Sicilia, Catania, Sez I, 18 Jan 2000, n 38, in *Corr. giuridico* 2000, 388, with note by A Di Majo, 'Danno ingiusto e danno risarcibile nella lesione di interessi legittimi'; in *Danno e responsabilità* 2000, 306, with note by *v* Carbone, 'Rivincita del cittadino e fine di un privilegio: prime condanne della PA a risarcire la lesione di interessi legittimi'; in *Foro it* 2000, III, 196, with note by L Carrozza and F Fracchia, 'Art 35 d leg. 80/98 e risarcibilità degli "interessi meritevoli di tutela": prime applicazioni giurisprudenziali'.

[76] TAR Lombardia, Sez III, 23 Dec 1999, n 5049, in *Corr giuridico* 2000, 388, with note by A Di Majo, 'Danno ingiusto e danno risarcibile nella lesione di interessi legittimi'; also TAR Friuli Venezia Giulia, 19 giugno 2000, n 514, in *Giust civ* 2000, I, 3351 (but here the court declined jurisdiction and thus any remark on fault is *obiter*).

(c) Breaches of Community Law

The Italian case law concerning liability for breaches of Community law is rather limited despite the fact that the *Francovich*[77] case was decided following references under the (then) Article 177 of the (then) EEC Treaty by two Italian first instance courts.[78] Cases have mostly concerned the application of the *Francovich* decision to workers having seen their rights under the 80/987/EEC directive forfeited by the late implementation of the said directive. At first the *Corte di cassazione* held that the Parliament could not be liable and compensation only followed because the statute having finally implemented the directive was retroactive in its effects.[79] Lately, however, the Court overturned its previous rulings and aligned itself with the *Brasserie du Pêcheur v Federal Republic of Germany* and *R v Secretary of State for Transport, ex p Factortame Ltd (No 4)*[80] decision by the European Court of Justice which was extensively quoted in the judgment.[81]

Other cases of breach of Community law are probably now covered by the case law referred to in the previous paragraph. The very limited scope allowed to fault, which is translated into a mistake which cannot be considered innocent, is consistent with the requirements laid down in *Brasserie du Pêcheur v Federal Republic of Germany* and *R v Secretary of State for Transport, ex p Factortame Ltd (No 4)*.[82] Some problems could arise in the future if the courts continue their recent tendency of making an annulment action a condition precedent of any damages action.[83] Such a rule would be consistent with the European Court of justice decision in *Brasserie du Pêcheur v Federal Republic of Germany* and *R v Secretary of State for Transport, ex p Factortame Ltd (No 4)*.[84] However, the more recent *Metallgesellschaft* decision seems to take a less generous stance towards national rules making annulment actions a condition precedent for liability actions.[85]

---

[77] Joined cases C-6 and 9/90 *Francovich and others/Italian Republic* [1991] ECR I-5357.

[78] The case law involving Community law has been extensively analysed by G Giacalone, 'La giurisprudenza della *Corte di cassazione* in materia di diritto comunitario (rassegna di giurisprudenza civile e penale della Suprema corte dal 1991 al 2000)', in *Giust civ* 2001, II, 155 (first part) and 271 (second part).

[79] Eg, Cass, Sez lav, 18 Oct 1995, n 10617, in *Resp civ prev* 1996, 309, with note by R Caranta, 'In materia di conseguenze della mancata tempestiva trasposizione di una direttiva comunitaria nell'ordinamento italiano'.

[80] Joined cases C-46/93 and 48/93 *Brasserie du pêcheur and Factotame IV* ECR I-1029, points 75 ff.

[81] Eg, Cass, Sez lav, 11 June 1998, n 5846, in *Giust civ* 1998, I, 2469, with observations by G Giacalone.

[82] Joined cases C-46/93 and 48/93 ECR I-1029.

[83] TAR Campania, Napoli, Sez I, 8 Feb 2000, n 603, in *Urbanistica e appalti* 2001, with note by R Caranta 'Il ritorno dell'irresponsabilità'; also, but with less force, Cons St, Sez IV, 22 marzo 2001, n 1684, in *Giur* 2001, .

[84] Joined cases C-46/93 and 48/93 ECR I-1029, point 84 f.

[85] Joined cases C-307/98 e C-410/98, nyr.

3. *English* Angst

French and Italian lawyers are used to reasoning by way of broad categories and general principle. They may be however ready to make room for exception in discrete areas. Common lawyers work on precedent and much more narrowly construed rules. This is very much so in the field of liability. Nominate torts take the place of general provision such as Article 1382 of Code Napoléon or Article 2043 of the Italian civil code.

Concerning governmental liability, English courts have steered clear from any equation between illegality and tort. 'The basic premise is that an invalid or ultra vires administrative act does not per se entail fault on the part of the administrative authority.'[86] In the Commonwealth, the High Court of Australia went to some length in affirming a similar stance. In *Beaudesert Shire Council v Smith* the Court recognised that 'unlawful, intentional and positive acts' could be actionable in tort.[87] However, in *Lonrho Ltd v Shell Petroleum (No. 2)*, Lord Diplock spoke against following such a path.[88]

Today the law is that 'Illegality without more does not give a cause of action.'[89] In *X (Minors) v Bedfordshire County Council* Lord Browne-Wilkinson forcefully made the case that 'The breach of a public law right by itself gives rise to no claim for damages. A claim for damages must be based on a private law cause of action.'[90]

Even in Australia *Beaudesert* is no longer good law. After having been distinguished a number of times, most notably by the Privy Council in *Dunlop v Woollahra Municipal Council*,[91] it was overruled by the Australian High Court in *Northern Territory v Mengel*.[92]

Something more than an illegality is thus needed to hold a public organisation liable. What more depends on each specific tort. The following analysis will be confined to the torts most relevant in the field of governmental liability.[93]

---

[86] Andenas and Fairgrieve, 'Sufficiently Serious? Judicial Restraint in Tortious Liability of Public Authorities and the European Influence', in Andenas (ed), *English Public Law and the Common Law of Europe* (London: Key Haven, 1998), 285, 296: also P Craig, *Administrative Law* 4th edn (London: Sweet & Maxwell, 1999), 845.

[87] (1966) 120 CLR 145, 156.

[88] [1982] AC 173 (HL) 187–8.

[89] *Three Rivers District Council v Bank of England (No 3)* [2000] 2 WLR 1220 (HL) 1268 (Lord Hobhouse).

[90] [1995] 2 AC 633 (HL) 730; also 768; and *Three Rivers District Council v Bank of England (No 3)* [2000] WLR 1220 (HL) 1230 (Lord Steyn).

[91] [1982] AC 158 (PC).

[92] (1995) 69 ALJR 527.

[93] According to Lord Browne-Wilkinson in *X(Minors) v Bedfordshire County Council* [1995] 2 AC 633 (HL) 730, 'Private law claims for damages can be classified into four different categories, viz: (A) action for breach of statutory duty simpliciter (ie, irrespective of care-

(a) Breach of Statutory Duty

Under given conditions the breach of a statutory provision can lead to liability.[94] As far as governmental liability is concerned, English courts have applied these conditions so as not to allow this tort to evolve into anything close to *Beaudesert*. According to a dictum by Lord Browne-Wilkinson in *X(Minors) v Bedfordshire County Council*, 'The basic proposition is that in the ordinary case a breach of statutory duty does not, by itself, give rise to any private law cause of action.'[95] The first obstacle is that only provisions conferring duties and not just powers are relevant with reference to the tort of breach of statutory duty.[96] Secondly, if the relevant statute is silent as to the remedies available in the case of breach, liability can arise only when the provision infringed can be shown to have been passed with the intent to confer a right on the person complaining of the breach or to a limited class to which the claimant belongs (this is something which the Germans refer to as *Normzwecktheorie*).[97]

As far as the distinction between duties and powers is concerned, reference can be had to *Stovin v Wise*, a car crash case to which we will have to revert later. The claim based on breach of statutory duty failed in the Court of Appeal.[98] Kennedy LJ, with whom all the other judges concurred, held that the highway authority had the power but not a duty to remove the obstacles to the visibility which had concurred to cause the accident.[99]

The *Normzwecktheorie* is an ingenious device to place on the (silent) legislator's shoulders the responsibility for policy choices made by courts. It is a device that is almost necessary under positivist constraints denying courts any power to make policy choices. For all the talk about the 'true intent of the legislator' or the 'true construction', however, everything boils down to judicial preferences. For instance, in *X(Minors) v Bedfordshire County Council*, a case concerning children welfare and education to which we will have to revert later, the House of Lords disposed of the claims based on various social security statutes just by claiming that 'Although regulatory or welfare legislation affecting a particular area of activity does in fact

---

lessness); (B) actions based solely on the careless performance of a statutory duty in the absence of any other common law right of action; (C) actions based on a common law duty of care arising either from the imposition of the statutory duty or from the performance of it; (D) misfeasance in public office, ie, the failure to exercise, or the exercise of, statutory powers either with the intention to injure the plaintiff or in the knowledge that the conduct is unlawful'; his Lordship later denies category C any autonomous relevance, stating that 'the careless performance of a statutory duty does not in itself give rise to any cause of action in the absence of either a statutory right of action [...] or a common law duty of care' (732).

[94] Generally KM Stanton, *Breach of Statutory Duty* (London: Sweet & Maxwell, 1986).
[95] [1995] 2 AC 633 (HL) 731.
[96] The distinction is relevant with reference to negligence actions too; consider however *Anns v Merton London Borough* [1978] AC 728 (HL) 755 f and 759 (Lord Wilberforce).
[97] For a comparison of the German and British ideas Markesinis *et al*, op cit, 23 ff.
[98] [1994] 1 WLR 1124.   [99] 1130.

provide protection to those individuals particularly affected by that activity, the legislation is not to be treated as being passed for the benefit of those individuals but for the benefit of society in general.'[100]

English courts have chosen to be very conservative in applying *Normzwecktheorie in the field of governmental liability at least. A number of rules for the 'construction'* of relevant statutes or 'pointers' have been developed in the course of time.[101] The overarching principle is one of effectiveness. Damages must be granted if there is no other remedy available for the breach considered. Breaches cannot be left without remedies.[102]

This rationale easily leads to defeat claims for damages where, as is the case in the situation we are dealing with now, judicial review is available. A number of cases illustrate this point.[103]

In *Bourgoin sa v Ministry of Agriculture* the defendant authority had refused the claimant a licence to import poultry in breach of Article 30 (now Article 28) of the then EEC Treaty.[104] As far as the claim for breach of statutory duty is concerned, the core of the legal question was squarely laid down by Mann J of the Queen's Bench:

The debate before me was whether the form of protection for the rights conferred by article 30 is solely a proceeding by way of judicial review for a declaration (as the defendant contended) or whether there is also available an action for damages for breach of statutory duty (as the plaintiffs contended).[105]

Mann J doubted whether judicial review was an adequate remedy and this the more so since at that time interim relief was not available against the crown. Moreover, he could 'see no reason in principle why the breach of a duty should not be the subject of proceedings both for judicial review and for damages for breach of statutory duty.'[106] The decision was reversed by the Court of Appeal (Oliver LJ dissenting). The majority of the court held that judicial review afforded an adequate remedy.[107]

In *O'Rourke v Camden London Borough Council*[108] the plaintiff presented himself as homeless to the local authority, which provided him with temporary accommodation. Pending consideration of his application, he was however evicted and the local authority failed to provide him with

---

[100] *X(Minors) v Bedfordshire County Council* [1995] 2 AC 633 (HL) 731 (Lord Browne-Wilkinson); see further 747.
[101] *Cutler v Wandsworth Stadium Ltd* [1949] AC 398 (HL) 407 (Lord Simonds).
[102] Eg, *X(Minors) v Bedfordshire County Council* [1995] 2 AC 633 (HL) 731.
[103] Also *Murphy v Brentwood District Council* [1991] 1 AC 398 (HL) 490 (Lord Oliver).
[104] [1986] 1 QB 716 (QB and CA).
[105] [1986] 1 QB 716 (QB) 727; also (CA) 752 f (Lord Oliver).
[106] [1986] 1 QB 716 (QB) 729.
[107] [1986] 1 QB 716 (CA) 785 (Parker LJ) 801 (Nourse LJ).
[108] (1998(AC 188 (HL).

alternative accommodation.[109] The action in damages was dismissed in the House of Lords. The leading judgment by Lord Hoffmann, with whom all the other law Lords concurred held that the Housing Act 1985 was part of a scheme of social welfare providing housing assistance to individuals for the benefit of society in general; no private law action therefore laid on the 'true' construction of the statute and breaches had to be remedied by way of judicial review.[110]

Without going any deeper into the case law, suffice it here to say that, 'outside the area of workplace legislation [...] private law causes of action are very rarely discovered or invented'.[111] 'In future, where Parliament fails to specify a particular remedy for breach of a public duty, the presumption will be that judicial review is the normal and exclusive means of enforcement. It is difficult now to see any scope for extending the application of the tort of breach of statutory duty in the public field.'[112]

Illegality does not *per se* give rise to liability under English law. In fact, where illegality can be challenged by way of judicial review proceedings, damages claims will normally fail.

(b) Negligence

From the point of view of civil lawyers, negligence could be easily mistaken for the general principle of non-contractual liability, with which they are familiar. This is not so. Not every negligent action causing harm opens the way to a claim in damages. Common lawyers rather speak about categories of negligence.[113] Even if the categories of negligence are nothing more than examples of some general conception, according to a well-know dictum by Lord Atkin in *Donaghue v Stevenson*, 'To seek a complete logical definition of the general principle is probably to go beyond the function of the judge, for the more general the definition the more likely it is to omit essentials or to introduce non-essentials.'[114]

In the past decades the pendulum has shifted many times from opposite casuistic and strongly principled approaches. In *Home Office v Dorset Yacht*[115] Lord Reid summed up the previous developments by stating that:

---

[109] The previous case law concerning housing benefits has been reviewed by R. Carnwath, 'The Thornton Heresy Exposed: Financial Remedies for Breach of Public Duties' [1998] *PL* 407.

[110] 193 ff; critically R Carnwath, 'The *Thornton* Heresy Exposed: Financial Remedies for Breach of Public Duties' [1998] *PL* 407, 414 ff.

[111] Markesinis *et al*, op cit, 14.

[112] Carnwath, 'The *Thornton* Heresy Exposed', 407, 419.

[113] Eg, *Murphy v Brentwood District Council* [1991] 1 AC 398 (HL) 461 (Lord Keith); this approch is not limited to English courts: in Australia it was shared by *Council of the Shire of Sutherland v Heyman* (1985) 157 CLR 424, 481 (Brennan J).

[114] [1932] AC 562 (HL) 580.

[115] [1970] AC 1004 (HL).

About the beginning of this century most eminent lawyers thought that there were a number of separate torts involving negligence, each with its own rules, and they were most unwilling to add more. They were of course aware from a number of leading cases that in the past the courts had from time to time recognised new duties and new grounds of action. But the heroic age was over; it was time to cultivate certainty and security in the law; the categories of negligence were virtually closed [...]. In later years there has been a steady trend towards regarding the law of negligence as depending on principle so that, when a new point emerges, one should ask not whether it is covered by authority but whether recognised principles apply to it.[116]

In later cases the emphasis was very much on precedents rather than on principles. In *Caparo Industries Plc v Dickman* the claimant, having accomplished a takeover and feeling it had been deceived as to the real value of the purchased, sued inter alia the auditors of the latter company; Caparo claimed that the auditors had negligently carried out their task and made an incorrect report; the claimant maintained that it had acted on that report when buying the shares at a substantial loss as it later appeared.[117] Caparo had no contractual relationship with the auditors; the action had to be in tort and the cause of action chosen was negligence. The action was dismissed by the House of Lords which, expressly disavowing earlier decisions, 'emphasised the inability of any single general principle to provide a practical test which can be applied to every situation to determine whether a duty of care is owed and, if so, what is its scope'.[118]

Commenting upon the general features of the tort of negligence, Lord Bridge further elaborated:

What emerges is that, in addition to forseeability of damage, necessary ingredients in any situation giving rise to a duty of care are that there should exist between the party owing the duty and the party to whom it is owed a relationship characterised by the law as one of 'proximity' or 'neighbourhood' and that the situation should be one in which the court considers it fair, just and reasonable that the law should impose a duty of a given scope upon one party for the benefit of the other.[119]

This has not to be treated like a precise definition of the tort, one base on general principle. Nothing more than lip service is paid to the idea of a general principle of negligence liability. It is Lord Bridge again saying:

---

[116] 1026 f; also 1038 (Lord Morris): 'precedents do not fix the limits of what may be called duty situations: they illustrate them'; contrast 1042 ff (Viscount Dilhorne), where the emphasis is laid on precedents: 'among the thousands of reported cases not a single case can be found where a claim similar to that in this case has been put forward. No case in this country has been found to support the contention that such a duty of care exists in the common law'; and further 'The absence of authority shows that no such duty now exists. If there should be one, that is, in my view, a matter for the legislature and not for the courts' (1045). The approach of the majority in *Dorset Yacht* was further elaborated upon in *Anns v Merton London Borough* [1978] AC 728 (HL) 751 f (Lord Wilberforce).
[117] [1990] 2 AC 605 (HL).   [118] 617 (Lord Bridge).   [119] 617 f.

Whilst recognising, of course, the importance of the underlying general principles common to the whole field of negligence, I think the law has now moved in the direction of attaching greater significance to the more traditional categorisation of distinct and recognisable situations as guides to the existence, the scope and the limits of the varied duties of care which the law imposes.[120]

The casuistic approach hinders the development of open-ended heads of negligence liability, and this so very much so in cases where mere economic loss is at stake.[121] The reference to a situation in which 'the court considers it fair, just and reasonable that the law should impose a duty of a given scope upon one party for the benefit of the other', while not by itself preventing the creation of new duties, allows for a considerable restraint.[122] Actually, the latter proviso has been at the heart of many later cases concerning specifically governmental liability.[123] The more defendant-friendly trend was indeed at the heart of the *Murphy v Brentwood District Council* to which we will have to revert in due time.[124]

These days cases where harm flows from the adoption of an illegal decision, which themselves normally involve solely economic losses, are not usually litigated in negligence. Something more than simple negligence coupled with illegality seems to be required.

(c) Misfeasance in Public Office
Misfeasance in public office is characterised by both illegality and intention. It is concerned with the deliberate and dishonest abuse of power by a public officer.

In *Bourgoin sa v Ministry of Agriculture*, the Court of appeal stated that targeted malice is not required. It is sufficient that the act was done knowing that it will cause harm.[125]

---

[120] 618; also 628 (Lord Roskill); their Lordiships quoted with approval the *dictum* by Brennan J in *Council of the Shire of Sutherland v Heyman* (1985) 157 CLR 424, 481; Lord Oliver and Lord Jauncey were not so sanguine on the overall approach to the tort of negligence; they rather stressed that just forseeability of damage without proximity between the tortfeasor and the damaged person is not enough to establish a duty of care.

[121] *Caparo Industries Plc v Dickman* [1990] 2 AC 605 (HL) 618 (Lord Bridge); but the same approach was followed in cases concerning physical damage to persons: eg, *X (Minors) v Bedfordshire County Council* [1995] 2 AC 633 (HL) 751 (Lord Browne-Wilkinson).

[122] Markesinis *et al*, op cit, 14 f. and 39: 'all these concepts are fluid enough to justify whatever result the judge has decided to reach'; 'the concepts used are only smokescreen for a heavy dose of judicial social engineering'. In the case law also *Barrett v Ministry of Defence* [1995] 1 WLR 1217 (CA) which held it not fair to consider the Ministry of Defence liable for failing to enforce regulations aimed at discourage drinking among sailors.

[123] This even though the requirement itself is by no way of exclusive application to governmental liability cases: T Weir, *A Casebook on Tort*, 9th edn (London: Sweet & Maxwell, 2000), 16.

[124] [1991] 1 AC 398 (HL).

[125] [1986] 1 QB 716 (CA) 775 ff (Oliver LJ).

This does not mean misfeasance can be easily established. In *Jones v Swansea City Council*[126] the claimant had been given permission to change the use of some premises rented to her by the local authority. The claimant's husband was at that time a majority councillor. Granting of the permission was fiercely and vocally opposed by a minority councillor who vowed to have it withdrawn if and when he came to power, which happened on the next elections. The claimant sued the council for damages claiming that the withdrawal had been motivated by the malicious intent of causing harm. The action failed in the House of Lords because proof was not given that all the councillors having voted for the withdrawal had acted out of malice. As Lord Templeman put it, 'The moral of this story is that a councillor and any close relative to a councillor should avoid any business transactions with the council.'[127]

The decision shows the difficulties facing the claimant even in most blatant cases to prove malice.[128]

Misfeasance in public office has been recently analysed by English courts all the way up to the House of Lords in *Three Rivers District Council v Bank of England*.[129] The case falls under the second category proposed here and will be therefore dealt with later in this paper. Suffice here to say that the House of Lords had somewhat watered down the intention requirement. Subjective reckless indifference both as to the illegality of the decision taken and as to its consequences is sufficient to establish liability.[130]

(d) Eurotort

Meeting Community law requirements in English law of torts has not been an easy task. As early as 1974, in Application de *Gaz sa v Falks Veritas Ltd*, a case between private parties, Lord Denning MR had ventured to envisage a new cause of action for breach of Community law.[131] The existence of any such a Eurotort was later forcefully denied by the Court of Appeal in *Bourgoin sa v Ministry of Agriculture*.[132] According to the majority of the Court, the defendant authority could be held liable only if misfeasance in public office was established.[133]

---

[126] [1990] 1 WLR 54 (CA); [1990] 1 WLR 1453 (HL).

[127] [1990] 1 WLR 1453 (HL) 1455.

[128] Furthermore, actions against public authorities are doomed to fail when the unauthorised acts of the officers are so unconnected with their authorised duties as to be independent of and outside them: *Racz v Home Office* [1994] 2 AC 45 (HL).

[129] *Three Rivers District Council v Bank of England (No 3)* [1996] 3 All ER 558 (QB); [2000] WLR 15 (CA); [2000] WLR 1220 (HL); the decision by the Queen's Bench was considered by C Hadjiemmanuil, 'Civil liability of regulatory authorities after the *Three Rivers* case' [1997] PL 32.

[130] *Three Rivers District Council v Bank of England (No 3)* [2000] WLR 1220 (HL) 1232 and 1235 (Lord Steyn), 1270 (Lord Hobhouse), and 1275 (Lord Millet).

[131] [1974] 1 Ch 381.

[132] [1986] 1 QB 716 (CA) 775 (Oliver LJ).   [133] 788 ff (Parker LJ).

In the years since *Bourgoin* was decided, however, the European Court of Justice has developed a highly sophisticated case law concerning the Member States' liability for breach of Community law.

In *Francovich v Italian Republic*[134] the Court of Justice introduced a principle of liability that has been refined by subsequent decisions.[135] In the light of the *Francovich* decision English courts have doubted whether *Bourgoin* was correctly decided.[136] The idea of a Eurotort has been finally vindicated by the judgments handed down in the *Factortame* litigation.[137]

Faced with dwindling fish stocks, the EEC—as it then was—had set national fishing quotas. The British Government had passed new legislation aimed to protect British fishing communities by preventing foreign nationals from fishing against the United Kingdom's quota. The new statute introduced new nationality, residence, and domicile requirements for the registration of vessels. Previously registered vessels had to seek registration again and thus had to comply with the new requirements. A number of boats failing one or more of the requirements were refused registration. Their owners sought judicial review but were not immediately granted interim relief. Later they asked for damages and their action was one of two claims leading to the ruling by the Court of Justice in *Brasserie du Pêcheur v Federal Republic of Germany* and *R v Secretary of State for Transport, ex p Factortame Ltd (No 4)*.[138]

The decision followed two preliminary references from a German court and the Queen's Bench respectively. The Court of Justice affirmed *Francovich* and held that Member States can be liable due to the infringement of Community law provisions where three conditions are met, namely, the rule of Community law breaches is intended to confer rights on the aggrieved person, the breach is sufficiently serious and there is a direct

---

[134] Joined cases C-6 and 9/90 *Francovich and others v Italian Republic* [1991] ECR I-5357.

[135] Also Joined cases C-178, 179 and 199–190/94 *Dillenkofer v Federal Republic of Germany* [1996] ECR I-4845, and Case C-392/93 *R v HM Treasury, ex p British Telecommunication plc* [1996] ECR I-1631.

[136] *Kirklees Metropolitan Borough Council v Wickes Building Supplies Ltd* [1992] 3 WLR 170 (HL) 188 (Lord Goff); it was not even quoted in *R v Secretary of State for the Home Department, ex p Gallangher* [1996] 2 CMLRep 1996 (CA) 851 (the claim for damages for unlawful expulsion failed because breach of Community law was not substantial—Gallangher was heard after, instead of before, the deportation order was made, but the order was maintained—and could not be connected to any damage as a matter of causation).

[137] *R v Secretary of State for Transport, ex p Factortame Ltd (No 5)* [1999] 3 WLR 1062 (HL); *R v Secretary of State for Transport, ex p Factortame Ltd (No 5)* [1998] EuLR 456 (CA); *R v Secretary of State for Transport, ex p Factortame Ltd (No 5)* [1997] EuLR 475 (QB); an authoritative commentary of the decisions of the lower courts is to be found in E García de Enterría, 'Le denouement de l'affaire "Factortame". La responsabilité civile du Royame-Uni' in *Mélanges en hommage à Michel Waelbroeck* (Bruxelles: Bruylant, 1999), 355; also A Cygan, 'Defining a sufficiently serious breach of Community law: the House of Lords casts its nets into waters' (2000) 25 *ELR* 452.

[138] Joined cases C-46/93 and 48/93 *Brasserie du pêcheur and Factortame IV* ECR I-1029.

causal link between the breach and the damaged sustained. The Court further held that in case the Member State enjoys wide discretionary powers the breach can be held to be sufficiently serious when the Member State manifestly and gravely disregarded the limits on its discretion. The Court went on to point out situations where a breach could be held sufficiently serious.

When the case came back to England, courts adopted the definition laid down by the Court of Justice for the tort of breach of Community law. In the House of Lords it was held that:

Before a member state can be held liable, a national court must find (i) that the relevant rule of Community law is one which is intended to confer rights on individuals; (ii) the breach must be sufficiently serious; (iii) there must be a direct causal link between the breach and the loss or damage complained of.[139]

English courts have so far debated whether the second requirement was met by the action of the British government. There was no discussion as to the first requirement since the question had already been solved in the affirmative by the Court of Justice and deliberation concerning the causation issue was postponed to a later stage. Since Britain enjoyed wide discretionary power in the matter, liability was conditional on the claimants establishing that the government had 'gravely and manifestly disregarded the limits on the exercise of its powers' or, said otherwise, the breach had been serious and manifest.[140] All the courts up to the House of Lords quite rightly held that the legislative action by the British government had met the second requirement. They denied that the breaches could amount to excusable mistakes, and this the more so since the European Commission had made clear from an early stage that it considered the proposed legislation inconsistent with various provisions of the EC Treaty and the British government decided not only to go on but to proceed quickly and in a way which left little scope for interim relief.[141]

B. Administrative Decisions One of Many Events Leading to Damage

Illegal decisions and omissions can be just one of many circumstances leading to damage. In the vigilance cases for instance, insufficient vigilance alone could not lead to any harm. Loss arises primarily because of the

---

[139] *R v Secretary of State for Transport, ex p Factortame Ltd (No 5)* [1999] 3 WLR 1062 (HL) 1072 (Lord Slynn); also 1082 (Lord Hope).

[140] *R v Secretary of State for Transport, ex p Factortame Ltd (No 5)* [1999] 3 WLR 1062 (HL) 1073 f (Lord Slynn); 1081 (Lord Hoffmann).

[141] The House of Lords has taken a slightly more nuanced position as to the relevance of the EC Commission opinion than the one shared by the lower courts: *R v Secretary of State for Transport, ex p Factortame Ltd (No 5)* [1999] 3 WLR 1062 (HL) 1078 (Lord Slynn) 1085 (Lord Hope).

behaviour of individuals and companies under vigilance. What could be called the 'principal tortfeasor' is usually insolvent. In any event, those wronged may prefer to try satisfying themselves with the public purse. Judicial review is usually no effective remedy since damages normally accrue a long time after some of the administrative decisions where taken and due to a long series of both decisions and omissions. Moreover, annulment of the decisions involved in no way can mitigate the prejudice. Illegality is now more in the foreground.

1. French Courts Not to Condone (Serious) Mistakes

French administrative law is still in many respects closely related to the most archetypal models of a coherent set of rules specifically designed to suit the centralised and authoritarian government of the State. More particularly, the cultural mode of what the Germans later called the *Polizeistaat* still makes people to consider it quite normal to have most if not all public and private activities under close scrutiny, vigilance or control by the State or other public law entities. This has set a fertile breeding ground on which liability for failures in the performance of vigilance missions has been allowed to grow and ultimately to thrive.

(a) Supervision of Private Activities

A long standing case law concerning supervision of various economic activities by organs such as the *Commission bancaire*, the *Commission des opérations de Bourse*, and the *Conseil national du crédit* has it that liability can be established only when *faute lourde* is present.[142]

The *leading cases* are four decisions handed down by the *Conseil d'Etat* in 1946 following the so called *affaire Stavinsky*.[143] In the early 1930s the *Caisse de Crédit municipal de Bayonne* issued bonds worth many millions of French francs; the money thus collected, instead of being lent to the general public, was in reality siphoned away with the complicity of the management of the bank. When the scheme collapsed and the *Caisse* went bankrupt many investors sued both the local authority and the State, whose organs were given various powers of control over the local financial institution. Concerning the liability of the local authority, the *Conseil d'Etat* held it responsible of *faute lourde* for not having supervised the management of the *Caisse*, for not having checked its budget and accounts; indeed, the whole scheme was successful only due to the negligence if not complicity of the

---

[142] See respectively CE 12 Feb 1960, *Kampmann*, Rec 1960, 107; CE 22 June 1984, *Sté Pierre et Cristal*, Rec 1984, *tables*, 731; CE 14 Feb 1973, *Ass diocésaine d'Agen*, Rec 1973, 141.

[143] CE 29 Mar 1946, *Caisse départmentale d'assurances sociales de Meurthe-et-Moselle et autres*, Rev dr publ 1946, 490, concl Lefas, annotation by GJ.

Mayor and the councillors of the *Commune*.[144] As to the liability of the
State itself, the *Conseil d'Etat* held that the choice of the wrong people to
manage the *Caisse*, the fact of keeping them in place, and the delay in starting an investigation into the abnormal operations undertaken by the local
bank, all together amounted to *faute lourde*.[145] In the end, the *Commune*
and the State were held each responsible for the loss corresponding to the
25 per cent of the bonds subscribed by the claimant, the remaining 50 per
cent being left on the shoulder of the claimant itself held to have been
imprudent in subscribing the bonds. Two other decisions handed down the
same day and concerning two other claimants raise the liability of the State
to 35 per cent and 30 per cent respectively, albeit without giving any explanation for the difference, probably due to the different and possibly earlier
phase when the bonds were subscribed.[146]

These precedents have been constantly followed in later case law,
concerning actions brought both by depositors and by the institutions
under supervision.[147]

The case law placing liability on the ground of *faute lourde* lays down
that simply showing illegal decisions by the authority responsible for supervision is not enough to make it liable. The equation between *illégalité* and
faute does not play here. Grave and/or reiterated breaches of the law and—

[144] CE 29 Mar 1946, *Caisse départmentale d'assurances sociales de Meurthe-et-Moselle c
Ville de Bayonne*, Rev dr publ 1946, 501, concl Lefas, annotation by G J: 'Considérant [. . .
] qu'il résulte de l'instruction que l'autorité municipale a commis une faute grave en ne surveil-
lant pas, contrairement aux dispositions de l'article 578 du décret du 31 mai 1862, l'administration du Crédit municipal; que le Conseil municipal s'est abstenu de toute contrôle efficace
des budgets et des comptes de gestion que lui étaient soumis en vertu de l'article 580 du décret
précité; que [. . .] l'action frauduleuse du sieur Stavisky n'a été rendue possible que par les
agissements répréhenibles, sino par la complicité du maire et par la négligence des conseillers
municipaux qui, par application de l'article 2 de la loi du 24 juin 1851, représentaient la ville
au sein du Conseil d'Administration; que ces fautes sont de nature à engager la responsabilité
de la commune.'

[145] CE 29 Mar 1946, *Caisse départmentale d'assurances sociales de Meurthe-et-Moselle c.
Etat*, Rev dr publ 1946, 503, concl Lefas, annotation by GJ: 'considérant que les agissements
criminels du sieur Stavisky et de ses complices n'ont été rendus possible que par la faute lourde
commise par le préfet des Basses-Pyrénées dans la choix du personel dirigeant du Crédit municipal de Bayonne los de sa création en 1931 et dans le maintien en fonction de ce personnel,
ainsi que par la négligence prolongée des différents services de l'Etat qui sont chargés du
contrôle de ces établissements publics communaux, et qui n'ont procédé que tardivement aux
investigations de toute nature que l'amplitude anormale des opérations du Crédit municipal de
Bayonne leur commandait de faire; que les sociétés réquerantes sont fondées à soutenir que ces
fautes sont de nature à engager la responsabilité de l'Etat.'

[146] CE 29 Mar 1946, *Sté l'Epargne Méridionale française et autres*, and CE 29 Mar 1946,
Sté La Continentale du Gaz, both in Rev dr publ 1946, 504 and 505, concl Lefas, annotation
by G J.

[147] Also CE, Ass, 27 Dec 1948, *Commune de Champigny sur Marne*, Rec 1948, 493; CE 6
Mar 1953, *Ville de Béziers*, Rec CE 1953, 119; CE 5 Dec 1958, *Commune de Dourgne*, Rec
1958, 606; 17 Jan 1969, *Bagot*, Rec 1969, 28; CE 20 June 1973, *Commune de Châteauneuf-
sur-Loire*, Rec, 1973, 428.

more generally—an overall malfunctioning of the supervisory services are necessary to find the authority liable.

Here again, however, the tendency to lessen the hurdle put on the claimant is slowly creeping up.[148] Two recent decisions by the *Cour administrative d'appel* in Paris, which have not been so far reported in full, appear to have distinguished those activities put under the generic of label of supervision into different phases. On the one hand, a purely administrative phase, on the other a judicial (or rather quasi-judicial) one. The requirement of *faute lourde* is applied only to the latter phase, starting from the moment a disciplinary proceeding has been started.[149]

A momentous shift in the rules traditionally applied to supervisory activities has been caused by the fallout from the infected blood *affaire*. For some time after it had been know that usual methods for scanning and processing blood and blood products was not sufficient to ensure remove of risk of contamination by some highly dangerous viruses, HIV the most prominent among them, the Health ministry failed to issue appropriate orders to make sure that only blood and blood products which had underwent more up-to-date processing were left on the market. A number of haemophiliacs, having contracted HIV due to the many blood transfusions their illness compelled them to undergo, sued the French State for damages.

Three cases reached the *Conseil d'Etat*, known respectively as *M G*, *M D* and *M et Mme B*.[150] The facts and the legal background were considered at length in the conclusions by the *Commissaire du gouvernment* Monsieur Legal. He started by pointing out that a 1991 statute provided for a procedure designed to give those having become HIV positive due to one or more transfusions what was called *une aide de solidarité*. The *Commissaire*, looking into the *travaux parlementaires* having led to the adoption of the statute, held that the statute itself did not intend to exclude any concurrent remedy in tort.[151] He accepted that the case was to be treated as one concerning supervision, but then referred to the general trend in sanitary cases to drop the requirement of *faute lourde*.[152] The *Conseil d'Etat*

---

[148] See also, with reference to vigilance on the respect of seaworthyness regulations, CE 13 Mar 1998, *M Améon*, in *Act jur Dr adm* 1998, 461; in this case the State was found not liable since negligence was not established and possibly mistaken decision authorising certain work on the ship had no casual link with the accident at sea where the ship sank.

[149] CAA Paris, 30 Mar 1999, *M El Shikh*, and CAA Paris, 13 July 1999, *Groupe Dentressangle*, concerning respectively the *Commission bancaire* and the *Commission de contrôle des assurances*, both commented in *Act jur Dr adm* 1999, 883. Note however that these decisions have been cast in doubt by the recent judgment of CE 30 November 2001, *Kechichian* AJDA 2002 136, in which the *Conseil d'Etat* reverted to a regime of *faute lourde*. For further discussion of these developments, see Ch 8, M Andenas and D Fairgrieve, 'Misfeasance in Public Office, Governmental Liability and European Influences'.

[150] CE, Ass, 9 Apr 1993, *M G*, *M D*, *M et Mme B* (three decisions), in *Rev fr dr adm* 1993, 583, concl H Legal.   [151] *Rev fr dr adm* 1993, 583, 586.

[152] 590 ff; cases on vigilance in other sectors are not recalled.

followed the conclusions of its *Commissaire*, and held that, by failing to
take any measure to forbid the use of blood which had not been processed
in ways to avoid the risk of contamination from the moment in which it
knew that there were serious risks of contamination, the State had incurred
liability on the ground of (simple) fault.[153]

The same evolution is maybe incipient with reference to those supervisory or police powers aimed at the prevention of disasters. A recent decision by the *Cour administrative d'appel* in Lyon found both the State and a
local authority having authorised the opening of a camping close to a river
liable for the damages following to a flooding. In doing so, the court placed
itself on the ground of *faulte simple*.[154]

Illegality as such, even when present, is of peripheral relevance to the
cases concerning the contaminated blood and flood *affaires*. The overall
functioning—or, rather, malfunctioning—of the supervisory services is
rather at stake. The choice to abandon *faute lourde* does not mean that any
illegality is equivalent to a tort, because illegality is of little interest. Public
law is referred to in order to ascertain the powers of the supervisory authority. Once the powers are defined, their exercise is assessed against general
standards of diligence having little to do with legality issues.

(b) Tutelle

Common lawyers are familiar with regulatory authorities supervising individuals and, more often than not, firms. They are less used to public authorities supervising other public authorities. This is however what happens in
France. The phenomenon is more apparent with reference to local government, which is much different from the English model of self-government.
Article 73.2 of the Constitution provides for State control about the way
departments and communes exercise their administrative powers; these
powers are collectively referred to as *tutelle*: the term itself conveys the idea
that local authorities are not considered to be persons of full age and capacity.[155] In the best Napoleonic tradition, an emanation of the State, the
prefect, resides in any department to this end.[156] According to tradition,
tutelle comprises many powers; at times prior approval is necessary before

---

[153] CE, Ass, 9 Apr 1993, *M G, M D, M et Mme B* (three decisions), in *Rev fr dr adm* 1993,
600: 'il appartenait à l'autorité administrative, informée à ladite date du 22 novembre 1984,
de façon non équivoque, de l'existence d'un risque sérieux de contamination des transfusés et
de la possibilité d'y parer par l'utilisation des produits chauffés qui étaient alors disponible sur
le marché international, d'interdir, sans attendre d'avoir la certitude que tous les lots de
produits dérivés du sang étaient contaminés, la délivrance des produits dangereux.'

[154] CAA Lyon, 13 May 1997, *M. Balusson et autres*, D 1998, jur, 11, n Ch Schaegis; J
Moreau 'Responsabilité administrative et sécurité publique', in *Act jur Dr adm* 1999, num
spéc, 96, 97.

[155] J-C Hélin, 'Le contrôle de légalité des actes locaux en France' *Act jur Dr adm* 1999, 767.

[156] M Verpeaux, 'La Constitution et les collectivités territoriales' *Rev dr publ* 1998, 1379.

a decision taken by the local authority is brought into effect; at other times, the delegate from the central government is empowered to stay, annul or substitute decisions taken by the administrative bodies under *tutelle*; even the local council themselves can be dissolved as a way to restore legality. At times, *tutelle* extends beyond mere legality. A decision taken by a local council can be overturned by the State on grounds of expediency.[157] Lately, most powers of *tutelle* have been cancelled. As a rule, today, in most but the most sensitive matters (such those having to do with the keeping of law and order), all the prefect can do is to challenge decisions taken by the local authorities in front of the administrative courts.[158]

The question has arisen as to the liability (if any) of the State when exercising its supervisory powers.[159]

The case law of the *Conseil d'Etat* is still firm in holding that, as a rule, liability can be established in case of gross negligence (*faute lourde*). The rule has been recently confirmed in the *Ministre de l'Intérieur c/ Commune de Saint Florent et autres*.[160] Some communes in Corsica had instituted a consortium to realise projects of common interest. The consortium bought some land and started to build structures to host a big country fair. Many administrative decisions taken to execute the project were adopted by an organ of the consortium which was not competent; further they were taken without any preliminary assessment as to both the convenience of the overall idea and the availability of the necessary resources. In the end, the consortium owed millions of French francs and was liquidated. The participant communes were left to shoulder the debts. Not having the resources to meet such high debts, most of the communes went to the local administrative court asking for damages against the State. They claimed that the State was responsible for having failed to stop in an early phase the constant flow of illegalities and the unlawful decisions taken by the consortium. The *Tribunal administratif* of Bastia applied the principle of *faute lourde* (gross negligence) and held the State liable for part of the damage. The *Cour administrative d'appel* of Marseille confirmed the finding of

---

[157] P Soublet, 'Le contrôle des acted des collectivités locales' *Rev adm* 1992, 443.

[158] M Verpeaux, 'La Constitution et les collectivités territoriales' *Rev dr publ* 1998, 1379; many voices, even in the political sphere, have however recently called for the reinstatement of general preventive control on the decisions taken by the local authorities: M Dreifuss, 'Vers une meilleure effectivité du contrôle des contrats des collectivités locales' *Rev dr publ* 1999, 828.

[159] Some of the cases arising from the *Stavisky affaire* had some profiles concerning *tutelle*: for instance CE 29 Mar 1946, *Caisse départmentale d'assurances sociales de Meurthe-et-Moselle c Etat*, *Rev dr publ* 1946, 503, concl Lefas, annotation by G J.

[160] The decisions by the *Cour administrative d'appel* of Marseille and by the *Conseil d'Etat* are both reported, respectively in *Rev fr dr adm* 1999, 1032, concl J-C. Duchon-Doris, and *Rev fr dr adm* 2001, 152, note P Bon; the first instance decision by the *Tribunal administratif* of Bastia has not been reported but the relevant informations can be gathered from the conclusions by J-C. Duchon-Doris.

liability but, following the conclusions of the *Commissaire du Gouvernement* J-C Duchon-Doris, based liability on the ground of *faute simple*.[161] The *Conseil d'Etat* reversed the decisions of the appellate court and reinstated the decision of the first court, albeit reducing to the liability of the State from one third to on fifth of 13.698.810 French francs.[162]

Given the protracted inaction of the supervisory authority, all the niceties concerning the ground of liability, whether *faute lourde* or *faute simple*, had no real impact on the final outcome of the claim for damages in the three courts. In any of them, the State was held liable.[163]

At times, the distinction between *faute* and *faute lourde* is more relevant to the outcome of a case. In the case *Commune de Roquebrune-Cap-Martin*, the commune had granted permission to develop some coastal area, including the building of both holiday houses and a hotel; the permission was invalid, since the area was protected from development, and annulled by the administrative courts on the initiative of some private party; the developer successfully sued the commune for damages consisting in the expenses incurred in relying on the permission which was later quashed. At that point, the communes sued the State arguing that, among other things, the prefect had failed to ask for the annulment of an earlier decision upon which the permission was based. The claim failed in the *Conseil d'Etat* which held that, in the instant case, it was not possible to say that, by not referring the first decision issued by the commune to the administrative courts, the prefect had been guilty of *faute lourde*.[164]

Faute lourde is not always required with reference to liability for the fail-

---

[161] CAA Marseille, 21 Jan 1999, *Ministere de l'Intérieur c/ Commune de Saint Florent et autres*, in *Rev fr dr adm* 1999, 1042, concl J-C Duchon-Doris.

[162] CE 6 Oct 2000, *Ministere de l'Intérieur c/ Commune de Saint Florent et autres*, in *Rev fr dr adm* 2001, 152, note P Bon, 'La responsabilité du fait des actes de tutelle'; in *Act jur Dr adm* 2001, 201, note M Cliquennois; the relevant passage of the decision is the following: 'que le préfet de la Haute-Corse, en s'abstenant pendant trois années consécutives de déférer au tribunal administratif neuf délibérations dont l'illégalité ressortait avec évidence des pièces qui lui étaient transmises et dont les conséquences financières étaient graves pour les communes concernées, a commis compte tenu des circonstances particulières de l'espèce, dans l'exercice du contrôle de légalité qui lui incombait, une faute lourde de nature à engager la responsabiltié de l'État.'

[163] According to P Bon, 'La responsabilité du fait des actes de tutelle' *Rev fr adm* 2001, 152, 153, 'la problématique faute lourde—faute simple ne fait que nourrir des controverses doctrinales stériles et n'a pas forcément pour le justiciable l'importance qu'on leur prête'; it is however submitted that the distinction was of little relevance only because gross negligence was anyway present in the case.

[164] CE 21 June 2000, *Ministre de l'Équipement, des Transports et du Logement c/ Commune de Roquebrune-Cap-Martin*, in *Rev fr dr adm* 2000, 1096, n P Bon 'La responsabilité du fait des actes de tutelle'; the relevant passage of the decision is states: 'Considérant que la circumstance que le préfet des Alpes-Maritimes s'est abstenu de déférer au tribunal administratif le plan d'occupation des sols de la Commune de Roquebrune-Cap-Martin sur le fondement du quel a été délivré le permis de construire litigieux, ne revêt pas le caractère d'une faute lourde, seule de nature à engager en pareil cas la responsabilité de l'État envers la commune'.

ure to properly exercise powers of *tutelle*. In *Sté de gestion du port de Campoloro et Sté fermière de Campoloro*, two firms which were creditors of the local commune had sued the State arguing that it had not been diligent enough to prompt the commune into paying. The action failed in the *Conseil d'Etat*, which remarked that the prefect had written many times to the commune to ask for the payments to be made and had even seized the court competent with reference to local financial matter to force the commune to set aside the money necessary to the payments.[165] The fact the *Conseil d'Etat* used the words *'le préfet n'a commise aucune faute'* is enough to conclude that *faute lourde* is not required (and, of course, it was *a fortiori* to be excluded on the facts of the case).[166]

Tutelle activities are highly formalised. The cases usually turn on administrative decisions taken and—more often than not—around decisions not taken. They can be easily analysed in terms of illegal acts or omissions. The choice between *faute* and *faute lourde* is one between a situation where an illegal action or inaction is enough to establish liability, and one where something more is needed. What more could be termed negligence, but it is often made of reiterated illegal acts and/or illegally protracted inaction.

One last remark concerning the constitutional background allowing the State to be liable to local authorities for the damages they have created themselves with their illegal behaviour. *Tutelle* is rooted in the idea that local authorities are not alone responsible for the efficient self-government of their respective communities; the State is always present, looking over the shoulders of local authorities with the aim, in theory at least, to protect local communities; if the State fails, local communities are harmed and local authorties can sue.

2. Italian Courts Coming To Terms With Liability

On 16 September 1959, at 6.45 pm a residential building collapsed in Barletta, a town in the Southern Italy region of Apulia. Fifty-eight people died and many more were injured. The building had originally been a one-floored row of garages. Then, in 1957, a firm had asked the local authority permission to build three more flat floors on the top of it. Permission was granted after the project submitted by the firm had been reviewed by the technical building commission of the local authority; the commission only required some minor aesthetic changes. The project was in breach of

---

[165] CE 10 Nov 1999, *Sté de gestion du port de Campoloro et Sté fermière de Campoloro*, in *Rev fr dr adm* 2000, 1096, n P Bon 'La responsabilité du fait des actes de tutelle'.

[166] P Bon, 'La responsabilité du fait des actes de tutelle' *Rev fr dr adm* 2000, 1096, 1100: 'Il est clair que, si le Conseil d'État avait entendu maintenir l'exigence traditionnelle de la faute lourde, il aurait affirmé que le préfet n'a commis aucune faute lourde.' So much for the ability to infer legal rules from the silences of the French courts!

many existing building regulations and was ridden with obvious mistakes in the way engineering calculations had been made. The project was further incorrectly executed, resulting in breach of the licence that had been granted. Even before the building was completed, however, the local authority issued a certificate stating that it was fit for human dwelling. An action for damages was brought by some of the victims and their relatives against the local authority. It 'snailed' all the way up to the *Corte di cassazione* which handed down its judgment in 1978.[167] The court, on what it claimed to be the true construction of relevant statutes, held that all the powers conferred on local authorities were aimed to protect the general interest to a more harmonious development of town and villages, and this both from the socio-economic and the aesthetic points of view, minding also the further general interest to minimal hygienic conditions of dwellings. The relevant provisions were not minded to confer any rights to specific individuals. According to the established national catchwords, only *interessi legittimi* but not *diritti soggettivi* flew from those rules, and this also due to the discretionary nature of many of the powers vested into the local authority.

One could say that the local authorities have a duty to the general public to allow only beautiful and sterilised dwellings, never mind if they fall down killing some dozen specific and named individuals. The court totally failed to appreciate that, even if the tragic story was riddled with illegal decisions, public law remedies were of no help to those harmed.

The same approach characterised the first judgments concerning the (non)liability of those bodies charged with supervising financial institutions. The only uncertainty centred on whether damages actions brought by depositors and investors had to be struck out as inadmissible because dealing with *interessi legittimi* or simply to fail because no civil law liability could attach to supervising authorities.[168]

A first change of mind took place at the beginning of the 1990s. A liabil-

---

[167] Cass, Sez un., 17 novembre 1978, n 5346, in *Giust civ* 1979, I, 17, with critical annotation by A Postiglione 'La tutela della salute nell'urbanistica e la responsabilità della pa nel caso di rovina di edificio'.

[168] Eg, Cass, Sez un, 29 Mar 1989, n 1531, in *Giur it* 1990, I, 1, 440, with note by F Vella, 'Proposta di avvio della procedura di liquidazione coatta amministrativa nei confronti delle imprese di vigilanza e responsabilità degli organi di vigilanza', and in *Banca, Borsa e Tit Cred* 1990, II, 425, with note by n Marzona, 'Limiti (attuali) e prospettive del raccordo tra tutela del risparmio e funzione di controllo', and Cass, Sez un., 14 Jan 1992, n 367, in *Giur. it.* 1993, I, 1, 1795, with note by F Satta 'La lesione di interessi legittimi: variazioni giurisprudenziali sull'inammissibilità del risarcimento e principi comunitari'; in *Resp civ prev* 1993, 332, con nota di R Caranta, 'Problemi di responsabilità degli organi di vigilanza sui mercati mobiliari'; in *Giust civ* 1992, I, 2727, with note by C Santoriello, 'Nuovi orientamenti in tema di ripartizione della giurisdizione fra giudice ordinario e giudice amministrativo', and in *Banca, Borsa e Tit Cred.* 1992, II, 393, with note by n Marzona, 'Le posizioni soggettive del risparmiatore secondo il giudice della giurisdizione: una difficile tutela'.

ity action was brought personally against a former Minister for the Industry, commerce and crafts, Mr Altissimo. That is in itself a rare occurrence; it is true that under Article 28 of the Italian Constitution all public servants are individually and personally responsible for breaches of individual rights; civil actions are however usually brought against public bodies whose solvency is not in doubt.[169] The minister was the authority then responsible for supervision of financial institutions other than banks. A number of claimants claimed that he had revoked the authorisation to one of such institution due to serious mismanagement, but, at the same time, he had allowed it to transfer its activities to another company being part of the same financial group. The latter company had later collapsed leading to financial losses for the claimants. Mr Altissimo defended himself claiming that as a supervisory authority he enjoyed wide discretionary powers; even if he had been mistaken in the use he had made of his powers, the depositors could only claim a breach of *interessi legittimi* not sounding in damages. The *Corte di cassazione* departed from its earlier case law and adopted an approach we will meet again concerning the performance of operational tasks. It held that in principle the public authority has to comply with the *neminem laedere* principle even when it exercises discretionary powers. More pointedly, and with a shift from the aforementioned principle we need not to be concerned with here, the *Corte di cassazione* held that depositors could claim a *diritto soggettivo* of theirs had been breached if they could show that the Minister had acted or failed to act in ways falling outside the limits of his discretionary powers.[170] The case was then referred back to a lower court for a new trial and the same approach was followed in subsequent decisions.[171]

So far the case law was in line with the more general approach holding the civil courts could not be called to investigate the way public authorities had used their discretionary powers, discretionary powers being linked with *interessi legittimi* whose breach could not sound in damages. In a way, public law limited the depth of judicial inquiry concerning liability actions. When in 1999 the *Corte di cassazione* overruled the principle that no claim for damages could arise from the breach of *interessi legittimi*, the conditions were laid down for further developments in the case law concerning the liability of supervisory authorities.

---

[169] M Clarich, 'The Liability of Public Authorities in Italian Law' in J Bell and AW Bradley *Governmental liability: A Comparative Study* (London: UKNCCL, 1991), 207, 233 ff.

[170] Cass, Sez un, 2 June 1992, n 6667, in *Resp civ prev* 1993, 576.

[171] Cass, Sez un, 27 Oct 1994, n 8836, in *Giust civ* 1995, I, 1295; in *Banca, Borsa e Tit cred* 1995, II, 525, with note by C Scognamiglio, 'Responsabilità dell'organo di vigilanza bancaria e danno meramente patrimoniale'; Cass, 27 July 1998, n 7339, in *Foro it.* 1999, I, 2001, with note by A Palmieri, 'Il comunicato mistificatorio costa caro all'amministrazione (ma incombe la responsabilità per omessa o cattiva vigilanza).'

This is what happened with the sudden twist taken by one of the cases springing from the Cultrera crack when it surfaced again in front of the *Corte di cassazione*. A company controlled by Cultrera asked the public for money to finance the development of some tourist facilities on prime seafront estates. To do so under the relevant legislation in force at the time, it had to have a brochure detailing the conditions of the operation approved by the CONSOB, the Italian financial market watchdog. The brochure was submitted to and approved by the CONSOB and the company was thus allowed to press the public for money. The brochure was riddled with false statements, most prominent among them one claiming that the real estates were already the property of another company of the same group. In due time the entire scheme collapsed and the angry depositors turned themselves against the CONSOB. The first time the case reached the *Corte di cassazione*, the Court held that the liability action had to fail because investors could claim only *interessi legittimi* as to the way the CONSOB used its powers and send the case back to a lower court to be dismissed.[172] The lower court considered the powers delegated to the CONSOB by the legislature to be limited to a rather formal control that the brochure was filled with all the information required by the law and not to include any verification as to the correctness of the same; it then dismissed the case claiming that it could not be shown that the CONSOB had acted outside its powers. The case came back to the *Corte di cassazione*—a usual occurrence in Italy—and this time the Court reversed its previous approach (this is less usual). It claimed that the CONSOB had the power to check the reliability of the information given in the brochure and that anyway liability of supervisory authorities was not limited to cases were they acted outside the limits of their discretion. Quite on the contrary, they could be liable also for failing to perform the tasks assigned to them in the public interest.[173]

The case has been sent back once more to the trial judge which will have to assess which damages were inflicted upon the investors because the CONSOB failed to notice that the brochure contained false statements (which was apparent from the documents which the supervisory authority

---

[172] Cass, Sez un, 14 Jan 1992, n 367, in *Giur it* 1993, I, 1, 1795, with note by F Satta, 'La lesione di interessi legittimi: variazioni giurisprudenziali sull'inammissibilità del risarcimento e principi comunitari'; in *Resp civ prev* 1993, 332, con nota di R Caranta, 'Problemi di responsabilità degli organi di vigilanza sui mercati mobiliari'; in *Giust civ* 1992, I, 2727, with note by C Santoriello, 'Nuovi orientamenti in tema di ripartizione della giurisdizione fra giudice ordinario e giudice amministrativo', and in *Banca, Borsa e Tit Cred* 1992, II, 393, with note by n Marzona, 'Le posizioni soggettive del risparmiatore secondo il giudice della giurisdizione: una difficile tutela.'

[173] Cass, 3 Mar 2001, n 3132, in *Resp civ prev* 2001, 562, with note by Caranta, 'Responsabilità della CONSOB per mancata vigilanza e futuri problemi di giurisdizione', e in *Giust civ* 2001, I, 907, with note by G Giacalone, 'Prospetto non veritiero e responsabilità della Consob.'

had received) and also failed to take any action whatsoever after the false statements were denounced in the national press.

This decision firmly roots liability of supervisory authority in the law of negligence. Public law provisions are relevant to define the scope of the powers conferred to those authorities. Once powers are defined, it is up to the courts to assess whether they were exercised with due care to the benefit of investors

3. English Court: Not Ready To Follow (For Now?)

English cases falling under this category concern two different factual situations. On the hand we have unduly licensed buildings that later turn out to be defective. On the other hand we have decisions dealing with the consequences flowing from what is claimed to be insufficient supervision of financial institutions.

Unsound foundations have sparked one of the most spectacular judicial changes in the last years. The first relevant decision by the House of Lords is *Anns v Merton London Borough Council.*[174] Lessees under long leases of structurally defective flats brought an action in damages for negligence against the local authority claiming that the defects were due to negligence by the defendant in allowing the builders to construct the block upon foundations which were only 2 feet 6 inches deep instead of 3 feet or deeper as required by the deposited plans, alternatively in failing to carry out the necessary inspections sufficiently carefully or at all, a result of which the structural movement occurred. The case went to the House of Lords as a preliminary point of law. Lord Wilberforce stated that, in order to establish whether in a given situation the defendants owed the claimants a duty of care:

it is not necessary to bring the facts of that situation within those of previous situations in which a duty of care has been held to exist. Rather the question has to be approached in two stages. First one has to ask whether, as between the alleged wrongdoer and the person who suffered damages there is a sufficient relationship of proximity or neighbourhood such that, in the reasonable contemplation of the former, carelessness on his part may be likely to cause damage to the latter—in which case a prima facie duty of care arises. Secondly, if the first question is answered affirmatively, it is necessary to consider whether there are any considerations which ought to negative, or to reduce or limit the scope of the duty or the class of person to whom it is owed or the damages to which a breach of it may give rise.[175]

---

[174] [1978] AC 728 (HL).
[175] *Anns v Merton London Borough* [1978] AC 728 (HL) 751 f; reservations as to the correctness of this test have been expressed in many subsequent cases: *Murphy v Brentwood District Council* [1991] 1 AC 398 (HL) 461 (Lord Keith) and more references there.

The House of Lords held that a situation of sufficient proximity exists between the public authority and the owners and occupiers of the houses. That was not enough to decide the case.[176] To define the scope of the duty of care owed to the claimants, Lord Wilberforce referred to the policy (or discretionary) and operational dichotomy first introduced in *Dorset Yacht v Home Office*,[177] a decision which will be analysed later; his Lordship made clear that the distinction is rather a matter of degree, since even operational decisions can allow for some elements of discretion.[178] In the end, 'A plaintiff complaining of negligence must prove, the burden being on him, that action taken was not within the limits of a discretion bona fide exercised, before he can begin to rely upon a common duty of care.'[179]

Anns was one of the few decisions by the House of Lords which was later to be departed from by the same court.[180] Defective foundations were again litigated in *Murphy v Brentwood District Council*.[181] The House of Lords held that no duty of care was placed on the public authority to protect buyers from purely economic losses due to latent defects in buildings. A principle of negligence liability was considered to be limited to cases where there is 'physical damage to person or to property other than the property which gave rise to the damage and where there was no reasonable opportunity of discovering the defect which ultimately caused the damage'.[182] Proximity had to be dealt with differently in cases where pure economic damage is present. It was deemed not sufficient to establish a prima facie duty of care.[183] The decision was very much influenced by the fact that, as a rule, under both the Defective Premises Act 1972 and the common law, a builder does not owe any duty of care in tort in respect of the quality of his work.[184] It was impossible to hold the local authority liable for defects where the builder was not.[185]

Vigilance cases indeed call for the existence of an 'immediate' tortfeasor which in the end is found wanting.[186] Public law issues were remarkably

---

[176] *Anns v Merton London Borough* [1978] AC 728 (HL) 753 f (Lord Wilberforce).
[177] [1970] AC 1004 (HL).
[178] 755 ff; public law is almost absent in Lord Salmon's speech, which was the only other fully reasoned judgment in that case.
[179] 755.
[180] In *D and Estates Ltd v Church Commissioners of England* [1989] AC 177 (HL), the House of Lords went out of its way trying to reconcile *Anns* with pre-existing case law.
[181] [1991] 1 AC 398 (CA and HL).
[182] *Murphy v Brentwood District Council* [1991] 1 AC 398 (HL) 492 (Lord Jauncey).
[183] Ibid, 487 (Lord Oliver).
[184] *D and F Estates Ltd v Church Commissioner of England* [1989] AC 177 (HL); liability of the builder was again ruled out in *Department of the Environment v Thomas Bates and son Ltd* [1991] 1 AC 499 (HL).
[185] *Murphy v Brentwood District Council* [1991] 1 AC 398 (HL) 481 (Lord Bridge).
[186] '[t]he injury of which the plaintiffs complained in *Anns* was not "caused" by the defendant authority in any accepted sense of the word. The complaint was not of what the defendant had done but of what it had not done. It had failed to prevent the builder of the flats from

absent from the reasoning in Murphy. The question 'whether, if personal injury were suffered by an occupier of defective premises as a result of a latent defect in those premises, liability in respect of that personal injury would attach to a local authority which had been charged with the public law duty of supervising compliance with the relevant building bylaws or regulations in respect of a failure properly to carry out such a duty', was however expressly left open by the House of Lords.[187]

Claims concerning the supervision of financial institutions have so far failed in English (and Commonwealth) courts. The Privy Council has decided the leading cases. In Yuen Kun Yeu *v* Attorney-General of Hong Kong[188] the claimants, having lost money due to the insolvency of a registered deposit-taking company, sued the Commissioner of Deposit-Taking Companies in Hong Kong claiming damages for negligence and alleging that the Commissioner knew or ought to have known, had he taken reasonable care, that the company's business was being conducted fraudulently, speculatively and to the detriment of depositors. The Privy Council reviewed all the classical authorities relating to the tort of negligence and tackled the proximity requirement: 'The primary and all-important matter for consideration [...] is whether in all the circumstances of this case there existed between the commissioner and would-be depositor with the company such close and direct relations as to place the commissioner, in the exercise of his function under the ordinance, under a duty of care towards would-be depositors.'[189] A relevant factor was considered to be whether the aim of the relevant legislation was the protection of individual depositor. The Council held that legislation was passed with the aim of protecting the public at large rather than conferring rights on individuals and, consequently, that the Commissioner owed no statutory duty to individual depositors. In these circumstances, 'it would be strange that a common law duty of care should be superimposed on such a statutory framework'.[190] Proximity was further to be excluded since the Commissioner had no control on the day-to-day management of the deposit-taking company.[191]

---

erecting a sub-standard structure': *Murphy v Brentwood District Council* [1991] 1 AC 398 (HL) 483 (Lord Oliver); 'If, then, the law imposes upon the person primarily responsible for placing on the market a defective building no liability to a remote purchaser for expenditure incurred in making good defects which, *ex hypothesi*, have injured nobody, upon what principle is liability in tort to be imposed upon a local authority for failing to exercise its regulatory powers so as to prevent conduct which, on this hypothesis, is not tortious?' 489 (Lord Oliver). The situation is possibly different in other common law jurisdictions: IND Wallace, 'The *Murphy* Saga in Australia: *Bryan* in Difficulties?' (1997) 113 *LQR* 355.

[187] *Murphy v Brentwood District Council* [1991] 1 AC 398 (HL) 457 (Lord Mackay) 463 (Lord Keith); according to Lord Hoffmann in *Stovin v Wise* [1996] AC 923 (HL) 947, 'the tone of their Lordships' remarks on this question was somewhat sceptical'.
[188] [1988] AC 175 (PC). [189] [1988] AC 175 (PC) 194 (Lord Keith).
[190] [1988] AC 175 (PC) 195 (Lord Keith).
[191] [1988] AC 175 (PC) 195 f (Lord Keith).

In *Davis v Radcliffe* the Privy Council disposed of a similar case brought against the Treasurer of the Island of Man and members of the Finance Board.[192]

At times regulatory authorities enjoy legislative immunity from negligence claims. This is the case of the Bank of England under the Banking Act 1987. Cases against the Bank of England must plead torts different from negligence. This is what happened in *Three Rivers District Council v Bank of England*.[193] Some 6,000 depositors who had lost their assets due to the collapse of the BCCI brought an action in damages against the Governor and the company of the Bank of England. They claimed that the Bank was liable for misfeasance in public office in that it had either wrongly granted a licence to BCCI or had failed to revoke the same licence when it knew, believed or suspected that the credit institution was due to go bankrupt. Alternatively, they pleaded that the Bank of England had acted in breach of Community law.

The claim for misfeasance failed both in the Queen's Bench and the Court of Appeal because intention to harm the claimants could not be pleaded on the facts assumed to be true by the claimants.[194] On appeal the House of Lords undertook a comprehensive review of earlier authorities. It held that:

The case law reveals two different forms of liability for misfeasance in public office. First there is the case of targeted malice by a public officer, ie conduct specifically intended to injure a person or persons. This type of case involves bad faith in the sense of the exercise of public power for an improper or ulterior motive. The second form is where a public officer acts knowing that he has no power to do the act complained of and that the act will probably injure the plaintiff. It involves bad faith inasmuch as the public officer does not have an honest belief that his act is lawful.[195]

The House of Lords further held that subjective reckless indifference both as to the illegality of the decision taken and as to its consequences is sufficient to establish liability.[196] On this basis the facts as pleaded could disclose a cause of action but indeed to establish liability for misfeasance of public office and thus holding a supervisory authority liable is still very much an uphill struggle.[197]

---

[192] [1990] 1 WLR 821 (PC).
[193] *Three Rivers District Council v Bank of England (No 3)* [1996] 3 AllER 558 (QB); [2000] 2 WLR 15 (CA); [2000] 2 WLR 1220 (HL).
[194] *Three Rivers District Council v Bank of England (No 3)* [2000] 2 WLR 15 (CA) Auld LJ dissenting.
[195] Ibid, 2 WLR 1220 (HL) 1231 (Lord Steyn).
[196] Ibid, 2 WLR 1220 (HL) 1232 and 1235 (Lord Steyn), .
[197] Ibid, 2 WLR 1220 (HL) 1235 (Lord Steyn) referring to the strict requirement governing the tort under consideration.

No action was found to lay as far as the breach of Community law was concerned. The majority of the Court of Appeal (Hirst and Walker LJJ, Auld LJ dissenting) rather artificially distinguished a Becker-type liability and a *Francovich*-type liability,[198] the difference being based on the assumption that a directive, once transposed in the national legal order, ceases to be the immediate source of rights enforceable by individuals in domestic courts.[199] The distinction, it is respectfully submitted, is untenable considering the well established case law of the Court of Justice requiring Member States to take specific implementing measures to make sure individuals are well-aware of the Community origins of the rights they derive from directive.[200] The chosen distinguishing hindered the majority of the Court of Appeal from going on and seeing whether the action of the regulatory agency was in line with the provisions of the directives. Moreover, the majority of the Court of Appeal held that the provisions of the directive were not aimed at conferring rights on individuals so that no liability could be established for their breach.[201]

In the House of Lords, no difference between liability types was accepted. Lord Hope held that:

although the appellants' case under Community law is put in different ways and is based on both types of liability, the conditions which the plaintiffs must satisfy in order to establish a right to damages against the Bank under each route are so closely analogous that they can be taken to be, at this stage of the case, the same. The critical questions in this appeal [...] are whether the Directive of 1977 entails grant of rights to individual depositors and whether the content of those rights is identifiable on the basis of the provisions of the Directive.[202]

The House of Lords unanimously held (but not without a lengthy debate) that the relevant Community law was not aimed at conferring individual rights upon the depositors but rather to harmonise the banking sector.[203]

This conclusion is open to doubts, but the House of Lords deemed

---

[198] The reference being respectively to the ECJ decisions in Case 8/81 *Becker v Finanzamt Münster-Innenstadt* [1982] ECR 53 and in Joined cases C-6/90 and 9/90 *Francovich v Italy* [1991] ECR I-5357.

[199] *Three Rivers District Council v Bank of England (No 3)* [2000] 2 WLR 15 (CA) esp 77 ff.

[200] C-29/84 *Commission v Germany* [1985] ECR 1661, para 18; detailed analysis in S Prechal, *Directives in European Community Law* (Oxford: UOP, 1995) 89 ff.

[201] *Three Rivers District Council v Bank of England (No 3)* [2000] 2 WLR 15 (CA) 84 f; contrast 134 ff (Auld LJ); Auld LJ's approach was followed but led to opposite conclusions in *Three Rivers District Council v Bank of England (No 3)* [2000] 2 WLR 1220 (HL) 1239 ff (Lord Hope) and esp 1271 ff (Lord Millet).

[202] *Three Rivers District Council v Bank of England (No 3)* [2000] 2 WLR 1220 (HL) 1242; also 1258.

[203] Ibid, 2 WLR 1220 (HL) esp 1257 (Lord Hope); Lord Millet put more emphasis on the specific provisions of the directive rather than on the overall aim of the directive itself (1271).

unnecessary any referral to the European Court of Justice under Article 234 (formerly 177) of the EC Treaty.[204]

Claims concerning the supervision of financial institutions cases in England turn around and usually fail on the application of the *Normzwechtheorie*. Questions as to the legality of the measures taken and of the overall action of the supervisory authority are not decisive. They are however one of the issues to be assessed when misfeasance is pleaded.

B. Cases Relating to the Performance of Operational Tasks or the Provision of Services to the Public

Illegality is quite in the background when harm flows from the way in which an operational task is performed or a service is provided to one member of the public. Of course, decisions concerning the provision of resources and staff to a given branch of the administration are relevant to the average performance of administrative tasks. Individual cases of medical malpractice or malfunctioning of a rescue service, for instance, cannot however be simply dismissed as the statistically necessary outcome of limited resources. Statistics need unlucky people but specific aspects concerning the way the task was performed or the service was provided in the individual case usually deserve to be taken into consideration; aspects relating to the individual situation normally bear heavily on the unsatisfactory result.

1. Ever Extending the Liability of the French Government

As a rule, when French authorities are given powers to be exercised for the benefit of the public at large, they are supposed to meet standards laid down by the courts themselves. If they fall below those standards, the requirement of fault is considered to have been met and they are held responsible for the damages accrued.[205]

These standards have nothing to do with legality or other public law issues. When the courts speak about fault (*faute*), they mean negligence.

---

[204] Ibid, 2 WLR 1220 (HL) 1258 (Lord Hope): 'I am of the opinion that it would not be appropriate for a reference to be made to the European Court on the critical question in this case, which is whether the Directive of 1977 entailed the granting of rights to individual depositors and potential depositors. I consider that this matter, on which I understand your Lordships to be unanimous and on which we have had the benefit of very full and helpful submissions both orally and in writing from both sides, is acte claire'; ibid, 2 WLR 15 (CA) 85 (Lord Hirst and Lord Walker) decided not to refer as a matter of discretion and considering that all the parties had asked to Court not to refer.

[205] Indeed, liability rules allow French administrative courts to 'standardise' 'the organisation and functioning of the different public services': M-A de Latournerie, 'The Law of France', in Bell and Bradley, op cit, 207.

(a) Liable as Private Individuals Are

In France administrative courts have jurisdiction also with reference to situations that are in no way different to those concerning relationships as between individuals. This is the case, for instance, of surgical or other medical operations. Here again, the trend is to abandon the requirement of gross negligence and, at times, even mere negligence is not required.[206] Concerning the health services, and specifically the performance of *actes médicaux*, the requirement of *faute lourde* was dropped in 1992.[207] *Faute simple* is normally read with reference to standards of properly working health services (*faute dans l'organisation du service*); the health service is easily held responsible due to the application of rules referring to *faute résultat*: if things went wrong it is up to defendant to show that this was not due to any shortcoming in the organisation of its services.[208] In this field liability can also be attached simply to the fact that no information as to the potential risks were given to patients prior to the operations.[209]

(b) Emergency Services

The case law concerning emergency services has long been one of the preserves of *faute lourde*. Indeed, since the 1905 *Tommaso Grecco* decision (which will be mentioned below), French administrative courts had paid attention to the specific difficulties in dealing with emergency situations.[210]

Things, however, have dramatically changed over the past ten years, with the result of making it easier for claimants to get damages.

The turning-point occurred at first in respect of the ambulance service. Mr Theux had suffered severe head injuries while playing rugby. The emergency service arrived immediately on the spot and, due to the serious condition of the victim, asked for an ambulance helicopter that took off but, due to the incoming darkness, desisted from achieving the rescue operation. The rescue party on land was informed after 15 minutes and decided to use a road ambulance that took some hours to arrive to an hospital with the necessary surgical facilities. Mr Theux, who in the end was left permanently

---

[206] J Waline, 'L'évolution de la responsabilité extracontractuelle des personnes publiques', in *Etudes et documents du Conseil d'Etat* 1994, 459; C Pollmann, 'L'étendue du contrôle de cassation du Conseil d'État en matière de responsabilité extra-contractuelle des personnes publiques', *Rev dr publ* 1996, 1653, 1658.

[207] CE, Ass, 10 Apr 1992, *M et Mme V, Rec CE* 1992, 171.

[208] The emergence of this trend is charted by M Paillet, *La faute du service èublic an droit administratif français* (Paris: LGDJ, 1980), 201 ff.

[209] Recently CE 5 Jan 2000, *Cts Telle*, and CE 5 Jan 2000, *Assistance publique—Hôpitaux de Paris*, both discussed by M Guyomar—P Collin in *Rev fr dr adm* 2000 137.

[210] CE 10 Feb 1905, *Tommaso Grecco*, D 1906, III, 81, concl Romieu; the conceptual framework at the time was still a little bit uncertain: M Deguergue, *Jurisprudence et doctrine dans l'élaboration du droit de la responsabilité administrative* (Paris: LGDJ, 1994), 210 ff.

disabled, sued the emergency service both for the failure to use a helicopter and the delay in informing those on the spot of the aborted flight. The action was rejected by the lower courts which applied the *faute lourde* requirement. The action failed also in the *Conseil d'Etat*; however, following the conclusions of the *Commissaire du gouvernement* Stahl, the supreme French administrative court placed itself on the ground of *faute*, thus effectively abandoning the requirement of *faute lourde*.[211]

As usual, the reasons for departing from earlier case law are not discussed in the judgment. Indeed, they are not even mentioned and, since the action is dismissed anyway, the change in the case law is made apparent only from the fact that the *Conseil d'Etat* refers to *faute* instead of *faute lourde*. The conclusions of the *Commissaire du gouvernement*, however, make clear that the reference to the *faute lourde* is today considered out of pace with common sensibility.[212] The same conclusions state that the requirement of *faute* is malleable enough to meet the exigencies which justified the recourse to *faute lourde*, namely to avoid emergency services working in difficult conditions being held responsible for any mistake. The *Commissaire du gouvernement* suggests that in assessing were the rescuers were negligent it will be necessary to consider the difficulties implied in the rescue operation as well as the circumstances—first among them the urgency—under which the rescue was performed.[213] With a remarkable opposition to the English way, the *Commissaire du gouvernement* maintains that the courts will give a harder look to the planning phase of rescue operations rather than to the specific rescue operations, the latter only being conducted under the constraint of urgency.[214]

---

[211] CE 20 June 1997, *Theux*, in *Rev fr dr adm* 1998, 82, concl J-H Stahl; the relevant passage of the decision held: 'Considérant qu'eu égard aux conditions météorologiques et de visibilités existant vers 21 h 25 le jour de l'accident, la décision de renoncer au transport du malade par hélicoptère n'a pas constitué une faute de nature à engager la responsabilité du centre hospitalier; que la circonstance que M Theux n'a pu être opéré qu'à 2 h 30 du matin est imputable, non au retard de quelque minutes avec lequel le SAMU de Toulouse aurait prévenu les sapeurs-pompiers de Masseube de l'impossibilité du transport du blessé par hélicoptère mais aux difficultés de son transport par la route en raison de la gravité de ses blessures; Considérant qu'il ensuite de là qu'en l'absence de toute faute du centre hospitalier régional [. . .] M. Theux n'est pas fondé a se plaindre [. . .]'.

[212] *Rev fr dr adm* 1998, 82, 86: 'Nous croyons en effet que le régime de la faute lourde, héritage d'un ancien principe d'irresponsabilité, est maintenant perçu par les justiciable comme une limitation injustifié de la responsabilités des personnes publiques.'

[213] *Rev fr dr adm* 1998, 82, 87.

[214] *Rev fr dr adm* 1998, 82, 87: 'La ligne de partage entre faute et erreur non fautive pourrait d'ailleur varier selon que la défaillance à l'origine du dommage résulte de l'organisation ou de l'exécution des secours; l'exigence sera plus forte vis-à-vis de l'organisation des secours, du moins lorsque sera en cause la planification préalable des opération, hors de la contrainte d'urgence. L'exigence nous paraît devoir être moindres pour les tâches d'exécution des secours, pour lesquelles la contrainte de l'urgence s'avère prégnante.'

The same evolution has taken place with reference to fire fighting.[215] In the case of *Mme Michaux*,[216] Madame Michaux and her insurer sued the Local Council of Hannappes on the basis that the fire fighters called to put out the fire at Madame's home had not been able for more than half an hour to start the engine of the water cannon they had brought on the place. The relevant passage of the decision by the *Conseil d'Etat* runs:

Considérant qu'il resulte de l'instruction que le pompiers du Service départemental d'incendie et de secours des Ardennes n'ont pu mettre en marche la moto-pompe transportée sur les lieux qu'avec un retard compris entre trente et quarante minutes; que, dès lors qu'il n'est pas établi que la défaillance de ce matériel soit imputable à un cas fortuit, ce retard est constitutif d'une faute de nature à engager la responsabilité de la commune.[217]

The reasoning is dense as is always the case with French judgments. The fact, however, that faute only is mentioned as a pre-condition of liability, indicates that the requirement of gross negligence has been dropped.[218]

In the end, considering the situation when the fire fighters arrived on the spot, the *Conseil d'Etat* thought appropriate the finding of the *tribunal administratif* holding the commune liable for the added damages due to delay in the rescue operation; added damages were held to be equivalent to 20 per cent of the costs for rebuilding the house.[219]

The same evolution is taking place with reference to the prevention of emergency situations. As already recalled, a recent judgment by the *Cour administrative d'appel* in Lyon has found both the State and a local authority having authorised the opening of a camping close to a river liable for the damages following a flood;[220] their authorisations were considered to have been negligent since a similar flood had occurred

---

[215] See also, with reference to high sea rescue operations, CE 13 Mar 1998, *M Améon*, in *Act jur Dr adm* 1998, 461; in this case the State was found not liable since no negligence was shown in the way the emergency service had acted.

[216] CE 29 Apr 1998, *Commune de Hannappes*, in *Rev dr publ* 1998, 1012.

[217] Ibid, 1012, 1013: 'considered that the instruction has established that the fire fighters were able to start the engine of the water cannon which they had brought with them only after thirty to forty minutes; that, since no proof was given that the default was due to circumstances outside the control of the fire fighters, the delay amounts to a fault sufficient to establish the liability of the local community' (author's tranalation).

[218] X Prétot, 'La responsabilité des services d'incendie et de secours', in *Rev dr publ* 1998, 1001, 1007 ff.; according to the author, the delay was in any event sufficient to establish a find of *faute lourde*.

[219] CE 29 Apr 1998, *Commune de Hannappes*, in *Rev dr publ* 1998, 1012, 1013: 'que, compte tenu de l'état de l'avancement du sinistre lors de l'arrivée du service d'incendie et de secours, cette faute a eu pour effet d'aggraver les dommages causés par le feu à la maison de Mme Michaux; que le tribunal administratif n'a pas fait une inexacte appréciation de cette aggravation en mettant à la charge de la commune de Hannapes [sic] la réparation de 20 per cent de ces dommages.'

[220] CAA Lyon, 13 May 1997, *M. Balusson et autres*, D 1998, jur, 11, n Ch Schaegis.

many decades before and the ground of liability was *faute* rather then *faute lourde*.[221]

(c) Cases of Strict Liability

At times, fault is not even necessary. For instance, in the case of exceptionally dangerous roads, the State is responsible for the accidents even if no blame can be laid on it (as in the case of insufficient maintenance).[222]

The requirement of fault has been abandoned even with reference to some operations of the health service. The leading case is Bianchi.[223] Mr Bianchi had developed serious neurological problems. To ascertain the origin of his troubles, he underwent a vertebral arteriography. When he woke up from the anaesthetic, he was gravely handicapped and had lost use of his limbs. No fault was found in the way the medical operation had been performed. Despite this the Hospital authority was found liable by the *Conseil d'Etat*. The French supreme administrative court held that, where a medical operation necessary to the diagnostic or the cure of an illness is inherently dangerous, but the chances of the danger materialising are extremely low and there is no reason to believe the concerned person is more at risk than anyone else, the health authority is responsible for the additional harm directly inflicted to the person who has been treated in the hospital, provided that the harm itself was grave in the extreme.[224]

Here again the reasons for the development are apparent from the conclusions of the *Commissaire du gouvernement Serge Daël*. He claims that the principle of equality is the real foundation of governmental liability. The same idea of *responsabilité pour faute* is but an expression of the equality principle and a remedy to the *rupture de l'égalité devant les charges publiques*.[225] Public law is however, and more generally, interested in restoring equality when it has been abnormally altered.[226]

---

[221] J Moreau, 'Responsabilité administrative et sécurité publique', in *Act jur Dr adm* 1999, num spéc, 96, 97.

[222] The leading case is CE, Ass, 6 July 1973, *Dalleau*, *Rec CE* 1973, 482; this condition however is not an easy one to establish: CE, 5 June 1992, *Cala*, in *Rec* 1992, 225.

[223] CE, Ass, 9 Apr 1999, *Blanchi*, in *Rev fr dr adm* 1993, 573, concl S Daël.

[224] 'Considerérant, toutefois, que lorsqu'un acte médical nécessaire au diagnostic ou au traitement du malade présente un risque dont l'existence est connue mais dont la réalisation est exceptionnnelle et dont aucune raison ne permet de penser que le patient y soit particulièrement exposé, la responsabilité du service public hospitalier est engagée si l'exécution de cet acte est la cause directe du dommage sans rapport avec l'état initial du patient comme avec l'évolution prévisible de cet état, et présentant un caractère d'extréme gravité'; in the end, ff 1.500.000 plus interests were awarded.

[225] Also M Deguergue, *Jurisprudence et doctrine dans l'élaboration du droit de la responsabilité administrative* (Paris: LGDJ, 1994), 137 ff.

[226] Conclusions to CE Ass, 9 Apr 1993, *Bianchi*, by S Daël in *Rev fr dr adm* 1993, 573, 577: 'la responsabilité pour faute n'est que le cas le plus évident de rupture de l'égalité devant les charges publiques. La faute pouvant et devant être évitée tout dommage est réputé anormal et constitue une rupture du principe d'égalité compensée par une indemnité. Hors le cas de faute,

A more recent decision has extended this fairly generous case law to medical acts that were in no way necessary and were performed under specific request from the injured person or his/her legal representatives. The parents of Djamel Mehraz, a boy aged 5 of North African origin, had him admitted to the Hôpital Joseph-Imbert in Arles to have him circumcised. Anaesthesia was practised and during the intervention the child's heart failed. He entered a comatose state and never recovered. After one year he died. The boy' mother sued the hospital for damages. The *Conseil d'Etat*, following the conclusions of the *Commissaire du gouvernement*, decided not to distinguish Bianchi and accepted the liability of the hospital where the surgery was performed.[227]

A robust case law is now developing concerning contamination due to blood transfusion. It has already been recalled that this issue has been debated concerning cases of supervisory negligence. The State has been held liable when contamination has taken place after a given moment in 1984, when the danger was finally known.[228] At times, however, damages action are brought with reference to predating transfusion and they are brought against the hospital having performed the transfusion rather than against the authority charged with supervision of the safety of the blood and blood products. The usual defence has of course been that proof cannot be given that contamination actually happened during the period the concerned person stayed in a given hospital; it could very well depend on other causes, such as sexual intercourse. This defence has usually failed. For instance, in the recent decision by the *Tribunal administratif* of Grenoble in the *Sayord* case, damages were sought against a local hospital following contamination by hepatitis C.[229] The court retained the liability of the defendant institution considering that no proof was given by the defendant that the blood transfused was not infected and that no indication existed as to other possible sources of contagion.[230] No better result would have been achieved if

---

le juge est appellé à porte des apprèciation plus délicates sur l'anormalité du dommage, entraînant rupture de l'égalité, et à repartir ainsi les dommages en deux catégories: ceux qui sont légitimement supportés par la victime et ceux qui sont pris en charge par la collectivité [. . .]. En ce sens, rien n'interdit ni exige absolument de dégager de nouveaux cas de responsabilité sans faute.'

[227] CE 3 Nov 1997, *Hôpital Joseph-Imbert d'Arles*, in *Rev fr dr adm* 1998, 82, concl *v* Pécresse; the reasons given are quite the same as those given in CE, Ass, 9 Apr 1993, *bianchi*, in *Rev fr dr adm* 1993, 573, the only difference being that the word '*patient*' has taken the place of the word '*malade*'.

[228] CE, Ass, 9 Apr 1993, *M G, M D, M et Mme B* (three decisions), in *Rev fr dr adm* 1993, 583, concl H Legal.

[229] Tribunal administratif de Grenoble, 21 Feb 2000, *M Syord*, in *Act jur Dr adm* 2000, 665, concl. Sogno, where a number of references to further cases concerning HIV contagion can be found.

[230] Tribunal administratif de Grenoble, 21 Feb 2000, *M Syord*, in *Act jur Dr adm* 2000, 665, 666, 'en l'absence, d'une part, de preuve de l'innocuité du sang administré à M Syord, et en

the defence had pleaded that at the time the transfusions were made there was no way of detecting hepatitis in blood samples. Applying the risk theory, transfusion centres are held to be strictly liable for the defective quality of the blood supplied to their patients.[231]

Strict liability also applies to *Dorset Yacht* type cases, the rationale being that the public has to shoulder the cost of rehabilitation programs which are thought to be in the general interest.[232]

Lately generous liability rules have been extended to other troubled youth assistance measures. David Clatot was placed under the authority of the local social services after having been found guilty of some petty crimes; social services placed him with a foster family for the weekends and during the summer holidays; at a '*fête de village*' one August night Clatot, who was a known troublemaker, had a fight with Michel Fraticola, 2 years his elder, and killed him; Fraticola's parents sued the social services for damages. The *Cour administrative d'appel* in Bordeaux, following the conclusions of its *commissaire du gouvernment Peano*, held the *Département de l'Aude* responsible for the damages due to the criminal act of M Clatot since it was not able to give the proof that the foster parents were not in the position to avoid what had happened.[233] The reasoning here is not based on strict liability, rather on an inversion of the onus of proof. The result, however, is to make a find of liability much easier. To a common lawyer can be of some interest to know that the financial burden argument was addressed by the *commissaire du gouvernement* but quickly dismissed observing that it is not pertinent with reference to public law liability.[234]

In some discrete sectors, strict liability has been the way to allow redress without going all the way in criticising the way the police enforces law and order. The *Couitéas* decisions, concerning a specific refusal to act has already been mentioned.[235] More generally, however, local authorities and now the State are held liable for damages to persons and property due to

---

l'absence, d'autre part, de toute autre sérieux facteur de risque, la contamination ne saurait résulter que des transfusions et administrations des produits sanguins subies par M Syord'; from the point of view of the '*innocuité*' it was fatal to the defendant authority not to be able to name three of the people who had donated the blood transfused to the claimant.

[231] Tribunal administratif de Grenoble, 21 Feb 2000, *M Syord*, in *Act jur Dr adm* 2000, 665, 667: 'eu égard tant à la mission qui leur est [. . .] confiée par la loi qu'aux risques que présente la fourniture de produits sanguins, les centres de transfusion sont responsable, même en l'absence de faute, des conséquences dommageable de la mauvaise qualité des produits furnis'; also CE, Ass, 26 May 1995, *N'Guyen, Rec CE* 1995, 221.

[232] The rule was first laid down by CE 19 Dec 1969, *Établissements Delannoy, Rec* 1969, 595; the rule has been recently applied to minors which have not been sentenced but are under investigation and have been placed into the care of some institution: CE 5 Dec 1997, *Pelle, Rec* 1997.

[233] CAA Bordeaux, Plén, 2 Feb 1998, *Consorts Fraticiola, Rev dr publ* 1998, 579, concl Peano. [234] 584.

[235] Had the refusal been illegal, liability would have been established under the rule equating illegality and fault: CE 21 Aug 1948, *Husson et Dame Chiffre, Rec* 1948, 173.

street violence (so called *faits des attroupements*). Under Article L 2216–3 of the *Code général des collectivités territoriales*, the State is liable for damages inflicted to persons and property by rioting mobs, be it with the use of weapons or not.[236]

2. Almost No Privilege for the Italian Government

Liability cases arising from the performance of operational tasks and the provision of services to the general public usually fall under the jurisdiction of civil courts. Normally courts do not have recourse to the idea of *interessi legittimi* when no formal administrative decision is challenged and what is asked are just damages. Even the fact that the defendant public authorities may enjoy discretionary powers does not, as a rule, lead civil courts to strike out the action as inadmissible.

When faced with liability claims in this area, Italian civil courts have constantly applied the general provisions on tort liability laid down in Article 2043 et seq of the Civil code. Article 2043 provides for a general rule of negligence liability; the following provisions deal with the hypothesis of strict liability (occupier's liability, liability for dangerous things, animals and vehicles). At times courts have had to construe those latter provisions in ways to make them specifically applicable to public defendants. In one instance, Italian courts have shown the pro-defendant activism so specific to French courts.

Specific statutes have severely curtailed claimants' rights in the field of unlawful expropriation.

(a) Of Roads and Animals

Courts have resisted the pressure put on them by claimants to bring roads under the strict liability rules on premises. A long-standing case law lays down that the State or other public bodies responsible for roads cannot be said to 'occupy' them.[237] They are liable according to the general rules on negligence liability.[238] Many cases concern liability for incidents due to

---

[236] 'L'Etat est civilement responsable des dégâts et dommage résultant des crimes et délits commis, à la force ouverte ou par violance, par des attroupements ou rassemblements armés ou non armés, soit contre les personnes, soit contre les biens'; the disposition has been clarified by CE, Ass, 20 Feb 1998, *Sté Etudes et construction de sièges pour l'automobile et autres*, in *Act jur Dr adm* 1998, 1029, note I. Poirot-Mazères; also J Moreau 'Responsabilité administrative et sécurité publique', in *Act jur Dr adm* 1999, num spéc, 96, 98 f.

[237] eg, Cass, 4 Dec 1998, n 12314, in *Giur i.* 1999, 1362; Cass, 10 June 1998, n 5772, in *Giur it* 1999, 1180; an eccentric decision is Cass, 20 Nov 1998, n 11749, in *Resp civ prev* 1999, 733, with note by *v* Rapelli, 'Proprietà pubblica delle strade e presunzione di responsabilità della pa.'

[238] This construction was validated by the Constitutional court: Corte cost. 10 May 1999, n 156, in *Giust civ* 2000, I, 649, with note by S Vitale, 'La responsabilità civile della PA per i danni derivanti da beni pubblici al vaglio della Corte costituzionale: un'occasione sfumata'; in

insufficient maintenance or to obstacles on the roads. The defendant authority is not allowed to plead in their defence that maintenance costs exceed the resources allocated to them, nor can they defend themselves by claiming that they enjoy discretion as to when and how to conduct the works. The general rule is that their discretion is curtailed by the principle of *neminem laedere*.[239] In the end, it is up to the courts to decide if the authority was negligent in not doing work or in doing it in a defective or insufficient way. Damages to be paid can be reduced in case of contributory negligence, for instance because the claimant exceeded the speed limits.[240]

According to a statute passed in the late 1970s with the aim to reinforce wildlife protection, animals in the wild are no more *res nullius*; instead they belong to the State.[241] This way illegal hunting can be prosecuted in the same way as theft. Under Article 2052 of the Civil code, owners and custodians of domestic animals are strictly liable for the damages caused by their animals. The question arose whether the State was also strictly liable for the damages caused by wildlife, usually damages to cultivated fields and orchards but at times even car accidents. Here again the *Corte di cassazione* has many times held that some form of control over the animal is necessary to apply the strict liability rule laid down in Article 2052 Cod civ. The State 'ownership' of wild animals is considered to be *sui generis* and entails no control, so that the State can be liable only if negligence is proven.[242] It is however fair to say that some recent decisions go a long way in imposing on the State onerous measures to prevent damages by wildlife if it is to escape even negligence liability.[243] Moreover, many Regions have passed statutes providing for compensation to be awarded to those, mainly peasants, having suffered harm from wildlife; compensation is normally independent from any negligence on the part of the local authority.[244]

Resp civ prev 1999, 1265, with note by I Peila 'Il concetto di insidia (o trabocchetto) ha superato il vaglio della Corte costituzionale'.

[239] Eg, Cass, 18 May 2000, n 6463, in *Giust civ Mass* 2000, 1053; Cass, 29 Mar 1999, n 2963, in *Resp civ prev* 1999, 1265, with note by I Peila, 'Il concetto di insidia (o trabocchetto) ha superato il vaglio della Corte costituzionale'.

[240] Eg, Cass, 11 Jan 1988 n 35,in *Giust civ Mass* 1988, *fasc* 1.

[241] L. 27 Dec 1977, n 968.

[242] Eg, Cass, 12 Aug 1991, n 8788, in *Giur It* 1992, I, 1, 1795, with observations by F Centofanti; Cass, 15 Mar 1996, n 2192, in *Danno e Resp* 1996, 591, with note by D RESTA 'La PA e i danni cagionati dalla fauna selvatica'.

[243] Cass, 13 Dec 1999, n 13956, in *Giur it* 2000, 1594, with note by OB Castagnaro 'Osservazioni sul criterio di imputazione della responsabilità per danni prodotti dalla fauna selvatica'; many cases concern car accidents provoked by wild animals, expecially boars, which display a remarkable tendency to suddenly cross roads; the problem is not so much to establish as to pinpoint the authority responsible: contrast Giudice di Pace of Torino, three decisions dated respectively Mar 8, 2001, Feb 18, 2001, and July 27, 2000, all reported in *Giur it* 2001, 1634, with note by A Ronco 'Il cinghiale e l'automobile.'

[244] Eg, Cass, Sez un, 29 Nov 2000, n 1232, in *Giur it* 2001; Cass, Sez un, 10 Aug 1999, n 587, in *Danno e Resp* 1999, 1096, with note by C Maresca 'Gli uccelli e l'uva: le Sezioni unite

When refusing to apply strict liability rules to public defendants in the aforementioned situations, Italian courts do not refer to the existence of discretionary powers or to the necessity not to overburden the public purse. They rather point out to the specific conditions of some goods making it impossible to apply rules designed with privately owned goods in mind. Thus, the rules on the occupier's strict liability for damages apply with full force when damages occur on premises over which the public authority has the same kind of power as a private owner.[245]

(b) One Judge-made Instance of Strict Liability

Italian civil courts have applied the ordinary rules laid down in the Civil Code to liability actions arising in an operational context. They have been attentive not to impose strict liability rules in respect of activities that could be distinguished from apparently similar private activities. They haven't imposed any heavier burden on public authorities by reason of their role in society.

There is only one exception to this rule, and it was rather the work of the Constitutional court. The Court first held that when damages were caused in the framework of a compulsory inoculation programme, compensation was due even if no fault can be attributed to the way the vaccination had been performed (for instance because the person suffering harm was one of the very few allergic to the vaccine and there was no way to foretell this condition). The reasoning of the Court was that the public at large had to shoulder the costs for the collateral damages of a programme conducted in the general interest.[246]

The analogy between this reasoning and the rules imposing compensation for expropriation is apparent.

The rule laid down by the Constitutional court was later embodied in a statute,[247] but the Court spoke again to say that the same rule applied to

---

tornano sugli animali famelici'; Cass, Sez un, 30 Dec 1998, n 12901, in *Riv giur ambiente* 1999, 504, with note by M Deledda 'Ancora in tema di risarcibilità dei danni cagionati dalla selvaggina: un ennesimo revirement della Cassazione'; Cass, Sez un, 27 Oct 1995, n 11173, in *Giur it* 1996, I, 1, 570.

[245] Eg, Cass, 26 Jan 1999, n 674, in *Giust civ Mass* 1999, 159; also Trib Potenza, 11 June 1998, in *Foro it* 2000, I, 902 (the latter case arose from the window of some court offices collapsing over a judge).

[246] Corte cost 22 June 1990, n 307, in *Resp civ prev* 1991, 73, with note by D Poletti, 'Danni alla salute da vaccino «antipolio» e diritto all'equo indennizzo'; in *Giur. cost.* 1990, 1874, with note by F. Giardina, 'Vaccinazione obbligatoria, danno alla salute e «responsabilità» dello Stato'; in *Foro it* 1990, I, 2694, with observations by A Princigalli and with note by G Ponzanelli 'Lesione da vaccino antipolio: che lo Stato paghi l'indennizzo!'.

[247] L 25 Feb 1992, n 210; the title is: 'indennizzo a favore dei soggetti danneggiati da complicanze di tipo irreversibile a causa di vaccinazioni obbligatorie, trasfusioni e somministrazione di emoderivati'; the statute covers both inoculations and blood transfusion; compensations were later reduced by L 20 Dec 1996, n 641.

inoculation programme which, even if not made compulsory, had been sponsored by the State.[248]

In a case concerning HIV contamination following surgery, the Court has recently refrained from extending its ruling and imposing full compensation in cases, not falling under any statutory provision or covered only up to a given limit, where harm was unrelated to any public sponsored program.[249]

(c) Unlawful Expropriation

Claimant's rights have been severely curtailed in the field of illegal expropriation. Faced with unlawful taking of private land, civil courts have refrained from ordering the public administration to give the land back to its owner when public work had been built on it. Instead, they have awarded compensation.[250] The legislature has intervened many times to limit compensation to amounts marginally exceeding the sums due for lawful expropriation and these interventions have finally withstood the scrutiny of the Constitutional court (if not of the European court of Human rights).[251]

3. English Governmental Liability (Belatedly) Coming of Age

Negligence has been the tort of choice concerning liability flowing from the execution of operational tasks and the provision of services to the general public. At times, breach of statutory duty too has been pleaded. Quite surprisingly from a Continental point of view, specific public law issue have emerged in the English case law on the matter.[252]

---

[248] Corte cost 26 Feb 1998, n 27, in *Resp civ prev* 1998, 1352, with note by Caranta, 'Danni da vaccinazione e responsabilità dello Stato'.

[249] Corte cost 22 June 2000, n 226, in *Giust civ* 2000, I, 2800.

[250] The *leading case* is Cass, Sez un, 14 Feb 1983, n 1464, in *Foro it* 1983, I, 626, with note of G Oriani, 'Prime osservazioni sulla cd occupazione appropriativa da parte della pa'; many other cases have followed: eg, Cass, Sez un, 21 July 1999, n 483, e in *Giur it* 1999, 2158, with note by G De Marzo, 'Occupazione appropriativa, annullamento del decreto d'espropriazione e decorso del termine di prescrizione'.

[251] Corte cost, 30 Apr 1999, n 148, in *Urbanistica e appalti* 1999, 603, with note by De Marzo, 'Occupazione appropriativa: il nuovo criterio risarcitorio supera indenne il vagli di costituzionalità'; Corte cost, 4 Feb 2000, n 24, in *Resp civ prev* 2000, 82, with note by S Verzaro, 'Sul risarcimento del danno da occupazione acquisitiva: ancora la Corte costituzionale, ancora discutibile, ma con qualche chiarimento'; the Italian rules and case law on the matter have been severely criticized by the European court of Human rights: cases *Albergo Belvedere* and *Carbonara e Ventura* decided on 30 May 2000, both reported in *Riv it dir pubbl comunitario* 2000, 1086, with note by S Bonatti 'Il crepuscolo dell'occupazione acquisitiva'.

[252] Andenas and Fairgrieve, 'Sufficiently Serious? Judicial Restraint in Tortious Liability of Public Authorities and the European Influence' in Andenas (ed) *English Public Law and the Common Law of Europe* (London: Key Haven, 1998) 285, 301, have made clear that 'there is a whole swathe of routine activities pursued by public bodies for which the existence of a

(a) The Story up to X *and* Stovin

The leading case is the House of Lords' decision in *Home Office v Dorset Yacht*.[253] Some Borstal boys took advantage of the lack of vigilance on the part of their supervisors to escape from the island where they were confined. In the process they stole and later damaged a yacht moored offshore. The claimant sued the Home Office alleging negligence in supervising the boys. The defendant pleaded that it owed the claimant no duty of care with respect to the detention of the boys, or to the manner in which they were treated, employed, disciplined, controlled or supervised. The issue of the discretion enjoyed by the defendant authority also arose.

It has already been mentioned that in *Home Office v Dorset Yacht* negligence was dealt with as a question of principle rather than precedent.[254] As far as discretion was concerned, the House of Lords held that:

there may, and almost certainly will, be errors in judgement in exercising such a discretion and Parliament cannot have intended that members of the public should be entitled to sue in respect of such errors. But there must come a stage when the discretion is exercised so carelessly or unreasonably that there has been no real exercise of the discretion which Parliament has conferred. The person purporting to exercise his discretion has acted in abuse or excess of his power. Parliament cannot be supposed to have granted immunity to persons who do that.[255]

The point was more fully elaborated in the speech by Lord Diplock.[256] His Lordship began by recognising that courts are ill-suited to substitute their views as the appropriate exercise of discretion.[257] Administrative decisions or omissions could be challenged only when they fell outside the statutory limits imposed upon the authority's discretion. In the instance, actions by

---

statutory framework makes little or no impact. They include teachers driving a football team to a match in the school minibus, staff serving school lunches, nurses dressing a patient's wounds in a hospital managed by a local health authority.' This position has yet to make effective inroads into the case law.

[253] [1970] AC 1004 (HL).

[254] [1970] AC 1004 (HL) 1026 f (Lord Reid) 1038 (Lord Morris).

[255] 1031 (Lord Reid); his Lordship further remarked that the instant case did not raise any issue of discretion since the officers in charge of the boys had failed to comply with the orders given to them; see also 1037 (Lord Morris): 'liability should not be held to result from what might be an error of judgment on the part of someone making a decision which is within his powers and his discretion to make.'

[256] Especially 1067 ff.

[257] 'The conflicting interests of the various categories of persons likely to be affected by an act or omission of a borstal trainee which has as its consequence his release or his escape are thus different kinds'; 'there is no criterion by which a court can assess where the balance lies between the weight to be given to one interest and that to be given to another. The material relevant to the assessment of the reformative effect on trainees of release under supervision or of any relaxation of control while still under detention is not of a kind which can be satisfactorily elicited by the adversary procedure and rules of evidence adopted in English courts of law or of which the judges (and juries) are suited by their training and experience to assess the probative value' (1067).

the Home Office could be reviewed only where 'the system adopted was so unrelated to any purpose of reformation that no reasonable person could have reached a bona fide conclusion that it was conductive to the purpose. Only then would the decision to adopt it be *ultra vires* in public law.'[258]

Liability cannot therefore be established in case of *intra vires* administrative action.[259] Moreover, policy considerations can lead courts to deny the same existence of a duty of care and thus any liability in negligence.

In the end, while in theory '[a]t first glance a pursuer who alleges that a public authority has been negligent should be in a position no different to anyone seeking damages', in the real world 'difficulties may flow from the mere fact that the defender is a public authority.'[260]

Later cases showed how serious were the hurdles those willing to sue public authorities in damages must face.

In *Hill v Chief Constable of West Yorkshire*[261] the mother of the last of a long series of victims of a serial killer brought an action in her daughter's name against the local police authority. She claimed that they had negligently failed to identify and apprehend the murderer. The question of law was, in the words of Lord Keith:

whether the individual members of a police force, in the course of carrying out their functions of controlling and keeping down the incidence of crime, owe a duty of care to individual members of the public who may suffer injury to person or property through the activities of criminals, such as to result in the liability in damages, on the ground of negligence, to anyone who suffers such injury by reason of breach of that duty.[262]

To answer the question, his Lordship emphasised that:

A chief officer of police has a wide discretion as to the manner in which the duty is discharged. It is for him to decide how available resources should be deployed, whether particular lines of inquiry should or should not be followed and even whether or not certain crimes should be prosecuted. It is only if his decision upon such matters is such as no reasonable chief officer of police would arrive at that someone with an interest to do so may be in a position to recourse to judicial review. So the common law, while laying upon chief officers of police an obligation to enforce the law, makes no specific requirements as to the manner in which the obligation is to be discharged. That is not a situation where there can readily be inferred an intention of the common law to create a duty towards individual members of the public.[263]

---

[258] 1068 (Lord Diplock).

[259] A discussion in the light of more recent cases is to be found in Andenas and Fairgrieve, 'Sufficiently Serious?', 285, 298 ff.

[260] D Brodie, 'Public Authorities and the Duty of Care' [1996] *Juridical R* 127.

[261] [1989] AC 53 (HL).   [262] 59.   [263] 59.

As to the merits of the case, *Home Office v Dorset Yacht*[264] was distinguished in that the Borstal boys had been in the custody of the defendant authority and committed their crime in the act of escaping therefrom, while the serial killer was apprehended only after the murder of Miss Hill.[265] A separate and concurrent ground to deny any liability was however linked to the second stage (the first being proximity/forseeability) of Lord Wilberforce's two stage test in Anns, that is 'whether there are any considerations which ought to negative, or to reduce or limit the scope of the duty or the class of person to whom it is owed or the damages to which a breach of it may give rise'.[266] From this point of view, Lord Keith held that police investigations, which involve 'matters of policy and discretion' should go on unhindered from the possible future tort actions to avoid a 'detrimentally defensive frame of mind.'[267]

Policy reasons to exclude any negligence liability have featured rather prominently in the case law until fairly recently.

In *X (Minors) v Bedfordshire County Council* the House of Lords heard a number of cases concerning both actual or suspected child abuses and failure to properly address some other children's special educational needs.[268] Before going into the detailed analysis of the different cases, Lord Browne-Wilkinson discussed at length the specific questions arising with reference to tort actions relating to the performance of statutory duties to come to the conclusion that 'a common law duty of care cannot be imposed on a statutory duty if the observance of such duty of care would be inconsistent with, or have a tendency to discourage, the due performance by the local authority of its statutory duties'.[269] Forseeability and proximity having been conceded by the defendant authorities, Lord Browne-Wilkinson turned to consider whether it was fair, just and reasonable to impose a duty of care. Referring to *Hill v Chief Constable of West Yorkshire*[270] his Lordship held that the requirement was not confined to cases concerning pure economic loss.[271] He denied that it was fair, just and reasonable to impose a duty of care in the cases under consideration. Besides the difficulties in disentangling the liabilities of the different authorities involved in many of the cases, his Lordship invoked the difficulties of the tasks imposed on the administration, the fear of inducing cautious and defensive approaches, and the existence of alternative remedies in the form of statutory

---

[264] [1970] AC 1004 (HL).
[265] [1989] AC 53 (HL) 62 (Lord Keith).
[266] *Anns v Merton London Borough* [1978] AC 728 (HL) 751 f.
[267] [1989] AC 53 (HL) 63; also 64 f (Lord Templeman).
[268] [1995] 2 AC 633 (CA and HL).
[269] 739.
[270] [1989] AC 53 (HL).
[271] [1995] 2 AC 633 (HL) 749.

complaint procedures.[272] It was conceded that liability claims could stand only with reference to unsound psychological advice to the parents of children with learning disabilities.[273]

Claims based on breach of statutory duty were also disposed of. Lord Browne-Wilkinson held that:

the Acts in question are all concerned to establish an administrative system designed to promote the social welfare of the community. The welfare sector involved is one of peculiar sensitivity, involving very difficult decisions how to strike the balance between protecting the child from immediate feared harm and disrupting the relationship between the child and its parents. Decisions often have to be taken on the basis of inadequate and disputed facts. In my judgment in such a context it would require exceptionally clear statutory language to show a parliamentary intention that those responsible for carrying out this difficult functions should be liable in damages if, on subsequent investigation with the benefit of hindsight, it was shown that they had reached an erroneous conclusion and therefore failed to discharge their statutory duties.[274]

The door was left open only to vicarious liability of the administration for negligence action of its employees and this with reference only to the cases relating to shortcomings in dealing with children having special educational needs.[275]

Policy considerations again were at the root of the different views expressed in *Stovin v Wise*.[276] Mr. Stovin collided with a car driven by Mrs Wise who failed to give him priority at a junction; the failure was partly imputed to a bank on private land adjoining the road which hindered the view of incoming vehicles having right to precedence. This made that particular crossroad dangerous and the highway authority had taken steps to have the bank removed or lowered but failed to pursue them. The case centred upon the liability of the highway authority that had statutory powers to compel the owner of the land to allow works aimed at preventing accidents. Negligence liability of the highway authority had been introduced in 1961 in case of unreasonable failure to properly maintain the

---

[272] 749 ff. and 761 ff; critically eg, SH Bailey and MJ Bowman, 'Public Authority Negligence Revisited' [2000] *CLJ* 85, 94 ff.

[273] 763.

[274] 747; his Lordship further contends that 'It is true that the legislation was introduced primarily for the protection of a limited class, namely children at risk, and until April 1991 the legislation itself contained only limited machinery for enforcing the statutory duties imposed. But in my view those are only pointers in favour of imputing to Parliament an intention to create a private law cause of action. When one turns to the actual words used in the primary legislation to create the statutory duties relied upon in my judgment they are inconsistent with any intention to create a private law cause of action.'

[275] 751 ff and 763 f; Bailey and Bowman, 'Public Authority Negligence Revisited', 85, 98 ff.

[276] [1996] AC 923 (HL); for commentaries J Convey, 'Public or Private? Duty of Care in a Statutory Framework: *Stovin v Wise* in the House of Lords' (1997) 60 *MLR* 559, and MC Harris, 'Powers into Duties—a Small Breach in the *East Suffolk* Wall?' (1997) 113 *LQR* 398.

roads under their responsibility. The situation was however different in *Stovin* since the obstacle to the circulation was not on the road but on the land adjoining it. The claim for negligence went all the way up to the House of Lords where it failed. The majority view was voiced by Lord Hoffmann, with whom both Lord Goff and Lord Jauncey concurred. Lord Hoffmann held that negligence liability for omissions could be engaged only in very exceptional circumstances;[277] his Lordship further contended that this rule was not to be departed from in case the defendant was a public authority; quite on the contrary, 'the liability of a public authority in tort is in principle the same as that of a private person but may be restricted by its powers and duties'.[278] Lord Hoffmann argues that even in case of statutory duties, when no discretion is present, the common law is wary of imposing liability for their breach or for the failure to discharge them; the same should be a fortiori true in case of mere powers.[279] In the end, according to this position:

the minimum preconditions for basing a duty of care upon the existence of a statutory power, if it can be done at all, are, first, that it would in the circumstances have been irrational not to have exercised the power, so that there was in effect a public law duty to act, and secondly, that there are exceptional grounds for holding that the policy of the statute requires compensation to be paid to persons who suffer loss because the power was not exercised.[280]

The case failed on both counts, since, according to Lord Hoffmann, 'the question of whether anything should be done about the junction was at all times firmly within the area of the council's discretion' and that the highway authority was not 'under a public law duty to do the work';[281] moreover, a legislative intent to provide compensation cannot be deduced from the relevant legislation.[282] In the end, 'Drivers of vehicle must take the highway network as they find it. Everyone knows that there are hazardous bends, intersections and junctions. It is primarily the duty of drivers of vehicles to take due care.'[283]

This analysis was forcefully countered by Lord Nicholls, with whom Lord Slynn concurred. Lord Nicholls too accepted that in principle negligence liability for omissions is rather the exception than the rule. Normally, bystanders have no duty to act to help others. Failure to help is thus not tortious. His Lordship however pointed out that things are different with administrative authorities. Referring to the highway authority, he observed that 'The council was more than a bystander. The council had a statutory power to remove this source of danger, although it was not under a statutory

---

[277] 'There are sound reasons why omissions require different treatment from positive conduct' (943).
[278] 947 (emphasis in the text).   [279] 951.   [280] 953.
[281] 957.   [282] 958.   [283] Ibid.

duty to do so.'[284] Praising Anns[285] for having dispelled the belief that no liability could attach the exercise of statutory powers, Lord Nicholls pointed to the necessity of 'coherent, principled control mechanism' to limit new areas of potential liability.[286] Faced with the approach envisaged in Caparo,[287] Lord Nicholls accepted it for want of better tools but was fast in pointing out its shortcomings; he noted that 'The basic test of fair and reasonable is itself open to criticism for vagueness. Indeed, it is an uncomfortably loose test for the existence of a legal duty.'[288] His Lordship held that the features of the case made it fair and reasonable to impose a duty of care on the defendant authority. Those features included the fact that physical injury was at stake, that road users were 'dependent on highway authorities fulfilling their statutory responsibilities', that the authority concerned knew of the danger, that it was in the power of the authority to remove the source of the danger, and the absence of effective remedies in public law.[289] Lord Nicholls also stressed that superimposing a duty of care to the statutory framework in a case such as *Stovin v Wise* did not defeat the aim of the legislator. Parliament wanted highway authorities to make safe driving condition. A 'concurrent common law duty would not impose on the council any greater obligation to act than the obligation already imposed by its public law duties. The common law duty would impose, not a duty to act differently, but a liability to pay damages if the council failed to act as it should.'[290]

(b) Barrett *and After*

'[B]y being too ready to accept at face value policy arguments against the existence of a duty of care, the courts ha[d] been steadily building an immu-

---

[284] 931; later it stated that 'Individuals may suffer loss through the carelessness of public bodies in carrying out their statutory functions. Sometimes this evokes an intuitive response that the authority ought to make good the loss. The damnified individual was entitled to expect better from a public body. Leaving the loss to lie where it falls is not always an acceptable outcome. The authority did not create the loss, but it failed to discharge its statutory responsabilities with reasonable care. Had it behaved properly, the loss would not have occurred' (933). Again, 'Unlike an individual, a public authority is not an indifferent onlooker. Parliament confers powers on public authorities for a purpose. An authority is entrusted and charged with responsabilities, for the public good. The powers are intended to be exercised in a suitable case. Compelling a public authority to act does not represent an intrusion into private affairs in the same way as when a private individual is compelled to act' (935).

[285] [1978] AC 728 (HL); as was pointed out by Convey, 'Public or Private? Duty of Care in a Statutory Framework: *Stovin v Wise* in the House of Lords' (1997) 60 *MLR* 559, 566, 'The spirit of *Anns* shines through Lord Nicholls's speech.'

[286] [1996] AC 923 (HL) 931.

[287] [1990] 2 AC 605 (HL).

[288] [1996] AC 923 (HL) 933; his Lordship further observed that 'no better or more precise formulation has emerged so far, and a body of case law is beginning to give the necessary further guidance as courts identify the factors indicative of the presence or absence of a duty'.

[289] 940.

[290] 936; also 940.

nity from suit for the benefit of public authorities that politicians would not have dared propose for incorporation in a statute.'[291] In later cases, however, English courts seem to have abandoned those positions more favourable to defendant public authorities. This may be the effect of some European Court of Human Rights decisions, such as the Osman case.[292] The result is however come at by carefully departing from the earlier decisions which were examined in the previous section.

The first relevant case is the House of Lords' decision in *Barrett v Enfield London Borough Council.*[293] The defendant authority had taken care of the claimant when he was an infant and placed him with various families and institutions. The claimant alleged that the council had failed to exercise reasonable care in the choice of the placements that lead to a troubled personality. The Court of Appeal struck out the claim holding it disclosed no cause of action.[294] In doing so it relied on *X(Minors) v Bedfordshire County Council.*[295] Even if the situations were not identical, since in Barrett the local authority had taken the child into care, the Court held that the same policy considerations militated to exclude any duty of care.[296] In the House of Lords, Lord Browne-Wilkinson predictably did not change his position as laid down in *X(Minors).*[297] Only, referring to the ECHR's decision in Osman,[298] he allowed the appeal holding that the case had to proceed to trial to find out what precisely the facts were before discussing 'the difficult issues of law.'[299] Lord Slynn, on the contrary, distinguished the situation in *Barrett* from the one in *X(Minors)* noting that in the former 'the child was taken into care'.[300] His Lordship could then come to the conclusion that the considerations militating against the recognition of a common law duty of care were not present in the case under decision.[301] As to the standard of care applicable, Lord Slynn referred to the principle stated in *Bolan v Friern Hospital Management Committee,*[302] a principle limiting the liabilities of those engaged in the medical profession with reference to the standard skills possessed by those in the same profession.[303] Lord Hutton too distinguished *Barrett* from *X(Minors).*[304] As to the standard of care applicable, his Lordship held that:

---

[291] Bailey and Bowman, 'Public Authority Negligence Revisited', 85, 121 f.

[292] *Osman v UK* (1998) 5 BHRC 293.

[293] [1999] 3 All ER 193 (HL); Craig and Fairgrieve, '*Barrett*, Negligence and Discretionary powers' [1999] *PL* 626.

[294] [1998] QB 367 (CA).

[295] [1995] 2 AC 633 (CA and HL).

[296] Reference was also had to Lord Hoffmann's speech in *Stovin v Wise* [1996] AC 923 (HL) 953, holding that only in exceptional circumstances a common law duty of care could be imposed on a statutory framework not expressly or by implication providing a statutory duty.

[297] [1995] 2 AC 633 (CA and HL).   [298] *Osman v UK* (1998) 5 BHRC 293.

[299] [1999] 3 All ER 193 (HL) 195 ff.   [300] 208.

[301] Ibid.   [302] [1957] 1 WLR 582.

[303] [1999] 3 All ER 193 (HL) 212.   [304] 228 f.

When the decisions taken by a local authority in respect of a child in its care are alleged to constitute negligence at common law, the trial judge, bearing in mind the room for differences of opinion as to the best course to adopt in a difficult field and that the discretion is to exercised by the authority and its social workers and not by the court, must be satisfied that the conduct complained of went beyond mere errors of judgment in the exercise of a discretion and constituted conduct which can be regarded as negligence.[305]

Barrett was followed by a momentous decision by the House of Lords, seven law Lords sitting, in *Phelps v Hillingdon London Borough Council*.[306] Phelps dealt again with a series of cases where it was pleaded that different local authorities had failed to provide appropriate educational services to pupils with limited learning abilities due to dyslexia in all instances but one, where the problem was muscular dystrophy. Breach of statutory duty was held not to lay due to the 'general nature of the duties imposed on local authorities' and to the existence of alternative remedies by way of appeal and judicial review.[307] As far as negligence claims were concerned, Lord Slynn quickly dismissed the existence of any public law question of justiciability and squarely placed the case in the category of liability for professional services. This allowed his Lordship to move from the *Caparo* test requiring it to be fair, just and reasonable before imposing any duty of care,[308] to the question 'whether there is any overriding reason in principle why a professional should not owe a duty of care' and 'why, if the duty is broken', 'the authority as employer or principal should not be vicariously liable'.[309]

Liability becomes the rule, rather than the exception, when his Lordship holds that 'it is long and well-established, now elementary, that persons exercising a particular skill or profession may owe a duty of care in the performance' of their tasks.[310]

The reference to *Bolan v Friern Hospital Management Committee*[311] as laying down the standard of care applicable allows Lord Slynn to deny the existence of any policy reason militating against extending the liability of the professional to the local authority.[312] The standard is indeed generous

---

[305] 230.

[306] [2000] WLR 776 (HL).

[307] 789 (Lord Slynn).

[308] *Caparo Industries Plc v Dickman* [1990] 2 AC 605 (HL); this case was indeed quoted by Lord Slynn at 790 and applied in a liberal way at 791 f.; it was given deeper consideration by Lord Clyde, who in any event held the test to have been passed (808 f).

[309] [2000] WLR 776 (HL) 790.

[310] Ibid; Lord Nicholls's speech is built along the same lines: 802 ff.

[311] [1957] 1 WLR 582.

[312] The demise of policy consideration is analysed by Fairgrieve, 'Pushing back the Boundaries of Public Authority Liability. Tort Law Enters the Classroom' [2002] *PL* 288, 294 et seq.

enough to allow room for innocent mistakes due to the complexity of the task imposed on the public authorities.[313]

Barrett was followed in *S v Gloucestershire County Council*,[314] another child abuse case where the child was already in care of the defendant authority.[315]

Barrett may bring about some changes to the case law concerning emergency services too.[316] Following *Hill v Chief Constable of West Yorkshire*[317] the Court of Appeal had struck out negligence claims against the police for failing to properly inspect a shop after an burglar alarm had been activated,[318] against the fire brigade for failing to show up timely on premises where fire had broken out,[319] and against the coast guards in relation to rescue at sea.[320]

In *Kent v Griffths* the claimant suffered an asthma attack at home.[321] An ambulance was called but it took an unreasonable amount of time to get to the claimant's home who consequently suffered a respiratory arrest which caused brain damage. No reason was given for the delay. The defendant relied on the case law following Hill to have the claim struck out. Woolf MR, who gave the only speech, recalled that those precedents were not without critics and observed that, following the ECHR's decision in *Osman*,[322] the House of Lords could be induced 'to adopt a more restrictive approach to the exclusion of liability to categories of cases without first ascertaining their precise facts'.[323] His Lordship then distinguished Kent from other emergency services cases holding that, 'as there were no circumstances which made it unfair or unreasonable or unjust that liability should exist, there is no reason why there should be not liability if the arrival of the ambulance was delayed for no good reason'.[324]

---

[313] [2000] WLR 776 (HL) 792; also 809 (Lord Clyde); concerning direct liability, Fairgrieve, 'Pushing back the Boundaries of Public Authority Liability. Tort Law Enters the Classroom' [2002] *PL* 288, 291–3 points out that the other members of the House of Lords were less positive concerning direct liability of the administrative authority.

[314] [2001] 2 WLR 909 (CA) 932.

[315] 938 (May LJ).

[316] A discussion of some of the cases recalled immediately after in the text in R Mullender 'Negligence, public concerns and the remedying of wrongs' [1997] *CLJ* 14.

[317] [1989] AC 53 (HL).

[318] *Alexandrou v Oxford* [1993] 4 All ER 328.

[319] *Capital & Counties plc v Hampshire County Council* [1997] QB 1004.

[320] *OLL Ltrd v Secretary of State for Transport* [1997] 3 All ER 897.

[321] [2000] 2 WLR 1158 (CA); T Hickman '"And That's Magic!"—Making Public Bodies Liable for Failure to Confer Benefits' [2000] *CLJ* 432.

[322] *Osman v UK* (1998) 5 BHRC 293.

[323] [2000] 2 WLR 1158 (CA) 1168; the House of Lords' decision in *Barrett v Enfield London Borough Council* [1999] 3 All ER 193 was quoted.

[324] [2000] 2 WLR 1158 (CA) 1172.

Wide differences have emerged as to the way French, Italian, and English courts deal with legality issues when deciding governmental liability cases. Those differences are but the result of very different approaches to public law issues in general. Some comparative remarks are possible when this wider picture is taken into account.

A. *Public Law v Private Law*

Public law illegality and private law liability would have made a structurally beautiful albeit incorrect title for this contribution. Since the 1873 *Blanco* decision by the Tribunal des conflits French law has firmly rooted governmental liability in public law.[325]

This has allowed French administrative courts to develop a liability system adequate to the realities of public powers enjoying exorbitant powers in the day-to-day management of the society. Constitutional principles at times dating from the 1789 French revolution, such as that of the *égalité devant les charges publiques*, have been instrumental in allowing compensation in cases where no illegality nor fault were present.[326] It has been claimed that the right to compensation in case of damages due to the construction of public works is at the roots of further developments in governmental liability.[327]

Strict liability has made possible to public authorities to act in the general interest, at the same time offering compensation to those adversely affected by administrative decisions.[328]

Wide powers have come coupled with an effective liability system ready to contribute to redress any abuse. Ready to admit liability when no illegality was present but citizens' rights were limited in the general interest, it was but an easy step to come to the general conclusion that detrimental exercise of exorbitant powers always demanded some form of redress. If possible, damages from illegal action were an easier candidate for redress than damages due to legal decision taken by public powers within the discretion conferred upon them by Parliament.

---

[325] TC 8 Feb 1873, *Blanco*, D 1873, II, 20; M Deguergue, *Jurisprudence et doctrine dans l'élaboration du droit de la responsabilité administrative* (Paris: LGDJ, 1994), 92 ff.

[326] Art 13 of the Revolutionary Human Rights Declaration provides: 'Pour l'entretien de la force publique, et pour les dépenses d'administration, une contribution commune est indispensable: elle doit être également répartie entre tous les citoyens, en raison de leur facultés.'

[327] M Deguergue, *Jurisprudence et doctrine dans l'élaboration du droit de la responsabilité administrative* (LGDJ Paris 1994) 100, speaking of *'priorité de la responsabilité sans faute, qui a vite débordé le cadre des dommage de travaux publics';* for more references see ibid 101 and 145 ff.

[328] P Fombeur, 'Les évolutions jurisprudentielles de la responsabilité sans faute', in *Act jur Dr adm* 1999, num spéc, 100.

French law on governmental liability thus stands for the proposition that public bodies have special, at times exorbitant, powers and duties. Correspondingly, they may incur liabilities that have no correspondent in private law.[329]

The practical outcomes of this position differ markedly with reference to situations where loss flows from an illegal administrative decision and to situations where administrative decisions are far removed in the background, the prejudice flowing from the way a given task is performed or a service is provided. As to the first situation, most liability questions are already solved when considering whether the decision was legal or not. **If the decision is indeed unlawful, only questions relating to causation and to the quantification of damages are left to be solved, normally applying the same criteria derived from private law.** It has already been recalled that French courts don't content themselves with the finding of some illegality. They get into the shoes of the public administration both to check if, set aside some purely procedural and formal illegality, the decision taken by the authority was in the end sound,[330] and, in case of (substantive) legitimate expectations, the chances to get some benefit were serious enough to entitle the claimant to compensation.[331]

Concerning the provisions of services to the public, to which cases concerning supervisory agencies can at times be compared, public law has another important influence to play. The standard applied to defendant public authorities is more stringent than the one applied to private defendants. The fact that they have a public mission to discharge is fully relevant to the definition of the obligations whose breaches sound in damages. Even if, as a rule, the general provisions of the Code civil find no application to governmental liability, in most cases the rule affirmed in administrative law is that every fault is sufficient to give rise to liability.[332]

Having rooted liability in public rather that in private law, French courts have more recently arrived at accepting liability even in cases where no reproach whatsoever can be vented to the public administration. The

---

[329] This point has been taken up by Bradley and Bell, 'Governmental liability: a preliminary assessment' in Bell and Bradley, op cit, 2 f.

[330] CE 14 July 1964, *Prat-Flottes et Sté des instituts de plein air*, Rec 438.

[331] CE 24 Jan 1996, *Collins*, Dr Adm 1996, no 112, and CE 23 Mar 1994, *Syndicat intercommunal à vocation unique pour l'étude et la réalisation du golf de Cognac*, D 1994, somm 123, obs Ph Terneyre.

[332] J-C Duchon-Doris, conclusions to CAA Marseille, 21 Jan 1999, *Ministre de l'Intérieur c/ Commune de Saint-Florent et autres*, in Rev fr dr adm 1999, 1032, 1038: 'On peut donc affirmer, à l'entrée dans le XXIe siècle, que le droit administratif, en matière de responsabilité, s'agissant de de la très grande majorité des activités de la puissance publique, repose sur un principe comparable à celui du code civil selon lequel toute faute engage la responsabilité de son auteur'. French administrative courts have long overcome their initial diffidence towards the private law idea of fault: M Deguergue, *Jurisprudence et doctrine dans l'élaboration du droit de la responsabilité administrative* (Paris: LGDJ, 1994), 160 ff.

decisions by the *Conseil d'Etat* in both *Blanchi*[333] and *Hôpital Joseph-Imbert d'Arles*[334] can be explained only from the perspective of specifically public law concepts such as the one of equality/*égalité*.[335]

A public law approach to liability makes it easier to accept responsibility when things done in the general interest go wrong. Even financial burden preoccupations lose some of their bite when it is considered that the general public rather than some individual have to shoulder the costs of things done in the general interest when they go wrong.[336]

Of course, it could be debated whether we are here still discussing about non-contractual liability or we have rather entered the field of social security law.

English law has endeavoured to keep public law illegality and governmental liability apart. Relationships have however been uneasy at best.[337]

In *Home Office v Dorset Yacht* Lord Diplock held that no liability could attach to intra vires decisions.[338]

Considering negligence actions against public authorities in *Anns v Merton London Borough Council*[339] Lord Wilberforce held that:

the local authority is a public body, discharging functions under statute: its powers and duties are definable in terms of public not private law. The problem which this type of action creates, is to define the circumstances in which the law should impose, over and above, or perhaps alongside, these public powers and duties, a duty in private law towards individuals such that they may sue for damages in a civil court.[340]

This said, the analysis proceeds alongside the policy/discretionary and operational dichotomy, which has its underpinnings in public law, to come to the conclusion that 'A plaintiff complaining of negligence must prove, the burden being on him, that action taken was not within the limits of a discretion bona fide exercised, before he can begin to rely upon a common duty of care.'[341] Having tried to separate the legality and liability questions, English courts fall back to lengthy discussions of public law points.

---

[333] CE, Ass, 9 Apr 1993, *Bianchi*, in *Rev fr dr adm* 1993, 573, concl S Daël.

[334] CE 3 Nov 1997, *Hôpital Joseph-Imbert d'Arles*, in *Rev fr dr adm* 1998, 82, concl *v* Pécresse; the reasons given are quite the same as those given in CE, Ass, 9 Apr 1993, *Bianchi*, in *Rev fr dr adm* 1993, 573, the only difference being that the word 'patient' has taken the place of the word 'malade'.

[335] Consider again the conclusions to CE, Ass, 9 Apr 1993, *Bianchi*, in *Rev fr dr adm* 1993, 573, by S Daël.

[336] Financial burden arguments are normally disposed of very expeditiously in France: eg, the conclusion of *Commissaire du Gouvernement* Peano to CAA Bordeaux, Plén, 2 février 1998, *Consorts Fraticiola*, *Rev dr publ* 1998, 579.

[337] See also Andenas and Fairgrieve, 'Sufficiently Serious?', 285, 288 ff.

[338] [1970] AC 1004 (HL) 1068.   [339] [1978] AC 728 (HL).

[340] 754.   [341] 755.

The same is true of *Hill v Chief Constable of West Yorkshire*.[342] Lord Keith is quite attentive in stressing the wide discretion enjoyed by police officers when investigating a murder case. Recalling the classic public law standard, he claims that 'It is only if his decision upon such matters is such as no reasonable chief officer of police would arrive at that someone with an interest to do so may be in a position to recourse to judicial review.'[343]

Public law issues were remarkably absent from the House of Lords decision in *Murphy v Brentwood District Council*[344] which reversed *Anns*.[345] All the discussion in *Murphy* was rather centred on the scope of negligence liability for pure economic loss.[346]

In *X (Minors) v Bedfordshire County Council*, the dichotomy of public law and private law featured prominently in the leading speech by Lord Browne-Wilkinson.[347] According to his Lordship:

The question is whether, if Parliament has imposed on statutory duty on an authority to carry out a particular function, a plaintiff who has suffered damage in consequence of the authority's performance or non performance of that function has a right of action in damages against the authority. It is important to distinguish such actions to recover damages, based on a private law cause of action, from actions in public law to enforce the due performance of statutory duties, now brought by way of judicial review. The breach of a public law right by itself gives rise to no claim for damages. A claim for damages must be based on a private law cause of action.[348]

This said, his Lordship has no difficulty in maintaining that 'a common law duty of care may arise in the performance of statutory functions'.[349] Then, in a passage reminiscent of the policy/discretionary and operational dichotomy proposed by Lord Wilberforce in *Anns v Merton London Borough Council*,[350] Lord Browne-Wilkinson distinguishes between '(a) cases in which it is alleged that the authority owes a duty of care in the manner in which it exercises a statutory discretion; (b) cases in which a duty of care is alleged to arise from the manner in which the statutory duty has been implemented in practice.'[351]

As far as the issue of discretion is concerned, Lord Browne-Wilkinson repeats the old saying that no authority can be held liable for doing what the Parliament has authorised.

Therefore if the decisions complained of fall within the ambit of such statutory discretion they cannot be actionable in common law. However if the decision complained of is so unreasonable that it falls outside the ambit of discretion

---

[342] [1989] AC 53 (HL).   [343] 59.
[344] [1991] 1 AC 398 (CA and HL).   [345] [1978] AC 728 (HL).
[346] Critically R O'Dair, '*Murphy v Brentwood District Council*: A House With Firm Foundations?' (1991) 54 *MLR* 561, 562–4.
[347] [1995] 2 AC 633 (HL) 730.   [348] 730.   [349] 735.
[350] [1978] AC 728 (HL) 754.   [351] [1995] 2 AC 633 (HL) 735.

conferred upon the local authority, there is no a priori reason for excluding all common law liability.[352]

His Lordship dissociates himself from Lord Diplock's reasoning in *Home Office v Dorset Yacht*.[353] Lord Diplock referred to the public law distinction between *ultra* and *intra vires* decisions.[354] Lord Browne-Wilkinson believes it is neither helpful nor necessary 'to introduce public law concepts as to the validity of a decision into the question of liability at common law for negligence. In public law a decision can be ultra vires for reasons other than Wednesbury unreasonableness [...] (eg breach of the rules of natural justice) which have no relevance to the question of negligence.'[355]

For all the pain taken in segregating actions in damages from public law concepts,[356] even Lord Browne-Wilkinson could not do without such a central idea of English administrative law as the *Wednesbury* unreasonableness.[357] In *Associated Provincial Picture House Ltd v Wednesbury Corporation*[358] Lord Greene MR, with whom all the other members of the Court of Appeal concurred, laid down the principle forbidding courts to go into the merits of administrative decisions. Courts can be allowed to interfere with administrative decisions only in so far has the administrative authority has come to a conclusion 'so unreasonable that no reasonable authority could have ever come to it'.[359] The official yardstick of judicial review is thus applied to damages claims. In the end, Lord Slynn held quite sensibly in *Barrett v Enfield London Borough Council*[360] that the idea of *ultra vires* referred to by Lord Diplock in *Home Office v Dorset Yacht*[361] 'is very much the administrative law test' (unreasonable-

---

[352] 736; see also 761.   [353] [1970] AC 1004 (HL).
[354] [1970] AC 1004 (HL) 1068.

[355] [1995] 2 AC 633 (HL) 736; see also C Lewis, *Judicial Remedies in Public Law*, 2nd edn (London: Sweet & Maxwell, 2000), 438 f; Lord Browne-Wilkinson is worried that characterising the action for negligence in the exercise of statutory powers as a public law claim could lead to the mistaken assumption that the action had to be brought in judicial review proceeding; according to P Cane, 'Suing Public Authorities in Tort' (1996) 112 *LQR* 13, 16 f, all the passage is meant to say that procedural infringements are not enough to substantiate a negligence action.

[356] Andenas and Fairgrieve, 'Sufficiently Serious?', 285, also underlines that 'Ironically, this final variant of public law filters owes its existence to Lord Browne-Wilkinson's desire to severe the link between public law notions of invalidity and private law actions in tort.'

[357] In *Stovin v Wise* [1996] AC 923 (HL) 953, a case concerning the failure to exercise a statutory power, Lord Hoffmann refers to irrationality, the label substituted to unreasonableness by Lord Diplock in *CCSU v Minister for the Civil Service* [1985] AC 374 (HL).

[358] [1948] 1 KB 223 CA.

[359] 234; his Lordship further contends that 'The power of the court to interfere in each case is not as an appellate authority to override a decision of the local authority, but as a judicial authority which is concerned, and concerned only, to see whether the local authority have contravened the law by acting in excess of the powers which Parliament has confided in them.'

[360] [1999] 3 All ER 193 (HL).

[361] [1970] AC 1004 (HL) 1068.

ness) used by other members of the House of Lords in that and other cases.[362]

Needless to say, such hurdles make it very difficult to sue public authorities in negligence.[363] A more coherent approach was voiced only in the Lord Hutton's speech in *Barrett v Enfield London Borough Council*.[364] His Lordship held that:

Where a plaintiff claims damages for personal injuries which he alleges have been caused by decisions negligently taken in the exercise of statutory discretion, and provided that the decisions do not involve issues of policy which courts are ill-equipped to adjudicate upon, it is preferable for the courts to decide the validity of the plaintiff's claim by applying directly the common law concept of negligence rather than by applying as a preliminary test the public law concept of Wednesbury unreasonableness [...] to determine if the decision fell outside the ambit of statutory discretion[365].

Lord Hutton, echoing the position of Lord Slynn, also gave indications as to the standard of care to be applied in a case the like of Barrett. The appropriate standard was not to be a too demanding one.[366]

Finally, public law was disposed of quickly and deftly in *Phelps v Hillingdon London Borough Council*.[367] Lord Slynn was fast to bring the cases in the operational area, so that no public law issue could arise and the case was adjudicated on the basis of the common law liability of those providing professional services to the public.[368]

English courts have been able to deal with government liability without addressing public law questions to a very limited extent only. Actually, with the possible exception of some of the most recent decisions,[369] courts have had first to overcome the public law hurdle by holding that the case under scrutiny was justiciable; only afterwards they are free to start with their private law considerations (such as those whether it is fair, just, and reasonable to impose a duty of care).[370] Indeed, it has been said with reference to

---

[362] [1999] 3 All ER 193 (HL) 210; however, immediately after his Lordship shared 'Lord Browne-Wilkinson's reluctance to introduce the concepts of administrative law into the law of negligence' (210).

[363] This was extrajudicially recognised also by Lord Browne-Wilkinson: for references and discussion, see Andenas and Fairgrieve, 'Sufficiently Serious?', 285, 306 f.

[364] [1999] 3 All ER 193 (HL).   [365] 225.   [366] 230.

[367] [2000] WLR 776 (HL).

[368] 790 and 795; the same can be said of Lord Nicholls's speech, while Lord Clyde gave the problem deeper thought (810 f).

[369] According to Fairgrieve, 'Pushing back the Boundaries of Public Authority Liability. Tort Law Enters the Classroom' [2002] *PL* 288, 298–9, cases such as *Barrett v Enfield London Borough Council* [1999] 3 All ER 193 (HL) and *Phelps v Hillingdon London Borough Council* [2000] WLR 776 (HL) points to a 'movement away from invalidity as a precondition for an action in negligence against public authorities'.

[370] Eg, Lord Slynn's speech in *Barrett v Enfield London Borough Council* [1999] 3 All ER 193 (HL) 209–11; Andenas and Fairgrieve, 'Sufficiently Serious?', 285, 292.

both *X(Minors) v Bedfordshire County Council*[371] and *Stovin v Wise*[372] that 'the priority of public law considerations over private law principles is clear'.[373]

B. Justiciability

In *X(Minors) v Bedfordshire County Council*, Lord Browne-Wilkinson had to consider another key concept of administrative law: justiciability.[374] He had to admit that 'if the factors relevant to the exercise of the discretion includes matters of policy, the court cannot adjudicate on such policy matters and therefore cannot reach the conclusion that the decision was outside the ambit of the statutory discretion. Therefore a common law duty of care in relation to the taking of decisions involving policy matters cannot exist.'[375] Only if and when the administrative decision is justiciable, 'the ordinary principles of negligence apply'.[376]

Such approach is totally foreign to French administrative law. There is no area where liability actions cannot be brought. Even the emergency services are not granted blanket immunity. Concerns not to excessively hinder useful activities are rather dealt with by imposing more lenient standard of care on the public authorities performing difficult tasks.[377] The now gone Italian case law denying any liability for the infringement of *interessi legittimi* could maybe considered as an attempt to deny justiciability. It was more probably due to the desire of civil courts to leave difficult cases involving decisions by public authorities to the administrative courts. Those cases where justiciable in front of the latter courts, even if no remedy in damages was available there.[378]

---

[371] [1995] AC 633 (HL).

[372] [1996] AC 923 (HL).

[373] Convey, 'Public or Private?', 559, 564; also Andenas and Fairgrieve, 'Sufficiently Serious?'; 'In order to maintain judicial restraint [. . .] the English courts have introduced extra elements to the ingredients of negligence actions against public authorities.'

[374] Also *Barrett v Enfield London Borough Council* [1999] 3 All ER 193 (HL) 211: 'Where a statutory power is given to a local authority and damage is caused by what is done pursuant to that power, the ultimate question is whether the particular issue is justiciable or whether the court should accept that it has no role to play. The two tests (discretionary and policy/operational) [. . .] are guides in deciding that question. The greater the element of policy involved, the wider the area of discretion accorded, the more likely it is that the matter is not justiciable so that no action in negligence can be brought.'

[375] [1995] 2 AC 633 (HL) 738.

[376] 739; his Lordship held that some of the claims in the cases then discussed were indeed justiciable.

[377] This since the very old decision of CE 10 Feb 1905, *Tommaso Grecco*, D 1906, III, 81, concl Romieu.

[378] Above A 1bi; Cane, 'Suing Public Authorities in Tort' (1996) 112 *LQR* 13, 17 f, however, distinguishes justiciability in the *GCHQ* sense—referring to *Council of Civil Service Union v Minister for the Civil Service* [1985] AC 374 (HL)—and justiciability in the *Beds CC* sense; this distinction could be used to characterise the old Italian case law.

The English position has been further elaborated by Lord Slynn in *Barrett v Enfield London Borough Council*,[379] who thought it wrong to come to the conclusion that 'if an element of discretion is involved in an act being done subject to the exercise of overriding statutory power, common law negligence is necessarily ruled out'.[380] Later in the same speech his Lordship held that:

A claim of negligence in taking a decision to exercise a statutory discretion is likely to be barred, unless it is wholly unreasonable so as not to be a real exercise of the discretion, or if it involves the making of a policy decision involving the balancing of different public interests; acts done pursuant to the lawful exercise of discretion can, however, in my view be subject to a duty of care, even if some element of discretion is involved.[381]

Taken together Lord Browne-Wilkinson's speech in *X(Minors)* and Lord Slynn's speech in *Barrett*, it looks as if the 'no go' area for courts is that of policy/non-justiciable decisions (usually taken at the stage when the authority decides whether or not to exercise its discretion and, if the positive applies, how); other decisions, and especially implementation and/or operational decisions, are justiciable even if some element of discretion is present.[382]

In some cases the existence of 'no go' areas for concurrent common law duties have been doubted. In his dissent speech in *Stovin v Wise*[383] Lord Nicholls stated that 'an area of blanket immunity seems undesirable and unnecessary. It is undesirable in principle that in respect of certain types of decisions the possibility of a concurrent common law duty should be absolutely barred, whatever the circumstances. An excluded zone is also unnecessary, because no statutory power is inherently immune from judicial review.'[384] What is peculiar here is that public law is for once called into action to extend the range of tort liability rather than to restrain it.

B. Policy v Discretion

The approach by English courts to liability cases having public authorities as defendants is uneasy at best. One reason may be the excessively wide and thus confusing conception of discretion as so far elaborated in the common law world.[385] Lord Slynn was quite right to point out in *Barrett v Enfield*

---

[379] [1999] 3 All ER 193 (HL).   [380] 210.   [381] 211.
[382] Also Craig and Fairgrieve, '*Barrett*, Negligence and Discretionary powers', 626, 631 ff.
[383] [1996] AC 923 (HL).   [384] 938.
[385] Andenas and Fairgrieve, 'Sufficiently Serious?', 285, 309, point out that 'the notion of "discretion" is of notoriously amorphous qualities when applied in a legal context'. In many continental law systems, however, it is a notion much more clearly defined; the analysis of the issue in *X (Minors) v Bedfordshire County Council* [1995] 2 AC 633 (HL) was far from: Cane, 'Suing Public Authorities in Tort' (1996) 112 *LQR* 13, 15 f.

London Borough Council,[386] that 'even knocking a nail into a piece of wood involves the exercise of some choice or discretion'.[387]

More restricted and precise is the concept of policy.[388] It is again Lord Slynn who says that

> Where a statutory power is given to a local authority and damage is caused by what is done pursuant to that power, the ultimate question is whether the particular issue is justiciable or whether the court should accept that it has no role to play. The two tests (discretionary and policy/operational) [...] are guides in deciding that question. The greater the element of policy involved, the wider the area of discretion accorded, the more likely it is that the matter is not justiciable so that no action in negligence can be brought.[389]

Policy rather than discretion is at the core of Lord Hutton's speech in the same case. Considering the judgements of both Lord Reid and Lord Diplock in *Home Office v Dorset Yacht,*[390] Lord Hutton held that:

> The courts will not permit a claim for negligence to be brought where a decision on the existence of negligence would involve the courts in considering matters of policy raising issues which they are ill-equipped and ill-suited to assess and on which the Parliament could have not intended that the courts substitute their views for the views of ministers or officials.[391]

It is doubtful whether Lord Hutton's speech introduced a further qualification to what Lord Slynn said. In Lord Hutton's opinion, 'It is only where the decision involves the weighing of competing public interests or is dictated by considerations which courts are not fitted to assess that the courts will hold that the issue is non-justiciable on the ground that the decision was made in the exercise of statutory discretion.'[392] In a way, both Lord Slynn and Lord Hutton, with whom the other Law Lords concurred, finally managed to bring back discretion, policy and justiciability to more precise contours, making it impossible for public authorities to shelter behind vague administrative law concepts and to go free from any liability even in case of behaviour flying in the face of common sensibility.[393]

---

[386] [1999] 3 All ER 193 (HL).   [387] 210.

[388] We deal here with 'executive policy' rather than with the 'judicial policy' relevant, for example, with reference to existence of a duty of care under *Caparo Industries Plc v Dickman* [1990] 2 AC 605 (HL) 618 (Lord Bridge).

[389] *Barrett v Enfield London Borough Council* [1999] 3 All ER 193 (HL) 211; in the same judgment Lord Hutton referred to discretion, holding that 'the fact that the defendant's relationship with the claimant arose from the exercise of statutory power does not prevent the claimant from claiming that the defendant owed him a common law duty of care, unless the defendant is entitled to contend that the claim is barred because it alleges negligence in the exercise of a discretion given by statute' (217); later, he too elaborated on policy: see below.

[390] [1970] AC 1004 (HL).   [391] [1999] 3 All ER 193 (HL) 220.   [392] 222.

[393] Lord Hutton was however very careful to point out that any court decision to the effect that a given matter is 'unsuitable for judicial determination' will require 'a careful analysis and weighing of the relevant circumstances' (225).

Lord Hutton's more precise description was later adopted by Lord Slynn in *Phelps v Hillingdon London Borough Council*.[394] Similar reasoning was also to be found in the speech by Woolf MR in *Kent v Griffths*, the delayed ambulance case.[395] Here again it was held the unreasonable time the ambulance had taken to get the patient had nothing to do with matters of policy or with the allocation of scarce resources; thus it was fully justiciable.[396]

All these contortions are probably the result of the traditional self-restraint characterising judicial review of administrative action in Britain. In Germany discretionary acts are subject to judicial review to a far greater extent than in English law.[397] For instance, proportionality and legitimate expectations are everyday working tools for German courts. Discretion is no taboo. In France, 'the adjudication of administrative liability largely mirrors judicial review of administrative legality.'[398] Here again, no administrative activity is considered non-justiciable and at times judicial review positively go to the limit where courts substitute their appreciation to the one shared by the administration (cases where the so-called *contrôle maximum* is possible).[399]

French administrative courts are not short-circuited even if the public authority still maintains some power to assess the merits of a given case. Courts circumvent this power by contenting themselves to consider the chances enjoyed by the claimant. If these chances are serious enough (an eminently subjective evaluation indeed) some compensation is granted anyway.[400]

Even in Italy, discretion is not always an impassable obstacle on the way to liability. This is done by civil and administrative courts using two different and alternative techniques.

Civil courts, mainly competent with reference to 'operational' cases, just short circuit the problem. A now long-standing case law applicable to the provision of services, to the performance of operational tasks and to the many supervisory cases simply states that, even when vested with discretionary powers, public authorities are to behave with due diligence. Lip

---

[394] [2000] WLR 776 (HL) 790 'It is only where what is done has involved the weighing of competing public interests or has been dictated by considerations on which Parliament could not have intended that the courts should substitute their views for the views of ministers or officials that the courts will hold that the issue is non-justiciable on the ground that the decision was made in the exercise of statutory discretion.'

[395] [2000] 2 WLR 1158 (CA) 1166.   [396] 1171.

[397] Markesinis *et al*, op cit, 23.   [398] Ibid, 53.

[399] A general overview in A De Laubadère, J-C. Venetia, and Y Gaudemet, *Traité de droit administratif*, 14th edn (Paris: LGDJ, 1996), 645 ff.

[400] Again CE 24 Jan 1996, *Collins*, *Dr Adm* 1996, no 112, and CE 23 Mar 1994, *Syndicat intercommunal à vocation unique pour l'étude et la réalisation du golf de Cognac*, D 1994, somm 123, obs Ph Terneyre.

service is paid to discretion, then it is up to the courts to lay down the standards public authorities have to comply with.[401]

Administrative courts have taken a different approach. They are now starting to fully accept a very refined concept of discretion elaborated by Massimo Severo Giannini, one of the most accomplished administrative law scholars for the period following the Second World War. Discretion is given a narrow meaning and confined to instances where public bodies are empowered to balance different public and private interest one against the other.[402] Discretion is thus rather close to the English idea of policy.

The balance between conflicting interests is often done at the normative or general rather than at the adjudicatory level. To avoid discrimination and preferences, both the legislation and the case law public bodies have introduced principles which run the opposite way to the English rule against the fettering of discretion.[403] In adjudicating specific cases, public bodies' decision-making powers are often bound (*compétence liée* in French legal jargon) or depend on technical evaluation as to the conformity of the given situation to the requirements laid down in the applicable rules.[404]

Technical evaluation, be it referred to scientific, medical, artistic or other fields, has nothing to do with discretion;[405] it is in principle amenable to judicial review and administrative courts can now have recourse to expertise to check the evaluation made by the administration.[406] It is fair to say

---

[401] Eg, Cass, Sez un., 2 June 1992, n 6667, in *Resp civ prev* 1993, 576 (a vigilance case); Cass, 29 Mar 1999, n 2963, in *Resp civ prev* 1999, 1265, with note by I Peila, 'Il concetto di insidia (o trabocchetto) ha superato il vaglio della Corte costituzionale' (a case concerning road maintenance).

[402] GF Scoca 'La discrezionalità nel pensiero di Giannini e nella dottrina successiva', in *Riv trim dir pubbl* 2000, 1045.

[403] Art 12 L 7 agosto 1990, n 241, states that every time administrative organs confer benefits on citizen, they must first state and make accessible to the public the criteria according to which the benefits will be granted; a long-standing case law has laid a principle according to which examination boards charged with selecting would-be public servants, or promoting them to higher position, have to set and make accessible to the interested persons the standards against which the candidates would be rated before starting the examination: eg, Cons St, Sez V, 1 Mar 2000, n 1071, in *Foro amm* 2000, 870; the same applies to selection in public procurement procedures: eg, Cons St, Sez V, 24 Nov 1997, n 1372, in *Foro amm* 1997, 3058 (sm); generally A Police, *La predeterminazione delle decisioni amministrative* (Napoli: ESI, 1997).

[404] There is an organisational aspect deserving to be briefly mentioned: while rules and programs, where the conflicting interests are balanced in a very general way, are adopted by organs which have been directly or inderectly elected, individual decisions concerning specific cases are taken by public servants: Arts 51 and 53 L. 8 June 1990, n 142, concerning local government, and Arts 3 and 14 D Lgs 3 Feb 1993, n 29; generally Caranta, 'Politica e amministrazione nella Costituzione', to be published in *Studi in onore di U Pototschnig*.

[405] A seminal work was F Ledda, 'Potere, tecnica, sindacato giudiziario sull'amministrazione pubblica', in *Dir proc amm* 1983, 371.

[406] Artt 7 and 16 L 21 July 2000, n 205; Cons St, Sez IV, 26 June 2000, n 3600, in *Cons St* 2000, I, 1503; F Ciontioli 'Consulenza tecnica d'ufficio e sindacato giurisdizionale della discrezionalità tecnica' in F Caringella and M Protto (curr), *Il nuovo processo amministrativo* (Milano: Giuffré 2000), 908.

that Italian administrative courts have still some way to go in the direction of second-guessing what would have been the correct solution had the competent body acted along the best possible technical methods, but they have started moving in that direction.[407]

What is left open, is the question of liability in the field of really discretionary (or policy) decisions, those involving the balance between conflicting interests. Such decisions are in principle amenable to judicial review. The review is however in a way rather incidental. Courts do not assess the merits of the decision. Beside matters of form and procedure, they are usually concerned with the reasons given. On the ground of *eccesso di potere*, Italian administrative courts review if the reasons laid down in the decision are sufficient to justify it, consistent with one another, apt to explain the difference with cases where another outcome was arrived to and so on. It is not a very objective kind of review, and is by no means free of judicial preferences: in the end it all boils down to the question whether the courts think the decision taken is reasonable or not. If they don't, the decision is annulled.[408]

This leaves the question of liability open. A decision was mistaken, indeed illegal. As it was said before, this does not yet mean that no other equally harmful decision could be legally taken. So far, most Italian administrative courts do not go into the merits of the case. They prefer to send the matter back to the authority having taken the decision for a new assessment and liability actions are rejected. Most courts don't even assess whether the claimant stood good chances to have a favourable decision.[409]

Here lays the most relevant difference between the approaches of French and Italian administrative courts. French courts first apply the equation between illegality and fault; a prima facie liability case thus established can then be reversed if harm (including *perte des chances*) cannot be linked to the admittedly illegal decision taken by the public authority. Italian courts refuse the equation and start looking for certainties concerning the harm (generally not being content with lost chances only). In a way, the Italian approach is closer to the now receding English tendency to analyse most issues under the heading of the existence of the duty of care, rather than

---

[407] Concerning governmental liability TAR Toscana, Sez I, 21 Oct 1999, n 766, in *Foro amm.* 2000, 2264; in *Foro it* 2000, III, 196, with note by L Carozza and F Fracchia 'Art 35 d leg. 80/98 e risarcibilità degli "interessi meritevoli di tutela": prime applicazioni giurisprudenziali', and TAR Lombardia, Sez III, 6 Nov 2000, n 6259, in *Giust civ* 2001, I, 863; given the very limited value of the respective claims, no expertise was however ordered by the courts in these cases.

[408] A critical reassment in F Ledda, 'Variazione sul tema dell'eccesso di potere', in *Dir pubbl* 2000, 447.

[409] Cons St, Sez IV, 2 June 2000, n 3177, in *Foro amm.* 2000, 2096, with remarks by R Iannotta; other decisions, however, are more in line with the French model: TAR Toscana, Sez II, 13 aprile 2000, n 660, in *Foro amm* 2000, 3679.

looking to other elements such as the breach of the duty, causation, and harm.[410] A minor difference is that, given the equation, French courts do not look further to see whether also fault-negligence is present; Italian courts can rule out liability in case of excusable mistake.

D. *Operational Cases*

On the Continent questions as to justiciability and discretion do not normally surface with reference to cases concerning the performance of operational tasks or the provision of services to the public. In those cases questions about the illegality of a formal administrative decision are not at the centre of the litigation. When the provision of services to the public is at issue or in cases concerning the performance of operational tasks (and here 'operational' and not 'discretionary' is the adjective given a broad meaning) French administrative courts do not bother about discretion. Nor are they concerned with questionable immunities or no-go areas for the judge. They just check whether administrative activities were up to the standards to be expected from a public body, standards they themselves lie down.

The same idea of some form of public law immunity was repelled by the *Conseil d'Etat* already in 1905 in the well-known case of *Tommaso Grecco* (or *Tomaso Greco* according to other reports) case.[411] The claimant had been hit in his home by a bullet fired while the police and private citizens were trying to kill a rampaging bull through the streets of Souk-el-Arba. His claim in damages was resisted by the interior ministry claiming that police operations could not be subject to judicial scrutiny. This idea was outright rejected by the *Conseil d'Etat* following the conclusions of its *Commissaire du gouvernment Romieu,* who claimed that it was up to the courts to say in which circumstances liability could be attached to the acts of some public authority.[412] The claimant's action was dismissed only because, in the

---

[410] The English case law on this problem is analysed by Craig and Fairgrieve, '*Barrett, Negligence and Discretionary powers*' [1999] *PL* 626, and more recently by Fairgrieve, 'Pushing back the Boundaries of Public Authority Liability', 288, 297.

[411] CE 10 Feb 1905, *Tommaso Grecco*, D 1906, III, 81, concl Romieu. The case has been dealt with recently by Deguergue, *Jurisprudence et doctrine dans l'élaboration du droit de la responsabilité administrative* (Paris: LGDJ, 1994), 90.

[412] The conclusions by Romieu are quite clear in this respect: 'on ne voit pas en vertu de quel texte ou de quel principe du droit le citoyen lésé par un vice d'organisation ou de fonctionnement du service public, par la faute grave de ceux qui le dirigent ou qui en sont les agents d'exécution, serait privé du droit d'obtenir réparation du préjudice souffert, par le seul motif que l'acte incriminé serait un acte de commandement ou que la mesure critiquée serait une mesure de police [...]. Ce qui est vrai c'est que toute erreur, toute négligence, tout irrégularité (même de nature à motiver une annulation pour excès de pouvoir) n'entraînera pas nécessairement la responsabilité pécuniaire de la puissance publique. Il appartient au juge de déterminer, dans chaque espèce, s'il y une faute caractérisée du service de nature à engager sa

circumstances of the case, no negligence was attributable to the police and it was even doubtful whether the bullet which hit Mr Grecco had been fired by the police.[413]

Concerning for instance the operation of the national health service, French administrative courts have no problem in checking whether the service provided was up to the standards they themselves set the public administration.[414]

Italian civil courts, having jurisdiction concerning most of the 'operational' cases, quite simply hold that, even when vested with discretionary powers, public authorities are to behave with due diligence.[415]

English courts, on the contrary, have shown a questionable tendency to refrain from adjudicating liability claims by applying tools forged with reference to judicial review to situations where no formal administrative decision is challenged. Too wide an idea of discretion has brought courts to twist public law and private law questions into unsteady compromises. In *S v Gloucestershire County Council* May LJ had to strike this rather complex balancing act:

> In considering whether a discretionary decision was negligent, the court will not substitute its view for that of the local authority upon whom the statute has placed the power to exercise discretion, unless the discretionary decision was plainly wrong. But decisions of, for example, social workers are capable of being held to have been negligent by analogy with decisions of other professionals people.[416]

E. Duties v Powers

The English tradition sharply distinguishes between duties and powers. Breach of statutory duty cannot be pleaded in case of mere powers.[417] Negligence liability is accepted with greater circumspection if ever with

responsabilité et de tenir compte à cet effet, tout à la fois de la nature de ce service, des aléas et des difficultés qu'il comporte, de la part d'initiative et de liberté dont il a besoin, en même temps que de la nature de droits individuels intéressés, de leur importance, du degré de gêne qu'ils sont tenus de supporter, de la protection plus ou moins grande qu'ils méritent et de la gravité de l'atteinte dont ils sont l'objet'.

[413] CE 10 Feb 1905, *Tommaso Grecco*, D 1906, III, 81, 82.

[414] If possible even more stringent is the approach followed by Italian courts moving by the idea that liability of the national health service to those admitted to the hospitals is contractual in nature: eg, Cass, 16 May 2000, n 6318, in *Resp civ prev* 2000, 940, with note by M Gorgoni 'L'incidenza delle disfunzioni della struttura ospedaliera sulla responsabilità "sanitaria"; also G Iudica, 'Danno alla persona per inefficienza della struttura sanitaria', in *Resp civ prev* 2001, 3.

[415] Eg, Cass, Sez un., 2 June 1992, n 6667, in *Resp civ prev* 1993, 576 (a vigilance case); Cass, 29 Mar 1999, n 2963, in *Resp civ prev* 1999, 1265, with note by I Peila, 'Il concetto di insidia (o trabocchetto) ha superato il vaglio della Corte costituzionale' (a case concerning road maintenance).

[416] [2001] 2 WLR 909 (CA) 932.

[417] Eg, *Stovin v Wise* [1994] 1 WLR 1124.

reference to powers.[418] From a different perspective, it can be said that Common lawyers are very wary to accept liability for omissions rather than for positive acts.[419] Referring to Lord Nicholls's dissenting speech in *Stovin v Wise*,[420] it has been submitted that 'the public law obligation is to refrain from acting unreasonably in the public law sense; not, as Lord Nicholls held, to "act as a reasonable authority"'.[421]

This position is possibly heavily influenced by the private law character of tortious liability. It is quite surprising to a Continental lawyer. Administrative authorities here are bestowed with powers that they have the duty to exercise when the conditions laid down by the legislator are present. Their position is described rather as one having some shades of both powers and duties.

A less insular approach shines through Lord Nicholls's dissenting speech in *Stovin v Wise*.[422] He too accepted that in principle negligence liability for omissions is rather the exception than the rule, but claimed that things can be different with administrative authorities. Referring to the position of the highway authority in that case, he observed that 'The council was more than a bystander. The council had a statutory power to remove this source of danger, although it was not under a statutory duty to do so.'[423]

Administrative law on the Continent is much in tune with Lord Nicholls's position. Administrative authorities are not endowed with powers just to sit idly. They have a duty to act.[424] Consequently, omissions

---

[418] *East Suffolk Rivers Catchment Board v Kent* [1941] AC 74 (HL) laid down the rule that the mere failure to exercise a power could not give rise to liability; the validity of this proposition was doubted by Lord Wilberforce in *Anns v Merton London Borough Council* [1978] AC 728 (HL) 755; in *Stovin v Wise* [1996] AC 923 (HL) 933 the House of Lords was quite divided on the subject. Also SH Bailey and MJ Bowman, 'Public Authority Negligence Revisited' [2000] *CLJ* 85, 97 ff; T Hickman, '"And That's Magic!"—Making Public Bodies Liable for Failure to Confer Benefits' [2000] *CLJ* 432, 435.

[419] Cases of nonfeasance are at times dealt with separately: eg, Craig and Fairgrieve, '*Barrett*, Negligence and Discretionary powers', 626, 628 f.

[420] [1996] AC 923 (HL) 928.

[421] Convey, 'Public or Private?', 559, 567.

[422] [1996] AC 923 (HL) 928; his Lordship's approach was the one preferred by Bailey and Bowman, 'Public Authority Negligence Revisited', 85, 112, and 116 f.

[423] 931; later it stated that 'Individuals may suffer loss through the carelessness of public bodies in carrying out their statutory functions. Sometimes this evokes an intuitive response that the authority ought to make good the loss. The damnified individual was entitled to expect better from a public body. Leaving the loss to lie where it falls is not always an acceptable outcome. The authority did not create the loss, but it failed to discharge its statutory responsabilities with reasonable care. Had it behaved properly, the loss would not have occurred' (933); Again, 'Unlike an individual, a public authority is not an indifferent onlooker. Parliament confers powers on public authorities for a purpose. An authority is entrusted and charged with responsabilities, for the public good. The powers are intended to be exercised in a suitable case. Compelling a public authority to act does not represent an intrusion into private affairs in the same way as when a private individual is compelled to act' (935).

[424] The traditional position is criticised by S Arrowsmith, *Civil Liability and Public Authorities* (London: Sweet & Maxwell, 1992) 183, and, more recently, by Craig, op cit, 869.

are not dealt with differently from positive acts. As was observed with reference to the French situation, but the same can be said with reference to other European legal systems, omission 'is a frequent cause of liability and there are no signs in the case law that it would, in any intellectual sense, be treated in a different way than negligent acts'.[425] Indeed, inaction is in itself *une faute du service public de nature à engager sa responsabilité.*[426]

Delay also can be sufficient to establish liability.[427] For instance, the French *Conseil d'Etat* had no hesitations in holding a local authority liable for the accrued fire damages to a building during the inordinate amount of time spent by the fire fighters in starting the recalcitrant engine of a water cannon, and this on the unspoken assumption that fire fighters have what the English would call a (private law) duty to act with reasonable expedience in fighting fires.[428]

F. Domesticating Community Law

Community law—and more generally European law—has been quite instrumental in allowing major inroads in the English law on tortious liability. It has been point out that 'Public bodies are especially vulnerable under Community law for they, unlike private individuals, may be bound by Directives even if they have not been implemented into local law (as we must now call it), and the state may itself be liable for failure to implement them. These are extraordinary innovations in English law.'[429]

English courts have 'domesticated' Member States liability by creating, or, rather, resurrecting, a new cause of action. The idea of adapting an existing tort, which has been forcefully voiced at the academic level,[430] has yet to make inroads into the case law. Existing torts in the field of governmental liability are widely at variance with the Community requirements.

In *R v Secretary of State for Transport, ex p Factortame Ltd (No. 5)* Lord Hope said:

It is a novel task for the court in this county to have to assess whether a breach is sufficiently serious to entitle a party who has suffered loss as a result of it to damages. The general rule is that where a breach of a duty has been established and a causal link between the breach and the loss suffered has been proved the injured party is entitled as of right to damages. In the present context however the rules are

---

[425] Markesinis *et al*, op cit, 57; also, with reference to Germany, 60.

[426] Deguergue, *Jurisprudence et doctrine dans l'élaboration du droit de la responsabilité administrative* (Paris: LGDJ, 1994), 195.

[427] More cases are given by Deguergue, op cit, 196 ff.

[428] CE 29 Apr 1998, *Commune de Hannappes*, in *Rev dr publ* 1998, 1012.

[429] Weir, *A Casebook on Tort*, 15.

[430] It has been suggested that Community requirements could be usefully extended to domestic litigation: Craig, op cit, 849: also Andenas and Fairgrieve, 'Sufficiently Serious?', 285, 316 ff.

different. The facts must be examined in order that the court may determine whether the breach of Community law was of such a kind that damages should be awarded as compensation for the loss. The phrase 'sufficiently serious' and 'manifestly and gravely' which the European Court has used indicate that a fairly high threshold must be passed before it can be said that the test has been satisfied.[431]

It is respectfully submitted that this difference should not be overestimated. The sufficiently serious breach requirement applies only where wide discretionary powers exist. Even if the divide still deserves to be much elaborated upon, decisions like *Francovich*,[432] *Hedley Lomas*,[433] and *Dillenkofer*,[434] show that breach of Community law is actionable per se in many cases.[435] Other differences are indeed present, and are rather much at the advantage of the claimant under Community law. Community law is much more generous than English law in so far as the protective character of the infringed provision (*Normzwecktheorie* or right requirement) is considered. Up to now, no decision by the Court of Justice on Member States' liability has found this requirement wanting. Under Community law, no lengthy inquiry into the legislative intention is made. It is sufficient that the citizen can derive some benefit from the application of a given provision. Conferring rights does not need to be the only or even main purpose.[436] Community law rights are a by-product of direct effect and the Court of Justice has been notoriously generous in defining the requirements for direct effect.[437]

It would be mistaken to address the purpose of the Community provision question in the same way it is addressed by English court with reference to the tort of breach of statutory duty.[438] From this point of view it is

---

[431] *R v Secretary of State for Transport, ex p Factortame Ltd (No 5)* [1999] 3 WLR 1062 (HL) 1083.

[432] Joined cases C-6 and 9/90 *Francovich and others v Italian Republic* [1991] ECR I-5357.

[433] Case C-5/94 *R v Ministry of Agriculture, Fisheries and Food, ex p Hedley Lomas (Ireland) Ltd* [1996] ECR I-2553.

[434] Joined cases C-178, 179 and 199–190/94 *Dillenkofer v Federal Republic of Germany* [1996] ECR I-4845

[435] *R v Secretary of State for Transport, ex p Factortame Ltd (No. 5)* [1999] 3 WLR 1062 (HL) 1085 (Lord Clyde) 'In some cases there may be no discretion left to the state, and where there is an absolute duty to act a liability for failure to act may more readily arise. In other cases there can be a degree of discretion and the wider the discretion the less readily should a claim for damages to be available.'

[436] This fact was noted but only in passing in *Three Rivers District Council v Bank of England (No. 3)* [2000] 2 WLR 15 (CA) 83 (Lord Hirst and Lord Walker); it was more elaborated upon by Auld LJ who held that 'A directive may have two or more purposes and, regardless of their relative importance, may impose obligations advancing both or all of them. In my view, it is an arid exercise to seek to attribute greater importance to one or other of the two purposes of immediate protection of depositors and progressive harmonisation' (*ivi* 112).

[437] Consider also *Three Rivers District Council v Bank of England (No. 3)* [2000] 2 WLR 15 (CA) 124 (Auld LJ).

[438] This mistake was quite rightly pointed out by Auld LJ in *Three Rivers District Council v Bank of England (No 3)* [2000] 2 WLR 15 (CA) 110 and 116 ff: 'It does not seem to me appro-

respectfully submitted that *Three Rivers District Council v Bank of England* may have been wrongly decided or, to say the least, a reference to the Court of Justice would have been highly appropriate. This very much so since it can be inferred from *R v Secretary of State for Transport, ex p Factortame Ltd (No 5)* that the question whether a Community law provision in intended to confer rights is to be answered by the Court of Justice.[439] The forecast that English 'courts will not readily accept that the Community provisions intended the creation of individual rights' proved right.[440] Reservations can be had as to whether it is for English courts to decide the issue.

Adapting English torts to Community law requirements would have been a momentous effort. The easiest way would probably have been to work on breach of statutory duty, relaxing some requirements and possibly tightening others. Indeed, this possibility has been voiced in the academic literature.[441] The requirement of a manifest and serious breach has been thought to be a sufficiently malleable tool and even the reference to the conferral of a right on the interested parties has been considered as leaving some leeway. It was already recalled, however, that so far the European Court of Justice has never held that the conferral of a right condition was not met. Further, the same range of application of the idea of 'manifest and serious breach' has yet to be properly defined. It is to be remembered that it was originally applied to sectors where there was legislative rather than administrative discretion, that is to complex choices of economic policy. If discretion were to be given such a delimited meaning, in most cases mere illegality will be enough to meet the manifest and serious breach requirement. This would be going a long way toward the *Beaudesert* principle. English courts have thought it better to have recourse to a new tort. The question now is whether this will be enough to considerably water down if not making outright impossible any spill-over of Community law solutions into the overall English law of governmental liability.[442]

The approach followed by French courts has been quite different. As the *Commissaire du gouvernement Goulard* said in his conclusions to the *Dangeville* case, '[l]'affaire qui vous est aujourd'hui soumise semblait vous

---

priate to pray in aid common law principles and public policy considerations going to the existence of a duty of care when determining as a matter of construction what, if any, obligations and corresponding enforceable Community law rights are to be derived from Community legislation' (116).

[439] *R v Secretary of State for Transport, ex p Factortame Ltd (No. 5)* [1999] 3 WLR 1062 (HL) especially 1082 f (Lord Hope).

[440] C Hadjiemmanuil, 'Civil liability of regulatory authorities after the *Three Rivers* case' [1997] *PL* 32, 42.

[441] Craig, op cit, 849: also Andenas and Fairgrieve, 'Sufficiently Serious?', 285, 316 ff.

[442] The prevailing academic opinion is that it will not: W Wade and C Forsyth, *Administrative Law*, 8th edn (Oxford: Oxford University Press, 2000), 764.

offrir l'occasion de juger [. . .] que toute décision ayant fait application de dispositions législatives incompatibles avec une directive est constitutive d'une faute de nature à engager la responsabilité de l'Etat.'[443] Also concerning breaches of Community law, the equation between illegality and fault necessary to establish liability is now firm.[444]

T his, however, it is still a far cry from always finding the State liable or fully liable. The *Arizona Tobacco Products* and *Philip Morris* case is again quite interesting. The *Conseil d'Etat* found the decisions illegal and in breach of Community law provisions enshrined in the Treaty and developed in directives, calling for the gradual elimination of State monopolies and forbidding Member States to set the price of tobacco products in a way discriminatory towards imported products. However, the *Conseil d'Etat* pointed out that non-discriminatory pricing was not inconsistent with Community law; it then proceeded to ascertain the level at which the French government could have set prices without breaching the Treaty. At the end, the tobacco producers, which had asked for 5.849.742,75 FF, just got 230.000 FF.[445]

This outcome is possible when courts are not afraid to get into the shoes of the administrative authorities. Compared with the approach followed by English courts, it has the remarkable advantage to limit the liability of public bodies by using elements of causation and harm that according to the case law of the European Court of justice are so far the preserve of national courts.[446]

III. CONCLUSIONS WITH REFERENCE TO THE ENGLISH WAY TO DEAL WITH TORT(S) AND ILLEGALITY

Common lawyers' difficulties in building a coherent system with tort and illegality are not only due to the way public law has been developed. To say the least, they are not made easier by the system of typical or nominated torts. The evolutions and convolutions concerning the torts of negligence and breach of statutory duty and their uneasy relationships represents very good cases in point. British courts, afraid of anything close to an equation between tort and illegality, began emasculating the tort of breach of statutory duty. Through dubious references to insaisissable legislative inten-

---

[443] Conclusions to CE, ass, 30 Oct 1996, *Sté Dangeville, Rev fr dr adm* 1997, 1067.
[444] CE, ass, 28 Feb 1992, *Arizona Tobacco Products GmbH et al, Act jur Dr adm* 1992, 210, concl M Laroque.
[445] Ibid.
[446] Joined cases C-46/93 and 48/93 *Brasserie du pêcheur and Factotame IV* ECR I-1029, point 65; Case C-5/94 *R v Ministry of Agriculture, Fisheries and Food, ex p Hedley Lomas (Ireland) Ltd* [1996] ECR I-2553, point 30.

tions,[447] statutory duties were almost invariably considered to be nothing more than public law duty whose breach could not sound in damage.[448] Then courts turned to consider whether the common law superimposed a (private law) duty of care on the public law statutory duty whose breach could amount to a tort of negligence. Open ended requirements, such as whether it is fair, just and reasonable to impose such a duty of care,[449] were applied again, at times reverting to divine legislative intentions. Having denied any legislative intention to confer a private law right when examining claims under the breach of statutory duty heading, courts normally came to the conclusion that superimposing a private law duty of care whose breach sounded in negligence was inconsistent with the statutory framework conferring the public authority with duties,[450] and—*a fortiori*—powers.[451] In *Stovin v Wise*,[452] Lord Hoffmann was quite adamant when, referring to omissions to perform a statutory duty, he held: 'If such a duty does not give rise to a private right to sue for breach, it would be unusual if it nevertheless gave rise to a duty of care at common law which made the public authority liable to pay compensation for forseeable loss caused by the duty not being performed.'[453]

Claims both in negligence and statutory duty were thus excluded, a remedy only laying in the admittedly rare occurrence of misfeasance in public office. Indeed, the same elements used to exclude breach of statutory duty (as for instance the availability of alternative remedies) have been called into action in this as in many other cases with the effect to deny the existence of a common law duty of care.[454]

---

[447] In *Re Island Records* [1978] Ch 122, 135, Lord Denning MR described the dividing line as 'so blurred and ill-defined that you might as well toss a coin to decide it'; Lord Carnwath has extrajudicially written of an 'elusive concept': R Carnwath, 'The *Thornton* Heresy Exposed: Financial Remedies for Breach of Public Duties' [1998] *PL* 407; also C Lewis, *Judicial Remedies in Public Law*, 2nd edn (London: Sweet & Maxwell, 2000), 450 f.; the orthodox approach is defended by KM Stanton, *Breach of Statutory Duty* (London: Sweet & Maxwell, 1986), 32 ff

[448] Claims for breach of statutory duty are usually dropped by the parties as their case reach higher courts: eg *Barrett v Enfield London Borough Council* [1999] 3 All ER 193 (HL).

[449] Critical remarks on this test are to be found in Lord Nicholls's speech in *Stovin v Wise* [1996] AC 923 (HL) 933.

[450] According to Markesinis *et al*, op cit, 14 f, in so doing the courts bring 'the public law test in the private law phase of the enquiry'.

[451] *East Suffolk Rivers Catchment Board v Kent* [1941] AC 74 (HL) laid down the rule that the mere failure to exercise a power could not give rise to liability; the validity of this proposition was put in doubts by Lord Wilberforce in *Anns v Merton London Borough Council* [1978] AC 728 (HL) 755; for a review of subsequent cases see MC Harris, 'Powers into Duties—a Small Breach in the *East Suffolk* Wall?' (1997) 113 *LQR* 398.

[452] [1996] AC 923 (HL).

[453] 952; Lord Nicholls too had to concede 'the difficulty of how much weight should be accorded to the fact that, when creating the statutory function, the legislature held back from attaching a private law cause of action' (934).

[454] At other times, the existence of alternative remedies is the ground for defeating any claim

The basic assumption seemed to be that remedies for breaches of public law should be found in public law itself rather than in tort. As far as judicial review is concerned, this is true only in cases where there is a specific administrative decisions or an omission to address a request for a specific decision made by the concerned party. Other 'soft' remedies such as complaint system and ombudsman can be appropriate with reference to a wider sphere of situations. However, if damages have accrued this is normally because other remedies were either not available or inadequate.[455] It has been remarked that 'There are situations where judicial review will not be adequate. A breach of a statutory duty causing physical harm to the individual cannot be rectified by judicial review. It is not then a question of nullifying decisions taken in contravention of statute, or compelling performance of a duty.'[456] As Lord Nicholls quite rightly pointed out in *Stovin v Wise*, *Anns*[457] 'articulated a response to growing unease over the inability of public law, in some instances, to afford a remedy matching the wrongs'.[458] His Lordship was quite right in stressing that 'the purpose of the statutory powers is to protect road users by enabling highway authorities to remove sources of danger, but public law is unable to give an effective remedy if a road user is injured as a result of an authority's breach of its public law obligations'.[459]

The attitude has much changed in later cases. In *Phelps v Hillingdon London Borough Council*[460] Lord Slynn addressed again the question 'does a common law duty of care exist in addition to any statutory duties' provided for by the legislator. His Lordship inferred from the *X (Minors) v Bedfordshire County Council*[461] that this was 'largely a question of whether a common law duty of care would be inconsistent with the due performance of the other duty'.[462] Here there is no prima facie case against finding a common law duty of care, and this contrary to what Lord Hoffmann held in *Stovin v Wise*.[463] Indeed, 'there may be cases where to recognise [...] a vicarious liability on the part of the authority may so interfere with the performance of the local education authority's duties that it would be wrong to recognise any liability on the part of the authority. It

for breach of statutory duty, while the ineffectiveness of the same alternative remedies is the reason for imposing a common law duty of care on the defendant authority: eg, *Phelps v Hillingdon London Borough Council* [2000] WLR 776 (HL) 789 and 790.

[455] Also R Carnwath, 'The *Thornton* Heresy Exposed: Financial Remedies for Breach of Public Duties' [1998] *PL* 407, 418 f. Such a failure was apparent in *The Dorset case*, decided with other in *X(Minors) v Bedfordshire County Council* [1995] 2 AC 633 (HL); this fact did not prompt specific attention by Lord Browne-Wilkinson, who thought that breaches should be remedied with the mechanisms set up by the relevant statutes (762 f).

[456] Lewis, op cit, 453.   [457] [1978] AC 728 (HL) 754.
[458] [1996] AC 923 (HL) 933.   [459] 940.
[460] [2000] WLR 776 (HL).   [461] [1995] 2 AC 633 (HL).
[462] [2000] WLR 776 (HL) 787.   [463] [1996] AC 923 (HL) 952.

must, however, be for the local authority to establish that: it is not to be presumed and I anticipate that the circumstances where it could be established would be exceptional.'[464]

Lord Slynn was also ready to admit that there are situations 'where other remedies laid down by statute (eg an appeal review procedure) do not in themselves provide sufficient redress for loss which has already been caused'.[465]

It would probably be naive to ask why courts refrain from finding breaches of statutory duty while at the same time seem now eager to impose common law duties of care. The answer is to be found in the fact that negligence is far a more malleable tool in the hands of courts. Both torts allow courts to decide when a duty whose breach sounds in damage is there; negligence also allows them to set, and differently to modulate according to various factual situations, the standard of care required from the defendant authorities.[466]

French *faute de service* (and German *Objectivierung des Verschuldens* leading to the recognition of *Organisationsverschulden* appreciated according to objective standards)[467] shows that demanding standards can be imposed unto the administrations while paying lip service to concepts like the one of fault.[468] The same can be said concerning the *neminem laedere* principle which is the tool of choice of Italian civil courts.[469]

It is, however, to be doubted whether civil law tools such like fault and negligence will be the most appropriate when the new trends in governmental

---

[464] [2000] WLR 776 (HL) 790 (Lord Slynn).

[465] *Phelps v Hillingdon London Borough Council* [2000] WLR 776 (HL) 790.

[466] Bailey and Bowman, 'Public Authority Negligence Revisited' [2000] *CLJ* 85, 130, attest to 'the flexibility and sophistication of the breach of duty mechanism'; also D Brodie, 'Public Authorities and the Duty of Care' [1996] *Juridical R* 127, 140, and Fairgrieve, 'Pushing back the Boundaries of Public Authority Liability. Tort Law Enters the Classroom' [2002] *PL* 288, 302–304. Two cases decided together by the Court of Appeal can be contrasted as way of example: *S v Gloucestershire County Council* and *L v Tower Hamlets London Borough Council* [2001] 2 WLR 909 (CA); negligence actions brought against a local authorities for having placed children with foster parents who later abused them were reinstated in the first case and struck out in the second. Craig, op cit, 849, has however remarked that the configuration of the tort of breach of statutory duty as a strict liability tort has been a (fairly recent) judicial choice which could and should be reconsidered.

[467] F Ossenbühl, *Staatshaftungsrecht*, 5th edn (München: CH Beck, 1998), 77.

[468] Caranta, 'From Fault to Illegality: Shifting Patterns in Governmental Liability', in A Gambaro and AM Rabello (eds), *Towards a New European Jus Commune. Essays on European, Italian and Israeli Law* (Jerusalem: The Hebrew University of Jerusalem, 1999–5759), 621. In France scholars have started wondering whether governmental liability has now definitively shifted towards social insurance patterns: E Souteyrand, 'La responsabilité de l'administration' in *Act jur Dr adm* 1999, num spec, 92; P Fombeur, 'Les évolutions jurisprudentielles de la responsabilité sans faute', in *Act jur Dr adm* 1999, num spéc, 100, 101.

[469] Eg, Cass, Sez un., 2 June 1992, n 6667, in *Resp civ prev* 1993, 576; Cass, 29 Mar 1999, n 2963, in *Resp civ prev* 1999, 1265, with note by I Peila, 'Il concetto di insidia (o trabocchetto) ha superato il vaglio della Corte costituzionale'.

liability will have to be applied to situations where damages flow directly from the adoption of the failure to adopt of specific administrative acts.[470]

It is admitted that this is a situation rarer in England than on the Continent. This notwithstanding, losing sight of public law concepts could end in finding public authorities liable in situations where their actions and omissions would have withstood judicial review.[471]

---

[470] This is not to say that this will happen soon; indeed, even in more recent cases English courts are very attentive in finding non pure economic loss: Fairgrieve 'Pushing back the Boundaries of Public Authority Liability', 288, 293 et seq; such loss is usually absent when harm flows from administrative decisions.

[471] The variance between the standards applied in negligence actions and in judicial review proceedings is highlighted by Craig and Fairgrieve, '*Barrett*, Negligence and Discretionary powers' [1999] *PL* 626, 641 ff; Cane. 'Suing Public Authorties in Tort' (1996) 112 *LQR* 13, 17, on the contrary, equates the *Wednesbury* and *Bolan* tests; the separation between legality standards and liability conditions is strongly advocated by Bailey and Bowman, 'Public Authority Negligence Revisited' [2000] *CLJ* 85, and by Hickman, '"And That's Magic!"— Making Public Bodies Liable for Failure to Confer Benefits' [2000] *CLJ* 432, 435.

11. A COMPARATIVE STUDY OF THE ENGLISH AND GERMAN JUDICIAL APPROACH TO THE LIABILITY OF PUBLIC BODIES IN NEGLIGENCE

*Ralph-Andreas Surma**

I. INTRODUCTION

On 28 October 1998, the European Court of Human Rights (ECHR) gave judgment in the case of *Osman v United Kingdom.*[1] At the heart of this dispute lay a decision by the Court of Appeal[2] to strike out an action against the police for damages in negligence for failing to prevent a crime.

In its reasoning the Court of Appeal relied primarily on the judgment of the House of Lords in *Hill v Chief Constable of West Yorkshire,*[3] which, on the basis of various public policy considerations, has in fact established an immunity for the police from actions for negligence in respect of their activities in the investigation and suppression of crime.[4]

The ECHR held that the decision of the Court of Appeal constituted a violation of Article 6 (1) of the European Convention on Human Rights (EConvHR)[5], not granting the claimants a sufficient hearing of their cause due to the refusal to let their action proceed to trial.

In 2001 the ECHR was faced with another English case from the same area of the law, the House of Lords' decision in *X (Minors) v Bedfordshire CC,*[6] concerning the failure of a local authority to protect children from serious neglect and abuse. No longer relying on Article 6 (1) of the EConHR, the ECHR came to the conclusion that the claimants had not

---

* M St (Oxon). Attorney-at-Law and Legal Counsel Jungheinrich-Group, Hamburg/Germany. The following chapter is an abridged and updated version of a thesis submitted for the Degree of M St in Legal Research to the University of Oxford in Trinity Term 1999.

[1] [1999] 1 FLR 193 (ECHR).
[2] *Osman v Ferguson* [1993] 4 All ER 344 (CA).
[3] [1989] AC 53.
[4] Cf B Markesinis and S Deakin, *Tort Law*, 4th edn (1999), 148.
[5] Rome, 4 Nov 1950; TS 71 (1953); Cmd 8969.
[6] [1995] 2 AC 633 (HL).

been afforded an effective remedy, resulting in a violation of Article 13 of the EConHR.[7]

In recent years there have been quite a few English decisions which denied liability of public authorities in negligence on policy grounds. Decisions which involved, for instance, building inspection services,[8] highway authorities,[9] social[10] and fire services,[11] along with more police and Crown Prosecution Service cases.[12] When policy reasons were raised, the courts often considered them as at least another independent ground upon which to reject imposing a duty of care and liability on public bodies.[13] Such a development was quite contrary to other countries' expansion of public and state liability.[14]

The aim of this article is to review critically whether the policy issues relied on by the English courts are apt to strike the right balance between the community's need for efficient administration and individual protection. As the cases of *Osman v UK* and *Z v UK* imply that English law in this area falls below European Human Rights standards, a comparative approach to the subject is adopted and, besides English law, the German law regarding public liability in negligence is examined.

Analysing this area of the law in England and Germany may be useful in a European context with regard to Article 288 (2) [ex Article 215 (2)] of the EC Treaty that refers to the general principles common to the laws of the Member States to define some of the conditions for the non-contractual liability of the Community. The same approach has been accepted to determine the Member States' liability for violations of Community law.[15] But more importantly, as will be shown, German cases with similar factual backgrounds to English cases often lead to opposite results, suggesting that German courts in general are more willing to impose liability on public bodies than their English counterparts. In doing so, they do not openly consider the policy arguments raised by the English courts. Instead, they follow a different approach being led by different concerns.

To prove this, the article includes not only a section about the state of

---

[7] *Z v UK* [2001] 2 FLR 612 (ECHR), para 111.

[8] *Murphy v Brentwood LBC* [1991] 1 AC 398 (HL).

[9] *Stovin v Wise* [1996] AC 923 (HL).

[10] *Barrett v Enfield LBC* [1998] QB 367; *Phelps v Hillingdon LBC* [1999] 1 All ER 421 (CA); *Beverly Palmer v Tees Health Authority* The Times, 6 July 1999 (CA).

[11] *Capital and Counties plc v Hampshire CC* [1997] QB 1004.

[12] *Elguzouli-Daf v Comr of Police of the Metropolis* [1995] QB 335; *Leach v Chief Constable of Gloucestershire Constabulary* [1999] 1 All ER 215 (CA).

[13] Eg, *Hill v Chief Constable of West Yorkshire* [1989] AC 53 (HL); *Elguzouli-Daf v Comr of Police of the Metropolis* [1995] QB 335; *Stovin v Wise* [1996] AC 923 (HL).

[14] Cf J Bell and AW Bradley, *Governmental Liability: A Comparative Study* (London: UKNCCL, 1991), 15.

[15] Cf joined cases C-60/90 and C-9/90 *Francovich and Bonifaci v Italian Republic* [1991] ECR I-6911.

the law in the two countries but also a chapter directly juxtaposing three English and three German cases. Notwithstanding a divergence in style and methodology, the reasoning by the courts in actual cases will further exemplify where the differences and similarities in the English and German judicial approach to the liability of public authorities in negligence lie.

Against this background follows a critical analysis of the persuasiveness and appropriateness of the policy arguments used by the English Courts to deny liability of public authorities in negligence. Afterwards, these policy concerns are contrasted with the German approach, in order to find an explanation for the different attitude towards public liability in the two countries.

II. THE COUNTRY REPORTS

A. *Some General Observations*

In every legal system an individual who has suffered loss due to the wrongful act of another will find rules that allow him to obtain compensatory damages if the necessary requirements for such a claim are met. These rules make up what is known as the law of torts in common law countries and as the law of delict in civil law countries. As part of private law, their primary purpose is to settle disputes between private parties.[16] Private persons, meaning private individuals as well as private legal entities, usually act for their own benefit; that appears to be one of the main reasons why in principle they are held liable for the damage they have caused.[17]

The position of public authorities is different. In contrast to private persons, their main function is to exercise statutory powers and duties in the public interest and to provide services for the welfare of society.[18] They often have a certain amount of discretion as to how to carry out these activities. Furthermore, their decisions are open to judicial review and can be challenged on the basis of the rules and principles of public law. The special nature of their tasks has consequently affected the scope of their non-contractual liability. It touches a border area of the law of torts and of administrative law. As a result, almost no legal system has completely subjected public bodies to the ordinary private law.[19] Nevertheless, while trying to fulfil their public function, public authorities do occasionally cause damage which can be attributed to erroneous or careless behaviour

---

[16] Bell and Bradley, op cit, 1–2.

[17] Cf *Rylands v Fletcher* (1868) LR 3 HL 330, 339–40, 341.

[18] Cf *Stovin v Wise* [1996] AC 923 (HL) 935; P Cane, *An Introduction to Administrative Law*, 3rd edn (Oxford: Oxford University Press, 1996), 233–4.

[19] Bell and Bradley, op cit, 4.

on their side. A person who has suffered loss wants to recover compensation from the tortfeasor, regardless of whether the tortfeasor is a private or a public body and regardless of the purpose of the harmful act. In most cases public officials and authorities are therefore not totally exempt from the rules of private law.[20] The extent to which they are held liable depends on where and how each legal system has struck the balance between the protection of the interests of the adversely affected individual and the patronage of public authorities for the public benefit.

In this area, as in many branches of the law, policy considerations occur more or less openly irrespective of the particular legal system. There is generally no fixed canon of them and they can probably be best described as open-ended concerns of public interest and welfare, not restricted to an individual case.[21] They are not legal rules but represent value-judgments which serve to obtain and justify a certain desirable outcome.[22] Thus, they are most often referred to when the standard principles of law do not point to a clear solution to a legal problem,[23] as in the case of public liability.

B. The English Law of Negligence with Regard to Public Authorities

In English law, a successful claim for damages in negligence requires three main elements: a duty of care owed by the defendant to the claimant, a breach of that duty, and the occurrence of a foreseeable and recoverable damage which was caused by the breach of the duty.[24] When these conditions are met, the defendant is liable regardless of being a private individual or a public body. The so-called 'rule of law' has established as a general principle that public officials and public bodies are formally subject to the same rules and may be held liable in tort in the same way and extent as private persons.[25]

The most obvious example of an identical liability of public bodies and private persons is when the former enter into relations with the citizen on a private law basis, just as any other private individual, and commit a tortious act. However, many of the functions of and services provided by public bodies are without equivalent in the private sector. This special posi-

---

[20] Ibid 4; for the UK: J Clerk and WHB Lindsell, *Clerk & Lindsell on Torts*, 17th edn (London: Sweet and Maxwell, 1995), 14.

[21] C von Bar, *Gemeineuropäisches Deliktsrecht*, vol 1 (Munich: CH Beck, 1996), 302–3.

[22] Bell, *Policy Arguments in Judicial Decisions* (Oxford: Oxford University Press, 1983) 23; id, *An Introduction to Administrative Law*, 3rd edn (Oxford: Oxford University Press, 1996), 116.

[23] Ibid, 24.

[24] WVH Rogers, *Winfield & Jolowicz on Tort* (15th edn) (London: Sweet and Maxwell, 1998), 90; KM Stanton, *The Modern Law of Tort* (London: Sweet and Maxwell, 1994), 27.

[25] *Mersey Docks and Harbour Board Trustees v Gibbs* (1866) LR 1 HL 93, 122, 128; cf. AV Dicey and ECS Wade, *An Introduction to the Study of the Law of the Constitution*, 10th edn (London: Macmillan, 1959), 193, 202–3.

tion is reflected in the way in which the courts have modified the application of the general features of the law of torts to public bodies. In the tort of negligence the concept of the duty of care is used as the most important device to control and limit liability, both in relation to public bodies and private persons.

1. Duty of Care

A person will only be held liable in negligence for a careless act if he owes the victim of his conduct a legal duty to take care. The concept of the duty of care is a complex notion that defies a clear definition. It is rather general in nature and has been subject to various formulations. Cases involving public bodies have played an important role in the emergence of the law of negligence as it stands today, often raising problems of general significance.

(a) The Present Law

After departing from a two-level approach set up by Lord Wilberforce in *Anns v Merton LBC*[26] a three stage test has been developed to examine the issue of the duty of care.[27] The formula was clearly laid down in *Caparo Industries plc v Dickman*:[28] It must be reasonably foreseeable that the conduct of the defendant will cause damage to the claimant. There must be sufficient proximity between the parties, and it must be fair, just and reasonable to impose a duty of care.

With regard to the fair, just and reasonable-approach, these expressions are not looked at separately. They describe a wide-ranging array of social, political or economical factors which are not based upon technical legal doctrine and are nothing else than 'shorthand expressions for policy'.[29] It is under this heading that the courts raise their policy arguments.

Although the three stage test is adopted in many cases, there is no universal approach to the question of when a duty of care is owed.[30] It is difficult to always distinguish the categories and keep them separate as they all incorporate arguments of the same nature and are consequently partly overlapping.[31] As Lord Bridge put it in *Caparo Industries v Dickman*:[32] 'the

---

[26] [1978] AC 728 (HL).
[27] Eg, *Governors of the Peabody Foundation Fund v Sir Lindsay Parkinson and Co Ltd* [1985] AC 210 (HL) 239–241; *Yuen Ken Yeu v Attorney General of Hong Kong* [1988] AC 175 (PC) 190–4; *Rowling v Takaro Properties* [1988] AC 473 (PC) 501.
[28] *Caparo Industries v Dickman* [1990] 2 AC 605 (HL) 617–18 (Lord Bridge).
[29] Markesinis and Deakin, 'The Random Element of their Lordships' Infallible Judgment: An Economic and Comparative Analysis of the Tort of Negligence from Anns to Murphy' (1992) 55 *MLR*, 619, 642.
[30] Cf *Davis v Radcliffe* [1990] 1 WLR 821 (HL) 826.
[31] *Caparo Industries v Dickman* [1990] 2 AC 605 (HL) 633 (Lord Oliver: 'facets of the same thing').
[32] Ibid, 618.

criteria are little more than convenient labels to attach to the features of different specific situations which the law recognises as giving rise to a duty of care of a given scope'. It thus seems to be of minor practical importance how the approach to the concept of duty of care is precisely formulated. Which decision will be taken with regard to the duty of care is in the end often a question of policy.[33] This becomes even more apparent when the defendants are public authorities. In considering whether they owe a duty of care there are various additional factors that the courts take into account.

(a) Duty Factors Relevant to Public Authorities

(i) Statutory duties and powers
Public bodies carry out duties and powers conferred upon them by statute. When there is no action for breach of statutory duty, the law of negligence applies in the same way to the performance of a duty as to the exercise of a power.[34] It is settled since *Merseyside Docks and Harbour Board Trustees v Gibbs*[35] that a public body can in principle owe a duty of care in the performance of statutory functions.[36] However, if on the construction of the statute no civil action arises, the mere careless exercise of a statutory power or duty is not sufficient to impose a common law duty of care. It can only be found under the ordinary principles of the law of negligence.[37]

A difficulty arises out of the fact that the exercise of a statutory power usually contains a certain amount of discretion. Discretion is also found to a lesser degree in statutory duties. It is conferred upon public bodies in areas where special skill or knowledge are required to let them decide what is best.[38] That is why the courts often do not want to substitute their judgement to that of the authorities, and regard certain decisions of the authorities as unsuitable for judicial resolution, especially when the allocation of scarce resources or the distribution of risks is concerned.[39] This issue of non-justiciability and discretion has led the House of Lords to embark on several slightly different approaches, almost on a case to case basis, in order to determine the imposition of a duty of care on public bodies when discre-

---

[33] *West Wiltshire DC v Garland* [1995] Ch 297 (CA) 311; Rogers, op cit, 111.

[34] Cf *Sutherland Shire Council v Heyman* (1985) 60 ALR 1 (HCA) 26 (Mason J); S Arrowsmith, *Civil Liability and Public Authorities* (Winteringham: Earlsgate, 1992), 186.

[35] (1866) LR 1 HL 93.

[36] Cf *X (Minors) v Bedfordshire CC* [1995] 2 AC 633 (HL) 735; P Craig, *Administrative Law*, 4th edn (London: Sweet and Maxwell, 1999), 858–9.

[37] *X (Minors) v Bedfordshire CC* [1995] 2 AC 633 (HL) 734–5; *Dorset Yacht Co Ltd v Home Office* [1970] AC 1004 (HL) 1030.

[38] Cf M Andenas and D Fairgrieve, 'Sufficiently Serious? Judicial Restraint in Tortious Liability of Public Authorities and the European Influence', in Andenas (ed), *English Public Law and the Common Law of Europe* (London: Key Haven, 1998), 285, 309.

[39] *Rowling v Takaro Properties Ltd* [1988] AC 473 (PC) 501.

tionary functions are involved. Examples can be found in *Anns v Merton LBC* by Lord Wilberforce,[40] in *X(Minors) v Bedfordshire* by Lord Browne-Wilkinson,[41] in *Stovin v Wise*[42] by Lord Hoffmann, and in *Barrett v Enfield LBC*[43] by Lord Slynn of Hadley and Lord Hutton.

Despite their variations such approaches all incorporate the consideration of policy arguments to determine the existence of a duty of care. This underlines the importance of such considerations for the liability of public authorities in negligence.

(ii) Liability for omissions and acts of third parties

Many cases against public bodies involve claims for the failure to confer protection or a benefit. In English law, there is in principle no liability for mere omissions to act.[44] This approach is also extended to public bodies[45] which are generally under no common law duty to exercise statutory powers. Exceptions will therefore only exist under special circumstances,[46] including relationships where the defendant is responsible for a state of danger or for the protection of the claimant who is unable to safeguard himself.[47]

Coinciding with the sphere of omissions are cases in which injuries were not primarily caused by public authorities but by a third person. Because of the unpredictability of human conduct and the problems linked to omissions, there is, vicarious liability apart, usually no liability for the acts of third parties.[48] There are exceptions in rare situations of a special relationship which are similar to the ones already mentioned.[49]

(iii) Statutory framework and statutory purpose

The framework of the statutory power is a significant aspect in determining whether a duty of care should be imposed or not.[50] If there are no indications within the statute of an intention to provide compensation, it will be difficult to establish a duty of care in negligence,[51] the law of negligence only being a last resort.[52] Similarly, when the conduct of the authority was

---

[40] [1978] AC 728 (HL) 755.

[41] [1995] 2 AC 633 (HL) 740.

[42] [1996] AC (HL) 923, 953.

[43] [1999] 3 All ER 193, 211, 222, 225 (HL).

[44] Rogers, op cit, 1998), 117.

[45] Cf *Stovin v Wise* [1996] AC 923 (HL) 943–4, 953–4 (Lord Hoffmann).

[46] Markesinis, 'Negligence, Nuisance and Affirmative Duties of Action' (1989) 105 *LQR* 104.

[47] *Sutherland Shire Council v Heyman* (1985) 60 ALR 1 (HCA) 28–9 (Mason J); cf R Bagshaw, 'The Duties of Care of Emergency Service Providers' [1999] *LMCLQ* 71, 85; eg, a school's responsibility to safeguard its pupils.

[48] *Smith v Littlewoods Organisation Ltd* [1987] AC 241 (HL) 270; RFV Heuston and RA Buckley, *Salmond & Heuston on the Law of Torts*, 21st edn (London: Sweet and Maxwell, 1996), 239.

[49] Cf [1970] AC 1004 (HL).

[50] Craig, op cit, 858 et seq.

[51] Cf *Stovin v Wise* [1996] AC 923 (HL) 953.

[52] Cf Cane, op cit, 245.

intended by statute not for the individual but mainly for the general public benefit, the imposition of a duty of care will be rare.[53]

(iv) The kind of the loss suffered

In general, the courts are more willing to allow recovery of compensation for personal injury, property damage and when other important personal interests are infringed. Economic interests are less well protected.[54] There are only very few cases where pure economic loss will be awarded if it is not consequential upon personal injury or property damage.[55]

(v) Immunities

General and complete immunities from liability are hardly ever found in the law and the only exceptions, as in the case of judges for example, are based on strong public interest considerations.[56] Otherwise the courts usually emphasise that for public bodies and their servants no blanket immunity exists.[57] Yet, there are areas of activity beyond judicial control. These include the aforementioned activities involving the exercise of discretion and mainly concern so-called policy matters in contrast to operational decisions. But it seems that even below the policy level, the courts have barred claims for damages against public authorities in certain domains on the basis of public policy arguments.[58] This might not always have been referred to as a partial immunity but it amounts to it and has been criticised by the ECHR in the *Osman v UK* case.[59]

(b) Other Elements of the Tort of Negligence

There are no special rules for public bodies with regard to the other elements of the tort of negligence such as breach of duty, causation and the assessment of damages. They follow the established principles.

C. The German Law

In German law there is no direct or exact equivalent to the English concept

---

[53] *X(Minors) v Bedfordshire CC* [1995] 2 AC 633 (HL) 731–2.

[54] Cf *Stovin v Wise* [1996] AC 923 (HL) 937; Rogers, 'Keeping the Floodgates Shut: "Mitigation" and "Limitation" of Tort Liability in the English Common Law', in J Spier (ed), *The Limits of Liability: Keeping the Floodgates Shut* (London: Kluwer Law International, 1996), 75, 83.

[55] Cf *Hedley Byrne and Co Ltd v Heller and Partners Ltd* [1964] AC 465 (HL); *Henderson v Merrett Syndicates Ltd* [1995] 2 AC 145 (HL); *White v Jones* [1995] 2 AC 207 (HL).

[56] JF Clerk and WHB Lindsell, *Clerk & Lindsell on Torts*, 17th edn (London: Sweet and Maxwell, 1995), 329.

[57] *Hill v Chief Constable of West Yorkshire* [1989] AC 53 (HL) 59; *Barrett v Enfield LBC* [1999] 3 All ER 193 (HL) 212.

[58] *Elgozouli-Daf v Commissioner of Police of the Metropolis* [1995] QB 335, 349–50 (Steyn LJ)—CPS; *Hill v Chief Constable of West Yorkshire* [1989] AC 53 (HL)—police; *X (Minors) v Bedfordshire CC* [1995] 2 AC 633 (HL)—social services. [59] [1999] 1 FLR 193.

of negligence as a separate tort. Being a civil law system, German law is not familiar with the notion of nominate torts. Instead, the law of torts is in principle embodied in the German Civil Code (*BGB*) and consists primarily of thirty successive articles, called paragraphs, which are found in the second book of the code as part of the law of obligations.

1. § 823 BGB

The first and most important of these tort provisions is § 823 BGB which lays down two general rules:

(1) A person who wilfully or negligently injures the life, body, health, freedom, property, or other right of another contrary to law is bound to compensate him for any damage arising therefrom.

(2) The same obligation attaches to a person who infringes a statutory provision intended for the protection of others. If according to the purview of the statute infringement is possible without fault, the duty to make compensation arises only if some fault can be imputed to the wrongdoer.[60]

In § 823 I BGB, negligence is referred to as a mode of committing a tortious act, as a form of fault. This represents the traditional and basic understanding of negligence in German law, which is defined in the second sentence of § 276 I BGB as not exercising the care required in ordinary social intercourse. When § 823 I BGB declares that careless conduct may render somebody liable in tort, it refers to acts as well as to omissions. Omissions, however, will only lead to liability if there was a legal duty to act.[61] Apart from statutory duties or the voluntary assumption of responsibility, a legal duty to act is most commonly derived from the so called *Verkehrssicherungspflichten*, which can only inadequately be translated as legal duties to maintain safety. These duties were developed by the courts on the basis that everybody who creates or controls a potential source of danger has to take the necessary precautions to protect others against the risks caused by his activity or his property.[62] Their impact goes beyond the sphere of omissions as the *Verkehrssicherungspflichten* determine which circumstances and relationships will give rise to a duty of care to safeguard the enumerated interests in § 823 I BGB and thus limit the scope of liability.[63] In German tort law, they seem to be the closest equivalent to the

---

[60] Translation of § 823 taken from Markesinis, *The German Law of Obligations: Volume II, The Law of Torts: A Comparative Introduction*, 3rd edn (Oxford: Oxford University Press, 1997), 12.

[61] Cf Palandt-H Thomas, BGB, 58th edn (1999), § 823 Rn 35.

[62] Ibid, § 823 Rn 58.

[63] Markesinis, *The German Law of Obligations, Volume II*, 75; MünchKomm-H Mertens, *BGB*, 3rd edn (1997), § 823 Rn 204.

English concept of a duty of care[64] and are often expressive of judicial policy.[65]

§ 823 II BGB gives rise to liability for breach of a protective statute or enactment. A statute is intended for the protection of others if it exists to defend not only general but also or solely individual interests.[66] In this sense the provision appears to be comparable to the English tort of breach of statutory duty, both requiring a protective nature towards a limited class of people. German law, however, does not also require a legislative intention in the context of the protective statute to create a civil remedy.

2. The German Law of State Liability

Although § 823 I and II BGB are the main German tort provisions and their wording does not include any limitation, they do not in general apply in the same way to private persons on the one hand, and public authorities and their employees performing public functions on the other.[67] Regarding public liability, there is a special claim for breach of official duty which is established in § 839 BGB in conjunction with Article 34 of the German Constitution (GG). This does not necessarily mean, however, that public bodies are not held liable in the same way, or to the same extent, as private persons. In fact, there is a provision in the German Constitution which could be described as the German rule of law. According to Article 20 III GG the executive and the judiciary are bound by law and justice. Correspondingly, any state activity can in theory be challenged in court; this is confirmed by Article 19 IV 1 GG which provides the right of the individual to have recourse to law where his rights are violated by public authority. In this context it is worth noting that the distinction between public and private law is a strong characteristic of German law.[68] Therefore, the remedy of judicial review or actions of annulment of administrative decisions have to be brought before the administrative courts, whereas only the civil courts have jurisdiction for claims for damages in tort actions against public officials and bodies.[69]

In Germany, public liability in tort is regarded as part of the wider-ranging law of state liability. The term state liability is not precise because not only the Federation (*Bund*) and the states (*Länder*) but also the other terri-

---

[64] von Bar, 'Limitation and Mitigation in German Tort Law', in Spier (ed), op cit, 17, 22.

[65] Markesinis, *The German Law of Obligations, Volume II*, 75.

[66] BGH ZIP (1991), 1597, 1598; MünchKomm-H Mertens, 3rd edn, *BGB* (1997), § 823 Rn 185.

[67] One exception in BGH NJW (1996), 3208, 3209.

[68] W Rüfner, 'Basic Elements of German Law on State Liability', in Bell and Bradley (eds), op cit, 249, 251–2.

[69] Bell and Bradley, 'Governmental Liability: A Preliminary Assessment', in Bell and Bradley (eds), op cit, 1, 3.

torial units and entities of public law, such as local authorities, are all subject to liability under the same principles. The rules of state liability law do not represent a coherent legal system united in one code. They are scattered in different statutes or have been developed by the courts. Besides public liability in § 839 BGB and Article 34 GG, they deal with compensation for other forms of public law measures,[70] which are of no interest for present purposes. Any special provisions in the states which used to make up the former German Democratic Republic are also not taken into consideration as § 839 BGB, in conjunction with Article 34 GG, is applicable there as well.[71]

3. The liability of Public Bodies for Breach of Official Duty

§ 839 BGB and Article 34 GG come from different areas of the law and came into force at different times. § 839 BGB, as part of the law of torts in the German Civil Code, came into force with the rest of the Code on 1 January 1900, while Article 34 GG is part of the German Constitution, which was promulgated on 23 May 1949. These provisions jointly constitute the foundation of the claim for damages against public bodies. They are interrelated and influence each other.[72] Although they are laid down in statutes, their elements have been interpreted, refined and adapted by the courts.[73] As a result the present German law concerning public liability has basically been developed through case law. Even though technically speaking judgments do not constitute a recognised source of law in civil law countries like Germany,[74] the actual influence of the courts on the law should not be underestimated. The following account mainly presents the current position of the Federal Supreme Court.

(a) § 839 BGB
§ 839 BGB reads as follows:

(1) If an official wilfully or negligently commits a breach of official duty incumbent upon him towards a third party, he shall compensate the third party for any damage arising therefrom. If only negligence is imputable to the official, he may be held liable only if the injured party is unable to obtain compensation otherwise.

(2) If an official commits a breach of his official duty in giving judgment in an action, he is not responsible for any damage arising therefrom, unless the breach of

---

[70] Eg, compensation for expropriation (*Enteignung*), sacrifice or denial damage (*Aufopferung*) or claims to remedial action (*Folgenbeseitigungsansprüche*).

[71] K Windthorst and HD Sproll, *Staatshaftungsrecht* (1994) 144; S Pfab, *Staatshaftung in Deutschland* (1996), 32.

[72] Ibid, 53.

[73] F Ossenbühl, *Staatshaftungsrecht*, 5th edn (Munich: CH Beck, 1998), 3–4.

[74] Cf von Bar, op cit, 303.

duty is subject to a public penalty to be enforced by criminal proceedings. This provision does not apply to a breach of duty consisting of refusal or delay in the exercise of the office.

(3) The duty to make compensation does not arise if the injured party has wilfully or negligently omitted to avert the injury by making use of a legal remedy.'[75]

The first section of this provision, if looked upon alone, imposes liability for breach of official duty only on the official acting on behalf of the public body and not on the public body itself. According to its wording, it holds the official personally liable for all the damage he caused by violating the duty he owed to the citizen. In this way § 839 I 1 BGB extends the ordinary tort liability established in § 823 I BGB, as, once the conditions of § 839 I BGB are fulfilled, the official has to compensate for any damage, in principle including pure economic loss, and not only for the infringement of certain enumerated interests;[76] thus the provision goes beyond the position of English law on the recovery of pure economic loss.

(b) Article 34 GG

When the official has breached his duties in the exercise of a public law or sovereign act, however, Article 34 GG shifts his personal liability arising from § 839 I 1 BGB onto the public authority in charge and makes it liable for the conduct of the official. Article 34 GG provides that:

If any person, in the exercise of a public office entrusted to him, violates his official obligations to a third party, liability shall rest in principle on the State or the public body which employs him. In the event of wilful or grossly negligent conduct, the right of recourse shall be reserved. In respect of claims for compensation or the right of recourse, the jurisdiction of the ordinary courts must not be excluded.[77]

Because of Article 34 GG, liability of the public body itself is the standard form of public liability. It leads to the assumption of an obligation on the part of the authority that leaves the official exempt from any liability to the third party.[78] It brings about a transfer of responsibility. This means that the public body is only liable if according to § 839 BGB the conditions for a personal liability of the official are met.[79] The public body will then be liable in exactly the same way and to the same extent as the official under § 839 BGB.[80] It is a form of indirect state liability[81] and thus differs from the direct and the vicarious liability of public authorities in England.

[75] For the translation cf Markesinis, *The German Law of Obligations, Volume* II, 14–15.

[76] Rüfner, 'Basic Elements of German Law on State Liability', in Bell and Bradley, op cit, 249, 250.

[77] For the translation cf Markesinis, *The German Law of Obligations, Volume II,* 903.

[78] BGHZ 4, 10, 45–6; B Bender, *Staatshaftungsrecht,* 3rd edn (1981), Rn 70.

[79] Cf BGHZ 34, 99, 109–10; Ossenbühl, op cit, 12.　　　　　　　　[80] BGHZ 4, 10, 46.

[81] Ossenbühl, op cit, 1998) 10; G Krohn, 'Zum Stand des Rechts der staatlichen Ersatzleistungen nach dem Scheitern des Staatshaftungsgesetzes' VersR (1991), 1085, 1085.

The personal liability of officials and public employees towards a third party continues in situations where they pursue ordinary private law activities. If they enter relations with a citizen on a private law basis on behalf of a public body and breach official duties owed towards the private party, Article 34 GG will not apply. Officials will be held liable under § 839 I 1 BGB. As a specific rule, it usually overrides the other more general tort clauses of the BGB.[82] It restricts the meaning of the term 'official', however, to civil servants as defined in public law (*Beamte*). Other government or administration employees are therefore liable according to the regular tort provisions.

The public authority is in these cases only held vicariously liable for its civil servants and employees.[83] This approach to fiscal liability corresponds with English law. The applicable provisions in the Civil Code are § 823 BGB and the provisions following it, in conjunction with § 831 BGB for acts of employees, or, for torts of organs, §§ 31, 89 BGB, which in fact represent a type of direct liability of the State. An official is able to avoid his personal liability on the basis of § 839 I 2 BGB if he can invoke the vicarious liability of the public authority as an alternative source of compensation for the claimant.[84]

(c). The elements of a claim under § 839 BGB, Article 34 GG

As enactments overriding § 839 BGB and Article 34 GG are exceptional and only found in a few specific statutes,[85] the two provisions will usually apply. A claim for damages under § 839 I BGB and Article 34 GG requires that an official in the exercise of a public office culpably breached an official duty he owed to a third party which suffered harm as a consequence of his conduct.

(i) The official

The wording of § 839 BGB limits liability to the acts of officials as defined in administrative law. In Article 34 GG this wording is extended to any person who is performing functions which are part of the sovereign activities of the public body,[86] not only including its employees but, under certain circumstances, also private enterprises or private individuals.[87] It is the nature of the activity which is decisive for the liability of the public body and not the legal position or status of the acting person.

---

[82] BGH DRiZ (1964), 197; Palandt-H Thomas, *BGB*, 58th edn, (1999), § 839 Rn 26, 85; but cf BGH NJW (1996), 3208, 3209.
[83] Windthorst and Sproll, op cit, 62.
[84] Cf BGHZ 85, 393, 395–6; OLG Köln VersR (1990), 898, 899.
[85] Eg, §§ 11 ff PostG.
[86] Windthorst and Sproll, op cit, 67.
[87] Cf Ossenbühl, op cit, 14–25.

(ii) Act in exercise of a public office
This element is satisfied whenever an act is based on a statute which
expressly designates a certain duty as an official duty in the exercise of a
public office.[88] Apart from these cases, the exercise of a public office generally encompasses any kind of sovereign conduct.[89] An activity can be
referred to as sovereign when public duties or functions are pursued with
public law means.[90]

In areas in which public bodies are able to choose between private law
or sovereign means to perform their public functions,[91] or when physical
acts (*Realakte*) are concerned, it can be more difficult to decide whether an
act was conducted in the exercise of a public office.[92] The courts therefore
rely on different criteria. If the form the act takes (*Rechtsform*), for
instance, is clearly a form used and established in the area of public law, the
exercise of a public office is presumed.[93] The same is true when the official
acts with the intention to execute public duties and the nature of the task
in question is indeed a public law one.[94] This last principle is especially relevant to classify physical acts of officials where the distinction between
forms or means of private and public law is of no assistance. There has to
be a special interrelation between the public duty pursued and the tortious
conduct.[95] The connection must be so close that the physical act can be
regarded as part of the sovereign activity of the public body.[96] On this basis,
the requirement of 'in the exercise' is not fulfilled, for example, when the
official acts purely out of personal motives.[97] If it should finally not be
possible to assign an official's act beyond doubt to public or private law,
there is a rebuttable presumption that it falls into the realm of public law.[98]

(iii) Breach of official duty
Official duties are the personal behavioural duties (*Verhaltenspflichten*) of
the official with regard to the exercise of his office. As such they constitute

---

[88] Cf BGHZ 60, 54, 56; BGH NJW (1981), 2120, 2121; eg, § 9a I StrWG NW or § 10 II
NS StrG.
[89] BGH NVwZ (1992), 92, 93; H Müller, *Das internationale Amtshaftungsrecht* (1991) 12;
P Dagtoglou, in *BKzGG* (1970) Art 34, Rn 86.
[90] Cf BGH NJW (1992), 972; Windthorst and Sproll, op cit, 76.
[91] Cf BGHZ 60, 54, 56; eg, the *Leistungsverwaltung*.
[92] MünchKomm-H Papier, *BGB*, 3rd edn (1997), § 839, Rn 146.
[93] Ossenbühl, op cit, 27.
[94] OLG Karlsruhe NJW (1994), 2033, 2034; cf Soergel-H Vinke, *BGB*, 12th edn (1998), §
839 Rn 56, 71.
[95] BGHZ 69, 128, 132–3; OLG Köln NJW (1976), 295.
[96] BGHZ 108, 230, 232; 42, 176, 179; H Papier in Maunz-Dürig, *Komm zGG* (1998) Art
34, Rn 131.
[97] Cf BGHZ 11, 181, 187; OLG Köln NJW (1970), 1322, 1324.
[98] MünchKomm-H Papier, *BGB*, 3rd edn (1997), § 839, Rn 146; Windthorst and Sproll, op
cit, 80.

in theory internal duties the official owes to the public body as his employer[99] and not to third parties.[100] They are nonetheless often identical with legal duties incumbent upon the state to the citizen[101] and—not least with regard to the effectiveness and wording of § 839 BGB—many of them are consequently ascribed an external effect as well.[102] Official duties are derived from all kinds and levels of legal provisions from community law to municipal law, including customary law and subordinate forms of law such as decrees and even instructions of the official.[103] In so far as the official has to follow orders of his superiors, he cannot be in breach of an official duty. When injustice is done to the citizen in such a case, it is the conduct of the superior that needs to be examined.[104]

There is no conclusive list of official duties either in § 839 BGB or in Article 34 GG. This vacuum has led the courts to create a multitude of official duties which often partly overlap.[105] The main official duty, which stems from the aforementioned Article 20 III GG, is to act lawfully.[106] The nature of this general duty is so wide and vague that it serves as a generic term for almost all of the official duties.[107] Among them is the duty to exercise discretion in a proper and lawful manner.[108]

Although German law frequently only refers to public functions in general, without distinguishing duties or powers, it does make the distinction between decisions involving discretion and 'bound decisions', i.e. acts without discretion. Once the conditions of the statute authorizing the exercise of discretion are met, discretion can comprise the choice whether to act or which decision to take.[109] Where the official acts within the ambit of his discretion, liability will not occur. That is true for German and for English law. It is acknowledged in both systems that discretion provides official bodies with a certain freedom to act. Yet, unlike the English courts, the German courts do not recognise an area of discretion which from the outset is beyond any judicial control. There is no reference to the allocation of resources or distribution of risks marking a boundary that might hint at a different, less policy oriented understanding of discretion in German law.

---

[99] MünchKomm-H Papier, op cit, § 839, Rn 189.

[100] Windthorst and Sproll, op cit, 83.

[101] Cf Papier, in Maunz-Dürig, op cit, Art 34, Rn 21.

[102] Ossenbühl, op cit, 42.

[103] Windthorst and Sproll, op cit, 84.

[104] Rüfner, 'Basic Elements of German Law on State Liability', in Bell and Bradley (eds), op cit, 249, 254.

[105] P Dagtoglou, in *BK zGG* (1970) Art 34, Rn 116 ff; Soergel-H Vinke, *BGB* (12th edn, 1998), § 839, Rn 136–46.

[106] BGHZ 16, 111, 113; cf BGHZ 60, 112, 117.

[107] Cf H Engelhardt, 'Neue Rechtsprechung des BGH zum Staatshaftungsrecht', NVwZ (1992), 1052 ff; MünchKomm-H Papier, *BGB*, 3rd edn (1997), § 839, Rn 191 ff.

[108] BGHZ 74, 144, 156; 75, 120, 124; 118, 263, 271.

[109] H Maurer, *Allgemeines Verwaltungsrecht*, 11th edn (1997), 121–2.

That does not imply that the courts are allowed to substitute their decision for the one of the public body. They can only review specific errors of the public body in the exercise of its discretion. In English law it nevertheless seems that even in justiciable areas of discretion, at least until recently, the misuse of discretion had to reach an obvious level of abuse before a duty of care was imposed.[110] In German law the courts used to have a similar point of view[111] but it is accepted now that it is sufficient that the official applied his discretion incorrectly, even if it did not amount to evident abuse.[112] The scope of evaluation granted to the courts includes an erroneous use of discretion (*Ermessensfehlgebrauch*), an exceeding discretion (*Ermessens-überschreitung*), no use of discretion at all (*Ermessensnichtgebrauch*),[113] or when the official did not realise that his discretion was limited to only one possible lawful decision (*Ermessensreduzierung auf Null* or *Selbstbindung der Verwaltung*).[114]

Other examples of official duties recognised to fall within § 839 BGB and Article 34 GG are the duty to act proportionally (*verhältnismässig*),[115] the duty to act without delay,[116] to act consistently,[117] the duty to provide correct information[118] and especially the duties not to commit tortious acts[119] and to comply with the public law duties to maintain safety (*öffentlich-rechtliche Verkehrssicherungspflichten*). These duties extend to all forms of conduct under public law and can also constitute duties to act.[120]

(iv) Duty owed to a third party

The official duty must be owed towards the claimant.[121] An official duty is owed towards a third party provided it exists in the interest of a limited group of people worthy of protection and not only in the interest of the community as a whole.[122] This same consideration occurs in the context of § 823 II BGB.[123] Three conditions have to be fulfilled for such a duty which

---

[110] Cf X *(Minors) v Bedfordshire* CC [1995] 2 AC 633 (HL) 736; *Stovin v Wise* [1996] AC 923 (HL) 953.

[111] BGHZ 4, 302, 313; RGZ 162, 273.

[112] BGHZ 74, 144, 156; 75, 120, 124; Palandt-H Heinrichs, *BGB*, 58th edn (1999), § 839, Rn 36.

[113] Ossenbühl, op cit, 46.

[114] BGHZ 118, 263, 271; BGH NVwZ (1994), 405, 405–6.

[115] BGHZ 18, 366, 368; 55, 261, 266; BGH NJW (1973), 894.

[116] BGHZ 30, 19, 26; BGH VersR (1992), 1354; BGH NVwZ (1994), 405.

[117] BGH NVwZ (1986), 245, 246; BGH NJW (1963), 644, 645.

[118] BGH NJW (1992), 1230, 1231; NJW (1994), 2087, 2090.

[119] BGH NJW (1992), 1310.

[120] Cf BGH NJW (1993), 2612, 2613; Windthorst and Sproll, op cit, 87, 97.

[121] Ossenbühl, op cit, 57.

[122] BGHZ 65, 196, 198; 74, 144, 146.

[123] Cf text accompanying n 66 above.

depend on its statutory framework and nature:[124] The official duty must generally be capable of including individual protection.[125] The claimant has to belong to the class of people protected by the duty and, finally, the damage suffered must fall within the protective ambit of the duty.[126] These formulas are quite open to interpretation by the courts and thus to implementation of policy and value judgments. What they convey is that an imposition of liability on the public body should in principle only be justified when the official duty establishes a somewhat proximate relationship between the claimant and the public body,[127] as for instance in administrative proceedings.[128]

Such a connection is not required where the public conduct breaches the official duty not to commit tortious acts and directly violates interests of the claimant enumerated in § 823 I BGB, which are of an absolute nature towards everybody. In such circumstances the affected claimant is always a third person within the meaning of § 839 I BGB.[129] This is somewhat parallel to the English view that in cases of personal injury or property damage mere foreseeability is often enough to satisfy the requirements of a duty of care.

With its emphasis on a relationship or connection between the claimant and the public authority, the element of a duty owed to a third party is in general reminiscent of the requirement of proximity in the duty of care concept in the English law of negligence.[130] It also recalls the importance of the protective purpose of statutory powers and duties.[131] Under both legal regimes such an element is in theory intended as a means to limit the liability of public bodies;[132] the German courts have however extended the third party effect of many official duties.[133]

(v) Fault

§ 839 I 1 BGB imposes liability only if the official has wilfully or negligently breached the official duty. The distinction matters because different rules apply depending on the kind of fault. In the case of negligent conduct, which is discussed here, § 839 I 2 BGB will apply and lead to an exclusion

---

[124] BGHZ 90, 310, 312; Ossenbühl, op cit, 58.

[125] F Schoch, 'Amtshaftung' *JURA* (1988), 585, 590.

[126] BGH NJW 1992, 1230, 1231; MünchKomm-H Papier, *BGB*, 3rd edn (1997), § 839, Rn 232.

[127] Ossenbühl, op cit, 58, 60; Windthorst and Sproll, op cit, 93.

[128] Cf also BGH NJW (1989), 99; J Martens, *Die Praxis des Verwaltungsverfahrens* (1985), 44 ff.

[129] BGHZ 69, 128, 138; BGHZ 78, 274, 279.

[130] Cf Rogers, 'Keeping the Floodgates Shut', in Spier (ed), op cit, 75, 83.

[131] Cf text accompanying n 38 et seq and n 50 et seq above.

[132] Ossenbühl, op cit, 59.

[133] Cf P Dagtoglou in *BK zGG* (1970), Art 34, Rn 158 ff.

of the liability of the official or public body if the injured party can obtain compensation otherwise.

Negligence is defined in general in § 276 I 2 BGB[134] and, unlike English law, subdivided into light, ordinary and gross negligence. As in English law, the required standard of care is objective.[135] Decisive is what standard could be expected from the average official who was acting in compliance with his duties in the same external circumstances as the defendant,[136] the latter's actual skill being irrelevant.[137] The claimant does not need to name or individualise the particular official who acted and fell below the necessary standard of care in order to succeed.[138]

(vi) Causation

The theory of equivalence or rule of *conditio sine qua non* requires for causation that the damage would not have occurred without the breach of official duty. This corresponds with the common law 'but for' test.

To keep this extensive concept of causation under control, the causal connection between damage and breach of duty has to be adequate. An adequate cause is one which generally is apt to enhance the objective possibility of or to produce such a consequence as has occurred.[139] It does not include conditions which according to objective human experience and common opinion cannot reasonably be taken into account.[140] This resembles the English law's use of the concept of foreseeability, particularly in the test for remoteness of damage in the tort of negligence.

Another feature of causation raised in the area of public liability is the concept of alternative lawful conduct.[141] When the damage would have occurred even in the case of lawful conduct of the official, the breach of duty is generally not deemed to be a sufficient cause of the damage.[142]

In relation to omissions, causation demands that—supposing there was a duty to act—the undertaking of the act omitted by the official would almost certainly have avoided the materialisation of the damage.[143]

(vii) Damages

§ 839 I 1 BGB in conjunction with Article 34 GG holds the public body

---

[134] Cf text accompanying n 61 above.
[135] MünchKomm-H Papier, op cit, § 839, Rn 279, 284; Bender, op cit, Rn 333, 334.
[136] Rüfner, 'Basic Elements of German Law on State Liability', in Bell and Bradley (eds), op cit, 249, 257.
[137] Müller, *Das internationale Amtshaftungsrecht* (1991), 18.
[138] RGZ 100, 102, 102–3; Ossenbühl, op cit, 62.
[139] Cf BGHZ 7, 199, 204.
[140] Palandt-H Heinrichs, *BGB*, 57th edn (1998), vor § 249, Rn 58–9.
[141] BGHZ 96, 157, 171.
[142] Cf BGHZ 36, 144, 154; but note OLG Oldenburg VersR (1991), 306, 307.
[143] Cf BGH VersR (1983), 1031, 1033; VersR (1984), 333, 335.

liable for any damage arising from the unlawful conduct of the official.[144] The sole condition is that the suffered damage represents the kind of loss that the official duty was supposed to prevent.[145] Nevertheless, the willingness of German courts to impose liability on public bodies does not appear to depend on the sort of damage claimed to the same extent as in English decisions. German law is not as limited in the situations in which pure economic loss can successfully be claimed in the area of public liability.

The assessment of damages is determined according to the general rules in §§ 249 et seq, §§ 842 et seq BGB with one difference: Public liability does generally not lead to compensation for damage in kind, as only monetary recompense can be awarded.[146] This is due to the fact that in most cases another public law act would be required to remedy the wrongful conduct of the official. Ordinary civil courts, however, which award the damage claims, have no jurisdiction to force public authorities to act in a particular way in the area of public law.[147] Moreover, liability in § 839 BGB, even when it is shifted upon the public body, remains focused on the person of the official himself who would be held liable in his capacity as a private person. A private person cannot perform public law acts.[148]

Apart from pecuniary losses, compensation for non-pecuniary losses may be claimed for pain and suffering in cases of personal injury, deprivation of personal liberty and severe infringement of someone's general right of personality on the basis of §§ 839, 847, 253 BGB, Article 34 GG.[149]

(d) Limitation of Liability

Even when the requirements of § 839 I 1 BGB and Article 34 GG are satisfied, public liability is subject to certain restrictions in German law. These restrictions are often expressive of the special role of public officials and bodies performing public functions. The most important limitations are found in the Civil Code itself in § 839 I 2 BGB, § 839 II BGB and § 839 III BGB, as well as in § 254 BGB dealing with contributory negligence. Public liability can also be, in exceptional cases, partly excluded or limited by specific parliamentary statute for reasons of general public interest, as long as it is not abolished altogether or significantly undermined.[150]

---

[144] Markesinis, *The German Law of Obligations, Volume II*, 903.

[145] Cf text accompanying n 126 above; OLG Oldenburg NVwZ-RR (1993), 593; Windthorst and Sproll, op cit, 112.

[146] Cf BGHZ 34, 99, 104–5; BGH NJW (1993), 1799, 1800; Palandt-H Heinrichs, op cit, § 839, Rn 79.

[147] BGHZ ibid; Rüfner, 'Basic elements of German Law on State Liability', in Bell and Bradley, op cit, 258.

[148] BGHZ 34, 99, 105; Ossenbühl, op cit, 11, 110.

[149] Cf BGHZ 78, 274, 279–80.

[150] MünchKomm-H Papier, op cit, § 839, Rn 332, 334–5.

(i) § 839 I 2 BGB

The provision of § 839 I 2 BGB is also referred to as the subsidiarity clause. It provides that as a rule the official is not held liable for negligent conduct if the claimant can claim the same damages from somebody else,[151] as in the case of the existence of a joint or different tortfeasor.[152] Thus, when somebody other than the official primarily caused the damage, which in English law is discussed under the liability for acts of a third party,[153] § 839 I 2 BGB will in theory relieve the public official of his liability,[154] if this problem has not already been dealt with through causation.

Although § 839 I 2 BGB was originally intended only for the protection of the individual official,[155] it equally applies to public bodies, reducing their financial burden,[156] when, due to Article 34 GG, they take over the official's liability.[157] Nonetheless, the German courts have modified and updated the scope of application of the subsidiarity clause by making use of a teleological reduction (*teleologische Reduktion*).[158] Accordingly, § 839 I 2 BGB is not applicable if it collides with the principle of equal treatment in respect of liability (*haftungsrechtlicher Gleichbehandlungsgrundsatz*), which has its foundation in Article 3 I GG.[159] This principle comprises those situations in which, exceptionally, the content of public law duties incumbent upon the official acting in a sovereign manner corresponds with the general duty of care imposed on everybody,[160] thus removing any justification for a different treatment of public bodies and private persons.

This is of relevance in two areas of great practical importance: First, it was established as a principle of equal treatment of users of the highway which does not allow any privileges for public officials or bodies acting in their public capacity in the case of ordinary driving,[161] unless they are claiming special rights such as in a police operation.[162] The second area concerns the public law duty to maintain road traffic safety (*öffentlich-rechtliche Straßenverkehrssicherungspflicht*) with regard to the condition of

---

[151] Markesinis, *The German Law of Obligations, Volume II*, 904.
[152] MünchKomm-H Papier, op cit, § 839, Rn 300.
[153] Cf text accompanying n 44 above.
[154] Cf LG Bielefeld ZAP-EN 1996 No 700; Staudinger-K Schäfer, *BGB*, 12th edn (1986), § 839, Rn 385.
[155] Cf text accompanying n 257 below.
[156] Cf BGHZ 13, 88, 104; Müller, op cit, 20.
[157] BGH NJW (1993), 1647.
[158] BGHZ 68, 217; Ossenbühl, op cit, 80.
[159] Windthorst and Sproll, op cit, 122.
[160] BGH NJW (1992), 2476, 2477; NJW (1993), 2612, 2613.
[161] Cf BGHZ 68, 217, 220–2; BGHZ 123, 102, 104.
[162] Then § 839 I 2 applies, cf BGHZ 85, 225, 228 f. Krohn, 'Zum Stand des Rechts der staatlichen Ersatzleistungen nach dem Scheitern des Staatshaftungsgesetzes', VersR (1991), 1085, 1089.

the roads.[163] Here, too, the scope of the public duty is identical with the general duty of care of anybody who owns, controls or creates a source of danger.[164]

The courts have further reduced the significance of § 839 I 2 BGB, not accepting every possible claim of the claimant against somebody else as an appropriate means of compensation within the meaning of the provision.[165] Public bodies are not discharged from their liability if this would be unreasonable and contrary to the intention of the rule.[166]

The largest category of claims which on that basis is no longer considered as an alternative way of compensation consists of private and public law insurance claims,[167] with the exclusion of the tortfeasor's compulsory car liability insurance.[168] The claimant earned these claims by using his own financial resources or through his work and performance;[169] they are often the result of private precaution. Moreover, according to German understanding, the insurance payment serves solely as a form of interim financing until the damage can finally be settled.[170] A claim for damages is subrogated by law to the insurer to the extent to which he has indemnified the injured person.[171] This *cessio legis* also indicates that neither the insurer nor the group of the insured as a whole shall in the end carry the loss unjustly suffered by one of their members, but that the tortfeasor must be held responsible for the damage he caused.[172] The insurer is only supposed to carry the risk of the enforceability of the claim for compensation.[173] He will therefore only bear the final loss when the tortfeasor is unable to pay,[174] which is not sufficient for § 839 I 2 BGB to apply.[175]

The English courts take a different view of the role of insurance. In principle it is established that the insurance status of the parties should be irrelevant to the question of liability[176] and that the insurability of the parties

---

[163] BGHZ 75, 134, 138; BGH NJW (1992), 2476; NJW (1993), 2612.

[164] BGH NJW 1993, 2612; S Lörler, 'Die Subsidiaritätsklausel in der Amtshaftung' *JuS* (1990), 544, 547.

[165] Cf BGHZ 91, 48, 54.

[166] Cf BGH NJW (1974), 1767; NJW (1974), 1769, 1770; Windthorst and Sproll, op cit, 125–6.

[167] BGHZ 70, 7 ff; BGHZ 79, 26; NJW (1981), 626; NJW (1983), 1668.

[168] Cf BGHZ 91, 48, 54.

[169] G Krohn, 'Zum Stand des Rechts der staatlichen Ersatzleistungen nach dem Scheitern des Staatshaftungsgesetzes', VersR (1991), 1085, 1088.

[170] Ibid; Ossenbühl, op cit, 83.

[171] In case of private insurance according to § 67 of the Insurance Contracts Act, in case of public insurance according to § 116 of the Code of Social Law, Part X.

[172] Cf BGHZ 70, 7, 11; 79, 26, 35; Krohn, op cit, 1085, 1088.

[173] Soergel-H Vinke, *BGB*, 12th edn (1998), § 839, Rn 213.

[174] Windthorst and Sproll, op cit, 126.

[175] Cf S Lörler, 'Die Subsidiaritätsklausel in der Amtshaftung', *JuS* (1990), 544, 546.

[176] *Lister v Romford Ice and Cold Storage Co Ltd* [1957] AC 555 (HL) 576–7; *Davie v New Merton Board Mills Ltd* [1959] AC 604 (HL) 627 (Viscount Simmonds).

is to be disregarded.[177] But, in the area of tort liability of public authorities, insurance is sometimes seen as an adequate means of protection for the claimant, since otherwise only the claimant's insurance company would benefit from the authority's liability.[178]

The German courts have been able to overcome the subsidiarity clause of § 839 I 2 BGB in the most frequent and important cases. In the areas where it still applies it is not necessary that the claimant has in fact obtained compensation from another source. The possibility of obtaining damages is sufficient to relieve public bodies of their liability.[179] This will, however, depend on the enforceability and reasonableness in the individual case.[180] If there are legal or factual grounds why the claimant cannot enforce the other claim in reasonable time, then it is not regarded as an appropriate form of compensation within the meaning of § 839 I 2 BGB, and the public body remains liable.[181]

(ii) § 839 II BGB

§ 839 II BGB confers upon judges exemption from civil liability for their activity in the context of giving judgments, unless their conduct amounts to a criminal offence. It thus establishes an immunity that is also found in English law. Apart from judges, no other group of officials or public bodies is given immunity in § 839 II BGB.

(iii) § 839 III BGB

According to § 839 III BGB there is no public liability if the claimant has wilfully or negligently failed to avert the damage by making use of any other legal remedy. Like § 839 I 2 BGB, this provision originally aimed at benefiting the individual official reducing the chance of his personal liability.[182] With the assumption of liability by the public bodies, the function of this rule is now seen in emphasizing that the claimant has no right to choose between primary and secondary legal protection,[183] as the latter is subsidiary to the former.[184] Primary legal protection means the possibility of judicial review and actions for annulment according to the rules of administrative law; secondary protection refers to actions for damages.

---

[177] Cf J Stapleton, 'Tort Insurance and Ideology' (1995) 58 *MLR* 820, 824.

[178] Cf *Stovin v Wise* [1996] AC 923 (HL) 955 (Lord Hoffmann).

[179] Ossenbühl, op cit, 85; Soergel-H Vinke, BGB, 12th edn (1998), § 839, Rn 218.

[180] BGHZ 2, 209, 218; BGH NVwZ (1993), 1228, 1229; P Dagtoglou in *BK zGG* (1970), Art 34, Rn 285, 287.

[181] BGH NJW (1993), 1647; BGHZ 78, 274, 279.

[182] Cf KA Bettermann, 'Rechtsgrund und Rechtsnatur der Staatshaftung' DÖV (1954), 299, 304; Soergel-H Vinke, *BGB*, 12th edn, § 839, Rn 229.

[183] Vgl BGHZ 98, 85, 91 f; H Maurer, *Allgemeines Verwaltungsrecht*, 11th edn (1997), 633.

[184] Windthorst and Sproll, op cit, 131; U Mayo, *Die Haftung des Staates im englischen Recht* (1999), 191.

Only after the claimant has made full, but unsuccessful, use of available primary legal protection against public law conduct is he entitled to secondary legal protection.[185] However, the primary remedies must be designed to cover or prevent the entire damage arising out of the breach of the particular official duty in order to come under § 839 III BGB.[186]

English law regards actions for damages in principle as on the same level with other remedies against unlawful conduct.[187] In the area of public liability, though, there is likewise the impression that the tort of negligence is seen as a remedy of last option.

(iv) Contributory negligence

In addition to § 839 III BGB the general rules on contributory negligence in § 254 BGB apply.[188] This provision includes in its two sections the conduct of the injured party before the occurrence of the initial harm as well as afterwards, in the sense of mitigation of damages. Contributory negligence of the claimant will in contrast to § 839 III BGB only lead to a reduction of his claim equivalent to his share of responsibility,[189] which in extreme cases may also exclude the claim entirely.

(e) Answerability as the Proper Party (Passivlegitimation)

Liability is generally imposed on the public body that entrusted the official with the office in the exercise of which he breached his official duties (*Anvertrauenstheorie*).[190] It usually constitutes a territorial entity, whereas in English law public bodies are mainly statutory corporations and sued as such.[191]

A. Summary

On the basis of the framework of the ordinary law of torts special rules exist or have been developed by the courts in England and Germany in relation to public liability in negligence. Whereas in English law public bodies and their employees may be liable, Article 34 GG has in German law established in

---

[185] Cf BGH NJW (1991), 1168; Ossenbühl, op cit, 92–3.

[186] Cf BGH NJW (1978), 1522, 1523; BGH VersR (1984), 947; G Eörsi, 'Private and Governmental Liability for the Torts of Employees and Organs', in A Tunc (ed), *Torts* (vol XI, International Encyclopedia of Comparative Law, 1975), 4–219; opposed by BGH NJW (1986), 1924

[187] Mayo, op cit, 191.

[188] BGHZ 68, 142, 151; BGH NJW (1987), 2664, 2666; H Engelhardt, 'Neue Rechtsprechung des BGH zum Staatshaftungsrecht', NVwZ (1989), 927, 932.

[189] Ossenbühl, op cit, 89.

[190] BGH NJW (1970), 750; BGH NVwZ (1992), 298; Windthorst and Sproll, *Staatshaftungsrecht* (1994), 140.

[191] Cf Cane, op cit, 19.

principle the primary liability of public bodies, thus also implying who to sue.

Both legal systems use a concept of duty to determine liability. In England it is the breach of a duty of care in the tort of negligence; in Germany it is the breach of an official duty owed to a third party in § 839 BGB. Within these concepts the courts make use of vague formulas, be it the *Caparo* test or the protective ambit of the official duty, leaving a certain amount of flexibility to decide whether a public body should be held liable or not. Whereas the reference to policy arguments is part of English law, such a direct way of considering them is not provided by German law.

Problems such as justiciability and discretion, omissions and liability for acts of third parties have caused the English courts great concern and reinforced a reluctant attitude towards liability of public authorities, which has sometimes even led to immunities for certain kinds of conduct. Except for judges, immunities are generally not found in German law, although a similar result can be reached when official duties are held not to be owed to third parties. However, not sharing the approach of their English counterparts, German courts have, instead of restricting public liability, restricted the effect of the means provided by statute to limit it.

III. THE ENGLISH AND GERMAN CASES

A. English and German Judgments

The present section will juxtapose three English cases involving the use of policy arguments to limit or deny liability of public bodies in negligence and three German cases with similar factual situations to demonstrate the different judicial approaches in the two legal systems in this area of the law.

The English and German cases opted for come from the same areas of responsibility of public bodies and mark a contrast in the way the courts dealt with them. They are presented in a summarised version with facts and reasoning, concentrating on the issues relevant to the topic of this article.

Each English case is directly followed by its German counterpart. A small section of explanatory notes is added to each pair of cases. Included are decisions of both the House of Lords and of the German Supreme Court as well as of the respective Courts of Appeal. In Germany there are several Courts of Appeal, each responsible for a certain geographical area. The *Oberlandesgerichte* as they are called consist of chambers of three judges, whereas the German Supreme Court (*Bundesgerichtshof*) is divided into Civil Senates comprising five judges. The amount of judges deciding a case in the highest civil courts in England and Germany is hence the same. In both countries they decide by simple majority.

There are some differences in style and structure between reported English and German judgments. In English judgments every judge involved in the decision, including a dissenting one, delivers his own judicial opinion under his name. The judgments usually contain a very full account of the reasoning by which a judge arrived at his conclusion. German judgments in civil matters are published as unanimous[192] and anonymous[193] decisions of the entire court, revealing neither the names of the judges nor whether there were any differences in opinion. They are usually much shorter than their English equivalents. Reported dissenting opinions are only found in the Federal Constitutional Court. Furthermore, the doctrine of binding precedent does not, in principle, exist in German law.[194] Previous case-law is cited by the courts either by way of example or to refer to an established practice of the court, of the Supreme Court in particular.[195]

B. The Cases

1. Liability of the Police for Failing to Prevent Crime

The first pair of cases deals with claims against the police for not preventing crime. The English case of *Hill v Chief Constable of West Yorkshire Police*[196] is contrasted with the German Supreme Court decision *BGH LM § 839[fg] BGB No 5* from 1953.[197]

(a) Hill v Chief Constable of West Yorkshire

The claimant was the mother of the last victim of the so-called Yorkshire Ripper. He had, prior to the killing of the claimant's daughter, committed twenty murders and assaults on young women in the police area of the defendant over a period of a little more than 5 years. It was claimed that during the police investigation of the series of crimes a number of mistakes were made and that it had to be assumed that the perpetrator would have been arrested before the murder of the claimant's daughter if the police had exercised reasonable care and skill.

The claimant claimed damages in negligence on behalf of the estate of her daughter for failure of the police to apprehend the murderer in time and thus prevent her daughter's death. The matter came before the court as an

---

[192] A Zeuner, 'Das Urteil in Deutschland', in Facoltà di Giurisprudenza—Universita degli Studi di F errara, (ed), *La Sentenza in Europa* (1988), 172, 175.
[193] Markesinis, *Foreign Law and Comparative Methodology: A Subject and a Thesis* (Oxford: Oxford University Press, 1997), 211.
[194] Zeuner, op cit, 172, 176.
[195] Cf Markesinis, *The German Law of Obligations, Volume II*, 10.
[196] [1989] 1 AC 53 (HL).
[197] Urt. v 30.4.1953—III ZR 204/52.

application by the defendant to strike out under RSC Order 18, 19 r on the grounds that the claimant's statement of claim did not reveal any cause of action.

The claim was struck out by the court of first instance which was upheld by the Court of Appeal. The House of Lords unanimously dismissed the claimant's appeal. It was held that the police in the course of their investigations owed generally no duty of care to individuals to identify or apprehend criminals.

The leading opinion was given by Lord Keith of Kinkel[198] and based on two separate grounds. The first was that there was not sufficient proximity between the claimant, or rather her daughter, and the defendant to impose a duty of care. In addition, there were compelling public policy considerations which in Lord Keith's opinion constituted an independent reason not to hold the police liable in negligence.

As regards proximity he thought that liability for the failure to prevent wilful injury by a third party could only arise if some special relationship existed between the defendant and either the victim or the wrongdoer, which was not the case. The identity of the murderer was not known to the police. The claimant's daughter was merely a member of a large undifferentiated class of potential victims.[199]

In relation to public policy Lord Keith raised mainly three groups of arguments against the imposition of liability on the police in the present circumstances.[200]

First, potential liability would not bring about a higher standard of care or motivation on the part of the police in carrying out their functions of investigating and suppressing crime. They already tried to perform their duties as best as they could. Liability would on the contrary be likely to cause a 'detrimentally defensive frame of mind' of the police interfering with their work.

Secondly, a recognised duty of care to apprehend a criminal would result in numerous lawsuits against the police. Some of them could make it necessary to review extensively the nature of a police investigation including decisions of policy and discretion. Yet, the courts would often regard such decisions as not being justiciable.

Thirdly, liability would lead to a serious diversion of manpower, time and scarce financial resources of the police from their main function of suppressing crime to the avoidance and preparation of litigation.

On the basis of these policy considerations Lord Keith went as far as to approve an immunity of the police from actions in negligence in respect of their activities in the investigation and suppression of crime.[201]

---

[198] *Hill v Chief Constable of West Yorkshire Police* [1989] AC 53 (HL) 57–64.
[199] Ibid, 62.   [200] Ibid, 63.   [201] Ibid, 64.

(b) BGH LM §839 [fg] BGB No 5

The claimant was the victim of a burglary that was committed by a gang of robbers. Some members of the gang were known to the police prior to the robbery of the claimant as having been involved in another burglary. Still, the two police officers that had found this out deliberately took no further action against the criminals to shield them.

The claimant successfully sued the respective *Land* that employed the two police men before the lower courts for breach of official duty according to § 839 BGB, Article 34 GG. The Supreme Court dismissed the defendant's appeal.

The Supreme Court focused in its judgment on the existence of an official duty and on whether this duty was owed to the claimant.[202] It held that the police officers had an official duty to take action against the members of the band of robbers they knew before those committed the burglary of the claimant or any other crime. Due to their knowledge of the severe crime already committed by the band and of the identity of some of its members who later took part in the burglary of the claimant, they had no discretion left in deciding whether measures against the criminals were necessary. In their capacity as policemen they had the duty to prosecute criminals and to prevent criminal acts. On the facts of the case their inactivity was not justifiable by any police considerations. There was a state of danger which made an intervention absolutely necessary.

This official duty to intervene was owed towards the claimant as a third party in the sense of § 839 I 1 BGB. The duty to prevent criminal acts was owed by the police not only in the interest of the community as a whole but also in the interest of any individual at risk of crimes which directly violate his protected interests or rights. As the duty arose out of the general duty of the police to avert dangers, it did not matter that the claimant, who was unknown to the police before the burglary, was only a member of an undetermined class of people possibly at risk, which basically comprised any citizen of the region. According to the court, a third party towards whom the police owed such duty was not only somebody who had already somehow emerged from the group of potential victims. This class of people had to be drawn considerably wider.

In the present case the police officers also breached their official duty not to abuse their office by their failure to act due to motives incompatible with the demands of proper police administration. This duty was equally owed to anybody who could be adversely affected by the abuse.

---

[202] BGH LM § 839 [fg] LM Nr 5, 644–5.

(c) Notes

The German decision factually differs from the *Hill* case because the police knew of the identity of the criminals and abused their powers. The cases nevertheless seem to be comparable. Other English cases have shown that the approach in *Hill* is also adopted when the identity of the offender is known to the police.[203] Moreover, the reasoning of the German court in its entirety suggests that, in contrast to English law, there is an official duty of the police to prevent criminal acts owed to possibly affected third parties whenever the police are in an obvious position to prevent serious crimes, and not only when they have abused the powers of their office. Such abusive conduct serves as an additional ground to impose liability. The decision is likely to have been the same if the police officers had simply carelessly forgotten to apprehend the criminals in time. The case is cited in recent decisions of the Supreme and other courts[204] when they refer in general to the official duty owed by the police to take action in the interest of individuals at risk of criminal acts likely to cause substantial damage.

The German Supreme Court did not raise any of the policy concerns of the *Hill* case. It also had no difficulties with the proximity issue although the claimant was a member of a large and undetermined class of people.

2. Liability of the Prosecution Service

The second pair of judgments is concerned with careless conduct of the prosecution service. The cases are *Elguzouli-Daf v Commissioner of Police of the Metropolis*[205] and *BGH NJW 1998, 751*.[206]

(a) Elguzouli-Daf v Commissioner of Police of the Metropolis

Under the heading of the *Elguzouli* case are in fact two cases involving similar facts. In the first case the claimant had been charged with rape and buggery and was taken into custody in September 1992. Forensic examination established that he could not have been the offender, but it took a total of 22 days until he was released. The claimant in the second case, who was arrested in October 1989, had been charged with handling explosives and remanded in custody. It was only at his committal proceedings 85 days later that the Crown Prosecution Service (CPS) offered no evidence against him and he was set free. Both claimants brought an action for damages in negligence inter alia against the CPS.

---

[203] Cf *Osman v Ferguson* [1993] 4 All ER 344 (CA); *Beverly Palmer v Tees Health Authority* The Times, 6 July 1999 (CA).
[204] Cf BGH NJW (1996) 2373, 2373; LG Landshut RuS (1994), 454, 455.
[205] [1995] QB 335.
[206] BGH, Urt. *v* 16.10.1997—III ZR 23/96.

The CPS successfully applied to strike out the claims of the claimants. The claimants' appeal was dismissed by the Court of Appeal in a unanimous decision which held that the CPS owed generally no duty of care to those it prosecuted.

Applying the principles laid down in *Caparo Industries Plc v Dickman*[207] to establish a duty of care, the judges of the Court of Appeal denied the element of proximity and that it was just, fair and reasonable to impose a duty of care on the CPS. Drawing an analogy to the *Hill* case,[208] the judges stressed in particular the weight of the policy considerations, similar in both cases, against the recognition of a duty of care. Steyn LJ giving the main judgment regarded them as 'compelling considerations, rooted in the welfare of the whole community, which outweigh the dictates of individualised justice,'[209] holding the CPS immune in general from liability in negligence.

His major concerns were that the imposition of a duty of care would lead to a defensive approach by the CPS to its duties and to a diversion of valuable resources away from prosecuting criminals to fighting civil actions.[210] The CPS was likely to be tied up in a great number civil law suits which would impair the whole criminal justice system.[211]

(b) BGH NJW (1998), 751

At the request of the prosecution service the County Court (*Amtsgericht*) issued an arrest warrant for the claimant in February 1990 on suspicion of defrauding his former employer. The claimant was arrested in Italy in March 1990 and remained in custody—meanwhile having been extradited to Germany—for almost two months. The arrest warrant was later formally annulled and the preliminary proceedings against the claimant were discontinued. The warrant of arrest was primarily based on the accusation of a former business partner. This allegation was false in the light of evidence available when the prosecution service requested the arrest warrant.

At the time of his arrest the claimant was managing director of the V company. He also had a consultancy contract with the P company earning him DM 50.180 per year. The P company terminated the contract with the claimant as soon as his arrest was publicised at the beginning of May 1990. In mid-May 1990 the claimant signed the dissolution of his managing director contract with the V company.

The County Court decided in April 1991 that the claimant was entitled to damages for the time in custody according to the Compensation for

---

[207] Cf [1990] 2 AC 605 (HL) 617–18.   [208] [1989] 1 AC 53f (HL).
[209] [1995] QB 335, 349.   [210] Ibid, 349.
[211] Ibid, 350.

Prosecution Measures Act (*Gesetz über die Entschädigung für Strafverfolgungsmaßnahmen—StrEG*). The claimant claimed his loss of income and the legal costs he had incurred. The ministry of Justice of the defendant *Land* which was in charge of determining the amount of compensation under the Act accepted only liability for parts of the legal costs of the claimant. The claimant then sued the defendant for loss of income and for his remaining legal costs. He also sought a declaration that the defendant had to compensate the further damages caused by the termination of the contract with P.

The District Court allowed the claim up to DM 4.228,45 to cover further legal costs of the claimant. The Court of Appeal awarded him in a part-judgment DM 160.990,78 for breach of official duty by the defendant covering loss of income as well as legal costs and granted the declaration. The appeal of the defendant was dismissed by the Supreme Court.

The Supreme Court[212] upheld the finding of the Court of Appeal that the investigating prosecutor had culpably breached an official duty by assuming that there was a 'compelling suspicion' (*dringender Tatverdacht*) of embezzlement against the claimant, which was a condition for the arrest warrant, and by requesting the latter.

The court acknowledged that some measures of the prosecution service, including the request for an arrest warrant, could not be reviewed by the courts on the merits but only whether there were reasonable grounds for taking them (*Vertretbarkeit* or *vertretbar*). The Court of Appeal had held that the assumption of a compelling suspicion against the claimant was untenable; this extended to the request for the arrest warrant. It had found that on the strength of other evidence available to the prosecution it was already obvious at the time of the request for the arrest warrant that the accusation against the claimant was implausible and unbelievable.

As the Supreme Court does not engage in fact-finding of its own, it was bound to the facts as found by the Court of Appeal and could only review that decision in respect of errors of law (*Rechtsfehler*), in particular whether the lower court had misjudged the meaning of the term *vertretbar*. Such errors of law were not apparent.

(c) Notes

In the German case the prosecution service was held responsible for inappropriate conduct at the time of the request for the arrest warrant whereas in the English case allegations were raised against the CPS for the time after the arrest. Still, in both cases evaluations and conclusions of the prosecutors lay at the heart of the claim.

German courts only very rarely acknowledge an area where their power

---

[212] BGH NJW (1998), 751, 752-3.

of review is restricted, as in principle all administrative conduct is justiciable in German law.[213] Discretion is one exception.[214] The same is true for certain functions and decisions of the prosecution service. The courts only review them according to their reasonableness, not their correctness. A decision is not reasonable (*unvertretbar*) when—taking the requirements of effective criminal justice into account—it is not comprehensible anymore.[215] Both the English and the German court are thus concerned to preserve an area of individual judgment and evaluation for a prosecutor. Yet, the German court grants less judicial freedom to the prosecutor, not raising any of the policy arguments put forward by the English court.

3. Liability of Highway Authorities

The third pair of cases concerns the failure of highway authorities to eliminate road hazards. The House of Lords was faced with this problem in *Stovin v Wise*[216] and the German Supreme Court in *BGH NJW 1980, 2194*.[217]

(a) Stovin v Wise

The claimant was seriously injured in a collision with the defendant's car that attempted to turn out of a dangerous junction on the claimant's left into a main road. Visibility was very limited at the junction because of a bank of earth topped by a fence on adjoining land owned by British Rail. Accidents had occurred at the junction at least three times before. Norfolk CC as the responsible highway authority knew of the dangerous situation. It had a statutory power, stipulated in the Highways Act 1980, to require British Rail, as the owner of the land, to remove the obstruction. Instead, it took the decision to cart off the earth bank at its own cost about a year before the claimant's accident happened. It asked British Rail for permission to do the necessary work but got no final response. The highway authority did not inquire again and the obstruction was not removed.

The defendant joined the highway authority as third party to seek a contribution for the damages payable to the claimant for his personal injuries. She alleged that the authority was in breach of a statutory duty under the Highways Act 1980 and liable to the claimant in negligence.

The High Court and the Court of Appeal both held that, although there was no action for breach of statutory duty, the highway authority was under a common law duty of care to improve the safety at the junction and

---

[213] Cf BGH NJW (1979), 2097, 2098.
[214] Cf text accompanying n 109 above.
[215] Cf BGH NJW (1989), 96, 97.
[216] [1996] AC 923.
[217] Urt. *v* 10.07.1980—III ZR 58/79.

liable to the claimant in negligence for its failure to exercise its statutory powers. These decisions were overruled by the House of Lords that allowed the appeal of the highway authority by a bare majority of three to two.

Lord Hoffmann giving the main opinion could only concede the possibility of liability for a failure to exercise a statutory power if the two minimum requirements of irrationality and exceptional grounds were fulfilled.[218] In his view, however, these conditions were not met in the present case. The highway authority had not acted irrationally because it was always in the ambit of its discretion whether anything should be done about the junction. There could also be no general reliance on road hazards being routinely removed. Nor had the claimant been arbitrarily deprived of a benefit provided to others.[219]

As to the lack of exceptional grounds requiring the imposition of liability on the highway authority, Lord Hoffmann referred to the range of policy arguments already known from the *Hill* and *Elguzouli* cases. As in *Hill* and *Elguzouli*, these considerations were so important to him that they alone were sufficient to deny a duty of care, even if the authority's behaviour was regarded as irrational.[220]

He feared that the imposition of a duty of care would lead to local authorities taking costly measures to avoid liability leaving fewer resources for other important social services.[221] A likely consequence of imposing liability was, he thought, that authorities would afterwards insist on better standards than were actually necessary, leading to unnecessary costs for the community.

Furthermore, as the standard of road improvements was a matter within the highway authority's discretion, the courts were not entitled or able to judge what was appropriate.[222] Drivers would have to take due care themselves and take the highway as they find it. Finally, accident victims would usually be able to rely on compulsory insurance for compensation.[223]

(b) BGH NJW (1980), 2194

The wife of the claimant who was driving his car wanted to turn left into a road. This road had two lanes which were separated by a central reservation upon which there was a hedge which had reached the height of 1.2m. The claimant's wife approached the central reservation which offered a gap for the turning traffic. As she tried to turn she collided with another car already driving on the left lane. The claimant claimed that his wife had not seen the other car in time only because the hedge on the central reservation was too high and had impeded her vision. Besides the owner of the other

---

[218] *Stovin v Wise* [1996] AC (HL) 923, 953.   [219] Ibid, 957.
[220] Ibid, 957–8.   [221] Ibid, 958.   [222] Ibid.
[223] Ibid.

car, he sued the city in which the accident had occurred for the damage to
his car.

The District Court dismissed the claimant's claim against the owner of
the other car but granted the claim against the defendant city to the amount
of one half of the assessed damages. Upon the defendant's appeal the Court
of Appeal rejected the claimant's claim against the city. The Supreme Court
allowed the claimant's appeal and sent the case back for trial.

The Supreme Court[224] held that the defendant city had breached its official duty to maintain road traffic safety. This public law duty, derived from
the Roads Act of the respective *Land*, had the same content as the general
legal duty to maintain safety (*allgemeine Verkehrssicherungspflicht*). Its
scope was determined by the importance of the highway in question and by
how often and by what kind of traffic it was used. The duty encompassed
all measures which were necessary to provide users of the highway with
roads in an adequately safe condition. Nevertheless, the road user had to
adapt his driving to the discernible road conditions and generally take the
highway as he finds it. Therefore, the local authority on which the duty was
imposed only had to take reasonable steps to remove those dangers which
could not be seen or seen in time by a user who exercised due care.

On the basis of these principles the defendant had to keep the height of
the hedge on the central reservation down to a level which did not seriously
impede the sight of the turning traffic. However, at the time of the accident
it was not possible to gain sufficient visibility of the left lane before turning.[225]

As § 839 I 2 BGB did not apply in the area of road traffic safety,[226] the
defendant could not rely on a possible liability on the part of the driver of
the car, the claimant's wife, in order to escape his own liability. The case had
to be sent back for trial to determine what weight was to be given to the
defendant's breach of duty in comparison with the contributory negligence
of the claimant's wife.[227]

(c) Notes

In the English case, the obstruction to visibility was on private property.
The hedge in the German case was part of the road which was property of
the defendant. This difference does not render the cases incomparable. The
main reason for the German defendant being responsible for the removal of
the obstruction was not his ownership of property but his statutory duty to
maintain road traffic safety, which admittedly is more than the statutory
power in *Stovin v Wise*. If the obstruction had been on adjoining private
property, then it is generally the duty of the owner of the property to avert

224   BGH NJW (1980), 2194–6.   225   Ibid, 2195.
226   Ibid, 2195; cf text accompanying n 161 above.   227   Ibid, 2196.

any danger arising therefrom to others. But also in German law the public authority has a right to ask for the elimination of a known danger on private property as part of its general duties to protect the public from danger. If the private person is not willing or unable to act, the relevant public authority will take the necessary action for him.[228]

Interestingly, both courts raised the same argument: The road user has to take the highway as he finds it. Yet, they drew different conclusions, the German judgment not sharing Lord Hoffmann's concerns on the authority's misconduct constituting an omission.

IV. EVALUATION OF POLICY ARGUMENTS

A. The Kind of Policy Arguments

The English judgments raised more or less the same policy arguments in cases involving very different kinds of public bodies or areas of their activities. The courts denying liability based their decisions on a core group of two considerations: First, potential liability would lead to public bodies and their employees taking a defensive approach to their work. Secondly, it would result in the diversion of scarce resources away from the primary functions of public bodies to avoiding litigation and taking defence measures. Both of these consequences would adversely affect the quality of their work.

Closely related to these concerns is the fear of a great number of lawsuits and vexatious claims, the so-called floodgates argument. It is raised in the police and CPS cases and often referred to as an argument against extending liability in the area of negligence in general. An 'avalanche' of claims would inevitably further reduce the available means of public bodies.

Another group of arguments focuses on the functions of the authorities. Whether it is the nature of police or CPS investigations,[229] the standard of road improvement,[230] or the delicate task of dealing with children at risk,[231] all these matters are regarded to be inapt for judicial evaluation, mainly due to their discretionary features.

Furthermore, judges argue that adequate protection for the claimants already exists by way of insurance or other remedies, as in the *Stovin* case,[232] rendering a negligence action unnecessary. Finally, there is a concern particularly in the area of child-care and education about the prob-

---

[228] Cf BGH NJW (1953), 1865.
[229] Cf *Hill v Chief Constable of West Yorkshire Police* [1989] AC 53 (discussed above).
[230] Cf *Stovin v Wise* [1996] AC (HL) 923.
[231] Cf *X (Minors) v Bedfordshire CC* [1995] 2 AC 633 (HL) 750 (Lord Browne-Wilkinson).
[232] [1996] AC (HL) 923 (discussed above).

lems of adjudicating a multi-disciplinary decision-making process, probably involving various responsible parties.

The German courts on the other hand have neither discussed nor addressed in their judgments any of the policy arguments summarised above, with the sole exception of partly limiting the judicial evaluation of certain decisions of the prosecution service. Examining the conditions set up by statute for a public liability claim, they stressed more claimant-oriented concerns: the individual at risk of crime, the protection of individual liberty and of users of the highway against hardly identifiable dangers, as well as the importance of being able to make a free and responsible adoption decision. These considerations are also expressive of judicial policy but the German courts outline different concerns.

B. Critical Review of the English Policy Arguments

The overriding function of the law of torts may be arguable. It seems to be uncontested, however, that one of its most important aims is to compensate victims for losses suffered because of wrongs committed by others.[233] Lord Browne-Wilkinson acknowledged in *X(Minors) v Bedfordshire CC*[234] that the policy of the law in principle requires wrongs to be remedied and only makes an exception for very significant reasons. That is why courts should only base their judgments on policy arguments when the latter are so evident that they leave no room for any doubt about their appropriateness.[235] Whether policy considerations can ever provide such certainty may be questionable due to their nature. In addition, policies are subject to change. This does nevertheless not preclude examining whether the policy arguments relied on in the English cases contain sufficient weight to justify not imposing liability. It makes such examination only the more necessary.

What is striking is that the English judges apply the policy arguments without referring to empirical or other kinds of evidence to support them. Not all of them may be suitable for proof. This cannot be said, however, of the defensive approach, the diversion of resources and the floodgates argument. These do raise factual or empirical issues, even though they may be difficult to assess.

1. Defensive Approach

The concern that potential liability would cause employees of public bodies to act in a defensive, too careful manner in carrying out their functions is a

---

[233] Markesinis and Deakin, *Tort Law*, 38, 41.
[234] [1995] 2 AC 633 (HL) 749.
[235] Cf *Spring v Guardian Assurance plc* [1995] 2 AC 296 (HL) 326.

two-sided argument. First of all, there is nothing wrong in principle with somebody acting more carefully, thus improving the standard of care, if this way harm to others can be avoided. One might also wonder why a duty of care should make public officials unnecessarily careful instead of encouraging them to exercise the ordinary standard of due care which would be sufficient to protect them against liability. As the individual employee will in practice in most cases not be financially responsible himself due to the vicarious liability of the public body,[236] it is not evident that he will constantly be looking over his shoulder.

Moreover, even the House of Lords does not use this argument in a uniform and consistent way. Whereas Lord Keith in the *Hill* case did not think a defensive mind would improve the standard of care or motivation of the police force,[237] it was presumed in *Stovin v Wise* that one of the likely consequences of liability in the *Anns v Merton* case[238] was that building inspectors insisted on better standards than necessary.[239] This has to be contrasted with the firm statement of Lord Reid in the *Dorset Yacht* case[240] who did not believe that British prison officers would be affected at all by such concerns. These examples only confirm the speculative character and the unpredictability of the argument.

2. Diversion of Scarce Resources

No other profession—including NHS hospitals—can successfully invoke this argument, nor can private individuals. Any kind of lawsuit or liability will involve the consumption of time, attention, and financial resources that could have been employed in a different way. Nobody has unlimited resources. This has nevertheless not lead to the exemption from liability of public bodies in other areas of tort law, or even for other kinds of their conduct, such as careless driving, where this consideration would be equally applicable with reference to more important functions.

It is not disputed that the financial situation of public bodies is tense. However, if public bodies took more care in the discharge of their functions in the first place, the question of compensation would arise less frequently, thus reducing their financial burden. Their financial situation cannot be attributed to the victims of their tortious conduct. Even in cases of a failure to confer a benefit or protection, there is a valid interest that those services are distributed evenly, many of them being intended for the individual as well as the collective welfare. It seems that the argument of limited and diverted resources has sometimes become an automatic response providing an easy shield for public authorities.

---

236   D Brodie, 'Public Authorities and the Duty of Care' [1996] *JR* 127, 140.
237   [1989] 1 AC 53, 63.   238   [1978] AC 728 (HL).
239   [1996] AC 923, 958.   240   1970] AC 1004, 1033.

3. Floodgates

The 'floodgates' argument is raised whenever it is feared that potential liability might get out of control. This has to be weighed against surveys which suggest that many people are discouraged from taking any legal action because of the risk of costly, long-lasting, and uncertain litigation.[241] Other areas of negligence in which a duty of care was imposed have revealed that litigation does usually not expand unreasonably.[242] Besides, despite the rising number of claims against public bodies in absolute terms, a lot of them are of a kind which will in fact only rarely occur.

Another concern of the floodgates argument is that many claims will be of a fraudulent nature.[243] Yet, there should be enough confidence in the courts that they are able to detect whether a claim is well-founded or of a dubious quality. For those who do not possess the means to sue rules as to cost and the limitation on legal aid will prevent the abuse of the judicial system.[244]

4. Special Nature of Function

When the courts single out certain areas of responsibility of public bodies as not being suitable for judicial re-examination, the question is whether they sometimes go too far when deciding what is not for them to evaluate. Looking at Lord Hoffmann's approach in *Stovin v Wise*,[245] for example, doubts arise. In his view the assessment of the necessary standard for road improvements would have to be left to the highway authority's discretion. Not only does this confer an implicit immunity upon the highway authorities in the area of improving the safety of the highway, but the immunity is conceded too easily. The minimum standard of safety required in order not to endanger traffic can certainly be determined with the help of expert witnesses, as it is primarily a matter of factual issues.

Furthermore, no professional in the private sector can escape liability by referring to the delicate task he is performing. Doctors, for instance, frequently have to make difficult decisions involving discretion, often at least indirectly affecting resources of hospitals, and they are not protected by an immunity from negligence actions.[246] It may be said that such an

---

[241] Cf findings of the Oxford Socio-Legal Studies Group in Markesinis and Deakin, *Tort Law*, 65.

[242] Markesinis and Deakin, in ibid, 22.

[243] Cf T Weir, 'Governmental Liability' [1989] *PL* 40, 57.

[244] J Wright, 'Local Authorities, the Duty of Care and the European Convention of Human Rights' (1998) 18 *OJLS* 5, 11.

[245] [1996] AC 923 (HL) 958.

[246] M Tregilgas-Davey, 'Osman v Metropolitan Police Comr: The Cost of Police Protectionism (1993) 56 *MLR* 732, 734.

argument overlooks the point that public bodies exercise statutory functions which do not exist in the private world. Yet, it could also be argued that the unique position of public bodies imposes special obligations to avoid causing harm to others.

5. Adequate Protection—Alternative Remedies

Alternative remedies often seem more attractive than a negligence action because they are less expensive, less time consuming and sometimes more informal. This argument can only be convincing, though, if the alternatives to a claim in negligence offer equivalent protection with regard to compensation and procedural conditions.

(a) Criminal Compensation Scheme and Local Government Ombudsman

The Criminal Injuries Compensation Scheme, for example, is mainly based on a tariff system. The compensation is usually substantially lower than in negligence awards and the limitation period after the injury occurred is only two instead of three years for personal injuries in ordinary damage actions.[247]

In cases falling short of the application of the Criminal Injuries Compensation Scheme and in some other areas of administrative misconduct the Local Government Ombudsman may recommend compensation. The payments are nevertheless also generally smaller .[248]

(b) Insurance

The question is the justification—in moral and legal terms—for the argument that the existence or possibility of insurance on the part of the claimant should relieve the tortfeasor from his liability. The complaint that it is not the function of public bodies to reimburse insurance companies that obtained the claimant's claim by way of subrogation is not convincing. First party insurance is a precautionary, and in many cases voluntary, measure taken to cover oneself against risks at the party's own expense. If insurance excludes a claim for damages, the tort victim is faced with the prospect of rising premiums, whereas the tortfeasor is not affected.

(c) Judicial Review

A further remedy is judicial review under order 53 of the Rules of the Supreme Court. This is a public law remedy primarily intended for annulling or declaring illegal acts of public authorities. A claim for damages

---

[247] Markesinis and Deakin, *Tort Law*, 49-50; cf Cane, *Atiyah's Accidents, Compensation and the Law*, 6th edn (London: Butterworths, 1999), 266–9.

[248] P Craig and D Fairgrieve, 'Barrett, Negligence and Discretionary Powers' [1999] PL 626, 636.

can be brought at the same time in such a proceeding but only if there is a private law wrong. Consequently, to establish the private law wrong the same requirements would have to be met as in an ordinary damage action, causing the same problems as in the area of liability of public bodies in negligence.

To conclude, it is not apparent that other remedies can equal the comprehensiveness of an action in negligence. In addition, there is no reason why a claimant should not have multiple ways of protection, as long as he is not overcompensated.[249]

6. Summary

The policy arguments relied on by the English courts represent the value choices those courts regarded to be in the best public interest. Many of their considerations may be as, or sometimes even more, relevant than the arguments against them. But it is only a 'may be'. Their coherence is not evident or definite. There are counter-arguments of weight against the application of each one of them. These have not been adequately discussed by the judges denying liability, let alone been disproved. The gravity of the defendant's fault and the seriousness of the claimant's harm[250] are usually disregarded, as well as the concerns of any dissenting opinions.

The courts thus failed in their decisions to comprehensively weigh the conflicting values, although such a balancing exercise is the essence of making use of policy considerations.[251] This substantially reduces their persuasiveness and aptness as a basis for judicial decisions and results in a too one-sided reasoning.

On this basis, it is submitted that the policy arguments applied by the English courts possess neither separately nor in combination sufficient weight to serve as a separate and independent ground to deny a duty of care of public bodies.

C. The German Approach

Although there are serious doubts about the use of policy concerns in the English judgments, these policy concerns are not far-fetched. However, the German decisions did not explicitly consider them but only approved of arguments more favourable to the claimants. This can be explained by a

---

[249] Cf *Barrett v Enfield LBC* [1999] 3 All ER 193 (HL) 228; J Stapleton, 'Duty of Care: Peripheral Parties and Alternative Opportunities for Deterrence' (1995) 111 *LQR* 301, 321.
[250] Cf *Osman v UK* (1999) 11 Admin LR 200 (ECHR).
[251] Bell, *Policy Arguments in Judicial Decisions* (Oxford: Oxford University Press, 1983) 23; cf R Summers, 'Two Types of Substantive Reasons: The Core of a Theory of Common Law Justification' (1978) 63 *Cornell L Rev*, 707, 716–25.

different general attitude towards public liability. It does not mean, however, that all the English concerns have been ignored by German law.

As the claim for breach of official duty has a statutory foundation in § 839 BGB and Article 34 GG there is a certain number of fixed elements the German courts have to examine. The wording of the subsidiarity clause in § 839 I 2 and of § 839 III BGB reflects that the alternative remedies concern, for example, has already been considered on the statutory level. The courts are moreover not prevented from discussing or taking into account other policy considerations. Statutory provisions are generally open to judicial interpretation which, when necessary, even allows the courts, within limits, to develop and supplement the law.[252] Thus, they are able to introduce value concepts or react to changing policies.

As has been shown in the second chapter, the law of public liability is an area in which the German courts have substantially made use of their interpretative powers and shaped the law. Policy considerations arise with regard to the requirement of the official duty being owed to a third party (§ 839 I 1 BGB) and to the interpretation of the subsidiarity clause (§ 839 I 2 BGB). The wording of these provisions suggests that they were introduced to limit the liability of public bodies, in addition to § 839 III BGB.

1. Duty Owed to Third Person

The German courts are able to take into account some of the same policy factors which are highlighted by the English courts in deciding whether an official duty was owed to an individual claimant. One example is the prosecution service which generally owes its duty to prosecute crimes only to the community at large.[253] It is likely that this conclusion was reached because of the nature of the prosecutors' activity and of the fear of an undesirable amount of legal actions against the prosecution service. Yet, the same concerns were apparently not relevant in other areas of conduct of the prosecution service or of the police, as the decisions discussed have demonstrated. If at all, the courts only opted for a reduced scope of judicial review.

Such concerns did also not prevail in other areas. Probably most astonishing was the position of the courts in the domain of state banking supervision where liability could result in vast amounts of damages. The Supreme Court held that, on the basis of the relevant statute, the state supervision of banks imposed an official duty owed to each individual owner or creditor of a deposit, thus rendering the State liable for damages.[254] Subsequently,

---

[252] Cf BVerfG NJW (1979), 305, 306.
[253] RGZ 154, 266, 268; BGH NJW (1996), 2373; OLG Düsseldorf NJW (1996), 530.
[254] BGHZ 74, 144, 147 ff; 75, 120, 122; cf in contrast *Yuen Kun Yeu v A-G of Hong Kong* [1988] AC 175 (PC).

the legislator intervened and added a new provision to the statute clarifying that the supervision of banks is only performed by the authorities in the general public interest.[255] Therefore, no official duty is owed to individuals anymore and the State is not liable. What becomes apparent is that German courts do not significantly restrict public liability by way of holding down the permitted circle of third persons. On the contrary, there has been a trend in recent years to expand the circle of third persons.[256]

(a) § 839 I 2 BGB

A claimant-oriented interpretation is also manifest in the subsidiarity clause in § 839 I 2 BGB, the other instrument provided by statute capable of shielding public bodies from liability in negligence in many cases. The Supreme Court has more and more reduced the scope of its application.[257] By disregarding it in the areas of traffic and road traffic safety, and by not accepting insurance claims as an appropriate alternative form of compensation within the meaning of the provision, the courts refuse to give dominant weight to the adequate protection argument. The German road traffic case is a concrete example.

This impression is strengthened by the way § 839 I 2 BGB is applied when it is still considered relevant. One of those situations is the involvement of another tortfeasor which has given the English courts so much concern. In theory, German law is very clear. As the claimant can claim his damages from the primary tortfeasor, the public body is not held liable for its negligent conduct according to § 839 I 2 BGB, leaving aside any problems of causation for present purposes. The primary or joint tortfeasor is moreover not entitled to claim any contribution from the public body.[258] Yet, it is not obvious that the public authority will in fact escape liability. As the other claim is not regarded as another form of compensation when it is not enforceable,[259] and since a claim is held to be non-enforceable when the other party cannot pay and is not likely to be solvent in the near future,[260] the effect of the provision is limited.

It is interesting to note that the courts have developed their approach towards the areas of non-applicability of § 839 I 2 BGB and the reduced acceptance of alternative claims only by a gradual process, culminating in the 1970s and early 1980s.[261] Before then, several kinds of insurance claims

---

[255] § 6 III KWG (1984 BGBl I 1693).
[256] Cf A Blankenagel, 'Die Amtspflicht gegenüber einem Dritten' *DVBl* (1981), 15, 17; cf Soergel-H Vinke, *BGB*, 12th edn (1998), § 839, Rn 20–1.
[257] Cf text accompanying n 155 et seq above.
[258] BGHZ 28, 297, 300–1; 37, 375, 380; 61, 351, 356 f.
[259] BGHZ 2, 209, 218; NVwZ (1993), 1228, 1229.
[260] BGH NJW (1979), 1600, 1601; NJW (1971), 2220, 2222; MünchKomm-H Papier, *BGB*, 3rd edn (1997), § 839, Rn 314.
[261] Cf text accompanying n 165 above; case law in Ossenbühl, op cit, 55.

were regarded as appropriate compensation in the sense of § 839 I 2
BGB.[262] Apparently, a period of expanding public liability occurred in
Germany and England at the same time. However, in contrast to the English
courts, the German courts did not subsequently change direction.

(b) § 839 III BGB

The reference to the priority of public law remedies expressed in § 839 III
BGB has also not proved to be a shield for public bodies to avoid liability.
It may indicate the principle that the public bodies' liability in tort is a last
resort,[263] however, in most instances, public law remedies will just come
too late to be able to avert the damage. The damage will already have
occurred before it was possible to take any public law action, leaving § 839
III BGB without effect.

(c) Reasons for the German Approach

When the German courts refuse to take a restrictive view on public liability, they are supported and influenced in their general direction by the main
academic authorities. For many of them the courts are still not going far
enough.[264] This conformity is expressive of the substantive difference in
viewing the role of public liability in Germany compared to English law.
The distinction between public and private law, between the 'mighty State'
and public power on the one side and the individual citizen in need of
protection on the other side, is, at least in the background, an apparent
feature of the German attitude towards public liability in general.

   Article 34 GG, following Article 131 of the Weimar Constitution, introduced the prime liability of the State or its bodies instead of the individual
official. It thus supplemented § 839 BGB but also changed that provision's
objective. The main purpose of Article 34 GG is seen as relieving the
claimant of the risk of the non-enforceability of his claim for damages and
to provide him with a solvent defendant.[265] On this basis § 839 BGB has
become an all-encompassing and effective means of protection for the citizen against tortious governmental harm.[266] This is deemed very important
as the citizen is in special need of protection when it comes to the exercise
of public power (*öffentliche Gewalt*) which provides the state with comprehensive and far-reaching opportunities of interfering with the rights of the
individual.[267] The individual is often dependent on the State and his offi-

---

[262] BGHZ 62, 394, 397; RGZ 138, 209; 145, 56; 161, 199.
[263] Cf text accompanying n 183 above.
[264] KA Bettermann, 'Rechtsgrund und Rechtsnatur der Staatshaftung' *DÖV* (1954), 299,
304; MünchKomm-H Papier, *BGB*, 3rd edn (1997), § 839, Rn 296–9.
[265] Papier, in Maunz-Dürig, *Komm zGG* (1998), Art 34, Rn 12; Ossenbühl, op cit, 10.
[266] Dagtoglou, in *BK zGG* (1970), Art 34, Rn 4.
[267] MünchKomm-H Papier, *BGB*, 3rd edn (1997), § 839, Rn 298–9.

cials and has no choice on whether to approach them or on which official to deal with. Such concerns are usually voiced in relation to the State in general, mainly without distinguishing between different kinds and levels of public bodies. Public liability, through Article 34 GG rooted in the Constitution, is thus seen as an indispensable element of the rule of law *(Rechtsstaatsprinzip)*,[268] especially with regard to the protection of the citizens' constitutional and civil rights.[269] This also indicates the substantial importance attributed in Germany to the deterrent effect of liability on the conduct of public authorities.[270]

Nevertheless, concern about a defensive approach by public officials has arisen in the context of Article 34 GG. This article is also seen as intending to protect the individual official from the risk of personal liability for negligent conduct which could otherwise adversely affect his work and his decisiveness. This protection would also indirectly benefit the State or public authorities since their efficient functioning largely depended on the performance and willingness of their officials and public employees.[271] Policy considerations of the kind put forward by English courts thus appear in the German legal discussion but they are only raised for the benefit of the individual official and not extended to justify an exemption from liability of the public body itself. The latter's liability is not believed to lead to a defensive approach by the official. English law uses this argument for officials and public bodies alike.

The same concerns about the likelihood of a defensive approach by public officials determined the original purpose of the subsidiarity clause in § 839 I 2 BGB. Created almost 100 years ago, and almost 50 years before Article 34 GG, its purpose was also to safeguard public officials against the risk of personal liability to maintain and promote their decisiveness and the efficiency of administration in general.[272] Since due to Article 34 GG liability is usually assumed by the State or public authority and the official is adequately protected, the provision of § 839 I 2 BGB is widely felt to be no longer necessary, except for the few remaining cases of personal liability of the official under § 839 BGB.[273] Despite introducing Article 34 GG, the Constitutional Assembly and later the legislator left § 839 BGB unchanged. The Federal Supreme Court acknowledged already in the 1950s that the original purpose, to shield the individual official, had lost its relevance

---

[268] Ossenbühl, op cit, 6; Papier, in Maunz-Dürig, *Komm zGG* (1998), Art 34, Rn 12.
[269] Papier, in ibid, Art 34, Rn 84.
[270] Ibid, Art 34, Rn 82; cf MünchKomm-H Mertens, *BGB*, 3rd edn (1997), Vor §§ 823–53, Rn 44.
[271] Windthorst and Sproll, op cit, 59–60; Dagtoglou, in *BK zGG* (1970), Art 34, Rn 2.
[272] Cf B Mugdan (ed), *Die gesamten Materialien zum Bürgerlichen Gesetzbuch für das Deutsche Reich* (1899), 1385–1403; RGZ 74, 250, 252; BGH NJW (1992), 2476; Ossenbühl, op cit, 79.
[273] Ibid, 79.

but—§ 839 I 2 BGB being valid law—recognised a new or extended purpose for the provision in the financial relief of public funds.[274] Yet, it was not happy with the clause and later called it antiquated.[275] The Supreme Court then, as has already been explained, started to restrict its application, as it became convinced that the aspect of financial relief of the State alone could not justify the application of § 839 I 2 BGB.[276] The liability of public authorities for damages was an important instrument for the protection of the individual citizen against unlawful conduct of officials,[277] and compelling reasons of public welfare in favour of the subsidiarity clause were not apparent.[278]

The legislator himself finally tried to abolish the subsidiarity clause in 1981 within an attempt to reform the law of state liability by incorporating and updating the present law in a comprehensive statute.[279] The act was later ruled unconstitutional by the Federal Constitutional Court due to lack of legislative competence of the Federation.[280] The reasons in favour of the law put forward by the Federal Ministry of Justice explicitly stated that a probable increase of public liability would be both negligible in comparison to the overall expenditure on social services and justified by the idea of compensation for wrongs committed by tortious public bodies.[281]

It is remarkable that not even the argument of scarce public resources or their diversion from important public functions has had an effect on the stand of the German courts and academic authorities. Public resources are likely to be as strained in Germany as in England. The functions of local authorities seem as widespread[282] and their income is made up of much the same sources as the one of English local governments, also being dependent on financial allocations from the Federation and the *Land* within the framework of local authority fiscal equalisation.[283]

These considerations demonstrate that the question whether public bodies themselves might be in need of protection against expanding liability is usually not given much weight in Germany. The present rules or the way they are applied are thought to be satisfactory in that respect. It can probably even be said that the State and its public bodies are regarded as less deserving of protection than the individual citizen or official.

---

[274] BGHZ 13, 88, 104.   [275] BGHZ 42, 176, 181.
[276] BGHZ 70, 7, 9; 79, 26, 29; cf Staudinger-K Schäfer, *BGB* 12TH EDN (1986), § 839, Rn 369.
[277] BGHZ 69, 128, 134; 79, 26, 29–30; 22, 383, 388.
[278] Papier, in Maunz-Dürig, *Komm zGG* (1998), Art 34, Rn 252.
[279] Cf ibid, Rn 89–96.
[280] Meanwhile the Constitution was changed, but the Federation has not yet made any further attempt to reform the law.
[281] Bundesministerium der Justiz (ed), *Zur Reform des Staatshaftungsrechts—Berichte, Modelle, Materialien* (1987), 377.
[282] Cf E Haschke, *Local Government Administration in Germany* <http://iecl.iuscomp.org/gla/literature/localgov.htm 6-7>.   [283] Ibid, 10–11.

Whether public liability is more bearable for public authorities in Germany because of a lower level of damages in comparison to English awards is difficult to assess. There is so far no empirical research on the amount of damages awarded in the area of public liability on a comparative basis. A direct comparison may prove difficult because of different methods of calculating compensation.[284]

(d) Summary

Some of the English policy considerations, such as the alternative remedies or the defensive approach concern, have also been raised in German law, either by § 839 BGB itself or in the context of determining the purpose of the statutory provisions. Yet, in the development of the interpretation of § 839 BGB and Article 34 GG these considerations were attributed a different and minor weight compared to the concern of individual protection, by the judiciary and the academic authorities, and they were not allowed to prevail. The body of case law of the Supreme Court to this effect, especially limiting the statutory restrictions on public liability in § 839 BGB, is assumed and often referred to by the German courts in their decisions without further discussion. This might explain why basically none of the English policy reasons were found in the selected German cases, as the Supreme Court had already laid down different priorities.

V. CONCLUSION

The comparison of English and German cases has shown that similar problems arise in the area of public liability in negligence in the two legal orders. The number of cases portrayed is admittedly too small to be representative. But the juxtaposition of the selected cases, together with the account of the present position of the law in the two countries, indicates a certain trend with regard to the extent of public liability in England and Germany.

The English 'Rule of Law' and the German Constitution both indicate that public liability, either established by ordinary or by specific rules, is an important means of control of public bodies. Against this common background, it is worth noticing that there was a period in the 1970s and early 1980s in which both English and German courts embarked on an extension of public liability. However, at the beginning of the 1990s the English courts departed from the common route and took a u-turn approach which did not occur in Germany. Moreover, the policy position of the German courts to expand liability has generally been supported by a widespread dissatisfaction in Germany with the present statutory rules in § 839 BGB, whereas

---

[284] Cf Rogers, 'Keeping the Floodgates Shut', 75, 81.

in England the issue of extending public liability in negligence has always been controversial.

In England, public bodies are in theory treated like any other tortfeasor. In practice, the courts have used the issue of non-justiciability, discretion and the concept of duty of care to limit and deny the liability of public authorities in negligence. They are often motivated by a general reluctance to hold responsible an authority, which acts for the benefit or protection of society, for merely not achieving this aim in individual cases.[285] Notwithstanding that the general pattern of restricting liability has more or less uniform, the House of Lords appears to use slightly different tests from case to case as to how to determine a duty of care with regard to public bodies. However, in many cases, which concern different kinds of public bodies and areas of their activities, the judges, be it in the House of Lords or the lower courts, openly agree on a number of similar policy considerations to let the public interest prevail within the fair, just and reasonable test. The whole issue of a duty of care ultimately depends on judicial views of policy.[286]

In contrast to the common law, the German courts are faced with a statutory claim for breach of official duty against public bodies established in the German Civil Code and the Constitution, introducing an indirect but primary liability of the authority. Applying the relevant provisions of § 839 BGB and Article 34 GG, they usually do not openly discuss policy arguments in their judgments. Nevertheless, there has not been a lack of judicial activity. The claimant is able to rely on a wide range of official duties owed to him which have been developed under the general public duty to act lawfully. The courts, led by the Federal Supreme Court, have by way of interpretation restricted the statutory means to limit the liability of public bodies in § 839 BGB. Non-justiciability is with few exceptions not accepted in German law. This does not mean, however, that German public bodies are without any protection against liability in negligence. Assuming the extent of public liability is greater in Germany, it has not lead to financial ruin of the public authorities. Yet, in the end the German approach is, like the English one, based on convictions deemed to be in the best public interest.

Although the two approaches have to be seen in their own context, they reveal how schemes of values and policy can influence and alter legal concepts. They also show how differently policy concerns can be perceived in different legal orders, in different circumstances and at different times; in one word how subjective they are. In weighing policy considerations judges come probably closest to exercising governmental and political functions.

---

[285] Cf *Stovin v Wise* [1996] AC 923 (HL) 952.
[286] Cf Rogers, *Winfield & Jolowicz on Tort*, 111.

Nevertheless, such considerations should only be applied in a judicial way, which means consistent with legal principles and concepts. When particular importance is attached to policy concerns in the area of public liability, a careful balance has to be struck between the countervailing interests, especially between the demands of an effective administration and the legitimate concerns of individual protection. To let the loss fall on the victim requires a careful analysis of the needs of society, especially in respect of the fact that the costs of public liability constitute only a very small proportion of public expenditure.

On this basis, the policy arguments used by the English courts are suitable neither to deny a duty of care nor to justify partial immunities irrespective of the individual case. First, these policy arguments cannot be regarded as having been convincingly balanced. Apart from any dissenting opinions, there is little or no discussion of the counter-arguments by the judges. Secondly, they are attributed excessive weight on their face value, without having been assessed or proven. Thirdly, if the English courts want to continue to limit the liability of public bodies, there are other and better ways for the courts to control liability in the areas of breach of duty or causation.

If one may speculate about why English courts are so hesitant to impose liability on public bodies, it seems that they are uncertain as to their role in deciding the extent of public liability. Judges often emphasise that it is not the function of the courts to determine how public funds should best be spent. They think it should be left to the legislator to make such a decision. In contrast to German courts, they cannot rely on a written Constitution to justify, or at least support, their judgments. In addition, unlike Parliament in England, the German legislator has given the courts an indication as to how it views their interpretation of the provisions. The attempt to create a comprehensive statute for state liability in the 1980s, including the abolishment of the subsidiarity clause of § 839 I 2 BGB, could be seen by the courts in Germany as an endorsement of their approach. Moreover, the legislator has also acted when it thought that the courts went too far in holding authorities liable, as in the area of state banking supervision.

In the light of recent European human rights decisions and English case law it is difficult to predict how English law will develop. The current situation is uncertain. There seem to be first signals that the approach of English courts, including their assessment of policy considerations, may change again. The decision of *Barrett v Enfield LBC*[287] and *Phelps v Hillingdon LBC*,[288] in the aftermath of the *Osman* case of the ECHR,[289]

---

[287] [1999] 3 All ER 193 (HL) 199–200, 213.
[288] [2000] 3 WLR 776 (HL), 777
[289] *Osman v UK* (1999) 11 Admin LR 200.

acknowledged that when the focus was essentially on policy concerns, on whether it is fair, just and reasonable to impose a duty of care, this could only be decided by a judge on a full trial of the matter, rather than in inter-locutory proceedings. The Court of Appeal has consequently taken the same view in *Beverly Palmer v Tees Health Authority*[290] and the education malpractice case of *Gower v Bromley LBC*.[291] The *Barrett* decision also conceded that the policy considerations so far relied on may not have equal force in all circumstances.[292] Whether this will lead to 'an important shift away from an unthinking accepting of such blanket policy factors',[293] remains to be seen. The English courts are not bound by the *Osman* or the *Z v UK* decision of the ECHR, which does not dictate the outcome of such cases, but only points out the way it considers appropriate to approach them. Yet, as *Barrett v Enfield LBC* has shown, the decision of *Osman* has not been without influence either. Especially after the implementation of the Human Rights Act 1998 cases such as *Elguzouli-Daf* may be decided in a different manner. To deny liability in striking out actions, the courts may be tempted to emphasise the issue of proximity to deny liability,[294] rather than the fair, just and reasonable test. The House of Lords in the *Barrett*[295] and the *Phelps*[296] case seemed to be arguing that actions against public author-ities could more properly be decided at the breach than at the duty level. This does not mean, however, that it will be easier for claimants to succeed.

No matter what direction the English courts will take, the process of European integration, the growing harmonisation of the laws of the Member States of the European Union and the influence of Community Law on national laws should in general increase the willingness of the national courts in Europe to approach their tasks on a comparative level. Looking—within their means—at the approach of neighbouring legal systems may give a stimulus to reflect critically about the own course of reasoning. They may as a result become either more convinced of the appropriateness of the present stand of 'their' law or receive valuable incen-tives for possible change. The exercise will be profitable in either case.

---

[290] *The Times*, 6 July 1999.
[291] CA, 29 July 1999.
[292] *Barrett v Enfield LBC* [1999] 3 All ER 193 (HL) 207–8, 227–9.
[293] Fairgrieve and Andenas, 'Tort Liability For Educational Malpractice' (1999) 10 *KCLJ* 229, 233.
[294] Cf *Capital and Counties plc v Hampshire CC* [1997] QB 1004; *Beverly Palmer v Tees Health Authority* The Times, 6 July 1999.
[295] [1999] 3 All ER 193 (HL) 230.
[296] [2000] 3 WLR 776 (HL) (Lord Clyde).

12. SUING CHILD WELFARE AGENCIES: A COMPARATIVE VIEW FROM NEW ZEALAND

Bill Atkin* and Geoff McLay**

I. INTRODUCTION

Complaints about the handling and investigating of claims of child abuse have surfaced frequently in the past few years. Many involve notifications of physical abuse or neglect which have apparently not been followed through by the relevant social welfare agencies,[1]or allegations that an agency chose not to remove a child in a dangerous situation in the hope of maintaining the child's family and that other less invasive measures would suffice.[2] Yet others arise where claims of abuse have been too readily accepted when they should not have been or the investigations have been wrongly conducted—a child removed from the family but the allegations or suspicions that led to the removal ultimately proving to be untrue[3] or some one else is found to be responsible for the abuse.[4] In another variant, a child placed with a family by social welfare agencies harms that family. Behind each complaint are very real human tragedies.

Accompanying this upsurge in complaints has been the attempt by dissatisfied families to bring civil proceedings against social welfare agencies they allege have failed them. In the United Kingdom, the House of Lords' *Bedfordshire*[5] decision appeared to have ended the chances of success for litigants in all but the 'dangerous child' cases. Then, remarkably in *Barrett*[6] the House of Lords, perhaps prompted by the European Court of Human Rights judgment in *Osman*,[7] reinterpreted *Bedfordshire* to allow

---

* Reader in Law, Victoria University of Wellington (Bill.Atkin@vuw.ac.nz). An earlier version of this chapter was presented to the 10th World Congress of the International Society of Family Law, Brisbane, July 2000.

** Senior Lecturer in Law, Victoria University of Wellington (Geoff.McLay@vuw.ac.nz).

[1] Essentially the allegation in *Prince v Attorney-General* [1998] 1 NZLR 262 (CA).

[2] The allegation in *X v Bedfordshire County Council* [1995] 2 AC 633.

[3] These are the facts of *B v Attorney-General* [1999] 2 NZLR 296.

[4] The facts of the Newham cases reported in *X v Bedfordshire County Council* [1995] 2 AC 633.

[5] *X v Bedfordshire County Council* [1995] 2 AC 633.

[6] *Barrett v Enfield London Borough Council* [1999] 3 All ER 193.

[7] *Osman v United Kingdom* [1999] 1 FLR 193 (1998) 5 BHRC 293 (ECtHR).

many of the claims that we had thought barred by *Bedfordshire* to proceed at least to trial. *Osman, Barrett* and now the European Court of Human Right in *Z v United Kingdom*[8] and *TP and KM v United Kingdom*,[9] in which the Court partially rejected *Bedfordshire*-style blanket immunities for welfare agencies, seem set to require the English courts to completely re-examine the issue and to develop law to replace those blanket immunities with a much more sophisticated approach.

Each case brought by children who might have avoided neglect or abuse by appropriate invention or by children, parents or families whose lives have been tainted by inappropriate intervention reflects very real human tragedy. The cases also inevitably bring into sharp focus the difficult and conflicting roles of social workers. There are stories of administrative good intentions gone awry, as inevitably sometimes must just happen. But there are also stories of under-resourcing of social welfare agencies or of mistaken reliance on unproved or even disproved social work practices.[10]

The purpose of this article is to look at some of the factors that might go into the judicial mix in trying to sort out an appropriate liability regime for social welfare agencies. It does so by directly comparing English case law with that from New Zealand. After examining the conflicting case law from those jurisdictions, we suggest a number of starting points from which courts might successfully begin the complicated process of mediating the need to give just compensation to those adversely but wrongly affected by social workers' decisions and the equal need to prevent litigation from over-whelming the primacy of child protection. Whatever ought to be the proper basis for allowing or rejecting such claims, we regard the New Zealand position as reached in the 1999 case, *B v Attorney-General*[11] as untenable and a warning to the English courts that before deciding particular cases, much thought needs to be given to the interaction of tort law on the one hand and family law on the other.

II. TORT AND FAMILY LAW: AN INEVITABLE TENSION?

Tort cases in which courts have been prepared at least to consider the possibility of negligence actions against state welfare agencies provide a striking example of the tensions between the common law and modern family law. The somewhat conflicting New Zealand Court of Appeal decisions in *Prince v Attorney-General* and *B v Attorney-General* and English decisions,

---

[8] *Z v The United Kingdom* (10 May 2001) Application No 29392/95 (ECtHR).
[9] *TP and KM v United Kingdom* (10 May 2001) Application No 28945/98 (ECtHR).
[10] This was, in essence, the allegation in *B v Attorney-General* [1999] 2 NZLR 296.
[11] *B v Attorney-General* [1999] 2 NZLR 296.

among them *Bedfordshire* and *Barrett* indicate the difficulty in articulating clear principles that can reconcile two very different branches of what is traditionally seen as 'private law'.

At the heart of the traditional view of the common law is the desire to remedy a wrong.[12] Tort law looks backward to assess what has gone wrong and ascribes responsibility to the party that has 'caused the loss'. The prime orientation of modern family law is to rebuild the family and protect children. Modern family law places great faith in welfare agencies to achieve these joint, if sometimes conflicting, goals. This conflict in goals is reflected in the inconsistent ways that courts have approached the question of welfare agencies' liability when the decisions that they have made to promote children's welfare turn out adversely for those children or their families.

While there is something very traditional about claimant children and families invoking the remedial function of the common law, there is something very untraditional about the kinds of the claims that they make in the social welfare context. English (and Commonwealth) common law has come only very lately to a separate law of governmental or state liability, preferring instead the mantra that the state is under the same duties as private individuals.[13] Such a proposition might make sense when a social worker causes a car accident, but it is not so convincing when the social worker is exercising the uniquely governmental function of whether to intervene in a family. An awareness that somehow governmental liability is different from ordinary tort law, especially when it involves the exercise of some form of discretion, has led to an extremely complex body of cases, of which *Bedfordshire* was until *Barrett* perhaps the leading authority.[14] That pre-*Barrett* case law somewhat unwisely sought to lay down general propositions about liability for government action without sufficiently examining the particular context of the governmental role in question. One of the most important aspects of *Barrett* is that it requires judges to look at the context in which the discretion is given to government officials and the context in which it is exercised. It is our view that, while family law and tort law clearly have different orientations, any perceived conflict between the two

---

[12] In the English Court of Appeal Sir Thomas Bingham referred to the remedying of wrongs being the first 'loyalty of the law', *X v Bedfordshire County Council* [1995] 2 AC 633, 663, reaffirmed by Lord Browne-Wilkinson, at 749.

[13] The leading Commonwealth exposition of this view is P Hogg and P Monahan, *Liability of the Crown*, 3rd edn (Toronto: Carswell, 1989).

[14] For a critical view of both *Osman* and *Barrett* and the commission decisions, see A Mullis, '*Barrett v Enfield London Borough Council*: a compensation-seeker's charter?' (2000) 12 CFLQ, 185. Mullis rightly raises the issue of the desirability of imposing legal liability, but to our eyes his critique of the cases, and especially of *Osman*, that the imposition of liability interferes in legitimate resource allocation decisions is simply not established on the facts of the cases, but of course might have been had the exclusionary rule not prevented a proper trial of whether a resource allocation issue had been involved.

is not a reason for granting a blanket immunity in the style of *Bedfordshire*, or the drawing of artificial or arbitrary distinctions between different claimants as the New Zealand Court of Appeal did in *B v Attorney-General*.

III. BREACH OF STATUTORY DUTY: MISSING IN ACTION OR
CORRECTLY SIDELINED?

All of the cases we discuss in this article occurred in the context of various family or child protection statutes. Often those statutes impose mandatory duties to protect the child's best interests. Strikingly, the cases give scant consideration to the 'tort' of breach of statutory duty. The general demise of the tort of breach of statutory duty is beyond this paper. We suggest, however, that its demise in this particular context is not necessary to be mourned, so long that is the Courts do not arbitrarily restrict negligence law.

A. Welfare Obligations Do Not Confer Private Benefits

The normal pre-requisite for a successful breach of statutory duty claim is that the statute conferred a benefit on an identifiable section of the public rather than merely providing a benefit to the general public. While the popular perception of social welfare legislation is that it does confer private benefits, albeit of a peculiar sort, on beneficiaries, English courts have been extremely reluctant to acknowledge that social welfare legislation is intended by Parliament to create a private benefit enforceable by private right of action. In *Bedfordshire* itself, Lord Browne-Wilkinson observed:[15]

> Although regulatory or welfare legislation affecting a particular area of activity does in fact provide protection to those individuals particularly affected by that activity, the legislation is not to be treated as being passed for the benefit of those individuals but for the benefit of society in general. The cases where a private right of action for breach of statutory duty have been held to arise are all cases in which the statutory duty has been very limited and specific as opposed to general administrative functions imposed on public bodies and involving the exercise of administrative discretions.

The English courts have thus gone quite close to observing that what at first blush appear to be privately enforceable rights are in fact simply laudatory goals for social welfare agencies to achieve. This, however, is in stark contrast to the acceptance by the House of Lords in *Barrett* that the oblig-

---

[15]   *X v Bedfordshire County Council* [1995] 2 AC 633, 731–2.

ations under the Children Act to provide for the welfare of a child in care are potentially enforceable in 'private' negligence law as opposed to the 'public' breach of statutory duty tort.

B. The Advantage of Common Law Negligence over Breach of Statutory Duty

The failure of the courts to directly recognise social welfare type duties as directly enforceable under the breach of statutory duty tort is not necessarily to be regretted. On the one hand, cases dealing with breach of statutory duty and its requirement that Parliament had intended a private right of action are notoriously incoherent and inconsistent. The search for parliamentary intention often proves elusive and becomes more of a way of stating a conclusion than articulating a reason.

On the other hand, breach of statutory duty might appear to be too absolute a weapon to employ against social welfare agencies. As Lord Browne-Wilkinson observed in *Bedfordshire*, liability under breach of statutory duty is often viewed as strict.[16] If the cases under consideration agree on anything, it is that some social welfare decisions will not give rise to liability, even if things turn out badly. Courts are concerned to preserve the element of discretion given by child welfare statutes to social workers to make appropriate decisions in particular cases even when acting under a statutory duty. Courts are also concerned to preserve the ability to say that a particular decision involves a policy that a private law court should not review. This 'high policy' concern has caused significant problems in common law negligence cases and there is no reason to believe that it would not cause the same problems in breach of statutory duty cases.

C. Are Private Remedies Needed when there are Mechanisms for Public Accountability?

Lord Browne-Wilkinson's conclusion in *Bedfordshire* that it was not just and reasonable to impose a duty of care on social workers in care and protection cases was, in his view, somewhat softened by the existence of so-called public remedies if the actions of the social workers had been inappropriate. Lord Browne-Wilkinson wrote:[17]

If there were no other remedy for maladministration of the statutory system for the protection of children, it would provide substantial argument for imposing a duty of care. But the statutory complaints procedures contained in section 76 of the 1980 Act and the much fuller procedures now available under the 1989 Act provide a means to have grievances investigated, though not to recover compensation.

---

[16] Ibid, 731–5.   [17] Ibid, 751.

Further, it was submitted (and not controverted) that the local authorities' ombudsman would have power to investigate cases such as these.

The New Zealand Court of Appeal in contrast, implicitly rejected the significance of the public remedies in the 'care and protection' cause of action.[18] The Crown had argued that complaints over the performance of Social Welfare could have been made through the ombudsman system or to the quasi-independent Commissioner for Children, an office expressly created to investigate issues of importance to child welfare.[19] Although, dissenting from the imposition of a duty of care, Henry J directly refuted the effectiveness of the kinds of public accountability discussed by Lord Browne-Wilkinson:[20]

[T]hose [methods of accountability] suggested by the [Crown], namely recourse to judicial review or by way of complaint to the Ombudsman, appear to be of marginal value; the significance of the Office of Commissioner for Children under the [1989] Act must be doubtful.

The role of public officers like the New Zealand Children's Commissioners is often advisory, and carries no powers to compensate. Vindication by, for example, the Ombudsman is seemingly little comfort to those who have suffered real loss. Ombudsman's reports are not perceived in the community as a real substitute for a court judgment.

In his speech in *Barrett*, Lord Slynn indicated a similar scepticism of the sorts of administrative remedies that Lord Browne-Wilkinson had proposed.[21] There is more in this proposition that public remedies will sometimes 'oust' private remedies than the space given it by either the *Prince* Court or the House of Lords in either *Bedfordshire* or *Barrett*. We suggest that there is a fundamental clash of values in the common law's backward looking compensatory approach and the forward looking, preventive model of ombudsmen schemes or the Commissioner for Children's office. There appears to a significant role for both to play in any system of public accountability.[22] Similarly in *Z v United Kingdom*, the European Court of Human Rights swept aside the United Kingdom's submissions that the availability of non-judicial remedies was, by themselves, a sufficient answer to the United Kingdom's obligation to provide

---

[18] *Prince v Attorney-General* [1998] 1 NZLR 262, 277 (CA).

[19] A recent prominent inquiry involved the failure of the Social Welfare to prevent the death of a child at the hands of his mother's partner and which made a number of severe criticisms of the performance of social workers. See Commissioner for Children *Final Report on the Investigation into the death of James Whakaruru* (Wellington, 2000).

[20] *Prince v Attorney-General* [1998] 1 NZLR 262, 289 (CA).

[21] See *Barrett v Enfield London Borough Council* [1999] 3 All ER 193, 208.

[22] The concepts of accountability is usefully reviewed in 'Accountability, administrative law and social work practice: Redressing or reinforcing the power imbalance' (1999) 21 *Journal of Social Welfare and Family Law*, 235.

remedies for breaches of the Convention. The United Kingdom had argued that as bodies such as the Criminal Injuries Compensation Board or Local Government Ombudsmen had been available to review the failure of the Council to protect children at risk, and in the case of the Criminal Injuries Compensation Board had actually given some compensation, the United Kingdom's obligation to provide a remedy for breaches of the Human Rights Convention had been discharged. The Court held that obligation of a Member State was to give an effective remedy.[23]

The Court indicated that administrative or quasi-judicial remedies, as opposed to judicial procedures, might in some circumstances be effective remedies but not given the seriousness of the allegations in *Z* that Bedfordshire County Council had systematically failed to protect children from mistreatment. Indeed it appears that the United Kingdom Government somewhat conceded that serious breaches of the Convention ought to be answerable in Court:[24]

However, the Government accepted that in the particular circumstances of this case they were insufficient alone or cumulatively to satisfy the requirements of Article 13. They conceded that there had been a serious violation of one of the most important Convention rights, that the CICB could only award compensation for criminal acts, not for the consequences of neglect and that any recommendation by the Ombudsman would not have been legally enforceable. They had been under the obligation, in this case, to ensure that some form of compensation was made available for damage caused by the breach of Article 3, whether by a broader statutory compensation scheme, an enforceable Ombudsman's award or through the courts.

IV. THE IMPACT OF EUROPEAN HUMAN RIGHTS JURISPRUDENCE

A. Introduction

In England, the outcome of these social workers cases now depends a great deal on European Human Rights jurisprudence. The European Convention on Human Rights has been applied with some vigour by the European Court of Human Rights in two recent decisions. Any common law rule that restricts the ability to sue social welfare agencies must be shaped by the European Convention on Human Rights. *Z v United Kingdom* was in fact the proceeding brought by the children in the *Bedfordshire* case. The children alleged that Bedfordshire social workers had failed to remove them from a dysfunctional family home that was not just neglectful but where conditions had been downright degrading. Its companion case, *TP and KM v United Kingdom*(reported in *Bedfordshire* as the *Newham* case) involved

---

23 *Z v United Kingdom* [2001] 2 FLR 612, para 108.
24 Ibid.

the removal of a sexually abused child from her mother on the basis, subsequently shown to be incorrect, that the mother's partner was the abuser.

B. *The Positive Obligation to Protect Children at Risk*

In contrast to the invocation by Lord Browne-Wilkinson of a blanket immunity that would completely prevent negligence suits, the Court emphasised that the Convention required the United Kingdom Government to act to protect children at risk. Article 3 provides that '[n]o one shall be subjected to torture or to inhuman or degrading treatment or punishment.'

The European Human Rights Commission had found that, given the special vulnerability of children, the United Kingdom was obligated to protect them from degrading treatment:[25]

The Court has held that the obligation on High Contracting Parties under Article 1 of the Convention to secure to everyone within their jurisdiction the rights and freedoms defined in the Convention, taken together with Article 3, requires States to take measures designed to ensure that individuals within their jurisdiction are not subjected to torture or inhuman or degrading treatment, including such ill-treatment administered by private individuals . . . The Commission considers that the protection of children who by reason of their age and vulnerability are not capable of protecting themselves requires not merely that the criminal law provides protection against Article 3 treatment but that, additionally, this provision will in appropriate circumstances imply a positive obligation on the authorities to take preventive measures to protect a child who is at risk from another individual . . . The Commission notes in this regard the international recognition accorded to this principle in Article 19 of the United Nations Convention on the Rights of the Child, which enjoins States to take all appropriate measures 'to protect the child from all forms of physical and mental violence, injury or abuse'.

Likewise, the Court found that it was simply established Convention Law that Article 3 gave rise to positive obligations on the State to prevent cruel or degrading treatment and that the failure to do so could result in a state being liable for damages.[26] The Court did acknowledge 'the difficult and sensitive decisions facing social services and the important countervailing principle of respecting and preserving family life'. The allegations against the Bedfordshire social services' repeated failure to intervene to protect the children were, however, beyond any such redemption as a genuine but ill-fated balancing of complex interests.

---

[25] *Z v United Kingdom* [2000] 2 FCR 245 (Eur Com HR) para 93, citing *A v United Kingdom* (1998) 5 BHRC 137 (ECtHR).
[26] *Z v United Kingdom* [2001] 2 FLR 612, para 73.

C. *The* Newham *Case*

In their respective companion report and decision on the *Newham* case, *TP and KM v United Kingdom*, both the Commission and the Court were considerably more understanding of the House of Lords' decision not to allow a cause of action to proceed on the basis that the child had been wrongfully removed. While it was clear that a removal decision might breach either the child's or the mother's right to family life under Article 8(1), the Commission accepted the importance of securing the safety of the child as a legitimate state role under Article 8(2).[27] Similarly, the Court accepted that a wide margin of appreciation ought to be granted to national authorities in protecting children's safety. That was not the end of the matter, however. A wide margin of appreciation was not necessarily appropriate in assessing subsequent decisions that affected parent's right of access to their children.[28] The Court indicated that the degree of access that the mother might be permitted, or directly apposite in this case, the procedure adopted in the removal and the subsequent return decisions might properly be scrutinised. The Court accepted:[29] 'whilst Article 8 contains no explicit procedural requirements, the decision making process involved in measures of interference must be fair and such as to afford due respect to the interests safeguarded by Article 8'.

D. Osman *and Blanket Immunities Preventing Suits Against the Government*

1. *The Reaction Against* Osman

Without a doubt the Court's prior decision in *Osman* created significant difficulties for both the Commission and the Court. In *Osman*, the Human Rights Court had held that granting a blanket immunity to Police that effectively immunised them from negligence actions based on their failure to protect citizens violated Article 6. The immunity, the Court held, violated potential claimants the right to have civil actions determined by a Court,[30]

---

[27] *TP and KM v United Kingdom* (10 Sept 1999) Application No 28945/98 (Eur Com HR) para 71. Art 8(2) provides: 'There shall be no interference by a public authority with the exercise of this right [to respect for family life] except such as is in accordance with the law and is necessary in a democratic society in the interests of national security, public safety or the economic well-being of the country, for the prevention of disorder or crime, for the protection of health or morals, or for the protection of the rights and freedoms of others.'

[28] *TP and KM v United Kingdom* (10 May 2001) Application No 28945/98 (ECtHR) paras 71–2.

[29] *TP and KM v United Kingdom* (10 May 2001) Application No 28945/98 (ECtHR) para 72 quoting from *W v United Kingdom* (8 July 1987) Series A 121-A, 28–9, paras 62 and 64.

[30] Art 6(1) provides: 'In the determination of his civil rights and obligations or of any criminal charge against him, everyone is entitled to a fair and public hearing within a reasonable time by an independent and impartial tribunal established by law.'

even given that Court could find no other violation of the Convention. The decision was the source of dismay for English academics and judges who largely rejected the Court's analysis as a failure to understand that in *Hill*,[31] the House of Lords had not applied an immunity to prevent the claimant from recovering in what would otherwise have been a valid action, but rather had denied that there was a cause of action in the first place.[32] Despite this criticism, the Human Rights Court's scepticism in *Osman* of the appropriateness of striking out cases against public authorities appeared to have considerable influence in subsequent cases in England.

In *Barrett* the House of Lords essentially distinguished the earlier *Bedfordshire* and thereby avoided the necessity of reconciling *Bedfordshire* with *Osman*.[33] None of the other Law Lords was prepared to join in Lord Browne-Wilkinson's criticism of *Osman*, preferring instead to simply reach the result that the Human Rights Court apparently mandated without directly considering it. The English Court of Appeal in the *Gloucestershire and Tower Hamlets London Borough Council* case dealt with *Osman* and used the Commission's report in *Z v UK* as confirming that the courts should be reluctant to recognise blanket governmental immunities.[34]

2. The European Court Abandons Osman or Rather the Osman Court's take on English Negligence Law

The Commission had applied *Osman* to the facts of *Z*[35] but had, perhaps,

---

[31] *Hill v Chief Constable of West Yorkshire* [1989] AC 53 (HL).

[32] See, eg, Lord Buxton, 'The Human Rights Act and Private Law' (2000) 116 *LQR* 48; Lord Hoffmann, 'Human Rights and the House of Lords' (1999) 62 *MLR* 159; Weir 'Down the hill—all the way?' [1999] *CLJ* 4; P Craig and D Fairgrieve, 'Barrett, Negligence and Discretionary Powers' [1999] *PL* 626; G Monti, '*Osman v UK*—Transforming English Negligence Law into French Administrative Law' (1999) 48 *ICLQ* 757; M Lunney, 'A Tort Lawyer's View of *Osman v United Kingdom*' (1999) *KCLJ* 238; M Lunney, '*Osman* in Action—Art 6 and the Commission Reports in *Z v United Kingdom and TP & KM v United Kingdom*' (2000) 11 *KCLJ* 119; C Gearty, 'Unravelling *Osman*' (2001) 64 *MLR* 159. The debate over *Osman* is inexorably bound up with the debate over the horizontal application of the Human Rights Act to the common law, the Buxton and Hoffmann articles show a strong correspondence between the force of opinion about *Osman* and the force of opinion about the appropriateness of horizontal application of the Human Rights Act. That debate is outside the scope of this article. For the most vocal proponent of direct horizontality, see Sir William Wade, 'Horizons of Horizontality' (2000) 116 *LQR* 217, the best summary of the more moderate indirect effect doctrine is M Hunt, 'The "Horizontal Effect" of the Human Rights Act' [1998] *PL* 423. See also A Lester and D Pannick, 'The Impact of the Human Rights Act on Private law: the knight's move' (2000) 116 *LQR* 380; N Bamforth, 'The True Horizontal Effect of the Human Rights Act 1998' (2001) 117 *LQR* 34.

[33] *Osman v United Kingdom* [1999] 1 FLR 193 (1998) 5 BHRC 293 (ECtHR).

[34] *S v Gloucester County Council; L v Tower Hamlets London Borough Council* [2000] 3 All ER 346, 371. Also citing the observations of Lord Woolf MR in *Kent v Griffiths* [2000] 2 WLR 1158, 1169 that *Osman* 'underlined the dangers of a blanket approach'.

[35] *Z v United Kingdom* [2001] 2 FLR 612, para 109.

not convincingly distinguished the mother from the daughter claimant in
TP and KM, holding that only the daughter's Article 6 rights had been
breached.[36] Perhaps as a result of the widespread English criticism, the
Court by a 12 to 5 majority simply confessed to have misunderstood
English law in *Osman*.[37]

Under its analysis of common law negligence, the Court held that the
English Court of Appeal in *Osman*[38] had not immunised what would otherwise been an actionable breach of a pre-existing obligations, but rather had
found that there was not pre-exiting obligation owed by the police at
common law to the Osman family. Similarly, *Bedfordshire* was viewed by
the Court not as immunising the social services against otherwise valid
claims, but in denying that the various Councils owed a pre-existing duty
in the first place and that there was therefore no possibly valid claim under
existing United Kingdom law.

3. The Court Rediscovers Article 13

Whatever the correctness of the critique of *Osman*, the point remains that
English Common law appears, from a Human Rights perspective, to
contain a significant gap in the legal mechanisms available to those children
who alleged that the United Kingdom had failed to protect them from
harm.[39] The Court had no intention of letting the United Kingdom off for
failing to provide an opportunity for the affected parties to vindicate the
alleged breach of their Convention rights. Rather than the contentious
Article 6, the Court preferred Article 13 which provides:

Everyone whose rights and freedoms as set forth in the Convention are violated
shall have an effective remedy before a national authority notwithstanding that the
violation has been committed by persons acting in an official capacity.

Article 13 had been raised in *Osman* but given its finding that the United
Kingdom was liable under Article 6, the Court had passed over any real

---

[36] The Commission argued that the mother's claim had been struck out in *Newham* because
she lacked sufficient proximity to the local council and hence the council owed no pre-existing obligation to her that was then subsequently immunised by the operation of public policy.

[37] *Z v United Kingdom* [2001] 2 FLR 612, para 100.

[38] *Osman v Ferguson* [1993] 4 All ER 344 (CA).

[39] The point was well made by Nuala Mole, adviser before the European Commission and
the European Court of Human Rights, for both the claimants in *Osman* and in *Z* and *TP and
KM* in Nuala Mole 'International Law, the Individual, and AW Brian Simpson's Contribution
to the Defence of Human Rights', in K O'Donovan and GR Rubin (eds), *Human Rights and
Legal History: Essays in Honour of Brian Simpson* (Oxford: Oxford University Press, 2000),
13, 26 (n 49): 'All of these eminent jurists [the critics of *Osman*] had difficulty with the Court's
findings that the decision of the Court of Appeal in *Osman* amounted to a procedural bar
rather than a definition of the content of the right. None has suggested what remedy should
have been available in English Law in order to satisfy Art 13.'

consideration of Article 6. The Court in Z now invoked Article 13 as the appropriate mechanism to require Member States to provide adequate enforcement mechanisms for alleged Human Right violations. The Court now interpreted Article 13 as requiring Member States to provide appropriate fora to inquire into the substance of complaints that Member States had violated their obligations under the Convention.[40] Since the blanket immunity rule in effect denied the *Bedfordshire* claimants any such court forum, the rule was in effect a breach of Article 13. In *TP and KM* the blanket immunity rule essentially prevented the mother from claiming a remedy for the Newhman Council's failure to observe acceptable procedures:[41]

the exercise of the court's powers to return the child almost a year later was not an effective remedy. It did not provide redress for the psychological damage allegedly flowing from the separation over this period.

The Court considers that the applicants should have had available to them a means of claiming that the local authority's handling of the procedures was responsible for the damage which they suffered and obtaining compensation for that damage.

E. Effect of Human Rights Jurisprudence on New Zealand and English Law

The extent to which human rights concerns filter through to case law in New Zealand remains to be seen. On the one hand, while English cases are seen as influential, there is an increasing divergence in the common law of different jurisdictions and certainly New Zealand courts will need to address the impact on the United Kingdom's European obligations, which New Zealand does not share, on English developments before adopting them into New Zealand law.[42] On the other hand, New Zealand judges may well view the English decisions as confirming that *Bedfordshire* type immunities are simply inappropriate as a matter of common law, especially since New Zealand judges once clearly led their English counterparts in recognising duties owed by both central[43] and local government.[44]

---

[40] *Z v United Kingdom* [2001] 2 FLR 612, para 108 and *TP and KM v United Kingdom* (10 May 2001) Application No 28945/98 (ECtHR) para 106.

[41] *TP and KM v United Kingdom* (10 May 2001) Application No 28945/98 (ECt HR), paras 108–9.

[42] The debate over whether *Barrett* ought to be considered unpersuasive for New Zealand because of its 'European' character has already featured in judicial review proceedings of the refusal of the New Zealand Government to grant legal aid to the appellants in *B v Attorney-General*, the *HB v Attorney-General* (15 Dec 2000) CP 92/00 High Court, Wellington, McGechan J.

[43] The most famous example is *Takaro Properties v Rowling* [1986] 1 NZLR 22, reversed by the Privy Council in *Rowling v Takaro Properties* [1989] AC 473.

[44] *Brown v Heathcote County Council* [1986] 1 NZLR 76 and *Invercargill City Council v Hamlin* [1996] 1 NZLR 515.

One of the oddest features of the negative reaction to *Osman* in England was that it came at a time when the Human Rights Act was about to make the Article 6 point irrelevant. The Human Rights Act clearly contemplates actions directly against pubic authorities that fail to meet their obligations under the now incorporated Convention. The real importance of *Osman* was that, under the European Convention, the Police might be liable for failing to protect citizens and its corollary that other Government agencies might also be liable for failing to protect citizens from harm. Indeed the United Kingdom Government appeared to acknowledge that the children in *Z* or the mother in *TP and KM* would have an action under the Human Rights Act had it the Act been in force.[45] The Court, after dealing with the United Kingdom Government's submission that a number of administrative remedies were available, recorded as telling the Government's acceptance that there would be a remedy under the Human Rights Act:[46]

[United Kingdom Government] pointed out that from October 2000, when the Human Rights Act 1998 came into force, a victim would be able to bring proceedings in the courts against a public authority for a breach of a substantive right and the courts would be empowered to award damages.

The application of human rights norms does not automatically make welfare agencies liable under tort law for social welfare decisions that turn out wrongly. What both decisions require is the careful identification of the reasons why a particular suit should not be allowed. The Human Rights Commission, for example, in *Z v United Kingdom*, had accepted that the United Kingdom had pursued a legitimate aim in trying to preserve the social worker's role from undue interference, but was not persuaded that a blanket denial of liability was necessary. The Commission wrote, for example, in relation to the Article 6 claim:[47]

The Commission accepts that this restriction pursued a legitimate aim, namely, to preserve the efficiency of a vital sector of public service . . . However, it is not satisfied that it was proportionate to that aim. It notes that the exclusionary rule gave no consideration to the seriousness or otherwise of the damage or the nature or degree of the negligence alleged or the fundamental rights of the applicants which were involved. As regards the multidisciplinary aspects of child protection work, this may provide a factual complexity to cases but cannot by itself provide a justification for excluding liability from a body found to have acted negligently. The risk that liability would open a floodgate of litigation from discontented parents or relatives is a speculative factor which is only of limited weight. The conflictual nature of child care work equally reflects the fact that it frequently concerns matters of

---

[45] See Mole, 'International Law, the Individual and AWB Simpson's Contribution to the Defense of Legal Rights', 27.
[46] *Z v United Kingdom* [2001] 2 FLR 612, para 107.
[47] *Z v United Kingdom* [2000] 2 FCR 245 (Eur Com HR), para 114.

fundamental individual importance. The Commission notes that the tests of foreseeability of damage and proximity serve already as limitations of the categories of plaintiffs who can legitimately claim against allegedly negligent local authorities and is not impressed by the argument that liability would render the social services more cautious in the exercise of their powers.

The Court in *TP and KM* similarly clearly believed that any responsibility to parents for disrupting their family life under Article 8 had to take into consideration the State Parties' obligations to protect the children under Article 3 from cruel and degrading treatment.[48] In the Court's view, the removal and subsequent measures were clearly aimed at protecting the 'health or morals' and the 'rights and freedoms' of the child. Accordingly they pursued legitimate aims within the meaning of paragraph 2 of Article 8.

In *Z v United Kingdom* the court was a little more reticent when expressing possible limitations on the liability of the State to prevent children suffering cruel and degrading treatment. At first blush, it is difficult to conceive of appropriate limiting factors to an obligation to prevent cruel treatment of children. But that is the wrong inquiry. The right inquiry is whether the system employed by the responsible authorities to detect and prevent abuse was appropriate given both the seriousness of obligations under Article 3 to prevent the abuse and the importance of other obligations under the Convention, especially to respect family life. But in its analysis of whether the facts of *Z* showed a breach of article 3, the Court put to one side 'difficult and sensitive decisions facing social services and the important countervailing principle of respecting and preserving family life' because 'the present case ...leaves no doubt as to the failure of the system to protect these children.'[49] The clear implication left is that in appropriate cases the countervailing duty would prevent the application of something akin to strict liability. Further it was clear from *Osman* that the positive obligations of state officials to protect others' lives might be triggered by state official's knowledge that the lives were under threat. The Court acknowledged that there was a clear difference between traditional Article 13 cases in which there was an allegation that a State official was directly responsible for cruel and degrading treatment and those where the State has failed to prevent others from cruel or degrading treatment. In state action cases it was appropriate to require Member States to carry out the investigations while in failure to act cases, but not the Court considered that Article 13 may not always require that the authorities undertake the responsibility for investigating the allegations.[50] There should, however, be

---

[48] *TP and KM v United Kingdom* (10 May 2001) Application No 28945/98 (ECt HR), 69.
[49] *Z v United Kingdom* [2001] 2 FLR 612, para 74.
[50] Ibid, para 109.

available to the victim's family a mechanism for establishing the liability of State officials or bodies for acts or omissions involving the breach of rights under the Convention.

A. The Need to Differentiate Cases

The nature of the particular decision that is alleged to have been negligently made is an important part in understanding the English and New Zealand court decisions in the area. New Zealand courts and the English courts, for instance, have identified a distinction between the decision to remove children from their parents (*Prince v Attorney-General*[51] and Bedfordshire)[52] and subsequent treatment of the child when in care (in *Barrett v Enfield London Borough* Council)[53] or the subsequent investigation of a complaint once child has been removed (*B v Attorney*-General).[54] While we will argue that distinctions have been applied inappropriately, there can be no one approach to common law liability in the family law context. This should not be a surprise. Attempts to articulate one simple, easy principle have proved illusory in other areas of negligence.

It is necessary to draw distinctions between different case groups, but those distinctions ought to reflect the values implicit in modern family law statutes. In particular common law liability ought not to be used to circumvent the priorities established by those statutes. The appropriate question for courts is not whether the negligent actions of the social workers occurred at a particular stage but whether the imposition of a private tort duty would cut across the statutory scheme of modern family law. The key question for family lawyers under such an analysis is what exactly the priorities of modern family law are.

1. A Short Diversion into New Zealand Family Law

New Zealand family law statutes are, however, notoriously confused in setting out priorities—the more recent family legislation in New Zealand often presents decision-makers with conflicting goals that are supposed to be observed when exercising various powers. The New Zealand Statute is not unique in this.

The Children, Young Persons and Their Families Act 1989 instituted a

---

[51] *Prince v Attorney-General* [1998] 1 NZLR 262 (CA).
[52] *X v Bedfordshire County Council* [1995] 2 AC 633.
[53] *Barrett v Enfield London Borough Council* [1999] 3 All ER 193.
[54] *B v Attorney-General* [1999] 2 NZLR 296.

dramatic new system for determining what outcomes should ensue for children in need of care and protection. Instead of relying on the apparent wisdom of professionals, social workers and other experts, primary decision-making was located in the so-called 'family group conference'. Such a gathering of members of the extended family, 'whanau' in indigenous Maori terminology, is charged with formulating plans for the future of an abused or neglected child. While the responsible social worker has a residual right of veto over a plan where, for example, it is thought not to protect the interests of the child, the policy thrust is to avoid top-down solutions imposed on the family.[55] The State should intervene primarily to facilitate the family's decision-making, not to take over the child's life. Use of the court structure is designed to be a last resort, usually where the family group conference has failed.[56]

At the time of the passage of this legislation, a somewhat strange confluence of Maori values and New Right ideologies occurred. Maori wanted the ability to make decisions for their own children. New Rightists believed in the minimalist State and individual responsibility. When the State was seen much more as a protective agency performing public services, the thought of suing the State itself was relegated in favour of a wider public interest. But the model of the minimalist State reverses this. If the State is now merely a professional facilitator for individuals and groups it lays itself open to greater accountability, including action through the courts. But when the genie is let out of the bottle, it is hard to restrict the temporal scope of claims. Events that occurred prior to the passing of the 1989 Act have also come under scrutiny and have led to litigation. Some of these cases we review later in the paper.

In the meantime, it is important to appreciate what tasks the State is given in child protection cases. For while the family group is central to the process, much else must happen before a matter is placed before the family group, and much may happen afterwards. Some of the principal steps set out in the legislation are:

- Under section 15, reports of abuse may be made to an official social worker or a member of the police. Such reports attract immunity from civil, criminal and professional proceedings.
- The social worker or member of the police must 'as soon as practicable' investigate the report.
- If the investigator 'reasonably believes' that the child is in need of care

---

[55] In 1999, three were 27,017 notifications of abuse, leading to 3345 family group conferences.

[56] Despite this, the level of courts order under the Act is high: 1551 in 1999.

or protection, the case must be referred to a care and protection co-ordinator, who in turn is obliged to convene a family group conference.[57]

- After consultation with the family, the care and protection coordinator must fix the time and place for the conference and must determine who should be invited to attend. Under section 22, the child has a right to attend unless this would be 'undesirable'. The child's parents, guardians and care-givers, and members of the 'family, whanau, or family group'[58] also have a right to attend unless the coordinator is of the opinion that such attendance would not be in the child's interests or would be undesirable for any other reason.
- Where a plan agreed to by the conference is acceptable to the authorities, the Department,[59] 'unless it is clearly impracticable or clearly inconsistent with the principles' of the Act, is required to give effect to the plan.[60] In some situations, this may involve placing the child in the custody or under the guardianship of the Department.

The Children and Young Persons Act 1974 which applied in both *Prince* and the *B v Attorney-General* which was replaced by the 1989 Act, can be compared:

- Where there was reason to suspect that a child was suffering or likely to suffer from ill-treatment or from inadequate care or control, or where the child's behaviour was causing serious concern, the Department was required to arrange for 'prompt inquiry' for the provision of assistance to the parties involved.[61]
- Where a member of the police or social worker reasonably believed that a child was in need of care, protection or control, a complaint could be made (but did not have to be made) to have the matter determined by the Children and Young Persons Court.[62]
- The Court had a range of order which it could make, including admonition, and placing the child in State care.[63]

The 1989 Act is replete with statutory obligations. Many of them however involve an element of judgment. In determining the reasonableness of a

---

[57] Sections 17 and 18, Children, Young Persons and Their Families Act 1989. It appears that often statutory family group conferences are not convened but instead 'family meetings' are held. The lawfulness of this approach may be questioned.

[58] 'Family' and 'whanau' are not defined in the Act, but 'family group' is defined to include an extended family, determined by biological and adoptive relationships as well as by significant psychological attachments not involving biological or adoptive links (s 2(1)).

[59] The Department of Child Youth and Family Services, formerly the Department of Social Welfare.

[60] Section 35, Children, Young Persons and Their Families Act 1989.

[61] Section 5(2), Children and Young Persons Act 1974.

[62] Section 27, Children and Young Persons Act 1974.

[63] Section 31, Children and Young Persons Act 1974.

report of abuse, a degree of assessment is required. Likewise, other decisions such as the membership of a family group conference are elastic. These are backed up by a range of 'principles', some conflicting.[64] For example, while the welfare and interests of the child are paramount and the child must be protected from harm, the child's relationship with the family, whanau or family group should be maintained and strengthened, consideration must be given to the stability of the family, and intervention into family life must be the minimum necessary for the child's safety and protection.

The statutory scheme is therefore a confused patchwork of duties, discretions and principles. The 1989 Act is not so different in this respect from the 1974 Act, except that the current law places much more weight on the importance of the family and 'family group'.[65] Getting the balance right in child abuse cases between safety and over-intervention in family life is always hard. It is even harder when the statutory framework is as described. To be looking over one's shoulder at the prospect of civil litigation such claims for damages simply adds to the pressures of a difficult situation. Failures can be readily understood and even excused. But does this mean that, absent bad faith, there should be general immunity? Are there not standards which even government officers are expected to meet? What if decisions are made in the face of obvious evidence pointing in the opposite direction, for example where a father accused of sexual abuse could not have been responsible because all access to the child had ceased?[66] In other words, when carrying out straightforward tasks which involve less of an element of assessment and judgment, should aggrieved parties be prevented from suing?

In *Prince v Attorney-General* (discussed later) the New Zealand Court of Appeal accepted that a duty of care could be imposed. One of the strongest reasons behind its decision was the lack of ambiguity in the statutory scheme—on the Court of Appeal's view the 1974 Children and Young Persons Act unambiguously required prompt inquiry of reports of abuse. Subsequent legislation also emphasises the importance of the family group and of cultural values. While the 1989 Act ultimately places the interests of the child above those of the family group or wider culture, the ambiguous relationship between the welfare of the child, the welfare of the family group and the values of the culture in which both exist have left New Zealand judges uneasy about whether common law liability should exist.

---

[64] Sections 5, 6 and 13, Children, Young Persons and Their Families Act 1989.

[65] In fact, in 1983 amendments were made to the 1974 Act which represent the first signs of a legislative recognition of the importance of the family group: ss 4A–4C.

[66] As in *Parkinson v Attorney-General* [2000] NZFLR 552 (HC).

2. *Courts Making Different Distinctions and Reaching Different Results*

Distinctions, however, are never free from an appearance of arbitrariness. The paradox of the New Zealand and English case law in care and protection cases is that courts while making essentially the same distinctions have reached the reverse results. In New Zealand, there appears to be liability for the failure to investigate a complaint while in England there is no liability (the European Convention to one side), if *Bedfordshire* is followed, for the decision to remove or not to remove the child from its family. The position is however reversed in the respective jurisdictions once that decision to remove has been made. In *B v Attorney-General* the New Zealand Court of Appeal held that social workers' common law duty did not exist after a decision was made to remove the child and did not extend even to an earlier incompetent investigation into the child's allegation that she had been abused by her father. In *Barrett v Enfield London Borough* the House of Lords held that social workers might be held liable for decisions they had made in regard to the welfare of a child once that child had been placed in care.

3. *Negligence Claims Brought by Parents or Families or Affected Third Parties*

Claims in this group can be broken into two subgroups. The first is where a family alleges that a social worker has failed in a duty to the family, independent of statute, which that social worker has breached by placing a 'dangerous' child with the family and that dangerous child has later caused harm to the family members. The second group involves cases where a parent alleges that the social workers' decision to remove a child from its normal family environment has compromised the parent's interests. The dangerous child cases are the clearest cases in which courts are prepared to hold that there will be common law liability. In these cases the judges typically see little conflict between the statutory scheme of the statute under which the social worker has been acting and the imposition of a private law duty of care. The disadvantaged parent cases on the other hand represent the situation in which courts have been most reluctant to impose a private law duty of care. Courts in these disadvantaged parent cases believe that the imposition of such a duty of care would cut across the statutory scheme under which the welfare agency is acting, the primary goal of which is the protection of child

(a) *The 'Dangerous Child'*
The two most prominent English dangerous child cases are the 1979 *Vicar*

of Writtle[67] case, and the much more recent decisions of the English Court of Appeal and the House of Lords in case of *W v Essex*.[68]

(i) The Vicar of Writtle—no discretion not to warn potential foster parents

The *Vicar of Writtle* case involved the failure of social services to alert a foster home that the child, whose care it had been entrusted with, was suspected of fire-raising at his school. Unfortunately, the child while in the claimant's care set the foster home on fire causing widespread damage. While the judge, Forbes J, acknowledged the welfare service had considerable discretion in the way that it dealt with children under its care, he held that there had been no exercise of that discretion. Indeed, there was a policy at the head office that information about a child's propensity to light fires would be important information for a prospective foster parent to know. The judge's analysis was very similar to Lord Reid's approach in *Dorset Yacht Club*,[69] where the legitimate exercise of discretion to rehabilitate the Borstal boys might have meant that the Home Office ought not to be liable if the rehabilitation were to go wrong. Far more important was the close relationship that the judge perceived between the social worker that placed the child and the foster home that accepted him.

(ii) W v Essex—Social Worker cannot mislead prospective foster parents

The English Court of Appeal decided in the *Essex* case not to strike out a statement of claim that alleged that a child that the defendant's social workers had placed with the family had sexually abused the foster parents' children. The Court of Appeal's decision was notable as the only one of three post *Bedfordshire* decisions involving actions against social workers to be allowed to proceed to trial, before the House of Lord's decision in *Barrett*. The other two Court of Appeal decisions, *Barrett*[70] itself and *H v Norfolk County Council*,[71] had involved respectively allegations about the way a child had been treated by the social welfare agency once in care, and an allegation that a child had been sexually abused by a foster parent. In both *Barrett* and the *Norfolk* cases, the English Court of Appeal held the cases governed by *Bedfordshire* and, as imposing a duty of care would cut across the statutory scheme of child protection, the claimants' claims ought to be struck out. In contrast, in the *Essex* case, the majority of the Court of Appeal focused on the relationship that existed between the social worker and the foster family, almost outside the statutory context. In the view of

---

[67] *Vicar of Writtle v Essex County Council* (1977) 77 LGR 656.
[68] *W v Essex County Council* [2000] 2 WLR 601 (HL).
[69] *Home Office v Dorset Yacht Co Ltd* [1970] AC 1004 (HL).
[70] *Barrett v Enfield London Borough Council* [1997] 2 FLR 167.
[71] *H v Norfolk County Council* [1997] 1 FLR 276.

Judge and Mantell LJJ, the assurances of the social worker that the child did not have a record of sexual abuse and the social worker's knowledge that the child would be accepted only by the foster parents if there were no record of sexual abuse gave rise to a *Hedley Byrne* reliance type of relationship.[72] In contrast, Stuart-Smith LJ in dissent held that the recognition of liability based on negligent misstatement would cut across the statutory scheme in a way that was impermissible after *Bedfordshire*. The correctness of the majority's approach has been underlined by the House of Lords' decision on appeal that not only the abused children might be able to claim against the social welfare agency, but that the parents also might be able to, at least, for the 'nervous shock' of discovering that the children had been abused. Lord Slynn wrote of the question of whether a duty might be owed to the parents:[73]

It seems to me that it cannot be said here that the claim that there was a duty of care owed to the parents and a breach of that duty by the defendants is unarguable, that it is clear and obvious that it cannot succeed. On the contrary whether it is right or wrong on the facts found at the end of the day, it is on the facts alleged plainly a claim which is arguable. In their case the parents made it clear that they were anxious not to put their children at risk by having a known sex abuser in their home. The council and the social worker knew this and also knew that the boy placed had already committed an act or acts of sex abuse. The risk was obvious and the abuse happened. Whether the nature of the council's task is such that the court should not recognise an actionable duty of care, in other words that the claim is not justiciable, and whether there was a breach of the duty depend, in the first place, on an investigation of the full facts known to, and the factors influencing the decision of, the defendants.

The House of Lords then left it open for trial whether the parents would be able to establish that they suffered harm under the requirements of nervous shock.

Judges in the 'dangerous child' cases tend to minimise the importance of the social worker's statutory discretion or role in 'rehabilitating' a troubled child and emphasise the reliance by the foster families. This can be contrasted with the care and protection cases where that same discretion forms the major barrier which any claim against social workers in this context must get over.

---

[72] *Hedley Byrne v Heller* [1964] AC 465 (HL). The Court of Appeal unanimously rejected the claimants' contention that there had been a contract between the social worker and the claimants which the social worker had breached, for a critique of the Court's refusal to find a contract, B Coote, 'Common Forms, Consideration, and Contract Doctrine' (1999) 14 *Journal of Contract Law*, 116.

[73] *W v Essex County Council* [2000] 2 WLR 601, 605 (HL).

(b) Claims by Disadvantaged Parents and Families

In contrast to the success of claims by foster parents for harm by a dangerous child, claims that the interest of parents (or the families) had been
compromised by negligent decisions by social workers have been notably
unsuccessful, with the limited exception of the European Court of Human
Rights' holding in *TP and HM*.

In the *Newham* case, which was heard together with the *Bedfordshire*
case by the House of Lords, the claimant child alleged that he had been
wrongfully removed from his mother by a social worker who suspected
(wrongly as it turned out) that the child was being abused by the mother's
partner. In Lord Browne-Wilkinson's view such a duty would cut across the
statutory scheme. Lord Browne-Wilkinson wrote in *Bedfordshire* that:[74]

The relationship between the social worker and the child's parents is frequently one
of conflict, the parent wishing to retain care of the child, the social worker having
to consider whether to remove it. This is fertile ground in which to breed ill feeling
and litigation, often hopeless, the cost of which both in terms of money and human
resources will be diverted from the performance of the social service for which they
were provided. The spectre of vexatious and costly litigation is often urged as a
reason for not imposing a legal duty. But the circumstances surrounding cases of
child abuse make the risk a very high one which cannot be ignored.

Unsurprisingly, parents who had sought to make the similar claim that they
had been deprived unnecessarily of their children by a social worker making
the wrong determination that the parent was abusing the child have been
unsuccessful. In the New Zealand case of *E v K*[75] Morris J struck out such
a claim by a father who had alleged that a social worker had wrongly determined that he had abused his child. Morris J accepted that there was a relationship of proximity between the social worker in investigating sexual
abuse allegations and the subject of those allegations. But he held that
policy would prevent the imposition of a duty of care. In particular, a duty
to a child abuse suspect might cut across the paramountcy principle that is
at the heart of modern family law. A duty of care might create a conflict of
interest for a social worker whose job under the 1974 Children and Young
Persons Act was to guard the interests of the child.[76] An appropriate analogy was with a private sector professional, including comparison to a
lawyer, who has an obligation to protect the interests of the client. We
partially agree with this 'conflict of interest' analysis—an important part of
whether there can be a duty of care ought to be the degree to which the
imposition of such a duty might place the prospective defendant in an
impossible position.

[74] *X v Bedfordshire County Council* [1995] 2 AC 633, 750–1 (HL).
[75] *E v K* [1995] 2 NZLR 239 (HC).
[76] *E v K* [1995] 2 NZLR 239, 249 (HC).

Care needs to be taken with comparisons to private sector professionals. They are perhaps a little misplaced in the case of social workers exercising statutory powers of removal as there are really no comparable private professionals that can exercise the kinds of powers with which social workers are entrusted.

Even with psychologists who might be said to be acting as private professionals employed to assist the social workers or indeed simply to treat the patient at hand, it is easy to be too absolute about the duty being owed only to the patient. As Morris J himself acknowledged, lawyers in a range of contexts can owe duties to non-clients.[77] Certainly in the education cases considered at the same time as *Bedfordshire*, Lord Browne-Wilkinson accepted that psychologists, employed by the local school authorities to assess children as to whether they had special educational needs, might owe duties to children they assess even though they were not strictly speaking their patients.[78]

Morris J's decision was essentially followed by Gallen J in the first instance decision in *B v Attorney-General*.[79] In *B*, a daughter had made an allegation to a school friend that her father had abused her. Upon hearing the allegations, social workers removed both the daughter and her sister from their father's care. A subsequent, and prolonged, hearing established that the child had not meant her allegations. The father and the daughters sued the Department and the psychologist employed to assist it, alleging that the conduct of the investigation had unnecessarily prolonged the length of the separation and greatly increased the family's legal costs in fighting the allegations. Gallen J acknowledged that the social worker's decision to remove the children from a parent accused of abuse, and the conduct of the subsequent investigation of that abuse, would foreseeably affect the father. However, it was inappropriate to allow a private law claim of negligence to be brought by the father because of the importance of safeguarding a child at risk.[80] His Honour also referred to the urgency with which social workers must work. We doubt that this factor was in fact a key one in *B*, since the father accepted that there could be no liability for the initial, protective

---

[77] Examples include the frustrated testamentary beneficiary cases but also include, in some instances, the failure to ensure that a non-client gets advice. See also Master Venning in *N v D* [1999] NZFLR 560. Lawyers may owe a duty to a third party when giving a solicitor's certificate: *Allied Finance v Haddow* [1983] NZLR 22 and in the family law context it was held that a lawyer advising one party on a matrimonial property agreement (under s 21 of the Matrimonial Property Act 1976) owed a duty to the other spouse: *Connell v Odlum* [1993] 2 NZLR 257 (CA). It ought to be noted that at least in commercial contexts the New Zealand Court of Appeal has emphasised in cases such as *Brownie Wills v Shrimpton* [1998] 2 NZLR 320 that in the absence of special circumstances there will be no duty to advise a non-client.

[78] See *Phelps v Hillingdon London Borough Council* [2000] 4 All ER 504 [2000] 3 WLR 776 where the House of Lords allowed the possibility of such a duty.

[79] [1997] NZFLR 550 (HC).

[80] *B v Attorney-General* [1997] NZFLR 550, 565 (HC).

decision to remove the children, but rather sued in relation to the on-going refusal to return the children.

An appeal failed.[81] The Court of Appeal did not deal directly with the claim brought by the father. Both the joint judgment of Keith and Blanchard JJ and the concurring judgment of Tipping J dealt with the father's claim in the same manner as that of the children. If the children could not succeed, the father certainly could not. But perhaps more importantly running the father's and the daughters' claims together obscured the different considerations that ought to apply to what are in fact very different claims.

These decisions however have to be contrasted with that of Master Venning in *N v D*.[82] Master Venning accepted that not only was the relationship between a psychotherapist and her patient's father, who was accused of abusing the patient, sufficiently proximate but, in contrast to Morris J's decision,[83] the duty of care should not be defeated by public policy. Master Venning sought to distinguish this case on the basis that in *E v K* the social worker had been performing a statutory power to protect the child from future abuse. In *N v D*, not only was the psychotherapist not acting in accordance with a statutory duty, but she had the gone beyond simply treating the patient to alerting another psychologist who was charged by the Family Court to prepare a quite separate report for a custody hearing. The Master concluded:[84]

In this case the plaintiff is the person that the defendant identified as having committed sexual abuse on the child. That allegation was passed on to third parties apart from the child's parents. The defendant intentionally passed the result of her findings on to the report writer in the Family Court proceedings. In those circumstances the defendant must have known, or should have known, that in passing on that accusation of sexual abuse it would impact upon the plaintiff as the person against whom the allegation was made. The relationship is direct and close.

The Master emphasised that, unlike the other two cases, the child was not at risk at the time the psychotherapist made her views known more widely. The Master also focused on the need, echoing Lord Bingham MR in the *Newham* case, for the affected parent to have a real remedy.[85]

We wonder whether it is appropriate to make such a distinction. Can it really be said that it is only a statutory duty that requires professionals to contact relevant authorities? We wonder whether Morris J's concern that the professionals not be charged with common law duties that might prevent them from properly protecting their clients ought also prima facie

---

[81] *B v Attorney-General* [1999] 2 NZLR 296.

[82] [1999] NZFLR 560.

[83] And we might add an extensive citation and analysis of *E v K* and *B* in the High Court on which we have ourselves drawn.

[84] *N v D* [1999] NZFLR 560, 564 (HC).

[85] *N v D* [1999] NZFLR 560, 564 (HC).

apply in cases outside the statutory scheme of the child welfare statutes. Certainly Morris J's concern not to create conflicting duties on child welfare professionals was echoed more recently by a Canadian judge who refused to impose a common law duty on a counsellor whom a family alleged had failed to properly treat a patient, leading the patient to make allegations of sexual abuse against her father.[86] Beames J reviewed a number of United States authorities in which courts had imposed liability on therapists to third parties, but rejected for similar reasons a private law duty in Canada. The judge there wrote:[87]

Notwithstanding the societal interests in preventing false accusations of abuse, I conclude that the detection and reporting of abuse are more important societal goals, and further, because the healing of victims may be dependent upon the maintenance of confidence between a therapist and patient and upon the undiluted duty of a therapist to the patient, it is only in the most compelling circumstances that a court should extend a duty of care from a therapist to those third parties who may be identified in the course of therapy as alleged perpetrators. Those cases which have found such a duty... have done so on a very limited basis, based upon the particular facts in the case. Amongst other factors, those cases where a duty has been found have involved the therapist either personally undertaking, or encouraging their patient to make, public accusations against the perpetrators.

However, we also wonder whether this prima facie reluctance to impose a duty might be countered in *N v D* by the other two factors that the Master mentioned. After all as the Master himself argued, in certain circumstances professionals have been held to owe duties to those others than their clients.[88] First this case was not an emergency one, the child was out of any immediate danger and the psychotherapist had treated the alleged victim for a long period of time before she made the allegations. Second, the psychotherapist chose to put herself outside the umbrella of the statutory scheme and its protection. We suggest that the conflict of interest analysis is perhaps the most important factor, but it cannot be the only factor in determining liability.

4.The Care and Protection Cases

(i) Introduction—one distinction, different results
It is possible to argue that the courts have adopted a consistent approach to suits brought by affected families, and have rightly focused upon the fear that allowing parents to bring suit in the second sub-category might cut

---

[86] *Gardner v Rusch* (1999) 179 DLR (4th) 336.
[87] Ibid, at para 36.
[88] See *N v D* [1999] NZFLR 560, 568 (HC).

across the statutory scheme of child welfare legislation. No such consistency is evident in care and protection cases.

Both New Zealand and United Kingdom courts have essentially adopted the same prime requirement, that a private law duty not 'cut across the statutory scheme' but the inconsistent results reached by those courts indicate that this phrase is less of a test and more a way of justifying the result that the court has reached.

Elsewhere, one of us has compared in detail the reasoning of the New Zealand Court of Appeal in *Prince* with that of the House of Lords in *Bedfordshire*.[89] We do not intend to describe in the same detail those two cases. Nevertheless, it will be necessary to repeat some of the arguments in that paper before considering more recent cases, *Barrett* and *B*.

In *Prince*, the New Zealand Court of Appeal was prepared to allow a claim that social workers had failed to investigate an allegation that the teenager Prince was being neglected by his adoptive parents. The Court of Appeal was prepared to let such claim go to trial on the basis that a duty of care to investigate such allegations would not cut across the statutory scheme of the Children and Young Persons Act 1974. But further, the majority argued, such a duty would in fact reinforce the duties placed by the statute on the Department of Social Welfare to guard the interests of children at risk. In doing so, the Court of Appeal purported to adopt the same approach as Lord Browne-Wilkinson had in *Bedfordshire*. Given the existence of different statutes in two different jurisdictions, it was quite conceivable that there might be liability under one regime but not under the other. However, an analysis of the Children Act 1989 and the Children and Young Person Act 1974 reveals almost identical statutory wording. The difference in results therefore cannot be explained simply by the observation that different statutes were involved. Rather the decision in *Prince* seemed to reflect a different weighing of the policy factors that Lord Browne-Wilkinson had thought so important in denying a duty of care in the *Bedfordshire* care.

The difference in approach is perhaps best exposed by comparing the different weighing of two policy factors: first, the difficulty of the social workers' job and the potential that liability might somehow promote defensive social work; and secondly the availability of administrative procedures through which the social worker's behaviour might be measured.

(ii) The Extraordinary Delicacy of the Social Worker's Task
Lord Browne-Wilkinson correctly termed the social worker's job as involving 'extraordinary delicacy' and expressed the not uncommon fear that the

---

[89] G McLay, 'Convicted killer can sue social welfare—Prince, the strange fate of Bedfordshire down-under' (1999) 11 *CFLQ* 75.

imposition of a duty of the care might adversely affect the way that social workers discharged the statutory duty. But rather than being focused on the performance of the statutory obligations to protect children, social workers would be focused instead on avoiding liability to the detriment of the children they were supposed to protect:[90]

The question whether there is such a common law duty and if so its ambit, must be profoundly influenced by the statutory framework within which the acts complained of were done...in my judgment a common law duty of care cannot be imposed on statutory duty if the observance of such a common law duty of care would be inconsistent with, or have a tendency to discourage, the due performance by the local authority of its statutory duty.

As discussed above, New Zealand Courts have been alive to this fear when adversely affected parents have brought suit. The New Zealand Court of Appeal, however, rejected this is as a reason for not imposing liability in *Prince*, indeed the New Zealand Court of Appeal was somewhat sceptical of the validity, in the absence of hard data, of this adverse deterrence argument. Writing for the majority Richardson J concluded:[91]

[the Crown] submitted that the imposition of a duty would or could cause the department and social workers to adopt a more cautious and defensive approach to their duties. He drew our attention to a considerable body of professional literature on that point and to the recognition of it in *Bedfordshire* case. But like lawyers and doctors, social workers are professionals. At that triggering step [the courts characterisation of the initial decision to investigate a complaint] (and at other steps) they should be expected to have shouldered willingly a standard of reasonable skill and care that the private sector counterparts were expected to discharge. And in the absence of any data as to potential claims based on the roles and responsibilities of department and social workers under the 1974 Act, which was replaced eight years ago by a very different legislative scheme, it would be unwise to give any particular weight to the rethought implications of allowing for a common law duty of care.

The force of the comparison between social workers' exercising powers to remove children and normal professional responsibility of others is that it dispels Lord Browne-Wilkinson's conclusion that the extraordinary delicacy of the social workers' task was any different from the delicacy which we associate with those professional groupings. As courts have been quite willing to impose duties on those professionals, the courts should not necessarily refuse to impose duties of care on social workers. There is some truth in this analogy. However, what the analogy cannot resolve is the source of the duty of care that is being imposed by the courts. Social workers involved in care and protection cases in fact exercise powers which are uniquely public,

---

[90] *X v Bedfordshire County Council* [1995] 2 AC 633, 739.
[91] While the New Zealand Court of Appeal in *Prince* accepted them relation to another cause of action based on the handling of Prince's adoption as a baby.

that is, the power to remove children from their families, and which have little or no private sector comparison. On the other hand, social workers involved in the subsequent care of children might be said to be doing something much more analogous to private sector nurses, or nannies or guardians.

Indeed, the Court of Appeal did not really identify the statute as being the source of the social worker's common law obligation, preferring merely to say that the common law duty simply reinforced the statutory obligations, rather than being derived from them. The majority expressed the point in the following way:[92]

[G]iven the important features of the 1974 Act which we had been emphasising, it cannot be said the common law duty of sheer in these terms would cut across the whole statutory scheme. At the early triggering step a specific positive duty rests on the Director-General. At that step it does not require participation with other agencies. The duty suggested does not conflict with any other duty by the department and its offices. On the contrary it enhances it.

(iii) B v Attorney-General—*the Court of Appeal restricts Prince*
Because of the way that *Prince* had been pleaded, the Court of Appeal had considered an allegation that the Social Welfare Department had failed to make any investigation into allegations that Prince's adoptive parents were neglecting him. The Court of Appeal's decision in *Prince v Attorney-General* was largely focused on that complete failure to investigate (what it termed the 'triggering stage') as opposed to the situation where investigation had gone wrong. The significance in *Prince v Attorney-General* of an allegation that there had been no investigation was that it ruled out any argument that the social workers involved had exercised any discretion which would justify the court in saying that the social workers had legitimately exercised their professional discretion.

Before the Court of Appeal's decision in *B v Attorney-General*, it was possible to argue that *Prince v Attorney-General* should not necessarily be restricted to situations where the social workers had failed to institute an investigation at all. The focus in Richardson P's judgment on the obligations of the Director-General to undertake an initial investigation might simply have been taken as a reflection of the procedural status of *Prince v Attorney-General*. The Court did not necessarily rule out the possibility of liability for inadequate investigations, and indeed appeared to imply that there might be liability in some cases. However, because it was a striking out application, the Court of Appeal needed to reach a definite conclusion only about the possibility of liability under the best possible scenario for the defendant.

<hr />

[92] *Prince v Attorney-General* [1998] 1 NZLR 262, 284 (CA).

B v Attorney-General, however, involved an allegation that the subsequent substantive investigation of a child's claim that her father had abused her had been negligently undertaken leading to a child and her sister being kept from their perfectly innocent father for over 18 months. It was the father's and his daughters' contention that, had the investigation been properly undertaken, the allegations would have been easily disproved. Rather than focusing on the obligations of the social workers to protect the interests of the child in any investigation, including an obligation not unnecessarily to deprive a child of her parents, the Court of Appeal restricted *Prince v Attorney-General.* The Court held that the duties the court had imposed in *Prince v Attorney-General* did not apply once investigations had moved beyond the initial triggering stage. Keith J writing for himself and Blanchard J concluded:[93]

The temporal issue is critical in the circumstances of this case. By contrast to be facts alleged in *Prince,* the facts complained of here occurred after the immediate triggering step. That step was the response by the department to the information provided by the mother of the friend of [the daughter] including the decision to arrange to prompt inquiry. By contrast, the criticised actions were various actions and failures occurring in the course of the investigation which followed and which continued beyond the initiation of the Court process.

This temporal distinction was in the Court's view key because of the scope of the duties imposed on the Director-General by section 5 of the 1974 Act. Keith J wrote:[94]

We have no doubt that the breaches of duty alleged in this case fall outside that initial period of positive statute obligations during which, in accordance with *Prince,* a common law duty of care may also arise. In this case the proceeds move rapidly from initial stage, involving a duty, to the operational stage of information-gathering and considering the exercise of statutory powers and then to the exercise of those powers. At this stage the department is exercising a discretion . . . the difficulties may be greater when a decision is made not to launch court proceedings. In some cases that decision may be so unreasonable as to amount to a failure of Department to do its duty. But we do not in this case have to give a precise definition to the line. The facts here lie clearly beyond it.

The distinction was drawn between the duty to institute an inquiry as part of the initial triggering stage and the subsequent conduct of that investigation during which no duty was possible. This distinction was possible because the Court of Appeal in *Prince v Attorney-General* left unclear the underlying source of the social worker's duty. While the Court of Appeal in *Prince v Attorney-General* had focused on the statutory duties imposed by

---

[93] *B v Attorney-General* [1999] 2 NZLR 296, 304 (CA).
[94] Ibid, 305 (CA).

section 5 of 1974 Act, it is unclear that the majority necessarily viewed the 1974 Act as the source of social workers' duty. Rather, the majority talks of the common law duty, however it arose, as reinforcing the statutory obligations of the social workers. The Court of Appeal in *B v Attorney-General* appeared to interpret the duty in *Prince* as being defined by the obligations in the 1974 Act. If, of course, the duty at common law had arisen independently of the statute, as *Prince* appeared to indicate, then there is no reason why that duty should be restricted to the obligations imposed by the statute.

From a tort law perspective a comparison of *Prince v Attorney-General* and *B v Attorney-General* leads to the odd proposition that, while social workers might be liable if they do nothing, they are not liable so long as they do something (unless what they in fact do is so unreasonable as to be in effect a failure to do anything at all). In essence the New Zealand Court had reached an odd position whereby social workers might be liable for non-feasance but not liable for misfeasance. This reflects a reversal of the normal common law rule that professionals in the absence of a special relationship owe no duty to act to protect others but do owe a duty to take reasonable care once they had decided to act to protect others.

From a family law perspective, the distinction also appears to us unsustainable. The initial investigation of abuse cases must be done in great haste, and a preliminary determination made quickly so as to prevent any further abuse. Yet at this stage the Court of Appeal in *Prince* seemed prepared to impose a duty. Bad decisions at this stage can be remedied in the next steps of the process. The element of haste is, however, far less apparent once the social worker has gone beyond that initial triggering stage. At the later investigatory stage, one can expect a degree of reflection on what is going on that is as reviewable by a court as the exercise of professional obligations in other fields. It is illogical that, had the investigation in fact been conducted, rather than not at all, in *Prince* the social workers should not be liable simply because they were beyond the so-called triggering stage. The oddity of the distinction is perhaps best illustrated by the reasoning of Potter J in the subsequent *Parkinson*[95] decision in the High Court. Despite the facts of *Parkinson* being very similar to those in *B*, the claimant father attempted to distinguish the case so that it could proceed. Potter J clearly viewed the investigation undertaken by the social workers of an allegation of abuse to be the same kind as in *B*. Her Honour wrote of the investigation:[96]

In *B* the Court considered that to impose a duty of care would prejudice the prompt and efficient exercise of the operational powers and discretions by the Department. In my view the conduct leading up to inquiry, the inquiry and the views that the offi-

---

[95] *Parkinson v Attorney-General* [2000] NZFLR 552.
[96] Ibid, 570.

cers formed in that inquiry, relate to the operational stage of information gathering in which the Court in *Prince* and *B* held no duty.

The oddity of this conclusion, which is a fair reflection of the holding in *B*, is that it represents a reversal of the normal understanding that operational decisions are the ones that are most appropriate for courts to assess, in comparison to high policy which is not.

Similarly, it seems wrong to us that there should be any formula along the lines suggested by Keith J that makes liability depend on whether an investigation can be termed as 'so bad' as not to be an investigation at all. This adds an unnecessary complication to what ought to be simply considered an inquiry as to whether the social workers had behaved according to normal professional standards. Any difficulty as to the delicacy of the social workers' task should be dealt with by the courts in the same way as with other professionals, by asking not if they got it completely right or completely wrong but whether they followed a reputable professional methodology in their investigations.

Why the Court of Appeal seemingly accepted such an approach in *Prince*, but rejected it in *B*, remains a mystery. It is true that the clash of interests that *B* involved was potentially more complicated than that in *Prince*. The Court needs to be much more subtle when reviewing a concluded investigation than a case of no investigation, but is such an inquiry really so much harder than other professional cases? One wonders whether the fact that the father was also bringing a claim meant that the Court was concerned about recognising conflicting duties, on the one hand the social worker's statutory duty to protect the children, while on the other a common law duty to the father. If it was, then these concerns remained unfortunately unexamined and undifferentiated from the children's case. Further, we do not believe that there is necessarily a conflict. The temporal distinction between beginning an investigation and conducting the investigation that the Court drew to deny liability might have been better employed to militate against any conflict of interest preventing the social worker from fulfilling the prime role of protecting the child. A duty to the father at the preliminary stage might interfere with social worker's duty to act urgently to protect the child. A duty to the father to conduct the subsequent investigation professionally may not carry the same risks to the child.

5. The House of Lords and the Proper Place of Discretion—Barrett v Enfield London Borough Council

(i) The English and New Zealand Courts change places
If New Zealand lawyers could have believed that after *Prince v Attorney-General* social workers might owe duties of care to children affected by

their decisions, after *Bedfordshire* English lawyers would have made the reverse prediction about the liability of English social workers in care and protection cases. For New Zealand lawyers, perhaps a little depressed by the restrictive approach of the Court of Appeal in *B*, the decision of the House of Lords in *Barrett*, released after *B v Attorney-General*, raised the prospect that the New Zealand courts were more conservative than their English counterparts. For English lawyers who had become accustomed to *Bedfordshire* being used to strike out a range of cases brought against social services, the decision in *Barrett v Enfield London Borough Council* must have been a revelation.

The claimant Barrett alleged that the social services section of Enfield London Borough Council had been negligent in a number of important decisions relating to how he was cared for during a childhood largely spent under its protection. The House of Lords held that, in contrast to *Bedfordshire*, the claim should not be struck out.

Again, the decision in *Barrett* is worthy of an extended paper in its own right.[97] For the purposes of this paper we want to compare the approach taken by the House of Lords to the crucial issue of whether a duty can be imposed when a social worker exercises a discretion in regard to a child in care. We believe that the approach of the House of Lords in *Barrett* is far closer to the New Zealand Court of Appeal's decision in *Prince v Attorney-General* than it is to its own previous holding in *Bedfordshire*. Indeed their Lordships' approach appears to be more consistent with the New Zealand Court of Appeal's approach in *Prince v Attorney-General* than the Court of Appeal's own decision in *B v Attorney-General*.

(ii) Barrett—the importance of distinguishing between professional discretion and governmental discretion

Ever since *Dorset Yacht Club*, common law courts have struggled with the problem of imposing a common law duty on public officials who exercised a discretion.[98] As we have seen, the House of Lords' perception that the task of social workers was extraordinarily complex played a major role in the House's striking out of the care and protection causes of action in *Bedfordshire*. *Bedfordshire*, is, however, only one of a series of cases in which the House of Lords and Privy Council have wound themselves into knots over how the courts ought to deal with discretion. The speeches of Lords Slynn and Hutton in *Barrett* are important advances in this general debate but we submit that their reasoning also significantly advances the approach adopted by the English Courts in care and protection cases. After

---

[97] See Craig and Fairgrieve, '*Barrett*, Negligence and Discretionary Powers' [1999] *PL* 626.
[98] See T Geuther, 'The Search for Principle—the Government's Liability in Negligence for the Careless Exercise of its Statutory Powers' (2000) 31 *VUWLR* 629.

Barrett, the fact that a defendant was exercising a statutory discretion appears to play at least three roles in a negligence case.

First, the fact that a discretion was exercised might rule out a claim under a justiciability rule that decisions involving matters of high policy are inappropriate to review at common law. Secondly, the fact the discretion has been exercised might be relevant when it comes to consider whether it is just and reasonable to impose a duty of care (as in *Bedfordshire* or seemingly in *B*). Lastly, whether a discretion has been exercised remains an important consideration in whether the duty of care has been breached (the standard case of professional liability or seemingly *Prince*). In *Bedfordshire*, Lord Browne-Wilkinson had placed the social worker's exercise of discretion clearly within the second role, and used the exercise of discretion as a reason to deny a duty of care. The significance of *Barrett* is to show how unlikely, but not impossible, it is that social workers would have exercised a discretion so as to make the claim non-justiciable. Certainly, it is now important to determine whether there are in fact issues of policy that a private law court should not review. There is seemingly no blanket exception of the type suggested by *Bedfordshire*. Lord Slynn wrote:[99]

In the present case, the allegations . . . are largely directed to the way in which the powers of the local authority were *exercised*. It is arguable . . . that if some of the allegations are made out, a duty of care was owed and was broken. Others involve the exercise of a discretion which the court may consider to be not justiciable—eg, whether it was right to arrange adoption at all, though the question of whether adoption was ever considered and if not, why not, may be a matter of investigation in a claim for negligence . . .

The fact that liability arises from the exercise of discretion is something that may defeat liability either at the duty stage or, to our minds, preferably at the breach stage, but only after the courts have heard the facts of the case. That *Barrett* had restricted the kinds of cases where it will not be just and reasonable to impose a duty of care was made plain by the English Court of Appeal in *S v Gloucestershire County Council* in interpreting Lord Slynn's observations quoted above.[100] That case involved allegations that a council had been negligent in the placing of children with a foster parent who subsequently abused the children. May LJ concluded that the negligence claims ought to go to trial, summarising the position after *Barrett* in the following way:[101]

(a) depending on the particular facts of the case, a claim in common law negligence may be available to a person who claims to have been damaged by failings of a local authority who were responsible under statutory powers for his care and upbringing.

---

[99] *Barrett v Enfield London Borough Council* [1999] 3 All ER 193, 212–13, quoted in *S v Gloucestershire County Council; L v Tower Hamlets London Borough Council* [2000] 3 All ER 346, 365.
[100] Ibid, 346 (CA).
[101] Ibid, 346, 369.

(b) the claim will not succeed if the failings alleged comprise actions or decisions by the local authority of a kind which are not justiciable. These may include, but will not necessarily be limited to, policy decisions and decisions about allocating public funds.

(c) the border line between what is justiciable and what is not may in a particular case be unclear. Its demarcation may require a more extensive investigation than is capable of being made from material in traditional pleadings alone.

(d) there may be circumstances in which it will not be just and reasonable to impose a duty of care of the kind contended for. Here again, it may often be necessary to conduct a detailed investigation of the facts to determine this question.

(e) in considering whether a discretionary decision was negligent, the court will not substitute its view for that of the local authority upon whom the statute has placed the power to exercise the discretion, unless the discretionary decision was plainly wrong. But decisions of, for example, social workers are capable of being held to have been negligent by analogy with decisions of other professional people. Here again, it may well be necessary to conduct a detailed factual enquiry.

(iii) Barrett—a disclaimer

Barrett and *Tower Hamlets* can be distinguished from *Bedfordshire, Prince v Attorney-General* and *B v Attorney-General*. Indeed, the House of Lords itself clearly distinguished *Barrett* from *Bedfordshire*. While *Bedfordshire* and *Newham* involved the decision to remove or not to remove the child from the family, *Barrett* involved an allegation that social workers had failed to take care in the way a child was treated while in care. *Barrett* could be distinguished by New Zealand courts on the basis that decisions relating to the subsequent care of children are conceptually different from decisions to remove a child from the parents. However, we submit, the House of Lords' approach to the role of social workers' discretion is highly relevant to both situations.

VI. CONCLUSIONS

Our conclusions can be summarised as follows:

- Three factors are necessarily involved in considering whether there ought to be a duty of care. The first is the statutory scheme under which the social workers and the psychologists are working. The second is the potential creation of a conflict of interest in recognising a duty of care to someone other than the child in care. The third is the time in the investigation that the alleged negligence has occurred.
- The fact that those involved in child welfare decisions have exercised professional discretion should not necessarily mean that a duty of care ought not to be recognised. Courts should be wary of arguments that

seek particular immunities for social workers or associated professionals simply on the basis that they exercised professional judgment. There may, as indicated by Lord Slynn, be some decisions that may not be justiciable but we doubt that there are many of these.

- The conflict of interest line of argument seems to us to be the most important reason for holding that sometimes it will not be just and reasonable to impose a duty of care. Social workers and psychologists, especially at the initial stage of the investigation, must not be placed in an untenable position where the child's safety is balanced against liability to others.

- The New Zealand Court of Appeal in *B* was right in seeking to distinguish between the initial stage of investigation and the associated decision to remove the child from the subsequent substantive investigation. However, the use it made of this distinction was inappropriate.

- In particular we believe that, in the absence of malice (including perhaps premeditation) that might bring into issue possible defamation or misfeasance in a public office actions, claimants other than affected children should not be able to sue during initial procedures (*Barrett* situations involving subsequent care are different). The potential danger to the child creates an urgency that might prevent the due professional weighing of the evidence.

- We believe that at this initial stage in accordance with *Prince* social workers ought to owe a duty to the child to investigate the claims.

- We believe that the Court of Appeal was wrong in *B* to prevent the children from suing the social workers and the psychologist involved merely because their alleged negligence occurred after the preliminary decision to remove the children had been taken and the investigation commenced.

- The fathers' claims in *B* and in *N v D* present the greatest difficulty for courts. On the one hand the same conflict of interest is present at the later stage as it was in the initial stage. Once the immediate safety of the child has been secured (which may sometimes mean an urgent removal of the child to a place of safety), the child is not in danger and there is no overwhelming urgency that might prevent a due balancing of the evidence. It is this balance that the Court of Appeal in *B* ought to have, but did not, address.

13. STATE EXTRA-CONTRACTUAL LIABILITY IN FRANCE, ENGLAND AND GREECE

Spyridon Flogaitis *

I. INTRODUCTION

Liability of public powers for wrongful acts is, normally, the last chapter to be developed in the framework of an administrative law system. This is at least the case with all three countries examined in this article: France, England and Greece.

This is only natural, since administrative law, that is the system of law regulating the organisation and action of administrative bodies, is the result of modern times, and the process of rationalizing public powers. France is undoubtedly the first country, which entered into that process. Although it is true that the rule of law, in the sense of subjecting everyone, including public bodies, to the law of the land, is an English invention, it is equally true that French jurisdiction was the first one to try in a systematic and coherent way to rationalize this process and organise it into a system. France is, therefore, a country that cannot be overlooked by a study like the present one.

England is the other angle of research. It is not very long ago that English law lay in the shadows of comparative public law research. And yet, in only a few years, English administrative law has acquired respectability as one of the most dynamic, and fast developing administrative legal systems, and one that is rich in ideas. The interest of comparative public lawyers has shifted, from comparing various continental legal systems amongst themselves, to comparing those systems with English administrative law.

I suppose the comparison with Greek law, the system of a small country in Europe, is only due to the nationality of the author of this article. Greece is not in fact a country, which could be characterised as one of the metropolises of modern legal thought. And yet, again, Greece is a very interesting country for its legal system and tradition. A country with no feudal past, created by succession from the Ottoman Empire thanks to a glorious

---

* Director of the European Public Law Centre, Athens, Greece.

Revolution, and which rebuilt its future entirely on the basis of the experience drawn from legal systems of Western Europe. The result is an original
mixture of legal cultures, which on occasion provides more satisfactory
answers to problems than the traditional, 'classic', legal systems.

Accordingly, this study will start with French law, continue with English
law, and finish with Greek law. Some comparative remarks will serve as
conclusion.

II. FRANCE

The story begins in Bordeaux at the end of the Third Empire. A wagon of
a tobacco manufacturer owned and managed by the State injured a small
girl in the street. This was an accident, which was meant to be the starting
point of the development of a comprehensive system of State liability in
France, and consequently, of a modern administrative law. Even if it has
been written that the resulting decision of the *Tribunal des Conflits* passed
unobserved at the time, it is definitely true that the founding fathers of what
is known as French administrative law, found in that decision the first
groundwork of a democratic development of a public law system applying
to the administration.[1]

That decision of the *Tribunal des Conflits* was rendered on 8 February
1973, and became known as the *Blanco* decision[2] from the name of the
applicant. It was at the beginnings of the Third Republic and a new democratic shift influenced the development of administrative law. The *Blanco*
decision established the rule that State liability cannot be decided on
grounds of private law. It was held that such liability ought to be governed
by public law and that liability of this nature is neither general nor absolute.
In this way, the old principle of the French Revolution, according to which
public administration is subject to the law in the sense of a special branch
of public law, was reaffirmed in the most solemn manner.

Today, the principles set forth by the *Blanco* decision are no longer
entirely valid, as public administration is ruled *only partially* by public law,
and State liability *is* in fact general and absolute. It is an irony that at the
turn of the century AV Dicey was teaching[3] that no administrative law
could ever develop in England, as in that country no public official can

---

[1] Amongst the literature on French Administrative Law in English language see especially
John Bell's edition of Neville-Brown and Garner, *French Administrative Law*, 5th edn (Oxford:
Clarendon Press, 1998).
[2] TC 8 Feb 1873, *Blanco*, concl David in M Long, P Weil, G Braibant *et al*, *Les Grands
Arrêts de la Jurisprudence Administrative*, 13th edn (Paris, Dalloz, 2001), 1 et seq.
[3] AV Dicey, *Introduction to the Study of the Law of the Constitution New York*, 10th edn
(London: St Martin's Press; Macmillan, 1959).

hide, in terms of liability, behind a '*droit administratif*'. At that time English law was still professing the maxim 'The King can do no wrong', the principle of State liability being established by an Act of Parliament as late as 1947,[4] ie in a new period of democratic shift, the times just after the war. At the same period of time, the principle of liability of public powers was also introduced in Greece when, in 1946, a public law rule to that effect was set out within the Introductory Law of the Civil Code.

A general rule of liability of public powers was, however, introduced in France only later, in 1905, with the decision of the *Conseil d'Etat, Tomaso Grecco*.[5] That decision essentially extended the principle of State liability to the acts of police, ie an area where actions are by nature difficult to be controlled. In this way the ambit of application of the principle of State liability was generalised.

It was exactly this distinction that attracted the attention of AV Dicey. According to Article 75 of the Constitution of the Year VIII, no action could be taken against a public official for his/her wrongful actions, unless special permission was granted by the *Conseil d'Etat*, a permission which was only very rarely granted in practice. The situation was redressed in 1870 through the abolition of that article. This abolition facilitated, if not prompted, the development of the case law starting just two years later with the decision *Blanco*.

In fact the principal decision was again handed down by the *Tribunal des Conflits* in 1873, the decision *Pelletier*.[6] In this decision, the basic distinction between personal fault and service-related fault was drawn. Later, the corresponding definitions were given by Lafferiere, *Commissare du Gouvernement*, who wrote:

the injurious act is personal, if it can be attributed personally to an administrator', it 'reveals the man with his weaknesses, his passions, his imprudence. The service-related fault is committed by the impersonal bureaucracy, a fault that cannot be individualized.[7]

The truth is that in most cases there is some public official to whom the fault can be individually attributed. Moreover, French public law acknowledged the notion of the cumulative faults through the 1911 decision *Anguet* of the *Conseil d'Etat*.[8] Nevertheless, the legal consequences of the coexistence of the two faults were explicitly drawn by the *Commissaire du Gouvernement* Leon Blum in the case *Lemonnier*. His conclusions are widely known and cited:

---

[4] Only a few years later a relevant thesis was published in France by Denis Levy, *La responsabilité de la puissance publique et de ses agents en Angleterre* (Paris: LGDJ, 1957).

[5] CE 10 Feb 1905, *Tomaso Grecco*, concl Romieu, in Long, *et al*, op cit, 86 et seq.

[6] TC 30 juill. 1873, *Pelletier*, concl David, in Long, *et al*, op cit, 8 et seq.

[7] TC 5 May 1877, *Laumonnier-Carriol*, concl Laferriere, Rec 437.

[8] CE 3 Feb 1911, *Anguet*, Rec 146, in Long, *et al*, op cit, 143 et seq.

If the personal fault was committed in the service or in the occasion of the service, if the means and the instruments of the fault had been at the disposal of the responsible person by the service, if the victim met the responsible person only because of the service, if in other words the service had conditioned the accomplishment of the fault . . . the fault is eventually detached from the service. . . . The service on the contrary is not detached from the fault . . .

This case law on the issue of coexistence of liability was favourable to the victims. Actually, the administration has unlimited resources and, therefore, injured individuals have invariably preferred to seek for damages against the administration rather than its agent. Since the decisions of the *Conseil d'Etat* in *Delville*[9] and *Laruelle*,[10] a rule has been applied that the public administration held liable for an injury has the right of recourse against its agent who was at fault.

Normally, in order to hold the administration responsible, proving an ordinary fault (*faute simple*) is sufficient. With the consolidation and extension of the principle of the liability of public powers, an ordinary fault of the administration could not always suffice to establish liability. The judge started asking for a 'manifest and particularly grave fault', or 'a fault of exceptional gravity', or finally 'a serious fault' (*faute lourde*).

With the development of the liability regime, the scope of application of the notion of serious fault was gradually restricted. This notion was useful for the extension of the domain of liability to sensitive and difficult areas, but later became problematic. This phenomenon could be clearly evidenced in the case of faults made in the medical service, where a serious fault was required as a condition for a long period of time but was later abandoned.

A serious fault is nowadays required in only three areas: the police,[11] the tax authorities,[12] and supervisory or regulatory activities.[13] In the case of control exercised by the State over the activities of a public body, it is admitted that when the authority under control is responsible for a mistaken activity, the State is also liable, albeit only in the case of a serious fault. The claim of liability for damages can be raised either by the injured individual or by the authority under control itself on grounds that no fault could have been made, if the controlling authority had properly exercised its powers.

If fault liability is the basis of French law, it is also well established that there are cases in which the public authorities have to remedy the injury caused to an individual without needing to prove any fault, be it simple or serious. It is the case of liability based on risk, otherwise liability without fault.

---

[9] CE 28 July 1951, *Delville*, Rec 447. 　　[10] CE 28 July 1951, *Laruelle*, Rec 447.
[11] CE 20 Oct 1972, *Ville de Paris c/Marabout*, Rec.664, AJDA 1972.597 concl Guillaume.
[12] CE 27 July 1990, *Bourgeois*, Rec. 242, AJDA 1991.53 note Richer.
[13] CE 29 Dec 1978, *Darmont*, Rec 542, D 1979.278 note Vasseur, Rec 664, AJDA 1979 no 11, 45, note Lombard.

There are circumstances in which case law or statute has laid down that the cost of the injurious results of an administrative action must be assumed by the community as a whole, following the general idea of the French public law known as the principle of the equality before public charges. The public administration has daily to take decisions and handle dangerous and difficult situations provoking abnormal damages either because of the risk taken or because of the importance of the activity concerned.

The scope of no-fault liability includes damages caused by the public works, damages caused by dangerous activities or situations and damages caused to the collaborators of public services.[14]

III. ENGLAND

The theory of state liability in English law constitutes the chapter of administrative law which is most imbued with concepts of private law. Seemingly, it merely constitutes a part of the theory of liability of civil law. This is so particularly in light of section 2(1) of the Crown Proceedings Act 1947, by virtue of which direct tortious liability of the Crown was first introduced into English Law. These provisions treat the Crown as a private person of full age and capacity. Individuals are able to sue public authorities for damages in tort or in contract; it is, in principle, the same law of tort or contract applied to public authorities as to private individuals. The truth is, however, that there is a purely public law part of state liability and it is exactly this part, stemming from case law or legislation, that sets apart the liability of an administrative authority not only in the event of a wrong being done but also on the basis of strict liability. The latter case exactly demonstrates the fact that the legislature or the judiciary take into account the particularities of the activities of public authorities, involving elements of an unusual risk or being of a particular nature, that does not require evidence of a wrong. Accordingly, there are solutions, which resemble also the solutions found in French case law and others that are entirely distinctive. Besides, it should not be underestimated that the English system of

---

[14] For the status of state liability in France see among others, *Repertoire Dalloz de Responsabilite de la Puissance Publique* (direction F Gazier and R Drag), Paris 1987); J Moreau, *La Responsabilite Administrative, Que sais-je?* (Paris: PUF, 1996); Douc-Rasy, *Les Frontieres de la Faute Personnelle et de la Faute de Service en Droit Administratif Francais* (Paris: GDJ, 1960); JC Maestre, *La Responsabilité Pecuniaire des Agents Publics* (Paris: LGDJ, 1962); *Repertoire Dalloz de Responsabilite de la Puissance Publique*, par Cl Gour ; M Paillet, *La Faute de Service Public dans le Droit Administratif Francais* (Paris: LGDJ, 1980); L Richer, *La Faute du Service Public dans la Jurisprudence du Conseil d'Etat* (Paris: Economica, 1978); P Amselek, 'La responsabilite sans faute des personnes publiques d'apres la jurisprudence administrative', in *Melanges Eisenmann* (Paris: Editions CUJAS, 1975), 233; JM Cotteret, 'La regime de la responsabilite pour risque en droit administrative', in *Etudes de droit public* (Paris: Cujas, 1964), 377.

administrative liability was historically a point of pride for Dicey and became the founding stone of its criticism against French administrative law. Due to its incremental public law element, state liability was, thus, never liberated from the global theory of liability and, consequently, the civil law manifestation of the system remained intact.

A. *Liability of Public Entities*

The liability of public entities was always founded upon civil law which determined the relationship between master and servant: according to the case law, when an employee is liable for a wrong committed in the course of his/her duties, the employer is also liable. Accordingly, the victim may bring a claim against the employer, the employee, or both of them at the same time. The Crown Proceedings Act 1947 has established the same principle for Crown servants or agents. According to this case law, one may draw a concept comparable to that of service fault *(faute de service)* of French administrative law. On the other hand, the legislature has on many occasions introduced strict liability of public entities.

1. *Service Fault*

The notion of service fault is not recognised as such in English administrative law. However, the case law arrives at similar results to those achieved by French case law through the implementation of the master-servant theory and of the Crown Proceedings Act 1947. In the former case, the administration not elevated to the status of the Crown is liable for wrongful actions of its agents on the basis of the civil law theory; in the latter case administrative liability is founded upon the legislation. In either case, the state endorses its liability because, at the end of the day, there is a deviation from the normal exercise of the service. This is why the immunity of the Crown for wrongful actions before 1947 was declared by the Committee on Ministers' Powers as a *lacuna* in the Rule of Law.

The Crown Proceedings Act 1947 sets out that the Crown is liable for torts committed by its agents provided that the agent himself/herself is liable. Accordingly, in English administrative law, unlike in France, service-related fault is in principle attributed to one or more servants personally; a fault attributed to the functioning of the service generally is not conceivable. Order 53 and the Supreme Court Act 1981 allow the applicant to join in an application for judicial review a single claim for damages. This is indeed an alternative to the possibility of initiating judicial proceedings according to the procedures set out by civil law. However, since the wrongful action must constitute an *ultra vires* act, the practice of granting damages within the application for judicial review becomes more widespread, thus possibly resulting in the acceptance of administrative liability more independently to the liability of a particular servant; this, in turn, stands for a move towards a more public law approach of the judiciary.

The service fault may be either one of the many torts, such as a property violation, false imprisonment, defamation, etc, or an act of negligence committed by an agent or servant when acting in the execution of orders by superior officials. The judge always makes reference to the torts specified by law and acknowledges the liability of the administration for any negligence of its servants taken within their competence according to a rule established by the House of Lords in 1866. The damaging act may be material or legal and the service fault is independent of the criminal character of the act. There are, however, applications of the Anglo-Saxon quasi-criminal principles of compensation that take into account the insulting conduct of the agent and not merely the damage caused by the administration.

Although, according to a rule established in English administrative law, *ultra vires* constitutes the only legitimate ground for liability, the French doctrine of independence of liability against the legality of the act also finds some application in England. English case law is generally founded upon the notion of substantive—and not purely formal—*ultra vires*; this in fact demonstrates a willingness to depart from the civil law mainstays of liability. At any rate, the exclusivity of the *ultra vires* doctrine remains essential since the act must cause damage: the *ultra vires* character of the act is a prerequisite. Like in France, apart from positive acts, wrongful omissions are also accepted by case law as a source of state liability.

Although service fault, even of a grave nature, cannot by itself justify administrative liability, diverse case law demonstrates a tendency to conceive the phenomenon of state liability and the degree of negligence in a different way. In fact, according to a very old case law of the House of Lords, the negligence of the authority to prevent the loss caused to citizens may constitute a legitimate ground to raise state liability. In fact, this negligence can give rise to liability if there is a statutory duty on the authority to act to that effect. Although the presumption that the Crown is not bound by statute unless an intent to be so bound is explicitly or implicitly set out still applies, the Crown can be held liable for breach of statutory duty. Negligence can also be the foundation for liability in the case of administrative discretion, when the power of the authority awarded by the Parliament is exercised in such a negligent or unreasonable way that it could be deemed not to have been exercised at all. In that sense negligence appears as a collateral to the principle of *ultra vires*. Thus, in the context of English administrative law, it is not necessary to prove that the administrative authority was obliged to exercise a duty of care in a satisfactory way. This is so exactly because the power does not depend on the condition of the civil law concept of liability but on the public law concept of *ultra vires*.

In the same spirit, which renders negligence as a necessary component for the existence of liability, there is also a case law releasing the administration of any liability when the act in question was authorised by law and the damage caused emerges as an unavoidable consequence of the will of the Parliament. Generally speaking, the evidence of the administrative fault must be subsumed by the individual, according to the common law of liability. In some cases, however, like inevitable damage, where a presumption of damages exists, the burden of proof is overturned against the administration.

2. Liability Without Fault

State liability without fault or strict liability also exists in English administrative law and has its origins in civil law. If its core is not to be found in a general principle of law, such as the equality before public burdens, it is largely identified in the notion of a particular *risk* caused by the administrative action.

The first case of strict liability recognised by legislation and case law in England is for pure and simple risk. The meaning of liability without fault as conceived in the case of an emergency risk was established in the case *Rylands v Fletcher* which set out a rather ambiguous rule, later interpreted in a diversified way: strict liability lies with a person who for his/her own purposes does or holds something causing an unusual risk.

On the other hand, the second category of liability without fault is that on the grounds of non-adherence by legal obligations on the part of the administration. This category substantively represents another application of the idea of a particular risk Although in the majority of relevant cases there is, in fact, liability caused by a wrongful action committed by the servant responsible to apply the law, the essence of this category of public law liability constitutes a variation of liability on the basis of risk.

Overall, it should be noted, however, that strict liability is currently mostly a matter of legislation rather than a matter of case law, which has not, indeed, been consolidated in a pure public law orientation. In any case, strict liability sometimes reveals a public law mentality in a chapter like administrative liability which is indeed the less independent *vis-à-vis* the civil law.

B. Liability of Agents

1. Personal Fault

The exemption of all Crown agents, who constitute the largest part of public servants in England, from any liability for torts that were not personal was until relatively recently, ie 1947, a weak point of the system of liability. The axiom 'The King can do no wrong' did not cover the King's servants, from ministers to simple employees, who were personally responsible. The liability of all high officials who had directly participated in causing the damage could also be joined. However, orders from higher officials could never be used as the ground of defence in the sense that neither the Crown nor its agents could possibly have authorised the cause of damage. In such a case of course there was always the right of the servant who was held liable consequently to demand the amount paid from his/her superior. On the other hand, the superior agent who instructed the subordinates to implement a decision in the exercise of his/her statutory duties was personally responsible for the execution of this competence. The Crown Proceedings Act 1947 brought in the cumulative liability of both the administrative authority and the agent personally. It is, therefore, up to the applicant to decide who to ask compensation from. But, unlike France, the applicant does not have the possibility to choose between two different juridical orders or juridical regimes.

According to law, the Crown is liable for torts committed by its 'servants or agents'. In English law, which is characterised by the fact that central public institutions are tantamount to an individual, the relationship between the Crown and its agents, the public servants, remains at a personal level. In the same way, the term 'agent' also comprises independent contractors, contrary to the common law rule concerning the general theory of liability of employer for the acts of its employees. In order to qualify as a 'servant' or 'agent' in the meaning of the law, the common law qualifications do not suffice. The Crown will be liable only for officers appointed directly or indirectly by the Crown, and being paid wholly by funds provided by the Parliament or out of certain funds certified by the Treasury. The result of this qualification is that there is no state liability for actions taken by agents of statutory corporations or the police who are paid out of local funds.

2. Ambit of Application of the Liability Rules

First of all, it is inconceivable to hold the state liable for Acts of Parliament since this would seriously hamper the fundamental notion of parliamentary sovereignty. In relation to state liability for judicial acts, the Crown Proceedings Act 1947 declares that the Crown is immune from liability for acts or omissions of persons exercising judicial functions in the course of a judicial process. With regard to the issue of the personal liability of judges, all judges whether of superior or inferior courts, including justices of the peace, enjoy full immunity from liability when acting *intra vires* (within jurisdiction), even in a malicious act. On the other hand, superior court judges are not liable in damages for an *ultra vires* (outside of the jurisdiction) act, provided that this was done in the honest belief that the act was within jurisdiction. Inferior court judges, ie judges of courts subjected to the control of the prerogative orders, seem to be in the position to be liable when acting outside of their jurisdiction although there are judicial dicta occasionally favouring the assimilation of protection for all judges, irrespective of their corresponding forum. In any case this judicial protection is not extended to the members of administrative tribunals, which are therefore considered even in this respect as part of the administration. However, certain tribunals, like the Mental Health Review Tribunal and the Commissioners of Customs and Excise, receive some protection in that respect.

Finally, it is noteworthy that specific legislation confers immunity from liability for the exercise of particular public powers. Two typical examples are the acts of state *(actes de gouvernement)* and the post services. In the field of acts of state one may refer, for example, to the provision of the Crown Proceedings Act 1947 limiting the liability of the state in a case of death or injury of a member of the army forces in the exercise of his/her duties only to the granting of a pension. On the other hand, the Post Office Act 1969, as amended by the Telecommunications Act 1981, establishes the rule that neither the Post Office not its employees can be held liable for damages caused by their professional activities. The Post Office may set up criteria to award compensation for non-fulfillment of registered posts however, only the authority and not employees could be held liable.[15]

C. Greece

The liability of public powers under Greek public law has its foundations in Article 4 para 5 of the Constitution, establishing the principle that Greek citizens have equally to contribute to the public charges in proportion to their means. Greek public law follows, in this sense, the rationale of the French public law and its principle of equality before the public burdens. Therefore, it is not possible for the legislator totally to deviate from the principle of State liability.

The Introductory Law of the Greek Civil Code of 1946 in Articles 105 and 106, determines the liability of public powers: the State and the other

---

[15] For the status of state liability in England see among others, GE Robinson, *Public Authorities and Legal Liability* (London: University of London Press Ltd, 1925); H Street, *Governmental Liability: A Comparative Study* (Hamden, Conn: Archon Books, 1975.); P Hogg, *Liability of the Crown*, 3rd edn (Toronto: Carswell, 2000); C Harlow, *Compensation and Government Torts* (London: Sweet & Maxwell, 1982); S Arrowsmith, *Civil Liability and Public Authorities* (Winteringham: Earlsgate, 1992). For recent developments in the English law of public authority liability, see Chapter 15: D Fairgrieve, 'Pushing Back the Boundaries of Public Authority Liability.'

public bodies are liable for any injury produced by an illegal administrative action or omission. Personal fault and responsibility is not required as liability operates objectively.

The positive administrative action or the omission of the public authority must take place in the course of the exercise of its unilateral activity through an administrative decision or a material act. The administrative action or omission should not, however, relate to the management of the private property of the administration.

The damage is understood in the terms of civil law and there must be a relation of *causa adequata* between the action or omission and the damage. The most important point is that in order to establish the liability of a public authority, the injurious action or omission must be illegal. However, on certain occasions, there is no field for application of the public law liability rules. This is so in the case that illegality relates to non-observance of a legal rule which does not establish any specific right of the injured individual, but was set out exclusively to serve public interest or the interest of the public powers or the interests of a third person.

A public body is only liable for actions or omissions that can be attributed to at least one of its agents. The public body that produced the injurious action or is responsible for the omission is still liable even if these activities are subject to the control of the State. The imputation of a material action or omission is more difficult, as this injurious event needs to be connected to the organisation and function of the public body as well as with events that took place during the performance of the service or on the occasion of the performance of the service in its normal and usual operation. This relation exists also when the agent acted against the directions given to him by his superiors.

With the exception of special circumstances under which a Minister can be liable jointly with a public body, the specific agent who acted illegally is also liable. This responsibility is not objective but subjective, ie in order for the agent to be liable it needs to be proved that he/she was in *dolus* or in negligence. Under the law, however, and with some exceptions, the agent is not personally liable towards third party but only towards the administration, which can raise a claim asking for the damage caused by personal actions or omissions to be repaired.[16]

IV. CONCLUSION

History is very important for legal systems, as it is very unlikely that legal

---

[16] For the status of state liability in Greece see among others, P Pavlopoulos, *Civil Liability of the State* (Athens, 1986); G Papachatzis, *Liability of the Administration from Illegal Acts* (Athens, 1947); M Stasinopoulos, *Civil liability of the State* (Athens, 1950).

reasoning can escape from tradition. This is the lesson from the above analysis.

All three legal systems try to give satisfactory answers to the same question: when and how public powers will be held responsible to repair the damage caused by their actions or omissions. The only system, which is not the result of thoughts and considerations going back in ages, is the Greek one. It is at the same time simple, as it serves the very mere principle according to which the illegal injurious action or omission of the administration ought to result to a damage repair.

I truly believe that this principle in its simplicity must be followed more widely by legal systems. The complexity of the French system supports this argument. In modern times, it is a democratic mainstay that public administration must repair the damages caused illegally, according to an objective rule, because only in this way the cost of compensation is borne by the society as a whole—going back to the very nice principle of French law of the equality before the public burdens.[17]

One thing has to be added about new themes in the area of liability of public powers: in modern times legal systems have expressed their interest in cases of liability by reason of precaution, otherwise the taking into consideration of scientific uncertainties and virtual risk. Now, legal systems have moved even further, towards prevention as a means to prevent and avoid the risk that could eventually lead to liability. It is an idea leading directly to interventions. This is an evolution of the law in all legal systems, let alone public international law.

---

[17] See P Devolve, *Le Principe d'Egalite Devant les Charges Publiques* (Paris: LGDJ, 1969); A Theocharopoulos, 'Equality of citizens before the public burdens and the civil liability of the state from civic state actions', *Melanges Vegleris* (1988).

14. UNITY OR DIVISION: THE SEARCH FOR SIMILARITIES IN CONTEMPORARY EUROPEAN LAW[1]

Basil Markesinis[2]

I. INTRODUCTION

There is a genre of historical writing, of which Le Roy Ladurie's *Montaillou*[3] is one of the best examples, that focuses on very small sections of society over a relatively short period of time. From this very detailed survey, attempts can and have been made to extrapolate wider conclusions for history. Whether one likes it or not, this is one more way of searching for the truth. It is not complete; nor flawless; yet it can be helpful if combined with other kinds of history—sociological, economic, diplomatic, narrative—in order to tell us something about the past and, perhaps, teach us something about the future.

Likewise with pictorial art. Looking at some paintings the observer can grasp the entirety of his subject easily, quickly, if in inadequate detail. The paintings of Claude Monet, known as *Les Nymphéas: Séries de paysages d'eau*, offer a good example of this kind of art. In the forty-eight paintings exhibited by Durand-Ruel in 1909, the colours of the horizontally depicted lilies is as remarkable as the artist's decision to portray the real world of trees and sky as vertical, pale reflections in the calm waters of his pond at Giverny. But, apart from the original decision to evoke the real world inverted and reflected in the spangled surface of the water, the enjoyment of the paintings lies on the absorption of the whole and not the understanding of the component parts or the search for some inner meaning. Staying with the imagery of paintings, the same cannot be said when looking at Piero de la Francesca's 'Flagellation'—arguably one of the most complex small paintings in the world. For much time is needed to take everything in and try to understand the relationship of the particular to the general. The appreciation of the

---

[1] This is an expanded version of an inaugural lecture delivered at University College London on 7 June 2001. It was first published in *Current Legal Problems*.

[2] Professor Basil Markesinis QC hc, LL D. (Cantab), DCL (Oxon), D. Iur hc, Ghent, Munich, Paris I (Panthéon-Sorbonne), FBA; Professor of Common and Civil Law, University College London; Jamail Regents Chair of Law, University of Texas at Austin.

[3] First published by Gallimard in 1978. Peter Linehan's *The Ladies of Zamora* (1999) is another example of local microhistory, though set in a wider context.

painting is thus progressively enhanced as its geometrical depiction of space adds admiration to the complex emotions that the sustained study of the picture generates. No one has ever doubted that both paintings are master-pieces; but the one, I always felt, is more approachable than the other. For the former depicts an idyllic picture whereas the latter taxes your mind even more than your eye as it forces you to understand the general from the particular.

Similar ideas can be entertained in the case of law. A concentrated look at legal problems can have some of the same advantages as the ones described above. To René David's pale reflections of the legal systems of the world[4] one can—and should—add a more focused effort to understand a foreign system and piece by piece come to terms with its complexity. *Montaillou* and the *Flagellation* are the parallels here. For in law, too, this approach can work only if one is content, at the beginning at least, to limit oneself to a focused attempt to understand one's subject, small piece by small piece. The danger of course is seeing the trees and missing the woods. But this is not worse than that of seeing the object of study in fuzzy contours and pale reflections and unable to describe precise forms and details. And any way, if one is conscious of the danger one can guard against it.

In law, the focused approach to a legal problem has an additional bene-fit that we do not find in our parallel historical or artistic examples. Put simply, it is that the study of a foreign legal system, especially through deci-sional law rather than through doctrinal writings, has the advantage of putting one initially at ease. For invariably in such studies one is starting the discovery journey by looking at litigated situations that are the same in most countries. Teaching and understanding law through cases also offers the inestimable advantage of making the student's experience of the world deepen as his study progresses in sophistication. For, as he reads the cases, he 'see[s] the variety and complexity of human life. [He] get[s] to know how things are done.... [He] encounter[s] every kind of human temptation and motivation. [He] becomes habituated to the fact that they are often strong arguments for diametrically opposed positions.'[5] The contrast with the world of geometry, architecture, and consistency, which academics so like to construct, could not be greater.[6] Thus, simply put, the comparative juxta-position of factually similar cases makes one feel at home. For the observer is comparing familiar situations and not confused by structures, terminol-ogy, or concepts that are either un-translatable or, if apparently easy to translate, they are misleading.

---

[4] Exemplified in his *Les grands systèmes de droit contemporains* (Paris, 1988).

[5] PBH Birks, 'Editor's Preface', in PBH Birks (ed), *What are Law Schools For?* (Oxford: Oxford University Press, 1996), xiii.

[6] On this see my 'Zur Lehre des Rechts anhand von Fällen: Einige bescheidene Vorschläge zur Verbesserung der deutschen Juristenausbildung', *Festschrift for Peter Schlechtriem* (forth-coming).

II. THE PROBLEM WITH CONCEPTS

By contrast, the reality (or illusion) of similarity is shattered once we move to concepts which is how comparative law has often been taught. Comparing *cause* to consideration leads to nowhere; juxtaposing termination for breach with *resolution judiciaire* reveals a yawning gap. Likewise with the concepts found in tort law. German tort law for instance makes great use of the notion of *rechtswidrigkeit*, which the Common law does not even know. What is unlawful in German law is to interfere—culpably and without lawful excuse—with one of the protected interests enumerated in section 823 I BGB. In other key provisions of the Code, illegality is determined by reference either to the content and purview of a particular statute (s 823 II BGB) or the open-ended notion of *boni mores* (s 826 BGB). But in all these instances the centrality of unlawfulness cannot be doubted. Though this may appear strange to us, it should not be surprising since much of the German thinking and conceptualism can here be traced back to Roman law, which also gave central place to the notion of *iniuria*. The same sense of surprise is engendered by the list of enumerated interests that are protected by the law, which form a key feature of section 823 I BGB. Again, none of this appears formally in the Anglo-American tort of Negligence, which is the approximate equivalent of the above-mentioned leading tort provision of the BGB. The comparison of two systems through their concepts is thus—at first instance at least—off-putting. This is because, look if you must, you cannot find the concept, notion, or architecture[7] you are looking for which is so self-evident to your foreign colleague.[8] By contrast, the two systems come much closer when you look at litigated cases and discover that the differences in result are diminished because, for instance, what the Germans do through a rigid list of protected interests we, in England, achieve through the more pliable notion of 'duty of care'.[9] For in the Common law, the notion of duty primarily performs

---

[7] By this I mean the systematic arrangement of the subjects. Thus the English tort of Nuisance appears as part of the French law of property (and related rights) and a search for it in a French tort treatise would produce little of interest to a Common lawyer. It is only when one reflects on the generic rubric of *troubles de voisinage* that one realises that what one system sees as rights another can, equally sensibly, examine under the heading of wrongs. History is, of course, responsible for this different optic which, however, does not affect the similarity of litigated cases nor of their outcome.

[8] The same is, of course, true if one compares French and English law. The cardinal Common law notion of 'duty of care' is thus totally absent from Art 1382 CC though in many decades ago Planiol and Savatier came close to recreating it for French law. See, Planiol, *Traité élémentaire de droit civil*, 11th edn, no 863 (Paris: LGDJ); Savatier, *Traité de la reponsabilité civile*, 2nd edn (Paris, 1951), 56–134. Examples such as these are particularly important since they show how close the different systems can be and that if they have come to follow different paths this does not mean that their differences are deep-rooted or insurmountable.

[9] Which, when we apply severely, we attract the wrath of Strasbourg.

the function of demarcating the range of relationships and interests that receive legal protection and which our German colleagues attempted to do through their list of protected interests. That neither system functions as purely as it is meant to do is inevitable since the neatness that can exist in the world of ideas is rarely found in the real world of litigation.

The same points can be made if we switch from comparing systems from different legal families to systems that belong to the same family, for instance English and American law. In this case the differences are not caused by different concepts because the systems, belonging as they do to the same legal family have, by definition, adopted the same legal vocabulary and broadly similar structures. Here, however, where there are differences, they are caused by a different constitutional background,[10] a different method of trial,[11] a different way of financing litigation,[12] a different philosophy of what are the State's responsibilities towards its weaker and needy citizens.[13] On all these points, American society takes different views than the English; and the law *in practice* is correspondingly different. Such exercises show us that we must start our work by means of a focused study of narrow, litigated cases; but we must also be ready to move forward to the next and most difficult phase of the enquiry by broadening our enquiry. This is where the wider understanding of the two societies that are being compared becomes necessary to explain remaining differences. But the human mind, having first been placed on a familiar base is now more ready than before to try exploring further the problem that confronts it. Indeed, having started with a welcome similarity, it is now probably unwilling to allow unexplored any differences that the comparison may have revealed.

The very brief discussion thus far suggests that the comparison of systems through their concepts can lead to confusion and inaccuracies. For different concepts may conceal similar solutions and philosophies; and similar concepts may hide differences, which flow from other structural differences. This is particular true of the law in the United States where, as stated, its differences from English (and often Continental European law) are not due to different rules of substantive law but to the kind of background differences to which I alluded earlier.

---

[10] For instance, the American Constitution guarantees the use of juries whereas in English civil trials they have all but disappeared. Likewise, the First Amendment gives speech rights massive prevalence over reputation rights, something which is not true in the English set-up.

[11] One is, of course, thinking of the use of civil juries and the way they affect the both the development of substantive law and the kind tactics employed by lawyers in the courtroom.

[12] The contingent fee system is not only one way of financing litigation (as contrasted to a legal aid scheme); it is also a system that has profound consequences on substantive law. On this see Professor John Fleming's remarks in *The American Tort Process*, (1988), *passim*.

[13] Here we note briefly the almost complete absence in the United States of a welfare state net for the needy and the ill. This inevitably (and one is tempted to add rightly to a point) makes the American tort awards more generous than the European.

III. FACTUAL EQUIVALENTS: A BRIEF CASE STUDY

In accordance with the above methodology, in this sub-section we shall look at one factual variant in two legal systems: the English and the French. Lack of space prevents us from including the German counter-parts; though the conclusions that one can draw from this system are not that different from those applicable to French law.[14] The factual variant deals with claims for negligent exercise of powers vested in social services meant to protect children in danger or with special needs.

In *X(Minors) v Bedfordshire County Council*[15] was one of two 'child-abuse' actions (consolidated and heard together with three other cases not discussed in this essay). It arose in connection with a claim that a local authority negligently and in breach of its statutory obligations failed to exercise its powers to institute care proceedings after it has received serious reports that the claimant/child had been the subject of parental abuse and neglect. The second case—*M (A Minor) v Newham London Borough Council*—was the mirror image of the first. For here the complaint was based on the negligent removal of child from maternal care on the basis of an unfounded belief that the abuse had taken place by the mother's cohabitee and the conclusion that the mother was unable to protect her child. The cases were tried on a matter of law, that is, on the basis that the facts were assumed to be as pleaded; and the House of Lords held that no action lay against the local authority either for its alleged violation of statute or for the tort of Negligence.

In the French equivalent of *X. v Bedfordshire*, the social services were held liable because of their negligence in the exercise of the powers vested in them for the purposes of protecting children in danger of family abuse. (This administrative duty is called *protection maternelle et infantile*.) In *Epoux Ouaras*[16] a 3-year-old girl had been sent, with the agreement of her parents, to stay with a foster family for three months. The foster family, which was not French, had been selected by an association devoted to children care. The child was seriously maltreated. Her parents were granted compensation. The *Conseil d'Etat* considered that the administration was at fault for not having verified the reliability of the foster family carefully.

Another French case offers a possible comparison with *Newham*. In *M et Mme Pillon*[17] the *Conseil d'Etat* held that a social service had committed no fault in not warning the authority able to institute care proceedings about the threat posed to the health of children entrusted in the care of a

---

[14] The next few sections make use of material contributed by Professor Jean Bernard Auby (and to a lesser extent myself) to a book we co-authored with Professor Dagmar Coester-Waltjen and Dr. Simon Deakin entitled *Tortious Liability of Statutory Bodies* (Oxford: Hart Publishing, 1999).   [15] [1995] 3 WLR 152.

[16] Conseil d'Etat, 23 Sept 1987, *Recueil des arrêts du Conseil d'Etat*, 290.

[17] Conseil d'Etat, 4 May 1983, n. 22811.

particular family. (Information collected by the agency pointed to such dangers, and the concern should have been even greater given that the family had refused permission to the social workers to enter their house and talk to the children.) It follows from these facts that had fault been found, liability would have ensued. To an English lawyer the facts as given would indicate the presence of fault, but we cannot labour this point too much given that the finding of fault depended on the facts in each case, and we do not have them before us as the court did. The outcome of the litigation, however, clearly shows how the controlling device of fault works in practice. However, one must also note the dangers that may arise from the fact that such determinations may only be possible *after* litigation has taken place. To an English lawyer this observation will not just be crucial, but also, arguably, a reinforcement for his view to dispose such disputes without the cost and delays of a full trial. Nevertheless, one must also repeat—perhaps with some degree of surprise—the paucity of French litigated examples, something which must indicate that in *practice* the potential liability rule has not opened the floodgates of litigation.

The factual examples I have chosen could not be narrower. Yet, as will be shown, the true value of my example lies not solely in its human interest which, of course, is great. It also lies in the fact that the arguments used in these cases for and against liability are broadly applicable over a wide range of state liability situations. This means two things. First, I can draw—and in this essay have drawn—supporting statements from cases dealing with factual permutations of my chosen example. Secondly, it means that if at some stage I reach a point where the systems diverge despite the factual similarity of the instances considered, I have to start looking into other areas of the law for explanations. Which area it is does not really matter. What matters is that the search (and the knowledge that comes with it) has now been broadened to include such topics as the law of damages, the law of social security, the law of procedure. Equally noteworthy is the fact that, equipped with the sense of security acquired by the knowledge that I am dealing with a familiar problem, I feel courageous enough to venture into these others areas of foreign law which, had I tried to tackle *de nuovo*, I might have found forbidding. It is my submission therefore that my proposed methodology draws you into the foreign system rather than allowing different conceptualism to put you off its study.

So let us proceed with my experiment. How did the French and English courts deal with my problem?

IV. THE REASONING OF THE COURTS

In the *Bedfordshire* decision the 'technical', legal arguments connected with tort liability[18] were limited to the enquiry whether the local authority owed a direct duty of care to the children.[19] Lord Browne-Wilkinson's remarks are brief on two of the usual requirements of liability—foreseeability and proximity—largely because the local authority (wisely) chose not to challenge the fact that they were satisfied in this case. Instead, he asserted (without discussion[20] and, some might argue, not so convincingly) that the requirement of 'fair, just and reasonable', essentially introduced into our system by the *Peabody*[21]and *Caparo*[22] judgments, also applied to cases involving physical harm to the person. This meant that if the court did not think that it was 'fair, just and reasonable' to discover a duty of care there would be no primary liability. To decide this issue Lord Browne-Wilkinson then switched his discussion to the policy arguments, which in his view negated the presence of any duty. In his Lordship's view these were basically four. First, imposing liability on the public bodies in question would make bad economic sense. Secondly, liability would inhibit the freedom of action of these bodies. Thirdly, it would be inappropriate for the courts to control elected bodies and tell them how to exercise their discretionary powers. Finally, the victims in these cases had alternative remedies, which make a tort remedy not only dangerous but also superfluous. This part of the judgment is the most crucial for present purposes.

---

[18] It would involve too great a digression into English administrative law rules to discuss the local authority's liability for breach of statute so the discussion in the text is limited to the tort of Negligence.

[19] The question of vicarious liability for the torts of its employees was, initially, left open. But it was finally decided in favour of the claimants in *Phelps v Hillingdon London Borough Council* [2000] 3 WLR 776 a decision of the House of Lords which, however, still left open the question whether the local authority could be *primarily* liable.

[20] [1995] 3 WLR 152 at 183. This was, indeed, accepted by the majority in *Marc Rich & Co. A G v Bishop Rock Marine Co. Ltd.* [1996] 1 AC 211—a case involving property damage. Two years later an attempt was made to transport this reasoning to cases of physical injury in *Perret v Collins* [1998] 2 Lloyd's Rep 255 but it was boldly repulsed by a unanimous Court of Appeal. Lord Justice Hobhouse (as he then was) had this to say (at 258) on this crucial issue: 'What the second and third defendants seek to achieve in this case is to extend decisions upon "economic" loss to cases of personal injury. It represents a fundamental attack upon the principle of tortious liability for negligent conduct, which had caused foreseeable personal injury to others. That such a point should be considered to be even arguable shows how far some of the fundamental principles of the law of negligence have come to eroded. The arguments advanced in this case [viz that the kind of wider policy considerations used in *Marc Rich* to justify the majority decision should also be used in this case and absolve the defendants from all liability] illustrate the dangers of substituting for clear criteria, criteria which are incapable of precise definition and involve what can only be described as an element of subjective assessment by the Court; such ultimately subjective assessments tend inevitably to lead to uncertainty and anomaly which can be avoided by a more principled approach.'

[21] *Governors of the Peabody Donation Fund v Sir Lindsay Parkinson & Co. Ltd.* [1985] AC 210, 241C, per Lord Keith. The idea can, however, be traced back to Lord Morris's judgment in the *Dorset Yacht* case in 1970.

[22] *Caparo Industries Plc v Dickman* [1990] 2 AC 605.

What about the French motivation? In *M et Mme Pillon*[23] the exact nature of the duty that should have made the social service more careful in the placement of children was not specified. On the contrary, in *Epoux Ouaras*,[24] the *Conseil d'Etat* referred to certain provisions, which, in the Public Health Code (*Code de la Santé Publique*) require that social services supervise the health of all children under a certain age. In short, almost the same brevity encountered in the reasoning of the judgments of the *Cour de cassation* is, again, the hallmark of the administrative jurisdiction, especially if its products are compared to the much longer and fuller judgments of the highest English courts. If the search for similarities is to proceed, one must begin to consult additional sources.

V. IN SEARCH OF A *RAPPROCHEMENT*

In one sense what is most remarkable about the comparison of these two systems is not that they (a) reach different results in these factually equivalent situations but (b) that they choose to motivate their judgments in such a patently different way. The English allusion to policy, with all its attractions and weaknesses (if it is attempted without empirical evidence to support it)[25] is thus notably absent from the French decisions. Closer examination of the systems, however, reveals that the second assertion—(b)—is only partially correct. This becomes clear once one moves away from the decisions themselves and starts looking at their supporting official as well as academic literature.[26] Here one finds evidence to support two observations. First, the English concerns can be found duplicated in France and can even be traced (though more tenuously) to judicial decisions. This, however, is a crucial assertion. For the more one can substantiate this point, the closer one can bring the two systems and challenge the illusion of difference and separateness. Secondly, further study of these policy arguments also reveals that, at the end of the day, they have faired differently in the two systems. The (final) rejection by French law of the English policy concerns thus leads us to the question why this has happened? The answer will be found at a different and deeper level of enquiry. And revealing as it does a

---

[23] Conseil d'Etat, 4 May 1983, No 22811.

[24] Conseil d'Etat, 23 Sept 1987, *Recueil des arrêts du Conseil d'Etat*, 290.

[25] This author at least thus has much respect for Lord Justice Buxton's reaction when presented by counsel with some policy concerns and retorted that '[t]here is no evidence to support any of these contentions. . . . In my respectful view, the Court should be very cautious before reaching or acting on any conclusions that are not argued before it in the way in which technical issues are usually approached, with the assistance of expert evidence', *Perrett v Collins* [1998] 2 Lloyd's Rep 255, 276–7.

[26] Whenever it is published for, unfortunately, the conclusions of the *Avocat général* and the *Commissaire du Gouvernement* are not always easily available.

different socio-political philosophy, once again leads us to assert a divergence and then to try to understand it. The absence of overt discussions, however, again makes the search difficult and any conclusion speculative. But one thing is clear. At this last stage (and deeper) level of our enquiry we are no longer comparing legal or legalistic arguments but competing philosophies about the role of the state in modern society. We shall deal with this aspect of the problem later on in section 6. Here suffice it to note that such core political, moral, or philosophical issues may be incapable of a right answer let alone one answer. Equally, one must note that what works for the specific problem discussed in this paper also works for other legal problems subjected to a similar kind of analysis.

A. Policy Reasons and Concepts in Decisions Involving the Liability of Public Bodies

As already stated, what most distinguishes common law judgments from French ones is not just their greater length but also their increasing willingness to confront *openly* the underlying policy issues. This makes the reading of Common law decisions not only more attractive but also more informative as to what is really happening not only during the secret judicial deliberations but also in the mind of the judge, himself. Last but not least, such greater frankness could make the argument of future cases more meaningful as counsel confront openly and with increasing evidence of an inter-disciplinary nature the issues that lie at the core of the dispute. For instance, the emphasis that the causation issue[27] has received in the French cases of wrongful life as a result of the recent *Perruche* decision[28] is a good illustration as any. And it contrasts sharply with the parallel American[29] and German[30] judgments which state quite clearly that they will not allow conceptual debates to interfere with the pursuit of justice.

---

[27] At its barest the argument is this. The doctor's negligence in failing to diagnose the mother's rubella did not cause the child's impairment but only allowed it to be born. Therefore the doctor should not be liable for anything towards the child. The best reply to this argument, suitable to the way the case was pleaded in French law, has come from Professor Michelle Gobert in 'La Cour de cassation méritait-elle le pilori?', *Les Petites Affiches*, 8 décembre 2000, 4.

[28] Decision of the *Assemblée Plénière* of 17 Nov 2000 published in *La Semaine Juridique*, No 50, 13 décembre 2000, 2293 et seq.

[29] *Procanik v Cillo* 478 A 2d 755 (1984) at 763. 'The philosophical problem of finding that such a defective life is worth less than no life at all has perplexed [many] distinguished members of this Court. We need not become preoccupied, however, with these metaphysical considerations. Our decision to allow the recovery [by the child] of extraordinary medical expenses is not premised on the concept that non-life is preferable to an impaired life, but is predicated on the needs of the living.'

[30] See, for instance, BGH 23 Oct 1951, BGHZ 3,261 where the court, after reviewing the various German theories about causation, said: 'The search is for [a] corrective that restricts the scope of the purely logical consequences to produce an equitable result. . . . Only of the

This (apparent) absence of policy factors in French decisions is even more obvious in the group of cases, which deal with the potential liability of the State and other bodies operating under statutory authorisation. Once again, the disputes I have in mind find factual parallels in both countries so, by studying them one can see how the two systems have dealt with similar problems. These cases involve such varied matters as the potential liability of the police for failing to prevent the commission of a crime or the negligent failure of the social security services to remove a sexually abused child from the care of its abusing relatives. Another example of contemporary significance is the possible liability of a school authority for failing to diagnose the learning problems of one of the children in its care and thus failing to provide it with the appropriate kind of training.[31] In all these cases Anglo-French law take different views; the English—until very recently—denied liability almost systematically; the French have not only allowed it; they also give the impression of taking it almost for granted. The difference in results is matched by a difference in motivation of the judgments. Once again, the Anglo-American judgments are replete with allusions to policy reasons justifying their results while their French counterparts resort to a myriad of concepts, some known to English law—for example, causation and contributory negligence—and others unknown—such a *faute lourde or égalité devans les charges publics*. Yet, once again, the true picture is not what appears to the naked eye but what is discovered after painstaking research hidden under the surface of a published decision. My general thesis thus remains unaltered even in the area of public law. It is what happens under the surface—what I later on call the 'core' of the problem—that really matters and it is this that shows whether the systems can converge or are destined to remain divergent until the underlying philosophy is re-assessed. A remarkable dissertation by my former pupil Dr. Duncan Fairgrieve, entitled *A Comparative Study of State Tortious and Delictual Liability in Damages in English and French Law*,[32] has recently shed new light on the issue at hand. It also provides additional supporting evidence for a thesis that I have been promoting for over thirty years. I am grateful to him for allowing me to draw here on his material and on his ideas in advance of their publication in book form.[33]

---

courts are conscious of the fact that it is a question here not really of causation but of the fixing of the limits within which the originator of a condition can be equitably be presumed liable for its consequences . . . will the danger of schematisation . . . be avoided and the correct results be guaranteed.'

[31] The leading English decision is *Phelps v Hillingdon London Borough Council* [2000] 3 WLR 776. For a factually parallel German decision see OLG Hamm, 11th Civil Senate, 23 Mar 1990, 11 U 108/89.

[32] To be published by Oxford University Press under the title, *State Liability in Damages: A Comparative Study* (forthcoming).

[33] The English translations of the French quotations are likewise his, unless otherwise stated.

Thus, in the factual scenarios here considered, two arguments have, above all, carried weight with English judges when deciding against liability. First is the fear that liability would impose a crushing financial burden on the State and, secondly, is the danger that the threat of legal action would make officials hesitant to act. We could almost call these English arguments since they do not figure in the French judgments. Yet both of them can, in fact, be found in France as well, though they must be sought in the interstices of the academic literature and not in the motivation of the judgments. With regard to the second of these arguments for instance Professor Chapus has admitted that:

Administrative authorities might be held back from acting with the speed that is sometimes required for fear of committing a fault and thus being the cause of damages liability. In other words, the risk of too frequent an imposition of liability would translate into a certain reluctance to act.[34]

Likewise, many argued that the easy imposition of liability would seriously deplete the reserves of the public purse. This view has thus been shared by Professors Weil,[35] Hauriou[36] and Touchard;[37] though it has been countered by other, equally eminent experts[38] as an illegitimate consideration, which should be ignored by the judge. Yet another group of commentators has claimed that, good or bad, these academic pre-occupations have actually influenced judges and thus determined judicial outcomes whether we like this or not. An unpublished (but widely influential) thesis by J. C. Hélin[39] has thus maintained that:

It is difficult to deny that the financial argument, invoked by the doctrine in order to restrict the ambit of liability, has been taken into account in the case law itself.

Equally fascinating are two other points. The first is how these policy reasons (against the imposition of liability) have surfaced in the French judgments in legal, conceptual clothes but are not immediately apparent to anyone who does not know what he is looking for. Dr Fairgrieve, for instance, a Common lawyer by training, applied common law techniques in analysing his raw French material. And what he has revealed is as remark-

---

[34] R Chapus, *Droit Administratif Général*, vol I, 13th edn (Paris: Montcrestien, 1999), para 1463.

[35] *Les Conséquences de l'Annulation de l'Acte Admininstratif pour Excès de Pouvoir* (Paris: A Pedone, 1952), 255.

[36] Case note on CE 29 May 1903, *Le Berre*, Sirrey 1904.3.121.

[37] The latter even going as far as suggesting that the judge should protect public funds. See, 'A propos de la responsabilité pour faute de l'Administration Fiscale' *RDP* 1992, 785 at 806.

[38] Such as Georges Vedel, *Droit Administratif*, 2nd edn (Paris, 1961), 281. Likewise, Clinquennois, 'Essai sur la responsabilité de l' Etat du fait de ses activités de contrôle et de tutelle' *Les Petites Affiches*, no 98, 16 Aug 1995, 4.

[39] *Faute de Service et Préjudice dans le Contentieux de la Responsabilité pour Illégalité* (Thesis, University of Nantes, 1969), 63.

able as it is encouraging for all those who like myself have for decades now[40] been arguing that the systems are very similar once you scratch below their surface of juridical reasoning and search for policy. The point must be emphasised over and over again; for decades of prejudice—legal and political—have been erected on the notions of separateness, difference, and ethnicity. Secondly, what gives the Fairgrieve thesis an extra dimension is the fact that the raw material it uses is widely available in France and yet, in another sense, it is little used by French administrative lawyers and entirely un-exploited by French public law comparatists. It thus took a Common lawyer's mind to draw it out and demonstrate its significance, especially for the purposes of comparative methodology. In the long run, this kind of work could, however, encourage French lawyers to apply this method to their own material. And this, not only as a way of testing the viability of their answers, but also as a way of demonstrating to outside observers of French law the system's richness and sophistication which can often be concealed behind its blandly phrased judgments.

Thus, the requirement that state liability be engaged only if there is a *faute lourde* is, very likely, one of these surreptitiously controlling devices based on the kind of policy reasons that have been openly invoked by the English courts. No wonder, those who condemn such defensive attitudes as something of a bygone era seriously doubt whether 'the administrative judge [should be allowed to] prioritise systematically and protect the finances of the State'.[41] This, it must be noted in passing, is a fascinating approach for it turns on its head Lord Hoffmann's very same argument used (in England) to achieve the opposite result, namely to allow the judge to use economic arguments to protect the state.[42] Be that as it may, this French use of the notion of *faute lourde* has led other influential commentators to express the hope 'that, in due course, the requirement . . . will cease to be part of the law'.[43] But, once again, whether one adopts or deplores the philosophy that allows judges to act as protectors of state finances, one cannot deny that Professor Deguergue[44] sounds convincing when she argues that:

All authors agree that the principal function of *faute lourde* is to lighten the liability of public bodies

---

[40] Thus, 20 years ago Professor Christian von Bar and I tried to do this for English and German law. See CB Mohr, *Richterliche Rechtspolitik im Haftungsrech* (Tübingen, 1981).

[41] Clinquennois, op cit, n 37 above.

[42] For instance in *Stovin v Wise* [1996] AC 923. Yet, one must also bear in mind that the Hoffmann approach can also be found in France. See, for instance, the views of Touchard, 'A propos de la responsabilité pour faute de l'Administration Fiscale' *RDP* (1992), 785 at 806.

[43] Roger Errera [1990] *Public Law*, 571.

[44] *Jurisprudence et Doctrine dans l'Elaboration du Droit de la Responsabilité Administrative* (1994), 638.

And, even if the use of this notion—*faute lourde*—were to weaken or it were to be seriously eliminated from some of the areas where it has been used, French law still has ways for, essentially, reintroducing it in some oblique form in order to keep liability within reasonable bounds. Thus, it is already accepted that not every minor malpractice such as simple errors constitutes *faute simple*; and that this distinction between *faute simple* and *erreur*, if properly applied, can avert a tidal wave of cases or an obliteration of public finances.[45] One specialist author[46] has thus expressed this thought in the following manner:

Finally, it is fairly clear in our country that the judicial mind is increasingly uncomfortable with the raising of the threshold of public liability achieved through the notion of administrative gross negligence. Since the protection that this notion accords to public authorities has been judged excessive, it will be up to the judge to decide whether to rely on it or not, without, however, either provoking a tidal wave of litigation or burdening public finances. For in that case the fault/error duo would supplant the ordinary negligence/ gross negligence alternative.

In French administrative law this wide-ranging discussion over the ambit and purpose of the notion of *faute lourde* shows, in my view, that the legal concepts in that country are as pliable as their English counterparts and can be made to bend to judicial views on policy. More importantly, the citations that I have given show that the French authors, themselves, accept this point. In my opinion, it requires only a small step further to accept that, in the light of the above, the concepts should be accorded some but not total respect or reverence. They are, as I keep saying, the tools that formulate judgments but not the reasons for them.

The same observations (about policy behind concepts) can, I submit, be made of the notion of causative theories in administrative law. To the extent that this is supportable by evidence it re-affirms my view, expressed in the context of the *Perruche* affair, that one should not take legal concepts too seriously.[47]

We thus note—in the context of the problem examined in this essay—the frank and illuminating observation of Professor Chapus who, referring to the use of the *théorie de causalité adéquate* in the context of (French) administrative law states that its:

judicial assessment is not mechanical. It is undertaken with a good deal of freedom and is influenced by common sense and subjectivity.[48]

---

[45] This has been admitted even by some *Commissaire du Gouvernment*. See, for instance, CE 29 June 1997, RFDA (1998), 87.

[46] Michel Paillet, *Responsabilité Adminsitrative* (Paris, 1996), para 259 (my translation).

[47] I stressed this point in my article, 'Réflexions d'un comparatiste anglais sur et à partir de l'arrêt Perruche' *RTD civ.* (1) Jan–Mar 2001, 77–102.

[48] R Chapus, *Droit Administratif Général*, vol I, 13th edn (Paris: Montchrestien, 1999), para 1414. Likewise, M Deguergue, *Jurisprudence et Doctrine dans l'Elaboration du Droit de la Responsabilité Administrative* (Paris: LGDJ, 1994), para 147.

Chapus continues with the observation that this is also the reason why the potentially more expansive theory of *équivalence des conditions* has, on the whole, met with less favour with French administrative courts, and, one could add, German courts, as well. Yet other authors have maintained that overall causative theories have received a restrictive application in order to minimise the burden on public finances.[49] Fairgrieve, in his aforementioned work, has gone further than repeat such statements. He has thus meticulously collected case law and references that show that 'the test of causation has been used to ward off large liabilities in sensitive areas such as planning, travaux publics, tax and regulatory activities'.[50]

The same protective philosophy can be found in other causative-related devices such an act of a third party or *faute de la victime*. Thus, where it can be proved that the third party conduct—some say faute—contributed to the injury suffered by the claimant, the administration will be expected to pay only the share of the damage which is due to them[51] (there being nothing equivalent to the English notion of joint and several liability). And where children have contributed to their hurt, their damages seem often to be reduced substantially, the apportionment process often, apparently, over-favouring the administration.[52]

B. *A Divergence in Fundamental Philosophy?*

So, approaching the case law of different countries in the above way leads us to a number of conclusions.

First, legal systems when compared through their decisional law reveal a considerable similarity of factual litigated instances. Beginning the comparison by using such material (instead of the *doctrine*) has the advantage of putting the reader at ease since he feels he is on familiar terrain and not lost in a jungle of legal notions and concepts. On the minus side, however, it must be admitted that this approach presents the drawback of having to do much original research before finding the obvious objects for comparison. No judge has the time to do that; but that is where academics can be of assistance both to their students as well as to their courts in helping then bridge the gap.

Secondly, when the comparison is pursued further, differences of concepts and reasoning become obvious. The need to explain them then becomes pressing and the researcher is pushed into a different and deeper

---

[49] C Guettier, *La Responsabilité Administrative* (Paris: LGDJ, 1996), 127-7.
[50] Unpublished thesis, 162; citations omitted.
[51] CE 28 Oct 1977, *Commune de Flumet* (1977), Rec 412; CE 14 May 1986, *Commune de Cilaos* (1986), Rec 716.
[52] S Rials, *Le Juge Administratif Francais et la Technique du Standard* (Paris: LGDJ, 1980) 331.

level of enquiry that involves him searching for the policy reasons of a particular judicial solution rather than for the verbal devices used to formulate them. This search, eventually, reveals that the policy debates that have dominated one system can also be found in the other; indeed, the little that has been cited above suggests a quite remarkable degree of duplication of ideas. But this material is discovered at different levels or in different sources, for example, academic writings (often in inaccessible journals rather than in the main treatises), preparatory papers leading to legislation, conclusions by advocates general. The one place from which they are missing from are the judicial opinions, themselves. The art of discovering the equivalent material is thus one which must be mastered but is not easily learnt. Even more intriguing (and difficult) is the task of tracing the impact that this material has had on the case law since the latter pretends to ignore it. The discovery of conclusive answers is by no means guaranteed; and, often, can only be attempted by talking to the real protagonists of litigation: judges and practitioners. But, at the very least, the pursuit of these aim gives the foreign observer a deeper and, it is submitted, more satisfying understanding of his own case law as he grapples with the difficulties of the foreign solutions.

Thirdly, intelligent questioning of this similar, policy-impregnated material leads one to the final and deeper level where one has to confront the core issues. At this level, legal arguments become subservient to political, economic, or moral ones, which now come to the fore. Inevitably, the key issues that have to be resolved here are not always susceptible to one answer; nor, indeed, are they always capable of receiving a right answer and certainly this cannot come from lawyers acting on their own. I have always felt this to be true of our system and was thus delighted when I came across the same idea expressed by some eminent French colleagues while criticising the over-legalistic dissection to which the important *Perruche*[53] decision was subjected to by most French jurists. These three French colleagues were thus, in my view right when they said that:[54]

the jurist cannot make use of the law and claim that it can solve [problems] by itself when, in reality, he can only (and does only) opt for an ontological, logical, or moral stance without being any more qualified than anyone else to do so. On the other hand, it falls upon him to create the tools and the techniques which make practicable in law the political solution he has decided to adopt. And that is no mean feat.

---

[53] The *Perruche* decision of the *Assemblée Plénière* of the *Cour de cassation* of 25 Nov 2000, dealing with a wrongful birth claim by a seriously handicapped child, is published in *La Semaine Juridique*, no 50, 13 décembre 2000, 2293.

[54] Article published in the *Monde* of 21 Dec 2000 by Professor de Béchillon and Olivier Cayla and Yan Thomas, both *directeurs d'études* at the *Ecole des Hautes Etudes en Sciences Sociales*, Paris (my translation).

It is thus at this final and third level that our illustrations from the Anglo-French administrative law finally find the reason for the diverging answers. The fear, for instance, of financially crushing deserving defendants, though genuinely entertained by both systems, in France gave way to a broader philosophical consideration. This underlying broader philosophy was not always different in France and England. The divergence developed[55] as the French State, in the late 1960s, was progressively seduced by the idea of equality, socialisation of risks, and social solidarity. Under this newer French philosophy the law tends to admit that when citizens suffer damage of a certain type and size it is the duty of the state to compensate them. This is so even if it is not possible to link them with something which could be called mal-administration. This vision explains why, in the recent past, several pieces of regulatory legislation were put into place in order to grant people compensation—from the state budget—for damages having sometimes no relation[56] to any administrative action or omission. The 1990 Act for victims of terrorist acts as well as the 1991 Act concerning people affected by transfusions of blood contaminated by the AIDS virus fall under this category.

Once the above 'philosophical stance' is noted—even if not accepted—one can see why French judges are likely to disregard the cost that a liability rule might entail for public authorities. More interestingly, the idea—so obvious in some English judgments—that such resources might be better used in another 'public' context, becomes equally irrelevant. For, in the kind of consumerist vision of public liability which has become predominant in French law since the late 1960s, compensating the damages suffered by citizens because of administrative activities can never be a wrong use of public money. On the contrary, it may even be seen as the best possible use of public money when it is viewed as serving the principle of equality by avoiding a result that means that people who have randomly been affected by administrative action remain without compensation.

The reader digesting the thoughts in the previous section may accept them as explaining the outcome of the French decisions. But the superficial reader—and for present purposes even educated English lawyers might fall into this category—may precipitously dismiss them as *totally* alien to the role of the state as it has come to be seen in England during the last twenty years. Certainly the views of some judges (such as Lord Hoffmann) and some academics (such as Tony Weir) would seem to espouse such a 'conservative' philosophy that is prepared to allow (if not encourage) judges to act

---

[55] While the underlying philosophy and concerns were similar, the legal solutions were likewise closer than they are today. Thus, see, P Weil, *Les Consequences de l' Annulation d'un Acte Administratif pour Excès de Pouvoir* (Paris: A Pedone, 1952) 255.

[56] Or at least without the need of demonstrating any relation.

primarily with the view of shielding the finances of the state. Yet something that comes close to the (new) French philosophy can also be found in England when one reads such documents as the First Report of the Select Committee on the Parliamentary Commissioner for Administration[57] or the views of other leading judges as Lord Bingham.[58] So, what really matters, is not to realise that the prevailing view is different in France and in England; even, less to exercise the political decision and choose between them. For the jurist, certainly the comparative jurist, what is much more important is to realise that these views and debates have, despite misleading appearances caused by different concepts and notions, their *exact* equivalents in England, France (and indeed Germany and Italy). A no less significant realisation would lie in the fact that the answer to this 'core' question is not one that can be given by lawyers or lawyers acting and thinking on their own. The previously quote views of Professor de Beschillon[59] and his colleagues thus come back to one's mind as containing a truth that is equally valid on both sides of the Channel and thus proves how similar we really are.

A not dissimilar kind of attitude would colour the view of a French judge towards the so-called inhibition argument.[60] For though it is not unknown in French theory of public liability, it certainly plays a secondary part. This is so because, apart from its fundamental compensatory function, public liability is also viewed as a way of disciplining the administration. In that role, it complements judicial review, by imposing payment of compensation, whereas the former provides for the annulment of illegal decisions.

Finally, would a French administrative judge refrain from imposing public liability because he thinks that it would mean that he has second-guessed the public body in the exercise of its discretion? Such an approach, which has found such an appeal in England, would hardly strike a French judge as a natural one. The reason is the following. In practice, in a large majority of cases in which the administration is held liable, the fault which has been identified is an illegality. Illegality, in other words, is the most ordinary form of administrative fault.

This strong relation between fault and illegality has the consequence that the adjudication of administrative liability largely mirrors judicial review of

---

[57] 'We agree that the priority in expenditure should be the improvement of services. Effective redress is itself a service improvement. It may be unfortunate that funds are spent in compensation. It cannot, however, be right to use such argument against schemes which justly reimburse the complainant for financial loss. The answer is not to avoid compensation but to avoid the original failure of service' (1994–5), HC 112, para 70.

[58] '[S]ave in clear cases, it is not for the courts to decide how public money is best spent nor to balance the risk that money will be wasted on litigation against the hope that the possibility of suit may contribute towards the maintenance of the highest standards.'

[59] See n 54 above.

[60] Namely, that the imposition of civil liability will make civil servants reluctant to act.

administrative legality. The judges' attitude, when faced with questions of discretion, is the same in both cases. This means that judges have no reason to think that accepting liability would especially impinge upon administrative discretion: they respect it, and review it to the same extent that they would otherwise do when reviewing questions of legality.

IV. WIDER CONCLUSIONS

Looking at foreign law the way I have in this short piece[61] is, as I have readily admitted, both difficult and time consuming. It takes time to read decisions in order to find factual equivalents that lend themselves to comparison. It takes even more of an effort to ensure that, having delved deeper into the procedural, constitutional, and political peculiarities of each system, you feel confident enough to emphasise their similarities and explain their differences. Finally, it takes Jovian patience to remain faithful to the overall cause of searching for and emphasising similarities in order to facilitate greater European integration without distorting the raw material you have discovered. This is particularly so as one becomes conscious of the difficulties of imparting this expertise upon those who really matter namely, the judges and the practitioners. For academics, with few exceptions, have both in England and France, approached comparative law in an excessively theoretical and abstract manner, unwittingly making it of little interest in the classroom and of even less use in the courtroom. The high priests of my subject bear a great responsibility for this sorry state of affairs.

If, despite the above, one perseveres, one realises that the core issues that confront our European systems are the same even though the answers they receive may be different. The next realisation is that if the answers differ it is not really because of the concepts or even the arguments used on the surface, but because of understandable and legitimate divergences at the core. As stated, however, at the core we do not find legal, certainly not legalistic, arguments. On the contrary, we here encounter political, moral, social, and economic issues. Because these issues are of wider import, lawyers alone cannot solve them. Moreover, and this is just as important, they are not issues that can be described as typically French, German, or English, since they appear across borders and thus by their very nature encourage comparison. Finally, individual systems—for instance the French—can and have themselves vacillated over what kind of answers is

---

[61] And with greater tenacity in the rest of my writings. Thus, see, *Foreign Law and Comparative Methodology: A Subject and a Thesis* (Oxford: Hart Publishing, 1997) and *Always on the Same Path: Essays on Foreign Law and Comparative Methodology* (Oxford: Hart Publishing, 2001).

appropriate to these fundamental questions. Thus, as swings and changes have taken place, so have the results of the judicial decisions altered.[62]

So the real differences between the systems do not lie at the surface where sets of similar facts lead to litigation—I call this the first circle—but at the core—and I call this the third circle. But what stops us from realising this phenomenon and, where necessary, addressing it in an intelligent way (especially if harmonisation of laws is our aim), are the arguments that take place in the second circle, where concepts, notions, and legal reasoning reign supreme. Unfortunately, it is here that most jurists have focused most of their energies. In keeping with nineteenth century ideas of state sovereignty, this has led them to a state-based case law. This, in turn, has led the same jurists to overemphasise (undoubted) differences rather than stress equally important similarities, and to stick jealously to the tools that their system has bequeathed them. But this is not what the twenty-first century requires given the move towards transnational legal regimes, be they in the human rights area or in the domain of commercial law. This emerging, new, and interdependent world cannot work with a legal science that is over-attached to parochial structures or local ways of doing business. It needs broad and flexible legal minds to import what is useful and to export what they, in their own countries, have done best. To do this, one must identify and confront the core issues and realise that they cut across national borders, offering great opportunities for a traffic in legal ideas.

The proper understanding of the systems thus require us to reduce the importance of the second circle and find and define the real issues that lurk in the third. In the controversial *Perruche* decision, where the *plenum* of the *Cour de cassation* had to decide whether to give *any* kind of damages in a wrongful life claim, the dominant theme was that of life, itself. However affected and diminished, our current thinking cannot accept it as 'damage' or as a 'harm'. And for as long as this remains true, compensation for 'being born' cannot and will not be sanctioned anywhere in the world. This is true and philosophically tenable though not as incontrovertible as courts functioning in a politically correct age would like us to believe.[63] At the same time, the same public opinion is not prepared to allow impaired children to suffer because eminent jurists such as Dean Carbonnier have argued that 'life, even if affected by misfortune, is always

---

[62] Think of the *concubinage* cases that divided that civil and criminal sections of the *Cour de cassation* throughout the 1950s and 1960s and how the Cour de cassation changed its stance in the 1970s you will understand my point in addition to discovering another example of how legal concepts—there the notion of *dommage légitime*—were distorted by policy considerations.

[63] Writers such as Herodutus, Sophocles, Shakespeare, and Nietzsche—to mention but a few—never managed to solve this underlying issue, so how can we expect a judge to do this for us? For fuller references see my article, 'Réflexions d'un comparatiste anglais sur et à partir de l'arrêt Perruche', *RTD civ.* (1) Jan–Mar 2001, 77–102.

preferable to nothingness'.[64] As I argued in my article in the *Revue Trimestrielle*[65] the *opinion savante* has no better claim to our loyalty than the *opinion souffrante*. Only academics, it seems to me, can aspire to such levels of intellectual arrogance. So, what *Perruche* did was to make sure—without entering the major philosophical debate—that the affected child had its extra needs taken care of in an adequate way.[66] Provided its damages are not (eventually) duplicated with those already given to the parents by the Court of Appeal which will finally put an end to this protracted litigation, the dignity of the French legal system will not be affected. I think this is the true meaning of *the Assemblée Plénière* of 17 November 2000. It is also the interpretation that brings the case—in its ultimate result—in line with American and German law because it looks at the core of the problem and is not distracted by the biased use of concepts. In France this dimension has, in my view, been missed. For most lawyers used the causation debate to block out of sight the fact that the court was trying to take care of the child and, at the same time, remain faithful to the prevailing view that impaired life was not less valuable than a healthy one.

The examples of tortious liability of statutory bodies, which have provided the main theme of this essay, must be approached in the same way, as the simple juxtaposition of English and French law will only reveal a false picture. For the equation made by French (but not English) law between illegality and fault makes French law appear doctrinally different and philosophically pro-claimant in a most extreme manner. Yet this is precisely the kind of opening statement which, though correct in one sense, does great disservice both to French and English lawyers. For, on the grounds that the differences between the two systems are so great, the statement almost inevitably implies that their further comparison is meaningless. It thus takes the works of Fairgrieve and his French counterparts (such as Hélin) to alter the first impression and show how the normative use of a multitude of concepts—such as *faute lourde, causalité, faute de la victime*, etc—go a long way towards reducing the differences which on paper seem so glaring. But this is still only the beginning of the kind of enquiry we need in order to make comparative law attractive as a discipline and useful to our courts. For the fact remains that in the eyes of those who have fashioned French administrative law, the economic concerns, which troubled their English counterparts, were only one part of the equation. What, in a sense, was paramount in their minds was to make a philosophical stand and

---

[64] Quoted by l'Avocat général Sainte-Rose in his conclusions in the *Perruche* case, *La Semaine Juridique*, no 50, 13 décembre 2000, 2293, 2307.

[65] 'Réflexions d'un comparatiste anglais sur et à partir de l'arrêt Perruche', *RTD civ.* (1) Jan–Mar 2001, 77–102.

[66] *M. le Conseiller rapporteur Sargos* makes, I think, this clear in his report to the court. See *La Semaine Juridique*, no 50, 13 Dec 2000, para no 49, 2302.

subordinate economic expediency to it. This stand was founded on the ideas of equality, risk-socialisation, and social solidarity: activities, which benefit us all must also, spread their costs among us all. Though we know that in France fashions change, one suspects that this edifice could become unstable only if the level of damages seriously endangered the financial viability of the 'deserving pockets' that meet these bills. My theory, however, works only on the basis of an *unproven* assumption that in this type of case[67]—unlike those involving medical malpractice—the level of damages awarded by French administrative courts is much lower than those that might be reached by English courts if they ever became sympathetic to these claims. I stress, however, *unproven*, for the collection of raw data on damage awards is an extraordinarily difficult task in French law and is still incomplete. And the assumption that my co-authors and I made in our *Tortious Liability of Statutory Bodies* was, in fact, the opposite, suggesting that the level of damages awarded in these cases could be equated to those found in personal injury litigation where some kind of parity can be established between English and French law.[68]

This (as yet unquantified) moderation of French law, coupled with the more concrete data one can collect from German law, might hold out some lessons for English law as it contemplates a more liberal stance in its post *Barrett* and *Phelps* phases. In one sentence this is: compensate but do not go overboard! Certainly, a number of dicta from *Phelps* could be collected to suggest that such a development of the law of damages might not be unwelcome to their Lordships.[69] Yet French law might make an even more important contribution to our legal theory if its underlying philosophy were ever to be adopted by our judges. For some such idea as that of social solidarity could well provide the underlying theme that could bring together the patchwork of remedies—given by ombudsmen, criminal injuries compensation boards, common law, etc—that are slowly being crafted in the penumbra of public law proper in our country. Of course, such a suggestion runs counter to Common law incrementalism, especially the English variant, and the system's aversion to fashioning wide and unifying principles. Yet is this not what happened to our private law of unjustified enrichment thanks to the combined tenacity of judge and jurist? And if it happened in one part of the law, and happened in the short space of 25 years or so, why cannot it also happen in the troublesome area where public

---

[67] Such as *Bedfordshire*, *Barrett*, or *Phelps*.

[68] These 'second thoughts' I am entertaining here about French law are personal and in no way bind my co-authors of *Tortious Liability of Statutory Bodies*. They also do not alter the validity of our (combined) thesis with regard to German law. For the German examples we quoted in our book show that the German awards, though not huge (especially by American standards), are not insignificant.

[69] Though how, for instance, a dyslexic child should be compensated for not having been given a proper education remains to be worked out.

law and tort overlap with such confusion? But this is my fifth inaugural lecture and, for my part, I feel I have done enough by raising this question and leaving it to be discussed by my successor in 9 years time!

In any event, tonight my main concern as a Professor of Comparative Law has not been to theorise in the borderline of tort and administrative law but to promote a better way of bringing together the different legal systems. For over 30 years in academic life I have tried to apply the approach I sketched here to the entire area of the law of obligations and, most recently, to expand it to include some areas of human rights. It is my belief, but not yet supported by adequate personal research, that this methodology can be applied successfully across the various areas of the law and across national borders. And if it can, it will I think suggest that despite formidable differences, the similarities that exist in the contemporary European systems are growing by the day. More importantly, the similarities are growing not because of Directives, model laws, or international treaties are regulating more and more of our life, but because growing urbanisation, industrialisation, interstate commerce, and travel, are attenuating local differences of behaviour and thought, and are assimilating human tastes, attitudes and values. In short they are affecting the core or third circle; and this, sooner or later, will force our lawyers to make their reasoning more open, more susceptible to interdisciplinary data, and more user-friendly. Such an approach will not only ensure greater mutual understanding; it will also ensure that good ideas, be they English or French, will travel faster and further. And the true comparatist can ask for nothing more.

PART IV:
COUNTRY REPORTS

15. PUSHING BACK THE BOUNDARIES OF PUBLIC AUTHORITY LIABILITY

Duncan Fairgrieve

Public authority liability is in a state of flux. There have been numerous decisions of the English courts in recent times with an increasingly important European law dimension of both Community law and human rights law provenance. Claims in the education sphere have been at the forefront of this litigation. The modern manifestation of the reasonable man, the London underground commuter,[1] would perhaps be unsurprised to learn that teachers owe a duty of care to children for their *physical safety* at school.[2] The existence of an enforceable right in damages for breach of duty to take care in educational matters might elicit a different reaction. Nonetheless, such claims have been made by aggrieved students around the world,[3] and have occupied considerable time of the English courts. The culmination of this process was the constitution of a panel of seven Law Lords in the case of *Phelps v Hillingdon LBC* to decide whether to recognise a tort for the untaught. The purpose of this paper is to analyse these recent developments, taking the important decision of the House of Lords in *Phelps* as the starting point for a broader discussion.

I. EDUCATION AND NEGLIGENCE:
THE CLAIMS IN *PHELPS V HILLINGDON LBC*

The House of Lords' decision in *Phelps v Hillingdon LBC* is of considerable significance for public authority liability in negligence. The case arose from four joined appeals concerning the alleged liability in negligence of Local Education Authorities (LEAs) for the provision of educational services for children. In *Phelps v Hillingdon LBC*, Ms Phelps alleged that an educational psychologist employed by the defendant local authority had negligently failed to diagnose her as suffering from dyslexia. At trial, the defendant was indeed found to be vicariously liable for the educational

---

[1] *McFarlane v Tayside Health Board* [2000] 2 AC 59, 82.
[2] *Van Oppen v Clerk to the Bedford Charity Trustees* [1990] 1 WLR 235.
[3] For a brief comparative law survey, see D Fairgrieve and M Andenas, 'Tort Liability For Educational Malpractice: the Phelps case' (1999) 10 KCLJ 229.

psychologist's negligence,[4] and the claimant was awarded just over £45,000 in damages for future loss of earnings, cost of tuition, and loss of congenial employment. This decision was overturned by the Court of Appeal on the basis that the psychologist was primarily employed to advise the school and the local authority and so had not assumed a personal responsibility to the claimant.[5] It was also held that policy reasons militated against a duty of care.[6] In support of the denial of a duty of care, reference was also made to the restrictive American cases concerning common law claims for educational malpractice.

In *G (A Minor) v Bromley LBC* the claimant, who suffered from muscular dystrophy, alleged that teachers at a special school for the physically disabled had failed to give him an appropriate education to cope with his disability, and that this caused a lack of educational progress, psychiatric injury, and financial expenditure. In the Court of Appeal, Lord Justice Auld held in a clear and powerful judgment that teachers are under a duty to exercise reasonable skill in responding to the educational needs of their pupils, and refused to accede to the defendant's application to strike out the claim.[7]

In *Jarvis v Hampshire CC*, a dyslexic young man sued Hampshire County Council in negligence and misfeasance in public office for what was admitted by one of the defendant's educational psychologists to have been 'a catastrophe of an education'.[8] He claimed compensation for the cost of remedial tuition and the loss of prospective future earnings. At first instance, the judge had refused to strike out the action in negligence, based both on vicarious liability for the alleged negligence of an educational psychologist and various teaching advisers in properly treating the claimant's dyslexia, as well as upon direct liability for the negligent manner in which the authority had operated an educational psychology service. The claimant appealed against the subsequent striking out of the action in negligence by the Court of Appeal.

Finally, the fourth case, *Anderton v Clwyd CC*, also concerned the failure to diagnose and treat dyslexia. The issue at stake was whether pre-action discovery should be ordered on the basis that the intended claim was for personal injury. The Court of Appeal had refused to grant such an order.[9]

---

4   *Phelps v London Borough of Hillingdon* [1998] ELR 38 (QBD).
5   *Phelps v Hillingdon LBC* [1999] 1 WLR 500.
6   Ibid, 522 et seq.
7   [1999] ELR 356.
8   *Jarvis v Hampshire CC* [2000] ELR 36.
9   *Anderton v Clwyd CC* [1999] ELR 1.

The House of Lords was offered a choice between two starkly differing views of public authority liability. Lord Justice Auld in the Court of Appeal in *G (A Minor) v Bromley LBC* had espoused an essentially liberal view of duties of care in the education sphere, arguing that teachers and education advisers should be subject to a duty to take care in their teaching and that the various policy factors which had traditionally defeated claims in negligence against local authorities 'should now be read in the light of *Barrett*', a reference to the case of *Barrett v Enfield LBC*[10] in which the House of Lords had been reluctant to accept the force of these public interest factors. On the other hand, the Court of Appeal in *Phelps v Hillingdon LBC* had adopted a far more restrictive approach, arguing that public policy was against the recognition of a duty, and that the vicarious liability of the local education authority for the acts of its educators would amount to a circumvention of its immunity from a direct duty in negligence by the 'backdoor' of vicarious liability.[11]

The House of Lords preferred the more liberal approach adopted by the Court of Appeal in *G (A Minor) v Bromley LBC*. Three substantial judgments were given by Lords Slynn, Clyde, and Nicholls.[12] The focus of these judgments was upon vicarious liability of the LEAs for the negligent acts of their employees,[13] but important statements were also made about the direct liability of LEAs.

A. Vicarious liability

The basic premise of their Lordships' analyses was that professionals owe a duty of care to the people they advise, and this similarly should apply to those engaged in the education process, be they psychologists, psychiatrists, class room, or special needs teachers.[14] Their Lordships rejected in a robust manner the policy concerns that had underlined the Court of Appeal's judg-

[10] [2001] 2 AC 550. On this case, see SH Bailey and MJ Bowman, 'Public Authority Negligence Revisited' [2000] CLJ 85; PP Craig and D Fairgrieve, 'Barrett, Negligence and Discretionary Powers' [1999] *PL* 626.

[11] *Phelps v Hillingdon LBC* [1999] 1 WLR 500 at 521. The Court of Appeal's decision in Jarvis v Hampshire CC was also very restrictive: [2000] ELR 36.

[12] Lord Jauncey concurred with Lords Slynn, Clyde, and Nicholls; Lords Lloyd and Hutton concurred with Lords Slynn, and Clyde; Lord Millett gave a very short judgment and agreed with Lord Clyde and Lord Slynn.

[13] It had been accepted by the parties, and this was confirmed by their Lordships, that the educational obligations imposed on local education authorities by statute could not give rise to a tort claim by way of breach of statutory duty: [2000] 3 WLR 776, at 789–90 (Lord Slynn) and 805 (Lord Nicholls).

[14] [2000] 3 WLR 776, at 790 (Lord Slynn), 802-4 (Lord Nicholls) 807–8 (Lord Clyde).

ment in *Phelps*.[15] The restrictive American case law on educational malpractice was held not to be decisive. Lord Slynn argued that the legislative and administrative background in England was very different.[16] Lord Clyde simply felt that a different view should be taken in English Law.[17]

As to the specific position of educational psychologists, their Lordships differed from the Court of Appeal in *Phelps*, deciding that the neither the fact that psychologists owe a duty to the authority to exercise skill and care in their employment nor that they are acting in the context of the local authority's statutory duties meant that a duty of care should be excluded.[18] However, the claimant pupil must show that the 'necessary nexus' existed between himself and the educational professional.[19] Where an educational psychologist is specifically asked to advise upon a child's education, and it is clear that the parents and the teachers will follow that advice, then Lord Slynn argued that prima facie a duty of care arises.[20] Lord Nicholls described this type of case as 'an example par excellence of a situation where the law will regard the professional as owing a duty of care to a third party as well as his own employer'.[21]

On the specific facts of the claim in *Phelps*, their Lordships upheld Garland J's finding at trial (and overturned the Court of Appeal's decision) that the educational psychologist in performing duties on behalf of the local education authority had breached a duty of care owed to the claimant which had led to compensable loss. In respect of the claim in *G (A Minor) v Bromley LBC*, the House of Lords approved the Court of Appeal's refusal to strike out the claim.[22] Similarly, in *Jarvis v Hampshire CC*, it was held to be arguable that the local authority was liable for the acts of the education officers in advising upon the claimant's education.[23] Finally, in the case of *Anderton v Clwyd CC* concerning the preliminary issue of discovery, Lords Slynn and Clyde held that the injuries of which the claimant complained fell within the definition of personal injury under sections 33(2) and 35(2) of the Supreme Court Act 1981 and thus ordered pre-trial discovery.[24]

The House of Lords' decision that educational professionals owe duties

---

[15] [2000] 3 WLR 776, at 792 (Lord Slynn), 804 (Lord Nicholls) and 809 (Lord Clyde).

[16] Ibid, at 792.

[17] Ibid, at 810.

[18] [2000] 3 WLR 776, at 791 (Lord Slynn) and 803 (Lord Nicholls) 810, 811–12 (Lord Clyde).

[19] Ibid, at 791. So that a casual remark or an isolated act would not give rise to a duty of care.

[20] Ibid, at 791.

[21] Ibid, at 803.

[22] *Phelps v Hillingdon LBC* [2000] 3 WLR 776, at 796–7 (Lord Slynn) and 813 (Lord Clyde).

[23] *Phelps v Hillingdon LBC* [2000] 3 WLR 776, at 799.

[24] [2000] 3 WLR 776, at 801–2 (Lord Slynn) and 813 (Lord Clyde).

of care to those they teach or advise has raised some eyebrows.[25] But the recognition of such a duty is not a revolutionary proposition. The House of Lords had already indicated in 1995 in *X(Minors) v Bedfordshire CC* that a school which accepts a pupil assumes responsibility not only for his physical well-being but also for his educational needs.[26] The reiteration of this point by a seven-judge panel in unequivocal terms is nonetheless significant, as is the disapproval of the Court of Appeal's belief that vicarious liability would introduce liability through the 'back door'.

B. Direct Liability

The issue of direct liability elicited a more nuanced response from their Lordships. It was the claimants' challenge to the decision in *X(Minors)* that a local authority owed no *direct* duty of care in the exercise of its statutory function to provide suitable education under the various Education Acts that had necessitated the constitution of a seven-judge panel. Although Lord Slynn did not think that the claim based on a direct duty was made out in the *Phelps* case, he would not as a matter of principle rule it out.[27] Indeed, his Lordship held that in respect of the claim in *Jarvis* it was arguable that the local authority was under a direct duty both in performing its functions under the Education Acts, and in operating an educational psychology service. The direct claim was so closely linked with the vicarious claim that his Lordship did not think it was right to strike it out.[28] In admitting the possibility of direct liability, Lord Slynn indicated that he was willing to overrule the House of Lords' decision in *X(Minors)*. On the other hand, Lords Nicholls and Clyde were more cautious, preferring not to make a decision as to whether a direct duty could arise until the facts of each case were determined at trial.[29]

Their Lordships therefore did not give a unanimous response to the question of direct liability. And yet it would seem that the courts' reticence in recognising a direct duty of local authorities in the exercise of social welfare functions is gradually being whittled away. This process of 'incremental demolition'[30] is likely to continue. It is hard to believe that the courts in the future will deny a *direct* duty on policy grounds alone: it would be incongruous to reject a direct duty on the basis of policy concerns which had been comprehensively dismissed in the context of vicarious liability.

---

[25] See, eg, J Greenwold, 'Lawyers in the Classroom: the New Law of Educational Negligence' (2000) *Education and the Law* 245.

[26] *X (Minors) v Bedfordshire CC* [1995] 2 AC 633, at 766.

[27] [2000] 3 WLR 776, at 795. [28] [2000] 3 WLR 776, at 799.

[29] [2000] 3 WLR 776, at 805 and 812–13.

[30] B Markesinis, 'Plaintiff's tort law or defendant's tort law? Is the House of Lords moving towards a synthesis?' (2001) 9 *Torts Law Journal* 168, 176.

How much practical relevance does the issue of direct liability actually have? As a local authority generally acts through its servants, an action may be based on vicarious liability.[31] However, vicarious liability does not cover all eventualities. An example of such a situation would be negligence relating not to individual acts, such as a diagnostic error by an educational psychologist, but to systemic failure in management or administration. Where no individual can be shown to be at fault, the ability to bring a claim for direct liability would be critical. Such situations have arisen in the medical sphere, for instance when a hospital's system for summoning medical assistance broke down during childbirth and lead to delay in the delivery of a baby.[32]

Equally, in the case of the egregious fault of an employee, such as the sexual abuse of a pupil by a teacher,[33] it may well be argued that this intentional act takes the employee beyond the scope of employment, and thus negates the vicarious liability of the employer.[34] In such a case, the only route open to the claimant would be direct liability, on the basis that the local authority was at fault, for instance in appointing an unqualified person or in failing to supervise the employee properly. However, there have recently been developments which might reduce the need for such a use of direct liability. In the case of *Lister v Hesley Hall Ltd*,[35] it was held that the employers of the warden of a school boarding house, who sexually abused boys in his care, could be vicariously liable for the torts of their employee. The crucial point was the close connection between the warden's torts and the nature of his employment.

C. Duty and Loss

An important aspect of education cases is the type of loss that is recoverable. Claimants have sought recovery of damages for a wide variety of loss, ranging from lack of educational progress to psychiatric injury. The House of Lords decision on this point was significant. Lord Slynn rejected the Court of Appeal's categorisation of the failure to ameliorate dyslexia in *Phelps* and *Jarvis* as pure economic loss. His Lordship held that 'psychological damage and a failure to diagnose a congenital condition and to take

---

[31] *Phelps v Hillingdon LBC* [2000] 3 WLR 776, at 795.

[32] *Bull v Devon AHA* [1993] 4 Med LR 117.

[33] For discussion of this point, see P Cane 'Vicarious Liability for Sexual Abuse' (2000) 116 LQR 21; B Feldthusen, 'Vicarious Liability for Sexual Torts', in N Mullany and A Linden, *Torts Tomorrow: A Tribute to John Fleming* (Sydney: LBC Information Services, 1998).

[34] Argument accepted in *Trotman v North Yorkshire CC* The Times 10 Sept 1998 (deputy headmaster of a special school sexually assaulted a handicapped teenager in his charge during a holiday abroad; the Court of Appeal held that these acts were outside the course of employment.)

[35] 2001] UKHL 22. The House of Lords overruled the decision in Trotman, ibid.

appropriate action as a result of which a child's level of achievement is reduced' could constitute recoverable loss in a negligence action.[36] It is important to look at this element of the judgment in more detail, distinguishing between two types of loss, psychological harm and the consequences of the failure to diagnose a congenital condition.

It was held that emotional or psychological harm could constitute damage for the purpose of the common law.[37] There was little discussion of this point in the decision, but it is submitted that Lord Slynn's statement is a remarkably liberal proposition. Traditionally, the common law has been wary of providing compensation for pure mental suffering.[38] Damages in negligence for personal injury commonly include a non-pecuniary element for pain and suffering, and compensation has also been granted for mental distress consequent upon property damage. But the English courts have been reluctant to countenance recovery for 'free-standing' mental distress, with the exception of psychiatric harm.[39] The judgment in *Phelps* seems to broaden this exception considerably. Inadequate education provision leading to mere 'psychological damage' would henceforth seem to be sufficient to ground a claim. Already, the effects of this liberalism in the House of Lords are being felt at a lower level. In a recent case concerning the alleged failure of a school to prevent the bullying of a child, Garland J held that 'a moderate depressive episode' could constitute the gist of a negligence action in education cases.[40]

The other arm of the purported loss as described by Lord Slynn in *Phelps* is the failure to diagnose a congenital condition. This brings us into new territory, if perhaps, less controversial than for the former type of loss. The argument supporting recoverability seems to be as follows. Dyslexia is a congenital condition of constitutional origin, the consequences of which it is possible to ameliorate by means of specialist educational provision. By analogy with medical cases,[41] the teacher or psychologist can be liable for the consequences of the failure to treat and improve the congenital condition, including the detriment to the child's level of educational attainment and career prospects. This reasoning would not be restricted to the case of dyslexia.[42] Dyslexia is just one of a number of specific learning difficulties for which educational provision is now made. Presumably, similar principles would apply to other specific learning difficulties, such as dyspraxia and attention deficit disorder.

---

[36] *Phelps v Hillingdon LBC* [2000] 3 WLR 776, at 791 and 801.   [37] Ibid, at 791.

[38] See N Mullany and P Handford, *Tort Liability for Psychiatric Harm* (London: Sweet & Maxwell, 1993) 43 ff; ead, *McGregor on Damages*, 16th edn (London: Sweet & Maxwell, 1997), para 90.

[39] *Hinz v Berry* [1970] 2 QB 40, at 42; *White v Chief Constable of South Yorkshire Police* [1999] 2 AC 455, 491.

[40] *Bradford-Smart v West Sussex County Council* [2001] ELR 138.

[41] Such as negligence in failing to diagnose and treat congenital dislocation of the hip: *Arkless v Leicestershire Health Authority* (CA, 22 Oct 1998).

[42] Indeed, in *G (A Minor)*, the claimant suffered from muscular dystrophy.

III. A NEW APPROACH TO PUBLIC AUTHORITY LIABILITY?

The decision in *Phelps* is an important application of the principles of negligence to the teaching of children. The impact of this case will not be limited to the education sphere. This decision both marks a different approach to claims in negligence and is illustrative of broader changes in the sphere of public authority liability. Placing this judgment in a wider context, various trends may be discerned.

A. Shift Away from Duty: A More Sceptical View of Policy Concerns

The concept of a duty of care has traditionally dominated the tort of negligence. And yet, there are many other important constituent elements of the tort of negligence. The recent cases on public authority liability can be interpreted as illustrating a shift away from the predominance of the duty concept.

Over a long period of time, the courts have repeatedly invoked a series of public policy concerns as militating against the imposition of duties of care on public authorities in the exercise of statutory functions.[43] Recently, there have been signs of a more liberal approach. The decision of *Barrett v Enfield LBC* first indicated a change in attitude.[44] The House of Lords showed a certain reluctance to accept the commonly invoked policy concerns to deny a duty of care, and refused to strike out an action in damages for the alleged negligence of social welfare providers in respect of a young boy who had been in their care.

The move away from the restrictive approach has been continued in *Phelps*. In fact, for a number of reasons, this decision may be seen as even more significant than *Barrett*. First, the impact of the decision in *Barrett* was limited by the fact that it concerned an application to strike out a claim. The House of Lords simply decided that the plaintiff had an *arguable* claim that it was just, fair, and reasonable to recognise a duty of care. The *Phelps* case was somewhat different. Although three out of the four appeals in *Phelps* were indeed interlocutory proceedings, the eponymous appeal, *Phelps v Hillingdon LBC*, had actually been to trial. The claim was not merely held to be arguable (as in *Barrett*); it was, in fact, considered to be fully justified and liability was upheld on the basis of concrete facts ascertained at trial. Second, in *Barrett* their Lordships carefully restricted their comments on the policy concerns to the particular circumstances of that case, and explicitly denied doubting the validity of the general policy

---

[43] See, eg, *Elguzouli-Daf v Commissioner of Police* [1995] QB 335; *Hill v Chief Constable of West Yorkshire* [1989] AC 53.

[44] [2001] 2 AC 550.

concerns as enunciated in *X(minors)*.[45] In *Phelps*, the challenge made to the policy concerns was more powerful. Not only was the language used of a particularly robust sort but also the views expressed seem to extend beyond the case at hand. It is not possible to examine here all these policy concerns in great depth, but three important considerations will be examined.

First, the *practical complexities* of actions in tort against public authorities have often been cited by the courts. Such actions often involve complex facts that have occurred many years prior to the bringing of the claim. To establish whether an action should succeed involves time-consuming litigation inevitably diverting resources—both financial and in terms of manpower—from the core activity of public service provision. But should this be a reason for denying a duty of care? Stuart Smith LJ in the Court of Appeal in *Phelps* seemed to think so.[46] The House of Lords disagreed. Lord Clyde argued that the mere fact that there may be practical difficulties in educational cases—such as the large number of witnesses—should not thwart otherwise deserving cases: justice should not be denied on the ground that a claim is of a complex nature.[47] It is difficult not to agree with this view. Evidently, any diversion of resources from frontline activities should be minimised. Where disproportionate legal costs are involved for small sums of compensation, it may well be thought preferable for alternative means of dispute-resolution to prevail, such as recourse to ombudsmen, mediation or settlement. However, it does seem wrong for the courts to preclude a whole class of actions due to their inherent complexity: the claimant cannot be blamed for the fact that his or her claim happens to concern intricate facts or issues which occurred some time in the past.[48]

Secondly, the risk of causing liability-avoiding *defensive practices* has also been invoked on many occasions. Although this concern has featured in numerous judgments,[49] it has by no means been unanimously accepted.[50] Doubt was cast upon this policy factor in the judgments in *Barrett*.[51] In *Phelps*, their Lordships were even more unhappy with this reason for rejecting a duty of care. Lord Clyde felt that rather than encourage a 'peculiarly' defensive attitude, a duty of care would probably increase standards.[52] It is

---

[45] Ibid, at 568.
[46] *Phelps v Hillingdon LBC* [1999] 1 WLR 500, at 522.
[47] [2000] 3 WLR 776, at 809.
[48] See the judgment of Lord Hope in *Three Rivers DC v Bank of England* [2001] UKHL 16 at para 106.
[49] Eg *Elguzouli-Daf v Commissioner of Police* [1995] QB 335, at 349; *Hill v Chief Constable of West Yorkshire* [1989] AC 53, at 63.
[50] See, eg, *Dorset Yacht v Home Office* [1970] AC 1004, at 1032-3; *Capital & Counties plc v Hampshire CC* [1997] QB 1004, at 1043-4.
[51] [2001] 2 AC 550, at 568, 589.
[52] [2000] 3 WLR 776, at 809. See also Lord Slynn's judgment: [2000] 3 WLR 776, at 792.

submitted that the doubts regarding this policy concern are justified.[53] Given that many public servants are protected by their employer from being financially responsible for negligence in the workplace,[54] it is uncertain how powerful the financial fear of liability actually is upon individual behaviour. This policy factor also rests upon questionable logic in the sense that it assumes that those persons subject to the legal duty will misread the standard of behaviour that is required of them and react in an overly cautious manner.

Finally, it has long been a fear of the courts that by recognising new duties of care, a *flood of unfounded claims would thereby be unleashed*. This policy concern is complex,[55] but in this context two manifestations of it can be discerned. First, the key aspect of this policy factor is the fear of a large volume of claims. In the Court of Appeal in *Phelps*, Stuart-Smith LJ was plainly worried by the potential 'proliferation' of education claims.[56] But the Law Lords did not share this concern. Lord Nicholls rejected the 'spectre of a rash of "gold-digging" claims'.[57] Lord Clyde said he did not believe a flood of claims would arise.[58] Despite this confidence, their Lordships provided only limited guidance as to how control mechanisms on liability should be formulated.

A second, and linked, consideration is that the courts will be overburdened with groundless or vexatious claims brought against public bodies. In *Phelps*, Lord Nicholls rejected this in broad fashion, with a phrase which it surely going to be used by a plethora of claimants attempting to break new ground in tort liability: 'Denial of the existence of a cause of action is seldom, if ever, the appropriate response to fear of its abuse.'[59] This is a significant statement. It challenges the predominance of the duty concept in shaping the limits of negligence.[60] If it is inappropriate to reject claims by

---

[53] For critique of this policy concern see Cane, *Tort Law and Economic Interests*, 2nd edn (Oxford: Oxford University Press, 1996), 241–3; B Markesinis, J-B Auby, D Coester-Waltjen, and S Deakin, *Tortious Liability of Statutory Bodies: A Comparative and Economic Analysis of Five English Cases* (Oxford: Hart Publishing, 1999), 78 ff; J Wright, 'Local Authorities, the Duty of Care and the European Convention on Human Rights' (1998) 18 *OJLS* 1, 10–11.

[54] Despite the fundamental English law principle of personal liability of public servants, protection from personal liability is provided by statute for the members and officers of local authorities (Local Government (Miscellaneous Provisions) Act 1976, s 39). Public bodies generally indemnify their employees for personal liability for acts within the course of employment through express stipulation in the employment contract, see *Burgoine v Waltham Forest LBC* (1996) 95 LGR 520.

[55] J Bell, *Policy Arguments in Judicial Decisions* (Oxford: Oxford University Press, 1983), 70 ff. WLR 776, at 792.

[56] *Phelps v Hillingdon LBC* [1999] 1 WLR 500, at 503, 516.

[57] [2000] 3 WLR 776, at 804.

[58] Ibid, at 809.

[59] Ibid, at 804. See also the comments of Lord Slynn: [2000] 3

[60] B Markesinis, 'Plaintiff's tort law or defendant's tort law? Is the House of Lords moving towards a synthesis?' (2001) 9 *Torts Law Journal* 168, 172–3.

denying a duty of care, then the courts will have to find other ways of tracing the contours of legal liability. However, the decision in *Phelps* was somewhat limited when it came to the discussion of the other elements of negligence liability. We will examine these elements in more detail, and look at the way in which they may be employed as control mechanisms to reduce the number of successful claims in the next section.

B. *Shift Away from Duty: Deconstructing the Duty Concept*

There has been a tendency in the past for the courts to merge disparate elements of the tort of negligence within the amorphous duty concept. This can be seen in two particular instances. First, in numerous public authority liability cases, it has been held that a duty should not arise because public servants were involved in difficult and delicate tasks, for instance social workers dealing with children at risk of abuse.[61] No one would deny the need to take account of the sensitivity of these tasks, and the desirability of allowing those who undertake them a margin of discretion. It is not self-evident however that these concerns should be used to exclude liability entirely. It would seem more appropriate to accommodate the difficulty of the task by modulating the standard of care.[62] The second example of this phenomenon is the injection of causal considerations into the duty concept. Stuart-Smith LJ in the Court of Appeal in *Phelps* argued that one of the policy reasons militating against a duty of care was that there were significant difficulties in attributing causation in these education cases.[63] Again, it is not obvious why these difficulties should *entirely* deny actionability. In the sphere of medical malpractice, attributing causation is a complex and technical matter,[64] and yet this has not prevented the recognition of a duty of care.

The cumulative effect of the cases of *Barrett* and *Phelps* has been to reverse this trend. Their Lordships emphasised that the complexity of decision-making is to be taken into account at the breach level,[65] and the difficulties in establishing a causal connection should not be allowed to stand in the way of the presentation of a proper claim.[66] The courts have thus undertaken a deconstruction of the duty concept, separating from it extraneous concerns and ensuring that issues which go to breach and causation are addressed as independent elements of the liability equation.

[61] *X(Minors) v Bedfordshire CC* [1995] 2 AC 633, 750.
[62] MJ Bowman and SH Bailey, 'Negligence in the Realms of Public Law-A Positive Obligation to Rescue?' [1984] *PL* 277, 306.
[63] *Phelps v Hillingdon LBC* [1999] 1 WLR 500, at 522–3.
[64] B Markesinis and S Deakin, *Tort Law*, 4th edn (Oxford: Oxford University Press, 1999), 289.
[65] *Phelps* [2000] 3 WLR 776, at 792, 809; *Barrett* [1999] 3 All ER 193, at 230.
[66] *Phelps* [2000] 3 WLR 776, at 791 and 809.

C. Re-assessing the Relationship between ultra vires and Liability in Tort

The relationship between public law unlawfulness and liability in negligence is a complex one.[67] An *ultra vires* administrative act that causes loss is not a *sufficient* condition of administrative liability.[68] Satisfying the conditions for annulment in a judicial review action does not equate with wrongfulness as expressed in the breach of a duty of care in negligence. A controversial question is whether it is a *necessary* precondition of liability to show that the administrative act is *ultra vires*. Must claimants prove public law invalidity as a prerequisite of liability in negligence of public authorities? If so, then given the restrictive heads of judicial review, this would constitute an effective control mechanism on liability.

In the landmark case of *X(minors)*, Lord Browne-Wilkinson initially rejected any role for *ultra vires*, denying that it was 'either helpful or necessary to introduce public law concepts as to the validity of a decision into the question of liability at common law for negligence'.[69] However, he went on to state that there could be no liability unless 'the decision complained of is so unreasonable that it falls outside the ambit of the discretion conferred upon the local authority'.[70] Lord Browne-Wilkinson's interpretation of this tenet was controversial. It is clear in his judgment that he envisaged a standard akin to *Wednesbury* unreasonableness,[71] which would in its orthodox interpretation involve showing that the public body's action was so unreasonable that no reasonable body could have taken it. Later in his judgment, Lord Browne-Wilkinson indicated that the requisite level of carelessness would only be committed by a 'grossly delinquent authority'.[72]

This resulted in a paradox. Whilst doubting the relevance of any public law notions of invalidity in the tort of negligence, Lord Browne-Wilkinson nonetheless ushered in a specific head of unlawfulness to play an important role in negligence actions against public authorities. The introduction of the *Wednesbury* principle into negligence actions was controversial.[73] It was

---

[67] Generally, see M Andenas and D Fairgrieve, 'Sufficiently Serious?', in M Andenas (ed), *English Public Law and the Common Law of Europe* (London: Key Haven, 1998); S Arrowsmith, *Civil Liability and Public Authorities* (Winteringham: Earlsgate, 1992); De Smith, Woolf and Jowell's *Principles of Judicial Review* (London: Sweet & Maxwell, 1999), ch 16.

[68] *X(Minors) v Bedfordshire CC* [1995] 2 AC 633, 730. Although this is being challenged by European Community law and human rights law, see M Amos, 'Extending the liability of the state in damages' [2001] LS 1.

[69] [1995] 2 AC 633, at 736.   [70] Ibid, at 736.

[71] Ibid, at 736 and 761. This standard of unreasonableness derives from Lord Greene's judgment in *Associated Provincial Picture Houses Ltd v Wednesbury Corporation* [1948] 1 KB 223.

[72] [1995] 2 AC 633, at 761.

[73] See J Wright, 'Local Authorities, the Duty of Care and the European Convention on Human Rights' (1998) 18 *OJLS* 1, 6.

unfair because it was a very high standard of unreasonableness to require,[74] and it was *inflexible* in the sense that it focused on the substance of the decision taken, neglecting actions concerning procedural violations[75] or the failure to take into account relevant considerations.[76]

In *Barrett*, the House of Lords took a different view of the role of unlawfulness. Lord Slynn confessed that he shared Lord Browne-Wilkinson's reluctance to inject administrative law notions into the law of negligence.[77] His Lordship argued that the test of invalidity was not conclusive: it is the normal conditions of a duty of care as set out in *Caparo Industries plc v Dickman*[78] that must be satisfied. Lord Hutton was even more explicit in asserting the autonomy of negligence from administrative law notions of invalidity. He held that the courts should apply the common law concept of negligence rather than stipulating *Wednesbury* unreasonableness as a precondition of liability.[79] Their Lordships seem to have intended to expunge public law concepts of invalidity from this area of the law. This approach was confirmed in *Phelps*. Lord Slynn again emphasised the primacy of the common law principles of negligence.[80] Lord Nicholls applied principles of professional negligence to this area of the law.[81]

The movement away from invalidity as a precondition for an action in negligence against public authorities is a welcomed rationalisation of this area of the law. This does not mean that the public law context will be neglected. Account will still be taken of the public law backdrop in shaping the duty of care,[82] and setting the standard of breach.[83] No duty may be recognised if it would interfere with the performance of the local education authority's statutory duties.[84] There is however one area in which the role of public law unlawfulness is not entirely resolved. In the case of a failure to exercise statutory powers, the courts are wary of imposing negligence unless it is shown that it was *irrational* for the authority not have exercised the statutory powers.[85]

---

[74] Andenas and Fairgrieve, 'Sufficiently Serious?', 306.

[75] P Cane, 'Suing Public Authorities in Tort' (1996) 112 *LQR* 13, at 16–17.

[76] See T Hickman, 'Making Public Bodies liable for Failure to confer benefits' [2000] CLJ 432, at 434.

[77] [2001] 2 AC 550, at 571–2.   [78] [1990] 2 AC 605.

[79] [2001] 2 AC 550, 586.

[80] An action should only be excluded where the impugned acts are not justiciable: [2000] 3 WLR 776, at 790.

[81] [2000] 3 WLR 776, at 802 ff.

[82] *Phelps v Hillingdon LBC* [2000] 3 WLR 776, at 810.

[83] Ibid, at 792, 809; *Barrett v Enfield LBC* [2001] 2 AC 550, 591.

[84] *Phelps v Hillingdon LBC* [2000] 3 WLR 776, at 790, 810.

[85] See *Stovin v Wise* [1996] AC 923, at 953. Lord Hoffmann also added the pre-condition that there must be exceptional grounds for holding that the policy of the statute was to confer the right to compensation on those who suffered loss if the power was not exercised. This controversial latter condition was no longer mentioned in the parallel case of *Larner v Solihull MBC* (CA, 20 Dec 2000).

D. *The Influence of European Human Rights Law*

No analysis of state liability can be complete without a consideration of the influence of human rights law.[86] To assess the effect of the European Court of Human Right's (ECtHR) case law on the tort of negligence, two recent cases must be examined, *Osman v UK*, and *Z v UK*. The ECtHR case of *Osman* arose from an application of the rule established in *Hill v Chief Constable of West Yorkshire*[87] precluding actions against the police for alleged negligence in the investigation and suppression of crime. A teacher had become obsessed with his pupil, and proceeded to harass the boy, his family and friends. Tragically, this course of events resulted in the teacher shooting and injuring two people, including the pupil, and killing two others. The police had been contacted on several occasions about the teacher's seriously aberrant behaviour, but failed to arrest him. A claim in negligence against the police was struck out by the Court of Appeal on the basis of the *Hill* rule.[88] The claim then proceeded to Strasbourg. The ECtHR found that the application of the *Hill* exclusionary rule in this case was contrary to the right of access to court enshrined in Article 6(1) of the European Convention on Human Rights (ECHR).[89] The exclusionary rule was disproportionate to the declared policy aims of maintaining the effectiveness of police. A plaintiff should be able to go to trial to argue on the merits that other policy considerations should prevail, such as the gravity of the defendant's fault and seriousness of injury.

The reaction of commentators was generally critical of the ECtHR's reasoning in *Osman*,[90] with some suggesting that the court had misconceived the rules for determining duties of care in English law, and others arguing that an essentially procedural protection had been transformed into a power to challenge the scope of substantive rights within contracting states, rights which were not protected independently under the Convention.[91] Once the Human Rights Act 1998 came into force, the domestic courts were obliged to take account of the ECtHR's interpretation of the convention rights.[92] Some members of the senior judiciary were crit-

---

[86] For a broader discussion of the impact of human rights law on tort law, see J Wright, *Tort Law and Human Rights* (Oxford: Hart Publishing, 2001).

[87] [1989] AC 53.

[88] *Osman v Ferguson* [1993] 4 All ER 344.

[89] *Osman v UK* [1999] 1 FLR 193.

[90] See, eg, M Lunney, 'A Tort Lawyer's View of Osman v United Kingdom' (1999) 10 *KCLJ* 238; Weir, 'Down Hill—All The Way?' [1999] *CLJ* 4; C Gearty, 'Unravelling Osman' (2000) 64 *MLR* 159. But cf L Hoyano, 'Policing Flawed Police Investigations: Unravelling the Blanket' (1999) 62 *MLR* 912.

[91] P Craig and D Fairgrieve, 'Barrett, Negligence and Discretionary Powers' [1999] *PL* 626, 630.

[92] Section 2(1) HRA.

ical of the decision in *Osman*,[93] but the decision has seemed to play a role—albeit almost invisible[94]—in the courts' recent shift to a more liberal view of public authority liability.[95]

Account must also be taken of the recent decision of the ECtHR in *Z v UK*.[96] *Z v UK* arose out of the House of Lords' decision in *X(minors) v Bedfordshire CC*, which has already been mentioned in relation to education negligence. Two other appeals in this case concerned the manner in which local authorities dealt with child abuse; the complaint in *X(minors)* being that the local authority had failed to take children into care quickly enough and left them with abusive and neglectful parents for too long. The House of Lords struck out the claim in negligence on the basis that it was not fair, just and reasonable to admit a duty of care.[97] When this case itself went to Strasbourg, the ECtHR concluded that the United Kingdom was in breach of Article 3 ECHR as the local authority had failed to provide the claimants with appropriate protection against serious long-term neglect and abuse, and was also in breach of Article 13 as the applicants had not been afforded an effective remedy for the breach of Article 3.

The ECtHR decided however that Article 6 had not been violated.[98] It was held that its own reasoning in *Osman* had to be reviewed in the light of the 'clarification' made by domestic courts that the fair, just and reasonable criterion was indeed an intrinsic element of the duty of care. In *X(minors)*, the applicants were not prevented in any practical manner from bringing their claims before the domestic courts. The House of Lords had undertaken a careful balancing of the policy concerns at the fair, just, and reasonable level. The inability of the applicants to sue the local authority flowed not from an immunity but from the applicable principles governing the substantive right of action in domestic law. The strike out procedure did not *per se* offend the principle of access to court.

It not possible here to provide an exhaustive analysis of the developments before the ECtHR, but a number of points should be made. It should be noted how adroitly the ECtHR has responded to the domestic disquiet about the *Osman* decision. Indeed, the decision in *Z v UK* is remarkable in

---

[93] Lord Browne-Wilkinson said in *Barrett v Enfield LBC* that he found the decision 'extremely difficult to understand', and described the state in which English law had been left in the wake of that judgment as 'very unsatisfactory'. See also Lord Hoffmann's extrajudicial comments: 'Human Rights and the House of Lords' (1999) 62 *MLR* 159.

[94] The issue was raised by counsel in a series of appeals before the House of Lords, but rarely featured in judgments, see however Lord Clyde's brief comment in *Phelps v Hillingdon LBC* [2000] 3 WLR 776, 808–9, and Lord Cooke in *Darker v Chief Constable of West Midlands* [2001] 1 AC 435, 455.

[95] See comments of Lord Woolf in *Kent v Griffiths* [2001] QB 36, 50.

[96] [2001] 2 FLR 612. See J Wright, *Tort Law and Human Rights*; J Miles, 'Human rights and child protection' [2001] *CFLQ* 431.

[97] [1995] 2 AC 633. A claim on the basis of breach of statutory duty was also struck out.

[98] [2001] 2 FLR 612, paras 95–101.

that it provides some satisfaction to all parties to the litigation. The applicants established the breach of important Articles of the Convention, and obtained significant compensation.[99] The Government can be satisfied by the fact that they avoided the breach of Article 6 ECHR, their main contention in the case.[100] Likewise, those commentators who had been most vociferous in their critique of *Osman*, will be pleased by this latest decision.

Even though the ECtHR appears to have retreated from the *Osman* decision in its disavowal of Article 6 in *Z v UK*, this does not necessarily undermine the more liberal approach to public authority liability in English law. First, the failure of the House of Lords explicitly to base the decisions in *Barrett* and *Phelps* upon *Osman*, allows these cases to enjoy a continued vitality, which might otherwise have been called into question. Secondly, the European Court in *Z v UK* did place some emphasis upon the recent developments in English tort law as underpinning its retreat from *Osman*;[101] indicating that these decisions were illustrative of a careful balancing of policy concerns which was sensitive to different factual situations, far from amounting to a blanket immunity denying access to Court contrary to Article 6 ECHR. This reasoning of the ECtHR can only support and encourage the English courts' more nuanced approach to policy concerns.

Indeed, it might well be argued that the decision in *Z v UK* will actually prove to be a further liberalising force. There are various possible ways in which the English courts may take account of the ECtHR decision concerning the breach of Article 13.[102] The minimalist response to the decision in *Z v UK* would simply be to say that an effective remedy is now provided by the Human Rights Act (HRA), under which the courts have gained a power to grant damages as a remedy for the breach of a Convention right by a public authority.[103] Although this may well be a valid response to the ECtHR decision,[104] one could also argue for a broader impact. It would make sense for human rights breaches to be remedied not only by the provision of damages under the HRA—which it is important to underline is perceived as a residual remedy[105]—but also through orthodox tort law by means of the continuing evolution of the fair, just and reasonableness limb

---

[99] The compensation accorded was the highest award so far for personal injury by EctHR.

[100] Indeed, they had conceded breach of the other Articles.

[101] Referring explicitly to *W v Essex CC* [1999] Fam 90, and Barrett.

[102] As they are statutorily obliged to do: ss 2(1) and 8(4) HRA.

[103] By virtue of s 8 HRA. See further M Amos, 'Damages for Breach of the Human Rights Act 1998' [1999] *EHRLR* 178; D Fairgrieve, 'The Human Rights Act 1998, Damages and Tort Law' [2001] *PL* 695.

[104] Note however that the HRA will not provide a remedy for those who sustained their injuries before 2 Oct 2000 and who will still be left without an effective remedy on the basis of *X(Minors)*. See discussion in J Wright, Tort Law and Human Rights, xxxiv.

[105] I Leigh and L Lustgarten, 'Making Rights Real: the Courts, Remedies and the Human Rights Act' [1999] *CLJ* 509, 527.

of the tort of negligence. Not only would this harmonised approach avoid the courts adopting a different response to the same factual circumstances—depending upon whether the remedy was based on the HRA or on the tort of negligence—but it would also encourage the process of weaving the Convention rights into domestic law,[106] by developing tort law in line with the new human rights considerations.

IV. CONTROLLING THE EXTENT OF LIABILITY

We have seen that the *Phelps* decision may be seen as illustrating a shift away from the duty concept as the overriding control mechanism in the tort of negligence. This decision is by no means an isolated example of this phenomenon. There is in fact a good deal of evidence that the courts are now more willing to recognise duties of care in the sphere of public authority liability.[107] Other control mechanisms will be needed in order to ensure that the claims are kept within reasonable bounds. In *Phelps* their Lordships made much of the fact that education claims should not be allowed to get out of hand,[108] but only limited guidance was given as to how the control mechanisms should be formulated. This question will be addressed in this section. The focus of the discussion will be upon the education sphere, but much of the discussion will also apply to public authority liability generally.

A. Breach of Duty

The standard of care in negligence is an objective one, and this expresses itself as a duty to take reasonable care.[109] For professionals the *Bolam* test of breach applies which means that claimants must show that the professional concerned did not exercise the skills of a competent professional and failed to act in accordance with the accepted views of a substantial reputable body of opinion.[110] The *Bolam* test of breach grants a measure of protection to professionals, by virtue of the deference the courts make to the standards the professions set.[111] So, in medical malpractice cases, it has

---

[106] A Lester and D Pannick, 'The Impact of the Human Rights Act on Private Law: the Knight's Move' [2000] 116 *LQR* 380, 383.

[107] See, eg, *S v Gloucestershire CC* [2001] 2 WLR 909; *Larner v Solihull MBC* (CA, 20 Dec 2000); *L and P v Reading BC* [2001] 2 FLR 50.

[108] [2000] 3 WLR 776, at 792 (Lord Slynn), 804 (Lord Nicholls).

[109] Generally, see Markesinis and Deakin, *Tort Law*, 155 et seq.

[110] *Bolam v Friern Hospital Management Committee* [1957] 1 WLR 582. There is some limited scope for the courts to review the reasonableness of the professional standards, see *Bolitho v City and Hackney Health Authority* [1998] AC 232, at 241–3.

[111] Cane, *The Anatomy of Tort Law*, 41; A Dugdale and KM Stanton, *Professional Negligence* (London: Butterworths, 1998), para 15.19.

often been remarked that showing negligence is a significant obstacle for claimants to overcome.[112] This protective element is also reflected in the judgments in *Phelps*. Lord Slynn stated that negligence should not be found too readily,[113] and Lord Clyde argued that the *Bolam* test is 'deliberately and properly a high standard'.[114]

In the education sphere, the *Bolam* test is likely to eliminate a good deal of claims for a number of reasons. First, in setting and applying the standard of care, it is recognised by the courts that teaching is not an exact science, and there are many appropriate ways of teaching children. This is particularly important in the special needs sphere, where the evolving attitude to diagnosis and treatment has encouraged a diversity of acceptable approaches.[115] Secondly, the standard of care will be tailored to the circumstances of the case, the role of the person involved and the task they were undertaking. So, a teacher will not be expected to act to the standard of an educational psychologist.[116] Account will also be taken of the fact that education professionals are exercising discretions conferred by statute in a sphere involving the taking of difficult decisions with limited time and resources.[117]

There are a number of concrete examples of the standard of care in negligence being used to thwart claims at trial in public authority liability cases generally. In *Swinney v Chief Constable of Northumbria Police*, a duty of the police to take care in their crime detection activities was recognised at a time when such duties were restrictively formulated, but the action ultimately failed at trial for lack of breach of the standard of care.[118] There are a number of similar examples.[119] However, these claims have only been dismissed once the defendants have financed a trip to trial. The crucial question that arises is whether defendants can repel claims on the basis of lack of breach without incurring the expense of going to trial. In order to answer this point, it is necessary to analyse some aspects of civil procedure. Under the Civil Procedure Rules 1998, a claim can be dismissed by means of a strike-out action *inter alia* if the statement of case discloses no reasonable grounds for bringing or defending the claim,[120] or by means of a

---

[112] Markesinis and Deakin, Tort Law, 159; RA Buckley, *The Modern Law of Negligence*, 3rd edn (London: Butterworths, 1999), para 15.06.

[113] [2000] 3 *WLR* 776, at 792.   [114] [2000] 3 WLR 776, at 809.

[115] *X(Minors)* [1995] 2 AC 633, at 763; *Phelps v Hillingdon LBC* [2000] 3 WLR 776, at 809.

[116] *Phelps v Hillingdon LBC* [2000] 3 WLR 776, at 803.

[117] See Lord Hutton's judgment in *Barrett v Enfield LBC* [2001] 2 AC 550, 591.

[118] *Swinney v Chief Constable of Northumbria Police* (No 1) [1997] AC 464 (strike-out action); *Swinney v Chief Constable of Northumbria Police* (No 2) The Times 25 May 1999 (at trial).

[119] Bradford-Smart v West Sussex CC [2001] ELR 138; *H v Isle of Wight Council* (QBD, 23 Feb 2001); *Larner v Solihull MBC* (CA, 20 Dec 2000).

[120] Rule 3.4(2)(a) CPR.

summary judgment if the court considers that the claimant has no real prospect of succeeding on the claim or issue and that there is no other reason why the case or issue should be disposed of at a trial.[121] A crucial difference with the previous regime of procedural rules is that evidence can now be adduced in support of either of these applications.[122] The courts are no longer restricted to the facts as enunciated in the claimant's statement of case: they may go further and examine concrete evidence such as witness statements.

The new approach under the CPR broadens the grounds on which a negligence claim can be dismissed, such as for lack of breach, rather than merely for want of an arguable duty of care. This is exemplified by the Court of Appeal decision in *S v Gloucestershire CC* concerning two joined appeals.[123] The claimants in both appeals claimed damages for the injuries caused due to sexual abuse by their foster-fathers. They both alleged that the local authorities had acted negligently in placing them with these foster parents and in the subsequent monitoring of their placements. In respect of the claim in *S v Gloucestershire CC*, May LJ refused to strike out the cause of action as his Lordship considered that the issues of duty and breach could not be decided until the facts had been determined at trial. In respect of the other joined appeal, *L v Tower Hamlets LBC and Havering LBC*, it was recognised that there was an arguable duty of care. However, after looking carefully at the facts as established by the evidence—which consisted mainly of documents disclosed by the local authorities—May LJ decided that the claimant had no real prospect of showing a *breach* of the standard of care. Summary judgment was thus given in favour of the defendants.

This case illustrates how the summary judgment procedure may be used as a means for dismissing actions for want of breach. There are, however, some restrictive conditions that must be satisfied before the courts can make such a summary judgment. In essence, these are that all substantial facts relevant to the allegations of negligence are before the court and that there is no real prospect of successfully disputing them.[124] This procedure might be one response to Lord Nicholls's desire for the courts to develop tools which allow for the weeding out of hopeless claims whilst at the same time ensuring that they have a sufficiently full factual picture of all the circumstances of the case.[125]

---

[121] Rule 24.2 CPR.   [122] See Rule 24.5 CPR.

[123] [2001] 2 WLR 909.

[124] [2001] 2 WLR 909, at 936. May LJ also recognised that there may be cases where a summary judgment could be given even if there was a gap in evidence, 'where the court concludes, for instance from the passage of time, that there is no real prospect of the gaps being filled', ibid.

[125] *Phelps v Hillingdon LBC* [2000] 3 WLR 776, at 804.

B. Causation

Many public authority liability cases raise very complex questions of causation. In education cases, it will often be very difficult for children to show that *but for* the educator's wrongful act he or she would have made better educational progress, obtained better results and enjoyed enhanced career prospects. As was pointed out by Lord Nicholls in *Phelps*, there are a myriad of factors which determine a child's educational progress, many of which the school has no control over, for instance emotional stress and the home environment.[126] Moreover, from an evidential point of view, the delay in bringing claims and the consequent absence or inadequacy of the records will pose a natural obstacle to actions.[127]

The educational sphere is not the only one in which difficulties may arise in establishing the causal link. In the social welfare sphere, the courts have underlined the difficulties of showing that local authorities' negligent treatment of children in care actually *caused* compensatable damage.[128] In medical cases, proving that negligence caused the victim's hurt is often a formidable obstacle for claimants to surmount.[129] In a recent case concerning the failure of a highway authority to provide for additional advanced warning signs at a dangerous road junction,[130] the Court of Appeal adopted a more liberal approach to duty than in previous cases,[131] underlining that it was possible to restrict claims through the use of breach and causation. Causation may also prove to be a formidable control mechanism in claims for damages under the Human Rights Act 1998. A strand of the case law of the European Court of Human Rights illustrates a strict approach to causation.[132]

There are, however, weaknesses in relying upon causation to dismiss actions. Due to the highly factual nature of determining the causal link, this question is generally not suited for decision at an early stage of proceedings.[133]

---

[126] [2000] 3 WLR 776, at 805.

[127] See J Greenwold, 'Lawyers in the Classroom', 245, at 249; M Harris, 'Education and Local Authorities' (2001) 117 *LQR* 25, at 28; B Markesinis, 'Plaintiff's tort law or defendant's tort law? Is the House of Lords moving towards a synthesis?' (2001) 9 *Torts Law Journal* 168 at 174.

[128] See *Barrett v Enfield LBC* [2001] 2 AC 550, at 574, 590.

[129] B Markesinis and S Deakin, *Tort Law*, 289.

[130] *Larner v Solihull MBC* (CA, 20 Dec 2000).

[131] Namely, *Stovin v Wise* [1996] AC 923.

[132] Law Commission and Scottish Law Commission, Damages under the Human Rights Act 1998 (Law Com No 266, 2000; Scottish Law Com No 180, 2000), para 3.58.

[133] *Three Rivers DC v Bank of England* [2001] UKHL 16, at paras 43 and 108; *Barrett v Enfield LBC* [2001] 2 AC 550, at 574–5, 590.

C. Duty and Loss: Damages for Poor Teaching?

We have already seen that the decision in *Phelps* was remarkably broad in terms of loss, allowing recovery for psychological damage and failure to diagnose a congenital condition, such as dyslexia. How much further should the duty on the part of the teachers extend? If damages may be obtained for the failure to ameliorate specific learning difficulties, how will the courts respond to claims that schools have failed to enhance the educational attainment of children without specific learning difficulties?

This question was addressed squarely by Lord Nicholls in *Phelps*. His Lordship argued that the law would be in an extraordinary state if teachers owed duties of care to some of their pupils but not others.[134] Teachers must owe a duty to all their pupils in the way they discharged their teaching responsibilities. Lord Nicholls gave an example of circumstances in which a claim might arise, where a teacher carelessly taught the wrong syllabus for an external examination, and provable financial loss follows.[135] This example is not likely to entail huge financial consequences. The proper syllabus can always be taught; the examination re-taken. In such a situation, the teacher's fault is unlikely to have the same long-term consequences as the failure to diagnose and treat a specific educational need, in which one can attribute a good deal of the problems of the child's educational career to an error in diagnosing and treating a specific problem. Lord Nicholls went on to lay down some tentative criteria for claims brought by children with ordinary educational needs. His Lordship contrasted general claims concerning the poor quality of teaching ('generalised educational malpractice' claims) in which liability should not arise, with claims that concern specific and identifiable mistakes.[136] It was left for courts in future cases to flesh out what is, at present, a rather vague distinction.

D. The Measure of Damages

Linked to the two previous sections is the question of the quantum of damages. This is a complex issue in education cases and one that has yet to be authoritatively addressed by the courts. Particular difficulties will arise in measuring the quantum of lost earnings and non-pecuniary loss.

In terms of lost revenue, it might be argued that in many cases it will be difficult for special needs claimants to show that the education failure ultimately caused the loss.[137] Given that those with certain types of educational special needs, such as dyslexia, can be tutored to overcome at least part of

---

[134] [2000] 3 WLR 776, at 804.   [135] Ibid, at 804.   [136] Ibid, at 804–5.
[137] See comments of Otton LJ in the Court of Appeal: *Phelps v Hillingdon LBC* [1999] 1 WLR 500, at 527.

their disabilities, it may even be thought appropriate for damages to be primarily devised for compensatory education such as private tutoring.[138] However, the House of Lords in *Phelps* upheld the decision of the Garland J in which an award was made for damages for future loss of earnings and loss of congenial employment despite the evident uncertainties about what the claimants prospects would have been if she had received appropriate teaching. But little guidance was given by the House of Lords about the appropriate method of calculation. This will no doubt be a future task for the courts even though—as with other cases in which children have been injured—a 'broad brush' approach is likely to prevail.[139]

Education failure leading merely to upset or minor behavioural problems is unlikely to be actionable.[140] But the House of Lords gave its approbation to the recovery of psychological damage, and this has already lead to dicta that 'a moderate depressive episode' could constitute the gist of a negligence action in education cases.[141] Determining the quantum of such loss will be a difficult task, and some parameters for the quantum of non-pecuniary damage will need to be settled.[142] The quantum of non-pecuniary loss in ordinary dyslexia cases is unlikely to be high; currently the guideline range for minor to moderate psychiatric damage is £500–£9,000.[143]

E. Public Funding

Education claims will invariably be expensive and complex. Many potential claimants will be unable to finance these privately. Some may try to gain public funding, but the evidence suggests that there will be substantial obstacles to cross. Under the legal aid rules, claimants making allegations of negligently caused injury are now no longer eligible for legal aid.[144] The

---

[138] Drawing inspiration from foreign law: Robert E Rains, 'Primer on Special Education Law in the US' (1998) *Education and the Law* 205, 222.

[139] *Coxon v Flintshire CC* [2001] EWCA CIV 302 (concerning child abuse).

[140] See the judgment of Bingham LJ in the Court of Appeal in *E (a minor) v Dorset CC* [1995] 2 AC 633, at 703.

[141] *Bradford-Smart v West Sussex CC* [2001] ELR 138.

[142] Analogous difficulties have been overcome by the courts in other spheres, for instance psychiatric harm.

[143] Judicial Studies Board, *Guidelines for the Assessment of General Damages in Personal Injury Cases*, 4th edn (London, 1998), 9–11. Note, however, that the Court of Appeal has held that in child abuse cases, it is doubtful whether the JSB guidelines should apply as the injuries 'fall into a wholly different category from psychiatric damage that follows other personal injuries' (*Coxon v Flintshire CC* [2001] EWCA CIV 302).

[144] Unless they relate to clinical negligence (see Para 1(a) of Schedule 2 of the Access to Justice Act 1999). There are also some exceptions to this exclusion in the case of proceedings against public authorities which involve serious wrongdoing, abuse of position or power, or significant breach of human rights or where there is a significant wider public interest: Scope of the Community Legal Service Fund: Lord Chancellor's Guidance (Lord Chancellor's Department, 2 Apr 2001), paras 7–10.

Legal Services Commission has stated however that *Phelps*-style claims will not be *automatically* excluded under the operation of this rule,[145] but they will instead be subject to the restrictive general criteria for the grant of legal aid.[146] An award for full legal representation will only be given if an attempt has been made to secure a conditional fee agreement and it is shown that this was not viable for the individual case.[147]

V. CONCLUSION

Recent cases illustrate a decisive move away from blanket exclusions of duties of care for public services. This shift towards a more 'consumerist vision of public liability'[148] is to be applauded.[149] It reflects developments in society: we live in an age of transparency, accountability, and standards-setting. This is illustrated in the education sphere by greater private sector involvement, enhanced parental choice, and partnership between 'education professionals' and parents.[150] It is therefore not surprising that the decision in *Phelps* is based upon the belief that the rules of professional negligence should be applied to teachers, and that it would be undesirable to draw a distinction between private and public sectors in the application of the rules of liability.

Litigation in the education sphere should however be minimised. The provision of risk management, training and better frontline services would help reduce the need for recourse to the courts, as supported by recent academic research conducted by educational psychologists.[151] Where things have gone wrong, some complaints may be better dealt with by the Local Government Ombudsman, which is a cheaper and quicker procedure than litigation,[152] even if the amounts recovered are likely to be less significant.[153] Despite these techniques, it should be acknowledged that the new approach to duties of care in the education sphere is likely to lead to a rise

---

[145] See Para 21.6 of The Funding Code—Decision Making Guidance (May 2001).

[146] In terms of prospects of success and cost–benefit. Ibid.

[147] Ibid, paras 10.2 and 21.6.

[148] B Markesinis, 'Plaintiff's tort law or defendant's tort law?', 168, at 178.

[149] For a different view, see A Mullis, 'Phelps v Hillingdon London Borough Council: A rod for the hunch-backed teacher?' [2001] *CFLQ* 331.

[150] J Greenwold, 'Lawyers in the Classroom', 245 at 252 et seq.

[151] G Williams, 'Professional negligence: issues for educational psychology services and case-work practitioners', Paper presented at the University of Birmingham Educational Psychologist professional training course (Nov 2001).

[152] Eg, Report 95/B/2431 cited in the Commission's Digest of Cases 1996, Section B: Education (London, 1997).

[153] Compensation for loss of future earnings would not be awarded. The actual cost of making the educational provision for the period during which the maladministration occurred has been suggested as an appropriate measure of quantum: Commission for Local Administration in England, Guidance on Good Practice 6: Remedies (London, 1997), para 22.

in litigation and an increase in costs for educational authorities both in terms of paying settlements and defending claims.[154] Is this, in Lord Browne-Wilkinson's words, the 'price which might have to be paid in the interests of justice'?[155]

[154] See the comments of a practitioner: J Goodman, 'The Final judgment on "failure to educate claims": a lawyer in every classroom?' Barlow, Lyde and Gilbert Briefing Note, Aug 2001.
[155] *X(Minors) v Bedfordshire CC* [1995] 2 AC 633, at 762.

16. LIABILITY OF PUBLIC AUTHORITIES AND PUBLIC SERVANTS: ISRAELI LAW

*Israel Gilead**

I. INTRODUCTION

Originally, the Civil Wrongs Ordinance (CWO),[1] allowed no action against the state in respect to any civil wrong.[2] This rule, based on the misplaced concept that 'The King can do no wrong', was remedied by the Civil Wrongs (Liability of the State) Law, 1952 (State Liability Law). The Law abolished the blanket immunity formerly enjoyed by the state, by providing that the state, subject to statutory exceptions, is to be regarded as any other corporate body for the purpose of civil tort liability.[3] This principle also applies to all governmental bodies other than the state: namely, municipalities and numerous statutory corporations that over time assumed functions and statutory powers formerly exercised by the state.[4] The statutory exceptions to the general rule of liability, as we shall see, are limited in scope and were thus interpreted, so the delicate task of setting the boundaries of governmental tort liability has been transferred to the courts.

In this regard a distinction should be made between the different capacities under which public authorities operate. When a public authority operates in a corporate or a proprietary capacity it is subject to the general law of torts in the same way as any other corporate body or private individual. This 'rule of equality' applies, for example, to a public authority with regard to safety in the workplace, motor vehicles, operation of State hospitals, and possession of dangerous premises. When the public authority operates in its unique governmental capacity, namely, exercising statutory powers, the analogy may break down, as no other 'private' corporation or individual exercises the same powers or conducts the same activities. The

---

* Dean, Bora Laskin Professor of Law, Faculty of Law, Hebrew University of Jerusalem.
[1] The Civil Wrongs Ordinance (CWO), enacted by the British Mandatory authorities in 1947, is, to this day, the heart of Israeli tort law. The CWO was promulgated by the British Mandate authorities on 28 Dec 1944 and became effective, after being amended, on 15 July 1947. Its original English version, known as the Civil Wrongs Ordinance, 1944, was replaced on 1 Oct 1968 by an official Hebrew version, the Civil Wrongs Ordinance (New Version).
[2] CWO (1944), s 4 (1).
[3] Section 2.
[4] Eg, The Broadcasting Authority, Airports Authority, Natural Reserves Authority, and National Insurance Institute.

question is whether in these exclusive fields of governmental activity special rules should apply. Israeli courts dealt with this question mainly in the context of negligence and breach of statutory duty, as most claims regarding exercise of statutory powers have been filed under these general torts.

As the exercise of statutory powers is also governed by administrative law (a field of public law), a question arises as to the interrelation between the rules of public law, applied by courts in their administrative capacity, and the rules of private law, applied by the courts in tort litigation.

Yet another question which arises is the extent to which public employees should be held personally liable for torts committed in the course of their employment. This issue relates to the nature of the public authorities' liability—whether it is vicarious, personal or both.

Section 2 introduces the notion of statutory immunities, the exceptions to the general rule of liability. Section 3 presents the interrelations between public law and tort law. Section 4 states the arguments for and against tort liability of governmental authorities. These policy considerations, in the final analysis, aid in marking the boundaries of liability. Section 5 presents the legal tools used by courts to control the scope of liability—the concepts and distinctions employed for the extension or the narrowing of liability. Sections 6 to 10 discuss the different phases in the development of the judicial approach toward governmental liability, including the effect of the Basic Law: Human Dignity and Freedom. Finally, Section 11 addresses the question of personal liability of public employees.

II. STATUTORY IMMUNITIES

A. General Immunities

The CWO provides for few immunities with general application: 'act under enactment' and 'scope of legal authority'. It also provides for a number of specific immunities protecting the 'judicial authority' and officials executing lawful arrest, search etc.[5] Other statutory provisions establish special immunities protecting, for example, the President, Parliament (Kenesset) Members and members of the diplomatic and consular corps. Different defences may overlap. Generally speaking, courts tend to interpret statutory immunities in a way that narrows their scope.[6]

---

[5] CWO, ss 24, 27. These defences, against assault and false imprisonment, can be found in Criminal Procedure legislation

[6] *Me'orer v Northern Galilee Regional Council* (1966) 20 (iii) PD (*Piskei Din*—The official reporter of the Supreme Court of Israel) 645—narrowing the scope of an immunity regarding damage caused due to cattle diseases.

B. Scope of Legal Authority

The CWO sets forth the principle that a public servant is personally responsible for any civil wrong he commits.[7] The exception: it shall be a defence 'that the act complained of was within the scope of his lawful authority or that it was done in good faith in the purported exercise of his lawful authority.' There is also an exception to the exception—the defence does not apply to 'an action for negligence'.[8] A corresponding defence is granted to the state, by the State Liability Law,[9] with regard to an act done within the scope of lawful authority, or *bona fide* in the purported exercise of lawful authority. Here, again, immunity is denied regarding 'negligence in connection with such an act'.

The scope and importance of these immunities[10] are substantially curtailed by the exclusion of negligence. Moreover, 'negligence' in this respect has been interpreted broadly to include not only actions based on the tort of negligence, but also actions based on any other tort, as long as they are founded on carelessness.[11] As a result, these defences can be employed only in cases of strict liability.[12] Intentional and malicious wrongs are excluded from the scope of the defence, either because negligence under Israeli law encompasses intentional and malicious behaviour[13] or because such behaviour is deemed to be unlawful, where the defence requires 'lawfulness'.[14]

C. Act Under Enactment

Under the CWO, in any action other than negligence it shall be a defence 'that the act or omission complained of was done or made under and in

---

[7] A 'public servant' is defined by the Interpretation Ordinance to include every employee whose duties are of a public nature, whether under the direct control of the government or otherwise. This broad definition includes employees of local authorities and of statutory corporations, as well as state officials and other employees of the state.

[8] CWO, s 7. A public servant is not responsible for a civil wrong committed by another public servant unless he expressly authorised or ratified such civil wrong (s 7(b)).

[9] See s 3.

[10] These provisions operate to negate liability and not merely as a procedural bar to recovery—See *Me'orer*, above n 5; *Galpand v Cohen* (1964) 18 (ii) PD 197.

[11] *Nanas v Fluro* (1986) 40(i) PD 210.

[12] A difficulty may arise when a public servant honestly, but negligently, believed that he was exercising his lawful authority although in fact he was not. May the servant rely on the defence even though he was in fact careless? It has been suggested that the answer should be negative.

[13] *Avrahami v City of Tel-Aviv* (1965) 19(i) PD 114; *City of Jerusalem v Gordon* (1985) 39 (i) PD 113.

[14] *Alon v Peled* (1963) 17 PD 2572. Negligent behaviour in and of itself is not unlawful (*Ra'ad v State of Israel* (1971) 25(i) PD 197, at 207).

accordance with the provisions of any enactment'.[15] This defence creates another source of protection for public servants,[16] though private citizens may also rely on it. Yet, like the 'lawful authority' defence, the act under enactment defence cannot be pleaded in cases of negligence.[17] This exception significantly narrows the scope of the immunity as the law usually presumes that a statute does not authorise the negligent exercise of statutory powers.[18] Another restriction on the scope of the defence lies in the requirement that the act be directly designed to achieve the purpose of the enactment. Collateral acts that are incidental to the authorized goal (eg, driving), are not covered by the immunity provided to the act itself.[19]

D. Narrowing the Aforementioned Immunities

The immunities discussed above are of limited importance as they do not provide protection against fault-based claims, only against strict liability claims. Furthermore, it appears that courts tend to restrict even this limited area of immunity. The term 'legal authority', for example, has been construed as the compliance of the specific authorising act with the rules of administrative law governing such acts. The existence of formal authorisation to execute such an act was considered a necessary but insufficient condition. For example, on the basis of this distinction, the state could be found liable for private nuisance caused by the operation of an airport. Although the state had the formal authority, by statute, to regulate take-offs and landings, if it exercised this power improperly it could not rely on the legal authority defense.[20] By limiting the defence, public law serves to extend tort liability.

E. War Operation

The state and soldiers are not civilly liable for an act done in the course of wartime operations by the Israel defence Force.[21] This provision has been interpreted narrowly to exclude non-combat military activities, even during

---

[15] CWO, s 6.

[16] An act carried out under a valid court judgment cannot constitute a civil wrong even though the judgment was later reversed by an appellate court—*Serna Movie Theater and Amusement Ltd. v Alkalai* (1991) 45(ii) PD 506.

[17] CWO, s 6; *Gesher Haziv v Israel Electric Co. Ltd* (1961) 15 PD 469, at 473.

[18] *Geddis v Proprietors of Bann Reservoir* [1878] 3 App Cas 430 (HL). In *Geddis* the statutory powers were granted to and exercised by individuals, not a public authority.

[19] *Me'orer v Northern Galilee Regional Council* (1966) 20 (iii) *Piskei Din* 645, at 656. The court did not refer directly to s 6 but to a similar provision under a specific enactment.

[20] *Moshav Bnei-Atarot v State of Israel* (1984) 38(iv) PD 30, at 44–8.

[21] State Liability Law, 1952, s 5 (the state) and 7B (soldiers).

war.[22] With regard to the first Palestinian uprising (the 'First Intifada') that took place during the 1980s and early 1990s, courts usually rejected the state claim that the enforcement of order by the military was a 'war operation', classifying it as 'police activity', thereby allowing many claims for bodily injury by injured Palestinians. This approach may change with regard to the second Palestinian 'Intifada' uprising (beginning in October 2000) since the conflict involves the autonomous Palestinian Authority and includes the exchange of fire between armed forces.[23]

F. Military Service

The state is not civilly liable for injury sustained by a person or for the death of a person, during military service or in consequence thereof.[24] A soldier responsible for causing such injury is also personally immune against tort liability.[25] This immunity has been extended to the police and other security forces as well. The major rationale underlying this immunity is that injury and death sustained in service, regardless of tort liability, are compensated by another source, namely special pension and rehabilitation laws. Moreover, equality and justice require that all those injured in service to be entitled to the same remedies regardless of whether their injury was the result of tortious behaviour.

G. Other State Immunities

The State Liability Law provides that the state is not civilly liable for defamation.[26] After the enactment of the Defamation Prohibition Law 1961, with its delicate and detailed balance between the protection of reputation and public interests, this blanket immunity seems obsolete and should be abolished. The State is also 'not liable as the owner of property vested in it solely by operation of law, so long as it has not taken possession thereof'.[27] Civil liability of the state is narrowed further by a provision stating that no duty is imposed upon the state by an enactment unless the enactment explicitly so provides.[28] This provision may narrow the state's liability for breach of statutory duty, as the enactment must explicitly impose a duty upon the state. Other specific and limited immunities of the state can be found in other statutes. The 'act of state' defence, which protects the state

---

[22] *Levi v State of Israel* (1986) 40(i) PD 477; *State of Israel v Ohana* (1988) 42(iii) PD

[23] For legal analysis of the different possible classifications of the conflict, see s IV of the report submitted by Dugard *et al* to the United Nations Economic and Social Council on 16 Mar 2001 ().

[24] State Liability Law, s 6 (injury) and 7 (death).   [25] Ibid, s 7B (enacted in 1989).

[26] Section 4.   [27] Ibid, s 8.

[28] Section 42 of the Interpretation Ordinance (New Version), 1954.

from liability for damage inflicted upon a foreign subject, is not mentioned in the CWO.

H. Judicial Immunities

The CWO provides that no action shall be brought against a member of any court or tribunal, or against a person performing judicial functions, including arbitrators, with respect to any civil wrong committed by such person in his judicial capacity.[29] The Court embraced a restrictive approach regarding the scope of the protected group, confining the operation of the defence to cases where the authority is involved in the resolution of a dispute (*lis*) between two or more parties through a judicial or quasi-judicial process.[30] This immunity, when it applies, is far-reaching. It protects the relevant persons against any wrong committed in judicial capacity, which clearly includes negligence, gross negligence and possibly bad faith.

It should be noted, however, that the above provision states that 'no action shall be brought' against judges. Unlike the other provisions of immunity discussed above, it neither provides a justifying defence nor negates civil liability. Being that this is only a procedural immunity, namely, one that bars personal claims against judges without negating their tort liability, it follows that the state, as an employer, may be held vicariously liable for the torts of the protected individuals. In other words, from the claimant's point of view the immunity can easily be circumvented by suing the state for any tort committed by a judge in the course of employment. Surprisingly, this question has not been tackled until recently, which suggests a widespread understanding that the immunity protects the state as well. Only in 2001 did a district court accept the view that the immunity is procedural. Consequently, the state can be sued for vicariously liability when torts are committed by judges.[31] Nevertheless, the district court considerably limited the scope of this liability by holding that the state can only be sued in severe cases of extremely gross judicial negligence. In the particular case, the Court categorised the alleged negligence of the judge in issuing a civil arrest order as simple and not as 'extremely gross', so that no vicarious liability was imposed. This decision raises difficult legal questions (eg, the distinction between 'simple', 'gross', and 'extremely gross' negligence), policy questions (eg, as to its effects on judicial independence and finality of judgments), and questions regarding the separation of powers (since in effect, judges determine the scope of their own immunity).

---

[29] CWO, s 8.
[30] *Yirmelovitz v Hovav* (1981) 35(iii) PD 766, at 769–71.
[31] *State of Israel v Friedman*, Jerusalem, 3/2001.

III. JUDICIAL REVIEW: PUBLIC LAW AND TORT LAW COMPARED

In the absence of applicable immunities courts have the authority to consider whether to impose tort liability on public authorities exercising statutory powers.[32] When they do so they are actually engaged in judicial review: they examine the decisions and the functioning of the executive in order to decide whether the latter exercised its powers properly. The imposition of tort liability is tantamount to a finding that the executive failed to function properly, and that the affected person is entitled to rectifying remedies against the authority. This venue of judicial review coexists with the judicial review conducted by administrative courts applying administrative law. The coexistence of two independent venues for judicial review raises various questions. The preliminary question is whether tort law is significant. Does it extend or deepen the scope of judicial review conducted by administrative courts? The answer to the question is undoubtedly positive for the following reasons:

A. Remedies and their Effect

Administrative law directly affects the functioning of the executive by issuing injunction orders instructing the administration how to act or limit their action. Yet, there are many situations where the administration functioned improperly but no effective remedy may be employed *post facto*—'What's done is done' (*fait accompli*). Usually, administrative law does not award monetary compensation for losses caused by the infringement of administrative rights.[33] In this regard, tort law has a great impact. It steps in to provide the remedy of compensation, to rectify past and future losses thereby covering a wide spectrum of cases where administrative judicial review is practically irrelevant. Moreover, since one of the aims of judicial review is to encourage the authority to function properly (through deterrence), it stands to reason that tort law may quite often prove to be a more effective deterrent than administrative law. The authority may take the risk of being ordered to change its ways if an injunction is issued, but it may hesitate to take such risk if it involves liability to pay substantial compensation.

---

[32] From this point forward, unless otherwise indicated, reference to public authorities is made in regard to their functioning as governmental bodies, as opposed to their corporate or proprietary capacity.

[33] Although it was held that, in principle, administrative courts are empowered to award damages (*Israel Electric Company v Malibu Israel* (1993) 47 (i) PD 662) this power is rarely exercised.

B. *Grounds for Intervention*

Tort law may provide grounds for judicial review where administrative law does not. Under administrative law the major traditional grounds for judicial review are actions that are *ultra vires*, irrelevant considerations, discrimination, arbitrariness and breach of natural justice. More recently recognised grounds are extreme unreasonableness and lack of proportionality. The major grounds for judicial review by tort law are the general torts of negligence and breach of statutory duty. The concept of negligence is not only wide enough to accommodate the above grounds for judicial review, it may also provide a cause of action in cases of simple, common unreasonableness that do not fit into the traditional administrative grounds for judicial intervention or into the 'extreme unreasonableness' requirement. The tort of breach of statutory duty may further extend the grounds of intervention unique to tort law by imposing strict liability on public authorities.

C. *The Reviewing Tribunals*

Judicial review via administrative law is conducted by the justices of the Supreme Court sitting as the first instance High Court of Justice, and by the administrative departments of district courts. Judicial review via tort law is conducted by magistrate courts and district courts sitting as civil courts of first instance. Generally speaking, first instance judges of administrative courts are higher ranking and more specialised than first instance judges who conduct judicial review through tort law.

IV. JUDICIAL REVIEW BY TORT LAW: POLICY CONSIDERATIONS

Given that tort liability may extend and deepen judicial review in the manner described above, the next question is whether such liability is desirable.

The following policy considerations have been introduced to support a restrictive approach to tort liability in general: excessive liability may lead, by creating a defensive frame of mind and inducing undesirable liability-preventive measures, to interruption, curtailment or even suspension of beneficial activities (overdeterrence); a flood of tort actions, including vexatious actions, may overburden the courts and consume precious and scarce societal resources (floodgate); uncertainty concerning legal risks may lead either to unjustifiably high prices of insured activities or to non-availability of insurance (failure to spread loss); unconfined liability may concentrate small or insignificant losses sustained by many on one or few tortfeasors who may collapse under the burden (loss concentration); imposition of burdensome liability on those who failed to meet the demanding objective standards imposed by law is unfair where the latter acted in good-faith, to the best of their ability (unfairness).

Most of these considerations apply to liability of public authorities. As the latter are involved in all aspects of human life, the risk of liability is substantial and may frequently outweigh the 'private' benefits, if any, derived by the administration from its activity. This may easily lead to public authorities' 'looking over their shoulder', increasing the amount of 'red tape', and 'deferral to higher authority' practices that negatively affect the quality and efficiency of the public service (overdeterrence).[34] The susceptibility of governmental authority to tort actions may lead to the opening of floodgates, with the ensuing social costs and overload of the courts, as well as to concentration of many small losses on one liable authority. There are, however, other policy considerations that apply only to governmental authorities that may justify a restrictive approach. With regard to loss-spreading, although the public authority is often considered the ultimate loss spreader, one should bear in mind that public budgets are always limited and that any tort award comes at the expense of other services provided to the public. The question then, is whether and when it is fair to allocate the scarce resources of society through decision-making process associated with tort liability, namely, one that prefers the interests of one group (tort claimants) over the interests of other groups (those ultimately deprived of alternative services as a result of reallocation of funds) or of the public at large. This question (fair allocation) is related to another important consideration—separation of powers. Courts should not, through intrusive judicial review, assume powers and responsibilities that the public entrusts within the executive branch. They should not 'second guess' administrative decisions. A related question is that of 'institutional justiceability'. There are some decisions concerning the exercise of statutory powers that would better be made by the executive and not by the judiciary because the former is institutionally better qualified and better suited to do so.

On the other hand, there are obviously strong arguments that support the imposition of tort liability on public authorities for negligent exercise of statutory powers or for breaching statutory duties. Tort liability may play

---

[34] The general theory of deterrence claims that the potential private tortfeasors, pursuing their own good, tend to externalise costs that their activity inflicts upon other parties, and that the role of tort law is to internalise these costs so that the full cost of such activity is taken into account. Public authorities, in contrast, are not assumed to act in pursuit of their own 'private' good but rather pursue the common good. If they do not, at the outset, externalise costs then, there is no need to internalise these costs through tort law. On the contrary, internalisation may lead to overdeterrence.

an important role in improving the quality of public service (deterrence) and in compensating those who incur the costs of activities that benefit the public (fairness and loss spreading). The fear of claim flooding should not lead to a complete closure of the floodgates. It must also be noted that judicial review of the executive is, to a certain extent, an integral part of the concept of checks and balances. Yet, the combined weight of the considerations against liability does support a restrictive approach. Ultimately, the real question is how to strike the proper balance between these conflicting considerations.

V. CONTROLLING LIABILITY: LEGAL TOOLS

The torts of negligence and breach of statutory duty provide a variety of legal tools to maintain liability within its desirable boundaries once a balance has been established between the pros and cons of public authorities' liability. In negligence, liability can be denied either by finding that the authority was not careless, or by the non-recognition of a duty of care. As to carelessness, liability can be restricted by setting a relatively low standard of due care, or even by requiring gross negligence as a precondition to liability. The duty of care may be denied on various grounds. First, by using the 'public duty' doctrine, which denies tort liability on the grounds that the relevant duty is owed to the public at large and not to the individuals who make up the public (in this context, a duty owed to everyone is duty owed to no one). Secondly, since it is necessary in establishing a duty, when the condition of proximity is unfulfilled, no duty will be recognised. Thirdly, duty may be denied with regard to certain types of losses (such as purely economic loss), certain types of activities (such as omissions or exercise of discretion), as well as for certain types of authorities (such as the judiciary or the prosecution) or certain types of claimants. The duty may also be denied based on a combination of grounds (omission causing pure economic loss). Similar legal tools may be used to restrict liability under Breach of Statutory Duty. The court may deny liability by interpreting the relevant statute as imposing duty that is only 'public duty', or as duty which was not intended to protect given types of claimants, of losses, or activities.

These legal tools enable the courts to widen or narrow the scope of tort liability of public authorities in accordance with the policy considerations that call for a balanced restriction of this liability. The following sections present how the above considerations and legal tools have shaped this complicated area of tort liability in its different phases of development.

VI. THE RESTRICTIVE APPROACH: UNTIL THE LATE 1970s

From independence (1948) until the late 1970s, Israeli courts basically followed the traditionally restrictive approach of the English common law with regard to the liability of public authorities.[35] It was held, for example, that a municipality was not liable for its failure to reconstruct a drainage canal which resulted in flooding and property damage,[36] and that officials of the Licensing Authority were not liable for failure to check whether a sold vehicle was insured.[37] The policy considerations justifying these restrictive decisions were overdeterrence, floodgate concerns, and the separation of powers. The legal tools employed to deny liability were the public nature of the duties owed by the authority in these cases ('public duty'), and denial of duty in cases of omissions, namely, where the authority did not actively create the risk but only failed to protect against this risk. Courts, however, did find public authorities liable for damage caused by road hazards, and rejected the distinction between misfeasance and nonfeasance in this regard.[38] Nevertheless these decisions can be reconciled with the restrictive approach. First, they involved bodily injury or property damage: interests that lie at the protected core of tort law. Secondly, as people justly rely on public authorities to maintain public roads in a safe condition, this legitimate reliance, which the authorities are aware of, changes the nature of the failure to maintain safe roads from an omission (nonfeasance) to a more active wrongdoing of creating and frustrating expectations.[39] As in cases of negligent misrepresentation and professional malpractice, legitimate reliance becomes an important factor in the expansion of liability, serving both as a justification and as a legal tool for imposing liability.

In the late 1970s, in some decisions, the courts seemed to reconsider the restrictive approach.[40] Liability was imposed on a municipality for failure to prevent the collapse of a building caused by nearby excavations.[41] This was a typical case of omission—failure to protect one individual from another, not a reliance case. Yet, the decision may still be reconciled with

---

[35] With regard to the liability of public authorities in their corporate or proprietary capacity, the 'rule of equality' has always been applied, holding the authorities liable in the same way as any other corporate body or private individual. See, eg, *Morad v Prust* (1963) 17 PD 36 (dangerous objects); *State of Israel v Giter* (1963) 17 PD 2073 (possessor of dangerous premises).

[36] *Sereg Adin v Mayor of Tel-aviv—Yafo* (1957) 11 PD 1110.

[37] *Sheha'da v Hilu* (1966) 20 (iv) PD 617.

[38] *State of Israel v Huati* (1962) 16 PD 209.

[39] *Maklef v Zilberberg* (1989) 43 (i) PD 137.

[40] In *Grubner v City of Haifa* (1975) 30 (i) PD 141 the Supreme Court upheld the decision of a municipality concerning the allocation of resources for safety in public parks. Nevertheless the Court seems to oscillate between the traditional restrictive approach and a more active, interventionist, approach.

[41] *Eyal v Fuksman* (1977) 31(iii) PD 349.

the restrictive approach as it deals with a specific and severe risk of bodily injury which the relevant authority was aware of. A true change in policy came only later.

VII. THE EXPANSION OF LIABILITY: FROM THE EARLY 1980S TO THE MID-1990S

In the early 1980s the Supreme Court, in a series of decisions, abandoned the traditional restrictive rhetoric and adopted instead an expansionist one. Yet, the decisions themselves, despite the rhetoric, can still be reconciled with a less expansionist approach. In a case dealing with the 'private' liability of a municipality as an operator of a swimming pool the Court rejected the English approach which viewed duties with general application as 'public duties' owed to no particular individual. The Court stated that statutory duties that protect the public at large may also protect each individual who makes up 'the public'.[42] This new ruling encroached upon both the 'public duty doctrine' and the notion of 'proximity' as tools for limiting liability. In the 1983 *Zohar* case the Court found a municipality liable for failing to monitor dangerous structures in an area accessible to the public, which resulted in a car being damaged.[43] Although the decision can be reconciled with former decisions concerning liability for failure to secure the safety of public roads,[44] the Court clearly took the opportunity to lunch a major attack on the restrictive approach. First, it undermined the policy considerations justifying the restriction by questioning the validity of overdeterrence, floodgate and separation of power arguments, commenting that it has never been proven that liability may demoralize and invalidate civil service. It then went on to discredit the legal tools used to restrict liability, characterising as 'obsolete' the distinctions between private and public capacity, acts and omissions, ministerial and discretional duties, operational and policy decisions, and *intra vires* and *ultra vires*. The Court stated further that the very existence of statutory authority and the concomitant ability to monitor and control risks may indicate the existence of a duty of care even where reliance is absent. The same approach was taken in the 1985 *Gordon* decision when the Court ruled that a municipality was liable for a mistaken arrest following unfounded charges which were brought against the claimant regarding his failure to pay parking tickets.[45] Here, again, the decision may be reconciled with a restrictive approach—liability was imposed for an infringement of a basic right by the misuse of the coer-

---

[42] *Va'aknin v Local Council of Bet-Shemesh* (1983) 37 (i) PD 113.
[43] *City of Hadera v Zohar* (1983) 37(iii) PD 757.
[44] See s 6, above.
[45] See *City of Jerusalem*, above n 12

cive power of the authority, power exercised in a clearly careless manner where no discretion was involved. But the Court, here as well, chose to use very strong rhetoric. Not only did it once again question the arguments of floodgate and overdeterrence, it also recognised, for the first time, that prosecutors could be sued for *negligent* prosecution rather than for *malicious* prosecution. Yet another new expansive development was the ruling that non-pecuniary loss, even when it is unrelated to physical damage, is recoverable under negligence.

These new breakthroughs paved the way for a major broadening of liability of public authorities. Moreover, the *Gordon* decision further strengthened two general liability-expanding concepts: the concept of *prima facie* duty of care, which states that in cases of carelessness the court should presume the existence of duty of care unless special considerations direct it otherwise, and the concept of *notional* duty of care that is hardly ever denied. These liability-expanding concepts clearly affect public authorities.

Other decisions in this period embraced the rhetoric of *Zohar* and *Gordon* and gradually extended the liability of public authorities. In three cases the Supreme Court recognised that the police could be held liable in negligence for: property damage caused by unlawful arrest and misinterpretation of a judicial writ,[46] failure of the border police to enforce a judicial writ prohibiting the departure of the claimant's husband, thereby letting him escape a divorce order and inflicting upon her non-pecuniary loss,[47] and failure to respond to an alarm system installed by the police.[48] Municipal Planning and Building committees were found liable in negligence for pure economic loss caused by awarding unlawful building permit in one case,[49] and for the unlawful suspension of such a permit in another case.[50] The above decisions, however, did not cope with the real 'test case'—the 'hard-core' problem—of a public authority's failure to properly exercise its discretion and protect a large public from the risks created by others. The *Levi* case,[51] discussed below, provided such an opportunity.

---

[46] *Buskila v State of Israel* (1984) 38 (iii) PD 169.
[47] *State of Israel v Suhan* (1988) 42(iii) PD 734.
[48] *R.G.M. Meret v State of Israel* (1990) 44 (iv) 272.
[49] *Kenny Houses v Local Planning and Building Committee, Netanya* (1992) 46(v) PD 737
[50] *Eyni Construction Co v Local Planning and Building Committee, Qrayot* (1993) 47 (2) PD 111. Liability was also imposed upon public authorities for negligent misrepresentation, but this kind of liability has always been considered equivalent to the liability of private individuals or corporations—see, eg, *City of Kiryat-Ata v Ilenco* (1988) 42(i) PD 190; *City of Bnei-Brak v Rotbard* (1991) 45(iv) PD 102.
[51] *State of Israel v Levi* (1994) 48 (iii) PD 45.

In the *Levi* case a private insurance company collapsed leaving beneficiaries
with no coverage. The district court found that the highly ranked Treasury
official in charge of the insurance industry was liable in negligence for failing to exercise properly his discretionary powers as the Commissioner of
the industry. Moreover, the Court ruled that this failure also amounted to
breach of statutory duty, despite the fact that the relevant statute did not
specify any mandatory obligations or even guidelines in this regard. In its
decision, the district court explicitly followed and applied the expansive
rhetoric of *Zohar* and *Gordon* also referring to the 'reliance factor', arguing that the public is entitled to rely on supervising governmental authorities to protect it from risks created by supervised activities. The state
appealed, arguing that the Commissioner exercised his statutory discretional powers properly.

The Supreme Court had the opportunity to allow the appeal on the
ground that the Commissioner had not been careless. Instead, as in the
Zohar case, the Court took the opportunity to change the course of liability, this time from an expansionist direction back to the more restrictive,
traditional approach. Actually, the *Levi* decision follows the pattern of
Zohar, but in an opposite direction.

The first step, under the title of 'pragmatic considerations', was to
embrace the policy considerations that support the restrictive approach,
those same considerations that *Zohar* and *Gordon* had criticised a decade
before. The arguments regarding the risks of overdeterrence and defensive
frame of mind, vast societal costs, opening of floodgates, and judicial invasion of executive powers gained new vigour under *Levi*. Moreover, the
Court in *Levi* reinvigorated the distinction between governmental and non-
governmental capacities of public authorities, and introduced the argument
of injusticiability, namely, casting doubt on whether tort law is well
equipped to review the ways in which the executive branch exercises its
discretionary powers.

After restoring the grounds of the restrictive approach the court restored
the legal tools that had been employed to restrict liability, the same tools
that were declared as 'obsolete' by *Zohar* a decade earlier. It embraced the
distinction between private and governmental capacity, between acts and
omissions and between discretional and policy decisions on the one hand
and other types of decisions on the other hand. Regarding omissions, the
Court drew a distinction between situations where the authority has the
means and the power to exercise effective or even conclusive control on
risks created by other factors, and situations where effective control is
limited the latter situation being less susceptible to liability. On a more
general level, the Court in *Levi* criticised and restricted the concepts of

prima facie duty of care and notional duty of care, concepts which had been utilised to extend liability under negligence in general, and liability of public authorities in particular.[52] The Court reintroduced 'proximity' as a necessary component of the duty of care, a component that by nature limits the class of potential claimants.[53] In this regard, it also stressed that the effect of the 'reliance' factor is limited. In the absence of proximity, individuals should not rely on the authorities to compensate them for general 'background' risks that should be borne by the public. It was also held that inappropriate exercise of statutory powers does not amount to breach of statutory duty unless a concrete duty specified by the statute has been breached.[54]

Interestingly, the Court in *Levi*, despite the sharp contrast between its rhetoric and the one employed in *Gordon* and *Zohar*, did not present its decision as a turnaround or a change of course, but rather as an evolution of existing case law. This was only possible because, as emphasised, the rhetoric of *Zohar*, *Gordon*, and following decisions greatly exceeded the actual decisions.

The most important restricting aspect of the *Levi* decision is the 'broad discretion' exception to liability. The Court ruled that when a public authority exercises broad discretion, it might only be held liable in extreme cases where its decision was extremely unreasonable. Broad discretion was characterised as a decision that requires balancing of competing social, political, and economic considerations with no guiding criteria or standards. The Court stressed that it is not the importance of the decision or its wide implications that render it immune to liability but rather the nature of the discretion exercised. This exception to liability was placed within the second component of the duty of care—the special public policy considerations that justify the negation of liability even where there is proximity between the parties.

Regarding the question at bar, the Court ruled that the Commissioner had exercised 'broad discretion' and was therefore protected by the exception to liability—special public policy considerations prevented the recognition of a duty of care to the frustrated beneficiaries of the bankrupt insurer. The Court added that the following decisions would also be protected by the exception: the closure of a bank, the fixing of interest rates, the freezing of loans, and the apprehension of criminals.

IX. THE AFTERMATH OF *LEVI*

The *Levi* decision has created uncertainty bordering on confusion. On the

---

[52] See I.1.3.   [53] Ibid.   [54] BSD.

one hand, *Levi's* rhetoric and the 'broad discretion' exception to liability did signal a change of course from *Zohar* and *Gordon* toward a more restrictive approach to the liability of public authorities. On the other hand, as mentioned, the Court in *Levi* did not overrule or criticise the *Gordon* and *Zohar* decisions, trying instead to integrate them into *Levi's* structure of liability. Moreover, we have seen that the expansive doctrines of prima facie duty of care and *notional* duty of care, identified with *Gordon*, have survived despite their criticism in *Levi*.[55] Post-*Levi* decisions of magistrate and district courts therefore seem to oscillate between *Zohar/Gordon* and *Levi*.[56] Generally speaking, it seems that the 'broad discretion' exception to liability has been followed, although courts may differ in their decisions with regard to what constitutes 'broad discretion'.[57] The Supreme Court, on its part, ruled that municipal Planning and Building Committees may be held liable in negligence to land owners for pure economic loss caused by an unreasonable delay in the decision-making process concerning the use and development of land.[58] Referring implicitly to the *Levi* decision, the majority stated that the question of liability of public authorities still requires further deliberation and discussion. Recently, the Court held that the state is not liable for damage caused by circumcision as it lacks the authority to control circumcisions.[59]

X. THE EFFECT OF THE BASIC LAW: HUMAN DIGNITY AND FREEDOM

The 1992 Basic Law: Human Dignity and Freedom states that every person is entitled to the protection of his life, body, and dignity, and that these

---

[55] See I.1.3.

[56] In *State of Israel v Drori*, eg, a magistrate court ruled that the State was liable in negligence for failure to enact regulations concerning remuneration of directors in state-owned companies. The court stated that the *Levi* decision is 'an exception' to the general trend regarding the liability of public authorities. The district court, on appeal, held that the State was not liable in tort, stating, inter alia, that the Levi decision, although not in line with former decisions, should be followed (1/98). Indeed, another district court decision, which dealt with the alleged failure of the State to enact regulations (concerning safety at the workplace), followed *Levi*, holding that the legislation process is protected by the 'broad discretion' exception to liability (*Oranim Silencer v State of Israel*—3/2000).

[57] Eg, in *State of Israel v Hushniya* (3/1998), a district court oscillated between the *Zohar* and *Gordon* decisions on the one hand, and *Levi* on the other. Finally, it decided to interpret the 'broad discretion' exception narrowly. It ruled that the discretion of the Ministry of Health in deciding whether to grant or deny an operating license of a hospital in east Jerusalem is not within the exception despite the fact that such a decision involves medical, budgetary, and organisational considerations.

[58] *Baruch and Tzipora Center v City of Tel-Aviv* (1999) 53 (iii) PD 517. As the case was remanded to the district court, the majority did not to discuss the *Levi's* 'broad discretion' exception in this context.

[59] *Ploni v Rabbi Ze'ev* (2001) 55 (v) PD 241.

rights as well as a person's property rights shall not be infringed. The law further states that every governmental authority is obliged to respect these rights. The Supreme Court, as has been mentioned, has stated that the Basic Law 'constitutionalised' these rights not only in the sphere of public law, but also with regard to private law: these rights now carry greater weight than in the past when they are balanced against conflicting rights of individuals or against public interests.

How does this Basic Law affect tort liability of public authorities? Tort law, in this regard, clearly balances individual rights against public interests. The overdeterrence and floodgate arguments against expansive liability, for example, obviously originate in the need to protect public interests. Does it follow that this Basic Law weakens the arguments that support restrictive approach and strengthen the expansive approach? Interestingly, the Supreme Court in *Levi* and in the other decisions discussed above made no reference to the Basic Law in this regard.

Although it may be said that this Basic Law may well strengthen the expansive approach, the justification, extent and direction of such expansion raise complex questions. First, life, body, dignity, and property in their strict sense have traditionally been at the protected core of tort law, with substantial weights attached to them.[60] Should these interests carry even greater weight? In other words, when, and on what grounds, should courts find that past balancing of the constitutionalised rights by tort law has become improper given the Basic Law? Secondly, should the rights to 'dignity' and 'property' be interpreted broadly, for example, by including *social rights* in 'dignity' and *economic interests* in 'property'? Such broad interpretation may lead to a further expansion of liability. Is this justified? When the 'constitutional' protection of individuals exceeds the core of the basic rights protected by private law, one may wonder why the interests of the public to avoid overdeterrence or flood of suits should not be protected as well. After all, the Supreme Court itself stated that by protecting public interests we protect the interests of the individuals who compose the 'public'.[61] Thirdly, the Law seems to impose on public authorities an affirmative duty to protect life, body, and dignity, but not property. It only forbids infringement of property rights. Does it follow that a public authority is or would be more susceptible to liability for an *omission* to protect life, body, and dignity than for *omission* to protect property? In what sense and why should 'dignity' be more protected than 'property'?

---

[60]   Dignity in this context means reputation and privacy.
[61]   See *Va'aknin v Local Council of Bet-Shemesh* (1983) 37 (i) PD 113.

XI. ON THE PERSONAL LIABILITY OF EMPLOYEES, AGENTS, AND ORGANS

The discussion so far has focused on the liability of public authorities without distinguishing between the liability of the authority itself as a legal
entity created by law, and the personal liability of the employees, agents or
organs through which such an entity exercises its functions and powers.
Having no physical existence, public authorities are liable in tort because
their employees, agents, or organs (public officials) acted or failed to act.
Such liability may be either vicarious or direct. It is vicarious where the
employee or the agent themselves are liable in tort and their liability is
extended to include the authority as their employer or principal. Liability is
direct where the person who commits the tort is considered to be an organ
of the authority, namely, that the conduct and/or the state of mind of such
person are deemed to be those of the authority. Consequently, in most cases
tort liability of a public authority is a derivative of the personal liability of
its employees, agents or organs.[62]

This personal liability is questionable. Public officials do not pursue their
own private interests. Rather, they serve the public in different capacities.
Given the vast powers of the authorities and their deep involvement in
almost all aspects of human life, public officials are exposed to significant
risks of personal liability without enjoying corresponding benefits.
Although public authorities usually stand behind their officials when they
are being sued providing legal protection and paying liability awards the
risk of being sued in person often results in a defensive frame of mind and
other negative symptoms of the over-deterrence phenomena. Moreover, it
seems unfair to burden public officials with the heavy load of liability when
they are acting bona fide but fail to meet the demanding objective standard
of due care. Another problem is that public officials are sometimes
subjected to threats made by those who want them to exercise their powers
in a favorable way. The threat is that they and only they, not the authorities, will be sued in person if they refuse to submit to these demands.

A reasonable solution to this problem is the extension of statutory
immunities protecting public officials without derogating from the liability
of the public authorities. A pending bill has adopted this solution. Under a
proposed 1999 bill no tort claim shall be filed against a public official for
an act or omission that took place in his or her course of employment. The
only exception is a malicious abuse of power. As this provision establishes
a personal procedural bar and not a substantive defence or justification, the
public authorities could be sued as being liable, vicariously or directly, for

---

[62] There may be cases, however, where the employee, agent or organ is not liable though the
authorities. This would be the case where the duty breached is owed only by the authority and
not its employee, agent, or organ.

torts committed by personally protected employees, agents, and organs. The bill went even further. In order to screen vengeful personal claims alleging that an official maliciously abused power, or *ex ante* threats to file such claims, the bill empowers the public authority, subject to approval by the Attorney-General, to issue a statement certifying that the sued public official was acting within the course of his or her employment. If such statement is not challenged, the public authority will substitute its official as the defendant, and the personal claim against the official will be denied.[63] On the other hand, to avoid over-protection of public officials and to induce them to fulfil their duties properly, the bill renders them liable to the authority in cases of extreme deviation from the due standard of public service. In such rare cases, a public official may be liable either to pay compensation for causing damage to the authority or to indemnify the authority for compensation paid to third party as a consequence of the official's misbehaviour.

XII. CONCLUDING REMARKS

The above review and analysis of Israeli law regarding the tort liability of public authorities leads to the following conclusion. In determining the scope and limits of liability, courts should seek the delicate balance between the conflicting policy considerations. Liability should be imposed in order to enhance deterrence, spread losses, and compensate those who incur the costs of the careless activities performed by the authorities. It should, however, be restrained where these benefits are outweighed by over-deterrence, burdensome social costs and the damaging effects of judicial intrusion into the realm of administrative sovereignty.

This balance may change with time. Moreover, the correct balance may differ from one country to another, given the differences in the structure and in the quality of the public services, the available resources, the legal environment, and the prestige and trustworthiness of public services. One should therefore be careful when drawing conclusions from the experience of other countries and in importing them into a different social and legal environment. Comparative analysis should therefore be conducted with great caution.

In the search for the best obtainable balance courts should examine the various characteristics of each case. It is suggested that some characteristics should be considered as enhancing liability, while others should be consid-

---

[63] This is true unless the issued statement does not ask for the denial of the personal claim. In this case the official and the authority would be co-defendants.

ered as restraining liability, and that conflicting characteristics should be balanced. For example, the court should examine the nature of the loss suffered. Bodily injury, physical damage to property, and consequential pecuniary losses are liability-enhancing characteristics. The same applies to infringements of the basic, core, human rights. In contrast, 'pure' economic or non-pecuniary losses that do not infringe basic rights call for a more cautious approach. The reason for this distinction is not necessarily a value judgement but rather the concern that comprehensive protection against such losses usually involves wide and indeterminate liability that by its nature leads to overdeterrence and burdensome social costs.

Another major characteristic that should be examined is the nature of the loss inflicting activity. That the public authority *actively* inflicted a loss, especially while exercising its coercive powers (arrest, taxation), is definitely a liability-enhancing characteristic. In contrast a 'pure' omission, namely a failure to protect the claimant from a risk actively generated by a third party (a tortfeasor, faultless person or natural occurrence), or failure to provide benefits, should be treated more cautiously. Here as well inclusive liability may lead to overdeterrence, huge social costs, etc. Within the realm of pure omissions, a distinction should be made between a failure to protect the interests of the claimant which frustrates expectations based on reasonable and legitimate reliance on the public authority, and a failure to protect the claimant's interests in the absence of such reliance. Reasonable and legitimate reliance is a liability–enhancing characteristic. Another distinction should be made between the failure to protect in situations where the authority has the ability and resources to do so, and situations in which such ability is limited. Actual and effective control is a liability-enhancing characteristic. Yet another distinction that should be made is between activities that involve broad discretion, and those that are technical or operational in nature. While the former raise the issue of separation of powers, and therefore call for judicial restraint, the latter do not.

Following this analysis there are some cases that will be easy to decide. An active infliction of bodily injury, which is caused while coercive powers are being exercised carelessly and where no discretion is involved, is obviously a liability situation. On the other hand, the failure to protect against a 'pure' non-pecuniary loss inflicted by a third party, in the absence of reasonable and legitimate reliance on the authority, where the authority's ability to control the risk is poor or costly, seems to be a no-liability situation. The difficulty lies in 'grey area' cases where some characteristics are liability enhancing but others are liability restraining. Examples of this include decisions that have both operational and discretionary aspects, cases where the legitimacy of the reliance is debatable, and pure omissions in situations of limited control that lead to physical damage.

Indeed, striking a balance between the conflicting considerations by using the above and other liability enhancing and liability restraining characteristics is not an easy task. But is there an alternative?

Tort law, as we have seen, provides ample legal tools to cope with this challenge, notably through the flexible and malleable concept of duty of care with all of its components. It is therefore suggested that courts should be less formalistic and more policy oriented in this regard.

Finally, it is most important to establish a reliable factual basis for analyses for both adjudication and academic discourse. How severe is the problem of overdeterrence, if it exists at all? Do liability-expanding decisions really lead to a flood of suits and to the overburdening of the courts? The answers to these questions may determine the scope of liability and should therefore be based on hard facts and not on unsubstantiated assumptions.

17. TORT LIABILITY FOR FEDERAL GOVERNMENT ACTIONS IN THE UNITED STATES: AN OVERVIEW

*Helene M Goldberg**

The United States inherited from Britain both its common law tradition and the concept of sovereign immunity. The United States is immune from suit except so far as it has waived its sovereign immunity. Waivers of sovereign immunity must be express and are strictly construed.[1] Against this backdrop of sovereign immunity, Congress and the Supreme Court have struggled to develop a system of remedies that would compensate for wrongs committed by the federal government but would not stifle the initiative and judgment needed for a vital government. The evolution of public tort law in the past half-century, through both controversial legislation and contested court decisions, reflects a nuanced approach to reconciling these competing goals. It also tells much about the structure of American government, the separation of powers between the judiciary and Congress, and the dynamic tension between the branches of government.

I. THE FEDERAL TORT CLAIMS ACT

Congress enacted the first coherent basis for federal government's liability for its torts in 1946, after two decades of debate. Prior to the enactment of the Federal Tort Claims Act (FTCA), recovery for federal government actions was available only through private legislation or a few isolated statutes allowing ex gratia payments. As it currently reads, the FTCA, codified in 28 USC §1346 and 28 USC §§2671 et seq, provides both a limited waiver of sovereign immunity and a procedural framework for pursuing claims against the United States.

A. *Waiver of Sovereign Immunity*

The Act waives sovereign immunity for acts or omissions of an 'employee of the government while acting within the scope of his office or employ-

---

* Atlantic Fellow in Public Policy at BIICL. At the time of writing Ms Goldberg is on sabbatical from the US Department of Justice, where she is director, Torts Branch. The views expressed in this article are the author's only and do not reflect the position of the US Department of Justice.
[1] *Smith v United States*, 507 US 197, 203 (1993).

ment, under circumstances where the United States, if a private person, would be liable to the claimant in accordance with the law of the place where the act or omission occurred'.[2] The FTCA provides the *exclusive* basis for tort claims against the United States; even tort claims against agencies that have statutory authority to sue and be sued in their own name are strictly governed by the FTCA.[3] As discussed below, however, individual government employees may be sued in their personal capacities for constitutional torts.

The FTCA's seemingly straightforward waiver of sovereign immunity raises three questions: (1) who is an employee of the United States; (2) when is he or she acting within the scope of his office or employment; and (3) how does one establish the basis for liability. The FTCA defines employee as including 'persons acting on behalf of a federal agency in an official capacity, temporarily or permanently in the service of the United States, whether with or without compensation'.[4] The term 'federal agency' 'does not include any contractor with the United States'.[5]

The question whether an individual is an employee of the United States for purposes of the FTCA is determined by federal, rather than state, law. As the two leading cases on this issue make clear, the decisive factor is the authority of the government to control the details of the individual's work. In *Logue v United States*,[6] the claimant sued the government based upon alleged negligence by a county jail that had contracted with the Federal Bureau of Prisons to house federal prisoners. The county was required to comply with federal regulations specifying treatment of the federal prisoners, but the United States lacked the authority to supervise the conduct of the jail's employees. In *United States v Orleans*, 425 US 807 (1976), the gravamen of the suit was action by a community organisation that received all of its funding from the federal government and, in fact, was created solely to carry out programs authorised by federal legislation.

In both cases, the Supreme Court determined that the entities were contractors, rather than federal employees, and that, therefore, the United States could not be sued for their actions. As the Supreme Court explained, the question 'is not whether the [entity] receives federal money and must comply with federal standards and regulations, but whether its day-to day operations are supervised by the Federal government'.[7]

By contrast, the question of whether an individual is acting within the scope of his or her employment is determined by state law. The basis for this

---

[2] 28 USC 1346(b).
[3] 28 USC §2679(a); *FDIC v Meyer*, 510 US 308 (1991).
[4] 28 USC §2671
[5] Ibid.
[6] 412 US 521 (1973).
[7] *United States v Orleans*, 425 US, at 815.

apparent anomaly is found in the language of the FTCA itself, which specifies that liability is to be determined 'in accordance with the law of the place where the act or omission occurred'.[8] The question of scope of employment is an element of the substantive respondeat superior law, and thus is governed by state law.[9] Generally, under most states' law, an employee's conduct is deemed to be within the scope of employment if the conduct is of a kind the employee is employed to perform, the conduct occurs substantially within the time and space limits of the employment, and the conduct is actuated, at least in part, by a purpose to serve the employer's business.[10]

And what is encompassed by the waiver of immunity, 'if a private person would be liable in accordance with the law of the place where the act or omission occurred?' The Supreme Court has consistently held that the source of substantive liability under the FTCA means state common law.[11] Thus, the FTCA does not waive sovereign immunity for claims arising from alleged violations of federal law, including federal constitutional law.[12]

B. Exceptions to the Waiver of Sovereign Immunity

There are a number of exceptions to the FTCA, codified at 28 USC §2680. The objectives of these exceptions were to ensure that important governmental activities would not be disrupted by the threat of damage suits, to avoid exposure of the United States to excessive or fraudulent claims and not to extend coverage of the FTCA for matters for which adequate remedies already existed.[13]

Perhaps the most important of the FTCA's exceptions is the discretionary function exception, which excludes all claims 'based upon the exercise or performance or failure to perform a discretionary function or duty on the part of a federal agency or an employee of the Government, whether or not the discretion be abused'.[14] In enacting this provision, Congress gave statutory support to the notion that separation of powers precludes judicial review of public policy decisions by the executive branch. The Supreme Court has examined the discretionary function exception on several occasions, refining and explaining the exception. It is now clear that the discretionary function exception encompasses governmental acts or omissions that (1) involve an element of judgment or choice (2) which is susceptible to policy analysis.[15]

---

[8] 28 USC §1346(b).
[9] See *Williams v United States*, 350 US 857 (1955) (per curiam).
[10] See Restatement (Second) Agency §228 (1958).
[11] See, eg, *United States v Muniz*, 374 US 150, 153 (1963).
[12] *FDIC v Meyer*, 510 US 471 (1994).
[13] *Kosak v United States*, 465 US 848, 858 (1984).   [14] 28 USC §2680(a).
[15] *Gaubert v United States*, 499 US 315, 325 (1991).

'Discretionary conduct is not confined to the policy or planning level.'[16] Indeed, as the Court explained in *Gaubert v United States*, a case challenging regulation of a savings and loan association:[17]

[i]f the routine or frequent nature of a decision were sufficient to remove an otherwise discretionary act from the scope of the exception, then countless policy-based decisions by regulators exercising day-to-day supervisory authority would be actionable. This is not the rule of our cases.

Any permissible exercise of policy judgment is exempt from the waiver of sovereign immunity, but 'when a suit charges an agency with failing to act in accordance with a specific mandatory directive, the discretionary function exception does not apply'.[18] Often, the key to determining the applicability of the discretionary function exception lies in the language of federal laws, regulations or directives governing the government's conduct. By definition, government standards that impose general responsibilities but leave discretion as to how to a federal employee is to accomplish his or her task are covered by the discretionary function exception. In order for directives to deprive an employee of discretion and hence render the conduct subject to suit, there must be 'no element of judgment or choice' and the employee must have 'no rightful option but to adhere to the directive'.[19] Thus, because under the Supremacy Clause[20] state law cannot control federal decision making, only federal directives will be considered for determining whether a federal official possesses the requisite discretion. Nor can the discretionary function exception be avoided by arguing that the agency lacks discretion to breach a duty imposed by state negligence law. As the United States Court of Appeals for the Ninth Circuit explained, '[s]uch a rule would collapse the discretionary function inquiry into the basic issue of negligence.'[21]

Properly applied, the discretionary function exception serves a vital role, ensuring that government decision-makers are free to balance competing policy considerations without the threat of tort liability based upon judicial second-guessing. Sloppy application of the exception can lead to either the failure to achieve this goal or to the use of the exception as an improper shield against negligence in the administration of government programs. Key to the correct application of the discretionary function exception is the careful identification of the challenged conduct. The Supreme Court's decision in *Berkovitz v United States* is instructive.[22] The parents of a child who had contracted polio from taking oral polio vaccine sued the United States,

---

[16] Ibid, at 325.   [17] *Gaubert*, 499 US at 334.
[18] *Berkovitz v United States*, 486 US 531, 544 (1988).
[19] *Gaubert*, 499 US, at 322.   [20] United States Constitution, Art VI, cl 2.
[21] *Kennewick Irrigation District v United States*, 880 F 2d 1018, 1030 (9th Cir 1989).
[22] *Berkovitz*, 486 US 531.

alleging that the government had been negligent in licensing the manufacturer to make the vaccine and in approving the release of the lot from which their child was vaccinated. The Court analysed each component of the plaintiffs' claim, finding that claims that the government failed to determine whether the manufacturer had complied with mandatory licensing standards were not barred by the discretionary function exception. A claim that the government had erred in its determination might be barred by the exception, however, if it involved policy judgment rather than merely application of objective scientific criteria.[23] Additionally, the Court held that plaintiffs' allegation that the release of the vaccine violated the government's policy of testing all lots of vaccine for safety survived a motion to dismiss, allowing discovery and fact development on whether the alleged policy was in fact mandatory.

Thus, in order to determine whether a claim will be barred by the discretionary function test, one must ascertain whether the actions upon which the claim actually is based involved discretionary decisions based on considerations of public policy. In *Fischer Brothers Sales, Inc v United States*,[24] or example, Chilean grape growers claimed that the Food and Drug Administration banned import of their grapes based upon negligent laboratory inspection, causing economic losses. The United States Court of Appeals for the Third Circuit held that the losses were caused not by the negligent inspection, but by the discretionary decision to impose the ban, and dismissed the claim.

Other key exceptions to the FTCA include claims arising out of 'assault, battery, false imprisonment, false arrest, malicious prosecution, abuse of process, libel, slander, misrepresentation, deceit or interference with contract rights'.[25] There is, however, an exception to this 'intentional tort' exception for claims arising out of assault, battery, false imprisonment, false arrest, abuse of process, or malicious prosecution by investigative or law enforcement officers.

C. The Administrative Claim Requirement and Statute of Limitations

In 1966, twenty years after the passage of the FTCA, Congress amended the Act to make the submission of an administrative claim a prerequisite to filing FTCA actions in court.[26] By requiring the submission and consideration of an administrative claim, Congress intended to encourage fair settlement of tort claims, and reduce unnecessary litigation.[27]

---

[23] Ibid, at 544–5.
[24] 46 F 3d 279 (3d Cir 1995) (en banc).
[25] 28 USC §2680(h).
[26] 28 USC §2675(a).
[27] S Rep No 1327, 89th Cong, 2d Sess, reprinted in 1966 US Code & Cong News 2515, 2516.

An administrative claim must be filed with the agency within 2 years of the claim's accrual, and the claimant must file suit within 6 months of the administrative denial of the claim.[28] The claim must provide written notification that includes sufficient information to allow the agency to investigate the claim and damages must be specified in a sum certain.[29] Damages awarded in FTCA actions may not exceed the amount of the administrative claim, except

where the increased amount is based upon newly discovered evidence not reasonably discoverable at the time of presenting the claim to the federal agency, or upon allegation and proof of intervening facts, relating to the amount of the claim.[30]

When does a cause of action accrue for purposes of the FTCA? The general rule under the FTCA is 'that a tort claim accrues at the time of the plaintiff's injury . . . '[31] When either the fact of the injury or its cause is not apparent, accrual will be delayed until the date the claimant knows, or in the exercise of reasonable diligence, should have known of both the injury and its cause. This 'discovery' rule, however, does not delay accrual of the claim until the claimant is aware that the injury was negligently inflicted.[32]

D. Claims Against Individual Government Employees

Nowhere is the interplay between the Supreme Court and Congress more dramatically displayed than in the area of claims against individual government employees. In *Westfall v Erwin*,[33] the Supreme Court slashed the immunity of federal employees for common law torts arising out of their official actions. Prior to the *Westfall* decision, it was widely understood that federal employees enjoyed absolute immunity from common law tort claims as long as they were acting within the scope of their employment.[34] In *Westfall*, however, the Supreme Court held for the first time that absolute immunity was available only if 'the challenged conduct is within the outer perimeter of an official's duties and "is discretionary in nature".'[35]

By adding the requirement that a federal employee's actions be 'discretionary in nature', the Court significantly restricted the previously recognised scope of absolute immunity for common law torts. At the same time, however, the Supreme Court invited Congress to review by legislation the

---

[28] 28 USC §2401(b).
[29] See, eg, *Ahmed v United States*, 30 F 3d 514 (4th Cir 1994).
[30] 28 USC §2675(b).
[31] *United States v Kubrick*, 444 US 11, 120 (1979).
[32] Ibid, at 123–4.
[33] 484 US 292 (1988).
[34] See eg, *Barr v Matteo*, 360 US 564 (1959) (plurality opinion). See also *Howard v Lyons*, 360 US 593 (1959).
[35] 484 US, at 296 (emphasis added).

standard it had adopted. The Court stated that 'Congress is in the best position to provide guidance for the complex and often highly empirical inquiry into whether absolute immunity is warranted in a particular context.'[36] The Court added that 'legislated standards governing the immunity of federal employees involved in state law tort actions would be useful'.[37]

Within 10 months, Congress responded to the Court's invitation by enacting legislation to overturn the *Westfall* decision. The legislation is officially titled the Federal Employees Liability Reform and Tort Compensation Act of 1988 but is known, for obvious reasons, as the Westfall Act. The Westfall Act restores the absolute immunity of government employees for common law torts arising from acts within the scope of their employment by requiring claimants in such cases to proceed exclusively against the United States under the FTCA.

The Westfall Act amends 28 USC §2679(b) to provide that the FTCA's remedy against the United States for negligent or wrongful acts by government employees acting within the scope of their employment 'is exclusive of any other civil action or proceeding for money damages . . . against the employee whose act gave rise to the claim. . . .' It is important to note, however, that does not apply to claims arising under federal statute or the federal Constitution.[38]

In the words of the House report on the Westfall Act,

the availability of suit under the FTCA precludes any other civil action or proceeding of any kind from being brought against an individual Federal employee or his estate if such action would sound in common law tort.[39]

Congress's purpose in enacting this exclusive remedy scheme was to render federal employees 'immune for personal liability' for actions within the scope of their employment, thereby 'return[ing] [them] to the status they held prior to the *Westfall* decision'.[40] Recognising this, the Supreme Court has made clear that this exclusivity applies even where an exception to the FTCA renders the United States immune from suit for claimant's claim.[41]

The Westfall Act's exclusive remedy provision is implemented by the Attorney General's issuance of a 'scope certification'—a certification that 'the defendant employee was acting within the scope of his office or employment at the time of the incident out of which the claim arose'.[42] In the event the Attorney General refuses to certify that the employee was acting within the scope of employment, the employee may petition the court

---

[36] 484 US, at 296. [37] Ibid.
[38] 28 USC §2679 (2)(A). See discussion below.
[39] HR Rep No 700, 100th Cong, 2d Sess 5 (1988) ('House Report'), reprinted in 1988 US Code Cong & Admin News ('USCCAN') 5949.
[40] Ibid, at 4, 1988 USCCAN, at 5947.
[41] *United States v Smith* 499 US 161, 163 (1991). [42] 28 USC §2679(d)(1).

to certify that the employee's actions were within the scope of employ-ment.[43]

Once a scope certification is made, the suit is 'deemed an action against the United States' under the FTCA and that 'the United States shall be substituted as the party defendant'.[44] Any such action 'shall proceed in the same manner as any action against the United States [under the FTCA] . . . and shall be subject to the limitations and exceptions applicable to those actions'.[45]

Although the statute is silent on the question of `reviewability' of the certification, the Supreme Court has now determined that the Attorney General's certification is subject to review by the district court.[46] Most courts have held that this review is *de novo*, but that the certification has the effect of shifting the burden of proof on the scope of employment issue to the claimant.[47]

II. CONSTITUTIONAL TORTS

A. Damage Remedies for Constitutional Violations

As noted above, the United States has not waived sovereign immunity for constitutional violations, and thus cannot be sued for damages for such violations. Nor is there a general statutory authorisation for liability of individual federal government employees for violations of constitutional rights.[48] Although a party may seek injunctive relief to protect against continuing prospective constitutional violations, there may be cases where individuals have suffered serious constitutional deprivations for which injunctive relief provides no remedy. It was in precisely such a case, *Bivens v Six Unknown Federal Narcotics Agents*,[49] involving a warrantless and destructive search of the claimant's home that the Supreme Court recog-nised for the first time a right to recover money damages from government employees personally for the violation of one's constitutional rights. In a decision reflecting the sharp disagreement over the role of the courts, the majority held that federal courts' jurisdiction over questions of federal law carried with it the ability to fashion a damage remedy for the violation of

---

[43] Ibid (3).   [44] Ibid (4).   [45] Ibid.

[46] *Gutierrez v deMartinez v Lamagno*, 515 US 417 (1995).

[47] See *Maron v United States*, 126 F 3d 317, 322 (4th Cir 1997).

[48] Title 42 USC §1983 provides a cause of action for constitutional deprivations committed by individual acting under colour of *state* law, but this does not apply to federal actors. Federal officials may be liable under other civil rights statutes that provide a cause of action for discriminatory actions, but these generally require a showing of class-based discrimination. See, eg, 42 USC §§1985, 1986.

[49] 403 US 388 (1971).

constitutional rights. The dissenters (Burger, CJ, Black, J, Blackmun, J) argued strenuously that the creation of such a remedy was a matter for congressional determination beyond the power of the Court, with Chief Justice Burger going so far as to propose a remedial scheme for Congressional consideration.[50]

Although *Bivens* arose in the context of the Fourth Amendment, nothing in the opinion limits the availability of a damages remedy for constitutional violations of the Fourth Amendment, and indeed the Court has extended the damages remedy to violations of the due process clause of the Fifth Amendment,[51] the Eighth Amendment,[52] and implicitly the First Amendment.[53] The *Bivens* Court did recognise two important exceptions to this right to recover money damages for violations of constitutional rights, however. A money remedy should not be inferred where there are 'special factors counselling hesitation' or an 'explicit congressional declaration' that money damages may not be awarded.[54] These 'escape valves' have provided fertile ground for the ongoing debate regarding the role of the courts in creating remedies for constitutional violations, and not always with logically consistent results.

In *Carlson v Green*,[55] the Supreme Court determined that the existence of a statutory remedy under the FTCA was not a 'special factor counselling hesitation' against creation of a damages remedy for actions claimed to be in violation of a prisoner's Eighth Amendment right to be free from cruel and unusual punishment. In 1974, following the Court's decision in *Bivens*, Congress amended the FTCA to allow recovery for common law claims for intentional torts by law enforcement officers.[56] Reading the legislative history of this amendment as indicating that Congress intended to create a parallel remedy, the Court held that the availability of relief complemented but did not replace the *Bivens* remedy. The majority found support for its holding in four factors: the deterrent effect of a *Bivens* remedy, the presumed availability of punitive damages against individual defendants,[57] the availability of a jury trial in a *Bivens* action,[58] and the dependence of an FTCA remedy upon state law.[59] Thus, concluded the Court, the 'FTCA is not a sufficient protector of the citizens' constitutional rights, and without a clear congressional mandate we cannot hold that Congress relegated

---

[50] 403 US at 422–3.
[51] *Davis v Passman*, 442 US 228 (1979).
[52] *Carlson v Green*, 446 US 14 (1980).
[53] *Crawford-El v Britton*, 523 US 574 (1999).
[54] *Bivens*, 403 US at 396–7.
[55] 446 US 14 (1980).
[56] 28 USC §2680(h).
[57] Punitive damages are not available under the FTCA. 28 USC §2674.
[58] Under the FTCA, fact-findings are reserved to the judge. 28 USC §2402.
[59] 28 USC §1346(b).

respondent exclusively to the FTCA remedy'.[60] In dissent, Chief Justice Burger railed:[61]

Until today, I had thought that *Bivens* was limited to those circumstances in which a civil rights claimant had no other effective remedy. Now it would seem that the implications of a *Bivens*-type remedy is permissible even though a victim of an unlawful official action may be fully recompensed under an existing statutory scheme. I have difficulty believing that the Court has thought through, and intends the natural consequences, of this test; I cannot escape the conclusion that in future cases the Court will be obliged to retreat from the language of today's decision.

Indeed, only three years later the pendulum had begun to swing back. In *Bush v Lucas*,[62] the Court refused to infer a *Bivens* remedy for alleged constitutional violations arising out of the federal employment relationship, which is protected by a comprehensive system of statutory safeguards. In reaching this conclusion, however, the Court seemed to engage in a legislative type decision-making.

The question is not what remedy the court should provide for a wrong that would otherwise go unredressed. It is whether an elaborate remedial system that has been constructed step by step, with careful attention to conflicting policy considerations, should be augmented by the creation of a new judicial remedy for the constitutional violation at issue. The question obviously cannot be answered simply by noting that existing remedies do not provide complete relief for the claimant. The policy judgment should be informed by a thorough understanding of the existing regulatory structure and the respective costs and benefits that would result from the addition of another remedy for violations of employees' First Amendment rights.[63]

In *Schweicker v Chilicky*,[64] the Court went even further, holding that Congress, in enacting the comprehensive Social Security review system, provided the only permissible remedies for wrongs resulting from the denial of Social Security benefits. Writing for a 6 : 3 majority in an opinion that sparked strong dissent, Justice O'Connor noted:

The concept of 'special factors counselling hesitation in the absence of affirmative action by Congress' has proved to include an appropriate judicial deference to indications that congressional inaction has not been inadvertent. When the design of a government program suggests that Congress has provided what it considers adequate remedial mechanisms for constitutional violations that may occur in the course of its administration, we have not created additional Bivens remedies.[65]

---

[60] *Carlson v Green*, 446 US, at 23.
[61] Ibid at 31 (Burger, CJ, dissenting) (citations omitted).
[62] 462 US 367 (1983).
[63] 462 US at 488.
[64] 487 US 412 (1988).
[65] Ibid at 423.

Thus, under this decision, even where a statutory remedy provides undeniably incomplete relief, a *Bivens* damage remedy may not be inferred. The majority did not discuss the apparent incongruity between this holding and the ruling in *Carlson v Green*, 8 years before.

In its most recent decision addressing the applicability of *Bivens*, *Correctional Services Corp v Malesko*,[66] the Supreme Court has completed the circle. In a sharply divided 5 : 4 decision, the Court refused to apply *Bivens* to provide a remedy for constitutional violations against a private corporation running a prison under contract with the federal Bureau of Prisons. The philosophical divide of the Court is demonstrated clearly by the framing of the question. The majority characterised the decision as a refusal to extend *Bivens* to new contexts, and held that such an extension would not serve the deterrent function of individual liability. By contrast, the dissent stated that 'the question presented in this case is whether the Court should create an exception to the straightforward application of *Bivens* and *Carlson*, not whether we should extend our cases beyond their "core premise"'.[67]

The *Malesko* decision may well reflect a fundamental hostility to any damages remedy for constitutional violations. Justice Scalia, joined by Justice Thomas, noted in his concurrence, '*Bivens* is a relic of the heady days in which this Court assumed common-law powers to create causes of action—decreeing them to be implied by the mere existence of a statutory or constitutional prohibition.'[68] At this juncture, however, the basic principle of individual liability for violations of constitutional rights is so well entrenched in the nation's jurisprudence that any change in the law is likely to be seen only at the margins.

B. Immunity Doctrines

Contrary to the *Bivens* majority's belief,[69] Justice Blackmun was indeed correct in predicting that the Court's creation of a damages remedy for constitutional torts would 'open [. . .] the door for another avalanche of new federal cases'.[70] In the 30 years since *Bivens* was decided, many thousands of federal employees have been subjected to suit based upon claims of constitutional violations. Significantly, only about 100 of these suits have resulted in final judgments against individual government employees.

Suits against individual federal employees are particularly disruptive of government operations. As the Supreme Court explained:[71]

---

[66] 122 S Ct 516 (2001).
[67] *Malesko*, 122 S Ct, at 521 (Stevens, J dissenting).
[68] Ibid, at 524.   [69] 403 US at 391 n 4.
[70] 403 US at 430.
[71] *Harlow v Fitzgerald*, 457 US 800, 814 (1982)(citations omitted).

claims frequently run against the innocent as well as the guilty at a cost not only to the defendant officials, but to society as a whole. These social costs include the expenses of litigation, the diversion of official energy from pressing public issues, and the deterrence of able citizens from acceptance of public office. Finally, there is the danger that fear of being sued will 'dampen the ardor of all but the most resolute, or the most irresponsible [public officials], in the unflinching discharge of their duties.

Thus, in order to balance the rights of those who have genuinely been deprived of constitutional rights by government employees with the need to protect government employees from unfounded and disruptive suits, courts have developed immunity doctrines specially adapted to constitutional tort litigation.

The Supreme Court has repeatedly recognized that some form of immunity is necessary to protect government employees from frivolous suits. For officials whose special function or constitutional status requires complete protection from suit, the Court has recognised the defence of absolute immunity. Legislators, in their legislative functions,[72] judges in their judicial functions,[73] and prosecutors in their prosecutorial functions,[74] are all absolutely immune from suit. The President also enjoys absolute immunity for actions taken during his presidency.[75]

Most government employees, however, are protected not by absolute immunity, but by a qualified immunity from suit. As originally formulated, the qualified immunity defence required a showing of both 'objective' and 'subjective' good faith. In *Harlow*,[76] the Supreme Court held that the subjective element of the good faith test was incompatible with the precept that insubstantial suits against government employees should not proceed to trial. An employee's subjective intent could easily be cast as a disputed fact question, thus precluding disposition of the case by summary judgment. Moreover, as the Court noted:

Judicial inquiry into subjective motivation . . . may entail broad-ranging discovery and the deposing of numerous persons, including an official's professional colleagues. Inquiries of this kind can be peculiarly disruptive of effective government.

In order to maintain the proper balance between claimants' rights and the proper functioning of government, the Supreme Court formulated a new test based solely upon objective factors. Under this new test, government employees performing discretionary functions, generally are shielded from

---

[72] *Eastland v United States Servicemen's Fund*, 421 US 491(1975).
[73] *Stump v Sparkman*, 435 US 349 (1978).
[74] *Imbler v Pachtman*, 424 US 409 (1976).
[75] *Nixon v Fitzgerald*, 457 US 731 (1982).
[76] 457 US 800, 814 (1982).

liability for civil damages insofar as their conduct does not violate clearly established statutory or constitutional rights of which a reasonable person would have known.[77]

The Court stressed that reliance upon the objective reasonableness of an official's conduct, measured by reference to clearly established law, should permit the resolution of insubstantial claims on summary judgment. Indeed, the Court instructed that discovery should not be allowed until the threshold issue of immunity is resolved.[78]

The Court's proscription of discovery prior to resolution of the threshold issue of immunity is central to the delicate balance struck between the ability of individuals to vindicate their constitutional rights and the protection of government employees from frivolous and disruptive suits. The immunity afforded government employees is

an immunity from suit rather than a mere defence to liability.[79] This immunity from suit would be effectively lost if a defendant were improperly subjected to the burdens of discovery or trial.[80]

Accordingly, the Court found that denials of qualified immunity on motions were immediately appealable. The availability and utility of this right of interlocutory appeal were severely constrained, however, when in 1995, the Supreme Court decided, largely for reasons of judicially economy, to bar interlocutory appeals of denials of qualified immunity on summary judgment insofar as the appeal challenged a determination that the pre-trial record contained material issues of fact.[81]

As the Supreme Court explained in *Anderson v Creighton*,[82] '[t]he operation of this [qualified immunity] standard . . . depends upon the level of generality at which the relevant "legal rule" is to be identified.' Reasoning that the 'clearly established rights' standard would be meaningless if it were applied on a general, abstract level, the Court held that a claimant may overcome an official's qualified immunity only if, in light of pre-existing law, the unlawfulness of the specific action upon which the claimant's claims are based was apparent. To do otherwise would destroy 'the balance that our cases strike between the interests in vindication of citizens' constitutional rights and in public officials' effective performance of their duties' by making it impossible for officials 'reasonably [to] anticipate when their conduct may give rise to liability for damages'.[83]

The operation of the qualified immunity standard is well demonstrated by the Supreme Court's opinion in *Wilson v Layne*.[84] In that case, representatives of the media accompanied federal law enforcement officers who,

---

[77] *Harlow,* 437 US at 818.   [78] Ibid.
[79] *Mitchell v Forsyth,* 472 US 511, 526 (1985).   [80] Ibid.
[81] *Johnson v Jones,* 515 US 304 (1995).   [82] 483 US 635, 639 (1987).
[83] Ibid, at 639 (citations omitted).   [84] 526 US 603 (1999).

pursuant to warrant, searched the petitioners' home for their son, a dangerous fugitive. The Wilson's son was not at their home, and after a protective search of the home, the officers departed. During the course of the search, media photographers took several photographs, which were never published. The Wilsons sued the law enforcement officers, alleging that the officers' actions in bringing members of the media to observe and record the attempted execution of the arrest warrant violated their Fourth Amendment rights.

In ruling on the defendants' defence of qualified immunity, the Court explained:[85]

A court evaluating a claim of qualified immunity must first determine whether the plaintiff has alleged the deprivation of an actual constitutional right at all, and if so, proceed to determine whether that right was clearly established at the time of the alleged violation.

The Court weighed the strong privacy interest in the sanctity of one's home against the proffered justifications for inclusion of the media—good public relations for the police and the need for accurate reporting on police issues. Finding the reasons insufficient for the intrusion, the Court held that it is a violation of the Fourth Amendment to bring members of the media or other third parties into a home during the execution of a warrant when the presence of the third parties is not in aid of the execution of the warrant.[86]

The Court then turned to the qualified immunity analysis. Surveying the body of law addressing this issue, the Court found that there were no cases of controlling authority in the petitioners' jurisdiction nor was there a consensus of persuasive authority such that a reasonable officer would have believed that taking members of the media along was unlawful. Rather, the law on the issue of 'media ride-alongs' was at the time of the incident 'at best undeveloped'.[87] Moreover, the court noted that between the time of the incident and its decision a split had developed among the federal courts of appeal. 'If judges thus disagree on a constitutional question, it is unfair to subject police to money damages for picking the losing side of the controversy.'[88]

C. Pleading Requirements

In order to ensure that federal officials receive the benefit of their qualified immunity from suit, it is essential that '[i]nsubstantial lawsuits . . . be quickly terminated by federal courts alert to the possibilities of artful pleading.'[89] Thus, the Supreme Court has repeatedly admonished lower courts to

---

[85] Ibid, at 609.   [86] Ibid, at 614.   [87] Ibid, at 617.
[88] Ibid.
[89] *Butz v Economou*, 438 US 507-08 (1978).

rely upon a 'firm application of the Federal Rules of Civil Procedure [to] ensure that federal officials are not harassed by frivolous suits'.[90]

To this end, most courts of appeal had required a heightened degree of specificity and completeness in constitutional tort complaints against government officials. Under these formulations, once immunity was asserted, the claimant must set forth his allegations with sufficient precision and specificity to negate the claim of immunity. Thus, theoretically the court would be able to determine the threshold issue of immunity before the defendant was forced to endure the burdens of discovery and further proceedings.

The state of the law regarding such heightened pleading standards now is at best in a muddle. In *Crawford-El v Britton*,[91] the Supreme Court reviewed a heightened proof standard imposed by the United States Court of Appeals for the District of Columbia Circuit in a case in which a prisoner alleged that a prison official had diverted his personal belongings in retaliation for the prisoner's criticism of the prison system. As the Supreme Court made clear in *Harlow v Fitzgerald*, 'bare allegations of malice' are insufficient to defeat an official's immunity.[92] Yet, in some cases, the subjective motivation of the government employee is an essential element of the claimant's cause of action. In certain circumstances, for example, an unconstitutional motive can transform an otherwise legal action into an abridgment of First Amendment rights. Such cases pose a difficult challenge for courts: because resolution of the claim is dependent upon proof of motivation, the cases are less susceptible to summary resolution, yet discovery and trial into the official's motivation are the very ills found so disruptive to sound government in *Harlow*. Moreover, 'an official's state of mind is easy to allege and hard to prove', *Crawford-El v Britton*.[93] In an attempt to deal with this problem, the District of Columbia Circuit formulated a rule requiring proof of improper motive by clear and convincing evidence.

By a bare majority, the Supreme Court reversed the court of appeals. Once again, the Court invoked a distinction between legislative and judicial authority, noting:[94]

the Court of Appeals adopted a heightened proof standard in large part to reduce the availability of discovery in actions that require proof of motive. To the extent that the court was concerned with this procedural issue, our cases demonstrate that questions regarding pleading, discovery and summary judgment are most frequently and effectively resolved either by the rulemaking process or the legislative process.

The majority was at pains to distinguish its reasoning in *Harlow* from its view of *Crawford-El*. 'Our holding in *Harlow*, which related only to the

---

[90] Ibid, *Harlow v Fitzgerald*, 457 US at 819–20 n 35 (1982).
[91] 523 US 574 (1998).   [92] 457 US, at 817.
[93] 523 US, at 585 (citations omitted).   [94] Ibid, at 595.

scope of an affirmative defence, provides no support for making any change in the nature of the claimant's burden of proving a constitutional violation.'[95] The dissenters were unconvinced, noting that any minimally competent litigant could convert an adverse decision into a motive based tort, and 'therefore subject government officials to some measure of intrusion into their subjective worlds'.[96]

In the majority's view, its decision in *Crawford-El* did not leave official defendants charged with motive based constitutional torts facing an inevitable trial.

When a plaintiff files a complaint against a public official alleging a claim that requires proof of a wrongful motive, the trial court must exercise its discretion in a way that protects the substance of the qualified immunity defense.[97]

Admonishing district court judges to ensure that defendants were not subjected to unnecessary and burdensome discovery or trial proceedings the majority noted several provisions of the Federal Rules of Civil Procedure that could be used to ensure that the protections of qualified immunity were not diluted. These included requiring a reply to the answer or a more definite statement from the defendant, resolving the legal issues of a qualified immunity motion before allowing discovery, and limiting both the scope and extent of discovery.

Whether the *Crawford-El* majority's instructions to district court judges to use their case management discretion will indeed protect official defendants from unnecessary and burdensome discovery and trial proceedings remains to be seen. What is clear, however, is that the decision has created substantial uncertainty in the lower courts about the continued viability of heightened pleading requirements in constitutional torts cases. Because the *Crawford-El* Court made expansive disapproving references to special procedural rules for qualified immunity cases but explicitly dealt only with a heightened *proof* standard, it is difficult to know whether prior Circuit precedent endorsing heightened pleading standards survive. Thus far, the Seventh,[98] Tenth,[99] and District of Columbia Circuits[100] have held that they do not; the First[101] and Ninth Circuits[102] continue to apply heightened pleading requirements.

---

[95] *Crawford-El*, 23 US, at 589.
[96] Ibid, at 605 (Rehnquist, CJ dissenting).
[97] *Crawford-El*, 523 US, at 597.
[98] *Nance v Vieregge*, 147 F 3d 589, 590 (7th Cir 1998).
[99] *Currier v Dorran*, 242 F 3d 905, 915-16 (10th Cir 2002).
[100] *Harbury v Deutsch*, 233 F 2d 596, 611 (DC Cir 2000).
[101] *Judge v City of Lowell*, 160 F 3d 67, 72–5 (1st Cir 1998).
[102] *Johnson v State of California*, 207 F 3d 650 (9th Cir 2001).

D. *Statute of Limitations*

As noted above, constitutional tort or *Bivens* actions are a judicially created remedy. Perhaps for this reason, Congress has never established a statute of limitations that would govern the period in which such actions may be brought. Faced with a similar gap with regard to civil rights actions brought under 42 USC §1983,[103] the Supreme Court has ruled that the state personal injury statute of limitations should govern the institution of §1983 actions.[104] This ruling did not fully resolve the question, however. Many states have different limitations periods for certain enumerated intentional torts and a residual statute for all other personal injury statutes. In order to avoid the many difficulties and imprecision involved in attempting to fit the square pegs of various constitutional violations into the round holes for enumerated personal injuries, the Supreme Court subsequently held that the residual or general personal injury statute of limitations should control.[105]

The statutes of limitations adopted by the different states vary markedly, from 1 year to 6 years for precisely the same type of conduct. In addition, for purposes of 42 USC §1983, courts look to state law to determine when the statute of limitations should be tolled. *Board of Regents v Tomanio*.[106] As the United States Court of Appeals for the Seventh Circuit explained:

The actual generosity of a statute of limitations depends not only on the nominal period within which suit must be brought but on provisions allowing that period to be extended for various reasons, so that if the federal court borrows just the period it may in fact be giving plaintiffs more or less time than the state that enacted the borrowed statute would have thought appropriate in the circumstances. [107]

State tolling principles vary as widely as the limitations periods themselves.

III. THE CONFLUENCE OF FTCA AND CONSTITUTIONAL TORT CLAIMS

Many cases present claims that may fairly be alleged both as common law torts and as constitutional torts. For example, a seizure that violates the Fourth Amendment may also involve a common law false arrest claim. In such a case, a claimant may seek damages against the United States for the

---

[103] This statute provides legal or equitable remedies for constitutional or other deprivations by persons acting under colour of state law. Because §1983 provides protections against constitutional violations, §1983 actions are frequently viewed as analogous to *Bivens* actions. As the discussion below indicates, however, there are some fundamental differences that may justify different treatment of the two types of actions.

[104] *Wilson v Garcia* 471 US 261 (1985).

[105] *Owens v Okure*, 488 US 235 (1989).

[106] 446 US 478, 486–7 (1980).

[107] *Lewellen v Morley* 875 F 2d 118, 121 (7th Cir 1989).

common law torts and against the individual government employees for the constitutional tort claims.[108]

The FTCA, while not extending to constitutional tort claims, does contain a provision that nonetheless may result in the dismissal of the constitutional tort claim. Pursuant to 28 USC §2676:

> [t]he judgment in an [FTCA] action . . . shall constitute a complete bar to any action by the claimant, by reason of the same subject matter, against the employee of the government whose act or omission gave rise to the claim.

Although some courts have interpreted this provision as requiring a judgment against the Government in the FTCA action, the prevailing view now is that either a judgment of dismissal or a judgment in favour of the claimant bars any further suit against the individual employees.[109] As the court of appeals explained in *Gasho,* the legislative history of this provision indicates that in enacting the judgment bar Congress intended to prevent both dual recoveries and multiple lawsuits. Accordingly, the court held:[110]

> That any FTCA action, regardless of outcome, bars a subsequent *Bivens* action on the same conduct that was at issue in the prior action. Our interpretation of §2676 serves the interests of judicial economy. Plaintiffs contemplating both a *Bivens* claim and an FTCA claim will be encouraged to pursue their claims concurrently in the same action, instead of in separate actions. This will foster more efficient settlement of claims, since evidence and proof in FTCA and *Bivens* claims often overlap.

Although governmental actions can give rise to both common law and constitutional claims, the courts have made clear that artful pleading may not transform mere negligence into a constitutional violation. As the Supreme Court explained in *Daniels v Williams*:

> Our Constitution deals with the large concerns of the governors and the governed, but it does not purport to supplant traditional tort law in laying down rules of conduct to regulate liability for injuries that attend living together in society.[111]

The Supreme Court underscored the distinction between common law torts and constitutional violations by holding that a claimant's allegation that an employer acted with malice in providing a negative reference that impinged upon the employee's ability to find suitable employment.[112] As

---

[108] Of course, claimant must comply with the administrative claim requirements applicable to the FTCA claim; there is no administrative exhaustion requirement for constitutional claims. *Hoosier Bancorp of Indiana, Inc v Rasmussen,* 90 F 3d 180, 183 (7th Cir 1996).

[109] *Gasho v United States,* 39 F 2d 1420 (9th Cir 1994).

[110] *Gasho,* 39 F 3d at 1437–8. *Accord Farmer v Perrill,* F 3d, 2001 WL 1672290 (10th Cir 2001).

[111] 474 US 327, 332 (1986).

[112] *Siegert v Gilley* 500 US 226 (1991). *Accord DeShaney v Winnebago County Dep't of Social Servs.,* 489 US 189, 203 (1989) (failure to protect from harm caused by third party does not implicate due process); *Brower v Inyo County,* 489 US 593, 596 (1989) (only intentional conduct rises to the level of a seizure under the Fourth Amendment).

the Supreme Court explained in *Baker v McCollan*, 443 US 137, 146 (1979):

Section 1983 imposes liability for violations of rights protected by the Constitution, not for violations of duties of care arising out of tort law. Remedy for the latter type of injury must be sought in state court under traditional tort law principles. Just as medical malpractice does not become a constitutional violation merely because the victim is a prisoner, false imprisonment does not become a violation of the Fourteenth Amendment merely because the defendant is a state official.

In order to state a cause of action for violation of the Eighth Amendment's prohibition against cruel and unusual punishment a claimant must plead deliberate indifference to a substantial risk of harm.[113] The Supreme Court has defined deliberate indifference as requiring a showing that the government official was subjectively aware of the risk.[114]

Moreover, government supervisors and other high level officials cannot be held vicariously liable for the constitutional torts of employees under their supervision.[115] While government supervisors may be liable for their own actions in failing to train or supervise their employees, liability will only attach where the supervisor's failure to train reflects a deliberate indifference to constitutional rights.[116]

IV. CONCLUSION

The American federal tort system is by no means perfect. The patchwork of statutory and judicially created remedies is at times incomplete and frustratingly unpredictable. Despite this, however, it strikes a fair balance between the need for redress of government wrongs and the necessity of a government workforce unafraid to exercise discretion responsibly.

---

[113] *Estelle v Gamble*, 429 US 97, 106 (1976) (only deliberate indifference to serious medical needs, and not negligence such as the mere failure to provide medical care, implicates Eighth Amendment prohibition against cruel and unusual punishment).

[114] *Farmer v Brennan*, 511 US 825, 829 (1994).

[115] *Rizzo v Goode*, 423 US 362, 371 (1976).

[116] *City of Canton v Harris*, 489 US 378 (1989).

18. COMPULSORY ALTRUISM AND PUBLIC AUTHORITIES

*Douglas Brodie**

Irrespective of the identity of the defendant a claimant asserting that a duty of care is owed by virtue of an omission to act faces an uphill struggle:

> The very parable of the Good Samaritan (Luke 10: 30) which was evoked by Lord Atkin in *Donoghue v Stevenson* . . . illustrates in the conduct of the priest and of the Levite who passed by on the other side, an omission which was likely to have as its reasonable and probable consequence damage to the health of the victim of the thieves, but for which the priest and the Levite would have incurred no civil liability in English law.[1]

The literature contains considerable discussion of the merits or otherwise of this position.[2] Traditionally, the focus has tended to be on the potential liability of a private individual. However, the defendant may be a public body and, in that case, should matters be viewed in quite the same light? Before exploring such questions it is important to recognise, given the plethora of statutory powers that exist, that many public bodies can be seen as potential rescuers. Should such a body fail to act, those who suffer loss as a consequence may feel aggrieved. A wide range of public bodies beyond the traditional rescue services have statutory powers to intervene to protect members of the public. One thinks, for example, of regulatory bodies such as the defendant in the case of *Davies v Radcliffe*,[3] local authorities with powers in relation to the construction of buildings[4] and Health and Safety inspectors who have power to prohibit the carrying on of dangerous businesses.[5] For many years the pivotal decision was *East Suffolk Rivers Catchment Board v Kent*.[6] It was viewed as holding that a statutory body does not owe a common law duty of care to exercise its statutory powers to protect you:

> Where a statutory authority is entrusted with a mere power it cannot be made liable for any damage sustained by a member of the public by reason of a failure to exercise that power. If in the exercise of their discretion they

---

* University of Edinburgh.
[1] *Dorset Yacht v Home Office* [1970] AC 1004, 1060 per Lord Diplock.
[2] In the context of public authority liability SH Bailey and MJ Bowman `Public Authority Negligence Revisited' [2000] *CLJ* 85 is a valuable contribution.
[3] [1990] 1 WLR 821.
[4] *Murphy v Brentwood DC* [1991] 1 AC 398.
[5] *Harris v Evans* [1998] All ER 522.
[6] [1941] AC 74.

embark upon an execution of the power, the only duty they owe to any member of the public is not thereby to add to the damages that he would have suffered had they done nothing.[7]

It does not appear that the House of Lords in *East Suffolk* would have arrived at a different conclusion had another statute been in issue. This seems to have been accepted as the correct position for many years until *Anns v Merton LBC*.[8]

I. ANNS AND ITS RATIONALE

In *Anns* the local authority inspectors were held to be under an obligation to give proper consideration as to whether to inspect the foundations and, if they chose to inspect, then this had to done with reasonable care and skill. For Lord Wilberforce consideration of the statutory background was central to any evaluation of the relationship between claimant and defendant: 'The factual relationship between the council and owners and occupiers of new dwellings constructed in their area must be considered in the relevant statutory setting—under which the council acts.'[9] Against that background local authorities were viewed as being 'public bodies operating under statute with a clear responsibility for public health in their area'.[10] The next question was how best to enforce this responsibility and part of the solution was to allow for private law remedies. *Anns* was, of course, notable in allowing recovery for pure economic loss and expounding the policy/operational dichotomy. Equally significant was the fact that it went much further than previous authorities in its rationale for finding that a duty of affirmative action existed. In *Dorset Yacht v Home Office* the basis for proximity had been the existence of a right of control over the prisoners and this led to the deduction that there was a duty to protect third parties who might be affected by a failure to control. However, the right to control was closely linked to the duty to physically detain the prisoners. Accordingly, the decision in *Dorset Yacht* would not, of itself, have led to the belief that a wide range of duties of affirmative action might be imposed on public bodies in the near future. What was remarkable about *Anns* was the inferences drawn from an examination of the statutory responsibilities placed on the local authority by the Public Health Act 1936. The existence of this legislation, which had the purpose of regulating house building and promoting health and safety, gave rise to a relationship of proximity embodying a duty of affirmative action. The fact that the actual content of the duty in *Anns*, with its emphasis on inspection etc, was perhaps not that

---

[7] Ibid, 102.   [8] [1978] AC 728.
[9] Ibid, 752.   [10] Ibid, 755.

dramatic was neither here nor there. In the wake of the decision it must have seemed that numerous other instances of regulatory legislation would also give rise duties of affirmative action. Nevertheless, it appears that affirmative action cases against public bodies after *Anns* were mainly building cases brought against local authorities and that a limited degree of creativity was displayed in the use of *Anns*. Why should this be? It is hard to say but, one factor may have been that, one group who would have seen themselves as potential litigants would be investors whose financial interests had been harmed and who may have believed that a regulatory agency should have intervened. In time such individuals would have to contend with the reaction against recovery for pure economic loss.

II. THE RETREAT FROM *ANNS*

In *Yuen Kun Yeu v A-G of Hong Kong* the Privy Council distinguished the situation it was confronted with from cases like *Dorset Yacht* and a salient difference was said to be the presence in the latter of the 'power to control the day-to-day activities of those who caused the loss and damage'.[11] Public bodies possess a wide range of powers of control and regulation and one might well ask why should any 'day-to-day' element be significant? Of course, the extent of any control that exists will be relevant to the question of the existence and content of the mooted duty. In *Dutton v Bognor Regis UDC* it was held that the local authority owed a duty of care to ensure that byelaws in respect of building work were complied with.[12] The extent of the local authority's control over building matters was regarded as decisive. The nature of that control was explored in some detail by Lord Denning:

the legislature gives the local authority a great deal of control over building work and the way it is done. They make byelaws governing every stage of the work. They require plans to be submitted to them for approval. They appoint surveyors and inspectors to visit the work and see if the byelaws are being complied with. In case of any contravention of the byelaws, they can compel the owner to remove the offending work and make it comply with the byelaws. They can also take proceedings for a fine . . .

He concluded that

the control thus entrusted to the local authority is so extensive that it carries with it a duty. It puts on the council the responsibility of exercising that control properly and with reasonable care.[13]

---

[11] [1988] AC 175, 196.   [12] [1972] 1 QB 373.
[13] Ibid, 392.

Had such reasoning been more generally utilised by the courts a significant number of public bodies would have been caught. One suspects that part of the explanation for the different approach in *Yuen Kun Yeu* was simply a desire to return to a traditional conservative approach in a case which concerned both pure economic loss and affirmative action; it concerned not just one, but two, aspects of negligence law where establishing a duty of care has always been problematic. A further dimension to the decision was the concern that an admission of liability

would surely be equally applicable to a wide range of regulatory agencies, not only in the financial field, but also, for example, to the factory inspectorate and social workers, to name only a few.[14]

Since then the case law has shown itself protective of regulatory bodies. In *Barrett v Ministry of Defence* the Court of Appeal reminded us that 'the mere existence of regulatory or other public duties does not of itself create a special relationship imposing a duty in private law'.[15] One should not be unduly surprised at this since part of the rationale for the setting up of regulatory agencies is to have decisions determined by a body with the appropriate specialist expertise. Such bodies

are created to engage in complex tasks that are specialised and require the exercise of judgment. The notion that precise standards can be used to control agency activity has long been questioned in the USA where most agencies in fact enjoy highly discretionary powers and regulate in pursuit of objectives that are stated in the broadest terms.[16]

Moreover,

where a body such as the judiciary provides the basis for accountability and control through judicial review, it may be objected that the judges are not competent in the relevant area . . . and that the legislature did not, in any event, intend that the courts rather than, say, the agency should decide this issue.[17]

On the other hand, it is possible to contemplate protecting such bodies from the full force of the law of negligence whilst, at the same time, not offering absolute immunity.

III. STOVIN V WISE[18]

In *Stovin* the House of Lords set out stringent criteria which have to be

---

[14] *Yuen Kun Yeu* [1988] AC 175, 198.
[15] [1995] 3 All ER 87, 94.
[16] R Baldwin and C McCrudden, *Regulation and Public Law* (London, 1987), 34–5.
[17] Ibid, 36.
[18] [1996] AC 923. For detailed analysis see J Convery 'Public or Private ? Duty of Care in a Statutory Framework: Stovin v Wise in the House of Lords' 1997 (60) *MLR* 559.

satisfied before a public authority owes a duty of care by virtue of having failed to act:

the minimum pre-conditions for basing a duty of care upon the existence of a statutory power, if it can be done at all, are, first, that it would in the circumstances have been irrational not to have exercised the power, so that there was in effect a public law duty to act, and secondly, that there are exceptional grounds for holding that the policy of the statute requires compensation to be paid to persons who suffer loss because the power was not exercised.[19]

Three features of this dictum call for comment at this juncture. First, the extent of protection given to public authorities where they are said to have failed to act is very considerable. In *Stovin* itself the claimant failed to persuade the Lords that section 79 of the Highways Act 1980 should have been resorted to. Secondly, the protection conferred consists, in part, of a public law hurdle. Thirdly, it prescribes a set of rules specific to situations where a public body has failed to act.

It should be said that it is far from inevitable that the shielding of public bodies from the full rigours of the law of negligence should involve a public law hurdle. It will be recalled that the immunity conferred by *Hill v Chief Constable of West Yorkshire*[20] inhabits the four walls of private law. However, the creation of the public law hurdle may be a reflection of judicial understanding of the private law/public law divide. The appropriate way to regulate public bodies may be thought to be by way of judicial review:

The gradual enlargement of the grounds of attack upon administrative decisions by judicial review would not have occurred if the courts had considered that every time a decision of an official or a tribunal was quashed an action for damages for negligence would potentially be available.[21]

The presence of a public law hurdle may also reflect a desire for coherence between public and private law. One might argue that if the claimant in *Stovin* could not have compelled the local authority to exercise its powers prior to the accident then it would be wrong, in a sense retrospectively, to penalise the authority in a negligence action for omitting to act. This argument would be at its strongest in a case where judicial review had, in fact, been sought but had not been granted. The defendant authority could regard the unsuccessful application as an endorsement of its stance and then argue that the courts should act consistently with that position thereafter. However, acceptance of that view would accord the principles of administrative law a higher status than those of the law of negligence. It is hard to

---

[19]   Ibid, 828, per Lord Hoffmann.   [20]   [1989] AC 53.
[21]   *Rowling v Takaro Properties* [1988] AC 473, 482.

see why this should be the case in a private law action. More prosaically, in the process, it would impose on a claimant a burden more onerous than the law of negligence typically does. After all, it is far from easy to be able to demonstrate that it would have been irrational, in the public law sense, not to exercise a power. This may be partly because a number of the precedents where the public law test of irrationality had been applied would have concerned situations where harm had not yet arisen; some of the judgments may have been, in a sense, hypothetical.[22] Decisions may well have been reached on the assumption that the situation was not dangerous or, at least, not as dangerous as the applicant had alleged. In stark contrast, an action in negligence can only be brought if harm has, in fact, arisen. In determining what the defendant should have reasonably foreseen an adjudicator would find it difficult to disregard what has actually happened. The question of reasonable foreseeability plays a crucial role in the law of negligence but one should not forget it is posed with the benefit of hindsight. Against this backdrop, I would suggest that *Stovin*'s advancement of the public law dimension comes at a very high price. Inserting public law concepts and language into a private law action can but complicate matters. However, a far more fundamental objection is that by imposing a pre-condition, to a negligence action, of a public law hurdle *Stovin* accords a higher priority to public law over private law.

Nevertheless, whilst the public law hurdle may be open to objection, it is much more difficult to dispute that one should be cautious in holding that a public authority should be liable, in any particular situation, for failing to act. A major difference between omission cases against an individual citizen and a public body is that claimants are far more likely to seek to 'pick on' the latter as a defendant. In *Stovin*[23] it was observed that 'the highway authority alone had the financial and physical resources, as well as the legal powers, to eliminate the hazard . . .' The private sector has nothing to fear here since there is no basis upon which any particular defendant can be singled out. However, the existence of statutory powers, whose exercise might have prevented/ameliorated the situation that has arisen, leads to claims that they should have been exercised by the public authority for the benefit of the claimant. All of that said, one must still seek to determine how much protection is appropriate and what form it should take.

---

[22] For instance, Lord Hoffmann observed in *Stovin* [1996] AC 923, 950 that 'A mandamus can require further consideration of the exercise of a power. But an action for negligence looks back to what the council ought to have done.'

[23] *Stovin* [1996] AC 923, 946 per Lord Hoffmann.

IV. THE AIMS OF THE LAW OF NEGLIGENCE

The public law hurdle distorts the operation of private law by virtually removing a failure to act by a public body from the scope of the action of negligence. The role of the concept of duty of care becomes almost superfluous. Justifying such a position would, it is submitted, require an exceptional case. After all, *Stovin* serves to deny the two central aims of the law of negligence—compensation and deterrence. The claim that the imposition of a duty of care contributes to the maintenance of high standards is a long standing one. There is no reason to doubt that this general stance is seen as apposite in relation to public bodies. Indeed in *Stovin* itself Lord Nicholls noted that 'if the existence of a duty of care in all cases, in the shape of a duty to act as a reasonable authority, has a salutary effect on tightening administrative procedures and avoiding another needless road tragedy, this must be in the public interest.[24] Thus it seems wholly appropriate to regard the imposition of a duty of care as a legitimate means of encouraging holders of powers under statute to exercise due care in deciding when and how to make use of them. It is undoubtedly more likely that a duty would be imposed where use of a power might have prevented personal injury. Of course, it may well be said that the extent to which the law of negligence actually deters bad behaviour is doubtful. However, that point could equally well be made in any negligence action. Concerns in the realms of over deterrence may also exist: 'It would not be surprising if one of the consequences of the *Anns* case and the spate of cases which followed was that local council inspectors tended to insist upon stronger foundations than was necessary.'[25] Such arguments may now carry limited weight in the absence of supporting empirical evidence.[26] In any event, there may well be something to be said for the additional pressure on public authority decision-making of a negligence action where personal injury has been suffered; perhaps in some contexts more than others. Any decision in law might prompt a review of an organisation's policy and, in extreme cases, result in legislation. It is, of course, the case that other mechanisms exist (for example, the local government ombudsman) to encourage local authorities to perform their responsibilities. However, a case-by-case approach can take these into account in determining whether a duty should be held to exist. What of the compensation function? A highly restrictive approach to recovery against public bodies diminishes not only the deterrent affect of the law of negligence but denies claimants the benefit of the compensation function. Damages are not always seen by the

---

[24] Ibid, 941.
[25] Ibid, 958, per Lord Hoffmann.
[26] *Arthur J S Hall v Simons* [2000] 3 All ER 673, 683.

courts as the most apposite remedy[27] but, nevertheless, it is usually felt to be the best the law can do.[28]

V. DISTINGUISHING BETWEEN ACTS AND OMISSIONS

A further issue raised by *Stovin* is whether it is appropriate, in the context of a negligence action against as public authority, to treat omissions on a different basis to positive acts. The task of identifying 'pure' omissions is less than straightforward. There are good reasons why, in the case of individual defendants, that task must be addressed given the concern that 'it involves a more serious restraint on individual liberty to require a person to act than it is to place limits on his freedom to act'.[29] Accordingly, concern over the autonomy of defendants requires that 'pure' omissions be identified. However, concern with individual liberty seems much less relevant in the context of public authorities since such bodies are established by the legislature to fulfil prescribed aims:

in some respects the typical statutory framework makes the step to a common law duty to act easier with public authorities than individuals. Unlike an individual, a public authority is not an indifferent onlooker. Parliament confers powers on public authorities for a purpose. An authority is entrusted and charged with responsibilities, for the public good. The powers are intended to be exercised in a suitable case.[30]

In the case of a public authority the more relevant question perhaps becomes whether the defendant has a statutory responsibility to regulate or supervise the area of activity within which the harm has arisen. Where such statutory responsibility exists the next question should be to determine whether a duty of care should be imposed. Unlike the case of private individuals one may doubt whether there is a need to isolate so called 'pure' omissions from omissions which are part of an on-going activity. The case law suggests that a relevant factor, in determining whether a duty of care exists, may be whether a public body can be regarded as having taken control. In *Dutton* it was said that

the negligence plainly occurred in the course of a positive exercise by the council of its powers. The moment it exercised its power . . . to make byelaws it assumed control over all such building operations within its area as were the subject of those byelaws. That assumption of control was a positive act and thereafter . . . any negligence in its exercise fell within the ambit of the decision in the *Geddis* case . . .[31]

---

[27] See, for instance, the speech of Lord Templeman in *Hill v Chief Constable of West Yorkshire* [1989] AC 53, 64.
[28] *M v Newham London BC* [1994] 4 All ER 602, 619.
[29] J Fleming, *The Law of* Torts, 9th edn (Sydney: Law Book Co, 1998), 163.
[30] *Stovin* [1996] AC 923, 935.
[31] *Dutton v Bognor Regis UDC* [1972] 1 QB 373, 403.

In the Scottish case of *Gibson v Chief Constable* a bridge had collapsed due to flooding.[32]. The fire service informed the police as to the condition of the bridge. Two constables had then proceeded to the north side of the bridge and positioned their Land Rover on that side with its blue light flashing and headlights illuminated so as to be visible and give warning to any persons approaching from the south side. They remained with their vehicle so positioned until late afternoon when they withdrew with their vehicle. At the time they did so they had received no information to confirm that any barrier or warning was in place on the south side of the bridge. Within a few minutes of their departure the car in which the pursuer was travelling made is approach from the south side and fell into the river. In holding that a duty of care was owed the actual practice of policing (and perhaps the expectations induced thereby) was important: the key background factor that pointed towards a finding that proximity existed was that

it is within common experience, at least in Scotland, that police officers, in emergencies and otherwise, take control of traffic or other road safety situations with a view better to safeguarding life and property. Such action is no sense dependent on any crime having been committed or on any crime being apprehended. It is a civil function in respect of which constables have authority, with attendant responsibility.[33]

Once the police had taken control of a hazardous road traffic situation they had put themselves into

a sufficiently proximate relationship with road users likely to be immediately and directly affected by the hazard as is sufficient for the purposes of the existence of a duty of care to such road users. That duty may extend not only to the manner of the exercise of that control but...to the relinquishment of it.[34]

In *Stovin* the Court of Appeal may have regarded the local authority as having taken control (even if only administratively); certainly the court was readily persuaded that they were not dealing with a 'pure' omission. It will be recalled that the case concerned whether any liability flowed from the fact that the authority had failed to take steps to ensure improved visibility at a road junction. The local authority had decided to take action and had entered into discussions with the owners (British Rail) with a view to purchase the land. At the time of the accident British Rail had not responded to the authority's proposal of some ten months previously. In the eyes of the Court of Appeal the failure to obtain the consent of British Rail 'could properly be regarded as a negligent method of performing a task which gave rise to obligations . . . '. As a consequence, the authority was not protected by the law on omissions:

---

[32] 1999 SCLR 661.   [33] Ibid, 674.   [34] Ibid, 676.

[It] decided positively to proceed by seeking agreement from British Rail, and its failure to pursue that course is not an omission on which it can rely to escape liability, any more than a car driver could escape liability simply because his breach of duty consisted in a failure to apply the brakes.[35]

At first sight the analogy does not seem sound; the driver is engaged in an on-going activity and the failure to apply the brakes is far removed from a 'pure omission'. However, the local authority undoubtedly had statutory responsibilities for road safety. They had also begun to act; even if road users would not have been aware of this.

Accordingly, should a public authority exercise its statutory functions and take control of a situation the distinction between acts and omissions may be rendered superfluous. However, one might go further and say that in the public authority context the distinction is without value. A better approach may be suggested by *Sargent v Secretary of State for Scotland* where a man was killed in a road accident.[36] He swerved to avoid a bus and his car left the road and fell 20 feet into a loch. Those bare facts are, in themselves, unremarkable. What gives rise to interest is the identity of the defender and the complaint made against them. The widow of the deceased sought damages against the local authority on the basis that there should have been a sign warning of the hazard of buses, a solid barrier, and traffic lights. Bearing in mind that a local authority has no power other than that conferred by statute one might say that the pursuer's complaint was that the local authority had failed to exercise its statutory powers. However, if that is a correct categorisation of the complaint then one would have expected that it be decided on the basis of the decision in *Stovin*. There is, though, no mention of *Stovin* in the judgment; nor does it appear to have been cited to the court. Instead the case was decided on the basis that the locus where the accident took place was hazardous and the accident was reasonably foreseeable. The defender was then held to be liable as they should have taken steps such as erecting signs, which would probably have prevented the accident. Lord Clarke did not regard the case as being about a failure to act. Instead it was treated as being about the maintenance of roads and Lord Clarke holds that a highway authority have a duty to take reasonable care to remove hazards from the road, to prevent reasonably foreseeable accidents arising therefrom.[37] The approach in *Sargent* is reflected in Lord Nicholls's judgment in *Stovin*:

A highway authority is liable in damages for failing to take reasonable care to keep the highway safe. But no sound distinction can be drawn

---

[35] [1994] 3 All ER 467, 480.
[36] 2000 Rep LR 118.
[37] See also the earlier decisions in *Smith v Middleton* 1971 SLT (Notes) 65 and *Fraser v Magistrates of Rothesay* (1892) 19 R 817.

between dangers on the highway itself, where the authority has a statutory duty to act, and other dangers, where there is a statutory power but not a statutory duty. The distinction would not correspond to the realities of road safety. On the council's argument a highway authority would be liable if it carelessly failed to remove a dead tree fallen onto the road, but not liable if it carelessly failed to act after learning of a diseased overhanging tree liable to fall at any moment. Such a legalistic distinction does not commend itself. It would be at variance with ordinary persons' expectations and perceptions.[38]

I would suggest that where a public authority is concerned the courts should, rather than seeking to identify pure omissions, look to see whether the authority in question has statutory responsibility to control, regulate, or supervise the relevant area of social or economic activity in the community. *Sargeant* may furnish a model through its categorisation of the behaviour in question as road maintenance.

VI. PUBLIC EXPECTATIONS

So far I have contended that both the public law hurdle and the distinction between acts and omissions should be departed from. This leaves unanswered the fundamental issue of determining the stance that should be adopted in a situation of the *Stovin* type. In his dissenting judgment Lord Nicholls referred to public 'expectations and perceptions'. Certainly, the public may well look to public bodies to protect them and, if they do not, to pay compensation should injury arise. It is perfectly conceivable that such 'general reliance' on a public body may lead to a duty of care being owed:

there will be cases in which the claimant's reasonable reliance will arise out of a general dependence on an authority's performance of its function with due care, without the need for contributing conduct on the part of a defendant or action to his detriment on the part of a claimant. Reliance or dependence in this sense is in general the product of the grant (and exercise) of powers designed to prevent or minimise a risk of personal injury or disability, recognised by the legislature of being of such a magnitude or complexity that individuals cannot, or may not, take adequate steps for their own protection. The situation generates on one side (the individual) a general expectation that the power will be exercised and on the other side (the authority) realisation that there is a general reliance or dependence on its exercise of power . . . [39]

---

[38] *Stovin* [1996] AC 923, 940.
[39] *Sutherland Shire Council v Heyman* (157) CLR 424, 464, per Mason J.

The potential of the concept of general reliance to extend the scope of the duties owed by public bodies is striking. However, the more pertinent question is when such general reliance is properly placed on a public body. Ultimately the question must be one of policy. It must be conceded that the concept of general reliance did not appeal to the House of Lords in *Stovin*. Lord Hoffmann thought that its application would require 'some very careful analysis of then role which the expected exercise of the statutory power plays in community behaviour'.[40] Nevertheless, the reasoning in *Heyman* has been influential of late in the Court of Appeal in *Perrett v Collins*[41] and *Watson v British Boxing Board of Control*.[42] The decision in *Perrett* is based upon the view that the fundamental concern of the law of negligence is with unreasonable behaviour that entails the risk of personal injury. However, the court also had a clear view as to the nature of the relationship between the individual citizen and bodies who act 'for the collective welfare'. In holding that a duty was owed, mention was made of the (general) reliance placed upon regulatory bodies by the general public:

any reasonably well informed member of the public, although not in possession of the detailed framework, would expect there to be such a regulatory scheme in force to ensure his safety when flying and would rely upon it. Furthermore, a member of the public would expect that a person who is appointed to carry out these functions of inspecting aircraft and issuing permits would exercise reasonable care in doing so.

Such reasoning is resonant of duty of care decisions of the 1970s such as *Dutton v Bognor Regis UDC* which adopted a collectivist stance. *Perrett* also provokes consideration of what would have happened in *Murphy v Brentwood* if the claimant had suffered personal injury or damage to his property. The Law Lords left the question open in that case.[43] *Perrett* would appear to point towards recovery. Lord Justice Buxton going so far as to say that

It was the fact that the damage in *Anns* ... had been wrongly classified as physical damage that led the House in *Murphy* to feel able to differ from the result that was based on that classification ...

When might reasonable reliance be held to have emerged from general dependence upon a public authority's statutory functions? In a case based upon specific reliance one might look for evidence of exchanges or conduct which could have led the claimant to rely reasonably upon the defendant.[44]

---

[40] *Stovin* [1996] AC 923, 954–5.
[41] [1998] 2 Lloyd's Rep 255.
[42] [2001] 2 WLR 1256.
[43] *Murphy v Brentwood DC* [1991] 1 AC 398, 457 per Lord MacKay, 463 per Lord Keith, 492 per Lord Jauncey.
[44] *Natural Life Health Foods v Williams* [1998] 2 All ER 577.

An equivalent approach in a case based upon general reliance might be thought to be the seeking of evidence that

an authority has habitually exercised a power and, in consequence, a person or class of persons has to the knowledge of the authority reasonably relied on the authority continuing to follow its normal practice.[45]

Were such an approach to be required in a case based upon general reliance the claimant's prospects of success might often be slim: 'If the "general expectations of the community" were to be the touchstone of liability, the proof of that fact would present considerable difficulty.'[46] It is, however, noteworthy that no evidence was sought to substantiate the notion of 'general reliance' which was seen as supporting the claimant's case in *Perrett*. It is submitted that this makes sense. It does not seem unreasonable to conclude that members of the public expect public bodies to utilise at least some of their statutory powers to protect them. Even if empirical evidence of the expectations of the public were forthcoming it seems unlikely that such evidence would reveal that the public had expectations of a sufficient degree of specificity to point towards a duty of care being owed in respect of a particular statutory power. What then is the role of general reliance? It is suggested that the concept may reflect, in broad terms, public expectations. The question of whether those expectations should result in a duty of care can only be determined upon further inquiry.

VII. A PRIVATE LAW APPROACH?

It is my contention that the rules governing a negligence action against a public authority should be firmly grounded in private law. The analysis of negligence is sufficiently flexible to provide protection for such defendants where appropriate. Protection through public law is not necessary but will inevitably complicate matters. It must also be said that the question as to whether a duty should be owed in respect of failure to exercise a statutory power does not permit of a general answer.[47] Nevertheless, in determining whether a duty of care exists certain factors are particularly likely to be taken into account. A number were suggested by Lord Nicholls in *Stovin*.[48]

---

[45] *Stovin* [1996] AC 923, 935.

[46] *Pyrenees Shire Council v Day* (192) CLR 330, 344.

[47] It is sometimes suggested that it will be much harder to show that a duty of care arises in respect of failure to exercise a power rather than a duty. It may be doubted whether this should be a factor of significance.

[48] In *Stovin* [1996] AC 923, 937 he states that 'Factors to be taken into account include: the subject matter of the statute (for instance, the regulatory power in *Yuen Kun Keu v Attorney-General of Hong Kong* [1988] AC 175, 195, was quasi-judicial, with a right of appeal); the intended purpose of the statutory duty or power (in *Governors of Peabody*

It would not be surprising if the occurrence of personal injury was to be seen as a particularly important factor. This was certainly the case in *Perrett*. The latter case may also suggest that statutory functions are more likely to give rise to a duty of care should they relate to situations 'of such magnitude or complexity that individuals cannot, or may not, take adequate steps for their own protection'.[49] In the *Pyrenees* case McHugh J referred to

those situations where individuals are vulnerable to harm from immense dangers which they cannot control or understand and often enough can not recognise. Controlling air traffic, fighting fires and inspecting the safety of aircraft are the examples that Mason J gave. In these and similar situations, I do not think that it is a fiction to conclude that members of the community rely on the relevant public authority, often endowed with extensive powers, to protect them from harm.[50]

One notes that in the Canadian case of *Swanson v The Queen*[51] the claimant recovered from a government agency on the basis that they had been negligent in not taking action against an airline they knew to be indulging in unsafe practices.

There is already some evidence to suggest that the Scottish courts may well be more than comfortable in taking on board factors peculiar to public authority liability in negligence at the stage of standard of care rather than at the stage of duty. In *Duff v Highland and Islands Fire Board* the view was expressed that

it is no doubt right that in operational matters much must be left to the professional judgement of the fire-fighters, but that can be achieved by applying a test analogous to the professional negligence test in determining what amounts to negligence. It is going too far . . . to suggest that operational judgement should be immune from challenge.[52]

Donation Fund v Sir Lindsay Parkinson Co Ltd [1985] AC 210 and *Murphy v Brentwood District Council* [1991] 1 AC 398, 408, public health measures were not intended to safeguard owners of buildings against financial loss); whether a concurrent common law duty might inhibit the proper and expeditious discharge of the statutory functions (such as the protection of children at risk, in *X(Minors) v Bedfordshire County Council* [1995] 2 AC 633, 749–51); the nature of the loss (whether physical injury or purely financial); the ability of the claimant to protect himself (in *Just v British Columbia* (1989) 64 DLR (4th) 689 a road user was injured by a rock falling onto his car); the adequacy of the public law remedies (*Rowling v Takaro Properties Ltd.* [1988] AC 473, 501–2 and *Jones v Department of Employment* [1989] QB 1, 22, 24–5); and the presence or absence of a particular reason why the claimant was relying or dependent on the authority (as in *Invercargill City Council v Hamlin* [1996] AC 624, and see the New Zealand Court of Appeal [1994] 3 NZLR 513, 519, 524–5, 530). This list is by no means exhaustive, and each case will turn upon the particular combination of factors present or absent.

[49] *Sutherland Shire Council v Heyman* (157) CLR 424, 464, per Mason J.
[50] *Pyrenees Shire Council v Day* (192) CLR 330, 370.
[51] 80 DLR (4th edn) 741.
[52] *Duff v Highland & Islands Fire Board* 1995 SLT 1362, 1363.

Such an approach can, for instance, make allowance for the fact that members of the emergency services will often have very little time to reflect before making very important decisions.[53] In *Gibson* Lord Hamilton indicated that the police would be treated in line with the foregoing cases when the question of standard of care was considered. Scholars of comparative law will be aware that the Canadian courts regard the concept of standard of care as a useful device through which one can balance the interests of a claimant against the interests of a defendant who is a public body. In *Just v British Columbia* the Supreme Court of Canada explained how the concept of standard of care might be applied where an action was brought against a public body:

let us assume a case where a duty of care is clearly owed by a governmental agency to an individual that is not exempted either by a statutory provision or because it was a true policy decision. In those circumstances the duty of care owed by the government agency would be the same as that owed by one person to another. Nevertheless the standard of care imposed upon the Crown may not be the same as that owed by an individual. An individual is expected to maintain his or her sidewalk or driveway reasonably, while a government agency such as the respondent may be responsible for the maintenance of hundreds of miles of highway. The frequency and the nature of inspection required of the individual may well be different from that required of the Crown. In each case the frequency and method must be reasonable in light of all the surrounding circumstances. The governmental agency should be entitled to demonstrate that balanced against the nature and quantity of the risk involved, its system of inspection was reasonable in light of all the circumstances including budgetary limits, the personnel and equipment available to it and that it had met the standard duty of care imposed upon it.[54]

It may be said that a decision for the claimant in a case like *Stovin*

would distort the priorities of local authorities, which would be bound to try to play safe by increasing their spending on road improvements rather than risk enormous liabilities for personal injury accidents.[55]

One might well accept that there is a risk that democratic decisions as to, for instance, allocation of resources will be disturbed. However, the point can be met without the creation of a public law hurdle. The dictum in *Just* quoted in the preceding paragraph indicates that, to some extent, such considerations may be taken into account at the stage of breach of duty. It is also the case that public authorities can protect themselves, to some extent by the taking of policy decisions. It may be objected that the policy/operational dichotomy itself is a public law device.[56] However, as

---

[53] *McCafferty v Secretary of State* 1998 SCLR 379 (N), 382.
[54] (1989) 64 DLR (4th ed) 689.
[55] *Stovin* [1996] AC 923, 958.
[56] Undoubtedly its origins are: Fleming, op cit, 213.

part of normal private law discourse it is perfectly legitimate to regard certain issues as non-justiciable; consideration of policy matters may be relevant at this juncture.[57] Thus if one could not get to hospital on time because there were not enough ambulances that would not be challengeable by means of a negligence action.

An important feature of this case is that there is no question of an ambulance not being available or of a conflict in priorities. Again I recognise that where what is being attacked is the allocation of resources, whether in the provision of sufficient ambulances or sufficient drivers or attendants, different considerations could apply. There then could be issues which are not suited for resolution by the courts.[58]

Applying the approach in *Caparo* would bring public authority cases into line with ones involving the traditional rescue services. Whilst the prospects of recovery in negligence may not be great the approach of the courts, where bodies such as the police, fire and ambulance services are concerned, is to apply the standard three stage test set out in *Caparo* to determine whether a duty of care is owed. The application of the test in such cases tends, albeit remaining in the realm of private law, to display certain features. Claimants may well find it difficult to establish proximity.[59] Furthermore, particular public policy factors are likely to be highlighted and, in some contexts (most notably cases involving the police) will tend to be seen as going against the existence of a duty of care. Again in such cases statutory provisions play a limited role. In the case of the police this is because 'the obligations of the police are rooted in the common law and not statute'.[60] Whilst matters may be somewhat different elsewhere the statutory framework is still likely to play a subordinate role. Thus in *Capital and Counties v Hampshire CC*, the statutory framework notwithstanding, the court decided that the fire brigade did not owe a duty of care to answer calls to fires or to take reasonable care to do so,[61] instead, by analogy with the police case of *Alexandrou v Oxford*,[62] the case was decided on the basis of a lack of proximity. There is much that might be said about the merits or otherwise of such decisions; the police cases, for example, might be thought to offer an excessive amount of protection to defendants. Nevertheless the framework within which decision-making takes place is purely private law one; public law concepts or thinking do not intrude. Again it is worth noting that the position of each branch of the emergency services is examined independently.

---

[57] *Phelps v Hillingdon LBC* [2000] 4 All ER 504, 536 per Lord Clyde.
[58] *Kent v Griffiths* [2000] 2 All ER 474, 484.
[59] See, for instance, both *Hill v Chief Constable of West Yorkshire* [1989] AC 53 and *Capital & Counties plc v Hampshire CC* [1997] QB 1004.
[60] *Kent v Griffiths* [2000] 2 All ER 474, 484.
[61] *Capital & Counties plc v Hampshire CC* [1997] QB 1004.   [62] [1993] 4 All ER 328.

Holding that a duty of care exists can be seen as consistent with negligence's role in deterring, and compensating for, dangerous behaviour. However, there are certain factors that may go against the establishment of a duty that may be particularly relevant in the case of public authorities. For instance, arguments based upon loss distribution need to be viewed with particular caution. In terms of spreading the loss across as wide a range of people as possible the existence of a public body defendant presents obvious temptations. The effect, however, of a finding for the claimant in a case like *Anns* is to force the local authority to recoup the money from local taxes or, perhaps, to claim against their insurance policy. In contrast, the consequence of the decision in *Murphy* is to put the responsibility of obtaining insurance cover on to householders. It is not immediately obvious which is the superior method of loss distribution. In some situations the answer may seem a good deal clearer; for example, in the context of actions mooted against other regulatory bodies. Take an action by an aggrieved investor against a regulatory body with powers over a securities market. Assuming that such a body is funded by central government the taxpayer will meet the cost of any award of damages. It may well be felt that this would be wrong. Distributing the loss over the widest group possible is not necessarily the best solution. In the Canadian case of *Kripps v Touche Ross*[63] the Superintendent of Brokers was alleged to have caused the pursuer's loss by failing to enforce the Securities Act. The court's view of the legislative scheme led to the denial of a duty:

It does not follow from a legislative decision to control the risk to which lenders are exposed that the scheme created for this purpose is intended to protect individual potential lenders from unreasonable risk of loss through advancing money on inadequate security. It is . . . inherently improbable that the legislature would create a scheme designed to protect all who might lend money on marketed securities against the danger of accepting as security something which proves to be inadequate, having regard to the risks to be expected when lending money at the rate of interest offered in a particular case. It seems more likely that the purpose of such a scheme will be to protect or improve the overall quality of the market by reducing hazards where and to the extent that the authority thinks feasible, having regard to the resources available, the range of securities being offered, and also the sorts of securities which appear most in need of scrutiny at any time.[64]

It is suggested that it would take a very strong case before a regulatory agency should be held to owe a duty of care in respect of purely economic loss.

It is also important to recall that a public bodies may well be a peripheral party.[65] One may also wish to consider who is the cheapest cost-

---

[63] 1992 94 DLR (4th edn) 284.   [64] Ibid, at 300–1.
[65] J Stapleton, 'Duty of Care: Peripheral Parties and Alternative Opportunities for Deterrence' (1995) 111 *LQR* 301.

avoider . Often it will not be the public authority. In a situation such as the one in *Anns* one would imagine that the cheapest cost-avoider would be the builder since if they follow the appropriate building regulations that is the simplest way to prevent problems arising. This leaves to one side questions of responsibility as between, for instance, builder and architect. If, on the other hand, matters are left to local authority inspection difficult questions arise. How many building sites should be inspected? How extensive should any inspection be? Sometimes the cheapest cost-avoider will be the consumer. It seems very unlikely that this would be so in a case like *Anns* or *Murphy.* This would be all the more so if one was dealing with a claimant who was not the initial owner or occupier. One recalls that in *Anns* that once the foundations were filled in there was no subsequent opportunity for inspection. Calabresi tells us that '[O]ften the cheapest way of avoiding accident costs is for several parties or activities to alter their behaviour somewhat.'[66]

VIII. CONCLUSIONS

The case law on public authority liability is hideously complicated. It may also obscure the fact that there are, in essence, two key questions to be addressed. First, what do we expect from public bodies and second, how should those expectations be enforced. It is the contention of this article that the law of negligence does have a role to play when a public body fails to act. Conaghan writes that

Given recent mounting revelations about the prevalence of child abuse in British children's homes, this may not be the best time to eschew private law in favour of a public regulatory system which has, historically at least, lamentably failed to safe-guard the interests of those who have come under its protection.[67]

Nevertheless, it is not obvious just how difficult it should be to sue a public authority where they have failed to protect you. It must be said that arriving at an across the board position does not seem possible. The existence of any alleged duty of care must depend on proper account being taken of the statute in question.

---

[66] G Calabresi, *The Costs of Accidents* (New Haven: Yale University Press, 1970), 259.
[67] J Conaghan, 'Tort Litigation in the Context of Intra-familial Abuse' (1998) 52 *MLR* 132, 155.

19. LIABILITY OF PUBLIC AUTHORITIES IN THE NETHERLANDS

Cees C van Dam*

I. INTRODUCTION

The Dutch law on the liability of public authorities can be classified in three categories: (1) liability for regulatory activities; (2) liability for judgments and (3) liability for administrative conduct (acts and omissions), legal acts excluded. In this section, I will make some general remarks on the first two categories, before focusing on the last category in the following sections of this chapter.

An important rule in the first category is that, according to Dutch law a public body is liable for the damage caused to third parties if an administrative court deems an order or a decree of this public body to be unlawful. Neither culpability nor foreseeability are required. This means that the public body is held liable, even in cases in which the administrative court has chosen a new line of ruling that was unforeseeable for the public body.[1] This is a stricter system than the system that follows from the *Francovich*— and *Factortame*—decisions of the European Court of Justice.[2] For that reason the European development did not really affect the Dutch law in this respect.

Liability for judgments is not a major issue in the Dutch law on liability of public authorities. It is very difficult to establish the liability of the State for incorrect judgments. Only if a court has neglected fundamental legal principles and no further appeal is possible, can the State be liable for the damage, especially on the basis of breaching its duty according to Article 6 ECHR.[3]

An important principle in the liability of public authorities in the Netherlands is the principle that is well -known by its French wording: *l'égalité devant les charges publiques*. The Dutch Supreme Court (Hoge

---

* Professor of Private Law, Vrije University, Amsterdam. Deputy Judge, District Court, Arnhem.

[1] Hoge Raad 31 mei 1991, NJ 1993, 112 (*Van Gog v Nederweert*).

[2] ECJ 19 Nov 1991, C-6/90 and C-9/90, Jur 1991, I-5357 (Francovich and Bonifaci); ECJ 5 maart 1996, C-46/93 and C-48/93, Jur 1996, I-1029 (Brasserie du Pêcheur and Factortame III).

[3] Hoge Raad 3 Dec 1971, NJ 1972, 137 (*X v State*); HR 17 maart 1978, NJ 1979, 204 (*X v State*); 26 Feb 1988, NJ 1989, 2 (*Franklin v The Netherlands Antilles*); Hoge Raad 8 Jan 1993, NJ 1993, 558 (*R v State*); Hoge Raad 29 Apr 1994, NJ 1995, 727 (*S v State*).

Raad) has applied this principle for instance in the case of a pig farmer who suffered severe economic loss because of an Order of the Minister of Agriculture. In this Order the use of swill (a kind of pig feed consisting of uncooked offal) was immediately forbidden in order to fight an outbreak of African swine fever. The Supreme Court deemed the Order of the Minister to be *unlawful* as far as it did not provide compensation for the very small group of farmers using swill, especially the claimant. The reason was that these farmers in fact paid the costs of measures that were taken in the public interest.[4]

II. FOCUS IN THIS PAPER: DUTCH DISASTERS

The main question in this paper is whether a public authority can be liable if it does not check whether operators of companies or establishments respect the terms of their licences and if it does not implement enforcement procedures. Two main accidents in 2000 and 2001 have caused this question to be of great importance in the Netherlands: the explosion on the premises of a company producing fireworks in Enschede in May 2000 and the fire in a café in Volendam on New Year's Eve 2001.

After a short description of these accidents, I will make some remarks on the statutory and unwritten duties of a public body to check and to enforce (sections III and IV). Then I will go into two main issues that may come up in this respect: the policy-defence of the public body (section V) and the burden of taking precautionary measures (section VI). Finally, I answer the question of attributability, ie whether a public body knows or ought to know about the risks in an establishment or a company (section VII).

On Saturday, 13 May 2000, a series of explosions occurred at the SE Fireworks company which stored and assembled fireworks in the city of Enschede, a city in the eastern part of the Netherlands close to the German border, causing the death of twenty-two persons and injury to almost 1,000 more. The incident inflicted extensive damage on a large area immediately surrounding the factory, including a residential area.[5] Questions were raised as to whether the operator was respecting the terms of his licence and whether enforcement procedures were being fully implemented. It is likely that the stored fireworks were heavier than was permitted and that it was stored in an unsafe way: the containers were too light and were not fire-resistant enough. It is also likely that the State and the City of Enschede did

---

[4] Hoge Raad 18 Jan 1991, NJ 1992, 638 (*Leffers v State*).
[5] The Oosting Commission was charged by the Dutch Government with investigating this accident, and their report was published in Feb 2001: De vuurwerkramp, Eindrapport, ISBN: 90-71082-67-9, 90-71082-68-7, 90-71082-69-5 and 90-71082-70-9.

not control whether SE Fireworks complied with the rules or enforced the operator to do so. One of the questions is whether this omission makes the State and the City liable for the damage of the victims.

The second severe accident took place in the early hours of 2001 in a café in Volendam, a small village north of Amsterdam. This café was called 'The Heaven' ('De Hemel'). Maybe that is why the owner did not set much store by the health and safety rules issued by the municipal authorities! On this New Year's Eve the ceiling of the café was covered with Christmas decorations. These were very dry and had not been treated to eliminate the risk of fire. To celebrate the New Year one of the young party-goers lit a sparkler and held it above his head, close to the bone-dry Christmas decorations. This caused a short but fatal fire that resulted in the death of fifteen persons. Many persons were injured; some of them very severely burned. All victims were between 15 and 25 years of age.[6] This event raised the question of liability of the Municipality of Volendam. The municipal executives knew that the café did not conform to the conditions of their licence, but they nonetheless decided to tolerate the situation. In the Netherlands it is beyond doubt that Volendam is liable for the damage of the victims and in fact the third-party insurer of Volendam has already admitted liability. The question is what is the basis for this liability?

It goes without saying that the operators of the factory and the café are liable for the damage of the victims' harm. But in both cases their own resources and the sum insured on their liability insurance policy was certainly not sufficient to compensate all the victims. That is why it is important to examine the liability of other parties, especially the local authorities. It is not easy to answer this question because the discussion in Dutch literature on this issue has started only recently and there is no court decision that can be used as a guideline in the discussion. This means that the answer has to be found by applying general Dutch principles of governmental liability and general principles of tort law.

III. STATUTORY DUTIES TO CHECK AND TO ENFORCE

In the first part of the twentieth century, a public body could only be liable for its acts and omissions if it had acted as a private person or a private body. If it had acted as a public body, it could not be liable for damage caused to others. That means that public bodies were immune from liability.[7] The Dutch Supreme Court abolished this rule in 1924,

---

[6] The Alders Commission was charged by the Dutch Government with investigating this accident; see Kamerstukken II, 2000–1, 27 575, no 5.

[7] Asser-Hartkamp III, De verbintenis uit de wet, 1998, no 281-4; Van Maanen en De Lange, Onrechtmatige overheidsdaad, 2000, 19 ff.

stating that public authorities can also be liable for damage if they exercise their public powers or duties.[8]

The main tool of the courts to judge the conduct of public bodies is the general tort law-provision in Dutch law which is Article 162 of Book 6 of the Civil Code (Burgerlijk Wetboek). According to this article there are three grounds for liability: the infringement of a right, a breach of a statutory duty, and a breach of a duty that follows from unwritten law. These three rules apply to every conduct of every person, private body, and public body.[9] For instance, a local authority is liable if it has drained polluted water into a river, because it breaches a duty of care owed to the persons living along this river.[10] The last two grounds are of special interest to formulate an answer to the central question in this paper.

Public bodies are, in general and under certain conditions, *entitled* to inspect the safety of public buildings and thus to enforce compliance with the licensing conditions. However, there is no general *statutory duty* to do so.

An example of a special statutory duty *to inspect and control* the compliance of companies with safety rules and the conditions laid down by licences can be found in the so-called Seveso-Directive that was enacted by the European Union after the major accident in a chemical plant in Seveso, Italy, in 1976.[11] This Directive is aimed at the prevention of major accidents that involve dangerous substances and the limitation of their consequences for man and the environment (Article 1). The Directive applies to establishments where dangerous substances are present in such a quantity that it causes the risk of a major accident (Article 2). Article 18 of the Directive provides a duty for the authorities to organise a system of inspections or other measures of control. Such inspections or other control measures must be sufficient for planned and systematic examination of the systems being employed at the establishment, whether of a technical, organisational, or managerial nature. The programme must entail at least one on-site inspection made by the competent authority every 12 months.

In Dutch law a special statutory duty *to enforce* compliance with safety rules and licensing conditions can be found in the Environment Conservancy Act (Wet Milieubeheer). This Act provides in Article 18.2 that an administrative body that is entitled to grant permits has a duty to take

---

[8] Hoge Raad 20 Nov 1924, NJ 1925, 89 (Ostermann).
[9] CC van Dam, Aansprakelijkheidsrecht, 2000, no 804–32; Asser-Hartkamp III no 286–9.
[10] Hoge Raad 20 Dec 1940, NJ 1941, 366 (Voorste Stroom V); Hoge Raad 19 Mar 1943, NJ 1943, 312 (Voorste Stroom VI).
[11] Council Directive 82/501, 24 June 1982, OJ 1982, L 230.1, replaced by Council Directive 96/82, 9 Dec 1996, OJ 1997, L 10.

care to enforce the legal rules with respect to the building and to the activity that is conducted within it. This is the only example of a codified duty to enforce legal rules. It has to be emphasised that this is not an absolute duty to enforce but a duty of care.

IV. UNWRITTEN DUTIES TO CHECK AND TO ENFORCE

As has been pointed out in the foregoing paragraph, in most cases there is no statutory duty to check compliance with safety rules and licensing conditions and to enforce these rules. In these cases the question arises whether a duty can be based on what follows from unwritten law. This question can be answered in accordance with the principles of supervisor's liability in other cases, such as the liability of parents, employers, and highway authorities.[12]

The main policy argument to establish a public body's duty to inspect, to control, and to enforce is reliance. Since it is forbidden to run a café or a disco unless one has a licence to do so, the public may rely on the local authority that issued a licence, that it more or less checks the safety of these places of entertainment and that it in principle enforces compliance with the applicable safety rules. In a comparable field, it has been ruled that watchdogs have a duty to supervise institutions, for example, banks and insurance companies in the interest of the public, more specific in the interest of the persons who foreseeably may suffer damage because of a lack of supervision.[13]

A second reason for a duty of public bodies is their surplus of knowledge about the safety of companies and places of entertainment. On the one hand, a public body has information or is entitled to inspect a building in order to get information about the safety risks. The public body is also, under certain conditions, entitled to enforce the safety rules. On the other hand, in most cases the potential victim does not have any information about safety risks and is, in general, not able or entitled to prevent, restrict or remove these risks.[14]

Another justification for a duty of a public body to inspect, to control, and to enforce safety rules can be found in the potential lack of distance between licensees and municipal executives. This lack of distance can for instance play a role if economic interests of a municipality (the wish to keep a company or an establishment within the borders of the city) interfere with

---

[12] Van Dam, nrs 1101 and 1401.

[13] District Court The Hague 13 July 2001, JOR 2001, 215 (*Stichting Vie d'Or v Pensioen-en Verzekeringskamer*). See also Hoge Raad 31 May 2000, NJ 2000, 555 (*Verzekeringskamer v Vie d'Or*).

[14] Van Dam, no 1101.

public safety interests. Tort law can provide the right incentives to balance the interests of the municipality, the establishment, the neighbours and the visitors in a fair way.

It can be concluded from the foregoing that, according to Dutch law, public bodies are not immune to liability with respect to their public acts or omissions. They are, in principle, under a duty to inspect, to control, and to enforce compliance with the safety rules. This duty is mainly based on unwritten law. At this point the question arises what can be said about the extent of this public body's duty. Like in most other legal systems, the extent of this duty has to be established by weighing two elements: on the one hand the magnitude of the risk (ie the probability of causing damage and the expected character and magnitude of the damage) and on the other hand the burden of taking precautionary measures and the character of the conduct and of the author of the damage.[15]

In this respect there are two main thresholds for establishing liability of a public body. First, the above-mentioned element of 'the character of the conduct and of the author of the damage', that comes back to the policy-defence of the public body (see section V). Secondly, a public body will defend itself by the argument of 'the burden of taking precautionary measures'. This defence is reflected in the question about what can be expected from a public body with respect to the control over, and enforce of, safety rules (see section VI).

V. THE POLICY-DEFENCE

One of the main defences of a public body against liability is that it ought to be free to make its own decisions. However, according to Dutch law, even if a public body exercises its discretionary powers, it is not immune to liability. The courts have four main tools to judge the conduct of public bodies.

First, a public act or omission is unlawful if the act or omission was so unreasonable that no reasonable body would have taken it. This kind of limited judicial review is comparable to what in English law is known as the 'Wednesbury-test'.[16]

Secondly, a public body is (of course) not allowed to abuse its powers or to use its powers in cases in which it was reasonably not allowed to do so.[17]

---

[15] Hoge Raad 5 Nov 1965, NJ 1966, 136 (Kelderluik). This decision reflects the same thought as has been expressed by the American judge Learned Hand in *United States v Carroll Towing Co* (1947) 159 F (2d) 169, 173. This formula has been more or less adopted in all the main European legal systems.

[16] *Associated Provincial Picture Houses Ltd v Wednesbury Corporation* [1948] 1 KB 223.

[17] Asser-Hartkamp III, no 289.

Thirdly, public bodies have to act in compliance with the so-called general *principles of good governance* (algemene beginselen van behoorlijk bestuur). If a public body does not do so, it breaches its duty of care.[18] Some of these principles are codified in the General Administrative Law Act (Algemene wet bestuursrecht). In these cases the duty of the public body is a statutory one. However, in Dutch law there is no significant difference between the breach of a duty of care and the breach of statutorty duty. The general principles of good governance imply amongst others that a public body is not allowed to use its power for another goal than for which it is given (this is what the French call 'détournement de pouvoir'), that a public body is not allowed to act arbitrarily or to abuse its powers, that a public body has a duty to act fairly and a duty to treat equal cases equally, that it has to give the reasons for its decisions and that it has a duty to be careful and to be reliable.[19]

Finally, citizens and companies can upheld fundamental rights against a public body. These rights can be found in the Dutch constitution as well as in many international treaties to which the Dutch State is a party, especially the European Convention on Human Rights.[20] In this respect it may also be argued that there is something as a fundamental right of safety. This can be concluded from a passage in the Commentary on the draft text of Article 174 of Book 6 of the Civil Code. This article provides a strict liability for the possessor of a defective building, including roads. The Minister of Justice stated in his commentary that in cases of liability of a highway authority the courts might take into account the restricted financial means of the authority. However, this does not imply that the level of maintenance may come under an acceptable level, or that the authority does not change a dangerous situation of which it has knowledge.[21] This means that restricted financial means of a public body are no justification for an unsafe policy.

Like most other legal systems Dutch law distinguishes between policy and operation. The Supreme Court confirmed the relevance of this distinction in the so-called *Diemen*-case in 1992.[22] In many cases it can be difficult *not* to confuse policy and operation. However, in the *Diemen*-case the difference was quite easy to make. Diemen, a small village near Amsterdam, decided to make a construction on a bus-lane in order to prevent other traffic to use this lane. The obstacle did not create problems for buses, but it did for motor cars. Drivers who tried to cross the obstacle drove their cars through a gap. Luckily this gap was not very deep but within a few months

[18] Asser-Hartkamp III, no 290a.
[19] Van Maanen en De Lange, 58 ff.
[20] See, eg, ECHR 28 Oct 1988, 87/1997 (*Osman v United Kingdom*).
[21] Parlementaire Geschiedenis Invoering Boek 6, 1394.
[22] Hoge Raad 20 Mar 1992, NJ 1993, 547 (*Diemen v Rep-Tax*).

some forty cars had landed in the gap. One of the victims, a taxi-driver, sued the Municipality of Diemen, alleging that the way that the obstacle had been constructed was unlawful.

The Municipality of Diemen defended itself by stating that the construction of the obstacle was a matter of policy. The Supreme Court did not agree with this point of view. It decided that, on the one hand, the Municipality's decision to make constructions in the bus-lane to prevent other traffic from using this lane was a policy decision. But on the other hand, the safety of the obstacle was an operational-issue that had to be judged according to the rules applicable in cases of physical damage. Although Diemen had taken a lot of safety measures, such as warning-signs, the Supreme Court decided that these measures were not sufficient and that Diemen therefore had breached its duty of care. This decision was not surprising given that almost forty drivers did not react properly to these warnings and drove into the gap.

All in all, the courts have many possibilities to judge the policy-conduct of public bodies. Despite these possibilities, there are not many cases in which this conduct has deemed to be unlawful.[23]

VI. THE BURDEN OF TAKING PRECAUTIONARY MEASURES

Until now, the question under which circumstances a public body breaches its duty to inspect and to control the safety of establishments and companies, has not been answered by a Dutch court. However, I will try to give an answer that is based on the general rules of the liability of public bodies in the Netherlands.

The decision of a public body to spend money on the inspection and control of the safety of establishments and companies has an important political dimension. Public bodies do not have an infinite amount of money to perform this duty. Thus one can argue that this decision is a matter of policy. This means that the courts can judge this decision with the tools that were mentioned in the foregoing section. It is therefore arguable that a public body is not allowed to make choices that lead to an unacceptably low safety-standard.

In this respect one can make a comparison with the liability of highway authorities. The safety-duty for highways and the duty for local authorities are to a large extent comparable, since in both cases there is a risk of physical damage that requires substantial precautionary measures. Both are non-

---

[23] Asser-Hartkamp III, no 290b-290d. Hoge Raad 29 Mar 1940, NJ 1940, 1128 (Heldenkermis); Hoge Raad 4 Jan 1963, NJ 1964, 202 and 204 (Landsmeer); HR 12 Mar 1971, NJ 1971, 265 (Westerschouwen).

feasance-cases in which safety measures can be much more expensive than in misfeasance-cases. And in both cases there is the problem of limited financial means of the responsible body.[24]

According to Article 162 of Book 6 of the Civil Code a highway authority has a duty to control the highway and to take enough safety measures, taking into account the nature and the amount of the risk on the one hand and the burden of taking these measures and the financial means of the body on the other. This rule is comparable with those in England and Germany.[25] Although I can not go into detail at this point, one can generally say that a highway authority can escape from liability for omissions if it can prove that it has a well-considered plan as to how to control the safety of the highway and that it operates this plan in a proper way.[26] For instance, according to a decision of the District Court of The Hague, a motorway authority complies with its duties by inspecting the motorway twice a day.[27]

In my view this standard can also be applied to a public body that has a duty to inspect the safety of public buildings. To avoid liability it must at least prove that it has, within its possibilities and means, made a plan as to how and how many times it aims at controlling the safety of public buildings (eg once a year) and that it in fact carries out this plan.

The last question that has to be answered with respect to the aspect of unlawfulness is whether a local authority can be held liable if it does not enforce compliance with licensing-conditions by licensees or, more generally, if it does not inspect the safety of public buildings. It seems to be that the local authorities in Enschede and Volendam (see above, section II) did know about the violation of safety rules by the owner of the fireworks-plant (Enschede) and of the café (Volendam) but did not try to enforce the owners to comply with the safety rules.

Although the Netherlands may be known as a country of tolerance and permissiveness, a public authority cannot, according to Dutch law, legally

---

[24] Van Dam, nrs 801–2, 1212. Art 174 of Book 6, Civil Code provides a rule of strict liability for damage caused by a defective building or a defective road. The applicable standard is comparable to that of the European directive on liability for defective products: a road is deemed to be defective if it does not provide the safety one may expect of that road. The Dutch courts are, until now, inclined to limit this strict liability to cases in which the road itself is defective; they decided that Art 6: 174 is not applicable in cases where things as branches, oil, or a tyre, were laying *on* the road. This line deviates from for instance the Belgian rule: Cornelis, Beginselen van het Belgische buitencontractuele aansprakelijkheidsrecht, 1989, no 287. Although it is arguable that this is not a correct interpretation of the Dutch provision, it implies that for things on the road, such as branches, oil, or tyres, liability has to be based on the general negligence-rule in Art 6: 162: see Van Dam, no 1212.

[25] See, eg, English law: *Haydon v Kent County Council* [1978] QB 343 and WVH Rogers, *Winfield and Jolowicz on Tort*, 14th edn (1994), 441. See, eg, German law: Bundesgerichtshof 1 July 1993, NJW 1993, 2802. and Münchener Kommentar-Mertens, § 823 N 256.

[26] Van Dam, no 1212.

[27] District Court Den Haag 20 Apr 1994, NJK 1994, 13 (*Van Goethem v Staat*).

state that it is purely a matter of policy whether it enforces the compliance with rules or not. Since 1998, the highest administrative court in the Netherlands, the Court Section of the Council of State (Afdeling Bestuursrechtspraak Raad van State) has ruled that public bodies have, in principle, a duty to enforce.[28] This means that a public authority has to explain its policy and to come up with strong arguments why it did not enforce compliance with (safety) rules. The decisions of the Council of State are related to a cabinet document in which the principle of enforcement was laid down. According to this document and to the jurisprudence of the Council of State, exceptions to this principle are possible (provided that the exception is restricted in time and in extent) in cases where (i) enforcement is evidently unreasonable, (ii) the protected interest is better served with non-enforcement and (iii) an important interest justifies non-enforcement.[29]

VII. KNOWLEDGE

Article 162 of Book 6 of the Civil Code requires that the unlawful act (see section III-VI) can be attributed to the author of the damage, in this case the public body. This requirement is fulfilled if it can be established that the public body knew or ought to have known about the risk.[30]

One of the questions that may arise in cases of governmental liability is: what does a public body know? The Supreme Court has ruled in several decisions that if one part of an organisation disposes of information, this knowledge can be attributed to the whole organisation. For instance, if a municipal official who is responsible for fire-prevention knows of a safety risk in a café, this knowledge can be attributed to the municipality as such.[31]

In many cases a public body receives information from third parties such as private citizens pointing out an abuse or reporting a dangerous situation. The Supreme Court has decided that in such a case a public body has a duty to act.[32] This means that it has to respond to the received information in a proper way by examining the extent of the risk and—if necessary—to take adequate measures to restrict or remove the risk. The receipt of the information does not in itself create liability for the public body but it deprives the public body of its defence that it did not know about the risk.

---

[28] Afd. Bestuursrechtspraak RvS 2 Feb 1998, AB 1998, 181; Afd Bestuursrechtspraak RvS 18 June 1998, AB 1999, 28; Afd. Bestuursrechtspraak RvS 12 Feb 1999, AB 1999, 321.

[29] Kamerstukken II, 1996-7, 25 085, no 2, 9 and 35-40.

[30] Van Dam, 2000, no 901.

[31] RPJL Tjittes, Toerekening van kennis, Offerhaus-kring, 2001; Van Dam, no 915.

[32] Hoge Raad 8 Jan 1999, NJ 1999, 319 (*Waterschap West-Friesland v Kaagman*); Van Dam, no 915.

Furthermore it has the burden of proving that it had reacted adequately to the complaint or the received information.

An unlawful act can be attributed to the public body not only if it was aware of the risk but also if it ought to have known about it. The question whether the latter is the case is absorbed by the question of unlawfulness whether the public body had to do check and control establishments and companies.[33] This question has been answered in section VI.

VIII. CONCLUSION

It can be concluded from what has been stated above, that Dutch law expects something of public bodies (see also section I). However, Dutch public bodies are still able to exercise their powers adequately. The question is why public bodies in the Netherlands are relatively relaxed as far as liability risks are concerned. One of the main answers is, that most of the Dutch local authorities have an adequate third-party insurance. This means that public bodies, like persons and private bodies, dare to take risks and are not seriously limited in their freedom to act or to omit.

The conclusion is that the Dutch do not seem to be afraid to open the floodgates of claims against public authorities. Maybe this has something to do with the fact that the inhabitants of the Netherlands think they know all about sluices and dykes. And that, in the end, they trust that there will always be a judge who knows where to put his finger in the dyke.

[33] Van Dam, no 820.

20. FROM INDIVIDUAL TORT FOR CIVIL SERVANTS TO QUASI-STRICT LIABILITY OF THE STATE: GOVERNMENTAL OR STATE LIABILITY IN GERMANY

Gert Brüggemeier *

Governmental liability in Germany is still 'official liability', *Amtshaftung*. This denotes a vicarious liability on the part of the state for wrongful acts by officials exercising governmental functions. The foundation of this vicarious liability is the tort of a civil servant, which is regulated in private law by § 839 BGB. But in contrast to common law vicarious liability, German constitutional law provides for an exonerating (for the civil servant) assumption of responsibility by the state in Article 34 of the Constitution, *Grundgesetz*. Governmental liability insofar is grounded on two pillars: private law and public law. The development from 'official liability' towards any form of state liability is correlated to the private law development from an individual person's responsibility to organisational or enterprise liability. That is why the presentation of governmental liability in Germany today has to focus on this relationship between private law and public law, on private enterprise liability and public state liability. Starting point for both is the German Civil Code—BGB—of 1896.

I. EMPLOYEE–EMPLOYER LIABILITY[1]

An employee is liable like any other under the main tort clause of § 823 (1) BGB. This requires

- injury to protected rights or interests;
- caused while acting within the scope of his/her employment;
- unlawfulness, ie no defences or excuses;
- fault (negligence or intent);
- actual damage arising out of the injury.

---

* Professor Dr Gert Brüggemeier, Director, Centre of European Law and Politics, Faculty of Law, University of Bremen.

[1] See more on this Otto and Schwarze, *Die Haftung des Arbeitnehmers*, 3rd edn 1998).

The employer, however, is in the BGB-tort law *not* under a regime of vicarious liability or under a doctrine of *respondeat superior*. The German law differs fundamentally from Anglo-American, Romanic, and Scandinavian laws in that the employer's responsibility is also subject to the principle 'no liability without fault'. The regime is neither one of strict liability nor of vicarious liability. The employer, incorporated or not, is liable under the following conditions, provided for in § 831(1) BGB:

- tort of an employee, acting within the scope of his/her employment;
- employer's own fault in selecting, supervising, etc.

The only move towards no-fault liability of the employer is that § 831 (1) (ii) contains a rebuttable presumption of employer's fault. In the case of incorporated employers the individual fault of the executives is attributed to the corporation. The corporation by its chief executive officer has to show exculpatory evidence.

On the basis of such a structure of employer–employee–liability the normal consequence is joint and several liability of master (under § 831) and servant (under § 823). The BGB originally posed the final burden of damage on the employee by granting the employer a right to indemnification (§ 840 (2)). This rule, however, has soon been derogated by the courts, especially by the labour courts (installed as a special branch of jurisdiction in 1927). The judiciary implanted in the employment contract an implied right of the employee to release from liability. Only in cases of gross negligence or intentional torts the damage is divided between employee and employer or totally shifted to the employee.

II. LIABILITY OF CIVIL SERVANTS

The only human being who received a special and privileged treatment in the BGB-tort law, which is well known for its abstract and generalised provisions—was the civil servant (*Beamter*). § 839 (1) (i) BGB provides:

If a civil servant wilfully or negligently commits a breach of an official duty towards a third party, he shall compensate the third party for any damage arising there from.

Interestingly though, § 839 differs noticeably from the main heading of German tort law—§ 823 (1) BGB with its enumerated protected interests. It resembles much more a general tort clause such as is found in the French Civil Code. The preconditions of a civil servant's liability are:

- official protective duty;
- [scope of protection];
- breach of the duty;

- fault;
- damage (this comprises material damage as well as pure economic loss).

On the other hand the historical lawmaker introduced several privileges for the civil servants. Guaranteeing the workability of public administration seemed to be a relevant concern of the legislator. This can be seen in the following points of law: (i) In cases of negligence the civil servant is only liable if there is no other responsible party. This other obligee can also be the state-employer under § 831 BGB (principle of subsidiarity). Most relevant examples are civil servant-doctors in public hospitals. (ii) Judges are generally immunised against liability, unless they commit a criminal felony. (iii) Plaintiffs loose their right to compensation, when they did not make use of legal remedies, which would have prevented the damage. (iv) As far as non-EU-citizens as claimants are concerned, their right to make the German civil servant liable is under the precondition of reciprocity; ie, that their home state recognises by bilateral agreement similar claims of German citizens.

III. (INDIRECT) GOVERNMENTAL LIABILITY

Up to this point the legal playing field has been civil tort law. But now we shift to the public law sphere. As far as the realm of state sovereignty is concerned and the public servant has exercised *sovereign power* when he injured a private party—the legal liability therefore is imputed to the state-employer. This imputation of liability has been introduced nation-wide for the first time by Article 131 of the *Weimar* Constitution of 1919. Article 34 of the *Grundgesetz* of 1949 followed this model. Article 34 (i) GG provides:

If someone, in the exercise of a public office entrusted to him, breaches his official duty towards a third person, responsibility will lie in principle with the state or the governmental body he is serving.

Governmental liability as provided for by Article 34 GG is indirect liability. The starting point remains in principle a tort of a public servant. In contrast to § 839 BGB, the notion of a tortfeasor in Article 34 GG is enlarged. It comprises every public servant, may he/she be a public worker, a public employee or a civil servant. But again, the crucial point is the public servant's acting within the scope of sovereign power. He or she must exercise a governmental function. In the so-called fiscal sphere, however, where public entities engage in market transactions, civil tort law still applies (§§ 823, 839, 831 BGB).

Having clarified this, the tort of the public servant has the well-known preconditions as laid down in § 839 BGB:

- official duty towards a third party;
- breach of this duty;
- fault;
- damage.

Here then as an exception the principle of *respondeat superior* applies. But in contrast to the Common law vicarious liability an exonerating assumption of liability of the public servant by the state takes place. Indirect governmental liability under Article 34 GG means the *exclusive external liability* of the state or governmental body. The state is only given a—discretionary—right to indemnification against the public servant when he/she acted with gross negligence or caused the damage intentionally.

IV. RISE OF (DIRECT) ENTERPRISE LIABILITY[2]

Let's look again at the development of liability in civil tort law. There is a dominant trend since the turn of the last century towards no-fault liability of organisations and enterprises in German law and elsewhere. I use the term enterprise liability to designate these two tendencies: strict liability and quasi-strict liability ('negligence without fault').[3]

Strict liability regimes (*Gefährdungshaftung*) have been introduced in Germany outside the BGB by special legislation to regulate the 'new risks' correlated to the process of industrialisation. The first has been § 25 of the Prussian Railway Act of 1838. More recent examples are the liability of manufacturers of pharmaceuticals (1976) or the EC products liability (1985).

The BGB tort law is governed by the concept of individual fault. As shown above also the employers' liability in § 831 BGB is also put under this regime. But especially for enterprises, be they incorporated or not, the element of fault has been eroded. The courts have introduced a duty of care. The addressee of this duty is the enterprise itself. *The enterprise* has to organise the intra- and extra-firm processes to make sure that no third person will be injured. Negligence turns into a notion of organisational fault that is to a certain degree depersonalised. Negligence becomes a matter of 'system failure'. Something went wrong, be it on the level of executives or on the level of employees and workers somewhere in the manufacturing process. The respective responsible person need no longer be identified.

---

[2] Cf in more detail, G Brüggemeier, *Prinzipien des Haftungsrechts* (1999) (ch E); *Common Principles of Tort Law* (London: BIICL, forthcoming in English 2002).

[3] Cf the famous analysis of AA Ehrenzweig, *Negligence Without Fault. Trends toward an Enterprise Liability for Insurable Loss* (1951).

But a further step has been taken by the courts on the path towards strict liability. They introduced a reversal of the burden of proof for organisational fault. This was originally restricted to products liability,[4] but is now extended elsewhere in organisational liability: eg environmental liability,[5] hospitals' liability.[6]

V. DIRECT STATE LIABILITY[7]

A. *Enterprise Liability Responsibility of the State*

A parallel development has taken place in governmental liability law that still has its roots in private law. The perspective shifted from the individual public servant to the governmental body itself. The 'official duty' of the civil servant, provided for by the wording of § 839 BGB, turned—more or less implicitly—into a duty of the public entity. It really does not matter any longer whether a public servant within the hierarchical structure of the governmental body personally committed a wrongful act. It is rather the question whether the respective governmental action was a violation of the public law rule governing the external relationship between the governmental body and the affected private individual or enterprise. The governmental body itself is under a duty to comply with the public law and to organise by its representatives the administrative processes appropriately. Governmental liability requires a violation of the public law regulating the activity of the respective public authority. This unlawfulness of the public act is going to replace the conventional element of breach of the official duty.

What is further required to establish governmental liability is fault? Sometimes individual fault on the part of a public servant may still be attributed to the public body. In most cases 'organisational fault' will suffice. Up to now there is no explicit shift of the burden of proof for organisational fault acknowledged in state liability law. But given the unlawfulness of the act some sort of presumption or of prima facie proof may help.

The scope of protection is rather far reaching. It depends on the context. In principle compensation of pure economic loss is available.

This governmental organisational liability corresponds to the private enterprise liability under § 823 (1) BGB. This case law developed quietly in this field of the law, diverging from the wording of both—the civil code and

---

[4] Cf the landmark decision BGHZ 51, 91 (fowl pest), NJW 1969, 269 annotated by Diederichsen.

[5] BGHZ 92, 143.

[6] BGH, JZ 1978, 275 annotated by E Deutsch; BGH, NJW 1982, 699.

[7] See in general F Ossenbühl, *Staatshaftungsrecht,* 5th edn (1998).

the constitution. It is basically incompatible with the doctrine of assumption of a public servant's responsibility that is still determining the German law of governmental liability (Article 34 GG, § 839 BGB).

B. Excursus: General Interest versus Particular Interest—Two Cases

Two cases may help to make this legal development clearer. The first case deals with the federal agency regulating and monitoring the insurance market. It had—until the deregulation of the insurance markets in the EC in 1994—the task of deciding the admission of companies and of controlling the content of the insurance contracts. Thus it had also to take into account the 'interests of the insured'. It worked as a 'watchdog' agency.

In 1972 the *Bundesgerichtshof* had to decide the following case:[8] A third party insurer of automobile owners became insolvent. The victim of a car accident could thus recover neither from an indigent car owner who caused the accident nor from his bankrupt insurance. The accident victim sued the federal government for compensation of his loss because of its allegedly negligent failure to control the solvency of the respective insurance company, thus relying on Article 34 GG and § 839 BGB. This raised two questions:

Does the statute establishing the federal agency protect the particular interest of a victim of a car accident who can get no payment from the insolvent car holder's insurance company?

Is the agency at fault?

The *Bundesgerichtshof* answered the first question in the negative. The protective purpose of the Act on establishing the agency aims at the general interest in the functioning of insurance markets. The particular interest of an individual creditor of insurance coverage to receive payment is only a 'reflex' of this public interest and thus beyond the scope of protection of the statute. As a consequence the fault question does not need to be answered.

Seven years later, in 1979, the *Bundesgerichtshof* had to consider cases of a similar federal agency charged with bank oversight. In one case it was a matter of illegal transactions undertaken by the bank.[9] In another it was a matter of insolvency of a bank.[10] Suit was brought by the customers of the respective bank against the federal government on the ground of negligent failure of the agency to supervise the bank. Here the *Bundesgerichtshof* interpreted the 'watchdog' agency as a sort of business police. Under the constitutional guarantees of the *Grundgesetz* the duty of the police is to defend the public *and* the individual citizens. The economic interest of the

---

[8] BGHZ 58, 96 = NJW 1972, 577.
[9] BGHZ 74, 144 = NJW 1979, 1354—Wetterstein.
[10] BGHZ 75, 120—Herstatt; but cf. also BGHZ 90, 310.

particular customers was thus within the scope of protection and not any longer regarded as a mere reflex of the public interest. Fault has been seen in insufficient supervisory measures of the agency.

Here then the German legislator reacted in 1984. It inserted into both statutes—on insurance and on bank regulation—the clear formula that the function of supervising these businesses is undertaken 'only in the public interest'. This however led to the—unresolved—question of the constitutionality of this amendment. The legislator cannot simply by federal Acts exclude constitutionally guaranteed rights of the citizens to a claim against the state.

This bundle of cases shows first that all the jurisdictions in the Western states have difficulties tackling the problem of compensation for remote pure economic losses[11], especially as far as governmental liability is concerned.

It secondly demonstrates to what extent the individual public servant has disappeared behind the veil of the governmental body.

VI. STATE LIABILITY ACT 1981

There was broad agreement on the structural weaknesses and policy defects in the existing German law of governmental liability. That is why in 1981 the federal legislator passed the so-called State Liability Act.[12] The new orientation towards the governmental body as responsible actor was clearly expressed in § 1(1):

If the public authority (!) breaches a duty of public law, entrusted to it towards a third party, the public body (!) shall compensate the third party for any damage arising there from.

The State Liability Act pursued a threefold approach to *direct* governmental liability:

- strict liability for failure of technical facilities;
- objective liability for unlawful official acts involving violations of fundamental rights ('constitutional torts');
- liability under a theory of negligence for other cases of monetary losses. In this context, as for enterprise liability, negligence generally means largely depersonalised organisational fault.

---

[11] Cf. EF Banakas, *Civil Liability for Pure Economic Loss* (London: BIICL, 1996); Bussani and Palmer (eds), *Pure Economic Loss*, 2001).

[12] BGBl. 1981 I, 553; see on this, Schwertfeger, JuS 1982, 1; Wochner, BB 1982, 1. Cf. also Recommendation No R (84) 15 on Public Liability, adopted by the Committee of Ministers of the Council of Europe of Sept 1984, and Explanatory Memorandum (Strasbourg, 1985).

[13] Art 74, No 25 GG.

But in 1982 the Federal Constitutional Court found this Act unconstitutional for reasons of competence. The federal legislator treated state liability as a matter of private law. The court found that it is a matter public law. Insofar the federal republic had no legislative competence. The procedural preconditions have however been provided in the meantime. By the 1994 reform of the *Grundgesetz* the competence to enact state liability has been shifted to the federal republic.[13] Its reform is still on the political agenda. The disappearance of former East Germany's governmental liability law and the effects of European Community law, in particular, have increased the pressure for change.

VII. NEW DEVELOPMENTS

A. Constitutional Protective Duties

This enterprise liability-like type of state responsibility for defective organisations has recently found a new field of application. The Federal Constitutional Court developed the concept of a state's duty to protection of individual interests springing from the fundamental rights of the constitution.[14] According to this concept, fundamental rights have also the function of guaranteeing protection to individuals against hazards from other sources than the state itself.[15] The organisation of public authorities should be adequate to fulfil this task. This subjective right of the citizen to protection gives thus rise to a subjective right to proper state organisation. This concept has led to a so-called theory of '*Untermaßverbot*',[16] which means that the state is under a duty not to do less than is needed for appropriate protection of the citizens. Allegedly insufficient state activity may give ground for governmental liability for organisational fault.

B. Europeanisation of Governmental Liability Law of Member States through the European Court of Justice

While the European Commission, with little success so far, has strived to create the basis for an EC law of enterprise liability in private law,[17] the

---

[14] Starting with BVerfGE 39, 1, at 42 = JZ 1975, 205 annotated byKriele; BVerfGE 46, 160; BVerfGE 49, 89, at 142; BVerfGE 53, 30, at 57.

[15] Cf Isensee, *Das Grundrecht auf Sicherheit* (1983); Hermes, *Das Grundrecht auf Schutz von Leben und Gesundheit* (1987); Robbers, *Sicherheit als Menschenrecht* (1987); Rebhahn, *Staatshaftung wegen mangelnder Gefahrenabwehr* (1997).

[16] Canaris, 'Grundrechtswirkung', *JuS* (1989), 161; id, *Grundrechte und Privatrecht. Eine Bestandsaufnahme* (1999); acknowledged by the Federal Constitutional Court: BVerfGE 88, 203, at 254.

[17] See Joerges and Brüggemeier, 'Europäisierung des Vertrags- und Haftungsrechts', in Müller-Graff (ed), *Gemeinsames Privatrecht in der europäischen Gemeinschaft*, 2nd edn. (1999), 301, 329–49.

European Court of Justice (ECJ) has, with greater success, developed an *original governmental liability* (of the EC/EU *and* member states) *for breach of Community law.*

The increasingly close-knit European Community and the ever-denser net of EC law have created the necessity of sanctioning violations of Community primary and secondary law on an EC-wide basis. The validity of Community law calls for more effective legal protection against and preventions of *violations of European law* on the part of (i) the EC and its organs, (ii) the member states and their institutions, and (iii) private actors. Liability in tort is playing an ever-greater role in this enforcement of European law.

Article 288 (2) EC provides with laconic brevity that the Community's extra-contractual liability for its organs and servants is to '(f)ollow general legal principles common to the legal systems of the member states.'[18] The relevant ECJ decisions on Article 288 (2) EC were at first guided by Articles 34(1), 40(2) ECSC Treaty, which presuppose fault on the part of the organ or servant. Since the 1970s, in contrast, the ECJ has looked more closely at violations of Community law. The Community's governmental liability under Article 288(2) EC has developed into objective liability for unlawfulness.[19]

With its decisions in the *Francovich* and *Bonifaci* cases on 19 November 1991, the ECJ opened up an entirely new dimension of Community governmental liability law:[20] where Community law is violated by a member state (in this case, through failure to adopt a directive despite the completion of breach of treaty proceedings under Article 226 EC), the disadvantaged citizen or enterprise may bring a damages suit before the national court against the respective member state if the following conditions are met:

- direct applicability of primary or secondary Community law,
- sufficient certainty that individual interests are protected under the respective Community law (protective purpose theory, *Schutznormtheorie*),

---

[18] See Heldrich, *Die allgemeinen Rechtsgrundsätze der außervertraglichen Schadenshaftung im Bereich der Europäischen Wirtschaftsgemeinschaft* (1961); Schermers, Heukels, and Mead (eds), *Non-Contractual Liability of the European Communities* (1988); Ewert, *Die Funktion der allgemeinen Rechtsgrundsätze im Schadensersatzrecht der EWG* (1991); W van Gerven and M Zuleeg (eds), *Remedies and Sanctions for the Enforcement of Community Law* (1996); Heukels and McDonnell, *The Action for Damages in Community Law* (1997).

[19] The leading case is ECJ, Case 5/71 Schöppenstedt [1971] ECR 975, 985 point 11: 'Sufficient qualified breach of a higher-ranking legal norm geared to protect the individual.' On older jurisdiction, see ECJ, joint cases 5/66 and 13/66 Kampffmeyer [1967] ECR 287; HP Ipsen, *Europäisches Gemeinschaftsrecht* (1972), 536, 539: 'objective fault'.

[20] ECJ, joint cases C-6/90 and C-9/90 Francovich *et al* [1991] ECR I-5357. The literature on the *Francovich* doctrine fills bookshelves throughout Europe! Here I would refer the reader to the current commentaries and textbooks.

- violation of Community law,
- presence of substantive (or non-material)[21] damage to a EU citizen (enterprise, employee, private person). 'Pure economic loss' is sufficient in principle.[22] The rule of full compensation applies.
- (direct) causation between the violation of Community law and the particular injury/damage.

In a series of subsequent decisions, most importantly the joint cases of *Brasserie du Pêcheur* and *Factortame III* of 1996,[23] the ECJ modified the *Francovich* doctrine while affirming it in principle. The modification primarily concerned the central precondition of liability that EC-law be violated. In the *Brasserie* decision, the ECJ once again took up the *Schöppenstedt* standard, formulating a 'sufficiently serious breach' of Community law. To be 'sufficiently serious', the decisive criterion is whether the state in question manifestly and gravely disregarded the limits of discretion.[24] An additional, separate element of fault was not required.[25] This indefinite formula allows the national courts the flexibility to distinguish among various arenas of member-state action. Particularly in arenas in which, in contrast to the clear cases of non-adoption of directives,[26] the member state is granted broad interpretive discretion for the legislative or administrative[27] measures it will take, the precondition of 'manifest and considerable overstepping of authority' is likely to be difficult to prove as a rule. The 'sufficiently serious breach' standard is flexible enough, in the cases of pure economic loss with which it is primarily concerned, to allow European and national courts to award compensatory damages only in extreme circumstances.

---

[21] ECJ, case 18/78 Mrs V [1979] ECR 2093, 2103, para 19.

[22] Most of the decisions based on the *Francovich* doctrine have involved pure economic loss!

[23] ECJ, joint cases C-46 and 48/93 [1996] ECR I-1029; see also the consequential national decisions: BGHZ 134, 30 = NJW 1997, 123—Brasserie du Pêcheur, and *R v Secretary of State for Transportation ex parte Factortame Ltd* [2000] LR (HL) 524.

[24] ECJ, id, I-1149, para 51. Member States possess broad discretion; a sufficiently qualified violation exists when the government organ involved has 'obviously and significantly overstepped' the limits of its authority (para 45).

[25] ECJ, id, I-1156, para 79. Cf. also PP Craig, 'Once more on to the Breach: the Community, the State and Damages Liability', in M Andenas (ed), *English Public Law and the Common Law of Europe* (London: 1998), 141.

[26] See especially for consumer law, the ECJ judgments in Case C-91/92 Dori [1994] ECR I-325 and Joint Cases C-178, 179 and 188-190/94 Dillenkofer *et al* [1996] ECR I- 4845.

[27] See the ECJ judgment in Case C-5/94 Hedley Lomas [1996] ECR I-2553; P Aubin, *Die Haftung der europäischen Wirtschaftsgemeinschaft und ihrer Mitgliedstaaten bei gemeinschaftsrechtswidrigen nationalen Verwaltungsakten* (1982).

VIII. SUMMARY

The German law governing state liability is characterised by uncertainties and a lack of coherence. There was a fresh new start in 1981 with the State Liability Act which however remained without success. The status quo is a diffuse mixture of traditional vicarious liability of the state and elements of quasi-strict state liability for organisational fault. The trend is towards no-fault liability. Insofar the EC-law is the role model: It is the *objective violation of national public law or Community law* that triggers liability of the member state or of the EC.